AMERICAN COURTS

PROCESS AND POLICY

Fourth Edition

Lawrence Baum
Ohio State University

HOUGHTON MIFFLIN COMPANY   Boston   New York

To Elena Baum and Maya Baum

Sponsoring Editor: *Melissa Mashburn*
Assistant Editor: *Lily Eng*
Senior Project Editor: *Susan Westendorf*
Senior Production/Design Coordinator: *Jill Haber*
Manufacturing Manager: *Florence Cadran*
Marketing Manager: *Sandra McGuire*

Cover design: *Judy Arisman, Arisman Design*
Cover image: *Rob Crandall/Folio*

Printed in the U.S.A.

Library of Congress Catalog Card Number: 97-72439

ISBN: 0-395-87105-0

123456789-QF-01 00 99 98 97

AMERICAN COURTS

Contents

Chapter 3 **Lawyers**   **59**

Chapter 4   The Selection of Judges   **101**

Chapter 5   **Judges**   **137**

Chapter 7   Trial Courts: Civil Cases   217

Chapter 8   Appellate Courts: The Process   263

Preface

Courts are a source of great fascination for people in the United States. The Supreme Court regularly captures headlines for decisions on public issues that range from presidential power to doctor-assisted suicide. The eagerness of some people to file lawsuits is chronicled by the mass media with a mixture of outrage and amusement. Criminal trials often attract widespread notice, and occasionally they garner a level of public interest that surpasses almost everything else in government.

Courts merit the attention they receive. While there is great disagreement about the impact of courts on the nation, without doubt they are an important force in American life. It would be impossible to comprehend government and society in the United States without taking the courts into account. This book has been written to provide a better understanding of courts in the United States, from the Supreme Court to the thousands of trial courts across the country.

One goal of the book is descriptive—to show how courts work and what they do. To achieve this goal, I will examine not only the courts themselves but also the people and institutions that help to shape them, including lawyers, litigants, and policy makers in the other branches of government.

A second goal of the book is to explain what courts do and how they relate to the rest of the political system. For instance, it is important to know that a high proportion of criminal cases are resolved through plea bargains, but it is also important to understand the forces that make plea bargaining so common. Throughout the book I consider explanations for such matters as the president's choices of federal judges and the positions that Supreme Court justices take on public issues.

The work of the courts is constantly evaluated by other policy makers, the mass media, and the general public. Much of that evaluation is negative. One consequence is an array of proposals for court "reform" to remedy what some people see as their failings. The text examines how these proposals are often adopted without a clear sense of their likely impact, resulting in considerable disappointment when that impact is less positive than expected. A third goal of this book is to help readers make informed judgments in evaluating both the courts as they are and proposals for court reform.

Features of the Revision

Like other institutions in government, the courts are constantly changing. This fourth edition of the book reflects the changes that have occurred in the four years since the last edition of the book was published. Among these changes are the following:

- The adoption by nearly half the states of "three-strikes" laws designed to ensure long sentences for repeat offenders (Chapter 6)
- A more assertive role for the Senate in selection of federal judges, a role reflected in President Clinton's difficulties in winning Senate confirmation for his nominees (Chapter 4)
- Growing pressures on judges to avoid the appearance of leniency in their treatment of criminal defendants (Chapters 4, 5, and 8)
- Increasing efforts by government and businesses to divert legal disputes from the courts to other forums, efforts that sometimes prevent individuals from taking their grievances to court (Chapter 7)

These changes are also reflected in the illustrative material in the book. As in the past, most of the exhibits and tables are updated or entirely new. Subjects of new exhibits include the plea bargain reached by skater Tonya Harding after the injuring of her rival Nancy Kerrigan (6.4), the complex body of litigation involving the tobacco industry (8.2), the lawsuit against McDonald's after its coffee burned a patron (7.5), and two heated election contests for judgeships (4.4).

Recent research has expanded our understanding of the courts a great deal. That research is incorporated throughout the book, and major new books are included in the bibliographies at the end of each chapter.

Contents of the Fourth Edition

The book is divided into nine chapters. Chapter 1 introduces the courts and the perspectives that I take in examining them. Chapter 2 describes the organization of the federal and state courts, discussing the structure of court systems and how they are administered. This chapter emphasizes the ways that court organization affects what courts do and shows why seemingly routine issues of court organization sometimes produce heated debate. Chapter 3 focuses on lawyers, who do much to determine how the courts actually operate. After examining the law as a profession, the chapter discusses the availability of lawyers to potential clients and the relationships between lawyers and clients.

Chapters 4 and 5 examine judges. The subject of Chapter 4 is the selection of federal and state judges. One major concern is the impact that the different systems for judicial selection have on the ways that judges are actually chosen and on the kinds of people who become judges. Chapter 5 discusses judges themselves. It begins by looking at judges' political activities, career experiences, and social circumstances and how those elements of judges' backgrounds affect their behavior. It then turns to judges' activities on the bench. Finally, it probes the quality of judges' work and considers means to strengthen their performance.

Chapters 6 and 7 look at the work of trial courts. Chapter 6 deals with criminal cases, focusing on the most important stages in the criminal process: decisions to prosecute suspects, plea bargaining, trials, and sentencing decisions. The chapter examines two major types of reform proposals, those designed to limit plea bargaining and to reduce judges' discretion in sentencing. Chapter 7 examines civil cases, focusing on decisions to initiate cases, the processing of cases in court, and patterns of outcomes in cases. One of the questions considered is the accuracy of the common image that Americans are quite eager, and increasingly eager, to take their grievances to the courts.

Chapters 8 and 9 deal with appellate courts. Chapter 8 examines the processes that occur in appellate courts, including choices to appeal unfavorable decisions, screening of cases by the courts themselves, and the process of reaching decisions. In its discussion of decision making, the chapter focuses on the question of why Supreme Court justices and other appellate judges make the choices they do. Chapter 9 examines appellate courts as policy makers. It discusses the policies made by appellate courts, including the "judicial activism" that is a matter of considerable debate. It then explores the ultimate impact of those policies on American society.

Acknowledgments

This fourth edition continues to reflect the help that a long list of people provided in my writing of the previous editions. I would like to thank those who assisted in this revision of the book. First of all, several scholars helped me to improve the book by suggesting changes from the third edition: Beth Henschen, Eastern Michigan University; Henry Glick, Florida State University; Edward N. Beiser, Brown University; and Mary Lee Luskin, Indiana University. In addition, a number of people assisted in my gathering of new information for this edition. Especially helpful were Sheldon Goldman, Elliot Slotnick, and—as always—my parents, Irving Baum and Ruth Klein Baum. In creating this edition, I benefitted even more than usual from the help of the people at Houghton Mifflin. For that help, I am pleased to thank Lily Eng, Melissa Mashburn, Mary Anne Stewart, Susan Westendorf, and Julie Lane.

L. B.

AMERICAN COURTS

1

An Overview of the Courts

January 1997 was an ordinary month in the American courts. There were no landmark decisions by the Supreme Court, no eagerly awaited verdicts in criminal trials. And yet the courts did some important things:

- A North Carolina jury awarded $5.5 million in punitive damages to the Food Lion grocery chain, which had sued the ABC television network and other defendants for deceptive methods in investigating the chain's practices.[1]
- The California Supreme Court ruled that an employer who wrote a letter of recommendation for a former employee could be held liable for failing to disclose charges and complaints of wrongdoing if the employee later engaged in related wrongdoing in a new job.[2]
- A federal district judge in New York ruled that protesters at an abortion clinic could not be held in contempt for violating a court order limiting their activities if their actions were based on "a sincere religious belief." In doing so, he limited the impact of a 1994 federal law intended to deal with obstruction of abortion clinics.[3]
- Another New York district judge ruled that a 1996 federal law prohibiting the sale of sexually explicit materials on military bases violated the First Amendment.[4]
- The Supreme Court held that someone who was convicted of a criminal offense in federal court could have a sentence increased for committing an additional offense, even though a jury had acquitted the defendant on that additional offense.[5]
- And the various state and federal trial courts disposed of more than 2 million cases through trials, negotiated settlements, and other means.[6]

All this activity makes the courts important institutions. And courts receive the kind of attention their importance merits. Newspapers and television news programs give substantial coverage to major events involving the courts. In the past few years, there has been a seemingly endless flow of television series and movies about courts and the people who work in them—as well as Court TV, a cable network established in 1991. Short of wars and other crises, few events in American history have been the subject of so much interest for so long as the trials of O.J. Simpson for the murders of Nicole Brown Simpson and Ronald Goldman. The prominence of American courts is symbolized by the television networks' splitting of their screens in February 1997 to show both President Clinton's State of the Union address and the verdict in the Simpson civil case.

Still, American courts are not very well understood. One reason is that the mass media often present incomplete and even inaccurate pictures of lawyers, judges, and cases. But the most fundamental source of this problem is that the range and complexity of the courts and their work make them very difficult to fathom. As a result, confusion about courts is widespread—not only among the general public but among political leaders as well.

This book is an effort to help in understanding courts in the United States. It has three related goals: to lay out a clear description of courts and their activities; to suggest explanations of these activities and of the behavior of people who work in the courts; and to offer ways of evaluating the work of courts.

In this introductory chapter, I provide an overview of the courts, outlining some ways of thinking about courts that may help in understanding them. Starting with the relationship between courts and law, the discussion then moves on to examine courts as institutions and their roles in government and society. The chapter also discusses the perspectives from which court processes and outcomes can be explained and the task of evaluating courts. Many of the topics discussed in this chapter will be examined more closely in the chapters that follow; the brief discussions in this chapter are intended to provide some background with which to begin.

COURTS AND LAW

Courts deal with law. The concept of law is complex, but it can be defined simply— adapting Herbert Jacob's formulation—as authoritative rules made by government.[7] The rules are authoritative in the sense that they are intended to bind government itself, people and institutions outside government, or both. The job of courts is to interpret law; in doing so, courts also make law.

Sources of Law

As illustrated by Exhibit 1.1, law comes from many places in government. The highest form of law is *constitutions*. The federal and state constitutions establish basic rules about the powers of government and the procedures by which government is to operate. State constitutions also contain a great many rules about the substance of government policy that one might not expect to find in a constitution. The Kentucky Constitution, for instance, includes a provision dealing with intersections of tracks belonging to different railroad companies.[8]

Whatever their subject matter, the legal rules in a constitution are the highest law for that level of government. State constitutions are superior to any other state laws. The federal constitution is superior both to other federal laws and to state laws— including state constitutions.

Second in the hierarchy are *statutes,* laws enacted by legislatures. (Laws passed by local legislative bodies are usually called *ordinances.*) Legislatures are free to enact statutes of any type, so long as their action is consistent with the relevant

Constitution

"No State shall . . . deny to any person within its jurisdiction the equal protection of the laws."

U.S. Constitution, Amendment XIV, Section 1

Statute

"It shall be an unlawful employment practice for an employer—

(1) to fail or refuse to hire or to discharge any individual, or otherwise to discriminate against any individual with respect to his compensation, terms, conditions, or privileges of employment, because of such individual's race, color, religion, sex, or national origin. . . ."

United States Code, Title 42, sec. 2000e-2 (a) (1994) (Title VII of the Civil Rights Act of 1964)

Regulation

"A recipient [of federal money] may administer or assist in the administration of scholarships, fellowships, or other forms of financial assistance established pursuant to domestic or foreign wills, trusts, bequests, or similar legal instruments or by acts of a foreign government which requires that awards be made to members of a particular sex specific therein; *Provided,* That the overall effect of the award of such sex-restricted scholarships, fellowships, and other forms of financial assistance does not discrminate on the basis of sex."

Code of Federal Regulations, Title 34, sec. 106.37 (1)(b)(1) (1996) (regulations for Title IX of the Education Amendments of 1972)

Executive Order

"Except in contracts exempted in accordance with Section 204 of this Order, all Government contracting agencies shall include in every Government contract hereafter entered into the following provisions:

'During the performance of this contract, the contractor agrees as follows:

'(1) The contractor will not discriminate against any employee or applicant for employment because of race, color, religion, sex, or national origin. . .' "

Executive Order 11246, sec. 202 (issued Sept. 24, 1965), as amended by Executive Order 11375 (issued Oct. 13, 1967)

Court Decision

"Yuri Veprinsky filed a charge with the Equal Employment Opportunity Commission in 1991 alleging that Fluor Daniel had discharged him from its employ on the basis of his national origin and religion, in violation of Title VII of the Civil Rights Act of 1964. He subsequently alleged in this lawsuit that Fluor Daniel had retaliated against him in several ways for filing the charge. The district court granted summary judgment in favor of Fluor Daniel on two of the retaliation claims. . . , relying in part upon our perceived holding in *Reed v. Shepard* . . . that post-termination incidents of retaliation are not actionable under Title VII . . . . Today we clarify our decision in *Reed* and hold that post-termination acts of retaliation that adversely affect the plaintiff's employment opportunities or are otherwise related to employment are cognizable under Title VII."

Decision of U.S. Court of Appeals for the 7th Circuit in *Veprinsky v. Fluor Daniel, Inc.,* 87 F.3d 881 (1996), at 882.

Exhibit 1.1   Examples of Language in Various Forms of Federal Laws Dealing with Discrimination

constitutional rules. While constitutions focus primarily on government, statutes generally are directed at society as a whole. Among their other purposes, statutes may prohibit certain kinds of conduct, such as damage to the environment, or provide benefits, such as Medicare.

Statutes typically are written in broad terms—in effect, outlining the law. An administrative agency that is responsible for carrying out a statute fills in the outline by adopting more detailed legal rules, called *rules* or *regulations.* In the federal minimum wage statute, the provisions for employees who receive tips take up about twenty lines. The regulations that interpret those provisions require more than three double-column pages.[9] Regulations stand below statutes in the hierarchy of law, in that they must be consistent with the statutes that they interpret.

Occupying multiple positions in the hierarchy are *executive orders,* laws made by chief executives such as presidents and governors. Some executive orders are based on statutes, so they are similar to administrative regulations. Other executive orders are based on the powers of the chief executive derived from the federal or state constitution, so they are similar to statutes.

Court decisions interpret all these forms of law. They also enforce the hierarchy of laws—most dramatically, when they determine whether a statute is "unconstitutional" because it conflicts with a relevant constitutional provision. In either instance, as noted earlier, they make law themselves. This function is particularly clear when courts write and publish opinions laying out the legal rules—often, new rules—on which their interpretations are based.

In some fields of law, such as contract and tort (which concerns primarily personal injuries), English and American courts first developed rules of law on their own. Even today, much of the law in those fields is contained in court decisions that were established independent of constitutions and statutes. Such independent, judge-made law is sometimes referred to as the *common law,* though the term has other meanings as well.

Courts make the ultimate judgments about the meaning of the specific laws they interpret. Those judgments can be overridden only by rewriting the law in question— that is, by amending the state or federal constitution or by enacting a new statute. Rulings about the common law can also be overridden through statutes. To the extent that the other branches of government do undertake such overrides, courts do not have the final word on the law.

Categories of Law

The law established by government policymakers ranges widely in its subject matter. Several distinctions can be made among categories of law, and a few are particularly important for an understanding of courts.

One distinction is between *public* and *private* law. Public law has been defined in different ways, but basically it involves the government acting as government—as opposed to other roles, such as property owner. Public law includes such matters as taxation, regulation of business practices, public welfare programs, foreign policy, and criminal justice. Law that does not involve government as government is private. Some common kinds of private law cases are those concerning disputes over personal injuries and provisions of contracts.

Another distinction is between *criminal* and *civil* law. Criminal law involves the prohibition of certain conduct and the threat of punishment for the prohibited conduct. Criminal cases are those in which individuals, or sometimes corporations, are prosecuted by government for alleged violations of criminal laws. Everything else is civil (though civil law sometimes has a narrower meaning). Much of the civil law also places prohibitions on conduct, but here the consequences of a violation ordinarily do not involve punishment as such. Most often, violators are required to compensate those who suffered losses as a result of the prohibited conduct. The same situation may bring both criminal and civil law into play. An alleged homicide, for instance, may lead to both a criminal prosecution by the state and a civil lawsuit for damages by the heirs of the victim. This, of course, is what happened after the murders of Nicole Brown Simpson and Ronald Goldman in Los Angeles.

Within these broad categories, law is often subdivided further. Criminal statutes deal with *felonies,* the more serious offenses, and with *misdemeanors.* Civil law covers a variety of fields, such as *contracts, property,* and *domestic relations.* As Chapter 3 shows, categories of law in practice are defined largely by the ways in which lawyers specialize in their work.

UNDERSTANDING COURTS
AS INSTITUTIONS

The judicial branch of government is composed of trial and appellate courts in both the federal system and the fifty state systems—altogether, thousands of courts. As institutions, these courts share some important traits. Most fundamentally, all courts interpret and apply the law in individual cases. To take another example, judges and lawyers play the central parts in nearly every court. Because of these shared traits and because courts are all in the judicial branch, people usually think of courts as a distinct set of institutions.

Yet this view of courts obscures two important realities: courts differ from each other in fundamental ways, and they have similarities with institutions other than courts. Both of these realities require some elaboration.

Differences among courts can be illustrated by comparing the U.S. Supreme Court with a municipal court, which exists in many states as a trial court for cases with relatively small stakes. This comparison highlights some important ways in which courts differ:

1. The municipal court is a *trial court,* while the Supreme Court is an *appellate court.* Cases are heard first in trial courts. When cases go to trial, the emphasis is usually on ascertaining facts, chiefly through the testimony of witnesses. Appellate courts review lower court decisions. They hear arguments that deal primarily with the application of the law to the facts that have already been ascertained at trial. A single judge presides in a trial court, and either the judge or a jury renders a decision. In appellate courts, cases are heard and decided by a group of judges. (Members of the Supreme Court and of state supreme courts are usually called justices rather than judges.)

2. Public proceedings in the two courts look quite different. Municipal court sessions typically involve action on large numbers of cases, which are often handled informally and speedily. Someone who walks into a courtroom probably will find it difficult to follow the action, and the overall impression is likely to be one of chaos. In contrast, public proceedings in the Supreme Court are conducted with considerable formality in a rather majestic setting. To the observer, the difference between the Supreme Court and a municipal court may seem like the difference between a well-staged show and a three-ring circus.

3. To continue the metaphor, the casts of characters in the two courts are also different. Lawyers who appear before the Supreme Court are likely to work in the most prestigious segments of the legal profession, while lawyers from those segments of the profession seldom appear in municipal courts. Similarly, most Supreme Court justices come from legal and political elite groups, but judges typically reach municipal courts from lower levels of the legal and political systems.

4. The two courts hear different kinds of cases. Municipal courts handle criminal and civil cases with relatively small stakes under state statutes and local ordinances. Common types of municipal court cases include small claims and misdemeanor criminal offenses (among them, traffic and parking violations, which are generally classified as misdemeanors in most states). The Supreme Court hears cases raising broad legal issues under the U.S. Constitution and federal statutes. Most of these cases concern civil liberties and government regulation of the economy. Nearly all cases heard by the Supreme Court were originally decided by some trial court, and occasionally a case that began in a municipal court is eventually decided by the Supreme Court. Even in such a case, however, the central issues generally change so much—from narrow factual questions to broad questions of legal interpretation—that the Supreme Court in effect decides a different case from the one that was heard in municipal court.

Taken together, these characteristics show basic distinctions between municipal courts and the Supreme Court. The more general lesson should be clear: courts do not constitute a homogeneous set of institutions.

A second and related point is that courts share attributes with institutions other than courts. Indeed, scholars such as Martin Shapiro have noted that a great many nonjudicial institutions are similar to courts in their functions, their operation, or both.[10] Some of these institutions are easy to identify because they look like courts and are labeled as such. The executive branch of government contains administrative tribunals, which hear appeals from decisions of agencies such as the Social Security Administration. These bodies resemble courts in the judiciary. The federal Court of International Trade, which originated as an administrative tribunal, changed relatively little when it moved from the executive branch to the judicial branch.

The private sector also contains institutions that resemble courts, many of which were set up as alternatives to courts in the judicial branch. An example is arbitration, in which two parties present their cases to an arbitrator for a decision. Arbitration has become increasingly common as a mechanism to resolve legal disputes such as those that arise between businesses. Some religious and ethnic groups use their own courts to resolve disagreements within their communities.

More broadly, some institutions that do not look or act like courts share important attributes with them. Indeed, both the Supreme Court and municipal courts have similarities with seemingly very different institutions in other branches of government. The Supreme Court is similar to Congress in many respects. Both set their agendas by selecting issues for consideration from a much larger body of requests. Both reach decisions through a series of group processes. Each establishes general policies on national issues, policies that must be put into effect by other people and institutions.

For their part, municipal courts have much in common with bureaucratic agencies that apply the law by processing large numbers of similar cases. Political scientist Michael Lipsky has made a more specific analogy, comparing trial courts with other "street-level bureaucracies" that deal directly with the public, such as police and welfare departments.[11] Like police officers and welfare workers, trial judges hold a great deal of power over the people with whom they interact and exercise considerable discretion in using this power. For instance, trial judges usually have a wide range of options and few clear standards in setting bail for criminal defendants. According to Lipsky, the behavior of each street-level bureaucracy is shaped by its limited resources and by official goals that are often difficult to achieve. In addition, each bureaucracy develops routines that allow the rapid processing of cases.

Thus it can be misleading to think of courts as a homogeneous and unique category of institutions. The differences among courts and their similarities to other institutions are noted throughout the book.

THE ROLES OF COURTS: FUNCTIONS AND IMPACT

A central goal of this book is to discern the roles that courts play in American government and society. In the process, two related questions are explored: what do courts do, and what impact do they have? In the chapters that follow, these questions are addressed in specific contexts; here I discuss them in more general terms.

The Functions of Courts

Courts engage in a wide variety of activities. These activities can best be understood in terms of their functions within government and society. The work of courts in the United States could be linked to a great many functions, but a few of these stand out as particularly important.

The first is *dispute resolution*. Civil cases explicitly involve disputes between at least one plaintiff (the party that brings the case) and defendant (the party against whom the case is brought). A great many criminal cases also arise from disputes between a complainant and the defendant. (A complainant is someone who calls a possible criminal case to the attention of the police or the prosecutor.) Thus courts provide a forum for the ventilation and resolution of disputes. In the great majority of civil cases that are filed in court, the parties themselves agree on a settlement prior to trial. Similarly, in most criminal cases, the defendant pleads guilty and thus settles at least one important aspect of the dispute. In other cases, of course, courts themselves determine how disputes are resolved by reaching decisions.

By establishing courts as a forum for dispute resolution, the government provides an important service for its residents. In this sense, courts are similar to other public institutions, such as health and fire departments. At the same time, the government is also serving its own goals. From the government's perspective, it is generally desirable to control and channel conflicts in a society and to help set the terms on which conflicts are resolved.[12]

This last point suggests a second function, *behavior modification.* Courts reward certain kinds of behavior and penalize others, with the goal of encouraging what is rewarded and discouraging what is penalized. This function is clearest on the criminal side of the law. Courts are part of a system for enforcement of the criminal laws, a system designed to reduce the incidence of certain activities by threatening serious penalties for those activities.

Similar purposes underlie the civil side of the law. Here the government allows lawsuits for damages against people who engage in certain types of behavior, hoping thereby to discourage such behavior. A negligent driver may face a suit brought by someone who has suffered an injury through the driver's actions. Or a business that violates the terms of a contract may be sued by the other party to the contract. In this sense, private individuals or groups who bring civil cases are acting unintentionally as agents of government.

The government sometimes goes to considerable lengths to link its behavior modification goals with the self-interest of potential litigants. To help deter false monetary claims against the federal government, Congress has given people an incentive to expose such claims: individuals can bring lawsuits in the name of government against people who allegedly have made false claims and recover a portion of the proceeds of the case.[13] To take a different kind of example, Congress encourages enforcement of drug laws by allowing law enforcement agencies to seize and retain assets such as homes and cars that are connected with drug offenses.[14]

A third function of courts, one tied to the first two, is the *allocation of gains and losses.* In criminal cases, courts impose penalties on defendants in the form of monetary fines, imprisonment, and even death sentences. In civil cases, courts often order transfers of money from one party to another. They also determine such matters as the custody of children and the control of corporations. In this process, civil courts frequently take something from one party and give it to another.

This allocation function is quite significant for its direct effects on litigants: each year millions of people gain or lose through their involvement in court cases. Beyond the individual level, courts can be thought of as allocating gains and losses between entire groups in American society, such as creditors and debtors in contract cases, or insurance companies and injured people in accident cases. In doing so, courts may benefit some groups systematically at the expense of others.

A fourth function of courts, *policymaking,* is implicit in the first three. Policymaking can have many different definitions; here the meaning is the creation and application of authoritative rules. Of course, the other branches of government are also heavily engaged in this function.

The distinction between creating new legal rules and applying existing rules seems clear in itself, and it helps to distinguish different kinds of policymaking in the courts. A state supreme court may create a new rule for liability in accidents caused by defective products; a trial jury then may apply that rule in determining whether an individual can recover damages for an injury from the manufacturer of a product.

In practice, however, the distinction between creating and applying legal rules is not always a sharp one.[15] In announcing a seemingly new rule, a court sometimes says that it is simply refining or clarifying the rules that already exist, and Supreme Court justices sometimes have heated disagreements in their opinions about whether the Court has changed the law. For their part, trial judges or jurors who seem to be applying legal rules to individual cases in a routine way may implicitly be creating new rules with their decisions. A judge who regularly imposes the maximum allowable sentence on individuals who are convicted of burglary is thereby helping to determine the law of burglary in practice.

Of the four functions just described, the first three are dominated by trial courts. This is because the great majority of court cases are terminated at the trial level— through a settlement, through a choice by the initiating party not to pursue the case, or through the acceptance of the court decision by all the parties. Thus, most of what courts do in resolving disputes, modifying behavior, and allocating gains and losses is done by trial courts. Appellate courts hear a small proportion of all cases, so they play a more limited part in performing these functions directly. Because of their roles in policymaking, however, appellate courts are institutions of considerable significance.

The Impact of Courts

Just how important *are* the courts for American society? Observers have expressed a wide range of views on this question. Some scholars and commentators write about government policymaking without paying much attention to courts, as if their activities were insignificant. In contrast, others have depicted the courts as a dominant force. According to former federal judge and Supreme Court nominee Robert Bork, "It is arguable that the American judiciary . . . is the single most powerful force shaping our culture. There are other claimants to the title, to be sure, but the judges' preeminence seems clear."[16] The difference between these two views suggests how difficult it is to pinpoint the courts' importance. Still, their impact can be explored.

At the outset, it is useful to distinguish between trial courts and appellate courts, which are important in somewhat different ways. Trial courts gain their impact chiefly through the large numbers of decisions that they make in individual cases. Each year millions of individuals are subject to court action involving such matters as criminal offenses, divorces, auto accidents, and traffic and parking violations. Some kinds of decisions, such as those about child custody or imprisonment, have an enormous impact on people's lives. And what courts do in these cases affects still more people—those who resolve matters out of court—because predictions of what a court would decide help to determine the bargaining positions of people who negotiate about a dispute.

Appellate courts exert influence primarily through the broad impact of the legal rules they proclaim. This impact follows from the doctrine that a court's interpretation of the law is binding on courts below it in the judicial hierarchy. Thus a state supreme court ruling on the obligations of landlords to tenants can affect decisions on landlord-tenant relationships in every court in the state. A ruling by the U.S. Supreme Court on the definition of obscenity affects every state or federal judge who hears an obscenity case. And because appellate courts influence what courts below them do, they also affect what happens outside of court. A Supreme Court decision on obscenity can help determine the language that legislatures put into obscenity laws, the ways that police departments enforce them, and even the content of published material.

Important as these effects are, they should not be exaggerated. For one thing, courts are only one part of the larger set of institutions that make government policy in an area. In deciding a criminal case, for instance, a trial court is applying rules that the legislature established. The case came to court because of decisions by police officers and prosecutors. How much time a person spends in prison may be determined not only by the court's sentencing decision but also by a parole board's decision whether to release the convict.

The impact of appellate court decisions depends heavily on the actions of other policymakers. A Supreme Court decision on censorship of school newspapers or on the questioning of suspects by the police must be interpreted and applied by lower courts. Ultimately, administrative officials—such as school principals and police officers—determine the effect of such a decision in practice. And Congress or a state legislature might limit the impact of a decision or even overturn it altogether.

Furthermore, even though their concerns are broad, courts do not play a major part in all the areas of government activity. Most notably, foreign policy features little significant judicial activity. Courts have been a minor participant in the shaping of American trade policy, and they have had almost no effect on most international conflicts in which the United States has been involved.

A second limitation on the impact of courts applies to government in general. Government is only one of many forces that shape society, and it is not necessarily the most powerful. Important nongovernmental forces—including the family, the mass media, and the economy—all help determine the impact of court decisions on conditions such as race relations and criminal activity. Supreme Court justice Clarence Thomas has argued that the "rights revolution," the judicial creation and expansion of individual rights since the 1960s, has eroded "the ideal of personal responsibility" and thus has helped to foster criminal behavior.[17] Whether or not Justice Thomas is correct in his judgment, it seems unlikely that the courts' impact on criminal behavior could be as strong as the effects of family structure and economic conditions, to take two examples of other forces.

I emphasize limitations on the impact of courts because those limitations are sometimes given insufficient attention. But we should not lose sight of the impact that courts do have. Judicial activities directly affect a high proportion of people in the United States and affect many of them quite significantly. Court decisions also have important effects on the nation as a whole. Thus courts certainly merit the attention that we give them, and one cannot understand American government and society without understanding the judiciary.

EXPLAINING COURT PROCESSES AND OUTCOMES

One of the aims of this book is to explain both the processes by which courts operate and the outcomes of cases that are brought to court. Thus I will discuss explanations for such matters as the prevalence of plea bargaining in criminal cases, the outcomes of automobile accident cases, and disagreements among judges in appellate court decisions. These matters seldom have simple explanations, and our ability to explain them is often limited by insufficient information.

It is difficult to explain what courts do in general terms because different aspects of their work are best explained in different ways. But we can begin by thinking about general perspectives from which the processes and outcomes that take place in court might be understood. Most of these explanations fit within three broad categories, which can be called the legal, the environmental, and the personal.

The Legal Perspective

Courts work within a legal framework. Decisions by judges and juries involve the application of legal rules to the facts of specific cases. These rules are found in the federal and state constitutions, in the statutes adopted by legislatures, and in past court decisions. Court procedures are also governed by legal rules.

Judges, lawyers, and observers of courts disagree sharply about the importance of this legal framework in shaping what the courts do. Some people, including many judges, argue that courts do little more than follow the law. At the other extreme, some critics argue that the law is primarily a rationalization for judges and other people in the court system. According to this view, judges actually act on other bases, such as their attitudes about the policy issues involved in the cases they decide. The reality, I think, is somewhere between these two views.

The law is important in courts chiefly because judges and lawyers believe that they are in the business of applying the law. To a degree, this belief is embedded in American culture, with its strong emphasis on the rule of law. And lawyers undergo intensive law school training in legal reasoning, training that is reinforced by their later experience in the legal system.

For these reasons, courts generally are pervaded by an atmosphere in which people speak and think in terms of legal principles. As a result, the law channels and constrains activity in courts. Lawyers seek to win cases by showing that their clients' positions are consistent with the best interpretation of the law. In turn, judges seldom reach decisions that cannot be justified as interpretations of the applicable body of law, and their reasoning reflects their training in the law. Thus a New Jersey court ruled in 1994 that if a state law defined fish as "any marine . . . animal or plant," courts were obliged to follow that definition—even if we would not generally think of seaweed, for instance, as a fish.[18] In the same year, a California judge held that an apartment resident was required to give the landlord the thirty days' notice of moving that was specified in the lease even though the resident's death made it impossible for him to do so.[19]

The impact of the law is most apparent when it seems to overcome other considerations that move judges toward a different decision. In 1992, for instance, an Alaska court reluctantly ruled that a ship's captain could not be prosecuted for actions resulting in a massive oil spill in 1989.

> The unparalleled environmental devastation wrought by the grounding of the Exxon Valdez is hardly lost upon this court. But, while we may feel sorely tempted, as individuals, to recast the law in a mold better suited to our personal sense of justice, we are bound, as judges, to resist this temptation.[20]

Yet the law is an incomplete explanation of what courts do, for two fundamental reasons. First, the law frequently leaves considerable discretion to judges and juries. In some instances, legislatures create this discretion deliberately. State legislatures, for example, often give judges a wide range of alternative sentences to impose for a particular criminal offense in the belief that sentences need to be fitted to the characteristics of individual cases and offenders. Thus, in Nebraska, a judge can mete out a prison sentence that ranges anywhere from one to fifty years for first-degree arson or assault on a police officer.[21]

More often, discretion results from ambiguities in the law and its application. Jurors are asked to apply the law to the facts of a particular case, but if there are two or more plausible readings of the facts, conscientious jurors may reach different conclusions. Similarly, many provisions of constitutions and statutes contain vague language, such as "due process of law," which requires judges to choose among credible alternative interpretations. Even seemingly clear language is often difficult to apply to a specific situation, as the case in Exhibit 1.2 shows.

The other reason that the law fails to explain court activities fully is that the motivations of people in the courts go beyond simply trying to follow the law. Undoubtedly, most judges strongly believe that they *should* follow the law in deciding cases and supervising court proceedings. But judges also hold preferences about public policy issues and feel external pressures to handle cases in certain ways. These

EXHIBIT 1.2   The Virginia Supreme Court Disagrees over Application of a Statute

A police officer in Falls Church, Virginia, found a man in a parking lot, sleeping behind the steering wheel of his car, with the engine off but the key in the ignition. The officer concluded that the man was intoxicated, and the man was convicted of drunk driving under a statutory provision that makes it "unlawful for any person to drive or operate any motor vehicle . . . while such person is under the influence of any . . . self-administered intoxicant." Another statute defines a vehicle "operator" or "driver" as anyone who "drives or is in actual physical control of a motor vehicle upon a highway."

The defendant argued that, under the circumstances, he was not actually "driving" or "operating" the car and thus could not be convicted under the statute; ultimately, the state supreme court ruled on the issue. A four-member majority concluded that "because the presence of the key in the ignition switch in the off position did not engage the mechanical or electrical equipment of" the defendant's car, he did not "drive or operate" the car under the meaning of those terms in the statutes. But three judges dissented vehemently, arguing that "when a drunk is sitting in the driver's seat of a parked, operable motor vehicle, and he is alone and has inserted the key in the ignition switch, he is in 'actual physical control' of the vehicle" and thus falls under the statute. Thus, by a 4–3 vote, the conviction was overturned.

Source: Stevenson v. City of Falls Church, 416 S.E.2d 435 (Va. 1992).

factors affect the behavior of judges, even of judges who wish only to apply legal rules faithfully. Federal judge Patricia Wald pointed out some of these nonlegal factors:

> Despite much protestation to the contrary, a judge's origins and politics will surely influence his or her judicial opinions. Judges' minds are not compartmentalized: their law-declaring functions cannot be performed by some insulated, apolitical internal mechanism. However subtly or unconsciously, the judge's political orientation *will* affect decisionmaking.[22]

The limitations of the law as an explanation of court behavior are highlighted by disagreements among judges and among jurors. On the Supreme Court, whose nine members apply the same body of law to the same case, only a minority of decisions are unanimous—43 percent in the 1995–1996 term.[23] And there are so many conflicting interpretations of the law by federal courts that the Supreme Court has time to resolve only a portion of them. In one conflict that the Court did resolve in 1992, about forty federal district courts had addressed the issue of whether the Red Cross could require that any case brought against it in state court be moved to federal court, with only a small majority on one side of the issue; the Supreme Court itself decided the issue by a 5–4 vote.[24] Such disagreements reflect both the ambiguity of the law and the influence of other motivations on those who decide cases.

It is worth reiterating that legal rules offer a good guide to much of what courts do. Without a legal perspective, it is impossible to understand what happens in courts, and the law is often the best starting point for an explanation of court behavior. But it is only a starting point, and other perspectives must be considered in order to gain a more comprehensive understanding of courts.

The Personal Perspective

In its strongest form, the legal perspective assumes that people who make decisions in courts are motivated only by a commitment to the law. In contrast, what might be called the personal perspective allows for a broader range of motivations that can influence behavior. Judges, for instance, may act on the basis of their own values, self-interest, or personal needs. Thus the processes that occur in courts and the outcomes of cases can be seen in terms of the motivations of people who are involved in them.

A focus on individuals has proved very useful in the study of Supreme Court decision making. Many scholars view the Court's decisions primarily as reflections of one motivational factor, the justices' policy preferences. According to this view, divisions on the Court can be explained by differences in values, and the Court's collective position results from the sum of the nine justices' conceptions of good policy.

On the Supreme Court, as well as on other courts, judges' personal policy preferences and court policies are often described as either *liberal* or *conservative*. These labels require some discussion. On most issues that courts decide, the competing positions generally are given one label or the other; Exhibit 1.3 summarizes what are usually considered to be the liberal and conservative positions on some major judicial issues. One common thread binding together positions on many different issues is that the liberal position on most issues is the one more favorable to equality rather than to competing values such as the autonomy of businesses. In

Issue Area	Liberal Position	Conservative Position
Criminal cases	Relatively sympathetic toward defendants and their procedural rights	Gives greater emphasis to effectiveness of criminal jutice system in fighting crime
Personal liberties	More supportive of liberties such as freedom of speech and right to privacy	More supportive of values that may conflict with these liberties, such as public order and national security
Disadvantaged groups	More strongly supports expanded rights and improved status for groups such as African-Americans, women, and the poor	Gives relatively great weight to the costs of these expansions and improvements, such as the monetary costs of public welfare
Regulation of business	More favorable to government regulation on behalf of such goals as protection of the environment	More protective of the autonomy of businesses
Businesses vs. individuals	In economic conflicts, such as disputes between insurance companies and injured drivers, more likely to support the individual	Less likely to support the individual; more favorable to business

Note: Positions of liberals and conservatives should be read in relation to each other; for instance, liberals are more likely to support individuals in disputes with businesses than are conservatives.

EXHIBIT 1.3   Liberal and Conservative Positions on Some Common Judicial Issues

part because of this common thread, people tend to be consistent in their ideological positions. In other words, a judge with liberal views on one issue is likely to have liberal views on most other issues. For this reason, the terms *liberal* and *conservative* are useful in summarizing both a judge's general views and the direction of a court's policies.

A different motivation, self-interest, is highlighted by the *plea bargaining* that takes place in criminal courts. In plea bargaining, lawyers, defendants, and judges resolve cases through negotiation rather than through trials. Plea bargaining is prevalent chiefly because it offers important advantages to each group. Among other benefits, prosecutors avoid the risk of an acquittal at trial, defendants and their attorneys limit the severity of the sentence, and judges save the time that trials would require. Efforts to eliminate plea bargaining tend to fail because of this mutual self-interest in maintaining it.

An implication of the personal perspective is that courts should be understood as institutions with their own dynamics. We can think of the set of people who participate in a particular court as an organization or a work group.[25] All the participants bring their motivations to the work group, and court processes and case outcomes emerge from the interaction of these motivations. One result is that legal mandates can be distorted. Legislatures may establish a mandatory minimum sentence for an offense, only to discover that judges and prosecutors who disagree with such a requirement have found ways to avoid imposing it.

Another implication is that it often makes considerable difference who participates in the courts generally and in particular cases. The general recognition of this reality is reflected in the attention focused on appointments to the Supreme Court. People interested in the Court understand that even a single new justice can shift the Court's ideological balance and thus its policies. This is the primary reason that presidential nominees to the Court receive so much scrutiny in the Senate. Similarly, in courts where judges are chosen randomly to hear particular cases, the luck of the draw can produce celebration on one side and dismay on the other. In 1996, three judges on a federal court of appeals were chosen to hear an appeal in a major lawsuit against tobacco companies. The fact that all three were conservatives was treated as a major victory for the companies, even though the judges had decided nothing yet.[26]

It is not just ideology that makes individuals important in the courts. Among trial judges, for instance, there are substantial differences in such matters as the skills that judges bring to legal rulings and the extent of their intervention into the proceedings in jury trials. Liberal or conservative, some judges seek to minimize their involvement in the making of public policy, while others eagerly look for opportunities to do so.

The internal focus that underlines the importance of individuals also constitutes a limitation on the personal perspective; a narrow concentration on people within the courts may cause observers to lose sight of the broad forces that shape what courts do. A focus on individuals helps a great deal in understanding why a Supreme Court justice has selected the more liberal position of the two that are debated in a particular case. It is less useful in identifying a position that no justice has considered because it cannot be reconciled with federal law or because it lacks sufficient support outside the Court. Today, for instance, the Supreme Court could hardly rule that the Constitution prohibits federal minimum wage laws; that position and its broader implications are unacceptable to too many people in and out of government. Nor does the focus on individuals point to the social forces and political currents that help produce a liberal or a conservative Court in any given period. Thus the personal perspective must be supplemented with a broader perspective on court behavior.

The Environmental Perspective

The environmental perspective views courts in relation to the government and society of which they are a part, looking to the ways in which courts are affected by external forces.

Certainly courts are influenced by their environments in a number of ways. The values and perceptions of lawyers and judges are shaped by their experiences in

American society. Other branches of government influence courts by writing laws, by providing resources for the judiciary, and by selecting judges and other court partici- pants. Interest groups sponsor significant cases and influence judges' perceptions of the issues in those cases. Similarly, the state of the economy and social trends help determine what kinds of cases reach court and how judges and jurors think about them.

From this perspective, it can be argued that courts tend to mirror their society. But what exactly do they mirror? To some degree, they reflect the pattern of social values and attitudes in the United States. One reason is that dominant attitudes are likely to exert at least subtle pressures on courts; another is that judges and other court participants are likely to share these attitudes. For both reasons, to take one example, widespread concern about illegal drugs in the past few years has had a con- siderable effect on the courts. Many judges impose longer prison terms in drug cases. The Supreme Court gives more weight to government success in attacking illegal drugs than to the individual liberties that sometimes conflict with those efforts.

Courts also tend to reflect the distribution of economic and political power. Those segments of society that have the most power are generally in the best position to influence what courts do. Most lawyers and judges come from higher-status back- grounds. Those with the greatest economic resources are the most capable of bring- ing cases to court and presenting them effectively, and they also hold disproportionate influence over the writing of statutes that courts apply. For these reasons, one might expect, for example, that courts would serve the interests of business corporations more diligently than the interests of low-income individuals.[27]

Courts also respond to more direct pressures from their environments. Elected judges want to retain public support, and that goal may move them to take popular positions in their decisions. Even judges who hold their positions for life may alter judicial policies that have incited outrage in the other branches of government. Today, in an era when the work of the courts receives close attention, such pressures are especially likely to arise. Thus, in 1996 a federal district judge in New York reversed himself after his exclusion of evidence in a drug case led to strong criticism from President Clinton, congressional leaders, and the press.[28]

Although environmental influences are powerful, their impact is limited by the relative autonomy of courts. Through such mechanisms as the life terms of federal judges and the norms that restrict direct lobbying of judges and juries, courts are par- tially insulated from external pressures. In addition, people who become judges have undergone training in which they are taught that they should withstand pressures in order to follow the legal rules that apply to cases. This insulation is reflected in some actions by judges. Many federal judges have ordered school busing for racial inte- gration despite the great unpopularity of this policy; their life terms enable them to take this position, which is much more dangerous for elected members of Congress. To use a somewhat different example, a trial judge who receives strong advice from the mass media to impose a heavy sentence on a notorious criminal may well bend to that pressure, but the judge is quite unlikely to impose a sentence more severe than the law authorizes.

Thus, courts reflect society imperfectly. Strong currents of thought and power in American society inevitably affect courts, but other influences and motives also help determine what happens in the courts.

General Implications

The discussion so far has pointed out several different perspectives—each with its strengths and weaknesses—from which one can explain the behavior of courts. It has also indicated that court processes and the results of court cases are shaped by a good many forces, so that few significant court phenomena can be explained in simple terms.

The examination of courts in this book reflects these lessons. I give primary emphasis to the personal perspective, and especially to the motives of judges and other people in the courts, but the book employs the other perspectives as well. External influences on court processes and on the outcomes of cases receive considerable attention. And I take into account the legal framework within which courts work, a framework that in itself reflects social thought and power in complex ways.

EVALUATING COURTS

American courts are constantly evaluated. Indeed, it is almost impossible to write about Supreme Court decisions or criminal court processes without assessing the performance of those courts. This book contains a good deal of evaluation, addressing such issues as the quality of judges and the effectiveness of trials in discovering the truth. But, more often than not, my evaluations are tentative rather than firm. This reflects my feeling that there are fundamental difficulties in reaching conclusive judgments about the courts.

One difficulty is that it is frequently unclear what criteria should be used for evaluation. Almost any significant aspect of court outputs or processes can be assessed on two or more different bases, and the mere choice of a particular criterion may predetermine whether an evaluation is positive or negative.

Perhaps the classic example of this difficulty involves the work of trial courts in criminal cases, work that has received considerable scrutiny and criticism during this century. Using a distinction made by Herbert Packer, we might evaluate criminal courts on the basis of either a *due process* model or a *crime control* model.[29] In the due process model, which some political liberals support, courts are judged primarily by their procedural fairness to defendants and their care in reaching appropriate decisions in cases. In the crime control model, more popular in society as a whole, courts are judged primarily by their efficiency and effectiveness in convicting and punishing criminals. Clearly, a court that looks good according to one model might look quite bad according to the other. This is one reason for the great disagreement about how well criminal courts actually work.

It is important, then, to be clear about one's criteria for evaluating courts and to recognize that alternative criteria might lead to quite different conclusions. People who disagree in their evaluations often are talking past each other because they have based their arguments on different premises.

Agreement on criteria does not end the difficulties of evaluation, for the application of these criteria to a particular situation also tends to be problematic. This is especially true when the criteria are broad or vague, as is often the case. We might agree, for instance, that the task of trial courts in adjudicating civil cases is to do justice. But, the concept of "justice" is complex, and its meaning and application to specific circumstances are matters of almost continuous debate. Businesses that come to court to collect debts from individuals are generally quite successful. Is that a just result? Beginning with one conception of justice in the context of American society, we may view the success of businesses as just, on the ground that courts are properly requiring people to pay their debts. Starting with a different conception, we may view this result as unjust, on the ground that it allows an advantaged segment of society to exploit those who are often economically vulnerable.

It is not much easier to evaluate a court according to how well it interprets the law. What is a good interpretation of the Constitution when the relevant constitutional language is vague and several conflicting methods of interpretation are available? Legal scholars generally write commentaries on Supreme Court decisions in the style of movie reviews, presenting one point of view and ignoring the possibility that there are other legitimate viewpoints. But commentaries on a decision, like reviews of a movie, often differ sharply in their conclusions. Such differences are inevitable, given the ambiguity of legal interpretation.

Often a lack of information increases the difficulty of evaluation. For example, people in the legal profession probably could reach at least moderate agreement about what constitutes competence in a trial lawyer. But there are so many trial lawyers across the country that no single observer could make a definitive judgment as to how competent trial lawyers actually are. Thus there has been a long-standing debate on this issue, one that is unlikely to be resolved.

Even more problematic is evaluation of court decisions on the basis of their intended impact. Many people feel that the primary goal of criminal sentencing should be to limit the future incidence of crime, and one long-standing purpose of court decisions in personal injury law is to minimize the frequency of accidents. But at this point we know too little to determine what kinds of sentences or personal injury doctrines will best achieve these goals. For this reason, some of the strong judgments that people make about the work of courts in such areas are open to question.

Despite all these difficulties, we should not be deterred from making tentative evaluations of courts; their work is too important not to be evaluated. In most areas, however, these evaluations must proceed with considerable caution and modesty. To offer a definitive assessment of court activities when both the appropriate criteria and their application are uncertain has little value.

This is also true of efforts to describe and explain court processes and the outcomes of court cases, for there is a great deal that we do not know about courts— including some things that many people think we know.[30] Caution is always appropriate in examining the courts. However, our knowledge is considerable, and it is growing rapidly. The remaining chapters of this book lay out what we do know about these institutions that play so central a part in American life.

NOTES

1. Howard Kurtz and Sue Anne Pressley, "Jury Finds Against ABC for $5.5 Million," *Washington Post,* January 23, 1997, A1.

2. *Randi W. v. Muroc Joint Unified School District,* 929 P.2d 582 (Calif. 1997). In citations of court decisions, the first number is the volume of the court reports in which the decision and accompanying opinions are found. The abbreviated designation of the court reports follows that number. The second number is the page on which the decision and opinions begin; "582, 584–85" would indicate that the decision began on page 582 and that relevant material is on pages 584–85. If a reporter covers multiple courts, it may include within the parentheses an abbreviation for the specific court issuing a decision. In this instance, "P.2d" stands for the second series of the *Pacific Reporter,* one of the regional reports of decisions by state courts. "Calif." indicates that the decision was made by the California Supreme Court. For decisions of the U.S. Supreme Court, the official reporter of decisions is the *United States Reports,* designated "U.S." For recent Supreme Court decisions, I cite "L. Ed. 2d." That abbreviation stands for the second series of the *Supreme Court Reports, Lawyers' Edition,* one of the unofficial reporters of Supreme Court decisions.

3. *United States v. Lynch,* 952 F. Supp. 167 (S.D.N.Y. 1997).

4. *General Media Communications, Inc. v. Perry,* 1997 U.S. Dist. LEXIS 447 (S.D.N.Y. 1997).

5. *United States v. Watts,* 136 L. Ed. 2d 554 (1997).

6. See Court Statistics Project, *State Court Caseload Statistics, 1994* (Williamsburg, Va.: National Center for State Courts, 1995), 138.

7. Herbert Jacob, *Law and Politics in the United States* (Boston: Little, Brown, 1986), 6–7.

8. *Kentucky Constitution,* sec. 216 (*Ky. Revised Statutes,* 1988 ed.).

9. 29 *United States Code,* sec. 203(m, t) (1988 ed.); 29 *Code of Federal Regulations,* secs. 531.50–.60 (1996 ed.).

10. See Martin Shapiro, *Courts: A Comparative and Political Analysis* (Chicago: University of Chicago Press, 1981), ch. 1.

11. Michael Lipsky, *Street-Level Bureaucracy: Dilemmas of the Individual in Public Services* (New York: Russell Sage Foundation, 1980).

12. Austin Sarat and Joel B. Grossman, "Courts and Conflict Resolution: Problems in the Mobilization of Adjudication," *American Political Science Review* 69 (December 1975), 1213–17.

13. 31 *United States Code,* sec. 3730 (1988 ed.).

14. 21 *United States Code,* sec. 881(e) (1994 ed.).

15. Lynn Mather, "The Fired Football Coach (Or, How Trial Courts Make Policy)," in *Contemplating Courts,* ed. Lee Epstein (Washington, D.C.: CQ Press, 1995), 173–175.

16. Robert H. Bork, *Slouching Toward Gomorrah: Modern Liberalism and American Decline* (New York: Regan Books, 1996), 96.

17. "Thomas Critiques the 'Rights Revolution'," *Legal Times,* May 23, 1994, 23–24.

18. "Judges: If It's in the Water, It's a Fish," *National Law Journal,* March 7, 1994, 51.

19. "Dead or Alive, Tenants Owe 30 Days Notice," *San Francisco Chronicle,* January 20, 1995, A24.

20. Andrew Blum, "Alaska Appeals Valdez Reversal," *National Law Journal,* December 14, 1992, 9.

21. *Revised Statutes of Nebraska,* ch. 28, secs. 105, 502, 929 (1995 ed.).

22. Patricia M. Wald, "Some Thoughts on Judging as Gleaned from One Hundred Years of the *Harvard Law Review* and Other Great Books," *Harvard Law Review* 100 (February 1987), 895.

23. "The Supreme Court, 1995 Term," *Harvard Law Review* 110 (November 1996), 369.

24. *American National Red Cross v. S.G.,* 505 U.S. 247 (1992) and *Petition for Writ of Certiorari* in the case, at 10–11.

25. The concept of work groups is presented in James Eisenstein and Herbert Jacob, *Felony Justice: An Organizational Analysis of Criminal Courts* (Boston: Little, Brown, 1977), ch. 2.

26. Glenn Collins, "Panel Is Named for Tobacco Class Action," *New York Times,* March 26, 1996, C2.

27. See Marc Galanter, "Why the 'Haves' Come Out Ahead: Speculations on the Limits of Social Change," *Law and Society Review* 9 (Fall 1974), 95–160.

28. Don Van Natta Jr., "Judge Assailed Over Drug Cases Issues Reversal and an Apology," *New York Times,* April 2, 1996, A1, A10.

29. Herbert L. Packer, *The Limits of the Criminal Sanction* (Stanford, Calif.: Stanford University Press, 1968), ch. 8.

30. See Marc Galanter, "Reading the Landscape of Disputes: What We Know and Don't Know (and Think We Know) About Our Allegedly Contentious and Litigious Society," *UCLA Law Review,* 31 (October 1983), 4–71; and Michael J. Saks, "Do We Really Know Anything About the Behavior of the Tort Litigation System—And Why Not?" *University of Pennsylvania Law Review* 140 (April 1992), 1147–1292.

2

Court Organization

The federal judicial system is divided into twelve circuits, each with a court of appeals. By any measure, the Ninth Circuit is the largest. It contains nine states and two territories, stretching from Alaska to Arizona and from Montana to Guam. It is allotted twenty-eight judges to handle the eight thousand cases filed each year.

In 1997, the Senate approved a bill that would split the Ninth Circuit in two.[1] Because of the circuit's size, the Senate's action might seem to be a simple, "nonpolitical" matter of judicial administration: cutting a very large circuit down to two circuits of more manageable size. Indeed, supporters of the bill emphasized what they saw as the administrative advantages of splitting the circuit.

But, if this were just an administrative matter, the pattern of votes in the Senate would be difficult to explain. The provision to split the circuit was approved by a 55–45 vote, with every Republican voting in favor and every Democrat in opposition. As in past years, the strongest advocates of circuit division were senators from the Pacific Northwest, while the California senators vehemently opposed it. And over the years, interest groups such as the Sierra Club have participated in the debate over circuit splitting. Why should a seemingly neutral proposal become the subject of battles between parties, regions, and interest groups?

The answer is that the proposal to split the Ninth Circuit is more than a technical matter of administration. For many years, the Ninth Circuit Court of Appeals has been the most ideologically liberal of all the courts of appeals. Conservatives in the Northwest disapprove of the court's liberalism, particularly its broad interpretations of environmental protection laws—interpretations that they see as damaging to timber and other industries in their region. To a considerable degree they identify this liberalism with judges from California. In particular, they see California judges as less sympathetic toward the economic well-being of states such as Washington and Idaho than are judges from the Northwest. Thus a proposal to put California in one circuit and the Northwest in another is appealing to them, so appealing that one Montana senator blocked the confirmation of any new court of appeals judge for the Ninth Circuit for a lengthy period in an attempt to force approval of the circuit split.

For the same reasons, liberals in the Senate and elsewhere have strongly opposed division of the circuit, viewing it as "judicial gerrymandering for ideological ends."[2] Supported by Ninth Circuit judges and lawyers, they have attacked proposals to split

the circuit as unnecessary and as an illegitimate effort to influence the course of judicial policy. In the past, their efforts had been successful. And the outcome in 1997 was
uncertain, because the House had approved a bill to study the structure of the circuit
rather than splitting it immediately. But if the advocates of circuit division ended up
losing again in 1997, it was certain that their campaign would continue.[3]

The battle over division of the Ninth Circuit underlines the importance of court
organization. The structure and administration of individual courts and court systems
help to shape judicial policies and thereby make a difference to those who use the
courts and to those who are affected by court decisions. Thus even seemingly routine
matters of court organization are often the subject of political contention.

This chapter examines the organization of courts in the United States. I give primary attention to the mechanics of court organization. But I also consider the politics
of court organization: the debates that arise over organizational arrangements and the
impact of those arrangements. The first section of the chapter discusses general principles of court organization, the second section focuses on the organization of the federal court system, and the third examines regularities and variation in state court
systems.

GENERAL PRINCIPLES OF COURT ORGANIZATION

Before looking at the specifics of court organization, we need to consider two broader
subjects: the relationship between the federal and state court systems and general patterns in the organization of court systems.

Federal and State Court Systems

Perhaps the most important feature of court organization in the United States is the
existence of multiple court systems. There is a separate court system in each of the
fifty states, the territories, and the District of Columbia. The federal government has
its own court system.

Separation of Court Systems   The state systems are, of course, divided from
each other by geography. In contrast, the federal and state systems overlap geographically. Indeed, federal and state courts are often located in the same city. But the two
sets of courts are in separate and distinct organizations.

Cases ordinarily stay within a single system. A case brought to a federal court
almost always remains in the federal courts. Under certain circumstances, a case may
begin in a state court system and then move to the federal courts. For instance, some
cases go from a state supreme court to the U.S. Supreme Court. But relatively few
cases take that path.

Each system is organized and managed by its own government. The constitution
and statutes of Colorado determine the form of the Colorado court system. As a result,
the Colorado system need not take the same form as that of other states or of the federal court system. Indeed, court systems vary considerably in such characteristics as
the structure of trial courts and the methods used to select judges. Of course, the laws

that courts carry out also differ from one system to another. In part for these reasons, each court system develops its own distinctive ways of operating.

Federal and State Court Jurisdiction   The concept of *jurisdiction* refers to a court's power to hear cases; that concept is central to the organization of court systems. Rules of jurisdiction, set primarily by state and federal constitutions and statutes, determine what kinds of cases each court can hear. By doing so, they also indicate which court or courts are appropriate forums for any specific case. Jurisdiction may be based on several characteristics of a case, including its subject matter (criminal versus civil, for instance), the parties (for example, whether the federal government is a party), and its geography (where the parties reside and the location of the events from which a case stems). Jurisdiction can be considered a characteristic both of court systems as a whole and of individual courts. The jurisdiction of the Missouri court system is the sum of the jurisdiction of all the individual state courts in Missouri.

The dividing line between the work of federal and state courts is based on the jurisdiction of the federal court system. Federal courts may hear only those classes of cases that federal law puts within their jurisdiction. Everything else is within the jurisdiction of state courts. The U.S. Constitution outlines the scope of federal court jurisdiction, which is developed in more detail in federal statutes. Although the rules of federal jurisdiction are complex, most of the cases they admit to federal courts fall into three categories.

1. *Federal question jurisdiction* is based on the subject matter of cases. Federal courts are entitled to hear all civil and criminal cases that are based on the U.S. Constitution, on treaties with other nations, and on federal statutes.
2. *Federal party jurisdiction* consists of cases in which the federal government is a party. Nearly all cases brought by or against the federal government, a federal agency, or a federal officer can be heard in federal court.
3. *Diversity jurisdiction* is based on geography. Federal courts can hear cases in which there is a diversity of citizenship between the parties (if they are citizens of different states or if one is a citizen of a foreign nation), as long as the suit is for seventy-five thousand dollars or more.

Jurisdiction over a particular class of cases may be exclusive to a particular court, or it may be concurrent (shared by two or more courts). This distinction can also be applied to court systems as a whole. With some exceptions, such as criminal cases based on federal statutes, the jurisdiction of federal courts is concurrent with that of state courts. Thus, for example, most kinds of civil cases brought by the federal government can be heard in either state or federal courts.

Cases based on diversity of citizenship illustrate the workings of concurrent jurisdiction. When citizens of different states become involved in a controversy involving at least seventy-five thousand dollars, the plaintiff has the option of filing a case in either federal or state court. But, if the plaintiff chooses state court, the defendant can have the case removed to federal court. Thus either party can take an appropriate case to federal court.

Diversity cases also illustrate the politics of jurisdiction. Congress first established diversity jurisdiction in 1789 as a protection against state bias; it was feared that state courts would favor their own citizens against those of other states. The diversity jurisdiction has survived for two centuries, even though some people think that bias against out-of-state litigants is no longer a problem. In recent years, federal judges have sought to limit or eliminate the diversity jurisdiction because it adds a large and burdensome set of cases to their workload.

But Congress has responded to this campaign only by raising the minimum monetary amount in 1988 from ten thousand to fifty thousand dollars, and then in 1996 to seventy-five thousand. The main reason is that lawyers want to retain the option of bringing diversity cases to federal court. They like the choice between federal and state courts because it allows them to engage in "forum shopping" by choosing the court whose judges seem more likely to favor their clients. The 1989 battle in baseball between manager Pete Rose and Commissioner A. Bartlett Giamatti, described in Exhibit 2.1, illustrates this kind of forum shopping.

Most cases that fall under federal jurisdiction do end up in federal court. Yet only a small proportion of all court cases are tried in federal court, simply because the great majority of cases fit under no category of federal jurisdiction and thus go to the state courts by default. Every year, the largest group of cases throughout the country results from traffic and parking violations, and almost all of these fall under state law. Criminal law is primarily a state matter, and people charged with common crimes, such as burglary and assault, ordinarily are tried under state law. Similarly, most common types of civil cases, such as those that arise from personal injuries or contract disputes, are based on state law and involve citizens of the same state.

On the other hand, a disproportionate number of cases that raise major policy questions come to federal court: many of these cases arise under the U.S. Constitution or federal statutes, and only a federal court—the Supreme Court—can lay down legal rules that apply to the country as a whole. As a result, the federal courts are a good deal more important than the numbers of their cases alone would indicate.

General Patterns of Court Organization

Although American court systems are diverse, there are some general patterns in the structure of courts within systems and in the administration of courts.

Court Structure   The jurisdiction of a court system must be divided among courts within that system. At the federal level and within each state, constitutional provisions and statutes create a set of courts and establish the jurisdiction of each. Such jurisdiction is always divided along two lines, vertical and horizontal.

Vertically, some courts are designated primarily as trial courts and others as appellate courts. Put another way, a court's jurisdiction may be mostly trial or mostly appellate. Most systems in the United States make a further distinction: between first-level appellate courts, which hear appeals from trial court decisions, and second-level appellate courts, which hear primarily cases brought from first-level appellate courts. A strong hierarchical element exists in every system. Higher courts review the decisions of the courts below them. Their judgeships are also more prestigious (and, in most systems, better paying) than those on lower courts.

Horizontally, jurisdiction may be divided among different sets of courts at the same level. Such a division occurs primarily at the trial level. In most states, one set of courts is designated to try cases with larger stakes, while other courts try cases with

In March 1989, the office of the commissioner of major league baseball announced an investigation of Cincinnati Reds manager and former star player Pete Rose, based on allegations of gambling by Rose. After an investigator submitted a report to Commissioner A. Bartlett Giamatti, the commissioner scheduled a hearing for June 26 to allow Rose to respond to the report.

On June 19, Rose filed suit to prevent the hearing from taking place, arguing that Giamatti had shown bias against him. Rose could have brought the case in federal court under diversity jurisdiction because he was a citizen of Ohio, whereas Giamatti and his office were located in New York. Instead, Rose brought the case in Ohio state court. By doing so, he could have it heard by an elected judge in Cincinnati, where Rose was very popular. Indeed, Rose's attorneys brought the case at a time when emergency motions were to be heard by a judge facing election in 1990 rather than a later year.

That judge, Norbert A. Nadel, scheduled his announcement of a decision for June 25 and allowed the announcement to be televised. When Nadel "started the hearing with a microphone check," wrote an editorial writer, "you knew Pete Rose had the home-court advantage." And Nadel did rule in favor of Rose, issuing a temporary restraining order to delay Giamatti's hearing and discipline of Rose for two weeks while Nadel considered a preliminary injunction.

On July 3, Giamatti's lawyers asked to have the case removed to federal district court, using the right of a defendant to such removal on the basis of diversity jurisdiction. The case was then transferred from Cincinnati to Columbus, also in the Southern District of Ohio, where it would be heard by a nonelected judge who did not live in Cincinnati. Judge John D. Holschuh, assigned the case, scheduled a hearing to decide whether the federal court had jurisdiction. On July 31, he ruled that there was federal jurisdiction, and on August 17 the federal court of appeals for the Sixth Circuit refused to consider the jurisdictional issue.

On August 24, while a hearing on Rose's request for a preliminary injunction was pending. Rose reached an agreement with Giamatti under which he could drop his case and accept a permanent prohibition on participation in baseball that could be rescinded at some point.

On November 6, 1990, Judge Nadel was elected to a new term on the court of common pleas, winning the largest majority of any Hamilton County judicial candidate who faced opposition. In 1997, Rose announced that he would seek reinstatement to participate in baseball and indicated his interest in managing a team.

Sources: The chronology is based primarily on "Rose's Woes," *Cincinnati Enquirer,* August 25, 1989, A9. Additional information comes from *Rose v. Giamatti,* 721 F. Supp. 906 (S.D. Ohio 1989). The quotation is from "Paint the Robe Red," *Cleveland Plain Dealer,* June 27, 1989, 14B.

EXHIBIT 2.1   Diversity Jurisdiction and Pete Rose

smaller stakes. Certain courts may be given relatively narrow responsibilities, such as tax cases or domestic relations cases. Sometimes two or more sets of courts in a system hold concurrent jurisdiction over a particular type of case.

Related to horizontal jurisdiction is *venue,* which concerns the place and court in which a case may be brought. At the trial level, there are usually multiple courts of the same type that sit in different places. For instance, there are ninety-four federal district courts spread across the United States. Venue rules are complex, but generally the place in which a case may be brought depends on the location of the parties' residences and of the actions from which the case stems. Although venue seems like a technical matter, courts take it quite seriously. In 1989, for instance, a federal court of appeals overturned the convictions—after a three-month trial—of two officials of the Beech-Nut Corporation for distributing phony apple juice. The court made this decision on the ground that the officials had been tried in the wrong federal district.[4]

Sometimes a case can be brought in only a single place, sometimes in two or more places. In the latter situation, as in cases that could go to either a state or a federal court, the litigant can engage in forum shopping. When the five largest tobacco companies in the United States sued the federal Food and Drug Administration in 1995 to prevent the agency from regulating cigarettes as drugs, they did not bring the suit in Washington, D.C. Rather, they chose the Middle District of North Carolina, where the tobacco industry is important and federal judges might be sympathetic to the industry. Indeed, the case was assigned to a North Carolina judge who had ruled in favor of the tobacco industry in a previous lawsuit against federal regulators. (Ironically, the judge's 1997 decision was largely favorable to the federal government.)[5]

A special case of forum shopping involves motions by criminal defendants for a "change of venue" to avoid potential prejudice in the place where the alleged offense took place. Such requests seldom are granted. But in the prosecutions that followed the 1995 bombing of a federal building in Oklahoma City, the defendants were successful in their motion for a change of venue to Denver. The judge agreed that "there is so great a prejudice against these two defendants in the State of Oklahoma" that they could not obtain a fair trial there.[6] A shift to another state was possible because the defendants were charged with violations of federal law, and federal jurisdiction is nationwide. If the charges had been under state law, only Oklahoma courts would have had jurisdiction.

Civil litigants can also ask for a change of venue, but these requests generally are rejected as well. In 1996, an insurance company that had been sued in federal court asked to have venue transferred from Galveston to Houston. As justification, the company cited the absence of a commercial airport in Galveston. The Galveston-based judge to whom the case had been assigned pointed out that his courthouse was fairly close to one of Houston's airports. He noted also that the defendant

> is not embarking on a three-week-long trip via covered wagons when it travels to Galveston. Rather, Defendant will be pleased to discover that the highway is paved and lighted all the way to Galveston, and thanks to the efforts of this Court's predecessor, Judge Roy Bean, the trip should be free of rustlers, hooligans, or vicious varmints of unsavory kind. Moreover, the speed limit was recently increased to seventy miles per hour on most of the road leading to Galveston, so Defendant should be able to hurtle to justice at lightning speed.[7]

Not surprisingly, the motion for a change of venue was denied.

Court Administration   The actual operation of individual courts and court systems is called court administration. Power and responsibility for court administration are divided between courts and the other branches of government. Constitutional provisions and statutes determine such basic matters as the kinds of courts that a system includes and the places where court is held. To a great extent, the courts administer themselves. Individual courts have their own administrative structures to handle their business, and court systems have administrative bodies to help run these systems as a whole.

Many judges are traditionalists who resist centralized control over their work and show a reluctance to change well-established ways of doing things. According to one Colorado judge, "Courts would still be using quill pens if there were enough people raising geese."[8] One commentator suggested that "judges don't want to govern themselves, but they don't want anyone else to do it either."[9]

Traditional patterns of administration have been challenged in recent years by growth in court workloads and the failure of court budgets to keep pace with these workloads. Indeed, resource problems increasingly dominate the concerns of judges and court administrators. A variety of programs have been adopted to dispose of cases more quickly, primarily by providing more incentives and opportunities for pretrial settlement. Courts resort to ad hoc measures to overcome limited space. In 1997, for instance, a Virginia county set up trailers on its courthouse square and linked them to create a needed courtroom.[10] Judges increasingly lobby the other branches for larger budgets or legal changes that would reduce the flow of cases into court. It should be emphasized that both resource problems and efforts to cope with them can influence the handling of cases and their results. One recurring theme of this book is the impact of heavy caseloads on court processes and outcomes.

THE FEDERAL COURTS

The basic structure of the federal court system is relatively simple. The organization chart in Figure 2.1 shows a bewildering array of courts, but the bulk of the system's work is done by the three sets of courts in the center of the figure. The district courts serve as the primary trial courts of the system and the courts of appeals as the primary first-level appellate courts. The Supreme Court is the only second-level appellate court.

Paralleling the district courts and courts of appeals are several other courts that are specialized by subject matter. These courts, taken together, are also a significant part of the system.

Federal District Courts

For the great majority of cases, the district courts are the point of entry into the federal judicial system. Most cases go no further. Thus these courts are the primary center of activity in the federal system.

Geographic Division: Districts   There are ninety-four federal district courts, one in each judicial district. These districts cover the fifty states, the District of Columbia, and some of the U.S. territories. Every state has at least one district of its own. Twenty-six states have a single district. The rest of the states are divided into two or more districts, with three states (New York, Texas, and California) having four districts each.

Many districts are divided into divisions, in each of which the court holds

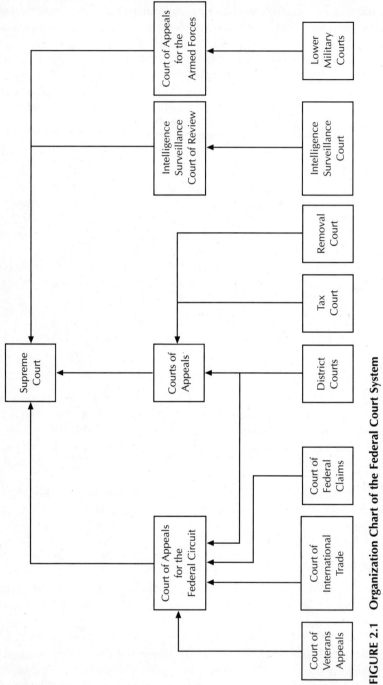

FIGURE 2.1   Organization Chart of the Federal Court System

Note: The lines and arrows show the routes of cases through appeals and Supreme Court grants of hearings. A few uncommon routes have been omitted.

proceedings. Even as routine a matter as the divisional structure of a district is sometimes controversial, as indicated by the proposal to create two divisions within the Maryland district. Prior to the creation of divisions, judges in the district sat only in Baltimore. Although lawyers in the Maryland suburbs of Washington, D.C., wanted a federal court in their area, Baltimore lawyers sought to keep all the judges in their city, and the district judges themselves preferred to stay where they were. Because of that opposition, Congress approved the division only after two decades of debate.[11]

Personnel   In federal district courts, as in other trial courts, cases are generally tried before a single judge, with or without a jury. Each district is staffed by at least one district judge, with a total of 649 judgeships in the ninety-four districts. A few districts have only one or two judges, while others have many. Twenty-eight judges are authorized for the Southern District of New York, which includes Manhattan. The districts in which Los Angeles, Chicago, and Philadelphia are located all have more than twenty judges.

District courts also make frequent use of visiting judges from other federal courts, especially from the courts of appeals above them. Even more important are senior (retired) judges from that district and from other courts. Their continued participation in cases has helped courts to keep up with growing caseloads, a problem aggravated when the president and Senate are slow to fill vacancies created by retirements—as they have been in recent years. Working full-time or part-time, senior district judges presided over 19 percent of all district court trials in 1995.[12]

In addition to district judges, each district employs two other kinds of judges, bankruptcy judges and magistrate judges. These three sets of judges are assisted by staff members, such as law clerks, secretaries, and probation officers. In numbers, district judges are overshadowed by the several thousand people who serve their courts in other positions. With these other personnel, the larger district courts are organizations of considerable size.

Jurisdiction and Business   Federal district courts have very broad jurisdiction. The great majority of federal cases are tried in them, with the remainder going to specialized courts. As a result, the business of the district courts is quite diverse.

Exhibit 2.2 shows the distribution by subject matter of cases brought to the district courts in 1995. The data in the exhibit indicate that each of the three major categories of federal jurisdiction accounts for a significant number of cases but that federal question cases predominate. It also demonstrates that district court cases span a broad range of legal and policy areas. As the exhibit shows, the caseloads of the district courts have grown substantially in the last two decades—by 83 percent between 1975 and 1995—though the pace of growth over that period was uneven. The numbers of criminal prosecutions have fluctuated over the past two decades, but the totals in 1975 and 1995 were about the same; essentially all the increase during that period derived from civil litigation. In turn, the preponderance of the growth in civil cases came under the federal question jurisdiction. Litigation by prisoners increased 130 percent, civil rights cases 150 percent.

The growing numbers of cases to be handled have led district judges and others to seek congressional help in coping with the heavier workload. In response,

1995 Cases

Type of Case	Number	Percentage
By source of jurisdiction		
Federal party cases	43,158	14.7
Federal question cases	199,277	67.8
Diversity cases	51,448	17.5
Other	240	0.1
By subject matter		
Criminal prosecutions	45,788	15.6
Prisoner petitions	63,550	21.6
Civil rights	36,600	12.4
Labor laws	14,954	5.1
Social Security laws	9,354	3.2
Torts	38,179	13.0
Contracts	49,434	16.8
Other	36,264	12.3

Total Cases Filed

Year	Number	% Change
1995	294,123	+10%
1990	266,783	−14%
1985	311,915	+58%
1980	197,710	+23%
1975	160,602	——

Note: The actual periods covered are fiscal years. Cases handled by bankruptcy judges and petty criminal offenses handled by magistrates have been excluded. Criminal cases are included in the federal question category. Figures given under "% Change" indicate change in the total number of cases over the preceding five years.

Sources: Administrative Office of the United States Courts, *Judicial Business of the United States Courts: Report of the Director* (1995) (Washington, D.C.: Administrative Office of the United States Courts, n.d.), 138–140, 195; *Annual Report of the Administrative Office of the United States Courts* (Washington, D.C.: Administrative Office of the U.S. Court) for earlier years.

EXHIBIT 2.2   Composition of Cases Filed in Federal District Courts in 1995 and Total Cases Filed in Selected Years

Congress has increased the number of district judges, most recently creating seventy-four new positions in 1990. Where new judgeships go depends primarily on need but also on power within Congress. In 1990, for instance, the chair of the House Judiciary Committee was from Texas. His efforts produced an increase from five to eleven in the number of new judgeships slated to go to Texas.[13]

Congress has also added substantially to the number of other court employees. Another important step taken by Congress has been to enhance the numbers and authority of two groups of decision makers other than district judges: magistrate judges and bankruptcy judges.

Magistrate Judges and Bankruptcy Judges   United States magistrate judges have been characterized as "subordinate judges." As such, they play important roles.[14] Magistrate judges are appointed to their posts by the district judges in their districts. Full-time magistrate judges serve for eight-year terms, part-time magistrates for four years. As of 1995, there were positions for 416 full-time and 81 part-time magistrate judges in the various federal districts. Federal law allows a considerable range of possible duties for magistrate judges. They may conduct many types of pretrial proceedings, rule on matters such as petitions challenging prison conditions, and (with the consent of the parties in most instances) try and decide civil cases and criminal misdemeanor cases. Depending on the type of case and other circumstances, a magistrate judge's decision can be appealed either to a district judge or to the court of appeals.

With a few exceptions, the judges in a particular district determine which of these duties are actually given to magistrate judges. As a result, there is considerable variation in their work from district to district. In general, however, they have come to perform a significant part of the district courts' work. Along with their extensive involvement in preliminary proceedings, they take final action in large numbers of cases. In 1995, for instance, magistrate judges disposed of seventy-three thousand misdemeanor cases through trial, dismissal, or the acceptance of a guilty plea.[15]

The status and role of magistrate judges have been enhanced considerably since the position of magistrate was created in 1968. Most recently, Congress in 1996 required that all minor misdemeanor cases be tried before magistrates. This enhancement is symbolized by the 1990 legislation that changed their title from "magistrate" to "magistrate judge." The position has become sufficiently attractive that some state judges have given up their positions to become magistrate judges. District judges have favored these changes, which allow magistrate judges to serve the district courts more extensively while remaining under the control of district judges.

In contrast, the appropriate status of bankruptcy judges has been the subject of great controversy.[16] As bankruptcy business grew, district judges increasingly delegated the actual processing of bankruptcy cases to referees (designated as judges in 1973). District judges were happy to do so, because these cases were time consuming and typically seemed uninteresting. As their responsibilities increased, bankruptcy judges sought higher status, including greater job security and recognition as judges. But district judges did not want their own status diminished by the designation of large numbers of bankruptcy judges as their equals or near-equals.

The result has been a series of conflicts between bankruptcy judges and district judges. In response to these conflicts, in 1978 and 1984 Congress adopted legislation that enhanced the status of bankruptcy judges while maintaining a clear distinction between them and district judges. The Bankruptcy Reform Act of 1994 continued that trend. In the current system, bankruptcy judges are adjuncts of the district courts, but they are appointed (for fourteen-year terms) by the courts of appeals rather than by district judges. Their decisions can be appealed to the district court or to a panel of bankruptcy judges, as determined by the district court and court of appeals.

The volume of bankruptcy cases grew rapidly in the 1980s, and the current level is about nine hundred thousand cases filed each year.[17] As a result, the number of bankruptcy judges has been increased (there are now 326 judgeships), and so has their impact. More and more, for instance, they help determine the fates of major corporations that go into bankruptcy proceedings.

The increasing importance of both magistrate judges and bankruptcy judges is one aspect of what some observers call the bureaucratization of the federal courts—a diffusion of effective decision-making power from judges on the major federal courts to other people. Of course, similar processes have occurred in the other branches of government: the size and responsibilities of presidential and congressional staff have grown enormously. But bureaucratization in the judiciary is especially problematical to many people, largely because of the traditional view that judges should make their own decisions. Indeed, one federal judge referred to bureaucracy as "the carcinoma of the federal judiciary."[18]

Three-Judge District Courts   The three-judge district court illustrates the use of judicial structure to serve policy goals.[19] This type of court, ordinarily composed of two district judges and one court of appeals judge, is set up to hear a single case. Its decision may then be appealed directly to the Supreme Court.

Under a series of statutes beginning in 1903, Congress required that certain kinds of cases be heard by three-judge courts. Its primary goal was to take decisions of great importance out of the hands of single district judges. For example, when state officials expressed unhappiness at the power of district judges to hold state laws unenforceable on constitutional grounds, Congress acted in 1910 to require three-judge courts in such cases. As such statutes accumulated, three-judge courts became increasingly common. In 1973, they heard 320 cases.

But with such frequent use, three-judge courts also became a burden on the federal court system. Not only did each case require that three judges from two levels of courts find the time to meet, but the provision for a direct appeal of their decision to the Supreme Court added to that court's workload. These burdens seemed to outweigh the original purposes of three-judge courts. In response, Congress eliminated most of the grounds for convening them in 1976, restricting them largely to suits that challenge the drawing of legislative districts and to certain civil rights cases.

Years later, however, Congress added one small piece to the jurisdiction of three-judge courts as a way to influence judicial policy. The federal court of appeals for the District of Columbia twice held that rules requiring cable television operators to carry local commercial stations were unconstitutional under the First Amendment. When Congress adopted a new statute regulating cable television in 1992, it included a provision under which challenges to the constitutionality of its new "must-carry" rules for local stations would go to a three-judge district court in the District of Columbia, with appeals to the Supreme Court, thus bypassing the

In 1994, former entertainer Sonny Bono, running as a Republican, won a U.S. House seat from California. In the same election, California voters approved an initiative measure that made illegal immigrants ineligible for most government benefits. Shortly afterward, a federal district judge in California issued an injunction that prevented the initiative from going into effect.

After Bono took his seat in the House, he introduced a bill under which applications for an injunction against a voter-passed ballot proposition on constitutional grounds would go to a three-judge district court rather than to a single judge. Bono and other supporters of the bill argued that a single judge, perhaps selected by litigants through forum shopping, should not be able to override a decision by a state's voters. Opponents countered that the bill would add to the burdens on the federal courts. But, the real disagreement was over ideology. Conservatives were unhappy because the California immigration initiative was one of several conservative measures approved by voters over the years, many in California, that judges had blocked. In turn, liberals saw the bill as a device to attack liberal court rulings. As a result, the House vote on the bill was strongly ideological. It passed by a 266–159 margin, winning all 230 Republican votes but only 18 of 136 votes from northern Democrats.

The bill was stalled in the Senate and thus did not become law. But conservatives' interest in this use of three-judge courts grew when another district judge issued an injunction against another initiative approved by California voters in 1996, this one prohibiting the use of affirmative action by the state. Representative Bono introduced his bill once against in 1997. The bill attracted 40 cosponsors, all Republican.

Sources: Congressional Record, 141 (daily edition), H9609–9627 (September 28, 1995); Sonny Bono, "How Judge-Shopping Squelches Democracy," *Orange County Register,* December 17, 1996, B8; other reports.

EXHIBIT 2.3   Sonny Bono Advocates a New Use for Three-Judge District Courts

court of appeals. This strategy worked: in 1993, and again in 1995, a three-judge district court upheld the must-carry rules by 2–1 votes.[20]

In 1995, the House passed a bill to add another piece to the jurisdiction of three-judge courts, a bill that illustrates particularly well the motivations behind structural changes in the judiciary. That episode is described in Exhibit 2.3.

Federal Courts of Appeals

If the district courts are the primary location of activity in the federal court system, the courts of appeals rank second. Most appeals from federal trial courts go to the courts of appeals. Because the Supreme Court accepts so few cases, these courts also represent the end of the line for nearly all litigation that reaches them. As a result, the courts of appeals are policymakers of considerable importance.

Geographic Division: Circuits   The basic geographic unit at this level is the circuit, and each circuit has a court of appeals. The twelve circuits are shown in Figure 2.2 on page 35. The District of Columbia is a circuit in itself. The states and territories are divided into eleven numbered circuits, each of which contains three or more states. The number of court of appeals judges in the circuits ranges from 6 in the First Circuit (New England and Puerto Rico) to 28 in the Ninth Circuit (the Pacific), with a total of 167 in the twelve circuits.

The controversy over possible division of the Ninth Circuit has been discussed at the beginning of the chapter. A similar controversy raged over division of the Fifth Circuit in the Deep South during the 1960s and 1970s.[21] The court of appeals had a majority that was sympathetic to claims of racial discrimination, and anti–civil rights senators favored a split because the new southeastern circuit seemed likely to be dominated by judges who were more conservative on civil rights issues. Pro–civil rights judges in the Fifth Circuit and their allies fought successfully against the division proposal for more than a decade; the court finally was divided in 1980, after concerns about civil rights had lessened.

Ordinarily, cases in the courts of appeals are decided by panels of three judges, which are not permanent but rather are rotated for each set of cases. Along with active judges from the circuit, these panels often include visiting judges (primarily district judges from the same circuit) and retired judges.

By majority vote, a court of appeals can hear or rehear a case *en banc,* a term that in most circuits means participation by the court's full membership of judges. However, this procedure is used only about a hundred times a year, across all the circuits.[22] It is employed primarily in cases of special importance and cases involving issues that have divided the court.

Geographic arrangements vary by circuit, with some courts sitting in a single city and others dividing their time among several cities. In most circuits, the judges themselves reside in different cities, complicating the task of scheduling hearings and conferences. In 1996, for example, the judges on the Ninth Circuit Court of Appeals resided in ten cities, including Phoenix, Arizona; Portland, Oregon; Billings, Montana; and Fairbanks, Alaska.

Like district courts, the courts of appeals employ a great many people other than judges. Each judge has three law clerks. Each court of appeals also has a central legal staff whose members have become subordinate judges in fact if not in name. The staff screens appeals and helps to decide those that it designates as routine, thereby saving judges' time. This development is examined more closely in Chapter 8.

Jurisdiction and Business   The courts of appeals have jurisdiction primarily over district court decisions. A dissatisfied litigant may appeal to the court of appeals after nearly any final district court decision and after some preliminary decisions in a case. Appeals from the decisions of three-judge district courts go directly to the Supreme Court, and appeals in patent cases go to the Court of Appeals for the Federal Circuit. The general rule is that litigants have the right to appeal district court decisions to some court. The only important exception is the rule that the federal government as criminal prosecutor may not appeal acquittals. Such an appeal is regarded as violating the constitutional prohibition against double jeopardy (putting a person in jeopardy of criminal punishment twice for the same offense).

The courts of appeals have two other sources of cases. First, they hear appeals from decisions of the Tax Court, which acts as a trial court for some tax cases. More important, orders of certain federal administrative agencies may be appealed directly to the courts of appeals without going first to the district courts. In 1995, such admin-

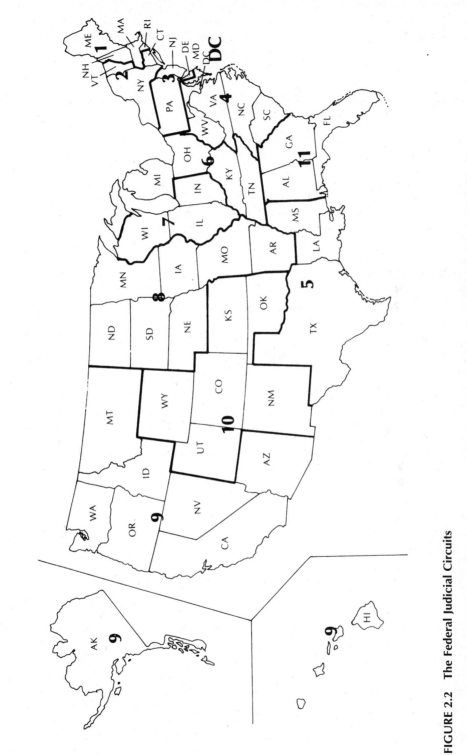

FIGURE 2.2   The Federal Judicial Circuits

Note: Not shown are Peurto Rico (First Circuit), Virgin Islands (Third Circuit), and Guam and the Northern Mariana Islands (Ninth Circuit).

istrative appeals made up about 7 percent of all the cases brought to the courts of appeals and 35 percent of the cases in the District of Columbia circuit.[23]

Caseloads of the courts of appeals have grown even faster than those of the district courts. Like the district courts, the courts of appeals have obtained congressional help in the form of additional personnel. Legislation between 1978 and 1990 increased the total number of judges from 97 to 167. And, as noted earlier, the courts of appeals have given their central legal staffs substantial responsibilities for decisions in some cases.

The Supreme Court

The Supreme Court is a single national court that decides cases with its full membership. The Court's size is determined by Congress, and the number of justices was changed several times in the nineteenth century. Some of these changes were motivated by the desire to affect the Court's policies. But there have been nine justices since 1869, and that number is unlikely to change. In contrast, the Court's staff has grown considerably and now includes more than three hundred people. The most important of these staff members are the justices' law clerks. Most justices now have four clerks, who perform such tasks as drafting opinions and screening requests to hear cases.

The Supreme Court's jurisdiction is almost entirely appellate. Cases come to the Court from several sets of lower courts. The two primary sources of cases are the federal courts of appeals and state supreme courts, but a case can be brought from a state system to the Supreme Court only if it contains an issue of federal law. A case that is initiated in a state court on the basis of state law sometimes develops a federal law issue, such as the procedural rights of a criminal defendant under the Constitution. Such cases are eligible for Supreme Court consideration, although they must go through the full set of appeals in state courts before the Supreme Court has jurisdiction to hear them.

With one minor exception—cases decided by three-judge district courts—the Supreme Court's appellate jurisdiction is discretionary. Thus, nearly all cases come to the Court not as appeals but as petitions for writs of certiorari. If the Court grants such a writ, this means that it calls up the case from the lower court for its consideration. If the Court denies the writ, as it does in the overwhelming majority of cases, the lower court decision is left standing.

The Constitution also gives the Supreme Court original (trial) jurisdiction over some cases involving states as parties and cases involving foreign diplomatic personnel; these cases are uncommon. When the Court does hear a case as a trial court, it delegates the task of gathering evidence and reaching a proposed decision to a special master, often a retired judge, who has been selected for that purpose.

Because the Supreme Court screens cases, and because its cases come from many sources, its agenda looks somewhat different from those of the lower federal courts. A large share of its decisions involve issues arising under the Constitution, and in the past quarter century it has concentrated heavily on civil liberties.

Like other federal courts, the Supreme Court has faced a growing caseload. The number of cases brought to the Court did not reach two thousand until 1961; since 1993, the Court has received more than sixty-five hundred cases in each term. Even though the Court can limit the number of cases that it hears, the increase in the numbers of certiorari petitions has added considerably to the Court's workload.

After several years of urging by the justices, Congress in 1988 eliminated nearly all of the Court's mandatory jurisdiction. As a result, the Court gained almost complete freedom to reject cases that the justices do not wish to decide. The Court itself has acted to lessen its workload by accepting fewer cases for full decisions. In recent years, even as the number of petitions for hearings kept growing, the Court reduced considerably the number of cases that it accepted. In its 1984–1987 terms, the Court accepted an average of 180 cases per term. In the 1992–1995 terms, the average was 99, a 45 percent drop, despite a continuing increase in the number of petitions for hearings.[24]

Specialized Courts

The district courts, courts of appeals, and Supreme Court can all be considered generalists in that they deal with a broad range of cases. The federal system also includes specialized courts, which have narrower jurisdiction. The characteristics and responsibilities of these courts are summarized in Exhibit 2.4. As the exhibit shows, there are two distinctions among them. First, some courts have their own permanent judges, while others borrow judges from the generalist courts. "Borrowed" judges are assigned to the specialized court for a limited period and serve on that court in addition to their regular duties on a district court or a court of appeals. The second distinction among the specialized courts is that some with their own judges are, like the generalist courts, established under Article III of the Constitution. Judges on Article III courts have lifetime appointments, and their salaries may not be reduced. Other specialized courts with their own judges are called legislative courts because they are established under Article I (which deals with the legislative branch); their judges lack these protections.

The specialized courts are hybrid institutions. In most respects they resemble generalist courts. But their focus on a relatively narrow set of issues also gives them characteristics that are more typical of administrative agencies. Such agencies frequently develop a strong point of view on the policy issues that they address. One reason is that agency officials with specialized responsibilities often develop narrow and parochial perspectives. Another reason is the special opportunity for influence that an interest group gains when an agency deals continuously with that group's area of concern. Specialization can have similar effects on courts. Indeed, according to one scholar, courts that are not generalists thereby "lose the one quality that clearly distinguishes them from administrative lawmakers."[25]

Partly for this reason, Congress has rejected a good many proposals to create specialized courts. But some proposals have been accepted, largely because they seemed to offer important advantages: the expertise of judges who specialize in a technical field such as tax law, the opportunity for a single court in a field to avoid the legal conflicts that develop among multiple courts, and reduced caseloads for generalist courts. And officials in the federal government or groups in the private sector sometimes seek the creation of a specialized court because they anticipate that the proposed court would rule more favorably toward them than would the district courts or courts of appeals. The cumulative result has been to make specialized courts a major

Court	Type of Judge	Level	Status Under the Constitution	Areas of Activity
Tax Court	Permanent	Trial	Article I	Federal taxes
Court of Federal Claims	Permanent	Trial	Article I	Claims against the federal government
Court of Veterans Appeals	Permanent	Trial	Article I	Veterans' benefits
Court of International Trade	Permanent	Trial	Article III	International trade issues
Court of Appeals for the Federal Circuit	Permanent	Appellate	Article III	Patents, trademarks, international trade, claims against the federal government
Foreign Intelligence Surveillance Court	Borrowed	Trial	—	Foreign intelligence surveillance warrants
Foreign Intelligence Surveillance Court of Review	Borrowed	Appellate	—	Foreign intelligence surveillance warrants
Removal Court	Borrowed	Trial	—	Deportation of suspected terrorists

Note: Military courts are not included.

EXHIBIT 2.4   Selected Characteristics of Specialized Federal Courts

part of the federal judicial system, handling issues as important as patent rights and international trade.[26]

One of these courts, the Court of Appeals for the Federal Circuit, illustrates both how such courts are created and what their potential effects can be. Congress established this court in 1982 by combining two existing courts, the Court of Claims and the Court of Customs and Patent Appeals (CCPA). The most important feature of the combined court is that it has jurisdiction over appeals from district courts in patent cases, which were formerly heard by the courts of appeals. Congress approved this transfer of jurisdiction largely because it would eliminate conflicts among courts of appeals over the standards used to determine whether a patent is legally valid.

But some people had favored creation of the new court because they wanted changes in patent law. Many courts of appeals had established high standards for patent validity, which meant that a large proportion of patents coming to court were found to be invalid. In contrast, in deciding a special set of patent cases, the CCPA had supported more lenient standards. Those who preferred lenient standards expected a new court with five CCPA judges among its twelve members to adopt such standards. Indeed, this occurred.[27] Thus the transfer of jurisdiction from generalist courts to a specialized court produced a fundamental change in judicial policy.

A quite different example is the Foreign Intelligence Surveillance Court, created in 1978.[28] Congress allowed wiretapping in the United States to obtain intelligence information about a foreign government or a person acting on behalf of such a government or engaging in such activities such as sabotage. A wiretap would have to be approved by one of seven federal district judges chosen by the chief justice. The judge who hears a particular wiretap request does so in a secret proceeding in a room at a Justice Department building, with an attorney representing the federal government but none representing the party for whom the wiretap is intended.

If the district judge denies an application for a warrant, the government may appeal to the Foreign Intelligence Surveillance Court of Review, which consists of three judges borrowed from the courts of appeals. But the Court of Review apparently has never met: although the Surveillance Court has required revision of some applications for warrants, it has not denied any applications except in one case where its jurisdiction was in question. Thus the government has won thousands of cases and lost only that one.[29]

Perhaps the government's record would be as successful if these cases were heard by a wide array of district judges in their own courts; the criteria by which warrant applications are assessed strongly favor granting them. But the use of a specialized court probably reinforces the government's advantage. The two chief justices serving since 1978, Warren Burger and William Rehnquist, have been conservatives who seemed inclined to choose judges with basically favorable attitudes toward the warrant program. Further, the frequent involvement of these judges in surveillance cases is likely to imbue them with sympathy for the federal officials with whom they interact in these cases.

In any case, members of Congress liked the record of the Surveillance Court enough that in 1996 they created a similar court, the Removal Court, to determine whether there is probable cause to find that a person is an alien terrorist and thus eligible for a deportation proceeding in a district court (the government also has to show a national security justification for using this special deportation procedure).[30] Proceedings before the Removal Court also would be secret. Congress provided that the chief justice could choose for the Removal Court judges who also sit on the Surveillance Court.

Federal Court Administration

The federal court system has a tradition of independence for individual courts and even individual judges. But the system also has a substantial and growing set of administrative structures.

Administration of Individual Courts   Individual federal courts have chief judges (called the chief justice in the Supreme Court). When a chief justice leaves the Supreme Court, the president makes an appointment to fill the vacancy, either elevating a sitting justice to that position (as was the case with William Rehnquist) or selecting a chief justice from outside the Court (as with Warren Burger). In lower courts, with some exceptions, the chief judge is simply the judge who has served on the court the longest.[31]

A chief judge has general administrative responsibility for a court. This responsibility covers such matters as assigning judges and panels to cases, supervising nonjudicial personnel, and budgeting. Chief judges of the courts of appeals also have some administrative duties related to the district courts in their circuits, and the chief justice has such duties for the federal court system as a whole.

The leadership of chief judges can affect the workings of their courts. Perhaps most important is their impact on intracourt relations. Chief Judge Harry Edwards of the court of appeals for the District of Columbia has been credited with reducing rancor on a court with a long history of feuding, while former chief judge Frank Battisti of the Northern Ohio district court engaged in a long and heated battle with colleagues over his leadership of the court.[32] Chief judges also hold some formal authority over their courts, such as the power to reassign cases from one judge to another. A recent battle between the chief judge of the Northern District of Texas and one of his colleagues, described in Exhibit 2.5, illustrates both the use of that power and the importance of the circuit councils, administrative bodies described in the next subsection.

Growth in federal court caseloads has demanded that chief judges and other judges give greater attention to administration of their courts. One consequence of that growth has been a substantial increase in personnel other than judges, from about one thousand in 1925 to twenty-eight thousand in 1995, an increase that requires judges to spend more time on personnel management.[33] Courts also have instituted mechanisms to process cases more efficiently and with less time required of judges. In 1990, Congress adopted the Civil Justice Reform Act, which required district courts to initiate plans to reduce expense and delay in civil cases. This legislation underlined the degree of concern about problems resulting from growing caseloads. It also underscored the ultimate power of Congress to impose administrative structures and procedures on the federal courts.

Administration of the System as a Whole   The administrative structure of the federal court system is largely a product of a statute called the Administrative Office Act of 1939.[34] This act created both the Administrative Office of the United States

Judge John McBryde of the Northern District of Texas, who sits in Fort Worth, has been regarded by some attorneys as unduly hostile and abusive in his courtroom style. The chief federal prosecutor in his district once said that "my assistants in Fort Worth deserve combat pay." In 1995, allegations of abuses by McBryde resulted in a decision by the district's chief judge, Jerry Buchmeyer, to reassign two cases from McBryde to himself. In one case, McBryde came into conflict with a federal prosecutor and district judge in Arizona, ultimately holding the prosecutor in contempt of court. In the other, he responded to a problem in the handling of the proceeds from a case settlement by castigating the district court's clerk in strong terms.

After Buchmeyer reassigned the two cases to himself, McBryde asked the judicial council for the Fifth Federal Circuit in New Orleans to return the cases to him. The circuit judicial councils, usually called circuit councils, are composed of judges from the circuit and have broad administrative authority over the circuit. The circuit council issued its own order reassigning the cases to Buchmeyer. The council also called McBryde's conduct in these cases "an impediment to the effective administration of justice."

McBryde then asked the Fifth Circuit Court of Appeals to return the cases to him. In July 1997, a court of appeals panel ruled that Buchmeyer and the circuit council had gone beyond their statutory powers in reassigning McBryde's cases, and it ordered that the two cases be returned to McBryde. The circuit council then announced its intent to seek Supreme Court review of the case, review that might clarify the supervisory powers of chief judges and circuit councils. Meanwhile, McBryde faced a separate disciplinary proceeding in which the circuit council would rule on charges that he engaged in abusive behavior toward lawyers and other court participants.

Sources: Reports in newspapers and legal journals; *In re: John H. McBryde, U.S. District Judge,* 117 F.3d 208 (5th Cir. 1997). The quotations are, in order, from Gary Taylor, "Texas Federal Judge Removed from Two Cases by 5th Circuit," *National Law Journal,* November 20, 1995, A6; and "One Federal Judge Does Battle with 19 Others," *New York Times,* May 1, 1996, A10.

EXHIBIT 2.5   *Judge McBryde* vs. *Judge Buchmeyer*

Courts and the Judicial Councils that serve each federal circuit (usually called circuit councils); it also expanded the responsibilities of a body called the Judicial Conference. The Administrative Office is responsible for the administration of the federal court system as a whole.

The Judicial Conference is made up of the chief judges of the courts of appeals and one district judge from each circuit. The chief justice of the Supreme Court presides. The conference develops rules of practice and procedure for federal courts, subject to Supreme Court approval. In 1994, for instance, the conference voted to continue a prohibition on television cameras in federal courtrooms after a three-year pilot program in a few courts.[35] It also takes positions on legislative proposals, and judges and judicial administrators lobby Congress on behalf of conference positions. In addition, the Judicial Conference puts together the proposed budget for the federal courts. The prestige of the Judicial Conference is suggested by an incident in 1989:

when Chief Justice William Rehnquist proposed legislation to limit death penalty appeals despite opposition from most conference members, their stance seriously weakened his position.

The circuit councils, established in 1939, were restructured and strengthened by congressional legislation in 1980.[36] Each of these councils is composed of judges from the court of appeals and district courts in the circuit; the chief judge of the court of appeals presides. By statute, each council has sweeping authority to "make all necessary and appropriate orders for the effective and expeditious administration of justice within its circuit," with the added proviso that "all judicial officers and employees of the circuit shall promptly carry into effect all orders of the judicial council."[37] (Court personnel have the same obligation to the Judicial Conference.)

The councils also have several more specific powers. Their most important and most controversial power, a product of the 1980 law, involves the disciplining of judges within the circuit. According to the statute, a council may investigate a complaint of misconduct against a judge. If that complaint is found to be justified, the council can take any appropriate action short of removing a judge from office. Such action can include a temporary order that no further cases be assigned to a particular judge or a recommendation that Congress consider impeachment. In 1986, the council for the Eleventh Circuit recommended impeachment of district judge Alcee Hastings after he was acquitted of conspiracy to receive bribes, and Congress removed Hastings through impeachment proceedings in 1989. In 1992, the council for the Fifth Circuit reprimanded district judge James Nowlin for consulting with a Texas state legislator, a fellow Republican and former legislative colleague, in drawing up Texas legislative districts. The council, however, found him innocent of "a corrupt or evil motive."[38]

This administrative structure creates a degree of centralized control over federal judges. In themselves, the disciplinary powers of circuit councils are a significant source of control. In general, however, the powers of the various administrative bodies are relatively limited. And the judges who serve on those bodies are reluctant to engage in coercion over their colleagues. Even with the enhanced powers of circuit councils, one district judge said that "the council just doesn't seem to influence my life."[39]

Congress retains ultimate administrative authority over the federal courts. It can alter the structure of administration as its members see fit. It can also intervene in specific administrative matters through such means as disapproving new rules of procedure or changing rules unilaterally, as it did with certain rules of evidence for criminal cases in 1994. Judges who prize their independence sometimes chafe at the control that Congress exercises, but the courts are left to govern themselves on most matters most of the time.

THE STATE COURT SYSTEMS

One characteristic of the states is variation in their government institutions. With the independent power that results from federalism, each state has created its own set of institutions through constitutional provisions and statutes. Inevitably, the results differ considerably. These differences are especially pronounced in state court systems. Indeed, hardly any generalization about these systems applies to all the states.

Yet state governments differ less than they might, because the states borrow ideas from each other and because they have been subject to common influences. This is true of state court systems. Traditionally, the most important shared characteristic of these systems was a quality that can be called fragmentation. More recently, there has been a nationwide movement to reduce this fragmentation through "court unification." To a degree, this movement has reduced variation among the states. But individual states have responded to the drive for unification in their own ways, so that today—as in the past—there is a pronounced diversity in state court systems.

Fragmentation and Unification

The traditional fragmentation of state court systems has both structural and administrative aspects. Structurally, the most important feature has been a multiplicity of trial courts. State and local governments set up new courts on an ad hoc basis to serve specific needs. As a result, most states eventually found themselves with many sets of trial courts. Many of these courts had very narrow jurisdiction, and the jurisdiction of different courts often overlapped in confusing ways.

The administration of the state court systems was also fragmented, with each court quite independent of the others. Court management and funding were divided between state and local governments, and administration of trial courts was handled primarily by the various local governments.

The effort to reduce this fragmentation through court unification began in the first decade of this century.[40] Legal scholar Roscoe Pound argued for the desirability of unification, gradually winning support from individual lawyers, state and local lawyers' groups, and the American Bar Association (ABA), the largest national group of attorneys. In 1913, lawyers established the American Judicature Society, which has been an important arm of the unification movement since that time. "Good government" groups, such as the League of Women Voters, have also joined in the effort.

The court unification movement has put forward a variety of policy proposals, but two general prescriptions stand out. The first is consolidation of trial courts into two sets of courts or, preferably, one. The second is centralization of court administration so that all courts are financed by state governments and administered by professionals under the supervision of the state supreme court.[41]

Several premises underlie these prescriptions. One is that the traditional fragmented system is highly inefficient and thus serves the public badly. Another is that control by the other branches of government, particularly local governments, weakens the judiciary. These premises are not universally accepted. Although fragmentation sounds like an undesirable quality, some people have argued that a fragmented system is more responsive to the needs of local areas and may even be more efficient than a unified system.

In practice, participants in the debates over unification take sides largely on the basis of their own situations and self-interest. Supreme court justices, for instance, tend to favor unification because it strengthens their own court's power over the judicial system. In contrast, judges on courts that might be consolidated or even eliminated through unification have a strong incentive to support the traditional system. And officials and residents of rural areas tend to oppose unification because they prefer to maintain local courts with which they are comfortable and over which they have some control.

Across the states, intermittent battles over court unification have raged for several decades. In this conflict, the opponents of consolidation hold the advantage of defending the status quo, and the backing of rural judges and officials provides them with considerable strength. But the unification movement has two offsetting advantages: the association of its prescriptions with widely accepted values, such as efficiency, and the prestige of many lawyers and judges who have been among the movement's leaders.

The outcome of these battles has varied from state to state. Across the states as a whole, proponents of court unification have secured enough victories to change the state court systems a good deal. For example, there is a continuing movement toward greater consolidation of trial courts. But the success of unification advocates is far from total: in many states, the traditionally fragmented system has changed relatively little. The current structure and administration of state courts reflect victories for both sides.

State Court Structure: An Overview

The wide variety of state courts fit into four general categories, two at the trial level and two at the appellate level.[42] Trial courts may be classified as *major* and *minor* courts, and appellate courts include *intermediate* appellate courts and *supreme* courts.

Major Trial Courts   For current advocates of court unification, the ideal trial court structure is a single type of court that handles all cases. Only about a half-dozen states fit that model even in a formal sense, and some of those break the single court into specialized divisions or departments.[43] Other states retain multiple sets of trial courts, ranging in number from two to ten. Thus the movement toward consolidation of trial courts is hardly complete.

Where multiple courts exist, they are usually divided into two categories. Sometimes these categories are labeled *general jurisdiction* and *limited jurisdiction,* but those terms are misleading since most courts in both groups are limited in the kinds of cases they can hear. The terms major and minor courts are preferable, if imperfect, because the chief distinction between the two types of courts is in the seriousness of the cases brought before them.

Most states now have a single set of major trial courts, commonly known as district courts, superior courts, or circuit courts. Typically, such a court conducts trials involving criminal offenses for which the most severe penalties are possible (felonies rather than misdemeanors) and civil cases involving relatively large sums of money. In many states, some special categories of cases are also heard in major trial courts: juvenile criminal offenses; domestic relations cases (primarily divorces); and probate cases (primarily the handling of wills).

In most states, major trial courts also have appellate functions, hearing appeals in at least some types of cases that are tried in minor trial courts. In many states, these appeals are de novo, meaning that the case is actually retried in the major court. As a result, a party who is unhappy with what may be a relatively informal trial in the minor court can go to the major court for a trial with a fuller set of procedural rights, such as a trial by jury.

Despite the campaign for consolidation, a few states retain multiple sets of major trial courts, with the jurisdiction of each based on geography and subject matter. Most often, one court with broad jurisdiction sits alongside another that hears a specific type of case, such as those involving taxes or probate. Even when there is a single court, it is often split into divisions according to the subject matter of the cases, with judges serving permanently or temporarily in a specialized division. This system is especially common in courts serving populous areas, which have enough judicial business and enough judges to allow such specialization. Thus, in many states the major trial courts are not quite as consolidated as they appear to be in organization charts.

Like federal district courts, major state trial courts are geographically dispersed. In some states, each county has its own court, while in other states the counties are grouped into circuits. In that system, each circuit typically has a set of judges who serve the whole area, traveling from county to county to hear cases.

Major trial courts have a great deal of business: in 1990, about 27 million cases were filed in these courts across the country.[44] This number is enormous compared with the number of cases filed in federal district courts.

The cases that come to major trial courts, as shown in Exhibit 2.6 for 1990, range widely. Nearly half involve traffic violations. Among the other cases, most are civil rather than criminal. Within the civil category, domestic relations cases stand out in frequency. The large number of juvenile cases, most of them criminal in content, is also noteworthy.

Minor Trial Courts   Below their major trial courts, most states still have minor courts, which handle less serious civil and criminal cases. These courts may also have jurisdiction over special categories of cases, such as juvenile criminal offenses. In several states, such as Michigan and Rhode Island, the minor courts handle the preliminary stages of felony cases as well. As a result, cases routinely move from one court to another before trial.

State systems became most fragmented at this level. The fragmentation of minor trial courts has been reduced a good deal over time, but only a few states, such as Kansas and Virginia, have a single set of minor courts. Other states retain multiple courts, sometimes a great many.

There are two common lines of division among sets of minor courts. The first is geographic, with urban areas often served by municipal courts and rural areas by county courts or justices of the peace. The second line of division is functional, as separate courts are frequently established to carry out specific duties. Jurisdictional lines are often confusing. Seemingly parallel courts, such as municipal and county courts, may have somewhat different jurisdiction. And in some states the jurisdiction of different courts overlaps.

In most states, minor trial courts are highly decentralized. It is common for every city of moderate population to have its own municipal court. In states that have retained justices of the peace, there are sometimes several hundred separate justice

Subject	Major Courts		Minor Courts	
Civil	34%		12%	
Family		11%		
Contract		5%		
Tort		3%		
Other		15%		
Criminal	14%		13%	
Felony		4%		
Misdemeanor		8%		11%
Drunk driving				1%
Other		2%		1%
Traffic	48%		74%	
Juvenile	4%		1%	

Note: Percentages for subcategories of cases are based on data from fewer than fifty states. In criminal subcategories. "Other" includes drunk driving cases for major courts and felony cases for minor courts, along with some miscellaneous cases.

Source: Court Statistics Project, *State Court Caseload Statistics: Annual Report 1990* (Williamsburg, Va.: National Center for State Courts, 1992), 10, 18, 33.

EXHIBIT 2.6   Subject Matter of Cases Heard by Major and Minor State Courts in 1990

courts. As a result, in 1994, there were more than thirteen thousand separate minor trial courts—along with more than two thousand major trial courts.[45]

The division of jurisdiction between major and minor trial courts varies among the states, but minor courts generally have more business. In 1990, minor trial courts received 73 million cases, more than twice the number in major courts, even though several states lack minor courts.[46] As Exhibit 2.6 shows, however, the work of minor courts is dominated by cases with relatively small stakes, particularly traffic offenses. The volume and composition of the business in minor trial courts make their operation distinctive. Because most cases involve small stakes and few are really contested, cases are typically handled in routine fashion. Often cases are processed and disposed of by administrative personnel rather than by judges. Even when judges handle cases, they may do so quite rapidly and informally.

Intermediate Appellate Courts   At the beginning of this century, state systems generally included only a single appellate court, the supreme court. But growth in the volume of appeals gradually caused state policymakers to create one or more intermediate appellate courts below the supreme court level. Today, thirty-nine states have intermediate courts as first-level appellate courts, most of them known as courts of appeals or something similar.

The structures of intermediate appellate courts vary in several respects. While some states have only a single court, others follow the federal model and provide separate courts for different regions. In a few states, one court hears criminal appeals and another hears civil appeals. In most states, intermediate courts sit in panels, either with judges permanently assigned to a particular panel or with rotating panel membership.

The jurisdiction of intermediate courts also varies. All share the function of hearing appeals from the decisions of major trial courts, although certain kinds of cases may go directly to the state supreme court. In some states, some or all appeals from minor trial courts go to the intermediate appellate court rather than to the major trial courts. In many states, appeals from at least some administrative agencies are heard by intermediate courts. In general, the jurisdiction of intermediate appellate courts is mandatory because of the doctrine that the parties to a case are entitled to one appeal. But the Virginia Court of Appeals has discretionary jurisdiction over criminal cases, and many other courts have discretion over narrower categories of cases.

Despite the mandatory jurisdiction of most intermediate courts, only a small fraction of the cases handled by trial courts reach them. In 1994, to take one example, state trial courts in Indiana received about 1.4 million cases, while the state's intermediate court received about two thousand.[47] Of course, the cases that do come to appellate courts generally have much larger stakes than average. Courts that can hear both civil and criminal cases receive substantial numbers of both, with the balance between civil and criminal business varying by state.

Supreme Courts   Whether or not it has created an intermediate court of appeals, every state has a court that serves as its supreme court. With a few exceptions, this court is actually called the supreme court or some variant of that name. In effect, Oklahoma and Texas each have two supreme courts; their supreme courts hear only civil cases, while their courts of criminal appeals serve as the final courts for criminal cases. In 1993, the chief justice of the Texas Supreme Court proposed merging his court with the Court of Criminal Appeals, but that action was not taken.

Supreme courts have between five and nine justices. (The Oklahoma Court of Criminal Appeals has three justices.) Even the larger courts generally sit en banc rather than in divisions or panels. Some courts hear cases not only in the state capital but in other cities as well.

The Louisiana and California supreme courts sit primarily outside the capital, residing in New Orleans rather than Baton Rouge and San Francisco rather than Sacramento. According to a former chief justice, the Louisiana court originally located in New Orleans because "there wasn't a road you could count on" until well into this century, and after that the court stayed in New Orleans "mostly from habit."[48] The California court seems simply to have a preference for San Francisco. In 1992, after the court had upheld a voter-mandated reduction in the legislative budget, some legislators threatened to punish it by moving its headquarters to Sacramento.[49]

A state supreme court, like its federal counterpart, is the final appellate court within its system. The functions of this court depend largely on the presence or absence of an intermediate state appellate court. Where that court exists, the supreme court is a second-level appellate court. As such, it receives most cases from the inter-mediate court and has discretionary jurisdiction over most of those cases. Typically, some classes of cases come from the intermediate court on a mandatory basis. Others bypass the intermediate court altogether, going directly from trial courts to the supreme court.

Because of their discretionary jurisdiction, these courts have considerable con-trol over their agendas. Indeed, in many states, the supreme court is highly selective in choosing cases to hear, granting hearings in less than 10 percent of the discre-tionary cases it considers. In 1994, Michigan and New Jersey had grant rates of only 4 percent.[50] Even so, because the range of state cases is so broad, a supreme court is likely to deal with a diverse set of legal issues in any given year.

In states without an intermediate appellate court, the functions and business of the supreme court resemble those of an intermediate court. Most cases come to such a supreme court from trial courts on a mandatory rather than a discretionary basis. But the supreme court of West Virginia has primarily discretionary jurisdiction, and the New Hampshire supreme court has adopted a rule under which it can refuse to hear cases. Thus these two states deviate the furthest from the general principle that liti-gants are entitled to one appeal.

Two Examples of State Court Structure

Two examples provide a clearer sense of state court structure. The states chosen, Illinois and New York, are both populous ones, with a great deal of judicial business. But they also represent two extremes of court organization. Illinois was the first state to consolidate all its trial courts, and only three other states have adopted the same fully consolidated structure. In contrast, New York is one of six states whose courts are at the lowest level of consolidation according to one set of criteria.[51]

Illinois   The simplicity of the Illinois court system, resulting from a full consol-idation of trial courts in 1962, is obvious from the diagram in Figure 2.3.[52] The highest court is the supreme court, which sits in Springfield, the state capital, and in Chicago. Cases come to the supreme court primarily from the intermediate appellate court, and its jurisdiction is mainly discretionary. The supreme court also hears appeals directly from trial courts in some types of cases, such as those with death sentences.

The intermediate appellate court, known in Illinois as the Appellate Court, hears all other appeals from trial courts. It also hears appeals from several administrative bodies, such as the Pollution Control Board and three boards dealing with labor rela-tions. This court is split into five divisions on a geographic basis.

The most noteworthy aspect of the Illinois system is the single set of trial courts, the circuit courts, which handle the functions of both major and minor trial courts. The trial court structure is not quite as simple as it seems, however, because the circuit courts may be subdivided. In Cook County (Chicago), which has nearly four hundred judges, the subdivision is quite detailed: the circuit court includes a county department with seven specialized divisions for functions such as probate and domestic relations, as well as a municipal department with six districts. Within these subdivisions, judges are assigned to hear particular categories of cases in a given time period. Some court-rooms are devoted to very specific types of cases, such as gun offenses.

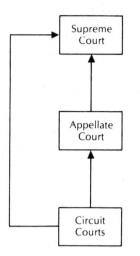

FIGURE 2.3   Organization Chart of the Illinois Court System

New York   As Figure 2.4 on page 51 shows, the New York court system is exceedingly complex.[53] In 1961, it underwent a partial consolidation, but a large number of separate courts and multitudinous routes for appeals were left standing. Efforts at further consolidation have been made from time to time but so far have not succeeded.

While the organization of Illinois courts can be described rather easily, any attempt to trace the position and functions of each New York court produces great confusion. Only at the top of the system, where the state's court of appeals is equivalent to the supreme court in most other states, is there much clarity. This court of appeals primarily hears cases brought from the intermediate appellate courts, but it also hears appeals from trial courts in cases involving only the constitutionality of a statute. Its jurisdiction is partly mandatory and partly discretionary.

At the intermediate appellate level, the structure begins to become complicated. Here jurisdiction is divided among the county courts and the appellate divisions and appellate terms of the supreme court. The county courts and the supreme court are also trial courts. (It is symbolic of the confusing structure of New York courts that the state has a lower court called the Supreme Court, and a supreme court called the Court of Appeals.) Where an appeal goes depends on the trial court from which it came, its subject matter, and the region of the state in which it was tried.

The New York supreme court is one major trial court, divided into eleven districts. It has unlimited trial jurisdiction, but it generally hears cases outside the jurisdiction of other courts. The county court, which is the other major state trial court, exists in each county outside the city of New York.

Minor trial courts are the most numerous, with hundreds of city, town, and village courts scattered throughout the state. Two Long Island counties also have district courts, and the city of New York has its own civil court and criminal court. Special courts exist for matters related to children (Family Court), for probate (Surrogates' Court), and for claims against the state (Court of Claims).

The contrast between this complex structure of minor trial courts and the simpler system in Illinois, where such courts are absent altogether, underlines the extent of the differences among the court systems of the various states.

Administration of State Courts

Like court structures, the administration of state courts varies considerably from state to state. In general, however, the efforts of the court unification movement and the pressures created by growing caseloads have strengthened central administration of individual courts and court systems.

Individual Courts   The chief judges of state courts are selected in a variety of ways. Like their federal counterparts, they hold administrative authority over their courts. Of course, that authority does not translate into anything like complete control. In this respect, state and federal courts are similar. The chief judges of state trial courts have the special problem that court clerks are elected in forty states, so that they and the employees they hire are largely autonomous. Clerks can often fight successfully against proposed changes in court operations.[54]

This is not to say that chief judges are powerless: they possess real power over the operation of their courts and the work situations of their fellow judges. A study of the circuit court in Chicago found that court subdivisions and individual judges hold a great deal of independence, but the chief judge's power to assign judges to particular subdivisions is a real source of control.[55] The presiding judge of the Los Angeles superior court (the major trial court) has taken such actions as eliminating night court and transferring judges to different courts against their wishes. One judge who complained about an action by the presiding judge was told by colleagues to "Cool it, or you're going to be sitting in Lancaster"—an outlying city with a small court.[56]

State Court Systems   Historically, the administration of state courts was fragmented along several lines. Individual courts operated independently of each other for the most part and with a minimum of control from the state supreme court. Legislative responsibility for the courts was divided between state and local governments; the standard reference to trial courts as "local courts" reflected this division of authority. Finally, authority for the governance of courts was split between the courts themselves and the other branches.

Supporters of court unification have sought to centralize administrative control and responsibility for court systems, primarily in the state supreme courts. Such centralization would shift power from lower courts to the supreme court, from local governments to the state government, and from the other branches to the courts. Largely because of opposition from those who would lose power, administrative centralization is far from complete across the country as a whole. Not surprisingly, the degree of centralization differs a great deal from state to state and from one area of court governance to another.

One area in which considerable centralization has occurred involves supreme court authority over lower courts.[57] Nearly every state now has professional court administrators under supreme court control, and in most states these administrators have substantial power over the management of lower courts. In every state but

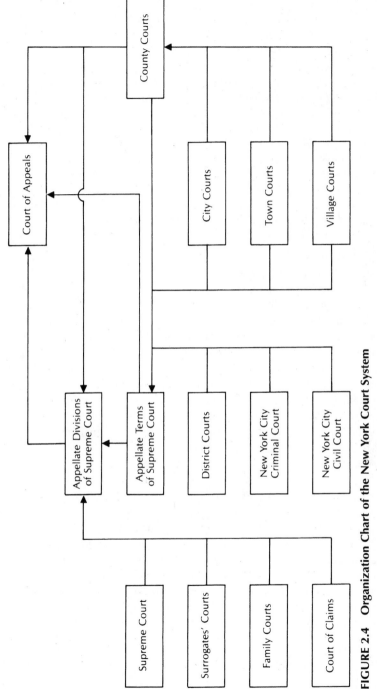

FIGURE 2.4   Organization Chart of the New York Court System

Note: Some of the routes of cases shown in the chart are uncommon, but very rare routes are not shown.

Sources: State of New York, *Report of the Chief Administrator of the Courts for the Calendar Year January 1, 1993—December 31, 1993* (New York: New York Office of Court Administration, 1994), 11; League of Women Voters of New York State, *The Judicial Maze: The Court System in New York State* (New York: League of Women Voters, 1988), 7.

California (where the legislature holds some of the power), the supreme court now has power to establish procedural rules for trial and appellate courts. These powers have been employed to differing degrees across the states, but they are used enough to bring about a considerable increase in centralized control over the courts.

Perhaps the most significant manifestation of supreme court authority has been the use of formal rules as means to speed the processing of cases in trial courts. Rising caseloads, funding shortages, and inefficiencies often combine to create long backlogs of cases to resolve. Mechanisms such as recommended time standards for the processing of cases are now common, and state chief justices sometimes engage in informal campaigns to encourage administrative innovations and other means of attacking case backlogs.

As supreme courts gain power over lower courts, conflicts are inevitable. One example was a 1991 battle between the Pennsylvania Supreme Court and the Philadelphia Traffic Court, a minor trial court. Acting on behalf of his court, supreme court justice Nicholas Papadakos sought a reduction in the traffic court staff. George Twardy, presiding judge of the traffic court, refused to go along. "Twardy said 'Go to hell' in effect," Papadakos reported after one meeting. Papadakos finally set up a panel under a supreme court order to make the staff cuts directly—thus partially taking over traffic court administration.[58] The outcomes of such conflicts vary, depending on the distribution of both legal and political power between supreme courts and lower courts.

Another area of significant change concerns the funding of trial courts, traditionally the responsibility of local governments.[59] Most state governments now provide substantial funding for trial courts, though few supply all of their funds. It is common for state governments to take primary responsibility for funding of some courts, while leaving others—typically, minor courts—for local governments to support. The growth of state funding reflects the financial difficulties of many local governments; the lack of greater growth reflects the financial difficulties from which state governments also suffer. Further, local governments sometimes prefer to maintain fiscal control over minor trial courts, including control over fines and fees paid to those courts.

One constant of court administration in the states is a degree of friction between courts and the other branches. Judges are accustomed to considerable autonomy from external control, and they sometimes balk at such control. A California trial court challenged state legislation allowing a county board of supervisors to close the courts on certain days in order to save money by putting court employees on unpaid furlough, arguing that the legislation violated the system of separation of powers. In 1996, the state supreme court ruled that the legislation was constitutionally acceptable.[60] Former New York governor Mario Cuomo and the chief judge of New York's highest court had a long battle over funding of the state's courts. At one point, the chief judge sued Cuomo and the state legislature for allegedly failing to meet a constitutional requirement to fund the courts adequately.[61]

Court Unification and Its Impact

The success of the court unification movement has differed from state to state, but the movement has secured considerable change in the structure and administration of court systems. Proponents of unification, of course, believe that these changes improve the functioning of state courts.

It is difficult to ascertain whether the improvements that are sought from court unification actually occur, in part because qualities such as efficiency are often very difficult to measure. One scholar took an imaginative approach to get around this difficulty, measuring the perceived quality of courts in each state in terms of the rate with which lawyers take cases to federal court under the diversity jurisdiction—in effect, rejecting the state courts. He found little relationship between this measure of quality and trial court consolidation or centralized court management, but he noted the limits of his approach as a way of getting at quality.[62] Other approaches would also have significant limits.

As a result, we know little about whether the improvements that are sought actually occur. Nor do we know much about other possible effects of changes in the state court systems. But a few judgments can be made concerning the impact of court unification.[63]

First, it is not certain that unification actually produces all the benefits that have been ascribed to it. Consolidating courts and centralizing authority do not necessarily improve the system's capacity to process and dispose of cases. Nor does unification appear to diminish the influence of other political institutions on the courts.

One reason is that unified and fragmented systems may differ less in reality than they do on paper. A consolidated set of trial courts, such as the Illinois circuit courts, may include divisions that are largely independent and judges who specialize in specific types of cases. Even in a system with a strong central authority, individual courts and judges retain a great deal of autonomy.

Perhaps more fundamentally, advocates of unification probably underestimate the strength of factors other than court structure. One example is the capacity of courts to process cases efficiently. Consolidation can improve efficiency by eliminating a situation in which some judges have too much to do and others too little. However, efficiency is also affected by the work habits and styles of individual judges and by the ways in which attorneys handle cases. If these factors work against efficiency, consolidation may accomplish relatively little.

Nor can structural changes shield courts from the intrusion of political considerations. For example, a shift from local to state funding may reduce court involvement in local politics but increase its involvement in state politics. As one commentator said, "No matter what the funding source, budgeting is politics."[64] And it is not clear that courts are in a stronger political position at the state level than they are locally.

Its intended effects aside, court unification—like other reforms—can have unexpected and sometimes undesirable consequences. The efforts of supreme courts in states such as Ohio and Kansas have improved efficiency in case disposition but also may have reduced the care with which cases are handled. The consolidation of a city and a county court (both of them minor trial courts) in Georgia increased costs for city residents and made court policies less consistent with their preferences.[65] Such unforeseen results are inevitable when major system changes occur. But we do not have a clear picture of the range of such results or the frequency with which they occur.

Even if there were better knowledge about the actual impact of court unification, definitive judgments about its desirability would be impossible because people disagree about the values that are associated with unification. Not everyone believes, for example, that the courts should be insulated from external politics. Though everyone presumably does agree that efficiency is desirable, the weight given to this goal in relation to others varies a good deal. In any case, we know so little about the actual consequences of unification that it would be folly to try to reach firm conclusions about its good and bad effects.

Thus there has been something of an irony in the history of the court unification movement. The movement developed a strong collective view about what a court system should look like, and it has engaged in a strong and sustained effort to move state court systems closer to that ideal. But the people laboring in the movement have little reason to be confident about the effects of the changes that they advocate. In this respect, the campaign for court unification is similar to many other campaigns for change in the courts.

CONCLUSIONS

The last two sections of this chapter have sketched the general patterns of organization in the federal and state court systems. In the process, they have illustrated two important themes: court organization is based on "political" as well as technical considerations, and organizational arrangements can have a substantial impact on the courts.

Although systematic evidence on the effect of court organization is limited, it should be clear that organizational features make a difference. Specialized courts may resolve policy issues differently from generalist courts, and a supreme court's possession of rule-making power may allow it to alter the ways in which trial judges process cases. Indeed, policymakers usually change the organization of courts as a means to change their operations or outputs. However, such changes do not always have the intended effects. In fact, they sometimes have consequences that were neither intended nor desired.

Because court organization is thought to make a difference, it is the subject of political conflict. Battles over state court unification have raged for several decades, and issues such as the diversity jurisdiction of the federal courts and division of the federal circuits have aroused considerable contention.

Of course, court organization is not static. As political realities and ideas about desirable arrangements change, so will those arrangements themselves. Both the federal and state court systems look different today from the way they looked half a century ago, and continued change is inevitable. This is particularly true when courts face strong pressures from their workloads and there is widespread dissatisfaction with the functioning of American courts.

FOR FURTHER READING

Barrow, Deborah J., and Thomas G. Walker. *A Court Divided: The Fifth Circuit Court of Appeals and the Politics of Judicial Reform.* New Haven, Conn.: Yale University Press, 1988.

Dubois, Philip L., ed. *The Politics of Judicial Reform.* Lexington, Mass.: Lexington Books, 1982.

Fish, Peter Graham. *The Politics of Federal Judicial Administration.* Princeton: Princeton University Press, 1973.

Hays, Steven W., and Cole Blease Graham Jr., eds. *Handbook of Court Administration and Management.* New York: Marcel Dekker, 1993.

Hellman, Arthur D., ed. *Restructuring Justice: The Innovations of the Ninth Circuit and the Future of the Federal Courts.* Ithaca, N.Y.: Cornell University Press, 1990.

Heydebrand, Wolf, and Carroll Seron. *Rationalizing Justice: The Political Economy of Federal District Courts.* Albany: State University of New York Press, 1990.

Posner, Richard A. *The Federal Courts: Challenge and Reform.* Cambridge, Mass.: Harvard University Press, 1996.

Smith, Christopher E. *United States Magistrates in the Federal Courts: Subordinate Judges.* New York: Praeger, 1990.

NOTES

1. Sources for this discussion include *Ninth Circuit Court of Appeals Reorganization Act of 1995,* Report of the Senate Committee on the Judiciary, to accompany S. 956, 1995; Symposium, "The Proposal to Split the Ninth Circuit Court of Appeals," *Montana Law Review* 57 (Summer 1996), 241–322; and the Senate debate on the 1997 circuit-splitting proposal, reported in the *Congressional Record.*
2. "Ninth Circuit Shenanigans" (editorial), *San Francisco Chronicle,* January 10, 1996, A18.
3. Rex Bossert, "Proposal to Split 9th Circuit," *National Law Journal,* March 31, 1997, A6.
4. John M. Doyle, "Court Reverses Convictions in Beech-Nut Juice Case," *Washington Post,* March 31, 1989, A5.
5. *Coyne Beahm, Inc., v. U.S. Food & Drug Administration,* 958 F. Supp. 1060 (M. D. N. C. 1997).
6. *United States v. McVeigh,* 918 F. Supp. 1467, 1474 (W. D. Okla. 1996).
7. *Smith v. Colonial Penn Insurance Company,* 943 F. Supp. 782, 784 (S.D. Texas 1996).
8. Rita Henley Jensen, "Computer Age Eludes the Courts," *National Law Journal,* May 30, 1988, 1.
9. Doris Marie Provine, "Governing the Ungovernable: The Theory and Practice of Governance in the Ninth Circuit," in *Restructuring Justice: The Innovations of the Ninth Circuit and the Future of the Federal Courts,* ed. Arthur D. Hellman (Ithaca, N.Y.: Cornell University Press, 1990), 271.
10. Victoria Benning, "Loudoun Plans Real 'Trailer Court'," *Washington Post,* March 20, 1997, D3.
11. Eric Pianin, "Md. Bar Governors Endorse Splitting U.S. District Court," *Washington Post,* November 27, 1987, B1, B5; Paul Duggan, "Senate Enacts Bill to Place U.S. Court in Md. Suburbs," *Washington Post,* October 1, 1988, B1, B2.
12. Darryl Van Duch, "Senior Judge Ranks Close Vacancy Gap," *National Law Journal,* July 22, 1996, A22.
13. Susan F. Rasky, "Congressional Poker Chips: Judges, Water, Oil and Beer," *New York Times,* October 29, 1990, A13.
14. Sources of information for the discussion of magistrates include Philip M. Pro and Thomas C. Hnatowski, "Measured Progress: The Evolution and Administration of the Federal Magistrate Judges System," *American University Law Review* 44 (June 1995), 1503–1535; and Christopher E. Smith, *United States Magistrates in the Federal Courts: Subordinate Judges* (New York: Praeger, 1990). The term *subordinate judges* is taken from Smith.

15. Administrative Office of the United States Courts, *Judicial Business of the United States Courts: Report of the Director* (1995) (Washington, D.C.: Administrative Office of the United States Courts, n.d.), 75.

16. Sources of information for the discussion of bankruptcy judges include Carroll Seron, *Judicial Reorganization: The Politics of Reform in the Federal Bankruptcy Court* (Lexington, Mass.: Lexington Books, 1978); and Lawrence P. King, "The Unmaking of a Bankruptcy Court: Aftermath of *Northern Pipeline v. Marathon,*" *Washington and Lee Law Review* 40 (Winter 1983), 99–120.

17. Administrative Office of the U.S. Courts, *Judicial Business* (1995), 33.

18. Patrick E. Higginbotham, "Bureaucracy: The Carcinoma of the Federal Judiciary," *Alabama Law Review* 31 (Winter 1980), 261–272.

19. Michael E. Solimine, "The Three-Judge District Court in Voting Rights Litigation," *University of Michigan Journal of Law Reform* 30 (Fall 1996), 79–145.

20. James C. Goodale, "D.C. Circuit Court Sticks It to Cable," *National Law Journal,* May 10, 1993, 13–14. The decisions were *Turner Broadcasting v. Federal Communications Commission,* 819 F. Supp. 32 (D.D.C. 1993), 910 F. Supp. 734 (D.D.C. 1995).

21. Deborah J. Barrow and Thomas G. Walker, *A Court Divided: The Fifth Circuit Court of Appeals and the Politics of Judicial Reform* (New Haven, Conn.: Yale University Press, 1988).

22. Judith A. McKenna, *Structural and Other Alternatives for the Federal Courts of Appeals* (Washington, D.C.: Federal Judicial Center, 1993), 177.

23. Administrative Office of the U.S. Courts, *Judicial Business,* 98.

24. These figures were calculated from data collected by the Supreme Court and published annually by *United States Law Week.*

25. Martin Shapiro, *The Supreme Court and Administrative Agencies* (New York: Free Press, 1968), 53.

26. Lawrence Baum, "Specializing the Federal Courts: Neutral Reforms or Efforts to Shape Judicial Policy?" *Judicature* 74 (December–January 1991), 217–224.

27. Gerald Sobel, "The Court of Appeals for the Federal Circuit: A Fifth Anniversary Look at Its Impact on Patent Law and Litigation," *American University Law Review* 37 (Summer 1988), 1087–1139; Robert L. Harmon, *Patents and the Federal Circuit,* 3d ed. (Washington, D.C.: Bureau of National Affairs, 1994), esp. 793–794.

28. Note, "The Foreign Intelligence Surveillance Act: Legislating a Judicial Role in National Security Surveillance," *Michigan Law Review* 78 (June 1980), 1116–1152.

29. "Intelligence on the FISA Court," *Legal Times,* April 14, 1997, 18, 20.

30. See Benjamin Wittes, "Will 'Removal Court' Remove Due Process?" *Legal Times,* April 22, 1996, 1, 16–17.

31. Sources of information for the discussion of court administration include Philip L. Dubois, "Court Executives for the Federal Trial Courts: Learning from the Circuit Executive Experience," *Justice System Journal* 7 (Summer 1982), 180–212; John T. McDermott and Steven Flanders, *The Impact of the Circuit Executive Act* (Washington, D.C.: Federal Judicial Center, 1979); John W. Macy Jr., *The First Decade of the Circuit Court Executive: An Evaluation* (Washington, D.C.: Federal Judicial Center, 1985); and Steven Flanders, "Court Executives and Decentralization of the Federal Judiciary," *Judicature* 70 (February–March 1987), 273–279.

32. Jonathan Groner, "Chiefly, Edwards Is a Calming Influence," *Legal Times,* July 8, 1996, 1, 15–18; Katherine L. Siemon, "Battisti Plans to Resign as Chief Judge," *Cleveland Plain Dealer,* July 8, 1989, 1A, 10A.

33. U.S. Bureau of the Census, *Statistical Abstract of the United States: 1996* (Washington, D.C.: U.S. Government Printing Office, 1996), 346.

34. The development and functioning of this structure are discussed in Peter Graham Fish, *The Politics of Federal Judicial Administration* (Princeton, N.J.: Princeton University Press, 1973).

35. Joan Biskupic, "Federal Court Camera Ban Continued," *Washington Post,* September 21, 1994, A3.

36. Michael J. Remington, "Circuit Council Reform: A Boat Hook for Judges and Court Administrators," *Brigham Young University Law Review* (Summer 1981), 695–736.
37. 28 *United States Code,* sec. 332 (d) (1988 ed.).
38. Roberto Suro, "Texas, in Redistricting Conflict, Seeks Delay in State Senate Vote," *New York Times,* February 14, 1992, A19; "Order and Report in In re: The Complaint of Lewis H. Earl against United States District Judge James R. Nowlin under the Judicial Conduct and Disability Act of 1980" (5th Cir. 1992).
39. Provine, "Governing the Ungovernable," 277.
40. The court unification movement and the politics associated with it are discussed in Henry R. Glick, "The Politics of State-Court Reform," in *The Politics of Judicial Reform,* ed. Philip L. Dubois (Lexington, Mass.: Lexington Books, 1982), 17–33.
41. Larry Berkson and Susan Carbon, *Court Unification: History, Politics and Implementation* (Washington, D.C.: National Institute of Law Enforcement and Criminal Justice, 1978), 2.
42. This discussion of state court organization is based largely on David B. Rottman et al., *State Court Organization, 1993* (Washington, D.C.: U.S. Department of Justice, 1995); and Court Statistics Project, *State Court Caseload Statistics, 1994* (Williamsburg, Va.: National Center for State Courts, 1995).
43. Carl Baar, "Trial Court Unification in Practice," *Judicature* 76 (December–January, 1993), 179–184.
44. Court Statistics Project, *State Court Caseload Statistics: Annual Report 1990* (Williamsburg, Va.: National Center for State Courts, 1992), 10.
45. Calculated from data in Court Statistics Project, *State Court Caseload Statistics 1994,* 8–59. *Court* can be defined in different ways, so these totals should be regarded as approximate.
46. Court Statistics Project, *State Court Caseload Statistics 1990,* 10.
47. Court Statistics Project, *State Court Caseload Statistics 1994,* 114, 140.
48. A. J. Liebling, *The Earl of Louisiana* (New York: Simon & Schuster, 1961), 12.
49. Vlae Kershner, "Willie Brown Backs Moving High Court from S.F. to Capital," *San Francisco Chronicle,* March 18, 1992, A13.
50. Court Statistics Project, *State Court Caseload Statistics 1994,* 129.
51. Victor E. Flango and David B. Rottman, "Research Note: Measuring Trial Court Consolidation," *Justice System Journal* 16 (1992), 68–69.
52. This discussion of the Illinois court system is based in part on Administrative Office of the Illinois Courts, *Annual Report of the Illinois Courts: Administrative Summary, 1995* (Springfield: Administrative Office of the Illinois Courts, 1996).
53. The discussion of the New York court system is based on State of New York, *Report of the Chief Administrator of the Courts for the Calendar Year January 1, 1993–December 31, 1993* (New York: New York Office of Court Administration, 1994); and League of Women Voters of New York State, *The Judicial Maze: The Court System in New York State* (New York: League of Women Voters, 1988).
54. Steven W. Hays, "The Traditional Managers: Judges and Court Clerks," in *Handbook of Court Administration and Management,* ed. Steven W. Hays and Cole Blease Graham Jr. (New York: Marcel Dekker, 1993), 230–233.
55. Herbert Jacob, "The Governance of Trial Judges" (paper presented at the annual conference of the American Political Science Association, San Francisco, August–September 1996).
56. B. J. Palermo, "The Judge with an Attitude," *California Lawyer* 12 (June 1992), 17.
57. See Rottman et al., *State Court Organization, 1993,* 113–134, 166–172.
58. Linda Loyd and Susan Caba, "New Panel to Cut Traffic Court Staff," *Philadelphia Inquirer,* May 30, 1991, 5B.
59. See Rottman et al., *State Court Organization, 1993,* 136–165; and Robert W. Tobin and John K. Hudzik, "The Status and Future of State Financing of Courts," in *Handbook of Court Administration and Management,* ed. Hays and Graham, 327–354.
60. *Superior Court v. County of Mendocino,* 913 P.2d 1046 (Calif. 1996).

61. Howard B. Glaser, "*Wachtler v. Cuomo:* The Limits of Inherent Powers," *Judicature* 78 (July–August 1994), 12–24.
62. Victor E. Flango, "Court Unification and Quality of State Courts," *Justice System Journal* 16 (1994), 33–55.
63. Glick, "Politics of State-Court Reform"; Thomas E. Henderson et al., *Significance of Judicial Structure: The Effect of Unification on Trial Court Operations* (Washington, D.C.: National Institute of Justice, 1984); Carl Baar, "The Scope and Limits of Court Reform," *Justice System Journal* 5 (1980), 274–290.
64. "Funding State and Local Courts: Increasing Demands and Decreasing Resources," *Judicature* 76 (August-September 1992), 89.
65. Josef M. Broder, John F. Porter, and Webb M. Smathers, "The Hidden Consequences of Court Unification," *Judicature* 65 (June–July 1981), 10–17.

3

Lawyers

President Bill Clinton is a lawyer. Clinton won re-election by defeating lawyer Bob Dole. Hillary Clinton and Elizabeth Dole are also lawyers. The president does not stand alone as a lawyer in the top levels of government; "in effect," says one scholar, "the legal profession has colonized the political domain in this country."[1] The activities of lawyers extend in other directions as well. Attorneys serve as labor union leaders, university presidents, and social critics and commentators.

Yet lawyers exert their greatest influence through their work as lawyers: representing clients in legal matters. That representation helps to determine the fates of criminal defendants, the custody of children, and the scope of civil liberties. Who is represented by lawyers and *how* they are represented make a great deal of difference for individual lives and the life of the nation. This chapter examines the law as a profession, giving primary emphasis to lawyers' representation of clients in the legal system.

The chapter has three parts. The first surveys the structure of the legal profession and the work that lawyers do. The second examines access to the services of lawyers. The final section explores relationships between lawyers and their clients.

THE LEGAL PROFESSION

To understand law as a profession, we need to look at several aspects of the profession. This section discusses the educational and licensing processes that determine who can practice law, the work of lawyers and the settings in which they work, specialization among lawyers, and the organization and regulation of the profession.

Entry into the Legal Profession

Like many other professions, the practice of law is regulated by the states. Most important, the states control entry into the profession: people cannot act as attorneys simply by labeling themselves as such. In order to represent clients other than themselves or to perform other work identified as that of lawyers, a person must be licensed to do so. Licensing, like regulation of other aspects of legal practice, is supervised by state supreme courts and is generally administered by boards of lawyers.

The legal profession as a whole has worked hard to limit what nonlawyers can do, seeking a broad definition of the practice of law and limiting that practice to licensed attorneys. The "unauthorized practice of law" by nonlawyers is a criminal offense in most states. Lawyers argue that limitations on nonlawyers are needed to protect people from unskilled practitioners, though critics respond that lawyers are most interested in protecting themselves against competition from other professional groups.

One recurrent battle is over the right to handle the settlement of real estate transactions. Despite strong urgings from lawyers, most states allow nonlawyers such as land title and escrow settlement companies to handle settlements. In 1995, for instance, the New Jersey Supreme Court ruled against lawyers on that issue even though it concluded that buyers and sellers would be well advised to obtain legal representation.[2]

As that example suggests, attorneys are on the defensive in their efforts to maintain barriers against legal work by nonlawyers. In practice, groups such as accountants and insurance agents provide a good deal of legal advice to clients. Thousands of "paralegals" work for law firms or on their own, doing tasks that do not constitute the practice of law as such but that lawyers might otherwise perform. And there has been a burgeoning of books and computer software programs to assist people in handling their own legal matters, such as wills.

Many people argue that opening up more legal work to nonattorneys would improve the access of nonwealthy people to needed legal services, access that is far from complete at present. But lawyers, who face greater competition among themselves with their growing numbers, can be expected to resist additional competition from nonlawyers.

Occasionally it is discovered that someone who is practicing law actually lacks a license. Some of these people do considerable harm with substandard legal work, but others are praised for the quality of their work. Of course, legal skills are not restricted to licensed attorneys. An attorney who had once served as a judge informed a Texas appellate court that the criminal defendant whom he represented had no basis for an appeal, but the defendant filed his own brief. That brief initially convinced the court to overturn his conviction; the court reheard the case and affirmed the conviction, but only by a 2–1 vote.[3]

Law School Training   In the nineteenth century, most American lawyers received their training through apprenticeship with practicing attorneys. Gradually the system of legal education evolved to the one with which we are familiar today: a structured law school curriculum that requires three years of full-time study or its equivalent.

This evolutionary process was both reflected in and strengthened by changes in the licensing requirements for attorneys. Today only four states—California, Vermont, Virginia, and Washington—permit prospective attorneys to bypass law school altogether and gain their training by apprenticeship. Three others—Maine, New York, and Wyoming—allow a combination of law school and law office training.[4] Even where these options exist, few prospective attorneys use them. In 1995, only about one hundred people took a state bar examination after following the apprenticeship route.[5] But some who do use these options pass the bar examination, and some of them achieve success as lawyers: in 1995, a New York lawyer who had flunked out of law school twice but who then passed the bar examination on his first attempt became a trial judge.[6]

Most states require not only that applicants graduate from law school but also that their school be accredited by the American Bar Association (ABA). The ABA's requirements for accreditation are highly detailed. Standard 304(b), for instance, mandates that "an academic year shall consist of not fewer than 140 days on which classes are regularly scheduled in the law school, extending into not fewer than eight calendar months."[7] In a few states, however, students from unaccredited law schools are eligible to practice under certain circumstances. Most students who take this route are in California, which has at least twenty-five law schools that are not accredited by the ABA (but many of which have state accreditation). In recent years, the ABA has been sued by the federal Department of Justice and by a Massachusetts law school that had failed to win accreditation; both charged that the ABA's accreditation requirements violated antitrust law. Under a 1995 settlement of the Justice Department lawsuit, the ABA has changed some of its accreditation procedures and has eliminated certain rules, such as its refusal to accredit law schools that are intended to make a profit and its required minimum levels for faculty salaries.[8]

Most law schools resemble each other in the general type of legal training they provide. The heart of their curricula is a series of classes on various areas of the law, such as contracts, property, criminal procedure, and constitutional law. The primary texts are the opinions of the appellate courts, which are intended to help students understand the substance of the law and to train them in legal analysis. The conventional form of teaching is the Socratic method, in which professors question students closely about the reasoning in opinions in order to illuminate particular cases and sharpen the students' thinking. One law professor has explained how this method achieved its dominance in law schools:

> Christopher Columbus Langdell of Harvard was one of the first advocates of the Socratic method of law teaching. His teaching style was so unpopular that Harvard's law school enrollment plummeted, and rumors circulated that Langdell might be fired. When law professors across American learned how much students despised the method, however, they immediately rushed to adopt it, and Langdell's job was spared.[9]

Both the content and the form of law school education have been criticized. The main complaint about content is that a focus on appellate court opinions does not give students much of the practical knowledge they need. Students learn little from such opinions about how to run a law office or try a case in court. Many new lawyers find that their education is just beginning when they leave school.

In response to this complaint, law schools have sought to diversify their curricula. Most now have clinical programs, in which students work with actual legal matters in order to gain such practical skills as interviewing clients and conducting negotiations over cases. As part of some programs, students may even make supervised appearances in court. But clinical programs still constitute only a small portion of the law school curriculum, and both faculty and students tend to view them as peripheral to the mainstream of a legal education.

A kind of hierarchy exists among law schools that is based on their prestige. The most widely respected, such as Michigan, Yale, Stanford, and Harvard, can be the most selective in choosing their students. In turn, because of their reputations and the abilities of their students, these schools provide the widest opportunities for graduates. Large law firms recruit disproportionately from the most prominent schools, and Supreme Court justices usually draw from them in choosing law clerks. Ultimately, graduates of these schools are the most likely to achieve eminence, such as positions on the Supreme Court itself. However, law schools with quite different levels of prestige have far more similarities than differences in what they teach and how they teach it.

Law students often incur substantial debts. In 1994, it was calculated that law school graduates used an average of 16 percent of their salaries to pay off debts.[10] These debts put considerable financial pressure on new lawyers, pressure reflected in high and growing default rates. They also reinforce the desire of most law students to find high-paying jobs after education.

Another effect of a law school education is that its intensive training influences students' attitudes and ways of thinking. In particular, law students are instilled with the tenets of legal reasoning. This socialization helps to account for the tendency of lawyers and judges to analyze issues in terms of the applicable rules of law, so that much of what they do can be understood from the legal perspective discussed in Chapter 1. There is some evidence that law school affects students' attitudes in other ways, especially by increasing their interest in the more remunerative types of law practice, but studies disagree about these effects.[11]

Licensing Requirements   The states vary a good deal in the conditions that a person must meet to become an attorney, but a predominant pattern does exist.[12] Nearly all states require good moral character. This requirement creates difficulties primarily for people who have been convicted of serious crimes, and several states prohibit the admission of people who were convicted of felonies.

The most important requirements are gaining a law school education, discussed already, and passing the bar examination. With some exceptions in Wisconsin, every prospective attorney must submit to a two- or three-day bar examination.[13] This test consists of essay questions on the laws of the state and, in all but four states, a multiple-choice Multistate Bar Examination, administered by a national testing service. All but seven states also include a short section on professional ethics, called the Multistate Professional Responsibility Examination, and some states have added a section designed to test practical lawyering skills. In nearly all states, the examination is offered in February and July.

Typically, about two-thirds of the applicants across the nation pass the bar examination each year; 70 percent passed it in 1995. But, success rates vary among the states—in 1995, from 90 percent in Nebraska and South Carolina to 54 percent in California. The examination in California is notoriously difficult. Among the people who failed it at least once are Governor Pete Wilson; Jerry Brown, a former governor and presidential candidate; and William Clark, who was both a member of the Reagan cabinet and a justice on the California Supreme Court.[14] Every state allows those who fail the bar examination to retake it at least once, and most allow unlimited retries. In 1991, an applicant passed the California bar examination on his forty-eighth try.[15] Until 1995, Pennsylvania's examination was regarded as one of the easiest to pass: under its rules, test takers were required only to achieve a passing score on the multiple-choice section of its examination and make a "good-faith effort" on the essay section. The examination was popular with lawyers who planned to practice in the District of Columbia, whose rules make it easy for a lawyer who has been licensed in another state to gain a D.C. license. But Pennsylvania now requires passing scores on both halves of its examination.[16]

The possibility of failure makes the bar examination a fearsome prospect for applicants. After completing law school, most take special "bar review" courses to prepare themselves for the test. The traumatic character of the examination is suggested by the test day in New York City in 1989. Ten minutes before the exam began, one prospective lawyer let out a "bloodcurdling scream." She was ushered out. As she returned twenty minutes later, another test taker stood up, cursed, and left the examination permanently.[17] In California, at least, the rules for the examination are enforced strictly. When a man at one test site in 1993 suffered a seizure, the five test takers who stopped their work to help him—including one who administered CPR—were denied any extra time to complete the test. Only later did the state administrators of the examination relent and take the loss of time into account.[18]

Attorneys who are licensed to practice in one state do not automatically gain the right to practice in other states. Indeed, in nearly half of the states, outsiders must pass all or part of the bar examination before doing business in the new state. In the others, a lawyer can be admitted to the bar on the basis of some period of experience in another state, most often five years. However, courts usually allow an attorney who is a resident of another state to participate in a single case.

Federal courts also establish their own requirements for the right to practice before them. In most instances, a lawyer need only be licensed in the state in which the federal court sits, but some courts have set up more stringent requirements. In ten federal districts, attorneys must pass a written examination or have a certain amount of trial experience before they can try federal cases.

The Size and Composition of the Legal Profession   The best-known fact about lawyers in the United States is the enormous growth in their numbers. Figure 3.1 shows just how rapid that growth has been. The 946,000 lawyers who were licensed in 1996 represented an increase of 326 percent since 1951 and 166 percent since 1971.

This growth, of course, results from massive increases in the number of new lawyers. In 1963, 11,000 people were admitted to the bar. In contrast, there have been more than 40,000 admissions in every year since 1979, and more than 50,000 in each year from 1991 through 1994 (the most recent years for which figures are available). This increase reflects a substantial rise in both law school enrollments and the proportion of law students who actually graduate.[19] The downturn in the job market for lawyers in the 1990s has produced a drop of more than 20 percent in the number of applicants to law schools, a very substantial decrease.[20] But the number of applicants and the size of law school classes remain at very high levels in historical terms.

Why are more people going to law school? One careful analysis suggests that a number of forces are involved.[21] For one thing, there is more legal work to be done. (If we control for population, the increase in the number of lawyers since 1951 has been about 140 percent rather than 326 percent. And interactions among people that might lead to legal work increase at a higher rate than population.)

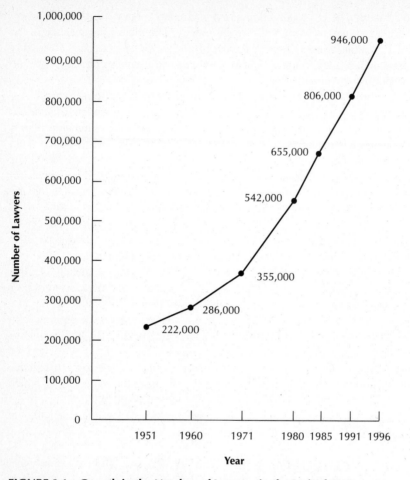

FIGURE 3.1 Growth in the Number of Lawyers in the United States.

Sources: Barbara A. Curran and Clara N. Carson, *The Lawyer Statistical Report: The U.S. Legal Profession in the 1990s* (Chicago: American Bar Foundation, 1994); M. A. Stapleton, "Lawyers Have Met the Enemy, and It Is Them," *Chicago Daily Law Bulletin,* September 13, 1996, 3.

Other contributing factors include the baby boom, which increased the pool of potential law school entrants; a growing perception of the impact that lawyers can have on society; and a sense, perhaps exaggerated, of the economic rewards available to attorneys.

Inevitably, this growth in the legal profession affects lawyers. It intensifies economic competition, which helps to explain the more aggressive marketing of legal services in recent years. The job market for new lawyers has also tightened.

Not surprisingly, in light of these developments, most attorneys—64 percent in a 1992 survey—think that there are too many lawyers.[22] The same view is widely held by nonlawyers, particularly those who think that lawyers encourage lawsuits and thus affect the economy negatively.[23] Such critics argue that the United States stands out among other countries in regard to the number of lawyers per capita. Former vice president Dan Quayle said that the United States has 70 percent of all the lawyers in the world. Other commentators have calculated much lower proportions, and one scholar concluded that the United States in 1987 ranked thirty-fifth among one hundred countries in the number of "law providers" per capita. As that term suggests, disagreement about the standing of the United States in this respect is based largely on differences in how one defines the equivalent of American lawyers in other nations.[24]

Until quite recently, almost all lawyers were white and male. In 1963, fewer than 3 percent of practicing attorneys were female, and in 1970, about 1 percent were black.[25] This pattern stemmed in part from restrictive practices by law schools and law firms. For example, few southern and border state law schools admitted black students until the 1950s, and many law schools throughout the country were equally restrictive for women. Until 1950, Harvard did not accept women as law students. Columbia had the same policy in 1922, when its dean (future Supreme Court chief justice Harlan Stone) justified the refusal to admit women by saying, "We don't because we don't."[26] Until at least the 1960s, most law firms were unwilling to hire women or members of racial minority groups.

As barriers have been broken and aspirations have risen, more women and non-whites have entered law school; the growth has been more substantial for women. Of the first-year students in the 1995–1996 academic year, 45 percent were women and 21 percent were minority group members.[27] Exhibit 3.1 shows the change that has occurred in the demographics of law school enrollments in recent years.

EXHIBIT 3.1   Enrollments of Women and Members of Racial Minority Groups in Law Schools

Year	Women		Minority Groups	
	Number	%	Number	%
1965–66	2,374	4.2	—	—
1975–76	26,020	23.4	8,703	7.8
1980–81	40,834	34.2	10,575	8.8
1985–86	47,486	40.0	12,346	10.4
1990–91	54,097	42.5	17,330	13.6
1995–96	56,923	44.0	25,554	19.8

Note: Enrollments are in programs leading to the J.D. degree in law schools approved by the American Bar Association. Percentages are enrollments of students in that group as a percentage of all students. Data on minority group enrollment are not available for 1965-1996. A few schools do not report minority group enrollment, so the numbers and percentages are slight underestimates.

Sources: American Bar Association, *A Review of Legal Education in the United States Fall 1995,* 67, 70 (Chicago: American Bar Association, 1996); American Bar Association, *A Review of Legal Education in the United States—Fall 1977,* 50—51 (Chicago: American Bar Association, 1978).

This trend guarantees that the proportion of lawyers who are not white men will grow substantially. It also means that women and members of racial minority groups increasingly will occupy important positions as lawyers. The presence of Sandra Day O'Connor, Ruth Bader Ginsburg, and Clarence Thomas on the Supreme Court symbolizes this trend. But, both women and minority group members continue to face discrimination within the legal profession at every stage from law school to appearances in court. The extent of discrimination against women has been documented in recent studies by the American Bar Association's Commission on Women in the Profession.[28]

Lawyers come primarily from families with higher than average economic status.[29] Aside from other factors, the cost of a college and law school education makes it easier for people to become lawyers if their parents are well-off.

The Work of Lawyers

The major activities of lawyers fit into several overlapping categories.[30] The first is litigation, handling cases in court and preparing for court appearances. This is the most visible part of lawyers' work, and television and movie portrayals of lawyers emphasize litigation. But litigation is only a small part of most attorneys' work, and many lawyers seldom or never go to court.

Similar to litigation is representation of clients—most often businesses—in the other branches of government. For example, lawyers represent clients in formal administrative proceedings before such agencies as the Federal Communications Commission and state public utilities commissions as well as in informal contacts with those agencies. Lawyers also lobby on behalf of clients in legislatures, seeking results such as an advantageous provision in federal tax law or a favorable city council ruling on a variance from zoning rules.

A third activity is negotiation, efforts to work out an agreement between a client and another party. Some negotiation occurs in the context of litigation, as lawyers seek to resolve cases prior to trial. Most serious criminal cases are ultimately resolved by the prosecution and the defense attorney through a plea bargain, and an even higher proportion of serious civil cases are settled by an agreement between the parties. Lawyers frequently negotiate to avoid litigation altogether, helping clients settle disputes at an early point or preventing disputes from developing in the first place.

Lawyers also engage in securing, providing security through the writing of documents. The most important of such documents are contracts, which are central to the functioning of the economy. Another common example is the will, which allows individuals to designate how their assets will be allocated after death. Wills illustrate the importance of securing, in that a properly written will can ensure that an estate is settled quickly and in the way that the writer wished.

The final activity of lawyers, counseling, involves helping clients find the most favorable course of action to handle a particular problem. Every area of the law entails a good deal of counseling. The primary task of many antitrust lawyers, for example, is to advise companies about whether certain decisions might lead to federal antitrust investigations or lawsuits by other companies. Similarly, tax lawyers provide advice on the tax consequences of different activities. One important aspect of counseling is helping clients to decide whether to file lawsuits and whether to accept negotiated settlements of cases. Counseling is linked to everything else that lawyers do. Almost inevitably, much of it goes beyond the realm of strictly legal knowledge.

Attorneys are often accused of encouraging lawsuits in order to create business for themselves, but this list of activities suggests a somewhat different conclusion. Although lawyers sometimes do stir up litigation, most of them spend the bulk of their professional time in other activities. In fact, much of what they do is intended to keep clients out of court by settling disputes, by preventing confusion that might lead to court battles, and by avoiding conduct that might expose someone to a legal challenge. As one scholar found in a study of consumer grievances, lawyers may even try to discourage action by potential clients who seem to lack a reasonable claim. "Rather than pour gasoline on the fire of indignation," the researcher concluded, "almost all of the lawyers interviewed in this study seem far more likely to use some type of fire extinguisher."[31]

Where Lawyers Work

Lawyers perform their activities in several different settings. Most are in private practice, but a significant and growing minority work in the business sector or for the government.

Private Practice   In 1991, 73 percent of all attorneys were engaged in private practice.[32] Although less dominant than it once was, private practice remains the primary form of work for lawyers.

Lawyers in private practice are members of a profession who are also engaged in a business. At least ideally, they do their work in accord with the standards of the legal profession. But they must also obtain enough work from clients and make a sufficient profit from that work to maintain a successful practice.

The private practice of law follows no single model. Some lawyers specialize narrowly, while others deal with a broad range of legal matters. Strategies to attract clients differ considerably. One important difference, linked to most others, is the size of the firms in which lawyers work.

Historically, most lawyers were solo practitioners. Over time, however, a growing number of lawyers have formed cooperative arrangements with colleagues. By 1991, 55 percent of the lawyers in private practice were involved in such cooperation, which can range from a simple sharing of office facilities by two attorneys to a highly structured firm employing several hundred lawyers.

This trend has resulted primarily from considerations of efficiency, since groups of lawyers can pool both the costs of a law practice and their personal expertise. It is also much easier for an inexperienced attorney to join an established group of lawyers than to start out alone, bearing all the costs of a legal practice and searching out sources of business. The advantages of practicing with other lawyers are reflected in incomes: lawyers practicing in large firms do far better than solo practitioners, with lawyers in small firms falling in between.[33]

All this being true, even today the majority of lawyers in private practice are solo practitioners or have only loose cooperative arrangements with other attorneys. Understandably, this kind of practice predominates in rural areas, and it is

City	Firm	Number of Lawyers
New York	Skadden, Arps, Slate, Meagher & Flom	1,150
Los Angeles	Latham & Watkins	764
Chicago*	Sidley & Austin	728
Milwaukee	Foley & Lardner	589
Houston*	Vinson & Elkins	523
Cleveland*	Baker & Hostetler	479
Pittsburgh	Kirkpatrick & Lockhart	446
Minneapolis	Dorsey & Whitney	412
Richmond, Va.*	McGuire, Woods, Battle & Boothe	382
Palo Alto, Calif.	Wilson Sonsini Goodrich & Rosati	370
Winston-Salem, N.C.	Womble Carlyle Sandridge & Rice	265
Rochester, N.Y.	Nixon, Hargrave, Devans & Doyle	258

Note: Cities are those in which firms have their principal offices; an increasing number of large firms list no principal offices, including the two largest (with 1,897 and 1,204 lawyers). In cities marked with an *, there is a larger firm that originated in that city but that no longer lists a principal office.

Source: "The NLJ 250," *National Law Journal,* September 30, 1996, C1–C22.

EXHIBIT 3.2   Largest Law Firms in Selected Cities, 1996

relatively common in medium-sized cities. Even in big cities, lawyers who serve individual clients in fields such as divorce are likely to work alone or in small groups.[34]

At the same time, a rapidly growing minority of lawyers practice in firms of substantial size. If we define large firms as those with fifty or more attorneys, there has been massive growth in both the number and size of large firms. Part of that trend, illustrated by Exhibit 3.2, is the spread of large firms from New York City to other large and medium-sized cities. Even in the current era, large firms hardly dominate the practice of law; of all the lawyers in private practice in 1991, 18 percent were in large firms.[35] But this segment of the profession has a significance far beyond its share of lawyers. Moreover, most characteristics of large firms are more extreme versions of those found in medium-sized firms. For both reasons, a closer look at large firms is useful.

Large Law Firms   The significance of large firms derives chiefly from their clienteles; they represent primarily business corporations, with an emphasis on major corporations. According to a 1996 survey, one large firm had done substantial work in the preceding year for at least 32 of the 250 largest industrial corporations, including Kmart, Pepsi, and Colgate-Palmolive.[36] Through their legal advice and action, large law firms affect the fortunes of the businesses they represent. They frequently provide advice and shape decisions on nonlegal matters as well, such as the economic consequences of a proposed merger between companies. Many law firms even have attorneys on the boards of major clients.

The services that large firms perform for their corporate clients frequently have a political tinge. Because their clients' interests are affected by legislation and administrative policy, particularly at the federal level, lawyers do considerable work to influence decisions in the legislative and executive branches. To provide this kind of representation, all of the twenty-five largest law firms in 1996 had offices in Washington.[37] Such representation occurs in the states as well: the nation's largest firm, working on behalf of a corporation that was fighting a hostile takeover, successfully lobbied the Kansas legislature to change corporation law in a way that helped protect against the takeover.[38]

Among the lawyers in large law firms, as in their smaller counterparts, the primary status distinction is between partners and associates. The distinction was so sharp at one New York firm that its "chief of protocol" refused to allow an associate to bring in his own furniture because it "had partner's legs, not being perfectly straight and squared off, and couldn't be used by an associate."[39] Attorneys generally enter firms as associates. If they remain with a firm for some period of time, typically five to ten years, they are considered for promotion to partnership status. (One New York lawyer, however, was made a partner in 1996 after twenty-five years as an associate.[40]) That status traditionally gives lawyers a permanent position in the firm and a share in its profits. In recent years, however, firms increasingly have lawyers who are made partners in title but who earn salaries rather than sharing in the firm's profits. (Some may be promoted to full partnership later.) Associates who are denied partnerships usually must leave the firm. But, in this respect too, firms are changing. Some lawyers who do not become partners are retained in permanent positions with titles such as "counsel" or "staff attorney."

Large firms seek to recruit the top-ranked graduates of the most prestigious schools. To attract these lawyers, large firms can offer high salaries, extensive support services, relative freedom from the difficult task of finding business, and—perhaps most important—the prospect of partnership. Competition among firms for graduates with the most impressive credentials is reflected in the upward spiral of salaries at the biggest firms. In 1996, one New York firm announced salaries of $92,000 for new associates.[41]

In exchange for the benefits of a large firm, associates typically work long hours under considerable pressure. At the extreme, the associates in the Houston office of one firm were reported to average 2,633 work hours in 1995—the equivalent of a little over 7 hours every day, including weekends and holidays.[42] The length of associates' workdays is a matter of legend, as illustrated by one story about a large-firm associate interviewing law students for jobs:

> One student asked if the associates ever do anything fun together. "Sure," the interviewer replied. "About two o'clock, we knock off for an hour and go play a game of racquetball." The student observed, "What a great way to break up the afternoon." The interviewer responded, "Afternoon?"[43]

The work that associates do is likely to seem uncreative and uninteresting, and few have much contact with clients. As one observer put it, "The work of young associates . . . is often so boring or trivial that many lawyers would refuse to do it if the money weren't so good."[44]

Attractive though it is, partnership is difficult to achieve. In most large firms, only a small proportion of associates become partners, the others leaving early or receiving a negative decision from the firm. In the early 1990s, the proportion went even lower—to one in ten in New York City's thirty largest firms.[45] The limited opportunity to win partnerships and other frustrations of associates' lives are reflected in the popularity of an anonymous but vocal associate called "The Rodent," whose work is described in Exhibit 3.3.

In large firms, there is considerable inequality among partners, even among those who share in firm profits. Relatively new partners enjoy neither the financial returns nor the power of senior partners, and at first their work may differ only marginally from what they did as associates. Over the course of their careers, however, partners come to do less strictly legal work. In the terms used by one lawyer, young partners and associates are "the grinders who do the work," while older partners are "finders," who attract clients, and "minders," who help manage the firm and take care of existing clients.[46] To earn their high incomes, senior partners charge clients the highest

EXHIBIT 3.3 The Rodent

In 1990, two associates at a Los Angeles law firm began a newsletter called *The Rodent,* which took a satirical look at law firms. The newsletter gained a following, achieving a circulation of about one thousand subscribers by 1994. The Rodent, as the author(s) became known, later began a column for legal newspapers and published a book in 1995.

The Rodent's publications express a highly cynical view of large law firms. In "The Firm," the prototypical firm that the Rodent depicts, associates work long hours under heavy pressure and difficult conditions to achieve the increasingly elusive goal of becoming partner. "Associates . . . are the ones who do all the work and grind out the legal product for the financial benefit of partners." The Firm focuses its efforts on making money to the virtual exclusion of other ends, such as high-quality lawyering and ethical practice. Its monetary goal is reflected in questionable billing practices and exploitation of associates and other nonpartners. A paralegal who worked himself to death was named "Employee of the Year"; one of the partners said that the paralegal "set an example not only for other paralegals but for all associates and staffers. If we had more employees like Andrew, The Firm would be a much better place and I'd be making a lot more money."

The popularity of *The Rodent* reflects its success in capturing the widespread frustrations of law-firm associates and the disillusionment of many with large firms. That popularity is one sign of what many lawyers see as undesirable trends in the legal profession.

Sources The Rodent, *Explaining the Inexplicable: The Rodent's Guide to Lawyers* (New York: Pocket Books, 1995); *The Rodent* (various issues); Saundra Torry, "From the Underground a Newsletter Rats on Greed," *Washington Post,* March 7, 1994, 7; Paul Reidinger, "Confessions of The Rodent," *American Bar Association Journal,* August 1995, 80–83. The quotations are, in order, from *Explaining the Inexplicable,* 54; and "McGonigle Named Employee of the Year," *The Rodent,* January/February 1996, 3.

rates for their time—in many firms, more than $300 per hour.[47] In one matter, former U.S. attorney general Griffin Bell, a partner in an Atlanta firm, charged E. F. Hutton $1,711 an hour for his services.[48]

The personnel of large firms include a great many nonlawyers, from administrators to clerical workers. Many firms have large staffs of paralegals, thereby enhancing considerably the volume of legal work they can perform.

The world of large law firms has changed a great deal in recent years.[49] Most fundamentally, that world has become less stable. For firms, the lack of stability stems largely from greater competition for legal business. Corporate clients increasingly "shop around" among outside law firms rather than maintain stable long-term relationships with firms, and they give more of their legal work to their own salaried lawyers.

One result is more aggressive marketing by firms. Another is the growing frequency of mergers between firms and hirings of partners from other firms, largely in an effort to add lawyers who can bring and attract business. Firms are now geographically more dispersed. Baker & McKenzie—the largest firm, with 1,897 lawyers in 1996—had lawyers in fifty-four cities, and three-quarters of its attorneys were outside the United States.[50] In this less stable situation, some firms grow rapidly and prosper; others fall behind, and some fail altogether. In 1994, for instance, the oldest firm in New York City closed down.

Instability at the level of firms has brought changes for their lawyers as well. As noted earlier, it has become more difficult for associates to achieve full partnership. With greater emphasis on bringing in legal business, those lawyers who do well at that part of the job are highly prized and get larger shares of firm profits. Partners who do not bring in substantial business may find their incomes reduced, and partnership no longer guarantees a lifetime job: firms increasingly fire partners. The financial pressures on large firms probably have reduced the average incomes of partners per hour worked, controlling for inflation.[51] Lawyers are more likely to move from one firm to another—some because their ability to attract business makes them prized "free agents," others because firms fire them, and others because their firms close.

Thus to the extent that the world of large law firms was ever genteel, it has become considerably less so today. In a 1997 survey of partners in the nation's 125 largest firms, many respondents expressed dissatisfaction with heavy workloads and pressures, and 83 percent said that private practice had changed for the worse. As the former chair of a large San Francisco firm concluded, "Life inside law firms ain't so much fun anymore."[52]

There is a certain irony in these changes: the pressures that big-firm attorneys increasingly face are similar to those that attorneys who work alone or in small firms have always faced.[53] Lawyers who practice outside large firms usually have to devote considerable time to attracting clients, and they often live with a great deal of economic insecurity. Practice in large firms is still different from other forms of private practice, but in some respects the differences are narrowing.

Business   About 10 percent of all lawyers work directly for businesses.[54] The long-term trend has been one of growth in the employment of "house counsel" as more businesses establish their own law departments and existing departments become larger. This growth has slowed in recent years, probably reflecting an increased concern with legal costs.

That concern also helps to explain the growth itself. Not only do businesses have more legal needs than in the past; increasingly, they prefer to use house counsel rather than outside lawyers. Corporations now spend more money on their own legal departments than on fees to outside law firms.[55] This trend toward in-house work has at least two sources. As noted, one is an interest in saving costs, an interest that has grown with the fees charged by big law firms. Estimates suggest that legal work done within a company costs one-third to one-half less than the same work done by outside law firms.[56] Another source is the greater control that companies can exert over the legal work done by their own employees.

Traditionally, house counsel concentrated on a company's routine and recurring legal work, and companies turned to outside law firms for less routine work such as litigation. Today, as businesses try to use outside law firms less, house counsel do more of their own litigation work—about one-third of that work, according to a 1990 survey of major legal departments.[57] General counsel, the heads of legal departments, manage and oversee the legal work done by outside firms. Even more than outside counsel, in-house lawyers are likely to participate in nonlegal decision making. Some general counsel in Chicago reported that they frequently advised on such matters as corporate acquisitions, labor negotiations, and even advertising campaigns.[58]

The dominant image of in-house legal departments contrasts strongly with that of large law firms: legal departments hire young lawyers with less impressive credentials and pay them less but give them greater security and shorter work hours. This image fits reality to a considerable degree, but the difference between in-house departments and large firms is not as sharp as it once was. One indication of that change is salaries: in 1994, the median level of compensation for heads of corporate legal departments was $222,000, and "non-supervisory" lawyers received a median of $86,000.[59]

Not all attorneys in the business world actually work as lawyers. Many can be found in fields such as banking and real estate, where their legal knowledge provides an advantage even if they are not practicing law as such.

Government   In 1991, about 11 percent of all attorneys worked for government in some capacity. Of these, about one-third were in the federal government, while the other two-thirds were scattered among the state and local governments. A small proportion worked in legislatures, and one-quarter were in the judiciary. In this discussion, I focus on those who serve in the executive branch.

Government engages in a good deal of litigation, both as a criminal prosecutor and as a plaintiff or defendant in civil cases. A considerable volume of "internal litigation" also occurs within government agencies, such as the Internal Revenue Service and the Social Security Administration, and lawyers represent the agency's position or serve as judges in these cases. And government agencies, like private parties, require expert advice on issues that involve legal questions.

The federal government employs about twenty-eight thousand attorneys. A substantial number of the federal government's lawyers work in the Department of Justice. The largest concentration of Justice Department lawyers is in the United States Attorneys' offices in the ninety-four federal judicial districts. U.S. Attorneys and their assistants represent the government in criminal prosecutions and civil litigation in the district courts. The Justice Department also has several divisions—Civil, Land, Antitrust, and Civil Rights, for example—that help set general department policy and advise the U.S. Attorneys. These divisions handle some civil litigation at the trial level and take over cases from U.S. Attorneys at the appellate level. Of particular importance is the Office of the Solicitor General, which must approve most federal government appeals to the courts of appeals and nearly all government appeals or petitions to the Supreme Court. The office itself handles litigation in the Supreme Court, thereby shaping the federal government's position on major legal issues.

Every other executive branch agency of significant size has a legal staff, and some—particularly the corps of lawyers in the Department of Defense—are substantial. These legal staffs advise agency officials and handle internal litigation within agencies. In a few instances, they also conduct litigation in court. Attorneys for the Internal Revenue Service, for instance, represent the government in the Tax Court.

Government legal services at the state and local levels are organized in a variety of ways, but in most states they are highly decentralized. The state attorney general and other state agencies may have substantial legal staffs, but most lawyers work for local governments in prosecutors' offices and other organizations. Some attorneys serve as prosecutors or city solicitors on a part-time basis, primarily in rural areas where government has little legal business.

The impact of government attorneys merits emphasis. Prosecutors play a critical role through their decisions about which cases to bring and how to handle them, a role that is examined in Chapter 6. Each state's attorney general influences government practices through advisory opinions on the law, and the legal advisers to federal agencies shape policy on both legal and nonlegal matters. Lawyers within the White House often play a critical role in developing presidential policy positions. Less visible lawyers in lower-level positions also can influence policy a good deal through their work in litigation.

Lawyers who work for government are chosen in several ways. Some, such as the federal attorney general, are appointed by the chief executive. But in most states the attorney general and county prosecutors are elected. Lawyers who hold lower-level positions are usually selected by their superiors.

The great disadvantage of government service is relatively low salaries.[60] But there are compensating advantages: opportunities to try cases and take on other major responsibilities much earlier than associates can do in law firms, the chance to participate in making public policy, and often high job security. Partly because of the tightening job market, these advantages have attracted an increasing number of lawyers to government in recent years.

For many lawyers, work in government is one part of a legal career. It is common for young lawyers to serve in government for a few years before moving to private practice or corporate law departments. As a result, a high proportion of government lawyers are inexperienced. Some lawyers come to government in midcareer to serve in high-level positions, often at salaries considerably lower than they had enjoyed before, and then return to private practice.

To a degree, government serves as a training ground for lawyers who go on to the private sector. One Chicago building houses a considerable number of criminal defense lawyers who migrated there from the court building a few miles west, where they had worked as prosecutors,[61] and such a shift from prosecution to defense is common. A more direct change of sides was undertaken in 1993 by the former top lawyer in the U.S. State Department, who had helped develop the legal rationales for economic sanctions against Libya and the American bombing of its capital: he was hired to represent the Libyan government in matters related to an airplane bombing for which Libyan terrorists were thought responsible. After a considerable outcry, he decided not to continue working for Libya, but four years later a disciplinary board found that his representation of Libya after working on the same matter in government violated an ethical rule for lawyers.[62]

Specialization in the Practice of Law

Lawyers are often thought of as generalists, as professionals who handle any kind of legal task for any client who comes to them. This image is largely and increasingly inaccurate: most lawyers specialize to a considerable extent. This specialization occurs along three lines.

The first is by type of activity. A small proportion of attorneys engage primarily in litigation. In contrast, many other lawyers seldom, if ever, go to court. Within large law firms, even trial lawyers may be "'paper litigators,' logging legal lifetimes taking depositions and exchanging motions." One lawyer became head of his firm's litigation group, with earnings of about $750,000 a year, without ever helping to pick a trial jury.[63]

The second form of specialization is by type of legal issue. In a complex legal system, no attorney can be an expert on everything. Largely for this reason, most lawyers devote themselves to a few fields or even to a single one. In a sample of Chicago lawyers, 22 percent practiced exclusively in one field, while another 39 percent gave more than half their time to one field.[64] Common specialties include tax law, criminal law, personal injuries, and real estate.

Finally, lawyers can specialize by type of client. Some lawyers serve the various legal needs of corporations. Others combine client specialization with legal specialization. Examples include lawyers who represent primarily personal injury plaintiffs (sometimes called trial lawyers) and those who represent criminal defendants. This combination helps produce some relatively narrow specialties, such as defense of white-collar criminal defendants or class-action suits by stockholders against corporations.

Patterns of specialization are influenced by social and legal developments, which are reflected in the needs of current and potential clients. For example, the growth in corporate bankruptcies in recent years has attracted more lawyers to that field. Some lawyers choose their specialties quite consciously. Others develop specialties largely by chance, based on such circumstances as the tasks they are given as associates in law firms.

The degree of specialization varies according to the setting in which lawyers practice. Lawyers in big cities are far more specialized than their rural counterparts. Surveys found that 70 percent of Chicago lawyers considered themselves specialists, compared with 56 percent in Springfield, Missouri, and 22 percent in rural Missouri.[65] Lawyers who practice alone are less specialized than those in large firms, partly because those firms can combine specialists in different fields to offer a broad range of services.

Because lawyers specialize, their perspectives and their self-interest differ. These differences often come to the surface on public issues. Today, for instance, lawyers who represent manufacturers strongly support proposals to limit legal liability for injuries caused by defective products, while lawyers who represent personal injury plaintiffs fight hard against these proposals. Because of differing needs and interests, most lawyers orient themselves primarily toward their own group of specialists rather than toward the legal profession as a whole.

The Two Hemispheres

> Washington has two distinct groups of lawyers. There's the "uptown" bar, feasting off the specialized and usually dry legal work generated by the Federal Government. And there's the "downtown" bar, a grittier group whose members are here because Washington, like any other city, has its share of mayhem and conflict thrusting people into the legal system.[66]

The reporter who made that distinction correctly perceived an important pattern in the practice of law. The various differences among lawyers that I have described are not random; rather, lawyers tend to cluster into what John Heinz and Edward Laumann called "the two hemispheres of the profession."[67]

These hemispheres are separated most sharply by the kinds of clients that lawyers represent. Some lawyers serve primarily large organizations, while others represent mainly individuals and small businesses. Relatively few do substantial work for both types of clients. As Exhibit 3.4 shows, this distinction between the "corpo-

EXHIBIT 3.4 A Comparison of Legal Practice on Behalf of Corporations and Individuals

	Primary Clients	
	Corporations	**Individuals**
Socioeconomic background of lawyers	Higher status	Relatively lower status
Law School attended	Relatively high percentage from elite schools	Primarily nonelite schools
Type of practice	Large firm or business legal department	Small firm or solo practice
Typical number of clients each year	Fewer	More
Control by clients	Higher	Lower
Prestige within profession	Higher	Lower
Income	Higher	Lower

Source: John P. Heinz and Edward O. Laumann, *Chicago Lawyers: The Social Structure of the Bar* (New York: Russell Sage Foundation, 1982).

rate" and the "personal" sectors is related to other important distinctions. Lawyers in the two sectors tend to specialize in different kinds of legal issues. Lawyers in the corporate sector are also far more likely to work in large firms (or, of course, for businesses themselves) rather than in solo practice or small firms. Lawyers in the corporate sector tend to serve a small number of clients over long periods of time, while those in the personal sector tend to serve a succession of clients on single matters. As I discuss later, one result is that attorneys in the corporate sector are generally subject to greater control by their clients.

Corporate lawyers are somewhat more likely to come from higher-status backgrounds and elite law schools, a difference reflecting the higher income and prestige of practice in the corporate sector. The gap in income has widened considerably since the late 1960s: lawyers in solo practice have suffered a substantial decline in real income.[68]

The distinctions between the two hemispheres should not be exaggerated, however. Indeed, in some respects, according to one scholar, "there's a continuum rather than a bifurcation."[69] But real distinctions do exist, and they have important consequences. Most lawyers and prospective lawyers aspire to enter the corporate sector. As a result, this hemisphere probably contains a disproportionate share of the most skilled lawyers. Furthermore, the good support services and other attributes of practice in the corporate sector are more conducive to effective legal work. For both reasons, the legal services provided in the corporate sector almost surely are superior, on the whole, to those provided in the personal sector. Hence, in the words of John Heinz, these two hemispheres make up "two systems of justice, 'separate and unequal.'"[70]

Organization and Regulation of Lawyers

As noted earlier, regulation of the legal profession is done almost entirely by state governments. For the most part, state legislatures have turned over to their supreme courts the power to regulate the legal profession, including admission of lawyers to the bar and disciplinary action. Most of the actual regulation is performed by lawyers themselves, under the supreme court's direction. About two-thirds of the states have an integrated bar, which means that all lawyers must belong to the state bar association; these associations are then given the primary role in professional regulation. In some states, the power of these mandatory associations and the level of required dues have brought about demands for reform or even abolition of these associations. Discontent has been particularly strong in California, but after a heated campaign lawyers in that state voted in 1996 by a 2–1 margin to maintain the mandatory association.[71]

The legal profession has a great deal of other organized activity. Its most important single group is the American Bar Association (ABA), to which 36 percent of the nation's lawyers belonged in 1996. The proportion of lawyers who belong to the ABA has declined in the 1990s, reflecting an economic squeeze on many lawyers that has affected membership in other lawyers' groups as well.[72] The ABA is divided into a number of sections, some based on specialized areas of practice. Both the ABA and its sections engage in a variety of activities. These include meetings and publications intended to improve the skills of members, as well as work in government on behalf of ABA positions on legal issues. The ABA also seeks to influence the selection of federal judges by rating potential or actual nominees.

The state bar associations, whether compulsory or voluntary in membership, usually resemble the ABA in organization and activities. There are also many city and county bar associations. In addition, each legal specialization has its own separate associations, some of which play significant roles within the profession and in politics. For example, the Association of Trial Lawyers of America, an organization of sixty thousand lawyers who represent plaintiffs in personal injury cases, exerts considerable impact on law and policy in its area of specialization. Perhaps most important, in recent years the association has fought against tort law "reform," a movement to change major legal rules about personal injuries in ways that favor defendants. For many lawyers, these specialized groups are more important than those that are open to all lawyers because they more fully represent their members' interests and serve their professional needs.

Lawyers' Lives[73]

There is a strong negative theme to much of what has been written about lawyers in the past several years. Lawyers have always been subject to criticism for their work and role in American society, but that criticism has become stronger, and public attitudes toward lawyers are more negative than in the past.[74] People within the legal profession write about changes that have made the profession a less positive force and less pleasant for its practitioners.[75]

Surveys of lawyers themselves indicate a considerable degree of dissatisfaction. In a 1994 survey of California lawyers, only 52 percent agreed that "if I were to pick a career, I would still choose to become an attorney"; 29 percent disagreed, with the other 19 percent taking a middle position. Other surveys of lawyers have disclosed even more negative attitudes toward the practice of law.[76]

In light of developments in the legal profession, such dissatisfaction is understandable. Between 1989 and 1996, the proportion of law school graduates who found legal work within six months dropped from 83 percent to 70 percent,[77] and fewer new lawyers obtain the positions they would prefer. Job security has declined for many established lawyers as well, and some face stagnant or declining incomes. Even lawyers in the most prestigious and remunerative segments of the profession face increased pressures on the job. According to one survey, half the lawyers in private practice reported that they worked at least twenty-four hundred hours a year, and 75 percent said that they felt substantial pressure and tension in their jobs.[78]

The extent and depth of lawyers' unhappiness should not be exaggerated. Certainly many lawyers do well in their practices and feel a high degree of satisfaction, and changes in the legal profession work in favor of some lawyers even while they make life more difficult for others. Moreover, there is always a tendency for people to remember the past in rosier hues than it merits. For that reason, both observers of the legal profession and lawyers themselves may exaggerate the negative impact of changes in recent years. But significant changes *are* occurring, and those changes have made some lawyers less happy with their work.

ACCESS TO LEGAL SERVICES

A lawyer's services can be helpful in many situations. We might expect people to seek out a lawyer whenever those situations arise—for instance, when they feel that their legal rights have been violated or when they need to make an agreement with someone. Yet many people who find themselves in these situations do not consult lawyers.

Why does this nonuse of lawyers occur? "Use of lawyers is an acquired habit," according to one legal scholar, and "most people never surmount the barriers of fear, ignorance, and unfamiliarity."[79] The primary fear is that going to a lawyer will worsen a situation rather than improve it. Besides, people may not know when a lawyer could help them or how to find an appropriate lawyer. Thus, even if legal services were free, by no means would everyone with a law-related problem go to an attorney.

But the monetary costs of legal services can add another important deterrent to their use. Most people who consider going to a lawyer lack a clear sense of how much a lawyer's help will cost them, but they often perceive that the cost will be more than they can afford or feel comfortable in paying. Indeed, standard rates for lawyers' services can make those services quite expensive. In the New York City area, even among lawyers who serve individual clients the most typical range of fees is $150–200 an hour.[80]

If there were no mechanisms to overcome this monetary barrier, the use of legal services by nonwealthy individuals would be quite limited and their use by people with low incomes virtually nonexistent. In turn, most individuals would have little ability to make effective use of the legal system and the courts; in practice, whatever legal rights they had would mean little. But, some mechanisms to address the problem of legal costs *have* developed, and they have grown considerably in number and scope over the last thirty years. Only after these mechanisms are considered can the impact of costs on access to lawyers be assessed.

Overcoming the Cost Barriers to Legal Services

The types of mechanisms that allow litigants to avoid the usual costs of legal services fall into two general categories. One consists of programs, primarily governmental, to meet the legal needs of the poor. The other includes an array of developments in the private sector that may reduce cost barriers for the population as a whole.

Criminal Defense Services for the Poor   There is a long history of efforts to provide free legal services to indigent criminal defendants, but until the 1960s these efforts were limited and unsystematic. Although low-income defendants in federal court and in most states gained a legal right to free services, this right was not implemented very effectively.

The primary impetus for strengthening this right was *Gideon v. Wainwright* (1963), in which the Supreme Court held that indigent criminal defendants in serious state cases must be provided with free counsel.[81] Although the Court's decision did not change the law in most states, it underlined the obligation to provide meaningful access to counsel. Spending for this purpose increased dramatically at all levels of government, and in 1990, governments spent about $1.7 billion for legal defense of the poor.[82] At least in felony cases, government-funded systems now represent most defendants.[83]

Across the country, two systems for defense of the poor predominate. The first is the public defender system, in which public employees (sometimes part-time) represent defendants. The second is the assigned counsel system. In this system, judges appoint private attorneys, usually from a list of volunteers, on a case-by-case basis to represent defendants. About one-quarter of the states have statewide public defender systems. Most other states employ both systems: public defenders' offices are used chiefly in urban counties, which have enough cases to make them practical, while most rural counties use assigned counsel. In a third system, used less often, a government unit contracts with lawyers or organizations such as bar associations to represent indigent defendants on a continuing basis.

Despite the great increase in financial support for defense of the poor, all of these systems suffer from serious monetary problems. These problems have been aggravated in recent years by growth in criminal cases and by the worsening fiscal problems of state and local governments. In the assigned counsel system, the problem lies in low hourly fees and limits on the maximum amounts allowed per case, both of which are quite widespread. These low fees discourage attorneys from seeking case assignments, although the depressed legal market of the 1990s has made such assignments more attractive in some places.[84] Low fees also discourage lawyers who do take assignments from giving sufficient time and effort to cases. In 1992, a federal court of appeals overturned a conviction that had put a Texas man on death row. In doing so, the court noted that "the state paid defense counsel $11.84 per hour. Unfortunately, the justice system got only what it paid for."[85] In the public defender system, the problem lies in the total funding provided to offices, funding that tends to be inadequate to meet an office's responsibilities. Consequently, public defenders are burdened with large caseloads, and they too may be unable to give sufficient attention to each case.

These financial problems have produced significant weaknesses in defense of the poor. In recent years, for instance, studies have found highly inadequate public defender systems in Tennessee and in Atlanta.[86] The most serious deficiency in providing assistance to indigent defendants occurs in death penalty cases. This deficiency results in part from the low fees paid to assigned counsel, and it worsened when Congress in 1995 cut off funding to centers that supply counsel in cases involving death sentences.[87] A 1996 federal law allows states to limit challenges to death sentences in federal court if the states meet certain criteria for adequate representation of defendants in state proceedings. Federal judges in California, Florida, and Tennessee quickly ruled that those states failed to meet the criteria, and the Indiana attorney general conceded that his state also fell short.[88]

Yet the average level of performance by assigned counsel and public defenders may equal that of privately hired defense attorneys.[89] Working-class and middle-class defendants, the primary users of privately hired attorneys, are limited in the quantity and quality of services they can purchase. And indigent defendants often receive very good legal services. This is particularly true of public defender systems, in which lawyers typically gain considerable expertise quickly through their specialization in criminal cases. One recent study, more positive than most, states its conclusion in its title: attorneys representing the indigent "Get the Job Done and Done Well."[90]

Civil Representation for the Poor   The first legal aid societies were set up in American cities in the late nineteenth century to provide legal assistance to low-income people in civil matters. The number and size of these societies grew in the twentieth century. The early legal aid societies accomplished a good deal, but they had only limited funding and often depended on volunteer staffing. As a result, they met only a small portion of the legal needs of the poor.[91]

In 1965, as part of President Johnson's War on Poverty, the federal government established its own program of legal assistance to the poor in civil matters. In 1974, after some evolution and political controversy, Congress created the Legal Services Corporation (LSC) to fund federal legal services to the poor on the civil side of the law.

LSC operates as an administrator of grants to more than three hundred local agencies that provide assistance directly to the indigent. Most of these agencies set up law offices to which clients can come for help. These offices have handled more than a million legal matters each year, encompassing a wide variety of problems that reflect the situations of the poor. Large as this number is, it represents only a small portion of the legal needs of the poor—less than 15 percent in New York state, according to a bar association study.[92] In 1994, 33 percent of the problems handled by Legal Services offices involved family matters, 22 percent housing, 16 percent income maintenance and health, and 11 percent consumer and personal finance issues.[93]

Most of the business of local agencies funded by LSC is fairly routine and is resolved without litigation. But attorneys in this program and its predecessor have used lawsuits and other activity for the broader purpose of shaping the law, sometimes through challenges to the legality of government practices. To support this work, Legal Services created special centers in fields such as youth law and consumer law.

LSC and the agencies that it funds have not been universally popular. Litigation to shape the law has aroused the greatest opposition, particularly from the government officials and private groups whose programs and practices are challenged by that litigation. Over the years, many restrictions have been placed on the kinds of cases that Legal Services can handle, and in the 1980s and 1990s there has been a series of battles over the LSC budget.

When the Republican party gained majorities in both houses of Congress in 1995, some members sought to eliminate the program altogether. Ultimately its budget was cut by one-third in 1996, and new restrictions to its activities were added. Among the most important restrictions was a prohibition on participation in class action lawsuits, in which a large class of people are joined together as litigants. Because of this prohibition, one Legal Services lawyer had to drop out of a Supreme Court case he was preparing to argue.[94] The budget cuts have led to the closing of some LSC offices, layoffs of attorneys, and in turn, reductions in the numbers and kinds of matters handled by local programs. Thus Legal Services can be expected to meet an even smaller proportion of the legal needs of low-income people than it did in the past.

Legal Services is not the only source of help for the poor in civil matters. Many lawyers donate a portion of their time pro bono publico (literally, for the public good) to meet what they see as a professional obligation.[95] A portion of this work is on behalf of the indigent. A few local bar associations have established pro bono requirements for their members, and in 1992 the Florida Supreme Court ruled that every lawyer in the state must do at least twenty hours of pro bono work in each year or pay $350. In 1993, the American Bar Association established a goal for law firms to give at least 3 percent of their lawyers' billable hours to service for the poor. Many firms formally accepted the ABA's challenge, but in the first year only one-third of those firms met the 3 percent goal.[96] The cuts in LSC funding will put greater pressure on other lawyers to assist the poor, but it is uncertain how much growth in that assistance will occur.

Advertising   Though the poor have the greatest difficulty in gaining access to lawyers' services, people with moderate incomes also may face substantial financial barriers to the use of attorneys. Government has done little directly to tear down these barriers, but several developments in the private sector have increased the availability of lawyers to people who are neither indigent nor wealthy. To some extent, these developments simply overcome people's fears about the cost of lawyers; to some extent, they actually reduce these costs.

Advertising by lawyers is significant in itself and a foundation for other developments.[97] Traditionally, state rules prohibited most forms of advertising by lawyers. In 1977, however, the Supreme Court struck down state prohibitions of advertising by lawyers as a violation of free speech rights.[98] Since then, state supreme courts and bar associations have adopted a great many rules limiting the forms of attorney advertising. The Supreme Court has upheld some restrictions and overturned others.

Lawyers were slow to begin advertising, but a growing minority use some form of advertising. A 1993 survey found that 16 percent of attorneys were in firms that used print advertising, and 15 percent placed display ads in the telephone yellow pages. Only 2 percent used television commercials, but spending on this highly visible form of advertising has grown enormously, to $126 million in 1993.[99]

The content of advertising varies a good deal; most is fairly restrained, but some lawyers take a more flamboyant approach. In one classic television ad, a Wisconsin lawyer named Kenneth Hur "played a convict whose final words to the chaplain from the electric chair were that he wished he'd called Mr. Hur's legal clinic."[100] Exhibit 3.5 describes the range of material and approaches in a sampling of advertisements in the telephone book yellow pages, to provide a sense of what advertising lawyers see as the most useful appeals to potential clients.

Lawyers also advertise to specialized audiences that include potential clients. In 1996, for instance, two New Orleans lawyers advertised their services in the Florida State University campus newspaper, seeking to reach students who were traveling to New Orleans for the Sugar Bowl game between Florida State and Florida. "If you get in trouble," the ad said, "we can help you out!"[101]

Lawyers sometimes solicit clients more directly. Some Maryland lawyers buy from the state court system lists of people who have recently been arrested for serious traffic violations and send letters to those people.[102] After a child died because of

Those lawyers who place display ads in the yellow pages take a variety of approaches, but certain themes frequently recur.

Costs

Many lawyers seek to assure potential clients that costs will be reasonable and manageable. A Chicago firm advertises "free first consultation" and indicates "credit terms available." A Phoenix firm calls itself "The Discount Accident Lawyers." Another Phoenix firm says that clients may "try us for free for 30 days. If you are not 100% satisfied, you pay us nothing." And firms that take cases on a contingency fee basis routinely point out that the client will owe no fees except for a share of what is won at trial or in a settlement.

Identifying with Clients

Some lawyers try to show that they share the perspective and views of potential clients. According to a Portland, Oregon, firm, "We're in your neighborhood and we're on your side." A Detroit lawyer says that "I don't represent drunk drivers—*I represent their victims.*" A San Antonio bankruptcy lawyer tells readers that "every day I am saddened when I see so many individuals who, like you, are honest people, but whose lives are made miserable" by inability to pay bills.

Credentials

Lawyers often point to credentials they have earned. A New York City lawyer points out that he has written "books and articles . . . on cases like yours," adding that potential clients are welcome to read them at his office. A Portland lawyer says that he is "Listed in 'The Best Lawyers in America.'" Two San Antonio lawyers state that they are both "licensed by the Supreme Court of Texas," a credential they share with every other attorney who is allowed to practice in the state.

Results

Ads sometimes cite favorable results achieved for clients in the past. A Milwaukee firm announces that its lawyers were "winners of Wisconsin's largest recovery ever in an injury case." A Los Angeles lawyer quotes a client: "Larry Parker got me $2.1 million." A San Antonio firm goes further, listing a dozen victories complete with citations to docket numbers or court opinions, though it cautions readers that "the results in your case depend on its facts and the law." Some ads are less cautious, addressing the issue of costs and prospective results simultaneously by assuring potential clients that there will be—in the words of a Phoenix firm—"no fee until we win!"

Striving for a Positive Image

In the minds of many Americans, the legal profession has fallen a long way from what it once was. A Chicago firm has responded by naming itself the "A. Lincoln Law Group." To the left of the firm name in its ad is a picture of the sixteenth president.

Sources: Selected telephone books distributed in 1995 and 1996.

EXHIBIT 3.5   Themes of Lawyers' Advertisements in Telephone Book Yellow Pages

apparent negligence by a day care center, an Alabama lawyer sent a wreath to the funeral home with a brochure and a note soliciting the parents' business.[103] Lawyers and their representatives have contacted the families of airline disasters within a few days to offer their services. Such actions have aroused considerable distaste and criticism, and in 1995 the Supreme Court upheld Florida's thirty-day moratorium on contact with accident victims or their families.[104]

The lawyers who advertise to the general public are those who seek business from individuals. Thus one study found that solo practitioners and those in small firms were the most likely to advertise in the yellow pages, while lawyers in large firms were the least likely.[105] The same is true of newspaper and television advertising. But large firms increasingly advertise in ways more appropriate to their needs. Most firms, for instance, distribute brochures about the firm and its services.[106] Large firms, like other lawyers, have always used techniques such as memberships in organizations to make contacts with potential clients. Holiday greeting cards are also common, and one lawyer-author points out a specific payoff from their use: couples with children often wait until after the holidays to seek a divorce, so a lawyer's Christmas card may come at a good time to obtain their business.[107]

Many lawyers are unhappy about the growth of advertising, feeling that it demeans the profession and serves consumers badly. Others argue that advertising has lowered fees and made lawyers more accessible to individuals. At present, we lack sufficient information to resolve these issues. But advertising clearly has become one important means for people to locate attorneys; one study found that 20 percent of the people who consulted lawyers after they had been injured in accidents found those lawyers through advertising.[108]

Legal Clinics and Prepaid Legal Services   In the 1970s, bar associations began to abolish minimum fee schedules, rules that prohibited lawyers from charging less than a certain amount per hour. In 1975, the Supreme Court eliminated these schedules altogether by ruling that they violated the antitrust laws.[109] This development, combined with the legalization of advertising, made possible the creation of legal clinics. As one author has defined them, these clinics are "firms that use advertising to attract a high volume of middle-income clients, and use technological tools and paraprofessionals to offer prices that are generally lower than those of traditional firms."[110] Clinics work primarily on legal matters that are relatively common for middle-income people, such as divorce and home sales, and advertising provides the means to attract people who need help with these matters.

Legal clinics burgeoned in the late 1970s and 1980s, led by two national firms with many local offices. But the numbers of lawyers who practiced in legal clinics were always relatively small; a 1990 study estimated that fewer than two thousand lawyers did so.[111] Clinics are now in a period of severe decline because of economic difficulties, partly a result of competition from firms and individual lawyers for the same types of legal business. This decline is symbolized by the shrinking size of one of the national firms and a decision by the other to shift its focus to personal injury cases.[112]

The term *prepaid legal services* refers to a variety of mechanisms under which a payment allows people access to a lawyer's services at some future time—in other words, insurance for those services.[113] Prepaid legal services were made possible by a series of court and legislative actions to remove traditional restrictions on legal insurance, beginning with a 1963 Supreme Court decision. As a result, prepaid legal services plans have become a significant part of the legal marketplace. It has been estimated that more than 17 million people are covered by some form of legal insurance.[114]

People obtain prepaid legal services primarily in two ways. Some are enrolled in group plans through their employers, either as part of their benefit package or by paying a monthly fee to participate. Others enroll in individual plans, some of which operate through credit unions or are sold to charge card customers. Companies such as Amway and Montgomery Ward market legal insurance plans.

The various legal insurance plans differ in what they provide. Some entitle their participants to a certain amount of a lawyer's time per year. One national program provides unlimited telephone advice and consultation, along with some other services. Some plans have open panels, which allow those enrolled to consult any attorney. More common are closed panels, under which people must choose from a specified group of lawyers.

Like legal clinics, the plans are used most often for the kinds of matters that are common among working- and middle-class people: marriage and divorce, real estate, landlord-tenant relations, and wills. With the decline of clinics, insurance plans have a much greater potential for expanding the availability of lawyers' services to individuals. But their growth has slowed in recent years, largely because companies became less willing to provide legal insurance as an employment benefit. That change reflects a general decline in employee benefits as well as a 1992 tax law change that makes legal insurance plans more expensive for employers.[115]

The Contingent Fee   Somewhat different from all these other developments is a long-standing system under which a lawyer's fee in a case is contingent upon its outcome.[116] Under the contingent or contingency fee system, a lawyer represents a client who has a legal claim for money without requiring an advance payment (except, in some instances, for the lawyer's expenses). If the client recovers money, either through a court decision or through a settlement with the other party, the attorney's fee will be a proportion of that sum. But if the client wins nothing, the attorney also receives nothing.

The contingent fee is used almost entirely in representation of individuals rather than institutions. It is employed most often in personal injury cases, where it is the predominant form of payment. One study found that contingent fees were used 97 percent of the time in this area.[117] The proportion the lawyer receives can vary, although a fee of one-third of the recovery is common. Lawyers often charge a higher proportion for a case that goes to trial.

The existence of the contingent fee increases the availability of attorneys to people who have legal claims. If a sizable advance payment were required, many people could not hire a lawyer, and if a significant fee had to be paid regardless of the outcome, this would strike many people as an unacceptable risk. However, as long as a substantial monetary recovery is likely, a person with a legal claim generally can find a lawyer to take the case on a contingent basis. Thus, for one important type of legal problem, the contingent fee overcomes much of the financial barrier to the use of legal services. One purpose of legal advertising is to inform individuals of the contingent fee and thus to allay their fears about the financial risks of litigation.

Nonetheless, the system has been criticized a good deal. In recent years, criticism has come primarily from people who think that the contingent fee has spurred a growth in personal injury litigation by giving lawyers strong incentives to bring cases. In recent years, groups representing defendants in personal injury cases have sought to reduce the level of contingency fees that lawyers can charge, and they have achieved some success in this effort.

The Overall Picture

The cost of legal services would seem to make it difficult for most people to take advantage of them; it would also seem to create a strong relationship between wealth and the ability to hire a lawyer. On the other hand, several mechanisms have been developed to overcome the usual financial barriers. In light of all this, what is the impact of costs on the use of lawyers?

The sharpest distinction is between individuals and large institutions. With the exception of those who are wealthy, individuals still face great constraints when they need to use lawyers for more than limited purposes. Some people under some circumstances can avail themselves of very good legal services—for example, the indigent criminal defendant in a city with an excellent public defender's office or the injured person who has a strong case involving a large potential recovery. By and large, however, nonwealthy individuals are limited in the quantity and quality of services they can obtain. They must refrain from using lawyers at times when legal help would be useful, and when they do employ an attorney, they may have to settle for less than the full level of the services they need. Nor can they afford to hire the most expensive attorneys.

These constraints have their clearest impact when people would like to take a case to trial but have no special help in paying the extensive lawyers' fees that usually result. As federal judge Shirley Hufstedler noted, a regular civil trial "is beyond the economic reach of all except the rich, the nearly rich or the person seriously injured by a well-insured defendant."[118]

If we leave aside the wealthy, the relationship between individuals' income and their ability to use a lawyer is not a simple one. Although people with higher incomes are in a better position to pay for lawyers' services, the constraints on the use of expensive services apply to the great majority of people regardless of income. The near-poor may now be in a weaker position than the poor, and the relative positions of low-income and middle-income people vary with such factors as the strength of a local Legal Services program and the availability of legal insurance. As a result, surveys of the public have not found a strong relationship between income and a person's use of lawyers to deal with legal problems.[119]

Of course, wealthy individuals are in a far better position than most other people to use lawyers' services. O.J. Simpson could spend virtually unlimited funds on his defense to murder charges. But a very small proportion of people are in that situation. Bill and Hillary Clinton are far better off economically than the average American, but even they were overwhelmed by the costs of lawyers' services resulting from the Whitewater investigation and other matters—nearly $4 million by early 1997.[120]

Large institutions such as corporations and the state and national governments can afford much higher levels of legal services. Large corporations are in a particularly strong position, both because of their wealth and because legal fees are tax-deductible as a business expense—in effect, a very large government subsidy. Thus major corporations can afford to pay a great deal for legal services, frequently millions of dollars a year.

Until fairly recently, large corporations seemed to feel no cost constraints at all. Law firms recognized the willingness of corporations to pay whatever they were charged without scrutinizing bills, and some responded by piling on charges that ranged from the legitimate but questionable (spending far more than necessary on a legal matter) to the dishonest (such as billing more hours than lawyers actually worked). A secretary at one of the largest firms in Los Angeles described her firm's traditional practices:

> We charged for everything. If we offered a client a doughnut, we would charge it to the bill. We would charge the client for soft drinks. We would charge for secretarial overtime. We made a profit on faxing and photocopying. Our lawyers were always padding their bills. I once saw a memo from one of the partners who said if you even *think* about a file, whether in your car, in the shower, or on the golf course, it gets a minimum fifteen-minute charge.[121]

Other billing practices are described in Exhibit 3.6.

In the past several years, corporations have increased their vigilance over legal costs. Perhaps the most important result, noted earlier, is an increasing reliance on in-house lawyers. Another sign of change is the development of companies to monitor

EXHIBIT 3.6   Some Reported Billing Practices of Law Firms

A California lawyer on three occasions billed a client for 50 hours of work in one day; a North Carolina lawyer billed clients more than 1,200 hours in one month (a thirty-one-day month has 744 hours).

A Chicago lawyer charged $25,000 for "ground transportation" while handling a case in San Francisco.

A New York firm, one of the country's largest, charged a client $85.01 for an outgoing fax that had cost the firm $7.51 in long-distance charges.

A lawyer in a San Diego firm moved into a hotel for a San Diego trial. Among the items charged to a client was $50 for money stolen from the hotel room.

A Los Angeles firm charged clients for the flowers it sent to their funerals.

Sources (in order): David Margolick, *At the Bar: The Passions and Peccadilloes of American Lawyers* (New York: Touchstone Books, 1995), 87 (50–hour day); The Rodent, *Explaining the Inexplicable: The Rodent's Guide to Lawyers* (New York: Pocket Books, 1995), 103 (1,200–hour month); Margolick, *At the Bar,* 87; Ralph Nader and Wesley J. Smith, *No Contest: Corporate Lawyers and the Perversion of Justice in America* (New York: Random House, 1996), 240; The Rodent, *Explaining the Inexplicable,* 115; Nader and Smith, *No Contest,* 234.

legal bills for businesses. Corporations are more willing to negotiate with law firms over charges and to challenge bills. As a result, they have gained some control over their legal expenses.

Still, large institutions spend very large sums for lawyers' services. The primary reason, of course, is that they are engaged in so many activities that require lawyers. But the ready availability of attorneys does provide a great advantage in utilizing the legal system. This advantage becomes most evident in a dispute between parties that differ in their access to attorneys. A working-class or middle-class individual may have great difficulty in combatting a large business or the Internal Revenue Service. The largest corporations probably are in the strongest position. In an antitrust dispute, even the federal government may be at a disadvantage against such a corporation, which can hire the most expert antitrust attorneys and assemble a much larger legal staff than the one available to the Justice Department.

This kind of advantage is also reflected in corporate influence on government policy. By employing attorneys as advocates in all three branches of government, large corporations can shape the development of the law. Where legal issues involve conflicts between corporations and sectors of society with less access to attorneys (as in consumer law), corporate interests generally have a greater capacity to achieve favorable rules of law.

There are exceptions. Legal Services lawyers have sometimes done quite well in securing judicial doctrines favorable to low-income citizens. Some interest groups and public interest law firms enjoy considerable success in obtaining rulings that favor relatively powerless segments of society, such as racial minority groups and consumers. On the whole, however, large institutions have the most ability to use lawyers to shape the law.

THE LAWYER-CLIENT RELATIONSHIP

Clients come to lawyers with legal problems or opportunities, seeking assistance in achieving their goals. In providing that assistance, lawyers play a variety of roles—those of "the gatekeeper who teaches clients about the costs of using the legal system, the knowledgeable friend or therapist, the broker of information or coach, the go-between or informal mediator, the legal technician, and the adversary bargainer-litigator."[122]

In allowing their lawyers to play these roles, clients put themselves in a dependent position. A client who hires an attorney turns over to that attorney some control over the course of events. As a result, a lawyer's ability and willingness to serve a client have much to do with the client's success in dealing with the legal system. An incompetent lawyer or one who does not represent a client's interests faithfully may do considerable damage to those interests.

Competence

Differences among lawyers in their skills have an obvious but important impact: the more competent an attorney, the better off are the lawyer's clients. That impact is especially visible in the courtroom, where the litigant with the better attorney may gain a clear advantage over the other party. This reality is disturbing. But differences in lawyers' skills are inevitable, and so we may have to tolerate their impact on the legal system.

Less tolerable is work by lawyers that falls below a minimal level of competence. When people give responsibilities to their lawyers, they typically assume that those lawyers have at least a moderate degree of ability. If that assumption is incorrect, the client may suffer grievously. A poorly drafted contract, inaccurate tax advice, and ineffective courtroom advocacy can all have very serious consequences.

Because lawyers are licensed only after intensive training and a lengthy examination, we might assume that few of them are incompetent. But, argues legal scholar Richard Abel, "it is absurd to pretend that any test of competence administered to someone at the age of twenty-five, no matter how well constructed, can ensure quality throughout a fifty-year career."[123] A number of critics have pointed to what they see as widespread inadequacies in the work of lawyers. One of these critics was federal judge David Bazelon. Referring to the constitutional provision that guarantees the right to counsel, Bazelon said that many criminal defense lawyers are "walking violations of the Sixth Amendment."[124]

In recent years, considerable effort has been devoted to improving lawyer competence through legal education. As noted earlier, many law schools have established clinical programs to give students more practical training, though these programs play only a limited part in the education of most law students. Some lawyers and educators have proposed more radical changes in law school education, but such changes will not come easily.

One major development is an increase in formal education after law school. Continuing legal education programs have become common as a means for lawyers to refresh and expand their knowledge. These programs use a variety of techniques, from formal courses to publications aimed at practical needs. In 1996, forty states required a certain amount of continuing education classwork for lawyers to renew their licenses.[125] A common requirement is fifteen hours of work per year. It is uncertain how much effect such requirements have on lawyers' competence, though they undoubtedly enhance the skills of some attorneys.

Another avenue taken by several states, such as Alabama and Minnesota, is to give official status to some legal specialties so that clients can identify lawyers who have expertise in particular fields. States certify specialists on the basis of experience or an examination. A 1990 Supreme Court decision allows attorneys to advertise as specialists on the basis of certification by private organizations,[126] and several specialized lawyers' groups have established such certification programs.

There have also been proposals for mandatory certification, under which lawyers could practice in certain fields only if they met certain requirements. But lawyers prize their freedom to practice in whatever fields they wish, and no state has adopted such a plan.

Faithful Representation

Everyone agrees that lawyers should work faithfully on behalf of their clients. But people also agree that there are limits to what lawyers should do for clients. The American Bar Association's Model Rules of Professional Conduct, widely used by the states as a benchmark for ethical conduct, require a lawyer to act "with zeal in advocacy upon the client's behalf," yet a lawyer is limited to "lawful and ethical measures" on behalf of the client.[127] The ethical limits on advocacy have been debated, but situations sometimes arise when lawyers clearly go too far. According to a 1990 indictment, for instance, three New York City lawyers committed such offenses as having a private investigator widen a pothole with a pickax to make it appear more dangerous and using the same person twice as an "eyewitness"—once for an accident that occurred when he was in prison.[128]

While inappropriate actions on behalf of a client represent a serious issue, more pervasive is the problem of inadequate adherence to a client's interests. According to the Model Rules, "the lawyer's own interests should not be permitted to have an adverse effect on representation of a client."[129] This is a concern because the self-interest of lawyers frequently fails to coincide with that of their clients.

One example concerns lawyers' fees. A lawyer who is paid on an hourly basis may have a financial incentive to devote more time to a case than a client needs. In contrast, a lawyer who is paid a flat fee has an incentive to resolve a matter by spending the minimum time necessary. The contingent fee system seems to meld the interests of lawyer and client, but it often creates a conflict of interest. The additional expenditure of time necessary to gain the maximum settlement for a plaintiff may not provide the lawyer with an adequate return to be financially worthwhile.

In situations that involve a conflict of interest, clients are at a disadvantage. Even though lawyers have a duty to elevate clients' interests over their own, in practice they have a strong temptation to follow the course of action most favorable to their own interests, especially because clients often have difficulty in evaluating a lawyer's decisions. As a result, clients do not always receive the most faithful representation from their attorneys.

The failure of some attorneys to represent their clients faithfully is illustrated by class action lawsuits. Lawyers sometimes bring class action suits on behalf of large numbers of people and then reach settlements that give them large fees while providing very little to members of the class they represent. In a large lawsuit against six large airlines for acting together to set fares, the lawyers representing airline travelers received $14 million while the travelers themselves received nearly worthless coupons for future flights.[130]

Some lawyers depart from their clients' interests in a much more extreme way: they behave dishonestly. Although many people think that lawyers are unusually prone to dishonesty, one legal scholar argued that "lawyers are about as honest as other people, given their opportunities. Unfortunately, they have many more opportunities than most people to be dishonest."[131] The two forms of dishonesty that seem most common among lawyers both reflect these opportunities.

One is the misuse of clients' funds. Attorneys entrusted with the proceeds of an estate or money to be placed in a trust sometimes "borrow" these funds for their own use, intending to pay back what they have taken. A few simply steal money— in some instances, a great deal of money. In recent years, for instance, lawyers in New York and Maryland have been accused of taking millions of dollars from clients and other victims.[132]

The second form of dishonesty involves fees. In a legal scholar's survey, "nearly all of the lawyers interviewed reported some amount of deception in practices relating to billing clients," deception that ranged from charging for nonessential work to billing for more time than the attorney worked.[133] Even more serious, lawyers sometimes accept money for services they never perform. As a result, the unsuspecting client may forfeit legal rights. For example, an attorney's inaction can cause a client to miss the deadline for filing a lawsuit.

One means to improve the ethical behavior of lawyers is education. Law schools now require their students to take some coursework dealing with a lawyer's professional responsibilities. Most states include a section on ethics on their bar examinations, and many require some study of ethics as part of continuing legal education. A knowledge of ethical rules is unlikely to deter lawyers who have larceny in their hearts, but it may prevent some lawyers from engaging in less obvious forms of unethical behavior through ignorance.

Variation in the Lawyer-Client Relationship

The character of the relationship between lawyer and client varies from situation to situation. Most important, some clients are in better positions than others to ensure that lawyers serve their interests. As Heinz and Laumann argue, corporations generally can exert considerably more control over their lawyers than can individuals.[134]

In the sector of the bar that serves individuals, lawyers typically represent clients on a one-time basis, and they have a great many clients. Heinz and Laumann found that, on the average, Chicago lawyers who represent individuals in nonbusiness matters such as divorce and personal injury have a hundred clients a year.[135] Thus no single client is particularly important to a lawyer's professional position or income, and the lawyer need not worry a great deal about incurring a client's disfavor.

For their part, few individual clients have an opportunity to scrutinize the performance of a lawyer over time or to develop independent expertise in the law. As a result, the client may find it difficult to obtain good representation for appropriate fees. For instance, a study by the New York City Department of Consumer Affairs found that lawyers in contested divorce cases frequently engage in questionable practices concerning fees, so that clients pay more than they expected without receiving satisfactory service. The problems found in the study were epitomized by one lawyer's explanation for not providing monthly bills to clients: he "told Consumer Affairs that he and his secretary make mistakes in the bill and that if clients scrutinized the bills and asked questions, he'd have to charge them for the phone calls."[136] Lawyers do not hold all the power in their relationship with individual clients, as Austin Sarat and William Felstiner demonstrated in their study of divorce.[137] But lawyers do have a great deal of freedom from control, and they have considerable capacity to exert control by shaping their clients' perceptions of their situations.

All this does not mean that lawyers for individuals typically fail to represent their interests effectively. Lawyers for criminal defendants and personal injury plaintiffs often display quite clearly the zealous representation that the ABA's code demands. It does mean, however, that individuals who are one-time clients of attorneys have relatively limited capacities to assess and control the performance of their attorneys.

The situation in the sector of the bar that serves institutions is rather different. Here some lawyers are employed by a single client, a business corporation. This arrangement gives the corporation a high degree of control because corporate executives can evaluate a lawyer's work over time and because the lawyer depends on the corporation for employment. Indeed, a number of court cases have arisen when lawyers were fired by their companies after they placed ethical responsibilities, such as refraining from illegal conduct, above the interests of their employers.[138] (Full-time government lawyers are in a similar situation in some respects, though their "clients" often are in other agencies and thus may have little direct control over them.)

Because of their independent status and their multiple clients, large law firms would seem to be in a much stronger position than lawyers who work for a single client. But large firms often provide continuing services to a set of corporate clients. These long-term relationships give clients a good chance to scrutinize and evaluate their lawyers' work, and they also require lawyers to satisfy their clients in order to maintain their business. Moreover, corporations are powerful institutions that can do much to affect the standing of a lawyer or firm.

How much control do institutional clients gain over the lawyers and law firms that represent them? Certainly that control is far less than total. In his study of medium-sized litigation, Herbert Kritzer concluded that "there is little evidence of significant control of the lawyer by the client, regardless of whether the client is an individual or an organization (even if that organization is a large insurance company on which the lawyer is highly dependent)."[139] It should be recalled that corporations, like individuals, are victims of outrageous and even dishonest billing practices.

Yet the dependence of lawyers in the corporate sector on their major clients means that those clients gain significant influence over lawyers' choices. To a considerable degree, for example, law firms structure their practices to serve major clients—even opening new branches to serve their needs better. Dependence on major clients makes lawyers reluctant to challenge what those clients want to do. According to one legal scholar, "there are strong forces at work that induce . . . lawyers to satisfy the managers in the company who hire them and can fire them. Sometimes this comes at the expense of ethical practice."[140] One example is the assistance that some large firms gave to savings and loan associations in continuing questionable practices in the 1980s. Three large firms have paid a total of $136 million in settlements with the federal Resolution Trust Corporation for their roles as representatives of two savings and loan institutions whose failures left the government with more than $3 billion in costs.[141] The influence of institutional clients on lawyers is symbolized by an incident that Heinz and Laumann relate, one that occurred after a major Chicago firm allowed some of its lawyers to spend time on pro bono work:

> All went well until a young lawyer reported to the firm that he had been assigned to defend a man accused of bank robbery. It happened that one of the principal clients of the firm was a major bank. The bank that was the firm's client had no connection with the bank that had been robbed . . . but the firm nonetheless ordered the young lawyer to withdraw from the representation of the defendant. . . . The reason for the firm's order to withdraw, apparently, was that bank robbers are the enemies of banks, and for the firm to permit one of its lawyers to represent a bank robber might therefore be seen as disloyalty to a major client.[142]

On the whole, then, institutions do achieve greater control over their attorneys than do individuals. Thus they gain one more advantage in their use of legal services. Not only do they get more and often better services, the services they get are more likely to be consistent with their interests.

Remedies

As noted already, education programs and certification of specialists have been used to improve the representation that lawyers provide to their clients. For people who feel that they have been badly served by their lawyers, there are more specific remedies: malpractice suits and complaints to disciplinary bodies. These mechanisms can provide redress to a disgruntled client, and their existence may deter lawyers from engaging in undesirable practices.

Malpractice Suits   Like other professionals, lawyers can be sued for malpractice on the ground that they failed to serve their clients adequately. Suits can also be brought by other people who claim that they have suffered losses because of a lawyer's representation of a client. In law, as in other professional fields, there is considerable disagreement about what kinds of actions constitute malpractice.

Although lawyers are frequently blamed for the growth in malpractice actions against physicians and others, they too have faced a burgeoning of such actions. Only a minority of all malpractice claims result in some kind of payment to the claimant.[143] But some jury verdicts and out-of-court settlements produce substantial payments, suggesting that attorneys made serious lapses in these cases. Both the increase in suits and the large verdicts and settlements have contributed to rising rates for malpractice insurance and some difficulties in obtaining insurance.

About half of all malpractice claims stem from litigation; the others result from aspects of office practice. Claims of alleged incompetence are far more common than claims of dishonesty. More than two-thirds of the claims relate to deficiencies in legal knowledge or poor office administration. In contrast, about 10 percent are related to intentional error—though a lawyer who makes a mistake may act to cover up the mistake. (One common allegation is that an attorney missed a deadline for legal action, but lawyers who miss deadlines sometimes deceive clients about what happened.)

One lawyer who represents people bringing malpractice suits has a simple explanation for the relatively large number of suits in recent years: "There are idiots out there practicing law."[144] Perhaps the large number of relatively new lawyers in recent years has increased the incidence of poor legal services. Almost certainly, clients are now more skeptical about the quality of legal work and more willing to seek redress when they feel that they have been badly served. In any case, the growth in claims is making lawyers more careful about their handling of cases and dealings with clients, and it may have at least a marginal effect in improving the quality of legal work.

Discipline   Clients or others who feel that a lawyer has acted unethically can complain to the agencies in each state that are responsible for disciplinary action against attorneys. Discipline is ultimately the responsibility of state supreme courts, but typically most of the disciplinary process is delegated to bar association committees or to lawyers' disciplinary groups established by the supreme court. In this process, a lawyer's conduct is assessed against standards adopted by the state supreme court, standards that are usually similar to those in the American Bar Association's Code of Professional Responsibility.

Most disciplinary proceedings begin with a complaint to the appropriate agency. The agency may set a complaint aside without further action or investigate it. After an investigation, it may file formal charges against the attorney and hold a hearing. Based on what it finds, the agency can then recommend disciplinary action, which may range from a private reprimand to permanent disbarment from legal practice in that state. The state's supreme court must make the final decision to impose disciplinary action.

The pattern of action by disciplinary agencies can be illustrated with data from Colorado in 1995. Colorado had about 17,700 active attorneys, 12,400 of them in private practice. A total of 1,550 "grievances" were filed against lawyers. The Office of Disciplinary Counsel determined that only 40 percent of the grievances that it considered merited full investigation. Ultimately, the supreme court suspended 34 lawyers from practice for some period and permanently disbarred 16 others.[145]

It is impossible to evaluate the disciplinary process on the basis of figures such as these. But that process has received a good deal of criticism, primarily on the grounds that too few complaints are given serious consideration and that the discipline applied to miscreant lawyers is too lenient. There is considerable support for this criticism: complaints often seem to be dismissed too readily, and sanctions for serious misconduct are not always heavy. As the example of Colorado indicates, however, many lawyers do receive severe sanctions. In the years from 1991 through 1995, each year an average of 780 lawyers in the United States were disbarred.[146] Contrary to most people's impression, however, disbarment is not necessarily permanent. In the 1991–1995 period, 206 disbarred lawyers—about half of those who applied—were readmitted to practice.[147]

In response to criticism, some states have made significant changes in their disciplinary systems. Among these states is California; most recently, after the disclosure that many disbarred lawyers are readmitted to practice, the state bar voted to allow for permanent disbarments of some lawyers.[148] But not everyone is satisfied. In 1992, one lawyer surveyed some recent disciplinary cases and asked, "What does it take to get disbarred in California?"[149] The sampling of cases in Exhibit 3.7 provides a partial answer to his question.

CONCLUSIONS

This chapter offers only a first look at lawyers. Discussions of their roles in specific areas of the court system, such as the criminal courts, provide a fuller picture of what lawyers do and how they fit into the judicial process.

Even this first look should make clear the importance of lawyers in both the legal system and American society. Lawyers provide the means by which individuals and organizations use the law to their benefit; in practice, legal rights are meaningful only to the extent that people can call on lawyers to assert those rights. And through their individual work and their organizations, lawyers play key roles in shaping the law.

Also clear are differences among segments of society in the use of legal services. The most fundamental difference is between the great majority of individuals and large organizations. For the most part, these two groups are represented by two different sectors of the bar, and the corporate sector that represents large organizations tends to serve its clients more fully than the personal sector.

The past few years have seen major changes in the legal profession. One key

A lawyer failed to act competently and failed to communicate properly with his clients in two lawsuits. In one case he agreed to dismissal of his client's lawsuit without consulting with the client. Sanction: one year of probation.

In one case, a lawyer failed to make necessary court appearances; the case was dismissed, but the lawyer told his client that the case was proceeding well. In another case, the lawyer failed to prepare a proposed order and file it in court. He had been disciplined three times in the preceding three years, twice for failing to meet conditions imposed on him in the first disciplinary order. Sanction: six months' suspension, probation for the remainder of five years.

A lawyer committed misconduct involving four clients; the misconduct included failure to perform legal services competently and to return unearned fees. He also failed to meet conditions of probation imposed in a prior case. He had a record of misconduct resulting in disciplinary actions that had begun in 1983. Sanction: disbarment.

Sources: Descriptions are paraphrased and summarized from descriptions in *California Bar Journal,* August 1996, 34; September 1996, 33; and June 1996, 28.

EXHIBIT 3.7   Selected Disciplinary Cases Resulting in Sanctions Against California Attorneys, 1996

source of these changes is the growing number of lawyers. That number will continue to increase for many years, and it will help spur further alterations in the work and situation of lawyers. Yet with all the changes that have come, much about the practice of law has remained remarkably stable. This stability reflects the deep roots of the ways that lawyers do their jobs. For this reason, most of the patterns described in this chapter are likely to endure well into the future.

FOR FURTHER READING

Galanter, Marc, and Thomas Palay. *Tournament of Lawyers: The Transformation of the Big Law Firm.* Chicago: University of Chicago Press, 1991.

Heinz, John P., and Edward O. Laumann. *Chicago Lawyers: The Social Structure of the Bar.* New York: Russell Sage Foundation, 1982.

Kelly, Michael J. *Lives of Lawyers: Journeys in the Organizations of Practice.* Ann Arbor: University of Michigan Press, 1994.

Kritzer, Herbert M. *The Justice Broker: Lawyers and Ordinary Litigation.* New York: Oxford University Press, 1990.

Landon, Donald D. *Country Lawyers: The Impact of Context on Professional Practice.* New York: Praeger, 1990.

Miller, Mark C. *The High Priests of American Politics: The Role of Lawyers in American Political Institutions.* Knoxville: University of Tennessee Press, 1995.

Pierce, Jennifer L. *Gender Trials: Emotional Lives in Contemporary Law Firms.* Berkeley: University of California Press, 1995.

Sarat, Austin, and William L. F. Felstiner. *Divorce Lawyers and Their Clients: Power and Meaning in the Legal Process.* New York: Oxford University Press, 1995.

Seron, Carroll. *The Business of Practicing Law: The Work Lives of Solo and Small-Firm Attorneys.* Philadelphia: Temple University Press, 1996.

Spangler, Eve. *Lawyers for Hire: Salaried Professionals at Work.* New Haven, Conn.: Yale University Press, 1986.

NOTES

1. Mark C. Miller, *The High Priests of American Politics: The Role of Lawyers in American Political Institutions* (Knoxville: University of Tennessee Press, 1995), 3.
2. *In re Opinion No. 26 of the Committee on the Unauthorized Practice of Law,* 654 A.2d 1344 (N.J. 1995). See Ann Davis, "Va. Bar Wants to Be There at Closings," *National Law Journal,* September 16, 1996, A6.
3. *Marlow v. State,* 886 S.W.2d 314 (Texas Ct. of App. 1994); see Gary Taylor, "Convict Beats His Own Attorney," *National Law Journal,* February 8, 1993, 43.
4. American Bar Association, *Comprehensive Guide to Bar Admission Requirements 1996–97* (Chicago: American Bar Association, 1996), 16–18.
5. "1995 Statistics," *The Bar Examiner* 65 (May 1996), 27.
6. Don Van Natta Jr., "Judge Passed Bar Despite Lack of Law Degree," *New York Times,* January 2, 1996, B2.
7. American Bar Association, Section of Legal Education and Admissions to the Bar, *Standards for Approval of Law Schools and Interpretations* (Indianapolis: American Bar Association, 1996), 32.
8. Margot Slade, "A Little Law School Does Battle with the A.B.A.," *New York Times,* February 4, 1994, B9; Ken Myers, "Settlement Will Mean Changes in ABA's Accreditation Process," *National Law Journal,* July 10, 1995, A15.
9. James D. Gordon III, "How Not to Succeed in Law School," *Yale Law Journal* 100 (April 1991), 1685, n. 3.
10. Ann Davis, "Graduate Debt Burden Grows," *National Law Journal,* May 22, 1994, A21.
11. Howard S. Erlanger and Douglas A. Klegon, "Socialization Effects of Professional School: The Law School Experience and Student Orientations to Public Interest Concerns," *Law and Society Review* 13 (Fall 1978), 11–35; Robert V. Stover and Howard S. Erlanger, *Making It and Breaking It: The Fate of Public Interest Commitment During Law School* (Urbana: University of Illinois Press, 1989).
12. This discussion of licensing requirements is based in part on American Bar Association, *Comprehensive Guide to Bar Admission Requirements 1996–1997.*
13. Data on the bar examination are taken from "1995 Statistics," *The Bar Examiner,* 23–38.
14. Jay Mathews, "California's Bar Exam Breaks More Lawyers Than It Makes," *Washington Post,* August 2, 1983, A2.
15. David Margolick, "At the Bar," *New York Times,* September 13, 1991, B9.
16. Saundra Torry, "Objections Sustained: The Grade Escape Route is Closed," *Washington Post,* August 8, 1994, Washington Business section, 7; Michael Wines, "At the Bar," *New York Times,* April 15, 1994, B10.
17. Joan M. Cheever, "A Scream and a Curse Open the Bar Exam," *National Law Journal,* August 7, 1989, 8.
18. Henry Chu, "Legal Samaritan Is Now on the Right Side of Law," *Los Angeles Times,* October 29, 1994, B7.
19. American Bar Association, *A Review of Legal Education in the United States, Fall 1995* (Chicago: American Bar Association, 1996), 67; Richard H. Sander and E. Douglass Williams, "Why Are There So Many Lawyers? Perspectives on a Turbulent Market," *Law and Social Inquiry* 14 (Summer 1989), 463.

20. Chris Klein, "Professor Saw Red over Lampoon by *Crimson* Newspaper Columnist," *National Law Journal,* March 17, 1997, A14.

21. Sander and Williams, "Why Are There So Many Lawyers?"

22. Fred Strasser and Bryan Greenwald, "Lawyers Reject Bush for Clinton," *National Law Journal,* August 10, 1992, S4.

23. Stephen P. Magee, "How Lawyers Sap the U.S. Economy," *Los Angeles Daily Journal,* February 29, 1991, 6.

24. Mark Hansen, "Quayle Raps Lawyers," *American Bar Association Journal* 77 (October 1991), 36; Ray August, "The Mythical Kingdom of Lawyers," *American Bar Association Journal* 78 (September 1992), 72–74. For other views on this issue, see Marc Galanter, "Pick a Number, Any Number," *Legal Times,* February 17, 1992, 26–28; Christopher Ocasal, "How to Count Japan's Lawyers," *Legal Times,* April 6, 1992, 22, 25; "The Legal Profession," *The Economist,* July 18, 1992, 3–18; and Ty Ahmad-Taylor, "Looking for a Lawyer? Dial Reykjavik (and Forget Jakarta)," *New York Times,* October 21, 1994, B13.

25. Cynthia Fuchs Epstein, *Women in Law* (New York: Basic Books, 1981), 4; Robert Benenson, *Editorial Research Reports: Lawyers in America* (Washington, D.C.: Congressional Quarterly, 1984), 535.

26. Epstein, *Women in Law,* 51.

27. American Bar Association, *Review of Legal Education, 1995,* 67, 70.

28. American Bar Association Commission on Women in the Profession, *Elusive Equality: The Experiences of Women in Legal Education* (Chicago: American Bar Association, 1996); Nina Bernstein, "Equal Opportunity Recedes for Most Female Lawyers," *New York Times,* January 8, 1996, A12; Jennifer L. Pierce, *Gender Trials: Emotional Lives in Contemporary Law Firms* (Berkeley: University of California Press, 1995).

29. Richard L. Abel, *American Lawyers* (New York: Oxford University Press, 1989), 87–90.

30. See Martin Mayer, *The Lawyers* (New York: Harper & Row, 1967), 29.

31. Stewart Macauley, "Lawyers and Consumer Protection Laws," *Law and Society Review* 14 (Fall 1979), 155.

32. Except where noted, all figures on the distribution of lawyers are taken from Barbara A. Curran and Clara N. Carson, *The Lawyer Statistical Report: The U.S. Legal Profession in the 1990s* (Chicago: American Bar Foundation, 1994).

33. Sander and Williams, "Why Are There So Many Lawyers?", 447–451, 474–475; Robert L. Nelson, "The Futures of American Lawyers: A Demographic Profile of a Changing Profession in a Changing Society," *Case Western Reserve Law Review* 44 (Winter 1994), 371–372, 394–395.

34. Donald D. Landon, *Country Lawyers: The Impact of Context on Professional Practice* (New York: Praeger, 1990), 24; John P. Heinz and Edward O. Laumann, *Chicago Lawyers: The Social Structure of the Bar* (New York: Russell Sage Foundation, 1982), 65.

35. Calculated from data in Curran and Carson, *The Lawyer Statistical Report,* 7–8. See also Marc Galanter and Thomas Palay, *Tournament of Lawyers: The Transformation of the Big Law Firm* (Chicago: University of Chicago Press, 1991), 123.

36. "Who Represents Corporate America?", *National Law Journal,* November 18, 1996, C3–C26.

37. "The NLJ 250," *National Law Journal,* September 30, 1996, C4–C8.

38. Jeff Lyon, "Chicago Law," *Chicago Tribune Magazine,* June 9, 1991, 16.

39. Lawrence Lederman, *Tombstones: A Lawyer's Tales from the Takeover Decades* (New York: Farrar, Straus and Giroux, 1992), 36.

40. Tom Schoenberg, "The Iron Man of Associate Ranks," *Legal Times,* April 29, 1996, 1, 17–18.

41. Ann Davis, "'First Years' Offered $92,000," *National Law Journal,* September 23, 1996, A4.

42. Chris Klein, "Who's Tops in Associate Toil," *National Law Journal,* August 26, 1996, A4.

43. Gordon, "How Not to Succeed in Law School," 1702.

44. Ruth Marcus, "Gloom at the Top: Why Young Lawyers Bail Out," *Washington Post,* May 31, 1987, C1.

45. Edward A. Adams, "Becoming Partner: The Impossible Dream," *National Law Journal,* June 22, 1992, 2. The figure was obtained from a survey by the *New York Law Journal.*

46. Robert L. Nelson, *Partners with Power: The Social Transformation of the Large Law Firm* (Berkeley: University of California Press, 1988), 69–70.

47. "Law Firm Billing," *National Law Journal,* December 2, 1996, B9–B12.

48. Morton Mintz, "Griffin Bell Set Hourly Fee at $1,711," *Washington Post,* January 30, 1987, F1, F2.

49. This discussion is based in part on Galanter and Palay, *Tournament of Lawyers,* and Nelson, *Partners with Power.*

50. "The NLJ 250," *National Law Journal,* C4.

51. Anthony T. Kronman, *The Lost Lawyer: Failing Ideals of the Legal Profession* (Cambridge, Mass.: Harvard University Press, 1993), 282.

52. Saundra Torry, "Attorneys Who Come In-House from the Cold," *Washington Post,* July 10, 1995, Washington Business section, 7. The survey is reported in Chris Klein, "Big-Firm Partners: Profession Sinking," *National Law Journal,* May 26, 1997, A1, A24, A25.

53. See Carroll Seron, *The Business of Practicing Law: The Work Lives of Solo and Small-Firm Attorneys* (Philadelphia: Temple University Press, 1996).

54. Curran and Carson, *The Lawyer Statistical Report,* 7; the proportions for government lawyers are from the same source.

55. James S. Wilber, "Support Staffing Ratios Remain High In-House in Spite of Automation," *National Law Journal,* May 20, 1991, S6.

56. Eve Spangler, *Lawyers for Hire: Salaried Professionals at Work* (New Haven, Conn.: Yale University Press, 1986), 71.

57. From table in *National Law Journal,* November 5, 1990, S8.

58. Jeffrey S. Slovak, "Working for Corporate Actors: Social Change and Elite Attorneys in Chicago," *American Bar Foundation Research Journal,* Summer 1979, 483.

59. "What Lawyers Earn," *National Law Journal,* July 15, 1996, C6.

60. This discussion is based in part on Spangler, *Lawyers for Hire,* ch. 4.

61. Anne Keegan, "Men of Monadnock," *Chicago Tribune Magazine,* March 3, 1996, 14–20.

62. Sharon Walsh, "Former U.S. Official Drops Libya as Client After Outcry," *Washington Post,* July 17, 1993, A1, A9; Saundra Torry, "State Department Lawyer Unethical in Pan Am 103 Case," *Washington Post,* July 1, 1997, A7.

63. David Margolick, "At the Bar," *New York Times,* September 9, 1988, B5.

64. Heinz and Laumann, *Chicago Lawyers,* 53.

65. Ibid., 54; Landon, *Country Lawyers,* 129.

66. Neil A. Lewis, "Washington's 2 Law Worlds Clash in Barry Case," *New York Times,* January 26, 1990, B11.

67. Heinz and Laumann, *Chicago Lawyers,* 319. This discussion of the "two hemispheres" is based primarily on Heinz and Laumann.

68. Sander and Williams, "Why Are There So Many Lawyers?" 474–475.

69. Murray Schwartz, quoted in Francis J. Flaherty, "The Myth—and Reality—of the Law," *National Law Journal,* August 6, 1984, 43.

70. John Heinz, quoted in ibid., 45. In this passage, Heinz was quoting a 1968 federal commission report on race relations in the United States.

71. Nancy McCarthy, "Lawyers Vote 2 to 1 to Keep California's State Bar Unified," *California Bar Journal,* July 1996, 1, 6.

72. Saundra Torry, "Shrinking Bar Associations Work to Make Their Case," *Washington Post,* July 8, 1996, Washington Business section, 7.

73. This title is borrowed from Michael J. Kelly, *Lives of Lawyers: Journeys in the Organizations of Practice* (Ann Arbor: University of Michigan Press, 1994).

74. Randall Samborn, "Anti-Lawyer Attitude Up," *National Law Journal,* August 9, 1993, 1, 20.

75. Examples include Mary Ann Glendon, *A Nation Under Lawyers: How the Crisis in the Legal Profession Is Transforming American Society* (New York: Farrar, Straus and

Giroux, 1994); Sol M. Linowitz with Martin Mayer, *The Betrayed Profession: Lawyering at the End of the Twentieth Century* (New York: Charles Scribner's Sons, 1994); and Kronman, *The Lost Lawyer.*

76. Nancy McCarthy, "Pessimism for the Future," *California Bar Journal,* November 1994, 1; Glendon, *A Nation Under Lawyers,* 85.

77. David Segal, ". . . and Aren't," *Washington Post,* October 11, 1996, A18.

78. American Bar Association, *The Report of "At the Breaking Point"* (Chicago: American Bar Association, 1991), 3–4.

79. Abel, *American Lawyers,* 129.

80. Seron, *Business of Practicing Law,* 117.

81. *Gideon v. Wainwright,* 372 U.S. 335 (1963).

82. Bureau of Justice Statistics, *Justice Expenditure and Employment,* 1990 (Washington, D.C.: U.S. Department of Justice, 1992), 3. Information on defense systems was drawn from Robert L. Spangenberg and Marea L. Beeman, "Indigent Defense Systems in the United States," *Law and Contemporary Problems* 58 (Winter 1995), 31–49; and Steven K. Smith and Carol J. DeFrances, *Indigent Defense* (Washington, D.C.: U.S. Department of Justice, 1996).

83. Roger A. Hanson, Brian J. Ostrom, William E. Hewitt, and Christopher Lomvardias, *Indigent Defenders Get the Job Done and Done Well* (Williamsburg, Va.: National Center for State Courts, 1992), 14.

84. Caryle Murphy and Patricia Davis, "Low Fees Cut Legal Services for the Poor," *Washington Post,* March 30, 1987, A1; Rosalind Resnick, "Associates Jump Ship, Go Public," *National Law Journal,* August 5, 1991, 10.

85. *Martinez-Macias v. Collins,* 979 F.2d 1067 (5th Cir. 1992).

86. David Margolick, "Volunteers or Not, Tennessee Lawyers Help Poor," *New York Times,* January 17, 1992, B10; Peter Applebome, "Study Faults Atlanta's System of Defending Poor," *New York Times,* November 30, 1990, B12.

87. Marcia Coyle, Fred Strasser, and Marianne Lavelle, "Fatal Defense: Trial and Error in the Nation's Death Belt," *National Law Journal,* June 1, 1990, 30–44; Marcia Coyle, "Death Resource Centers Reborn as Private Groups," *National Law Journal,* January 15, 1996, A9.

88. Marcia Coyle, "Florida Flunks Death Counsel Test," *National Law Journal,* September 30, 1996, A16.

89. See Roy B. Flemming, "If you Pay the Piper, Do You Call the Tune? Public Defenders in America's Criminal Courts," *Law and Social Inquiry* 14 (Spring 1989), 393–414; and Hanson et al., *Indigent Defenders.*

90. Hanson et al., *Indigent Defenders.*

91. See Emery A. Brownell, *Legal Aid in the United States: Supplement* (Rochester, N.Y.: Lawyers Co-Operative Publishing, 1961).

92. Kevin Sack, "Judge Pushes Lawyers to Give Services to Poor," *New York Times,* May 2, 1990, A13.

93. Sarah Neville, "Legal Services Faces Cuts in Funds, Authority," *Washington Post,* September 14, 1995, A21.

94. Eva M. Rodriguez, "Legal Aid Forced to Drop Cases," *Legal Times,* August 12, 1996, 1, 13, 14; Marcia Coyle, "Limits at LSC Compel Lawyer to Quit a Case," *National Law Journal,* July 8, 1996, A21.

95. See Robert A. Katzmann, ed., *The Law Firm and the Public Good* (Washington, D.C.: Brookings Institution, 1995).

96. David E. Rovella, "Can the Bar Fill LSC's Shoes?" *National Law Journal,* August 5, 1996, A26.

97. This discussion is based in part on American Bar Association Commission on Advertising, *Lawyer Advertising at the Crossroads* (Chicago: American Bar Association, 1995).

98. *Bates v. State Bar,* 433 U.S. 350 (1977).

99. American Bar Association, *Lawyer Advertising at the Crossroads,* 52. See also Lauren Bowen, "Advertising and the Legal Profession," *Justice System Journal* 18 (1995), 43–54.

100. Gail Diane Cox, "Battle on Legal Ads Comes Down to Class," *National Law Journal,* August 10, 1992, 44.
101. "Ill Legal Pitch," *Sports Illustrated,* December 30, 1996–January 6, 1997, 18.
102. Saundra Torry, "Not Everyone Can Abide the Letters of the Law," *Washington Post,* May 20, 1996, Washington Business section, 7.
103. David Margolick, *At the Bar: The Passions and Peccadilloes of American Lawyers* (New York: Simon & Schuster 1995), 170–171.
104. *Florida Bar v. Went For It, Inc.,* 132 L. Ed. 2d 541 (1995).
105. William E. Hornsby Jr., and Charles Dainoff, "Let the Yellow Pages Do Your Talking," *The Compleat Lawyer,* Spring 1992, 29.
106. Fred Setterberg, "Creating an Image," *California Bar Journal,* August 1989, 44–45, 49–51.
107. Margolick, *At the Bar,* 82.
108. Deborah R. Hensler et al., *Compensation for Accidental Injuries in the United States* (Santa Monica, Calif.: Rand Corporation, 1991), 134.
109. *Goldfarb v. State Bar,* 421 U.S. 773 (1975).
110. Lori Andrews, *Birth of a Salesman: Lawyer Advertising and Solicitation* (Chicago, ABA Press, 1980), 13.
111. Special Committee on Delivery of Legal Services, *Report on the Survey of Legal Clinics and Advertising Law Firms* (Chicago: American Bar Association, 1990), 134.
112. Mike France, "Legal Clinics: Lights Go Out for Storefronts," *National Law Journal,* December 12, 1994, A1, A24, A25; Randy Kennedy, "Groundbreaking Law Firm Shifts Its Focus to Personal-Injury Cases," *New York Times,* May 12, 1995, A16.
113. This discussion of legal insurance is based in part on William A. Bolger, Sandra De Ment, and Joanne F. Pozzo, eds., *Group Legal Service Plans: Organization, Operation and Management* (New York: Harcourt Brace Jovanovich, 1981); and Roger Billings, "Legal Services," in *Encyclopedia of the American Judicial System,* ed. Robert J. Janosik (New York: Charles Scribner's Sons, 1987), 645–652.
114. Saundra Torry, "Joining the Ranks of the Prepaid Services Attorneys," *Washington Post,* January 27, 1992 (Washington Business section), 5.
115. Mike France, "Dimmer Prospects," *National Law Journal,* December 12, 1994, A24.
116. One source for the discussion of the contingent fee is Patricia Munch Danzon, *Contingent Fees for Personal Injury Litigation* (Santa Monica, Calif.: Rand Corporation, 1980).
117. Herbert M. Kritzer, *The Justice Broker: Lawyers and Ordinary Litigation* (New York: Oxford University Press, 1990), 151.
118. Warren Weaver, "The Legal Profession Takes a Look at Itself," *New York Times,* February 10, 1974, sec. 4, 9.
119. Barbara C. Curran, *The Legal Needs of the Public: The Final Report of a National Survey* (Chicago: American Bar Foundation, 1977), 152–157; "Project: An Assessment of Alternative Strategies for Increasing Access to Legal Services," *Yale Law Journal* 90 (1980), 140–141; Bruce Campbell and Susette Talarico, "Access to Legal Services: Examining Common Assumptions," *Judicature* 66 (February 1983), 313–318.
120. Stephen Labaton, "Clinton Defense Fund Is Shrinking Rapidly," *New York Times,* February 28, 1997, A11.
121. Ralph Nader and Wesley J. Smith, *No Contest: Corporate Lawyers and the Perversion of Justice in America* (New York: Random House, 1996), 234.
122. Macauley, "Lawyers and Consumer Protection Laws," 152.
123. Abel, *American Lawyers,* 151–152.
124. Laurence Meyer, "Conference to Weigh Lawyer Competency," *Washington Post,* May 21, 1979, C1.
125. American Bar Association, *Comprehensive Guide to Bar Admissions Requirements 1996–97,* 70–71.
126. *Peel v. Attorney Registration and Disciplinary Commission,* 496 U.S. 91 (1990).
127. American Bar Association, *Model Rules of Professional Conduct* (Chicago: American Bar Association, 1995), 15. The language quoted here and in the next paragraph is from "Comments" that spell out the general requirements in the Rules themselves.

128. Dennis Hevesi, "8 at Law Firm Accused of Bribing Witnesses and Faking Evidence," *New York Times,* January 12, 1990, 28.
129. American Bar Association, *Model Rules of Professional Conduct,* 26.
130. Barry Meier, "Fistfuls of Coupons," *New York Times,* May 26, 1995, C1, C5.
131. James D. Gordon III, *Law School: A Survivor's Guide* (New York: HarperCollins, 1994), 109.
132. Edward A. Adams, "Lawyer's Flight Investigated," *National Law Journal,* February 4, 1991, 10; Ed Bruske, "Hard-Driving Md. Lawyer Drives Himself into Disgrace," *Washington Post,* January 24, 1990, B1, B5.
133. Lisa G. Lerman, "Lying to Clients," *University of Pennsylvania Law Review* 138 (January 1990), 705–720. The quotation is from p. 705.
134. Heinz and Laumann, *Chicago Lawyers,* 353–373.
135. Ibid., 70.
136. New York City Department of Consumer Affairs, *Women in Divorce: Lawyers, Ethics, Fees and Fairness* (New York: Department of Consumer Affairs, 1992), 23.
137. Austin Sarat and William L. F. Felstiner, *Divorce Lawyers and Their Clients: Power and Meaning in the Legal Process* (New York: Oxford University Press, 1995).
138. Lawrence Dubin and Donald Jolliffe, "Recent Discharge Cases Focus New Attention on Counsel as Employee," *National Law Journal,* May 20, 1991, S2, S4, S19.
139. Kritzer, *The Justice Broker,* 167.
140. Nader and Smith, *No Contest,* 136.
141. John B. Cushman Jr., "Paul, Weiss Law Firm to Pay U.S. $45 Million," *New York Times,* September 29, 1993, C1, C16.
142. Heinz and Laumann, *Chicago Lawyers,* 372–373.
143. Data on malpractice claims in this and the following paragraph are taken from William Gates, "Charting the Shoals of Malpractice," *American Bar Association Journal* 73 (July 1, 1987), 62–65; Ronald E. Mallen, "Malpractice at a Glance," *California Lawyer* 5 (July 1985), 34–35; and David Segal, "Lawyer vs. Lawyer: The Quiet Bar Fight," *Washington Post,* March 18, 1997, D1, D4.
144. Richard Pérez-Peña, "When Lawyers Go After Their Peers: The Boom in Malpractice Cases," *New York Times,* August 5, 1994, B12.
145. "1995 Annual Report of the Colorado Supreme Court Grievance Committee," *Colorado Lawyer* 25 (May 1996), 1–6. The cases in which action was taken at various stages in 1995, of course, were not exactly the same as those filed in that year. Some lawyers may have agreed to suspensions or disbarments that did not have to be imposed by the supreme court.
146. Ann Davis, "The Myth of Disbarment," *National Law Journal,* August 5, 1996, A25.
147. Ibid., A1, A24, A25.
148. Kathleen O. Beitiks, "Worst Offenders Now May Face Permanent Disbarment," *California Bar Journal,* October 1996, 1, 9.
149. Matthew J. Nasuti, "What Does It Take?" (letter), *California Lawyer* 12 (February 1992), 10.

4

The Selection of Judges

Judges are at the center of the judicial process. In the cases that come to court, judges preside over proceedings and make decisions. Indirectly, their decisions influence the outcomes of disputes and situations that never get to court. This chapter deals with the processes by which these important figures are selected, and the following chapter examines their characteristics and their behavior as judges.

The judicial selection process merits close consideration for several reasons. Because different people would behave in different ways as judges, the process by which some are chosen rather than others is critical. Further, the selection process influences judges' choices: the judge who faces re-election, for instance, may take that prospect into account in deciding cases. Finally, the selection process reveals some important realities about the courts, the larger political system, and the relationship between the two.

The selection of judges has been a matter of debate throughout our history as a nation. That debate has focused chiefly on formal rules for judicial selection, reflecting a widespread belief that formal rules have great impact on the results of the selection process. In reality, differences among the various formal systems used in the United States have more limited effects than many people think. Perhaps their most important similarity is that each formal system provides considerable room for the influence of other political institutions, including political parties and the other branches of government. Indeed, judicial selection is the point at which courts are shaped most directly by their political environments.

GENERAL ISSUES IN JUDICIAL SELECTION

Debates about methods for selecting judges are largely debates about what people want from the courts and how to achieve it. In these debates, two questions have been dominant.[1] The first is whether to give priority to judicial independence or to political accountability. Many people argue that judges should be selected in a way that maximizes their freedom from control so that they can apply the law in the way they think appropriate. But others contend that judges are important policymakers, so that they should be accountable to the people they serve—either directly or through the other branches of government.

The second question is how to obtain the most competent judges. Lawyers and judges differ about which selection system produces the best judges. These differences stem in part from disagreement over the kind of competence that is desirable. Some people seek only legal competence, a mastery of the law and legal procedures. Others see a broader understanding of politics and government policymaking as important for judges.

The United States differs from most other democratic nations in its emphasis on accountability in the selection process and its relatively limited emphasis on legal competence. In continental Europe, for instance, prospective judges typically receive special training as judges and then enter a professional corps that resembles a civil service system. In the United States, in contrast, elected officials and the general public play the central roles in putting judges on the bench and determining whether they stay there. And American judges attain office through a highly unstructured process, one in which no specialized training is required and judges on higher courts need have no experience at lower levels.

Within this general pattern, formal rules of selection vary considerably. The federal and state governments use several distinct selection systems, systems that differ in both the goals they emphasize and the ways they are designed to achieve these goals.

The mix of judicial selection systems in the United States has a strong historical element. Different systems have been popular in different periods, reflecting changes in people's views about goals and the best means to achieve them.[2] Until the 1840s, the federal government and most states gave power over judicial selection to the other branches of government—the chief executive, the legislature, or both. This approach reflected a desire to minimize direct popular control over the judiciary. And the federal government and most states gave judges lifetime terms in order to maximize their independence.

In the nineteenth century, a growing movement for popular control over government led to support for partisan election of judges who would hold terms of limited length.[3] For several decades from the 1840s on, most new states and many existing states adopted this system.

By the late nineteenth century, political parties had come into some disfavor. Because party leaders exercised so much power, many people came to see parties as barriers to popular control of government rather than as means to achieve it. Accordingly, nonpartisan elections gained support as a method for selection of public officials. The movement for nonpartisan elections had perhaps its greatest success in the judiciary: in the half century that began in the 1880s, most new states and several existing ones chose this system.

Early in this century, former president William Howard Taft and other prominent lawyers expressed dissatisfaction with all the existing methods of judicial selection, arguing that they provided for too little judicial independence and gave insufficient weight to legal competence. This feeling was reflected in the reform agenda of the American Judicature Society (AJS), founded in 1913, whose leaders sought a new method of judicial selection. The AJS helped devise a system in which a state governor would choose a new judge from a list of nominees provided by an independent commission, with the voters later having the chance to approve or disapprove the governor's choice.

Supporters of this new system had their first success when Missouri adopted it for some of its courts in 1940. For that reason it is often called the Missouri Plan, although its supporters prefer the term *merit selection.* Other states followed Missouri, at first slowly and then more rapidly.

Today the Missouri Plan remains the primary focus of debates over formal methods of judicial selection. Supporters seek its adoption by individual states and, in a modified form, by the federal government. They suffer a good many defeats, largely because voters are reluctant to give up their power to choose between judicial candidates. But, they have won enough victories that a large minority of states use the Missouri Plan for at least some of their courts. Since 1950, nearly all of the states changing their systems for selecting judges have adopted some variant of the Missouri Plan.

Most recently, Rhode Island in 1994 replaced legislative election of judges with the Missouri Plan for all its courts. This change was made through legislation for the state's trial courts, but a constitutional amendment and thus voter approval was required at the supreme court level. Rhode Island voters had rejected the Missouri Plan in 1986, but scandals involving the supreme court led 70 percent of the voters to approve the change in 1994.

Debates over formal systems of judicial selection have also reached the federal level. In 1977, President Jimmy Carter incorporated Missouri Plan–style commissions into his procedures for selecting lower-court judges, and after Carter left office, some senators continued to employ commissions to help them recommend candidates for judgeships. But there has never been a sufficient consensus to change the constitutional procedures for selecting federal judges, and these procedures continue to reflect the views about judicial selection that predominated two centuries ago.

THE SELECTION OF FEDERAL JUDGES

The formal rules for selection of federal judges are fairly simple. All judges are nominated by the president and confirmed by the Senate, with a simple majority of senators present required for confirmation. When the Senate is out of session, the president can sometimes make a *recess appointment,* under which a nominee takes the bench immediately, to be confirmed after the Senate returns. With the exception of the specialized courts established under Article I of the Constitution, such as the Tax Court and the Court of Federal Claims, federal judges hold their positions for life.

This means that vacancies on federal courts occur at irregular intervals: when a sitting judge resigns, retires, or dies—or, occasionally, when new judgeships are created. In turn, judges can influence which president gets to replace them through the timing of their retirements or resignations. New York district judge Jack Weinstein decided to retire shortly after the 1992 presidential election. "Even though Clinton is less liberal than I am," he said, "I thought Reagan and Bush had enough appointments, and I want a young person to have the opportunity to enjoy this job."[4] Weinstein was not alone in thinking about who would select his successor; there is evidence that judges are more likely to leave the bench when a president of their own party wins office.[5]

The actual selection process is considerably more complicated than the formal rules suggest. It also differs a good deal among the three major sets of federal courts.

The Supreme Court

Most people see the Supreme Court as unique among courts in its importance. This perception makes the selection of Supreme Court justices unique as well, both in the way that justices are chosen and in the mix of criteria used to choose them.

The Nomination Process   Every president must select hundreds of federal officials, but presidents make the great majority of these appointments in name only. A few appointments are deemed too important to delegate to subordinates, and foremost among these are positions on the Supreme Court. Thus, when a vacancy occurs on the Court, the president usually plays a very active role in filling it. One reflection of this role is the common practice of having a president meet personally with one or more potential nominees before making a final choice.

Presidents do not act alone. They usually get considerable assistance from Justice Department officials and from members of their own staffs to help in identifying and investigating candidates and in choosing among them. Before selecting Ruth Bader Ginsburg in 1993, Bill Clinton employed a corps of volunteer attorneys to gather information on forty-two potential nominees. The extent to which the president relies on others in selecting justices varies with the president's general style and interest in the Court. George Bush and Clinton have played more direct roles in the selection process than did Ronald Reagan.

A variety of individuals and groups outside the executive branch seek to influence the president's choice. Interest groups that are close to the administration may participate privately in the nomination process. If not, their positions will be taken into account as nominees are considered. The business community, for instance, is likely to influence choices by Republican presidents; civil rights groups have an impact on Democrats. Groups that lack ties to the administration sometimes seek to exert pressure through the mass media—by indicating, for instance, that they will fight against Senate confirmation of a particular candidate if that candidate is nominated. Presidents would prefer to minimize such pressure. For this reason, Bush chose both David Souter and Clarence Thomas within four days after their predecessors announced they were retiring. Clinton took five weeks to choose Stephen Breyer and three months to choose Ginsburg, and these long periods gave groups a chance to mobilize and exert pressure on the administration.

Other participants in the nominating process can include sitting members of the Court and people who would like to be nominated themselves. Sitting justices sometimes identify and endorse candidates for the Court. Aspiring justices occasionally take direct action to secure Supreme Court nominations. Warren Burger's successful campaign for a Nixon nomination as chief justice reportedly included a promise to retire in time for Nixon to name a successor.[6] Ruth Bader Ginsburg did no campaigning for a nomination, but her husband (apparently without her knowledge) worked to mobilize support for her.[7] People sometimes campaign indirectly, through decisions and public statements that they hope will appeal to presidents.

In 1981, Robert Bork accepted a judgeship on a federal court of appeals because Reagan administration officials told him that doing so would make him a strong candidate for the Supreme Court.[8]

Criteria for Nominations Presidential nominations to the Supreme Court have reflected many different criteria. The most important of these criteria fall into four categories.

The first includes what might be called the qualifications of prospective nominees: their *competence* and *ethical standards.* A nominee who falls short on either criterion may fail to gain Senate confirmation, and an unqualified candidate who does get confirmed but serves poorly on the Court may embarrass the appointing president. As a result, relatively few nominees are susceptible to attack on either ground. Indeed, most rate very high for their legal competence, and some have brought truly distinguished records to the Court.

The second category concerns the attitudes of the nominee toward issues with which the Court deals—that is, the nominee's *policy preferences.* Because Supreme Court decisions are so important, presidents seek appointees who share presidential views about policy. A liberal president, for example, wants to select justices who take liberal positions on most issues. As a result, administration officials usually scrutinize the views of potential nominees with considerable care. All the nominees since 1975 have been lower-court judges, primarily because their votes and written opinions as judges helped in predicting their behavior on the Court.

A president is not guaranteed that a justice will actually behave as expected. To take one example, David Souter has been considerably less conservative than George Bush hoped. But such unexpected developments are the exception rather than the rule. More typical is the early record of President Clinton's appointees. Both Ginsburg and Breyer have established themselves as moderate liberals, which appears to be what Clinton sought.

The third category of criteria might be labeled *reward.* Nominations often go to personal and political associates of the president. Most broadly, 90 percent of all nominees have come from the president's party;[9] one reason is the belief that such important prizes should be awarded to people within the party. Beyond party, more than half of those nominated to the Court have known the president personally.[10] Frequently, a nominee is a personal acquaintance who has also been a political ally. Former justice Byron White, a long-time friend of President Kennedy, had worked in the 1960 Kennedy campaign for president and then served in the Justice Department.

The final category is *pursuit of political support.* Some nominations are used to appeal to important interest or demographic groups. Most often a president tries to appeal to voters in a large demographic group by selecting a member of that group. For instance, President Bush's selection of Clarence Thomas in 1991 was intended to appeal to black voters—especially because Thomas would succeed the Court's only black justice, Thurgood Marshall.

Presidents differ in the weight they give to particular criteria, but in recent administrations policy preferences have had the highest priority. This certainly was true of Reagan and Bush, who emphasized finding strong conservatives. Although their selections often served other goals very well, those goals were clearly secondary. The preeminence of this criterion is symbolized by the declining importance of personal acquaintanceship as a basis for selecting justices. Lyndon Johnson was the last president to choose nominees whom he knew well.

The preeminence of policy preferences reflects the growing recognition that the Supreme Court plays a significant role in national policymaking. More directly, it reflects the current salience of Supreme Court policies to people whose support is important to presidents. George Bush's effort to appoint strong conservatives to the Court was in part a response to conservative groups in the Republican party, for which some issues before the Court—especially abortion—were critical. Bill Clinton's selection of moderate liberals, like many of his other decisions as president, has been an effort to balance the competing demands of groups on both sides of the ideological spectrum.

Senate Confirmation   The Senate confirms the great majority of the nominees that it considers, twenty-four out of twenty-eight since 1949, and usually with just a few negative votes or none at all. Yet confirmation is never automatic, and in the current era the Senate consistently gives nominees a close collective scrutiny. The most public form of this scrutiny is the hearings held by the Judiciary Committee, in which nominees are questioned at length and other witnesses are heard.

The combination of close scrutiny and a high rate of success reflects some basic realities about the confirmation process. Aware of the Senate's active role, presidents seek to choose nominees who are likely to win confirmation. Faced with a Senate controlled by the Republican party, Bill Clinton in his second term could not be expected to choose a strongly liberal nominee. For their part, senators generally begin with a presumption in favor of confirmation. Although that presumption usually holds up, it can be overcome under the right circumstances—or, from a nominee's perspective, the wrong ones.

Several circumstances can weaken a nominee's position.[11] Some circumstances relate to the specific nominee. One is strong and widespread opposition to the views of the nominee on legal issues, particularly if interest groups sharing that opposition mobilize against a nominee. Liberal senators and interest groups sought to defeat some Reagan and Bush nominees who seemed to have strongly conservative views on civil liberties issues, particularly Robert Bork in 1987 and Clarence Thomas in 1991.

Another unfavorable circumstance is a credible challenge to the competence or ethical behavior of a nominee. Nixon nominee G. Harrold Carswell was defeated in 1970 after opponents mustered evidence of his limited legal skills. Reagan choice Douglas Ginsburg withdrew in 1987 before his formal nomination because disclosures about his use of marijuana made confirmation unlikely. Evidence of ethical weaknesses is important in swaying moderate senators who would not oppose a nominee on ideological grounds alone.

Beyond the specific nominee, elements of the situation in which a nomination is made play a part in confirmation decisions. Inevitably, these decisions are affected by the partisan makeup of the Senate; nominees of a president whose party controls the Senate are in a relatively good position. Nominations may be more vulnerable near the end of a president's term or if the seat in question is seen as especially important. Presidents generally become weaker politically as their terms progress, and senators from the other party may want to keep a seat open in case their own party wins the next election. When the Supreme Court is closely divided between liberal and conservative justices, as it was in the late 1980s, contention over nominees tends to increase.

In the current era, nominees generally win confirmation by wide margins unless there are both widespread opposition to their views and questions about their competence or ethics. To take one example, liberal Democrats in the Senate were quite unhappy with what they perceived as Clarence Thomas's extreme conservatism, but Thomas still would have been confirmed easily had doubts not arisen about his competence and character. The exception to this rule was Robert Bork, defeated for confirmation despite his very high level of legal skills and the absence of serious concerns about his personal behavior. Exhibit 4.1 describes the confirmation decision on Thomas, along with the others since 1990.

The Lower Courts

The district courts and courts of appeals differ from the Supreme Court in their geographical decentralization. Further, judgeships on these lower courts are more numerous and, at least individually, less important than positions on the Supreme Court. For these reasons, the process and criteria for selection traditionally have differed radically from those for the Supreme Court. But these differences have been reduced as presidents and their administrations increasingly see lower-court judgeships as significant to their political and policy goals.

The Nomination Process   Presidents generally delegate the nomination of lower-court judges chiefly to the Justice Department. Presidents themselves have played a very limited part in the selection process, usually setting down general guidelines for subordinates to follow and intervening only in a few specific cases.

These patterns have been modified in recent years. The Reagan and Bush administrations involved the White House more directly in the selection process, a choice reflecting the importance of judicial appointments to those presidents. President Clinton has continued that practice, giving the most power over nominations to a "Judicial Selection Group" composed of Justice Department officials and White House staff members and headed by the White House counsel. The Justice Department has primary responsibility for district court nominations, the White House for the courts of appeals.[12]

In making their choices, the officials who act on behalf of the president are subject to a variety of pressures and constraints. The most important is the practice of senatorial courtesy. Under this practice, when a presidential nomination to a federal position within a state requires Senate confirmation, the Senate as a whole gives some deference to the wishes of the senators from that state—very strong deference to a home-state senator of the president's party, who is accorded something of a veto power.

The existence of senatorial courtesy provides home-state senators of the president's party with leverage that they can use to intervene in the original nomination process, since they hold so much power over the subsequent confirmation. Indeed, such senators often seek to dictate a nomination by submitting a name to the administration. But such names may be rejected if administration officials have strong reasons to disapprove a senator's choice. If senatorial courtesy grants cer-

David Souter, 1990

President Bush chose Souter, recently selected as a federal judge, to succeed liberal justice William Brennan. Liberals reacted to Souter's nomination with some concern because of its potential for strengthening the Court's conservative majority. But Souter had a very short record of positions on public issues, making him difficult to attack. His Senate testimony disclosed little more information about his views and gave some observers an impression of moderation. Souter was confirmed by a 90–9 vote.

Clarence Thomas, 1991

After the retirement of Thurgood Marshall, the Court's one remaining strong liberal, President Bush nominated Thomas, a federal judge with a highly conservative record before and after joining the bench. Opposition to Thomas built slowly, in part because some liberals thought that continued African American representation on the Court was desirable. But Thomas's Senate testimony, in which he disavowed some past statements of views, raised doubts about his legal skills and personal credibility. Allegations that he had engaged in sexual harassment of a former assistant produced a new set of hearings, which ultimately changed few senators' positions. Thomas was confirmed by a 52–48 margin.

Ruth Bader Ginsburg, 1993

After a long period of considering possible candidates, President Clinton nominated Ginsburg to succeed the moderate Byron White. As a law professor Ginsburg had taken liberal positions on legal issues and led the effort to expand women's rights through litigation, but as a federal judge her record had been fairly moderate. Though some senators and interest groups thought Ginsburg too liberal, there was little opposition to her nomination; she was confirmed by a 96–3 vote.

Stephen Breyer, 1994

President Clinton selected Breyer to replace Harry Blackmun, one of the two most liberal members of the Court. Breyer was known and respected by senators because of his service as a committee staff member prior to becoming a federal judge. He also appeared at least as moderate as Ginsburg. But his risky investment in the insurance syndicate Lloyd's of London seemed imprudent to some senators, and it raised questions about a possible conflict of interest in some past cases. These concerns and Breyer's liberalism caused some Republican senators to oppose him, but his confirmation was never in jeopardy. The vote was 87–9.

Sources: Various press reports and books.

EXHIBIT 4.1   Senate Action on Supreme Court Nominations, 1990–1994

tain senators veto power over nominations, the president's control over formal nominations gives administration officials a veto power as well.

A home-state senator who is not of the president's party usually has limited influence. If a state's two senators are from different parties, the senator from the president's party can monopolize influence over nominations. In some instances, that senator agrees to share some power. This has been true, for instance, of New York Republican Alfonse D'Amato and Democrat Daniel Patrick Moynihan.[13] If neither senator is a party colleague of the president, one or both senators may have some impact on nominations. But the administration shifts much of its attention to important public officials and leaders of its own party from that state.

The extent of a senator's power over nominations partly depends on the senator's power in the Senate. When the president's party controls the Senate, for instance, the majority leader and chair of the Judiciary Committee wield considerable influence. Thus it is not surprising that George Bush gave a district court nomination to someone who had served on the staff of Senator Strom Thurmond of South Carolina, ranking Republican on the Judiciary Committee. Nor is it surprising that this nominee was confirmed with unusual speed, despite some questions about his qualifications.[14]

A final element in the relationship between the president and the Senate—an element that shapes the whole process of selection—is the importance to the administration of control over lower-court nominations. Since the 1960s, there has been a general trend toward greater concern with the lower courts. This trend is best reflected in the Reagan and Bush administrations. Officials in those administrations saw the appointment of lower-court judges as an important mechanism for shaping policy. The Bush administration tried to require that Republican senators from the relevant state provide it with three names of possible district court nominees rather than the traditional one, though senators sometimes resisted that effort.[15] President Clinton has been more willing to share power with senators. That difference is reflected in his administration's asking senators for only one recommended nominee.[16]

As in the selection of Supreme Court justices, interest groups try to influence the president's choices. One such group is the American Bar Association (ABA), which has created a committee to rate candidates for federal judgeships. In the past, some presidents allowed the ABA committee to rate potential nominees before they were actually chosen, effectively giving it something of a veto power over nominations. The committee was allowed that role because presidents wanted to avoid choosing someone who then received a negative rating, which would lead to some embarrassment and that might even threaten Senate confirmation. But Reagan, Bush, and Clinton have refused to allow ABA prescreening. Republicans have been unhappy with the ABA committee because of what they perceive as a liberal bias in its evaluations, and in 1997 the Republican chair of the Senate Judiciary Committee announced that the ABA no longer would be given any special status in the confirmation process.[17] Still, the prospect of ABA ratings for nominees sometimes affects the nomination process.

In contrast with the Supreme Court, people who would like to become lower-court judges routinely campaign for those positions. Indeed, according to one student of the process, "rarely is it the case that a person who has not actively sought the nomination receives it."[18] One important kind of campaigning is amassing support from people and groups that are politically significant to the administration and home-state senators. Although some aspirants convey their interest indirectly, others go directly to the officials who have the greatest impact on nominations. Senators hear from large numbers of people who want judicial appointments.

Criteria for Selection   The criteria that influence Supreme Court nominations are also important for the lower courts. Until recently these criteria were given quite different weights for the lower courts, chiefly because of a general feeling that these courts were not of much consequence. The growing recognition that district courts and courts of appeals make significant policy has reduced the differences in the weight of particular criteria, but it has not eliminated them altogether.

Political reward has always been a crucial consideration in nomination decisions: judgeships are frequently used to recognize the efforts of those who support the administration and, even more, to recompense personal and political associates of home-state senators. Indeed, the best way to become a federal judge, one Senate staff member joked, "is that you should have the foresight to be the law school roommate of a future United States senator; or, that failing, to pick a future senator for your first law partner."[19]

The joke is an enduring one because of the large element of truth it contains. Senators often seek to reward lawyers who have served in their campaigns and otherwise aided their political advancement. Presidents and Justice Department officials use nominations for similar purposes. President Clinton in 1995 nominated Charles Stack for a seat on a court of appeals. Stack was a respected Miami lawyer, but the primary impetus for his nomination may have been his service as financial chair of the 1992 Clinton-Gore campaign in Florida—service that allegedly allowed him to insist on a court of appeals nomination when administration officials tried to steer him to a less visible position. Ultimately, opposition from Senate Republicans on several grounds induced Stack to withdraw from consideration.[20]

The pursuit of new or enhanced political support has also carried some weight in the nominating process. Although lower-court nominations are less visible than those for the Supreme Court, they too may be used to appeal to interest groups or sets of voters. As did Jimmy Carter before him, Bill Clinton has selected record numbers of female and nonwhite judges. For both presidents this record was motivated in part by the belief that enhanced diversity in the judiciary was desirable in itself, but it also reflected the desire to maintain support for these administrations among two groups that were important to it.[21]

In a sense, administration deference to senators constitutes another kind of pursuit of political support. Some presidents go beyond the dictates of senatorial courtesy as a way of seeking goodwill. A famous example comes from the Kennedy administration, which nominated some anti–civil rights district judges in the South in order to keep peace with powerful southern Democratic senators. Such actions have become less common because presidents are less willing to put people on the federal courts without regard for their policy views, but they have not disappeared. The Clinton administration has reversed the recent trend somewhat, particularly since the Republicans regained control of the Senate in 1994. Administration officials consult regularly with Judiciary chair Orrin Hatch during the nomination process, and they have withdrawn some nominations and potential nominations because of Senate opposition.[22]

Candidates' qualifications have traditionally been much less important for the lower courts than for the Supreme Court. As long as the lower courts were viewed as unimportant, participants in the process thought that little harm would result if people of limited merit served on them. As perceptions of the lower courts have changed, senators and administration officials give greater attention to the qualifications of the judges they select. But it remains true that some lawyers of questionable abilities and accomplishments, people who would not be considered seriously for the Supreme Court, are placed on the district courts and courts of appeals.

The most significant change in the criteria for selecting lower-court judges is the increasing emphasis given to policy preferences. Historically, administrations varied widely in their interest in the views of their nominees. But ideological screening of candidates for judgeships has become standard practice in the past three decades. In the Johnson administration, efforts were made to select southern judges who had some sympathy for civil rights. President Nixon was especially concerned about criminal justice issues, and prospective nominees during his administration were scrutinized for their views about law and order. In a more general way, President Carter sought to nominate judges with liberal views.

President Reagan brought to the presidency a strong commitment to blunt what he saw as excessive judicial liberalism by appointing conservative judges. The result was, in the words of one expert, "the most self-conscious ideological selection process since the first Roosevelt Administration."[23] President Bush himself may have been less concerned with judicial ideologies, but he continued Reagan's emphasis on the selection of conservatives. The goal, according to White House counsel C. Boyden Gray, was "to shift the courts in a more conservative direction."[24] One important reason was Bush's desire to retain the support of conservative Republicans, who cared a great deal about federal court policies.[25] By the time that Bush left office in 1993, a majority of federal judges were Reagan and Bush appointees. Their presence on the district courts and courts of appeals shifted the balance on those courts distinctly to the ideological right.

In contrast, President Clinton has not made as strong an effort to move the lower courts to the left. According to White House counsel John Quinn, "Our mission is not to counteract the conservative appointments of the Reagan and Bush years."[26] One reason is that judicial policy is a lower priority for Clinton than it was for the presidents from Nixon through Bush.[27] Another related reason is that the nomination of relatively moderate judges helps Clinton to maintain good relations with the Senate and assists him in getting his nominees confirmed, particularly with a Republican Senate majority. It also may have served the president in his effort to present a moderate image to the voters, though in 1996 Robert Dole still attacked Clinton's appointees as overly liberal and referred to them as "one of the root causes of the crime explosion."[28]

One way to gauge the ideological tenor of presidents' appointments is through the voting records of the judges they selected. A 1996 study found that the Reagan and Bush judges on the courts of appeals were no more likely than those of earlier Republican presidents to cast votes that could be characterized as conservative, but district judges appointed by Reagan and Bush *were* the most conservative cohorts. Up to that point, the Clinton appointees were more liberal in their voting behavior than the appointees of any Republican president, but they were distinctly less liberal than the Carter judges.[29] That finding supports the conclusion of most observers that—for whatever reasons—the Clinton administration has chosen a moderate course in judicial appointments.

Senate Confirmation   The traditional confirmation process for lower-court judgeships was linked to senatorial courtesy. If home-state senators did not indicate their support for a nomination, the Judiciary Committee did not consider it. In this way, the committee enforced the requirement that the Justice Department reach agreement with the home-state senators. If a candidate did have the support of the home-state senators, the committee and the Senate confirmed the nomination automatically rather than giving it collective scrutiny; this is the other side of senatorial courtesy.

The traditional process has been modified since the late 1970s. Home-state senators of the president's party still have something like an absolute veto power, but the support of those senators no longer guarantees easy approval by the Judiciary Committee and confirmation by the Senate.

This change seems to derive partly from a general decline in senators' deference to each other and partly from the growing recognition that lower-court judgeships are important. In any case, senators are now less willing to rubber-stamp the choices that an administration and the senators from the affected state have agreed on. Some nominees receive close scrutiny, often after interest groups have raised questions about them. The Alliance for Justice and other liberal groups played this role during the Reagan and Bush administrations, as the Free Congress Foundation has during the Clinton administration. It has become increasingly common for votes to be cast against confirmation, and several nominations have been defeated or withdrawn in the face of likely defeat. Exhibit 4.2 describes some of these cases.

In addition to those nominees who attract opposition as individuals, some nominees run into difficulties because of conflicts that have nothing to do with them personally. Any senator can put a "hold" on any legislative item, including a judicial nomination, and such action at least delays confirmation. In 1996, Republican senator Kay Bailey Hutchison of Texas put a hold on a Minnesota district court nomination that had been set for confirmation, reportedly in part because she was unhappy with the handling of a bill she was sponsoring. Democrat Paul Wellstone of Minnesota, who had sponsored the district court nomination, then put a hold on *all* pending legislation. Wellstone's pressure succeeded; a day later, the nominee was confirmed by unanimous consent.[30]

That Minnesota nomination was also caught up in broader partisan conflict between President Clinton and the Republican Senate. If they wish to block confirmation of judges, the Judiciary Committee chair can choose not to act on nominations and the Majority Leader can refuse to schedule their consideration on the floor. They are particularly likely to take such actions in a presidential election year, because vacancies that are not filled will remain for a new president—who might be of the same party as the Senate majority.

Despite the relative moderation of Bill Clinton's choices for judgeships, the Republican-controlled Senate in 1996 was even less willing to confirm nominees than its predecessors had been in the same situation. Only seventeen district court judges were confirmed, and *no* court of appeals nominees were confirmed.[31] Clinton's re-election gave him another four years to select federal judges. But the Senate continued its resistance to the president in the first half of 1997, confirming few nominees. The extent of this resistance was highly unusual, and it underlined the growing importance of federal judgeships in the current era.

Nominee	Year	State	Level	Charges by Opponents	Outcome
Kenneth Ryskamp	1991	Florida	CA	Racial insensitivity, hostility to civil liberties litigants	Defeated in committee
Edward Carnes	1992	Alabama	CA	Overly zealous advocacy to obtain death sentences, racial insensitivity	Confirmed, 62–36
Rosemary Barkett	1994	Florida	CA	Unwillingness to uphold death sentences as state judge	Confirmed, 61–37
Alexander Williams	1994	Maryland	DC	Insufficient competence, lack of candor in responding to questions from ABA and Senate Judiciary Committee	Confirmed by voice vote
R. Samuel Paz	1995	California	DC	As lawyer, represented people suing police for alleged brutality	Nomination withdrawn
Charles Stack	1996	Florida	CA	Insufficient competence, service as Clinton fundraiser, membership in discriminatory private club	Nomination withdrawn

Note: "Year" refers to final action on the nomination; "state" is the state of the nominee's residence; "level" refers to the court for which the person was nominated, district court (DC) or court of appeals (CA).

Sources: press reports; Sheldon Goldman, "Judicial Selection Under Clinton: A Midterm Examination," *Judicature* 78 (May–June 1995), 288–289.

EXHIBIT 4.2 Selected Lower Court Nominations That Aroused Opposition, 1991–1996

THE SELECTION OF STATE JUDGES

The history discussed at the beginning of this chapter has left states with a variety of formal systems for selection of judges. These systems work in practice to produce an even wider array of selection processes.

The Formal Rules

The formal systems used by the states can be placed in five categories:

1. *Gubernatorial appointment.* In this system, as the title indicates, the governor appoints judges. In nearly every state that uses gubernatorial appointment, the governor's choice must be confirmed. Usually, the confirming body is the state senate.
2. *Legislative election.* In this system, now used in only two states, the legislature elects judges.
3. *Partisan election.* Here voters choose between party nominees in a general election, with party labels indicated on the ballot. The nominees generally are selected through partisan primary elections.
4. *Nonpartisan election.* Under this system, voters choose between candidates in a general election, with no party labels indicated on the ballot. Usually, the top two candidates in a nonpartisan primary are placed on the general election ballot.
5. *Missouri Plan.* In this complex system, a commission is established to nominate candidates for judgeships. Most often, the commission includes lawyers who have been selected by their colleagues and nonlawyers selected by the governor. In many states, a judge also serves. When a judgeship needs to be filled, the commission produces a short list (usually three names) of nominees, and the governor makes the appointment from this list. After the judge has served for a short time, and at periodic intervals thereafter, voters are asked whether or not to retain the judge; there is no opposing candidate.

Exhibit 4.3 shows the distribution of these five systems among the states. The table excludes special selection systems that many states use for a few major trial courts or for some of their minor trial courts, such as the appointment of municipal judges by mayors.

Historical patterns in the popularity of different systems are reflected in their distribution across regions. Gubernatorial appointment and legislative election are found almost exclusively on the eastern seaboard, among the original thirteen states. Similarly, partisan election of judges is most common in the South and Midwest, whose states were formed when this system was most popular. Because they developed relatively late, nonpartisan election and the Missouri Plan have the weakest geographical patterns.

None of the five formal systems has only a single form. The details of the Missouri Plan, for instance, differ considerably from state to state. In addition, some states have combined features of different systems. For instance, although Ohio is classified as a nonpartisan election state, its system includes a partisan primary that precedes the nonpartisan general election.

Partisan Election	Nonpartisan Election	Gubernatorial Appointment	Legislative Election	Missouri Plan
Alabama	Arizona* (M)	California* (M)	South	Alaska
Arkansas	California*	Delaware	Carolina	Arizona*
Illinois (M)	Florida*	Maine	Virginia	Colorado
Indiana*	Georgia	Maryland (M)		Connecticut
Kansas*	Idaho	Massachusetts		(M)
Missouri*	Kentucky	New Hampshire		Florida*
New York*	Louisiana	New Jersey		Hawaii (M)
North	Michigan (M)			Indiana*
Carolina	Minnesota			Iowa
Pennsylvania	Mississippi			Kansas*
(M)	Montana (M)			Missouri*
Tennessee*	Nevada			Nebraska
Texas	North Dakota			New Mexico
West Virginia	Ohio (M)			(M)
	Oklahoma*			New York*(M)
	Oregon			Oklahoma*
	South Dakota*			Rhode Island
	Washington			(M)
	Wisconsin			South Dakota*
				Tennessee*
				Utah
				Vermont (M)
				Wyoming

Note: The states in this table are classified according to the system they use for the regular selection of judges rather than the system for filling vacancies in the middle of terms. These systems used only for minor trial courts or for a small number of major trial judgeships are not listed. An asterisk indicates that another system is also used in that state (in such cases, both systems are listed in the table). An "M" indicates that the system used in a particular state is a significant modification of that described in the text. States that have established nominating commissions for appointments through executive order rather than through constitutional or statutory provisions are classified as gubernatorial appointment states.

Sources: The Book of the States, 1996–97 Edition (Lexington, Ky.: Council of State Governments, 1996), 133–135; Lyle Warner, *Judicial Selection in the United States: A Compendium of Provisions,* 2d ed. (Chicago: American Judicature Society, 1993); state constitutions and statutes.

EXHIBIT 4.3 Formal Systems for the Selection of State Judges

Exhibit 4.3 shows another complication: many states use different selection systems for different courts. Indiana, for example, uses the Missouri Plan to choose appellate judges and partisan election to select nearly all its trial judges. The special systems for minor trial courts, not shown in the exhibit, complicate the picture even further.

The terms of state judges also vary a good deal. Rhode Island gives its judges life terms, and judges in Massachusetts and New Hampshire hold office until the age of seventy. Elsewhere judges have fixed terms. In many states, these terms are longer for appellate judges than they are for trial judges. The most common term length is six years, but some states give trial judges four-year terms, and most New York judges serve fourteen-year terms.

Some states have mandatory retirement ages or ages beyond which judges cannot seek new terms. The rule in Indiana is that candidates cannot run for county court judgeships if they will be seventy years old before beginning the new term. In 1996, one Indiana judge used an affidavit from his sister to secure a change in his official birthdate from December 31, 1926 to January 1, 1927, thus allowing him to run for re-election. Despite this extraordinary action—or perhaps because of it—he was defeated.[32]

Vacancies can occur during judges' terms because of resignation, retirement, or death. In states that do not use popular elections, such vacancies are usually filled by the method that is ordinarily employed to select judges. But in states with elective systems, the governor generally makes interim appointments. In some of these states, the selection is made from nominees of a commission like that used in the Missouri Plan. In most states with interim appointees, an appointee must face the voters fairly soon, even if the term has not expired.

The Operation of Elective Systems

Nearly two-thirds of the states elect some or all of their judges. The difference between partisan and nonpartisan ballots is one of several ways that formal rules for election differ. Because of these differences in rules and differences in political processes, judicial elections vary a good deal among states and even within them. Still, some general patterns exist.

Campaigns and Voters   Elections to judgeships vary enormously in their level of competition. At one end of the spectrum, a good many judicial candidates run unopposed; at the other end, some seats are contested fiercely in large-scale campaigns. In between these extremes are quiet contests that are barely visible to voters and that one of the candidates may win easily. Traditionally, only a small minority of judicial elections have involved fierce contests. Such contests remain exceptional today, but they have become increasingly common.

Because we think of judgeships as prized positions, it may be surprising that judicial candidates often run unopposed. One reason is that judgeships are *not* always attractive, especially to lawyers whose incomes far exceed judicial salaries. Because positions on supreme courts are the most attractive of state judgeships, they are most likely to be contested. Another reason for uncontested races is that, where one candidate has a great advantage, potential opponents may see no reason to run a futile campaign. Unable to attract willing candidates for some judgeships in 1995, the Conservative Party in New York (a significant third party) put two candidates on the ballot without informing them beforehand. One of the two later congratulated the voters for their "good sense" in defeating him.[33]

Quiet contests result in part from the limited amounts of money available to many judicial candidates. In North Carolina, for instance, candidates for the major trial court between 1988 and 1994 spent an average of less than two cents per voter.[34] As a result, judicial candidates often find it difficult to get their messages to voters.

Judicial candidates in all but a few states are also constrained by ethical rules that severely limit their discussion of policy issues. These rules stem from a fear that candidates who take positions on specific issues cannot later deal impartially with cases involving these issues. Because of the rules, candidates' speeches and materials tend to focus on such matters as career experience, endorsements by newspapers and interest groups, and family life. One Maryland candidate, lacking a child of his own, sent out a mailing with a picture of his wife and her young niece; if voters inferred that the candidate was the devoted father of a baby, that was their choice.[35]

The mass media could compensate for these limitations by devoting heavy coverage to the candidates and campaigns. But, newspapers and television news programs usually concentrate on races for high executive and legislative offices, giving only occasional attention to contests for judgeships.

Because of limited campaigns and media coverage, the general rule is that voters go to the polls knowing little about the candidates. The problem of learning about candidates is aggravated when voters face large numbers of judicial contests, as they often do in large cities. In a 1986 exit poll, for instance, the name of one judicial candidate in Houston was recognized by only 23 percent of the voters there; a Dallas candidate was recognized by only 19 percent of the local voters.[36]

Lacking much information about candidates, voters make use of whatever information they can obtain. A recognizable name can provide a handy cue, so candidates who are well known usually have a considerable advantage. The same can be true of candidates who are personally unknown but who hold a familiar name. In 1990, Chief Justice Keith Callow of the Washington Supreme Court was defeated by a lawyer named Charles Johnson, who had not bothered to campaign. The winner was assisted by his sharing both first and last names with a trial judge in Seattle, and the familiar sound of a name as common as Johnson undoubtedly helped as well. In 1994, another member of the Washington court barely defeated a challenger who did little campaigning but who also had an attractive name.[37] In 1991, two challengers to an Indiana trial judge named Donald R. Phillippe sought to enhance their chances by changing their own names to Donald R. Phillippe. The voters were spared considerable difficulty when an election board ruled that the new Phillippes had failed to meet legal requirements for getting on the ballot.[38]

Judicial campaigns sometimes depart from this pattern of limited activity and little substantive information, and the departures have become increasingly common in the past decade. Two examples are described in Exhibit 4.4. One key reason for this change is growth in levels of campaign funding. Another is a partial breakdown in the constraints against raising policy issues in judicial campaigns.

Increased campaign funding reflects a growing awareness by interest groups that they have a stake in the outcomes of judicial elections. Most important are groups concerned with personal injury law, groups that focus primarily on supreme court contests. On one side are the "trial lawyers" who represent injured parties. On the other side are the lawyers who represent defendants in these cases, as well

Hooper vs. Hornsby **(Alabama, 1994)**

Sonny Hornsby served as president of the Alabama Trial Lawyers Association, the group of attorneys representing people who sue for personal injuries. In 1988, he was elected chief justice of the Alabama Supreme Court, and the court developed a reputation for legal rulings favoring injured parties as against the businesses that defend against legal claims. In an earlier era, when Alabama was overwhelmingly Democratic, the Democrat Hornsby would have been safe from Republican challenge in a partisan election system. But Alabama had become increasingly competitive between the parties. Business groups recruited Republican Perry Hooper to run against Hornsby in 1994 and worked for his election, as well as that of pro-business Republicans who ran for other positions on the court.

The campaign for chief justice set an Alabama judicial record for the level of spending, as groups on both sides of the disputes in personal injury law poured money into the campaign. Campaign appeals from the two sides were not always genteel. After press reports that Hornsby had personally solicited campaign funds, one television commercial depicted him pressuring a lawyer for a campaign contribution. The lawyer responded, "Judge Hornsby, you do realize we have a case pending in your court, don't you? . . . All right, I'll get the money over to you right away."

The vote was so close that the result apparently hinged on whether some disputed absentee ballots were counted. Hooper challenged the ballots in federal court. Meanwhile, the state's Republican attorney general ordered Hornsby's salary cut off. The case finally was resolved in Hooper's favor after almost a year, and he was declared the winner by 262 votes.

Tsenin vs. Rothschild vs. Albers **(San Francisco, 1996)**

California's nonpartisan elections for trial judgeships usually feature an incumbent running unopposed. But some positions are contested, and the intensity of campaigning has increased in recent years.

In 1996, three lawyers ran for a San Francisco municipal court position that had no incumbent. All the candidates were liberal Democrats, but they battled each other with considerable ferocity in a well-funded primary election. Ron Albers attacked one opponent with mailers that proclaimed: "The San Francisco Bar Association rates candidate Kay Tsenin: barely qualified." (Tsenin had received a rating of "qualified," lower than the one given to Albers.) The campaign of the third candidate, Matthew Rothschild, posted signs in liberal neighborhoods reading, "The Republican Party Endorses Ron Albers for Judge."

Albers finished third in the primary, and Tsenin and Rothschild fought the general election campaign with the same ferocity shown in the primary. Rothschild was endorsed by the local Democratic organization, Mayor Willie Brown, and most other Democratic officeholders, helping to secure for him an advantage in fundraising. But Tsenin also did well in raising money, and the result was an unusually visible campaign.

The campaign was dominated by personal attacks. Both candidates were strongly criticized for past financial problems. Tsenin adapted the tactic that Albers had used against her in the primary, pointing out that the bar association had rated Rothschild as

EXHIBIT 4.4   Two Examples of Heated Judicial Election contests

"not qualified." She also argued that his lack of trial experience would make it difficult for him to do well as a judge. Rothschild called Tsenin a "landlord lawyer" who would be biased against tenants, a high proportion of San Franciscans.

Ultimately Tsenin won with 59 percent of the vote, apparently benefiting from the perception of her as an "outsider." Whatever else can be said about the campaign, it boosted the San Francisco economy: among them, the three candidates spent more than $400,000.

Sources: News reports. Quotation in Alabama contest is from Tom Baxter, "Political Ads Are Good Mean Fun on Alabama TV," *Atlanta Constitution,* November 6, 1994, A15. Quotations in San Francisco contest are from Jim Doyle, "Candidate for Judgeship in S.F. Assails Rival," *San Francisco Chronicle,* March 25, 1996, C2; Keith Donoghue, "Hallinan Says He'll Look Into Judicial Campaign Tactic," *Recorder* (San Francisco), March 27, 1996. 4; and Venise Wagner, "Tsenin Wins Nasty Muni Court Race," *San Francisco Examiner*, November 6, 1996, A26.

EXHIBIT 4.4   Two Examples of Heated Judicial Election contests

as the business and professional groups whose members are usually the defendants. These groups have been active in a great many states, and in some states they have fueled vast increases in the money available to supreme court candidates. In Texas, more than $50 million was spent on contests for appellate judgeships between 1988 and 1994.[39]

Candidates who raise policy issues in campaigns usually try to associate themselves with a conservative stance on criminal justice matters, a stance that accords with the views of most voters. Usually they do so in an indirect manner, one that does not directly conflict with the rules against taking positions on judicial issues. Candidates who can do so cite their experience as prosecutors or highlight endorsements from law enforcement groups. But some are more direct, announcing that they have taken or will take a pro-prosecution stance in criminal cases.

The personal injury issues that motivate monetary contributions often remain beneath the surface in judicial campaigns. Thus a 1996 candidate for the Georgia Court of Appeals bought television time to attack his incumbent opponent for an opinion reversing the conviction of a confessed child molester. But, as one commentator pointed out, "The personal injury lawyers who bankrolled Merritt's advertising campaign . . . were not really mad at Judge Andrews for coddling a child molester. They were mad at him for coddling insurance companies."[40]

Sometimes personal injury issues do become part of the public campaign. This is particularly true for candidates who support restrictions on lawsuits and on monetary damages, because these positions are perceived as popular ones. A commercial for an Ohio Supreme Court candidate in 1994 attacked her opponent for receiving substantial contributions from personal injury lawyers. The commercial depicted a $300,000 check to the opponent from the law firm of "Sue & Sue"; the check was signed by "Cheatem Good." Two years later the candidate was reprimanded by a judicial disciplinary panel for running this commercial on the ground that it had improper implications.[41] The possibility of disciplinary action is avoided when issues in personal injury law or other areas are publicized by independent groups supporting a candidate, groups that are not subject to the rules against raising of policy issues or to other limitations in what they can say.

Although large-scale campaigns and issue-based appeals have become more common, they remain exceptions to the rule. Especially below the supreme court level, elections with only a single candidate remain quite common, and most contested elections still involve limited activity and controversy.

The Situation of Incumbents   The continued predominance of quiet and uncontested judicial elections is linked to the situation of incumbent judges. When incumbents in any office run for re-election, they enjoy several advantages. Voters usually know them better than their opponents, they usually come from the majority party in their state or district, and they generally can raise more campaign funds than their opponents.

Incumbent judges enjoy several additional advantages. Some lawyers are reluctant to run against sitting judges, either because they feel that a reasonably competent judge should not have to face electoral challenges or because they fear having to try cases before a judge whom they challenged unsuccessfully. For similar reasons, the organized bar and individual lawyers tend to support incumbents.

Perhaps most important, the small scale of most judicial campaigns favors incumbents. Judges may not be nearly as well known as governors or legislators, but over time their names do become familiar to many voters. In contrast, challengers often begin as unknowns, and the near-invisibility of most campaigns makes it difficult to overcome this disadvantage. In this situation, voters are inclined to favor the candidate about whom they know a little over an opponent about whom they know nothing.

These advantages are reflected in an impressive rate of success for incumbents. Except for supreme court justices, high proportions of judges run unopposed for re-election. Over twenty-year periods, judges on the major trial court in Ohio were opposed only 27 percent of the time, those on the major trial court in Michigan 26 percent of the time, and those in California only 7 percent.[42] Judges who do face opposition win most of the time. The success rate for the Ohio and Michigan judges in contested races was more than 80 percent.[43]

Of course, some judges face strong electoral challenges, and some of these challenges are successful. In light of their advantages, what causes incumbent judges to suffer defeats?

Several conditions can make incumbents vulnerable. Judges sometimes are caught up in political tides against their political party. Judges who are charged with serious wrongdoing attract negative attention that may bring about their defeat. This was the case, to take one example, of a Las Vegas judge who was indicted in 1996 on federal charges related to allegations of corruption. Five months later he finished a distant third in a primary election for his seat.[44] Some judges lose re-election campaigns after developing a reputation for incompetence or bizarre behavior, often as a result of media attention. And voters may turn against a judge who adopts an unpopular line of policy, especially on an issue of widespread public concern. Even a single well-publicized and unpopular decision can make a judge vulnerable to defeat.

The growth in campaigns emphasizing policy issues largely reflects efforts by challengers to overcome the advantages of judicial incumbents. This is particularly true in criminal justice. Supreme court justices in states such as North Carolina and Louisiana have been attacked for alleged unwillingness to uphold death sentences, and trial judges frequently are charged with undue sympathy for criminal defendants. In Texas and California, organized groups seek to defeat judges whom they depict as liberals in this field. In one extreme case, a newspaper advertisement charged that an incumbent municipal judge in California had never sentenced a defendant to prison. The ad did not mention the fact that municipal judges had no power to sentence defendants to prison.[46] The rise of personal injury issues in Texas in the 1980s upset a traditional pattern in which supreme court justices were re-elected in quiet campaigns.[47] Issue-based challenges to incumbents fail more often than they succeed, but their successes are one source of the occasional defeats that incumbent judges suffer. They have contributed to a growing, if perhaps exaggerated, feeling of electoral vulnerability on the part of many judges.

Partisanship   As already suggested, partisanship can play a role in judicial elections. This role depends largely on a state's formal system. In states in which the candidates' party affiliations are listed on the ballot, voters have an additional piece of information on which to base their decision. Most voters identify themselves as Democrats or Republicans, and in an election in which they have little information they tend to support their own party's candidates because they have little reason to do otherwise.

Because party labels provide additional information to voters, they can complicate the positions of incumbents. A judge whose party is dominant may have little to fear from potential challengers; just as there are "safe" seats in Congress and state legislatures, there are judicial districts in which one party is usually assured of victory. But an incumbent whose party is in the minority may be vulnerable, and an unfavorable partisan tide can sweep an incumbent out of office.

The impact of party labels in partisan judicial elections is especially clear in the South. When the Democratic party was dominant in the region, Republican candidates had no chance to win judgeships in states that employed partisan elections. As Republican strength has grown, however, the party's judicial candidates have enjoyed increasing levels of success. This shift is reflected in defections of Democratic judges to the Republican party. In January 1996, for instance, ten Birmingham judges announced that they were joining the Republican party.[48]

In Texas, Republicans now hold a majority of seats on both the Supreme Court and the Court of Criminal Appeals, the state's highest court for criminal cases, after winning the preponderance of races in 1994 and 1996. After the 1996 election, one defeated Democratic incumbent on the Court of Criminal Appeals said that "I don't think a Democrat, in the next four years, is going to have a snowball's chance of beating a Republican" in a statewide judicial contest.[49] Republican candidates for trial judgeships have also done very well in cities such as Dallas and Houston.

The extent of this recent Republican dominance is suggested by what happened to Steve Mansfield, one of the party's 1994 candidates for the Court of Criminal Appeals. During the campaign, Mansfield admitted that he had not told the truth about some matters, including his claim that he had been born in Texas rather than Massachusetts. It was also disclosed that in 1986 he had been arrested in Florida for practicing law without a license. But Mansfield ran as a Republican, and the Republican tide of 1994 carried him into office over an incumbent Democrat. According to one observer, "If Steve Mansfield can get elected, anyone can."[50]

The candidates' party affiliations influence voters even if the party organizations play no role in the election process. But party organizations often do become involved. The prestige and power of judgeships make them alluring prizes. As a result, in states in which party organizations are strong and the political climate favorable, the parties may participate actively in the election.

New York and Illinois, which have partisan elections for judges, are two such states.[51] Democratic judicial candidates in Chicago are generally chosen by the party leaders, whose endorsement virtually guarantees victory in the primary election. Because Chicago is heavily Democratic, a victory in the Democratic primary is the major requirement for winning a judgeship. In New York State, candidates for trial court judgeships are nominated in party conventions or primary elections. Where a local party organization is strong in New York, it controls the convention or primary outcome. In counties in which one party dominates, the endorsement of that party's organization assures election. An incumbent from the minority party in a county is likely to suffer defeat if the other party's organization chooses to oppose the incumbent. Thus, one report concluded, "most judges in New York are chosen by elections that are almost totally controlled by political party leaders."[52]

Elections that are officially nonpartisan typically involve little partisanship in practice. Ordinarily, few voters know the party affiliations of the candidates, so their party loyalties have limited impact on their choices. As a result, partisan considerations are less likely to compete with the incumbent's advantage. In turn, fewer incumbents face opposition and suffer defeat in states that have nonpartisan elections. Further, party organizations are much less likely to involve themselves in the election process. Ohio is an exception: party organizations actively recruit candidates and support their candidates, and voters choose candidates partly on the basis of their party labels.[53] Ohio's use of a partisan primary, unique among states that elect judges on a nonpartisan ballot, encourages a degree of partisanship. In most states with a nonpartisan ballot, party organizations and partisan voting play limited roles in the election of judges.

Interim Appointment In nearly all states that elect judges, the governor fills vacancies between elections. These interim appointments are important because vacancies occur with some frequency and because appointees generally are successful in winning subsequent elections. As a result, at any given time a high proportion of the judges in states with elective systems will have gained their positions initially through appointments. For this reason, elective systems should be considered both elective *and* appointive.

The success of appointees in winning election is understandable: an appointed judge shares some of the advantages of long-time incumbents, and most appointees are too new to create enemies or to arouse concerted opposition. In some states, appointed judges from the minority party in their district can be vulnerable to defeat, but even in those states most newcomers hold their positions. In other states, they do extremely well. For example, over a twenty-year period no appointee to Michigan's major trial court was defeated.[54]

In some states, appointments have become the dominant element in formally elective systems. In Minnesota, the usual pattern is for supreme court seats to be filled by interim appointments; the appointees then run for election with no opposition. A lawyer who took the unusual step of challenging an incumbent justice in 1990 was foiled when the incumbent resigned—allowing the governor to make an appointment and, under Minnesota's rules, cancel the election. When the lawyer tried to run against another incumbent in 1992, the governor sought to extend the incumbent's term by two years. The lawyer then went to court, won a ruling that the governor's action was unconstitutional, and then won the election. Unusual as this sequence of events was, it does illustrate one generalization about judicial elections, the value of name recognition: the lawyer whose persistence ultimately won him a supreme court seat was Alan Page, very well known and well liked as a former star for the Minnesota Vikings football team.[55]

The Operation of Appointive Systems

Of the three nonelective systems of judicial selection, legislative election is so rare today that it requires no further discussion. But gubernatorial appointment and the Missouri Plan are of considerable importance, the former because it is commonly used to fill vacancies in states that elect judges and the latter because of its widespread and increasing use.

Gubernatorial Appointment   Only eight states give their governors the general power to select judges. But in states with elective systems, governors choose a significant number of judges through interim appointments. As a result, a large minority of all state judges originally were selected by a governor.[56]

In making their selections, governors can consult with a wide array of individuals and groups. The views of people who are politically important to the governor tend to get serious consideration. Legislators may also influence the governor's choices, particularly in states in which the senate must confirm nominees. In New Jersey, under a variant of senatorial courtesy in Congress, any senator from the county in which a nominee resides holds an informal veto power over the nominee's confirmation, and in making a choice the governor needs to take the home-county senators' views into account.

In some states, governors have allowed bar associations to screen potential appointees. In Mississippi, for instance, most governors have deferred to local bar associations in choosing interim appointees.[57] As the popularity of the Missouri Plan has grown, some governors with appointing power have set up similar nominating commissions and agreed to select judges from the commission's nominees. This practice gives the bar a role through the inclusion of lawyers on commissions.

The criteria that governors apply in making judicial appointments fall into the same general categories as those employed by presidents. To a considerable degree, appointments are used to advance political goals, especially by serving as rewards.

Most broadly, judgeships generally are reserved for members of the governor's party. Political allies, particularly those who have helped to advance a governor's career, have an advantage in winning appointments. This advantage is symbolized by the 1995 appointment of a Maryland lawyer to a trial judgeship eight days after a fund-raising golf tournament for the governor that she had helped to arrange.[58] And it does not hurt to have a long-standing association with the governor. When California governor Pete Wilson appointed a justice to the state supreme court in 1994, one commentator noted that he "most likely relied on a 30–year friendship with the honors-winning classmate he wisely chose to study with" in law school.[59]

The attractiveness of judgeships makes them powerful rewards to lawyer-legislators. "If there are any lawyers in the Legislature who don't want a judgeship," said one observer in California, "I don't know who they are."[60] With legislative term limits now operating in California and many other states, judgeships are even more attractive. Thus legislators may have an extra incentive to follow the governor's lead. On the other hand, in 1989, Governor William Donald Schaefer of Maryland appointed as judge a legislator who had been a strong critic of Schaefer, referring to him once as "Don the Con." Some observers suspected that Schaefer made the appointment to get a nettlesome opponent out of the legislature.[61]

Particularly in states where the courts play a highly visible part in policymaking, governors may seek to staff the courts with ideological allies. Thus, beginning with Ronald Reagan, recent California governors have worked hard to select judges who share their policy views. In one survey, self-described conservatives outnumbered liberals among Reagan's appointees to the major trial court by a 25–1 ratio, while liberals had a 7–1 advantage among the judges appointed by his Democratic successor, Jerry Brown.[62] Brown's own successor, George Deukmejian, was especially interested in selecting judges with conservative views on criminal justice issues. As a result, 65 percent of his appointees had experience as prosecutors.[63]

Governors also consider the apparent competence of potential judges, although the importance of this consideration varies a good deal by state and by level of court. Governors who voluntarily establish nominating commissions do so, at least ostensibly, to give more weight to candidates' qualifications.

Although governors usually have unilateral power to make interim appointments, most states with gubernatorial appointment as the regular selection method require that the governor's choices be confirmed by the state senate or, less often, another body. Few nominations fail to be confirmed, in part because governors avoid making nominations that might displease the confirming body. But the senatorial courtesy powers of New Jersey state senators have led to battles over some appointments. Occasionally nominees run into trouble in other states as well. In Maryland, for instance, a trial court nominee aroused strong opposition after allegations that he had used sexist, racist, and crude language in a discussion of legislation; ultimately, he withdrew his candidacy.[64]

A 1995 confirmation battle in Massachusetts reached a level of intensity comparable to that of some major battles over nominees to the U.S. Supreme Court. Republican governor William Weld nominated Charles Fried to the supreme court. Fried's accomplishments included service in the Bush administration as solicitor general, the chief advocate for the federal government in the Supreme Court. Massachusetts appointments must be confirmed by a body called the Governor's

Council. A campaign against Fried's confirmation developed, based primarily on conservative positions that he had taken as solicitor general. After heated hearings and considerable lobbying, Fried was confirmed when the council split 4–4 and the lieutenant governor broke the tie with a positive vote. Perhaps the most memorable aspect of this extraordinary battle was the explanation of the councilor whose decision to vote for Fried created the tie: "Charles Fried does not have horns and a long green tail. He's not a rapist, murderer, or pedophile."[65]

In states with gubernatorial appointment of judges, as in legislative election states, the general practice is to grant an additional term to a judge who wishes to continue in office. As a result, appointments to judgeships generally constitute lifetime appointments in practice. But some judges do fail to win reappointment. One denial of reappointment, described in Exhibit 4.5, tells a good deal about the politics of judicial selection.

Exhibit 4.5   A Delaware Judge Fails to Win Reappointment

The laws of Delaware have attracted a high proportion of large businesses to incorporate in the state, and the state's courts thus have considerable power over legal issues involving corporate activity. In 1994, Justice Andrew Moore was denied reappointment to the state supreme court; he was replaced by Carolyn Berger, a state trial judge. Berger formerly had worked with Skadden, Arps, a law firm that often represents companies seeking hostile takeovers of corporations. Moore had been a leading critic of hostile takeovers, and he had taken other positions favorable to stockholders as opposed to corporate management. He had been part of a court panel that ruled against an important Skadden client in a large-stakes case involving the takeover of Technicolor, Inc.

The nominating commission that was used to recommend candidates to the governor placed only Berger's name on its list of nominees, and Governor Thomas Carper decided to appoint her. The commission included a Skadden partner who represented that losing client, and a current and a former Skadden lawyer each had links to the governor. For that reason, there was considerable suspicion that the firm had used its influence to rid itself of a judge who was perceived to be unfriendly to its interests. On the other hand, a leading Skadden attorney supported Moore's reappointment, and some people argued that Moore lacked an appropriate judicial temperament.

Thus the reasons for Moore's replacement by Berger remain uncertain. In any case, a year later, a panel of the Delaware supreme court (one on which Justice Berger did not sit) reached a final decision in the Technicolor case, ruling in favor of the Skadden client.

Sources: Richard B. Schmitt, "Delaware Governor Picks Trial Judge to Succeed Moore on Supreme Court," *Wall Street Journal,* May 26, 1994, B7; Karen Donovan, "Shareholders' Advocates Protest Judge's Removal," *National Law Journal,* June 6, 1994, B1, B2; Diana B. Henriques, "Top Business Court Under Fire," *New York Times,* May 23, 1995, C1, C6; other newspaper reports. The supreme court decisions were *Cede & Co. v. Technicolor, Inc.,* 634 A.2d 345 (Del. 1993); and *Cinerama, Inc. v. Technicolor, Inc.,* 663 A.2d 1156 (Del. 1995).

The Missouri Plan   Twenty states now use some form of the Missouri Plan as the formal selection system for at least some of their courts. As noted earlier, several states that elect judges have also established truncated Missouri Plan systems (involving commission nomination and gubernatorial appointment) to fill vacancies between elections, and a number of governors have voluntarily adopted commission nomination processes for regular or interim appointments.[66]

As we would expect, lawyers and judges predominate among commissioners: a 1989 national survey of commissioners found that 59 percent were legal professionals. Nonlawyer commissioners tend to be high in socioeconomic status; the largest numbers are business executives or educators. Many are active in politics, and in the 1989 survey, 37 percent of those appointed by a governor had campaigned for that governor. The great majority were white men.[67] Commissioners are far from a random sample of the population in all these respects, and nominations may reflect the perspectives of the groups that are best represented.

Partisan considerations and political conflicts do influence the selection of commissioners. In Missouri, for example, different segments of the bar compete over who will be chosen. Some states require a close party balance within their commissions, but in some others the overwhelming majority of lay members share the governor's party affiliation. At one time, this was true of twenty-one of the twenty-five lay commissioners in Maryland and all thirty-two in Iowa.[68]

Theoretically, a commission's decisions are to be based only on the qualifications of potential judges. Inevitably, other factors enter into the process. Prominent among these factors is partisanship. Because some commissioners have strong party loyalties and ties, partisanship colors their consideration of candidates. Of course, personal considerations can also play a part. "There is considerable anecdotal evidence," according to one scholar, that the process of selecting nominees in Nebraska "has been manipulated to favor friends, law partners, and even relatives."[69]

In most states the governor appoints lay commissioners, and the appointment power provides some potential influence over the selection of nominees. Governors can usually achieve the results they want without direct pressure if the lay commissioners are sympathetic to the governor's goals, as many are. Several of the commissioners who responded to the 1989 survey "viewed their commissions as being controlled by gubernatorial appointees whose commission membership is a political 'thank-you' and who select whomever the governor wants."[70] In 1996, New York governor George Pataki appointed a close adviser to serve on the nominating commission for a position on the state's highest court. The commission included on its list a longtime friend of Pataki's who shared the governor's conservatism, and Pataki appointed his friend to the position.[71]

Of course, the governor also chooses among the candidates forwarded by the commission. Where the governor's influence over the commission is sufficient, at least one nominee for each seat will be highly acceptable. (Governors may go even further. One commissioner complained that "the governor has insisted the commission present him candidates of his choice; otherwise he refuses to appoint anyone."[72]) In this situation, the governor can use court appointments to serve the same ideological and partisan goals that they serve in gubernatorial appointment states. For instance, judgeships sometimes are used as political rewards. Partisan concerns appear to play a prominent role in Missouri.[73]

In nearly all states operating under the Missouri Plan, a judge needs to win a simple majority of votes in a retention election to remain in office. Most judges are in an excellent position to do so; in a retention election, all the ordinary advantages of incumbency are strengthened by the absence of an opposing candidate. The results are highly favorable to judges: the overwhelming majority of judges win, and generally by large margins. Between 1980 and 1990, the average proportion of positive votes for judges in retention elections (whether under the Missouri Plan or as part of another selection system) was 74 percent, and 99 percent of the judges were successful. Eighteen of the thirty-four defeated judges were in Illinois, which requires a 60 percent vote for retention. All but one of the eighteen received more than 50 percent of the vote.[74]

Impressive as this record of success is, it obscures an important trend: the proportion of negative votes has increased since the 1960s.[75] In Missouri, for instance, the average proportion of favorable votes dropped from 82 percent in 1972 to 73 percent in 1988—and then below 60 percent in 1990. In Missouri, at least, this downward slide was halted and even reversed somewhat in 1992 and 1994, but in 1992 a Missouri judge lost a retention election for the first time since 1942.[76]

Voters typically have little information about individual judges in retention elections, particularly in large districts and for appellate courts. As a result, the various judges on the ballot in a particular place tend to do about equally well. In St. Louis County, Missouri, voters responded to fourteen judges in 1994. The most successful candidate received 66.3 percent of the vote, the least successful 57.5 percent.[77] Thus the growing proportion of negative votes reflects a generalized reaction to judges, perhaps stemming from a decline in citizens' trust of political leaders as a group.[78]

Even with this growth in voter negativism, judges still win retention unless voters are given reasons to vote specifically against them. Judges who suffer defeats usually have aroused opposition from people who see their performance as substandard or who disagree strongly with their decisions. In recent years there have been a few well-organized campaigns against retention based on judges' positions on legal issues. In California, conservative groups spent an estimated $5.5 million against three supreme court justices in 1986, securing their defeats by large margins. The money came largely from opponents of the court's liberal positions on personal injury law, but the public campaign against the justices centered on their votes to reverse death sentences.[79]

In Florida, supreme court justices Leander Shaw in 1990 and Rosemary Barkett in 1992 drew opposition from groups that were unhappy with their support for protection of abortion rights under the state constitution and from groups that disapproved of decisions favoring criminal defendants. Barkett also faced strong opposition from the National Rifle Association. Ultimately, both Shaw and Barkett won retention, but each garnered only about 60 percent of the vote.[80] As described in Exhibit 4.2, Barkett later ran into opposition based on her votes in death penalty cases when President Clinton nominated her for a federal judgeship; she was confirmed by a 61–37 vote.

In 1996, Tennessee supreme court justice Penny White was defeated by a 55–45 margin in a low-turnout retention election after a two-month campaign against her by conservative and anticrime groups. These groups publicized votes by White that were favorable to criminal defendants in some cases, and that publicity was sufficient to cause her defeat.[81] This outcome underlines the increased vulnerability of judges who face retention elections when an organized opposition can tap strong public feelings on issues. Still, the great majority of judges do not face such opposition, and easy victories remain the dominant pattern.

The Impact of Formal Selection Systems

A great deal of effort has been expended on debates over alternative systems for the selection of judges. Has that effort been justified? In other words, how much do the various formal selection systems actually differ in practice? This question can be considered at three levels: the actual processes by which judges are selected, the characteristics of the people who are chosen as judges, and the behavior of judges and courts.

Effects on Selection Processes   On paper, the five major systems for selecting judges look very different. In practice, however, they function similarly in some important respects.

First, the chief executive typically has a great deal of impact, regardless of which system is in operation. Even in states with judicial elections, the governor selects a good many judges by filling vacancies. Because the governor's appointees usually win subsequent elections, interim appointment gives the governor considerable power to determine the membership of the courts. In Missouri Plan states, the governor makes the final choice from a commission's list. As we have seen, the governor often has considerable influence over the list itself. "In most states, and for most judges," a California judge noted, "the path to judicial office is through the governor's door."[82]

Second, in each system judges are likely to remain in their positions as long as they want. Few incumbents are removed by the voters in states with elective systems, and even fewer in states with the Missouri Plan. Governors nearly always reappoint incumbents. Judges now have less security in office than they did twenty years ago, but it remains true that only a small proportion are removed from office.

Finally, all judicial selection systems are political in the sense that considerations other than the merits of prospective judges come into play. The operation of the Missouri Plan underlines this reality. After New York replaced partisan elections for its highest court with a modified Missouri Plan, one legislator complained, "I think we have brought more politics into the process . . . than we ever did when judges were elected."[83] His remark may have been an exaggeration, but it reflects the fact that no system is truly "nonpolitical."

Of course, formal systems for choosing judges do have some effect. For example, a governor who directly appoints all judges has more power than one who only fills vacancies or one who works with nominating commissions. Similarly, voters have greater control over judges in a state that elects judges than in one in which the governor or the legislature chooses them. Political parties have a better opportunity to influence the selection process in a partisan election state than in one that uses the Missouri Plan. Judges are most likely to be removed from office in states with partisan elections. These differences are not trivial.

Yet the ways in which states select judges are a product of their political conditions and traditions as well as their formal systems. Thus the same formal system can work quite differently from one state to another. For example, in states with partisan traditions and strong party organizations, such as New York, partisan considerations would play an important part under any formal system. In states with a nonpartisan ethos or weak party organizations, the same system would be less partisan. This produces an irony: in states in which judicial selection is heavily permeated by partisanship, so that the Missouri Plan seems most attractive to reformers, the plan is least likely to minimize partisanship.

Effects on Characteristics of Judges   For those who debate methods of selecting judges, one central concern is the kinds of people who are selected. Supporters of the Missouri Plan, for instance, argue that it will strengthen the qualifications of judges, as reflected in characteristics such as educational attainments and legal experience.

Studies of state supreme courts from the 1960s to the 1980s suggest that the different formal systems actually produce similar mixes of judges.[84] These studies found that traits such as academic training and prior judicial experience differed little by selection system and that, as the most recent study concluded, most of the differences found in the backgrounds of justices "are due mainly to region, not selection system."[85] This does not mean that the various systems produce exactly the same results. Not surprisingly, for instance, legislators have the best chance to become judges in the few states in which the legislature chooses judges. But such differences are outweighed by similarities among the systems. Missouri's shift from partisan elections to the Missouri Plan did not have major effects on the kinds of people selected as judges.[86]

Formal systems might produce effects that have not yet been measured. For instance, the Missouri Plan might produce fewer judges who are actively involved in political party organizations. When better means to gauge the competence of judges are developed, we might find that some systems produce abler judges than others. But, because the various formal systems seem to operate less differently in practice than in theory, it appears unlikely that they produce judges who differ dramatically in any significant respects.

Effects on the Behavior of Judges   Ultimately, the most significant effects of formal selection systems—to the extent that there *are* effects—are on judges' behavior and court policies. Advocates of a particular system often argue that it produces better justice, but not everyone agrees on what better justice actually means. Leaving aside this question, we might expect selection systems to influence court behavior and policies for either of two reasons: the systems put different kinds of judges on the bench, or they subject judges to different kinds of influences once they reach the bench.

As just discussed, there is some reason to discount the first possibility. The second possibility, however, is an intriguing one. For example, judges who are subject to party nominations may take party interests into account in their decisions more than do judges who run in nonpartisan elections. Judges who are appointed by the chief executive might support the positions of the executive branch more often than those who are elected.

One possible effect that has received considerable attention is the effect of elective systems on judges' responses to public opinion. With the growing frequency of issue-based campaigns against incumbent judges, some commentators conclude that the prospect of election deters judges from taking unpopular positions on issues that voters care a lot about—especially criminal justice. In a 1995 Supreme Court decision, Justice John Paul Stevens argued against allowing trial judges to overrule jury recommendations against the death penalty.

> The "higher authority" to whom present-day . . . judges may be "too responsive" is a political climate in which judges who covet higher office—or who merely wish to remain judges—must constantly profess their fealty to the death penalty. Alabama trial judges face partisan election every six years. . . . . The danger that they will bend to political pressures when pronouncing sentence in highly publicized capital cases is the same danger confronted by judges beholden to King George III.[87]

Stevens's analysis might be questioned on the ground that few judges actually suffer electoral defeats. But judges, like legislators, may exaggerate the likelihood of defeat and take action to reduce that likelihood even when it is already small. Certainly elected judges have attested to their concern about scrutiny of their decisions by potential opponents and by the voters.[88]

But how different are elected and appointed judges in this respect? Missouri Plan judges also have to face the voters periodically. Although defeats in retention elections are rare, some judges worry about the impact of their decisions on future retention elections.[89] Even judges appointed by governors might be concerned that unpopular decisions would make a governor reluctant to reappoint them. Life tenure would seem to eliminate any concern with public opinion, yet even federal judges sometimes bend to political pressure when they are attacked for unpopular decisions.

This does not mean that election has no impact on judges' responsiveness to public opinion; almost surely, it does. But, there is only scattered evidence on the extent of this impact. The same is true of other possible effects of judicial selection systems. It does seem likely that differences among systems have a greater impact on some issues than on others. Of course, concern with re-election is more likely to surface in criminal justice than in contract law. Similarly, it may be that the role of political parties in the selection of judges has an impact primarily on those issues that affect the parties' fortunes most, such as legislative redistricting.[90] It also seems certain that the effects of formal selection systems are mediated by the political situation in particular states. Judges in a state with highly contested elections, for instance, would react differently to the prospect of election from judges in states in which incumbents seldom face opposition. But these differences, like the general effects of selection systems, require more systematic study.

CONCLUSIONS

In the United States, concern about the selection of judges has focused largely on choices among formal selection systems. That focus is apparent in the states, which change their formal systems with some frequency. The concern about formal systems stems from the belief that they make a difference. As we have seen, however, there are several interrelated reasons to think that the effects of formal systems have been exaggerated.

First, the actual operation of a formal selection system often differs from what its rules suggest. Elective systems can become largely appointive in practice. The Missouri Plan permits partisan politics to exert an influence.

Second, the different formal systems actually converge to a considerable extent in both their operation and their results. Chief executives play central roles in all the systems used in the United States. Systems as different in appearance as the Missouri Plan and partisan election produce similar kinds of judges.

Finally, a single formal system may work quite differently under different circumstances. The U.S. Constitution establishes the same rules for the selection of Supreme Court justices and district judges, but the two are actually selected in very different ways. Recent presidents have established somewhat different processes for the selection of lower-court judges and have chosen different mixes of people.

All this does not mean that formal systems to select judges make little difference. For one thing, the various systems used in the United States probably have some significant effects. More important, these systems do not represent the full range of possible systems. Rather, in contrast with the civil service–like systems that exist in much of the world, the various American systems share an emphasis on accountability rather than judicial independence. In this sense, it is not surprising that the American systems look somewhat similar in operation and seem to produce similar results.

These similarities merit emphasis. The federal government and every state government select judges in ways that ensure a linkage between those judges and other political institutions. The results are noteworthy: a high proportion of judges are people who have been politically active and who have connections with political officials, and the courts are relatively open to influence from their political environments.

Judicial selection systems, then, are significant. But in the United States their significance lies in their shared effects more than in their differences. These shared effects are explored in the next chapter.

FOR FURTHER READING

Abraham, Henry J. *Justices and Presidents: A Political History of Appointments to the Supreme Court.* 3d ed. New York: Oxford University Press, 1992.

Carter, Stephen L. *The Confirmation Mess: Cleaning Up the Federal Appointments Process.* New York: Basic Books, 1994.

Dubois, Philip L. *From Ballot to Bench: Judicial Elections and the Quest for Accountability.* Austin: University of Texas Press, 1980.

Maltese, John Anthony. *The Selling of Supreme Court Nominees.* Baltimore: Johns Hopkins University Press, 1995.

Phelps, Timothy M., and Helen Winternitz. *Capitol Games: Clarence Thomas, Anita Hill, and the Story of a Supreme Court Nomination.* New York: Hyperion, 1992.

Silverstein, Mark. *Judicious Choices: The New Politics of Supreme Court Confirmations.* New York: W. W. Norton, 1994.

Watson, George L., and John A. Stookey. *Shaping America: The Politics of Supreme Court Appointments.* New York: HarperCollins, 1995.

Watson, Richard A., and Rondal G. Downing. *The Politics of the Bench and the Bar: Judicial Selection Under the Missouri Nonpartisan Court Plan.* New York: John Wiley, 1969.

NOTES

1. See Philip L. Dubois, *From Ballot to Bench: Judicial Elections and the Quest for Accountability* (Austin: University of Texas Press, 1980), especially ch. 1.

2. This discussion is based in part on Evan Haynes, *The Selection and Tenure of Judges* (Newark, N.J.: National Conference of Judicial Councils, 1944), chs. 2–4; and Allan Ashman and James J. Alfini, *The Key to Judicial Merit Selection: The Nominating Process* (Chicago: American Judicature Society, 1974), 7–11.

3. Kermit L. Hall, "The Judiciary on Trial: State Constitutional Reform and the Rise of an Elected Judiciary, 1846–1860," *The Historian* 44 (May 1983), 337–354.

4. "Benchmark," *The New Yorker,* May 3, 1993, 34–35.

5. Deborah J. Barrow and Gary Zuk, "Turnover in the Lower Federal Courts, 1900–1987," *Journal of Politics* 52 (May 1990), 457–476; James F. Spriggs II and Paul J. Wahlbeck, "Calling It Quits: Strategic Retirement on the Federal Courts of Appeals, 1893–1991," *Political Research Quarterly* 48 (September 1995), 573–597.

6. John Ehrlichman, *Witness to Power: The Nixon Years* (New York: Simon & Schuster, 1982), 114–115.

7. Eleanor Randolph, "Husband Triggered Letters Supporting Ginsburg for Court," *Washington Post,* June 17, 1993, A25.

8. David G. Savage, *Turning Right: The Making of the Rehnquist Supreme Court* (New York: John Wiley & Sons, 1992), 136.

9. Robert Scigliano, *The Supreme Court and the Presidency* (New York: Free Press, 1971), 111; updated by the author.

10. Ibid., 95; updated by the author.

11. On the factors that shape Senate confirmation decisions, see John D. Felice and Herbert F. Weisberg, "The Changing Importance of Ideology, Party, and Region in Confirmation of Supreme Court Nominees, 1953–88," *Kentucky Law Journal* 77 (1988–1989), 509–530; and Jeffrey A. Segal, Charles M. Cameron, and Albert D. Cover, "A Spatial Model of Roll Call Voting: Senators, Constituents, Presidents, and Interest Groups in Supreme Court Nominations," *American Journal of Political Science* 36 (February 1992), 96–121.

12. Sheldon Goldman and Elliot Slotnick, "Clinton's First Term Judiciary: Many Bridges to Cross," *Judicature* 80 (May–June 1997), 254–255.

13. Wayne King, "As of Now, No Hispanic Nominees for Federal Bench in New York," *New York Times,* February 15, 1991, A16.

14. Neil A. Lewis, "Senate Is Quick to Approve Judgeship for Former Aide," *New York Times,* November 12, 1990, A10.

15. Sheldon Goldman, "The Bush Imprint on the Judiciary: Carrying on a Tradition," *Judicature* 74 (April–May 1991), 305; see Ruth Marcus, "GOP Senators, Bush Administration at Odds Over Judicial Appointments," *Washington Post,* November 23, 1989, A25.

16. Miller Center for Public Affairs, *Improving the Process of Appointing Federal Judges: A Report of the Miller Center Commission on the Selection of Federal Judges* (Charlottesville: University of Virginia, 1996), 5.

17. Harvey Berkman, "Hatch to ABA: You're Out. ABA: So What," *National Law Journal,* March 3, 1997, A6.

18. Harold W. Chase, *Federal Judges: The Appointing Process* (Minneapolis: University of Minnesota Press, 1972), 29.

19. Joseph C. Goulden, *The Benchwarmers: The Private World of the Powerful Federal Judges* (New York: Weybright and Talley, 1974), 23.

20. Joan Biskupic, "Appeals Court Nominee Says No Thanks," *Washington Post,* May 10, 1996, A17.

21. See Sheldon Goldman and Matthew D. Saronson, "Clinton's Nontraditional Judges: Creating a More Representative Bench," *Judicature* 78 (September–October 1994), 68–73; and Goldman and Slotnick, "Clinton's First Term Judiciary," 270.

22. Elliot E. Slotnick and Sheldon Goldman, "Congress and the Courts: A Case of Casting," in *Great Theater: The American Congress in Action,* ed. Herbert F. Weisberg and Samuel C. Patterson (New York: Cambridge University Press, forthcoming). See "Hatch Fires Warning Shot of Judges," *Legal Times,* November 18, 1996, 14.

23. Ezra Bowen, "Judges with Their Minds Right," *Time,* November 4, 1985, 77.

24. Neil A. Lewis, "Bush Travels Reagan's Course in Naming Judges," *New York Times,* April 10, 1990, A1.

25. See Joan Biskupic, "Bush Boosts Bench Strength of Conservative Judges," *Congressional Quarterly Weekly Report,* January 19, 1991, 174.

26. Neil A. Lewis, "In Selecting Federal Judges, Clinton Has Not Tried to Be the Anti-Reagan," *New York Times,* August 1, 1996, A12.

27. Goldman and Slotnick, "Clinton's First-Term Judiciary," 256.

28. Blaine Harden, "Criminal Justice Failing, Dole Says Eying Clinton," *Washington Post,* May 29, 1996, A8.

29. Ronald Stidham, Robert A. Carp, and Donald R. Songer, "The Voting Behavior of President Clinton's Judicial Appointees," *Judicature* 80 (July–August 1996), 16–20.

30. Greg Gordon, "Minnesota Judge Finally Approved After Wellstone Bogs Down Senate," *Minneapolis Star Tribune,* August 3, 1996, 10A.

31. "Too Many Federal Court Vacancies" (editorial), *New York Times,* February 14, 1997, A22.

32. Mike Magan, "What a Difference a (Birth)day Makes," *National Law Journal,* May 13, 1996, A8.

33. "Born to Run," *National Law Journal,* November 20, 1995, A4.

34. Theodore S. Arrington, "When Money Doesn't Matter: Campaign Spending for Minor Statewide Judicial and Executive Offices in North Carolina," *Justice System Journal* 18 (1996), 262.

35. Anna Borgman, "Candidate Accused of Fabricating a Picture-Perfect Family," *Washington Post,* November 1, 1996, B1, B7.

36. Johnson, "Voter Survey: Judges Unknown," *Texas Lawyer,* November 10–14, 1986, at 1, 8–9. Cited in Anthony Champagne and Greg Thielemann, "Awareness of Trial Court Judges," *Judicature* 74 (February–March 1991), 272.

37. Robb London, "For Want of Recognition, Chief Justice is Ousted," *New York Times,* September 28, 1990, B9; William S. Bailey, "Time to Change the Way We Pick Judges," *Seattle Times,* September 28, 1994, B7.

38. Gail Diane Cox, "Will the Real Phillippe Please Stand Up?" *National Law Journal,* April 8, 1991, 2.

39. *Rogers v. Bradley,* 909 S.W.2d 872, 882 n. 1 (Texas 1995). See Anthony Champagne, "Campaign Contributions in Texas Supreme Court Races," *Crime, Law and Social Change* 17 (March 1992), 91–106.

40. Stuart Taylor, "Campaigning for the Bench," *Legal Times,* July 22, 1996, 21.

41. James Bradshaw, "Judge Reprimanded over '94 Election Ad," *Columbus Dispatch,* December 7, 1996, 1D.

42. Philip L. Dubois, "Voting Cues in Nonpartisan Trial Court Elections: A Multivariate Assessment," *Law and Society Review* 18 (1984), 399; Lawrence Baum, "The Electoral

Fates of Incumbent Judges in the Ohio Court of Common Pleas," *Judicature* 66 (April 1983), 424; Susan B. Hannah, "Competition in Michigan's Judicial Elections: Democratic Ideals vs. Judicial Realities," *Wayne Law Review* 24 (July 1978), 1303.

43. Hannah, "Competition in Michigan's Judicial Elections," 1303; Baum, "Electoral Fates of Incumbent Judges," 424–425.

44. Jeffrey Cohan, "Indicted Judge Loses District Court Re-Election Bid," *Las Vegas Review-Journal,* September 4, 1996, 9B.

45. Sheryl Stolberg and Frederick M. Muir, "Judge Karlin's Win Baffles Black Leaders, *Los Angeles Times*, June 4, 1992, B1, B4.

46. Gail Diane Cox, "Jerry's Judges," *National Law Journal,* May 25, 1992, 31.

47. Patricia Kilday Hart, "Disorder in the Court," *Texas Monthly,* March 1988, 118–121; Peter Applebome, "Rubber Stamp Is Gone in Texas Judicial Election," *New York Times,* October 21, 1988, B7.

48. Kevin Sack, "10 Alabama Judges Stage a Mass Defection to the G.O.P.," *New York Times,* January 4, 1996, A8.

49. "Judge Not," *Texas Observer,* November 22, 1996, 32.

50. The quotation is from "Ex Parte Mansfield," *Texas Observer,* January 26, 1996, 24. See also "Q&A with Stephen Mansfield: 'The Greatest Challenge of My Life,'" *Texas Lawyer,* November 21, 1994, 8; Bruce Nichols, "Questions Follow Lawyer Elected to Appeals Court," *Dallas Morning News,* November 26, 1994, 1A. On the partisan changes in Texas, see L. Douglas Kiel, Carole Funk, and Anthony Champagne, "Two-Party Competition and Trial Court Elections in Texas," *Judicature* 77 (May–June 1994), 290–293.

51. On Illinois, see James Tuohy and Rob Warden, *Greylord: Justice, Chicago Style* (New York: G. P. Putnam's Sons, 1989), 45–49; on New York, see New York State Commission on Government Integrity, *Becoming a Judge* (New York: Commission on Government Integrity, 1988); and Matthew L. Hickerson, "Electing Little-Known Candidates as Judges," *New York Times* (Long Island Weekly), October 20, 1991, 1, 15, 20.

52. New York State Commission on Government Integrity, *Restoring the Public Trust: A Blueprint for Government Integrity* (New York: Commission on Public Integrity, 1990), 16.

53. See Lawrence Baum, "Electing Judges," in *Contemplating Courts,* ed. Lee Epstein (Washington, D.C.: CQ Press, 1995), 18–43.

54. Hannah, "Competition in Michigan's Judicial Elections," 1306.

55. Michael Abramowicz, "Page Puts On Big Rush in Minnesota Court Bid," *Washington Post,* October 24, 1992, G1, G4. See *Page v. Carlson,* 488 N.W.2d 274 (Minn. 1992).

56. See John Paul Ryan, Allan Ashman, Bruce D. Sales, and Sandra Shane-Du Bow, *American Trial Judges: Their Work Styles and Performance* (New York: Free Press, 1980), 124.

57. James J. Alfini, "Mississippi Judicial Selection: Election, Appointment, and Bar Anointment," in *Courts and Judges,* ed. James A. Cramer (Beverly Hills, Calif.: Sage Publications, 1981), 258.

58. Michael Abramowitz, "Judge's Opponents Make Issue of '95 Fund-Raiser," *Washington Post,* October 5, 1996, B3.

59. Philip Hager, "A Friendly Appointment," *California Lawyer,* July 1994, 41.

60. Larry Liebert, "Hoping for a Judgeship," *San Francisco Chronicle,* February 18, 1978, 12.

61. Robert Barnes, "Schaefer Names Foe to Judgeship," *Washington Post,* April 5, 1989, B5.

62. Philip L. Dubois, "State Trial Court Appointments: Does the Governor Make a Difference?" *Judicature* 69 (June–July 1985), 25.

63. Peter Allen, "Deukmejian's Judicial Legacy," *California Lawyer,* February 1991, 25.

64. Richard Tapscott and Charles Babington, "Arnick Drops Judicial Bid, Citing 'Media Frenzy,'" *Washington Post,* February 18, 1993, D1, D3; Patricia S. Florestano, "The Case of the Failed Nomination: Subtexts in a State Legislature," *PS: Political Science and Politics* 26 (September 1993), 507–510.

65. Peter J. Howe, "Win for Weld as Fried Gets Seat on SJC," *Boston Globe,* August 31, 1995, 1, 34; the quotation is on p. 1.

66. The operation of commissions is discussed in Joanne Martin, *Merit Selection*

Commissions: What Do They Do? How Effective Are They? (Chicago: American Bar Association, 1993).

67. Beth M. Henschen, Robert Moog, and Steven Davis, "Judicial Nominating Commissioners: A National Profile," *Judicature* 73 (April–May 1990), 329–333.

68. Ashman and Alfini, *Key to Judicial Merit Selection,* 77.

69. Steven L. Willborn, "Off the Mark: The Nebraska Supreme Court and Judicial Nominating Commissions," *Nebraska Law Review* 70 (Spring 1991), 300–301.

70. Henschen, Moog, and Davis, "Judicial Nominating Commissioners," 334.

71. "Mr. Pataki Picks a Judge" (editorial), *New York Times,* December 4, 1996, A22.

72. Henschen, Moog, and Davis, "Judicial Nominating Commissioners," 334.

73. Paul Wenske, "Dissension Rocks Missouri Justices," *National Law Journal,* May 27, 1985, 1, 26–28.

74. Robert C. Luskin, Christopher N. Bratcher, Christopher G. Jordan, Tracy K. Renner, and Kir S. Seago, "How Minority Judges Fare in Retention Elections," *Judicature* 77 (May–June 1994), 319–320.

75. William K. Hall and Larry T. Aspin, "What Twenty Years of Judicial Retention Elections Have Told Us," *Judicature* 70 (April–May 1987), 344.

76. Jonathan M. Moses, "BCCI Creditors to Challenge Settlement," *Wall Street Journal,* December 31, 1991, B4; William C. Lhotka and Tim Bryant, "Missouri Judge Voted Out for 1st Time in 50 Years," *St. Louis Post-Dispatch,* November 5, 1992, 6C. Results for 1994 were taken from Missouri Secretary of State, *Official Manual, State of Missouri, 1993–1994* (Jefferson City: Missouri Secretary of State, 1995).

77. Calculated from data in Missouri Secretary of State, *Official Manual 1993–1994,* 144. See William K. Hall and Larry T. Aspin, "Distance from the Bench and Retention Voting Behavior: A Comparison of Trial Court and Appellate Court Retention Elections," *Justice System Journal* 15 (1992), 801–813.

78. Hall and Aspin, "What Twenty Years Have Told Us."

79. This discussion of California is based in part on John H. Culver and John T. Wold, "Rose Bird and the Politics of Judicial Accountability in California," *Judicature* 70 (August–September 1986), 81–89; and John T. Wold and John H. Culver, "The Defeat of the California Justices: The Campaign, the Electorate, and the Issue of Judicial Accountability," *Judicature* 70 (April–May 1987), 348–355.

80. "State's Chief Justice Keeps His Seat," *Miami Herald,* November 7, 1990, 17A; Karen Branch, "Politics and Florida's Highest Court," *Miami Herald,* November 1, 1992, 6M; Andrew Blum, "Jurists, Initiatives on Ballot," *National Law Journal,* November 16, 1992, 31.

81. Tom Humphrey, "White Becomes 1st Appellate Level Judge to be Defeated in 'Yes-no' Vote," *Knoxville News-Sentinel,* August 2, 1996, A1, Paula Wade, "White First Casualty of Yes-No Option on Judges," *Memphis Commercial Appeal,* August 2, 1996, 1A.

82. Joseph R. Grodin, *In Pursuit of Justice: Reflections of a State Supreme Court Justice* (Berkeley: University of California Press, 1989), 3.

83. David Margolick, "Picking of Judges Assailed by Cuomo," *New York Times,* August 15, 1983, A1, B8.

84. Bradley C. Canon, "The Impact of Formal Selection Processes on the Characteristics of Judges—Reconsidered," *Law and Society Review* 6 (May 1972), 579–593; Susan P. Fino, "Similarities and Differences in the Backgrounds of State Supreme Court Justices" (paper presented at the 1983 meeting of the Midwest Political Science Association, Chicago, Illinois); Henry R. Glick and Craig F. Emmert, "Selection Systems and Judicial Characteristics: The Recruitment of State Supreme Court Judges," *Judicature* 70 (December–January 1987), 228–235.

85. Glick and Emmert, "Selection Systems and Judicial Characteristics," 235.

86. Richard A. Watson and Rondal G. Downing, *The Politics of the Bench and the Bar: Judicial Selection Under the Missouri Nonpartisan Court Plan* (New York: John Wiley, 1969), 205–219, 257–263, 282–286.

87. *Harris v. Alabama,* 130 L. Ed 2d, 1004, 1019 (1995) (Stevens, dissenting). See also Steven

P. Croley, "The Majoritarian Difficulty: Elective Judiciaries and the Rule of Law," *University of Chicago Law Review* 62 (1995), 726–742.

88. See Paul Reidinger, "The Politics of Judging," *American Bar Association Journal* 73 (April 1, 1987), 58.

89. Larry T. Aspin and William K. Hall, "Retention Elections and Judicial Behavior," *Judicature* 77 (May–June 1994), 306–315.

90. See Randall D. Lloyd, "Separating Partisanship from Party in Judicial Research: Reapportionment in the U.S. District Courts," *American Political Science Review* 89 (June 1995), 413–420.

5

Judges

The debates over systems for selection of judges and the battles over confirmation of Supreme Court nominees reflect the same central reality: judges are important individuals. Like other public officials, judges are subject to significant constraints, and one concern of this chapter is the tightening of some constraints. But they have a great deal of freedom to put their own stamp on their work. How they do their jobs and what decisions they reach largely reflect their own choices made from their own perspectives.

Thus, it makes a good deal of difference what kinds of people become judges, and the first section of this chapter focuses on judges' characteristics. The second section discusses several aspects of judges' behavior on the bench. The final section examines the quality of judges' performance.

JUDGES' BACKGROUNDS

There are few formal restrictions on who can become a judge. The U.S. Constitution establishes no requirements for federal judges. The great majority of states do have restrictions: among the requirements that exist in some states are U.S. citizenship, a period of residency in the state or district, and minimum or maximum ages.[1] The great majority of states require that judges be licensed as lawyers, and in 1994 a federal court of appeals ruled that this requirement did not violate the constitutional rights of two nonlawyer Nevadans who wanted to run for judgeships.[2] Many states also specify a length of time that a person must be a lawyer or, in some states, actually have practiced law to be eligible for a judgeship; the longest time required is ten years.

Some states that require most judges to be attorneys exempt their lowest courts from this requirement. One justice of the peace in New York State pointed out that although he was not a lawyer, members of the U.S. Supreme Court did not have to be lawyers either.[3] In practice, of course, only attorneys are considered for positions in the federal courts.

Aside from their profession, judges have another characteristic in common: at some point, each of them came to the favorable attention of the people who choose judges. In many states, the voters play an important part in that choice. But in the country as a whole, the people who have the greatest effect on the selection of judges are public officials who appoint judges directly and political leaders who influence candidacies and outcomes in judicial elections.

This shared characteristic provides a perspective from which to view judges' backgrounds. I examine three aspects of these backgrounds: judges' political activity, their career experiences, and their social circumstances. The discussion of judges' backgrounds gives special attention to federal judges, because we know the most about their characteristics. Exhibit 5.1 summarizes some important characteristics of the judges chosen by George Bush and Bill Clinton.

Political Activity

Most judges were active in politics prior to their selection. As Exhibit 5.1 shows, about 60 percent of the federal judges appointed between 1989 and 1996 had records of activism in a political party. Undoubtedly many others were involved in party politics in some way.[4]

This pattern is quite understandable. In a judicial election, a candidate who has already been involved in politics has an easier time building an organization and often has the advantage of name recognition among voters. Even more important is the value of political activity in winning the support of the public officials and political leaders who play key parts in every selection system.

These people tend to favor political activists for two reasons. First, a major goal in the selection of judges is to reward political supporters. Accordingly, those who have been allied with the selectors have the best chance to be chosen. Second, since most of the people who help to select judges are political activists themselves, most of their acquaintances are also activists. Even if the selectors cared only about the qualifications of potential judges, they would have the greatest confidence in people they already knew.

For the same reasons, a considerable proportion of all judges have personal ties with the officials who help to select them, especially state judges with governors. In a statement that is widely quoted, a judge and novelist put the matter succinctly: "a judge is a member of the Bar who once knew a Governor."[5] People who want to become judges often participate in politics solely as a means to develop these personal ties and the other advantages of political activism. As one federal judge said, "I saw politics only as a way of becoming a judge."[6]

The kinds of political activity that lead to judgeships differ somewhat depending on the level of the court. Members of the U.S. Supreme Court who participated in politics before their selection often played prominent roles in presidential campaigns. This was true of former Justice Byron White, who led a national volunteer organization for John F. Kennedy in 1960.

At the other end of the spectrum, many state trial judges were party activists at what is sometimes called the clubhouse level of politics. Attorneys may work for years in unglamorous local party jobs and contribute money to party coffers in order to obtain a judicial appointment or a party nomination to a lower court. This traditionally has been true in Chicago, to take one prominent example. And in Chicago, as in other places, links to powerful political figures have often led to the bench. When Mayor Richard J. Daley (father of the current mayor, Richard M. Daley) controlled

Characteristic	District Courts(%)	Courts of Appeals(%)
Political activity		
Past political activism	57.1	60.6
Member of the president's party	89.6	87.9
Career experience		
Experience as a judge	48.3	65.2
Judge at the time of appointment	43.2	59.1
Experience as a prosecutor	38.5	33.3
In private practice at the time of appointment	43.2	27.3
Firm of 100 or more lawyers[a]	21.9	38.9
Firm of 25–99 lawyers[a]	27.0	22.2
Firm of 5–24 lawyers[a]	36.5	38.9
Firm of 1–4 lawyers[a]	14.6	0.0
Economic status at time of appointment (net worth)		
$1 million or more	32.2	40.9
$500,000 to $1 million	27.4	31.8
$200,000 to $500,000	26.5	21.2
Under $200,000	13.9	6.1
Social background		
White	80.1	81.8
Male	74.8	75.8
Private undergraduate school	55.5	60.6
Ivy League undergraduate school[b]	14.5	15.2

[a]The percentages are of those engaged in private practice.
[b]Also included in the private undergraduate school category.
Source: Sheldon Goldman and Elliot Slotnick, "Clinton's First Term Judiciary: Many Bridges to Cross," *Judicature*, 80 (May–June 1997), 261, 269.

EXHIBIT 5.1   Selected Background Characteristics of Federal Court Appointees, 1989–1996

the Democratic organization, he secured a party endorsement for a lawyer named Joseph Gordon. According to one account,

> Gordon, a bright and highly regarded former law professor, would have been an outstanding member of any judiciary, but that had little to do with why Daley selected him. When Daley's youngest son, William, was having trouble with his grades at John Marshall Law School, Gordon tutored him privately. For this, Daley was grateful. He expressed his gratitude by making Gordon a judge.[7]

Of course, political activity in itself hardly guarantees a person's selection as a judge: there are far more lawyers active in politics than there are judgeships. To a considerable extent, the translation of activism into a judgeship is a matter of good fortune—of alliance with someone who ends up in a position to help select judges. After all, most rising state politicians do not become governors, just as most law school roommates do not become senators. But if political activity is not sufficient for selection, it is often necessary. "Take a popular lawyer who has not been active in party activities," said a former Democratic chair in Buffalo; that lawyer's "chance of being a nominee for a high court position is very slight."[8]

Career Experience

Except at the very lowest levels of the judiciary, nearly all of today's judges were educated in law school. But a wide variety of career paths can lead from law school to a judgeship. Exhibit 5.2 illustrates this diversity by describing the routes that some state supreme court justices took. As there are many ways of making useful contacts and establishing a reputation for competence, the diversity of career paths is understandable. But certain kinds of career experiences are especially common because they provide major advantages.

Private Practice   Like other attorneys, the great majority of judges engaged at some point in the private practice of law. Indeed, in most courts a high proportion of the judges came directly from private practice. As Exhibit 5.1 shows, more than 40 percent of federal district judges in recent years took that path. The proportion for state trial judges is probably about as high.[9] Another large group of judges moved from private practice into public office or lower-court judgeships before attaining their current positions.

Higher-court judges come primarily from practices that brought high incomes and substantial prestige. One imperfect way to measure success is in terms of firm size. Between 1989 and 1996, more than ten times as many lawyers who were appointed to the federal courts came from firms of twenty-five or more lawyers as came from solo practice. This ratio is striking because even today about half of all the attorneys in private practice are in solo practice.

For federal judges, we have more direct information on financial success. Among the appointees from 1989 through 1996, 62 percent had a net worth of at least $500,000, and 34 percent were millionaires. This level of wealth reflects both the financial rewards of high-status law practice and inherited wealth.

Lower-court judges are less likely to come from elite segments of the bar. State trial courts contain a broader cross section of private practitioners than do the federal courts of appeals. In a national study of major trial courts two decades ago, about 60 percent of the judges who came directly from private practice reported no specialization, a characteristic associated with solo practice and small firms.[10] One reason for this difference is that highly successful lawyers are much less likely to seek positions in lower courts, which carry only limited power and prestige. Another reason is that participants in judicial selection tend to demand higher levels of achievement, as measured by success as a lawyer, for higher courts.

Government Legal Practice   A great many attorneys practice law for the government at some point in their careers, and this is true of lawyers who become judges. Some spent the first few years after law school working for the govern-

Priscilla R. Owen, Texas
Law degree, Baylor University, 1977
Private practice,1977–94
Joined supreme court in 1995

Donald L. Corbin, Arkansas
Law degree, University of Arkansas, 1966
Private practice, 1967–80
State legislator, 1971–80
State court of appeals judge, 1981–90
Joined supreme court in 1991

David Harris, Iowa
Law degree, University of Iowa, 1951
Private practice, 1951–1962
County attorney, 1959–62
State trial judge, 1962–72
Joined supreme court in 1972

Alex J. Martinez, Colorado
Law degree, University of Colorado, 1976
Deputy state public defender, 1976–83
State trial judge, 1983–97
Joined supreme court in 1997

Yvonne Kauger, Oklahoma
Medical technologist, 1959-68
Law degree, Oklahoma City University, 1969
Private practice, 1970–72
Judicial assiatant, state supreme court, 1972–84
Joined supreme court in 1984

Harry Lee Anstead, Florida
Law degree, University of Florida, 1963
Private practice, 1964–76
State court of appeal judge, 1976–94
Joined supreme court in 1994

Note: A few pre–supreme court positions are omitted. Some individuals serve in government positions part-time while maintaining a private practice.
Sources: *Who's Who in American Law*, 9th ed. (New Providence, N.J.: Marquis Who's Who, 1996); *Judicial Yellow Book,* vol. 2, no. 2 (New York: Leadership Directories, Inc., 1997).

Exhibit 5.2   Career Paths of Some State Supreme Court Justices Serving in 1997

ment and then moved into private practice. Others came to the bench directly from government service.

A lawyer who works for the government has an advantage in coming to the attention of people who choose judges. Thus lawyers who work for the Justice Department are in a good position to be recognized and rewarded with a judgeship. At the state level, a prominent government lawyer such as an attorney general has the sort of visibility that helps in winning an election or an appointment to the courts. Government lawyers also have a good chance to develop the trial experience that is often deemed essential for a judge.

Criminal prosecution is the most common form of prior government service for judges. From 1989 through 1996, about 40 percent of the federal district court appointees had been prosecutors; that experience is also common, though less so, among state supreme court justices.[11] The figures reflect both the large numbers of lawyers who serve as prosecutors and the credibility of prosecutors as candidates for judgeships. This credibility stems partly from a prosecutor's advantage in projecting a "law and order" image that most voters favor, and the growing importance of criminal justice as an issue in judicial elections probably has enhanced prosecutors' advantage.

High Government Positions   For most judges who were politically active before reaching the bench, politics was an avocation (though often a very time-consuming one) rather than a career. But some people become judges after holding high positions in government outside the legal realm. These positions can be a brief way station or a person's primary career.

At the state level, one path to the judiciary is from the legislature. Because state legislators are in a good position to extract appointments from governors and to win judicial elections, the state courts include a liberal sprinkling of former legislators. In 1997, more than 10 percent of the state supreme court justices in the country had been legislators.[12] Federal judgeships below the Supreme Court are less attractive to members of Congress, except for those who tire of legislative life or suffer electoral defeat.

It is less common for a chief executive to become a judge. The only president to do so was William Howard Taft, who was defeated for re-election in 1912 and became chief justice of the U.S. Supreme Court in 1921, after a strenuous campaign for the position. Over the years, a number of former governors have become state supreme court justices. In Ohio, C. William O'Neill achieved the most unusual feat of heading all three branches of state government, serving as Speaker of the Ohio House of Representatives and then as governor before he became chief justice of the Ohio Supreme Court in 1970.

The Judicial Career Ladder   Judges in many countries serve within a kind of civil service system, attaining their first judgeships early in their legal careers and progressing upward through the ranks. The system in the United States is fundamentally different. Here most judges reach the bench at middle age or later, and service on one court is not required to obtain a seat on the court above it.

Still, in both the federal and the state court systems, it is common for judges to ascend upward.[13] One reason is the widespread feeling that service on a lower court helps to qualify a person for a higher judgeship. Besides, a prospective appointee's abilities and policy preferences can be gauged more easily from a judicial record than from most other career experiences. Where judges are elected, prior service on a lower court can give a candidate name recognition.

The federal court system shows an increasingly strong pattern of promotion. In recent years, nearly half of the district judges came directly from other judicial positions, primarily in the state courts. More than half of the new court of appeals judges rose from lower courts, primarily the district courts. At the top level, the last ten people appointed to the Supreme Court were serving as judges at the time, all but one (Sandra Day O'Connor) as members of a federal court of appeals. One federal judge suggested that "we may be evolving toward the European system of a career judiciary," though he noted that we still do not have people moving directly from legal training to judgeships.[14]

Social Background

Whatever people accomplish in their own lives, they begin with certain characteristics they cannot control. One is their parents' social and economic status. Others are race and gender. In each of these respects, judges, like other public officials, are far from a random sample of the population.

Social and Economic Status   Most judges come from families of higher-than-average status. This pattern reflects the advantages that relative wealth and high social status confer. A high family income helps a person to become a lawyer, most directly by making it easier to pay the costs of a college education and law school. Inherited social status affords some people an advantage in entering the most prestigious schools and law firms and in advancing their careers in politics and government.

High family status is most common among judges on the highest courts. The Supreme Court in particular has been populated mostly by people from high-status backgrounds, and to a lesser extent the same is true of lower federal courts. One indicator of family status patterns among federal judges is the schools they attended. From 1989 through 1996, about 56 percent of the federal court appointees had attended private undergraduate colleges. About 15 percent of these judges had gone to Ivy League schools for their undergraduate education and 19 percent for their legal education. As noted earlier, the high level of wealth held by many federal judges results in part from the substantial family wealth that some inherited.

Lower-court judges appear to be a more heterogeneous group, and in some localities there is a good deal of upward mobility into the state trial courts. It is not unusual for people from relatively poor families to make their way through law school (perhaps attending classes at night while working during the day) and then make themselves candidates for judgeships through legal work and political activity. A study in the 1970s of trial judges in the Baltimore and San Francisco areas found that roughly a third of them were the children of industrial wage earners and low-salaried workers.[15] And fewer judges at the lower court levels come from highly advantaged backgrounds.

In recent years, more people from relatively humble backgrounds have become judges. This change has occurred because college and law school educations are more widely available and because an elite social background has become less of a prerequisite for advancement in politics and law. But individuals from high-status families continue to hold advantages that are reflected in their representation on the bench.

Race and Gender   Until recently, the judiciary consisted almost entirely of white men. As late as 1977, about 96 percent of the judges on major state trial courts were white, and about 98 percent were male; more than 99 percent of the state supreme court justices in 1980–1981 were white and 97 percent male.[16] The Supreme Court was entirely white until 1967, entirely male until 1981.

These patterns resulted from several social realities. Poverty and discrimination limited the numbers of nonwhite citizens who could obtain college and legal educations. Largely because of admissions policies, women had a difficult time getting to law school. Women and members of racial minority groups who did manage to become lawyers found that many career and political opportunities were closed to them. After finishing near the top of her class at Stanford Law School in 1952, future Supreme Court Justice Sandra Day O'Connor discovered that no California law firm would offer her anything more than a secretarial position. Her experience was far from unique.

Women and members of racial minority groups have gained many more judgeships in recent years. In 1995, 15 percent of all federal judges and 18 percent of the state supreme court justices were women. Nonwhites occupied 14 percent of the seats on federal courts and 8 percent of the seats on state courts.[17] These increases reflect the changing composition of the legal profession, reduced discrimination in the profession, the greater political power of groups representing racial minorities and women, and changing attitudes of people who select judges. Some chief executives have used appointments to increase the diversity of the judiciary. At the federal level, Presidents Jimmy Carter and Bill Clinton stand out in this respect.[18] State governors have played similar roles. Appointments by Governor Rudy Perpich gave the Minnesota Supreme Court a female majority in 1991; this majority, the first ever for an appellate court, symbolized the changes that have occurred in the demography of the courts.[19]

White men continue to hold judgeships well beyond their proportion in the general population, and their numerical dominance probably will decline only at a slow and uneven pace. But the numbers of female and minority-group judges are certain to increase further, largely as a reflection of growing representation of these groups in the legal profession.

Changes in judicial elections might also increase the numbers of nonwhite judges. In 1991, the Supreme Court ruled that the Voting Rights Act applies to judicial elections.[20] That decision led to lawsuits challenging "at-large" election systems in which trial judges are chosen from a whole county rather than from smaller districts; at-large systems may tend to reduce the number of judges elected from minority groups.[21] Because of mixed results in these cases and the Supreme Court's evolving doctrine on race and election districts, the ultimate impact of the Voting Rights Act on the composition of the judiciary is uncertain.

The Impact of Judges' Background Characteristics

In their backgrounds, judges are not a random sample of the legal profession. They are even less representative of the general population. This reality has some symbolic importance, affecting the ways that people in different segments of society think and feel about the courts. It may also have practical importance. People with different backgrounds may develop different sets of attitudes toward political and social issues; in turn, judges' attitudes influence the decisions that they reach on the bench.[22]

A variety of background characteristics might affect judges' behavior. The legal training shared by nearly all judges undoubtedly influences their thinking about the issues that come before them. The past involvement of most judges in partisan politics may incline them to view some cases in terms of their effects on political parties and factions.

Especially interesting is the possible impact of social backgrounds, the characteristics that are beyond people's control. As we have seen, judges are distinctly higher in family status than the general population; whites and men also predominate in comparison with their numbers in the population. What difference do these characteristics make for the behavior of the judiciary?

What to expect is uncertain. Surveys of the general population show that opinions on policy issues differ between people of higher and lower economic status and between women and men; the differences between blacks and whites are even greater.[23] In some respects, these differences can be characterized as ideological, with greater conservatism among whites, men, and people of higher status. There is also reason to expect that judges will have greater empathy for people who share their own characteristics.

On the other hand, those people who achieve judgeships are likely to share certain experiences and perspectives no matter what their origins were. The person from a humble economic background who becomes a successful attorney and then a judge may develop values similar to judges who grew up in more advantaged circumstances. And those who select judges, whether voters or political leaders, may look for people with particular outlooks no matter what their origins were.

Studies of judges' race and gender have differed in their findings about the impact of these characteristics on decisions.[24] Across the sweep of issues that judges address, there do not appear to be dramatic differences in the behavior of men and women or of people from different racial groups. At the federal level, the absence of dramatic differences reflects the choices of presidents. Bill Clinton's preference for moderate liberals applies to the people he appoints from *all* groups. Thus Ruth Bader Ginsburg and Stephen Breyer have similar records on the Supreme Court because Clinton was looking for similar ideological positions when he chose them.

But there is some evidence that race and gender affect specific aspects of judges' work on the bench.[25] One example is sentencing. A study of Philadelphia determined that white judges treated white defendants somewhat more leniently than black defendants in deciding whether to impose a prison sentence, while no such difference existed for black judges. In contrast, male judges in Philadelphia seemed relatively lenient toward female defendants, perhaps because of "paternalism," while female judges treated women and men more evenhandedly.[26]

The differential experiences of men and women and of different racial groups can affect their perspectives in ways that are too subtle to measure across whole categories of cases. In a dispute over child custody, a female judge may see the consequences of spousal and child abuse as crucial, while her male colleagues may regard evidence of abuse as irrelevant.[27] Black judges who continue to face discrimination in their daily lives despite their exalted positions may view allegations of racial bias differently from judges who have never experienced that bias.[28]

There is little systematic evidence about the impact of social class. But it seems likely that the higher-status backgrounds of most judges subtly influence their work by affecting the perspectives that they bring to cases. One example, considered in Chapter 6, is the traditionally lenient sentencing of white-collar criminals. As judges themselves have noted, they tend to identify with defendants whose backgrounds and social circumstances are similar to their own. As I discuss in Chapter 7, business creditors who sue individual debtors are quite successful. This success results in part from judges' tendency to regard the creditor as the more respectable and responsible party. In turn, this perception is related to the family backgrounds and careers of most judges, which make it easier for them to identify with the owner of a business than with a low-income debtor.

The impact of race, gender, and class on the courts should not be overstated. There are probably more similarities among judges with divergent backgrounds than there are differences. But differences do exist. For that reason, the predominance of white men from higher-status backgrounds on the courts has had practical as well as symbolic importance.

Overview   In Chapter 4, I argued that differences among judicial selection systems in the United States are less significant than their similarities. In this section, I have made a similar point about judicial backgrounds: although judges differ a good deal, most share some important characteristics.

The two points are related. The traits shared by most judges result in part from the systems by which they are selected. If the United States followed the example of most other nations and chose judges through a civil service system, judges' partisan ties would be much weaker. Under such a system, judges would still be disproportionately male, white, and upper status in background but almost surely less so than they actually are.

To a degree, then, the systems used to select judges link the courts with the patterns of economic and political power in the United States. These systems favor those whose backgrounds and personal attainments give them relatively high status; they also favor people who are connected with the holders of political power. This is one important way in which the courts are shaped by the larger society in which they operate.

JUDGES ON THE BENCH

More than thirty thousand people serve as judges in the United States.[29] Their work as judges differs a good deal. The most striking difference is between trial and appellate judges, whose jobs are somewhat distinct. State and federal judges operate within different systems and hear different kinds of cases. Some judges are generalists who hear a wide range of cases, while others focus on single fields such as taxes and domestic relations. Although a majority of judges serve full-time, a large minority— primarily at the lowest levels of the state systems—are part-time. Of course, individual courts and judges develop their own ways of operating.

All this variation makes it difficult to generalize about the work of judges on the bench. But it is possible to sketch some patterns in the job of judge as well as some types of variation.

What Judges Do

Judges' work includes a wide array of activities, which can be separated into several categories.[30]

Adjudication   The term *adjudication* refers to formal decision making. This activity comes most readily to mind when we think about judges, and it is at the heart of what judges do. It also consumes the largest share of most judges' work time.

Adjudication varies in form along several lines. Perhaps most important, it looks somewhat different in trial and appellate courts. Trial court decisions are nearly always made by single judges. In contrast, appellate decisions are group products; even if judges do most of their work on decisions apart from their colleagues, they ultimately reach a collective decision. The timing of decisions also differs between the two levels. Trial judges frequently make and announce their decisions in open court, but appellate decisions are generally made outside the courtroom and announced later.

The most familiar decisions are those that directly resolve the merits of cases—whether a defendant is guilty or innocent, whether a lower-court decision is affirmed or reversed. But judges also make preliminary decisions on matters such as the admission of evidence and dismissal of criminal charges. Often these preliminary decisions resolve cases directly or indirectly.

In trial courts, different kinds of cases have their own typical forms of adjudication.[31] Trials in major criminal and civil cases are usually lengthy and formal, while cases with lower stakes may be processed in speedy and routine fashion. Appellate courts also distinguish between cases that require close judicial consideration and those that can be resolved in more summary fashion. These differences and other aspects of adjudication are examined more fully in later chapters.

Negotiation   In *negotiation,* judges seek to resolve cases without formal adjudication by encouraging the parties to reach settlements. The great majority of cases are terminated prior to trial through settlements, and a smaller proportion of appeals are settled between the parties. Settlements often occur without the judge's participation, but judges may play active roles in bringing them about.

Trial judges are more likely to involve themselves actively in negotiation of civil settlements. Opinion is divided on the legitimacy of judges' participation in plea bargaining, but there is a general consensus that their involvement in civil negotiations is appropriate. Appellate judges traditionally have not taken part in efforts to settle cases, but in recent years some courts have initiated settlement efforts.

As this discussion suggests, judges have some freedom to determine how much they will involve themselves in negotiation. But their freedom is not total. Court rules and customs may influence judges' roles in negotiation, and increasingly heavy caseloads in many trial courts make it almost mandatory for judges to encourage settlements in order to reduce backlogs. This is one important way that the judge's job has changed.

Administration   The administration of federal and state courts was discussed in Chapter 2, but it is worth emphasizing this part of judges' responsibilities. As the size of courts and the number of cases they handle have grown, so has the volume of administrative work needed for a court to function adequately. Support staff have increased in number, taking much of the burden of this work from judges, but supervision of the staff is itself a significant task.

Among the judges on a court, the chief judge has the primary responsibility for administration. Court management may consume the largest share of the chief judge's time. But no judge can escape administrative work altogether; this is particularly true of trial courts, where judges usually do most managerial work for their own courtrooms. Increasingly, some judges also are called on to help administer court systems as a whole.

External Relations   Most judges devote at least some of their work time to the larger political systems and communities of which they are part. These activities are of several types.

Some external relations are with the other branches of government. Judges depend on the legislature for budgetary resources, and they may work with legislators to gain support for their requests. They may also lobby governors and legislators on issues that affect them. Working through the Federal Judicial Conference, for instance, federal judges in recent years have supported proposals for additional judgeships and opposed proposals that would have brought new kinds of cases to federal courts.

Most judges also engage in what might be called general community relations. They often give talks to civic groups and interviews to the mass media. Some judges work with lawyers' groups and other organizations on matters of mutual interest. For elected judges, an important motivation for this activity is the desire to maintain and enhance electoral support. Community activities are one way to build the positive name recognition that helps incumbents gain re-election.

The Difficulties and Rewards of Being a Judge

The position of judge is like other jobs in that it has both positive and negative features. But the attractions and drawbacks of serving as a judge are both stronger than those of most other careers.

Many Skills Required, Little Preparation   My catalogue of judges' activities suggests that a good judge must possess a diverse range of skills. Effective judicial performance requires, among other things, a good knowledge of legal rules, the capacity to run trials, a talent for negotiation, and skill in managing court operations. This is a daunting set of requirements. To meet all of these requirements well, a judge needs an impressive set of personal traits. Inevitably, most judges fall short in some respects.

Judges' difficulties in performing their job well are aggravated by their lack of training. In nations with a career judiciary, aspiring judges study how to carry out the work of judges. In the United States, no such preparation exists. As a result, most judges begin their work with limited knowledge about what to do on the bench. As one judge put it, "We are overnight transformed from seasoned professional to rank amateur."[32] Another judge reported that "it took me a good seven years to find my sea legs in this turbulent environment."[33]

Appellate judges are not immune to these difficulties, even if they have experience at the trial level. Indeed, some Supreme Court justices—including people who had sat on other appellate courts—have noted the difficulty they faced in mastering their jobs as justices.[34] But appellate judges do their work largely in private, with an opportunity to consider decisions at length before making them. In contrast, trial judges sit in court proceedings more or less alone, having to preside and make rulings—often instantaneously. Trial judges who are unfamiliar with procedures or substantive legal rules are almost certain to make embarrassing mistakes early in their time on the bench.

Of course, a judge's prior experience helps to determine the difficulty of the learning process. An experienced trial lawyer is usually better prepared to become a trial judge than is an office lawyer who has seldom practiced in court. But even the most experienced lawyer finds that the judge's job is quite different.

Inevitably, novices on the bench turn for help to those who have more experience—other judges, members of the court staff, and lawyers who appear before them. Through this process, the perspectives and approaches of people who are already in the courts are passed on to new judges. A judge who starts off with a distaste for plea bargaining usually comes to accept it, partly because the colleagues and lawyers with whom that judge interacts generally accept and encourage it.[35]

In the past, new judges were given very little formal assistance. One appellate judge recalled that "when I joined the court, I was left to stumble, bumble, and do injustice to other people. I was given no manual, no orientation. . . . I was abandoned."[36] Increasingly, judges receive formal training and written materials to aid them. Still, the task of learning the judge's job remains difficult and largely unsystematic.

Stresses of the Job   Judges are likely to become frustrated by the gap between their abilities and training and the requirements of their position. Other characteristics of the judge's job add to its stresses.

Most fundamentally, judges have to make a large number of decisions with potentially serious consequences under less than ideal conditions. In a full trial, a judge often must hand down a series of procedural rulings with little time to consider them and with the prospect that an appellate court will find a ruling in error, perhaps overturning the trial verdict as a result. Both trial and appellate judges frequently must choose between two competing sides when it is not clear where the facts and the law point and when the decision may have enormous effects on people's lives.

It has always been true that some judges face caseloads that are heavier than they can manage easily, and this situation has become increasingly common as the volume of cases grows faster than the number of judgeships. Both trial and appellate judges find themselves scrambling to dispose of cases in order to prevent unacceptable backlogs. A survey of federal trial judges documented the impact of these pressures on them. One judge, expressing a widespread feeling, reported that "I am very much behind, cannot catch up, and I am frustrated and stressed because I cannot catch up."[37] One commentator has said that American judges "are coming to resemble harried bureaucrats."[38]

Just as caseloads have grown, so has scrutiny of judges' work from outside the court system. Increasingly, the mass media and interest groups observe judges at work and issue criticisms when they disagree with decisions. Judges receive the greatest scrutiny in criminal justice, where observers often castigate judges whom they see as unduly lenient.

Electoral campaigns against judges based on their decisions have become common, and some are successful. In the past few years, judges have been threatened with impeachment for the same reason. The judge who awarded custody of O.J. Simpson's two youngest children to Simpson in 1996 became the subject of a campaign to recall her from office.[39] The effects of all this scrutiny are suggested by the efforts that judges sometimes take to justify decisions that have received scrutiny—as in an Ohio judge's twenty-four-page opinion to explain an unpopular sentencing decision and a New York judge's agreeing to interviews in order to explain his acquittal in a police brutality case after the decision had aroused protests.[40]

Judges also have reason for more immediate fears. A federal district judge in Texas was killed in 1979, and a New York district judge in 1988; both murders resulted from their work as judges. Bombs have been sent to judges in several states, and in 1997 a man threw a firebomb at an Illinois judge in his courtroom.[41] In the same year, a California man was charged with hiring two people to bomb a county court building, allegedly as part of an effort to prevent himself from being tried in a pending case.[42] People with political grievances have threatened violence against judges.[43]

Inevitably, these pressures affect judges. In one extreme case, a judge's widow was granted survivor's benefits under the Connecticut workers' compensation law on the ground that the pressures of the judge's job had brought about his fatal heart attack.[44]

Freedom, Status, and Power   These negative elements of the judge's job might suggest that it is difficult to find people to fill judgeships. In general, this is far from the case. Governors and presidents who appoint judges usually find many eager aspirants for each position. Although some judges leave the bench because of their dissatisfaction, many remain for long periods. Despite signs of growing stresses on federal judges, during the 1980s only thirty judges left the federal courts for reasons other than health or age; the proportion of federal judges who resigned in that decade was one of the lowest in history.[45] In the state courts, many judges work very hard to win re-election. All this is especially striking because many—perhaps most—judges could earn more money in other positions. Clearly, the position of judge has powerful attractions.

One attraction is the degree of freedom that judges have in their jobs. Certainly they face constraints—not just from audiences outside the courts but also from the lawyers and judges with whom they work. Heavy caseloads create constraints of their own. On the whole, however, it is judges' freedom that stands out.

That freedom is reflected in work styles. Judges typically set their own work schedules, and they have considerable leeway in allocating their time among the various parts of their job. Judges' freedom also is reflected in differences in the positions they take on the same legal issues and even, in appellate courts, in the same cases. To a considerable degree, judges can apply the law as they see fit. Lawyers try to get their cases before one judge rather than another, and interest groups battle over the selection of judges, because they are well aware that different people on the bench would make different choices.

Another attraction is the status of the job. In the courtroom, judges are generally accorded great deference by court personnel, lawyers, and other participants. "No matter what their personality," one commentator noted, "when approaching the bench," lawyers "tend to sound like Eddie Haskell of 'Leave It to Beaver' talking to June Cleaver. They compliment the judge's appearance, lavish him with honorifics, pore over his decisions, praise his erudition, double over with laughter at even his lamest jokes."[46]

Outside of court, many people give automatic respect to a person who holds the title of judge. Successful lawyers may enjoy respect and status within their own profession, but in society as a whole, judges fare much better.

Along with a judge's status comes a considerable measure of power. Judges routinely make decisions that affect people's lives in important ways. Some decisions have broader impact on people throughout a state or the nation. Nowhere is that power more evident than in the federal district courts, where individual judges often make a mark through their handling of important issues. Exhibit 5.3 illustrates that point with some noteworthy examples in recent years.

If the responsibility for important decisions sometimes creates stress, it also allows judges to make a difference, to do what they see as good. And because judgeships *are* powerful positions, they attract lawyers who enjoy the exercise of power for its own sake. One study found that the "most pronounced" personality trait among judges was a need for dominance.[47] Judges may speak of the burdens of the powers they hold, such as criminal sentencing, but they frequently employ these powers with enthusiasm.

THE QUALITY OF JUDICIAL PERFORMANCE

Because judges have so much impact on individual lives and society as a whole, the quality of judges' performance is a matter of great importance. But it is very difficult to assess the performance of American judges as a group. For one thing, observers cannot agree on the criteria for assessment and how to apply those criteria. Polls of lawyers often produce substantial disagreement about the performance of a particular judge. For another, there are so many judges serving across the country that even active trial lawyers can have only a partial sense of the overall level of performance.

We should begin with reasonable expectations. With luck, the process of selecting judges favors people who would perform their jobs at a relatively high level. But the selection process is highly imperfect, and those who become judges are likely to vary considerably in their strengths and weaknesses. And judges cannot be expected to differ fundamentally from other people in their traits. Abraham Lincoln often quoted from a letter by Thomas Jefferson on this point: "Our judges are as honest as other men, and not more so. They have, with others, the same passions for party, for power, and the privilege of their corps."[48]

Reports about judges' activities regularly remind us that they are subject to the same foibles as other people. A baseball-loving California judge cut star player Barry Bonds's family support obligations in half and then asked for his autograph.[49] A Texas judge who put happy faces on all the court documents he signed failed to consider that it might be a bad idea to do so on an order informing a prisoner of his execution date.[50]

Harold H. Greene, District of Columbia

In 1978, Greene was assigned to handle the antitrust suit by the federal government against the American Telephone and Telegraph Company. He presided over the case for nearly two decades. Greene approved the 1982 agreements that split up AT&T, and he later ruled on a number of issues concerning the rights of the regional "Baby Bell" companies that resulted from the 1982 split-up. His rulings allowed the regional companies to engage in some new activities but prohibited others such as providing long-distance services and manufacturing telephone equipment. In 1994 he prohibited AT&T's proposed purchase of a cellular communications company on the ground that it would violate the original antitrust settlement. A 1996 statute ended Greene's role by establishing the structure of the telecommunications industry, but he had a great deal to do with the evolution of that structure.

William Wayne Justice, Eastern District of Texas

Justice has stood out for his decisions in a wide array of "institutional reform" litigation challenging the legality of practices by public institutions. His rulings on the Texas prison system in the 1980s required massive changes in the operation of the system and conditions for prisoners. He also has made major rulings on such matters as statewide school desegregation, rights of juveniles in reform schools, and bilingual education. Justice stands out so much from other Texas federal judges in his approach to institutional reform that litigants have gone to considerable efforts to get cases before him or away from him. Because of his rulings, some observers regarded Justice as the most powerful public official in Texas.

H. Lee Sarokin, District of New Jersey

In the 1980s and 1990s, Sarokin made a number of significant decisions on public policy issues. Among his rulings were ones in which he held that affirmative action considerations should override seniority in layoffs in some fire departments, that Kiwanis International could not disallow the use of its trademarks by a local chapter that accepted women as members, and that mass drug tests of police and firefighters constituted an illegal search. He handled a set of cigarette liability cases for ten years and presided over the first trial in which a tobacco company was found liable for health damage to a smoker. In 1992, the Third Circuit Court of Appeals removed Sarokin from another tobacco case on the ground that his criticism of the tobacco industry in an opinion detracted from the necessary "appearance of impartiality." Sarokin was elevated to a court of appeals in 1994 after a difficult confirmation battle that focused on his controversial rulings, but he retired two years later.

Sources: Newspaper reports; court decisions; *Almanac of the Federal Judiciary* (New York: Aspen Law & Business, 1996); Frank R. Kemerer, *William Wayne Justice: A Judicial Biography* (Austin: University of Texas Press, 1991).

EXHIBIT 5.3   Profiles of Some Federal District Judges

Keeping in mind both the need for realistic expectations and the difficulty of evaluating judges, it is still useful to consider what we know about their performance.

Several Areas of Performance

Judges can be assessed according to several criteria. Perhaps the most important are competence, commitment to the job, "judicial temperament," and impartiality.

Competence   Competence refers to a judge's general capability to handle the job effectively. Of all the qualities of judges, competence is perhaps the most difficult to define and measure. That difficulty is reflected in the widespread disagreement about the quality of work by Supreme Court justices, whose work is readily available for examination in written opinions.

Except at the lowest levels, all judges have received legal training. In that sense, they all have basic preparation for their jobs. But legal education does not guarantee competence as a judge any more than it guarantees competence as an attorney: law school classes and the bar examination do not cover all the skills required of a judge. For this reason, even very good judges often had to go through a period in which they performed poorly while they learned the task of judging.

Lawyers' observations offer evidence that there is wide variation in judges' competence. In local bar polls, most judges typically receive quite satisfactory ratings for their ability to do their jobs. Yet in a 1982 poll of American Bar Association members, a 51 percent majority agreed with the proposition that a significant proportion of judges are not qualified to preside over serious cases, and only 39 percent disagreed.[51]

What about nonlawyer judges, who remain fairly common at the lowest levels of the judiciary? In the view of many lawyers, lay judges are incompetent almost by definition. Undoubtedly, there is some basis for this view; some lay justices of the peace clearly lack the skills needed to do their jobs.

But the incompetence of nonlawyer judges has probably been exaggerated, in part because justices of the peace have become such familiar figures in American folklore. (It seems unlikely, for instance, that there really was a Texas justice of the peace who determined fines by leafing randomly through a Sears catalogue.[52]) Marie Provine, herself a former town justice in New York (perhaps the only person with both a law degree and a Ph.D. to serve in that position), concluded from an extensive study that lay judges differ little in their behavior from lawyers serving on the same courts. On the basis of her efforts to estimate judges' levels of competence, Provine argued that "lay persons are no less competent than lawyers as lower-court judges."[53]

Commitment   Along with its other effects, judges' relative freedom from direct supervision creates a temptation to give the job something less than a full commitment. Indeed, there is a widespread perception that many judges fail to work full-time.

In part, this perception rests on a misunderstanding: that a judge who is not in a courtroom is not working. Still, there is evidence that more than a few judges succumb to the temptation to keep short hours. In his annual report to the state bar in 1989, the North Carolina chief justice said that "I hear that in some districts, judges may be hard to find on Fridays"; the response was "knowing laughter from the lawyers."[54] In 1990, a reporter who had helped investigate the schedules of Massachusetts judges concluded that "the work force breaks down into two groups— judges who care enough to work a full day and those who don't." Focusing on the latter, he suggested that "the unspoken motto of the court system might well be: Get it done in the morning or put it off to another day." Later that year, the state's chief justice penalized five judges for failing to work full days.[55]

Yet offsetting the judges who make an incomplete commitment to the job are other judges—sometimes in the same courts—who work long hours to get their judicial work done. Those judges are exemplified by the federal district judge in Washington, D.C., who went into the hospital with a lethal cancer in 1993. He spent much of his time over the next few weeks in an effort to produce a decision in a complex case involving contracts for the building of local subway stations. The judge did issue the decision and a long opinion two days before his death.[56]

Judicial Temperament What lawyers call "judicial temperament" is one of those qualities that is difficult to define but easier to recognize. Judges have enormous power over the lawyers and litigants who come before them, and they receive a great deal of deference. Particularly in trial courts, they often face considerable stress. Judges with a judicial temperament maintain their composure and refrain from misusing their power by bullying the people who come before them or acting arbitrarily.

That is not necessarily easy. As one commentator explained, judges

> wear robes and sit up on a high bench. People stand up when you come in. Emotions are high. Attorneys can be obnoxious. It can really get on your nerves, and it takes a special kind of person to handle it.[57]

If this is true, many judges are indeed "special." They handle job pressures with calm and good humor, and they treat the people in their courtrooms with respect. It appears, however, that a substantial number of judges fail to meet this high standard. The worst cases, those that ultimately attract widespread attention, are indeed bad:

1. The Indiana Supreme Court publicly reprimanded a judge for jailing a lawyer who failed to appear at a hearing and then requiring the lawyer to make a court appearance for a client while wearing jail-issued clothing.[58]
2. A California judge received a similar reprimand from the state's Commission on Judicial Performance after playing sadistic jokes on two criminal defendants.[59]
3. The Illinois Courts Commission removed a judge whom it called "a mean-spirited judicial tyrant." Among other things, the judge told some defendants to "shut up" and improperly jailed people for contempt.[60]
4. The Florida Supreme Court removed a judge for a variety of abuses of power. The judge's offenses were typified by a case in which he added three months to a driver's license suspension after the defendant questioned the fairness of the sentence. The judge then asked the defendant whether he wanted the sentence reconsidered. After the defendant said, "yes sir," the judge added three more months to the suspension.[61]

In 1991, the chief judge of the Los Angeles Superior Court persuaded the court's executive committee to cancel most of the court's subscriptions to the *Metropolitan News-Enterprise*, a local legal newspaper. While the chief judge pointed to budgetary considerations, he had been subject to considerable criticism from the *News-Enterprise*; among other things, the newspaper had called him "a despotic twit."

Angry about the cancellations, which had a serious economic effect on his newspaper, the editor wrote a phony memo from the chief judge to his colleagues and put it on the chief judge's letterhead. Among other things, the memo announced that offices would be searched "to determine if copies of the Metropolitan News-Enterprise or any other contraband is present" and declared "a court emergency" under which the chief judge would remain in office beyond the end of his term. Court employee apprehended three *News-Enterprise* employees distributing the memo in the courthouse. They were taken to the chief judge's chambers and interrogated. Afterwards, the employees sued the chief judge for false arrest; in turn, he sued the *News-Enterprise* for libel.

The newspaper asked that the libel suit be thrown out on the ground that the memo was an obvious satire and thus could not be libelous. A state court of appeal did throw out the suit in 1994, agreeing that any reasonable person would recognize the memo as a fake. But one judge dissented. "Los Angeles' legal history," the dissenter wrote, "does not lack for examples of the occasional judge gone off the beam," and he described three judges who had behaved in bizarre ways. In a footnote, the dissenter added that "there is no disrespect intended here to judges in our sister county. Orange County, as indeed the state as a whole, has seen its share of 'colorful' jurists." He then recited several stories of odd judicial actions that were "common knowledge in these parts." "No," the dissenter said, "the majority has its rose-colored glasses on when it thinks people familiar with the local legal scene could not be taken in by the phony memo; stranger, much stranger, things have come from Los Angeles judges."

Sources: David Margolick, "At the Bar," New York Times, March 4, 1994, B12; *Patrick v. Superior Court*, 27 Cal. Rptr. 2d 883 (Cal. App. 4th Dist. 1994). The quotations are from pp. 889–893 of the court decision.

EXHIBIT 5.4   A Judge Sues for Libel

A case involving a tyrannical California judge offered an appellate court the opportunity to consider the overall standard of judicial behavior. That case is described in Exhibit 5.4.

Impartiality   One quality that everyone would want from a judge is impartiality between the litigants. No judge can be perfectly impartial, because all people hold views that would incline them in favor of some parties and against others. A judge who believes strongly in freedom of speech will have a kind of bias in favor of parties who bring free speech claims. A judge who believes that government engages in too much regulation of business will be skeptical toward efforts to enforce environmental regulations against companies.

But it is reasonable to expect that a judge be sufficiently open-minded to give a fair hearing to both sides. Thus many people find it troubling when judges take firm public positions on issues, like the California judge who served as chair of the Sierra Club Legal Defense Fund or the Washington State judge who went almost directly from his swearing in to an antiabortion rally at which he spoke.[62] A newly elected New York judge was ordered to get rid of a personalized license plate that read "GUILTY."[63]

It is especially troubling when a judge leans toward one side not because of the issues involved but because of who the parties are. The most obvious example is racial and gender bias. It appears that judges today are less likely to engage in direct discrimination against women and members of racial minority groups than in the past. The increased diversity of the bench has had an effect in itself, in part by sensitizing white and male judges to problems of bias. But blatant discrimination has hardly disappeared, as both systematic studies and anecdotal evidence indicate,[64] and there are still some judges who openly make ethnic and racial slurs.[65]

Another possible source of favoritism is the judge's political affiliations. Judges may be inclined to favor their political party either to maintain a critical source of support or as an expression of long-standing loyalties. In some states and cities—Chicago is a well-known example—judges usually can be counted on to support their party's interests in important cases. Judges are more likely to uphold legislative redistricting plans if those plans favor the interests of their own party.[66] As campaign contributions to judges grow, there has been concern about judges' ruling in cases in which contributors are litigants or lawyers.[67] But it is difficult to determine the impact of contributions on judges' decisions, and as yet we know little about this connection.

The worst form of partiality is bribery, the direct selling of decisions. It is impossible to ascertain the frequency with which judges accept bribes, but two conclusions seem safe: this kind of corruption touches only a small minority of judges, but it does occur. In recent years, bribery of multiple judges has been disclosed in Miami and San Diego.[68] Seventeen Chicago judges have been convicted on federal corruption charges in the 1980s and 1990s, primarily as a result of two FBI investigations.[69] One of the seventeen was found guilty of taking bribes to fix three murder trials. It was charged as well that the judge covered his tracks with a "compensatory bias" against some defendants who had *not* bribed him.[70] A judge who participated in the first FBI investigation speculated that as many as one-eighth of the judges in Cook County (encompassing Chicago and some of its suburbs) might be dishonest.[71] Even if that estimate is high and Chicago is unusual, the existence of even a very small proportion of corrupt judges is troubling.

Enhancing the Quality of Judging

In discussing the performance of judges, I have given special attention to the judges whose work is deficient in important respects. It is worth emphasizing that those judges are far from representative. Still, given judges' power, the inadequacies that do exist represent a real problem. The extent of these inadequacies might be reduced and the overall quality of judging enhanced along any of three lines: selecting better judges, removing inadequate judges, and improving the performance of sitting judges.

Selecting Better Judges   Perhaps the best way to improve the quality of judging is simply to put the most qualified people on the bench. For many lawyers and judges, the primary means to achieve that goal is adoption of the Missouri Plan. Advocates of the Missouri Plan see its nominating commissions as a device to identify the most promising candidates. They have won enough support that a majority of states now use some version of the Missouri Plan by law or in practice for at least some of their courts.

As suggested in Chapter 4, it is uncertain whether the Missouri Plan actually affects the quality of judges. In surveys taken in the 1960s, most Missouri lawyers indicated that the plan had raised the quality of the state's judiciary.[72] This finding is significant, but it seems unlikely that adoption of the Missouri Plan would affect the quality of judges in any dramatic way. Criteria other than qualifications affect the selection of judges under the Missouri Plan, and it is not clear that the performance of judges can be predicted very well from their records prior to their selection. It is also noteworthy that the background characteristics of Missouri Plan judges, including those related to their qualifications, are similar to the characteristics of judges selected under other systems.

Another approach is to raise judicial salaries so that good judges will have a greater incentive to remain on the bench and good prospective judges will be more interested in serving. Although judges' salaries typically are well above the average for the workforce as a whole, they are also substantially lower than the incomes of the most successful lawyers. That difference reduces interest in judgeships; people who serve on Missouri Plan nominating commissions collectively rated judges' salaries as the most important factor deterring potential candidates from seeking nominations.[73]

Thus better compensation might improve the quality of the judiciary by broadening the pool of candidates. On the other hand, judgeships would be more attractive to less competent people as well as to the most competent. In any case, it has proved very difficult to secure legislative approval for substantial increases in judicial salaries. If inadequate compensation does weaken the quality of the judiciary, that problem is likely to continue.

Removing Inadequate Judges   If it is impossible to ensure that only good judges will be put on the bench, an obvious remedy is to remove judges whose performance proves to be inadequate. As Exhibit 5.5 shows, a number of removal methods exist.

The simplest of these methods is refusal to grant a judge a new term in office. In practice, this approach works quite imperfectly. In states whose governors appoint judges, the normal pattern is that sitting judges are reappointed almost automatically. In states that use regular elections or retention elections, the voters generally have only limited information about a judge's performance. In part for that reason, incumbents have an excellent chance of winning, no matter how well or how badly they have performed. And most defeats of incumbents are for reasons that have little to do with the quality of their performance on the bench. Still, on occasion, a judge's bad performance is well publicized and results in an electoral defeat.

Federal judges and those in nearly all states are subject to impeachment proceedings. The procedure generally used is that judges can be removed if impeached (in effect, charged with an offense) by the lower house of the legislature and con-

Method	Where Available	Frequency of Use[a]
Defeat in regular election	About 3/5 of states[b]	A
Defeat in retention election	About 2/5 of states[b]	B
Recall by voters	A few states	C
Non-reappointment by governor	About 1/6 of states [b]	C
Impeachment by legislature	Federal; nearly all states	C
Legislative "address"	About 1/3 of states	C
Disciplinary action	All states	B
Compulsory retirement for disability	Nearly all states	B

[a]"A" means used with some frequency, "B" means used occasionally, "C" means almost never used.
[b]These three categories add up to more than 100 percent because some states use two different methods to select judges.
Sources: Marvin Comisky and Philip C. Patterson, *The Judiciary—Selection, Compensation, Ethics, and Discipline* (New York: Quorum Books, 1987), 149–232; other sources.

EXHIBIT 5.5   Selected Methods to Remove Judges from Office

victed by the upper house. For the most part, legislators seriously consider impeachment only where corruption or other criminal offenses are alleged, so this mechanism has little application to problems such as tyrannical behavior. Because the impeachment procedure is so extreme and so unwieldy, it is not always employed even where there are serious allegations of criminal conduct. The removal of a Pennsylvania Supreme Court justice through impeachment in 1994 was a noteworthy event because such action is so rare.[74]

The use of the impeachment power in practice can be illustrated with its history at the federal level.[75] The Constitution provides for impeachment in cases of "treason, bribery, or other high crimes and misdemeanors," with a House majority required for impeachment and a two-thirds Senate majority required for conviction and removal from office. But from 1789 through 1936, only nine federal judges were impeached, and only four were convicted by the Senate (a fifth resigned). After 1936, a half century passed with no impeachments.

Since then, however, impeachment has revived somewhat. In 1987, Congress removed Nevada district judge Harry Claiborne, who had been convicted of two counts of tax evasion in court. In 1989, two other district judges were removed: Walter Nixon of Mississippi, for perjury, and Alcee Hastings of Florida, for bribery and related offenses. The Senate limited the burdens imposed on senators by these three cases through the device of having committees rather than the full Senate hear the evidence. Judge Nixon challenged this procedure as unconstitutional, but the Supreme Court in 1993 held that this was not a question for the courts to settle.[76]

Faced with the limitations of other methods, since 1960 every state has adopted a new structure with which to investigate and act on complaints against judges. This is the judicial conduct commission, an agency within the judicial branch.[77] People can make complaints against judges to the commission (which usually includes judges, lawyers, and lay members) on such grounds as misconduct in office and failure to perform judicial duties.

Typically, the judicial conduct commission screens complaints, investigates those that have possible merit, and recommends disciplinary action to the state supreme court. Such action can take several forms, ranging from private admonition to removal or retirement. In assessing judges' behavior and considering sanctions, most commissions are guided by their state's version of the Code of Judicial Conduct, developed by the American Bar Association.

Only a small minority of complaints result in any kind of disciplinary action against judges, but such action does occur in a substantial number of cases. In a recent year, according to one count, 123 state judges received a private sanction, 65 were publicly censured or reprimanded, 20 were suspended from office, and 9 were removed altogether. Another 27 resigned or retired after complaints were made against them. The offenses committed by judges who were removed from office included deciding cases in which there were serious conflicts of interest, refusing to obey a chief judge's legitimate orders, and engaging in intentional abuse of a public defender. In several instances, a judge had committed offenses of multiple types.[78]

The vigor of judicial conduct commissions varies among the states, and many are regarded as unable or unwilling to respond adequately to misconduct. One of the commissions thought to be particularly weak is the Illinois Courts Commission.[79] Another is the California Commission on Judicial Performance. In a San Diego scandal involving substantial gifts from lawyers to judges, the most severe penalty was a private reprimand; in contrast, when some Philadelphia judges accepted gifts from lawyers or litigants, eight were removed from their positions.[80] In 1994, the California legislature and voters acted to limit the role of judges on the conduct commission and to make the commission's work more public. In both respects, it was following a national trend.

The federal courts do not have an equivalent system. But Congress in 1980 gave the judicial councils of the circuits the power to act as judicial conduct commissions for federal judges. Congress did not allow the councils to remove judges from office, chiefly because of doubts that such action would be constitutionally acceptable. In addition to lesser measures, however, a council can order that no further cases be assigned to a judge for a specified period of time, and it can send a case to the Federal Judicial Conference for a possible recommendation of impeachment by Congress. Circuit councils took that action in the cases of Walter Nixon and Alcee Hastings. The Judicial Conference recommendation that Hastings be impeached, which helped to spur congressional action, was controversial because Hastings had been acquitted of criminal charges. The circuit council made an independent examination of the evidence and concluded that Hastings had lied and used fabricated documents in his trial.[81] In contrast with these highly visible cases, several judges have quietly retired after complaints about them were made to circuit councils.

Improving Sitting Judges   Inevitably, the methods used to select judges and to remove inadequate judges are imperfect. For the most part, we have to live with the judges we have: a set of people whose performance varies considerably. This reality has become increasingly clear to people who care about the quality of the judiciary, so more attention is now given to improving the quality of judges' work.

One form of these efforts is organized educational programs. The Federal Judicial Center conducts such programs for federal judges. Nearly all the states now provide some kind of training for their judges, and there are also several national educational programs. The largest of the national programs is the National Judicial College in Reno, Nevada, established in 1963; sixty thousand judges (some from other nations) have attended classes at the college.[82] Only a few states require training for all their judges, but a large minority impose such requirements on nonlawyer judges and those who serve on specialized courts. These programs undoubtedly improve the skills of most judges who participate in them, but their overall impact is difficult to assess.

Some effort has also been made to provide help for sitting judges who are identified as having problems. Indeed, one function of the state conduct commissions is to warn judges of deficiencies that need correction. Some states have established programs to help judges who suffer from alcoholism and psychological problems.

Attempts to improve the performance of sitting judges, like efforts to select good judges and remove bad ones, have significant limitations. Inevitably, some of the judges whose performance is most deficient will be least willing to try to improve their work. Even judges who want to do better may be limited in their capacity to improve. Thus we will continue to have some judges who perform poorly, just as we have others who meet the highest standards.

CONCLUSIONS

This chapter has pointed to some generalizations about judges. For instance, certain background characteristics are widely shared. To take another example, most judges face the same kinds of stresses in their jobs.

But differences among judges stand out as much as similarities. Their values, their competence, and the ways they approach their jobs all vary a great deal. Thus it does make a difference which people sit on the bench, and the amount of energy devoted to the selection of judges is quite understandable. Heated election campaigns for state judgeships and bitter battles over confirmation of Supreme Court justices, still unusual but more common in recent years, reflect a growing awareness that individual judges have an impact.

Thus far I have discussed judges' work only in general terms. The next three chapters look more closely at judges as decision makers, at the individual characteristics and other forces that shape their behavior.

FOR FURTHER READING

Bass, Jack. *Taming the Storm: The Life and Times of Judge Frank M. Johnson, Jr., and the South's Fight Over Civil Rights.* New York: Doubleday, 1993.

Kemerer, Frank R. *William Wayne Justice: A Judicial Biography.* Austin: University of Texas Press, 1991.

Provine, Doris Marie. *Judging Credentials: Nonlawyer Judges and the Politics of Professionalism.* Chicago: University of Chicago Press, 1986.

Ryan, John Paul, Allan Ashman, Bruce D. Sales, and Sandra Shane–Du Bow. *American Trial Judges: Their Work Styles and Performance.* New York: Free Press, 1980.

Schmidhauser, John R. *Judges and Justices: The Federal Appellate Judiciary.* Boston: Little, Brown, 1979.

Tuohy, James, and Rob Warden. *Greylord: Justice, Chicago Style.* New York: G. P. Putnam's Sons, 1989.

Volcansek, Mary L. *Judicial Impeachment: None Called for Justice.* Urbana: University of Illinois Press, 1993.

NOTES

1. *The Book of the States, 1996–97 Edition* (Lexington, Ky.: Council of State Governments, 1996), 131–132.
2. *O'Connor v. Nevada,* 27 F.3d 357 (9th Cir. 1994).
3. "Evolution of Lay Judges: From Kitchens to Courts," *New York Times,* October 23, 1994, A44.
4. All statistics presented on the backgrounds of federal judges in the 1989–1996 period are from Sheldon Goldman and Elliot Slotnick, "Clinton's First Term Judiciary: Many Bridges to Cross," *Judicature* 80 (May–June 1997), 254–273.
5. Curtis Bok, *Backbone of the Herring* (New York: Alfred A. Knopf, 1941), 3.
6. Michael York, "George H. Revercomb, U.S. District Judge, Dies," *Washington Post,* August 2, 1993, D6.
7. James Tuohy and Rob Warden, *Greylord: Justice, Chicago Style* (New York: G. P. Putnam's Sons, 1989), 47.
8. Charles Anzalone, "Candidates in Pursuit of a Judgeship Must Learn Rules of the Game," *Buffalo News,* March 18, 1990, B1.
9. John Paul Ryan, Allan Ashman, Bruce D. Sales, and Sandra Shane–Du Bow, *American Trial Judges: Their Work Styles and Performance* (New York: Free Press, 1980), 125.
10. Ibid.
11. Susan P. Fino, *The Role of State Supreme Courts in the New Judicial Federalism* (New York: Greenwood Press, 1987), 52; Henry R. Glick and Craig F. Emmert, "Stability and Change: Characteristics of State Supreme Court Justices," *Judicature* 70 (August–September 1986), 108.
12. This proportion is based on data in *Judicial Yellow Book,* vol. 2, no. 2 (New York: Leadership Directories, Inc., 1997).
13. On the states, see *Judicial Yellow Book;* Glick and Emmert, "Stability and Change," 108; and Ryan et al., *American Trial Judges,* 125.
14. Richard A. Posner, *The Federal Courts: Challenge and Reform* (Cambridge: Harvard University Press, 1996), 20.
15. Joel S. Ish, "Trial Judges: Their Recruitment, Backgrounds and Role Perceptions" (paper presented at the 1975 meeting of the American Political Science Association in San Francisco, California), 4–6.
16. Ryan et al., *American Trial Judges,* 128; Glick and Emmert, "Stability and Change," 108.
17. Reynolds Holding, "Sitting in Judgment," *San Francisco Chronicle,* October 29, 1995, 4.
18. See Goldman and Slotnick, "Clinton's First Term Judiciary"; and Sheldon Goldman and Matthew D. Saronson, "Clinton's Nontraditional Judges: Creating a More Representative Bench," *Judicature* 78 (September–October 1994), 68–73.

19. David Margolick, "Women's Milestone: Majority on Minnesota Court," *New York Times,* February 22, 1991, B10.
20. *Chisom v. Roemer,* 501 U.S. 380 (1991).
21. Anna M. Scruggs, Jean-Claude Mazzola, and Mary E. Zaug, "Recent Voting Rights Challenges to Judicial Elections," *Judicature* 79 (July–August 1995), 34–41.
22. See, for instance, C. Neal Tate and Roger Handberg, "Time Binding and Theory Building in Personal Attribute Models of Supreme Court Voting Behavior, 1916–88," *American Journal of Political Science* 35 (May 1991), 460–480; and Martha A. Myers, "Social Background and the Sentencing Behavior of Judges," *Criminology* 26 (November 1988), 649–675.
23. See Howard Schumann, Charlotte Steeh, and Lawrence Bobo, *Racial Attitudes in America: Trends and Interpretations* (Cambridge: Harvard University Press, 1985); Carol M. Mueller, ed., *The Politics of the Gender Gap* (Beverly Hills, Calif.: Sage Publications, 1988); and Robert S. Erikson, Norman R. Luttbeg, and Kent L. Tedin, *American Public Opinion: Its Origins, Content, and Impact,* 2d ed. (New York: John Wiley and Sons, 1980).
24. Thomas G. Walker and Deborah J. Barrow, "The Diversification of the Federal Bench: Policy and Process Ramifications," *Journal of Politics,* 47 (May 1985), 596–617; David W. Allen and Diane E. Wall, "The Behavior of Women State Supreme Court Justices: Are They Tokens or Outsiders?" *Justice System Journal,* 12 (Fall 1987), 232–245; Sue Davis, "Do Women Judges Speak 'In a Different Voice'? Carol Gilligan, Feminist Legal Theory, and the Ninth Circuit," *Wisconsin Women's Law Journal* 8 (1992–1993), 143–173; Sue Davis, "The Voice of Sandra Day O'Connor," *Judicature* 77 (November–December 1993), 134–139.
25. Donald R. Songer, Sue Davis, and Susan Haire, "A Reappraisal of Diversification in the Federal Courts: Gender Effects in the Courts of Appeals," *Journal of Politics* 56 (May 1994), 425–439.
26. Susan Welch, Michael Combs, and John Gruhl, "Do Black Judges Make a Difference?" *American Journal of Political Science* 32 (February 1988), 126–136; John Gruhl, Cassia Spohn, and Susan Welch, "Women as Policymakers: The Case of Trial Judges," *American Journal of Political Science* 25 (May 1981), 308–322.
27. *Patricia Ann S. v. James Daniel S.,* 435 S.E.2d 6 (W. Va. Sup. Ct. 1993). See also *Office of Disciplinary Counsel v. Mestemaker,* 676 N.E.2d 870 (Ohio Sup. Ct. 1997).
28. See David Margolick, *At the Bar: The Passions and Peccadilloes of American Lawyers* (New York: Touchstone, 1995), 193–195.
29. Court Statistics Project, *State Court Caseload Statistics, 1994* (Williamsburg, Va.: National Center for State Courts, 1995), 96; Administrative Office of the United States Courts, *Judicial Business of the United States Courts: Report of the Director* (1995) (Washington, D.C.: Administrative Office of the United States Courts, n.d.), 42–44.
30. This list of categories is adapted from a list in Ryan et al., *American Trial Judges,* 6–7, and some of the material in this subsection was drawn from that source.
31. See Cornelius M. Kerwin, Thomas Henderson, and Carl Baar, "Adjudicatory Processes and the Organization of Trial Courts," *Judicature* 70 (August–September 1986), 99–106.
32. Judith S. Kaye, "My 'Freshman Years' on the Court of Appeals," *Judicature* 70 (October–November 1986), 166.
33. Harold J. Rothwax, *Guilty: The Collapse of Criminal Justice* (New York: Random House, 1996), 9.
34. See Albert P. Melone, "Revisiting the Freshman Effect Hypothesis: The First Two Terms of Justice Anthony Kennedy," *Judicature* 74 (June–July 1990), 6.
35. Milton Heumann, *Plea Bargaining: The Experiences of Prosecutors, Judges, and Defense Attorneys* (Chicago: University of Chicago Press, 1977), ch. 6.
36. Stephen L. Wasby, "'Into the Soup?': The Acclimation of Ninth Circuit Appellate Judges," *Judicature* 73 (June–July 1989), 10.
37. Lauren K. Robel, "Caseload and Judging: Judicial Adaptations to Caseload," *Brigham Young University Law Review* (1990), 11.
38. Mary Ann Glendon, *A Nation Under Lawyers: How the Crisis in the Legal Profession is Transforming American Society* (New York: Farrar, Straus and Giroux, 1994), 149.

39. B. J. Palermo, "O.J. Custody Judge Targeted," *National Law Journal,* April 28, 1997, A8.

40. See, respectively, Eileen Dempsey, "Judge Tells Why He Freed Convicted Mom," *Columbus Dispatch,* February 1, 1997, 4B; and Matthew Purdy, "Judge Explains His Acquittal of Officer in a Choking Death," *New York Times,* October, 9, 1996, A16.

41. "Firebomb Defendant Scolds Judges," *Chicago Tribune,* April 10, 1997, sec. 2, 4.

42. Tim Golden, "Police Say They Arrested Leader of a Bombing Plot," *New York Times,* February 4, 1997, A7.

43. See Martha A. Bethel, "Terror in Montana," *New York Times,* July 20, 1995, A13.

44. David Margolick, "At the Bar," *New York Times,* April 7, 1989, B5.

45. Emily Field Van Tassel, *Why Judges Resign: Influences on Federal Judicial Service, 1789–1992* (Washington, D.C.: Federal Judicial Center, 1992), 9.

46. David Margolick, "At the Bar," *New York Times,* January 6, 1989, B9.

47. C. Robert Showalter and Daniel A. Martell, "Personality, Stress and Health in American Judges," *Judicature* 69 (August–September 1985), 85.

48. Quoted in Charles M. Haar, *Suburbs Under Siege: Race, Space, and Audacious Judges* (Princeton, N.J.: Princeton University Press, 1996), 156.

49. Phillip Matier and Andrew Ross, "Barry Bonds' Judge Says He's Sorry," *San Francisco Chronicle,* August 20, 1994, A1, A13.

50. Gary Taylor, "This Smile's Not Contagious," *National Law Journal,* September 6, 1993, 39; *Drew v. Collins,* 5 F.3d 93 (5th Cir. 1993).

51. "Law Poll," *American Bar Association Journal* 68 (October 1982), 216.

52. Bennett Cerf, "A Texas Sampler," in *An Encyclopedia of Modern American Humor,* ed. Bennett Cerf (Garden City, N.Y.: Doubleday, 1954), 385–386.

53. Doris Marie Provine, *Judging Credentials: Nonlawyer Judges and the Politics of Professionalism* (Chicago: University of Chicago Press, 1986), 166.

54. "Never on Fridays," *National Law Journal,* November 6, 1989, 6.

55. John Aloysius Farrell, "Half-Day Justice," *Boston Globe,* September 23, 1990, 1, 34; Paul Katzeff, "Massachusetts Judges Investigated," *National Law Journal,* October 15, 1990, 2.

56. Michael York and Stephen C. Fehr, "Metro Wins Green Line Ruling," *Washington Post,* July 31, 1993, C1, C5.

57. Quoted in Pamela Coyle, "Bench Stress," *American Bar Association Journal,* December 1995, 61.

58. *In the Matter of the Honorable Donald C. Johnson,* 658 N.E.2d 589 (Ind. Sup. Ct. 1995).

59. Harriet Chiang, "Prankster Judge Is Chastised," *San Francisco Chronicle,* June 22, 1993, A15.

60. David Bailey, "Commission Dumps 'Mean-Spirited' Judge," *Chicago Daily Law Bulletin,* January 14, 1994, 1.

61. *Inquiry Concerning a Judge, No 91-415 Re: Gary G. Graham,* 620 So. 2d 1273 (Fla. Sup. Ct. 1993).

62. See, respectively, "Victories and News," *In Brief,* Summer 1994, 2; and Patti Epler, "Justice Sanders Reprimanded," *Tacoma News Tribune,* May 13, 1997, A1.

63. "Judge-Lawyer Feud Reaching Climax," *Columbus Dispatch,* December 13, 1995, 6A.

64. See, for instance, "Minnesota Supreme Court Task Force Report on Racial Bias in the Judicial System," *Hamline Law Review* 16 (Spring 1993), 477–877; "The Effects of Gender in the Federal Courts: The Final Report of the Ninth Circuit Gender Bias Task Force," *Southern California Law Review* 67 (May 1994), 745–1106; and Sheila Weller, "America's Most Sexist Judges," *Redbook,* February 1994, 83–87.

65. Lynne Duke, "Panel Faults Remarks by U.S. Judge," *Washington Post,* October 22, 1993, A14; "Mass. Judge Quits Prior to Hearing on Conduct," *Boston Globe,* May 29, 1993, Metro section, 1.

66. See Randall D. Lloyd, "Separating Partisanship from Party in Judicial Research: Reapportionment in the U.S. District Courts," *American Political Science Review* 89 (June 1995), 413–420.

67. See *MacKenzie v. Super Kids Bargain Store,* 565 So. 2d 1332 (Fla. 1990).

68. *United States v. Shenberg,* 89 F.3d 1461 (11th Cir. 1996); Peter Kaye, "It's Time to Judge the Judges," *California Bar Journal* May 1996, 8.

69. Bill Peterson, "Operation Greylord's Scorecard Nearly Complete," *Washington Post,* August 25, 1989, A5; Matt O'Connor, "Jury Plays Tape Until All Agree Shields Is Guilty," *Chicago Tribune,* September 29, 1991, sec. 1, 1–2.

70. Matt O'Connor, "Judge Maloney Found Guilty in Corruption Case," *Chicago Tribune,* April 17, 1993,1,6; *Bracy v. Gramley,* 138 L. Ed. 2d 97 (1997).

71. Mark Starr, "Stinging the Chicago Courts," *Newsweek,* August 22, 1983, 21.

72. Richard A. Watson and Rondal G. Downing, *The Politics of the Bench and the Bar: Judicial Selection under the Missouri Nonpartisan Court Plan* (New York: John Wiley, 1969), 257–263, 282–286.

73. Joanne Martin, *Merit Selection Commissions: What Do They Do? How Effective Are They?* (Chicago: American Bar Foundation, 1993), 14–20.

74. Bill Moushey and Tim Reeves, "Senate Convicts Larsen, Bars Him from any Office," *Pittsburgh Post-Gazette,* October 5, 1994, A1, A10; Charles Gardner Geyh, "Highlighting a Low Point on a High Court: Some Thoughts on the Removal of Pennsylvania Supreme Court Justice Rolf Larsen and the Limits of Judicial Self-Regulation," *Temple Law Review* 68 (Fall 1995), 1041–1077.

75. Mary L. Volcansek, *Judicial Impeachment: None Called for Justice* (Urbana: University of Illinois Press, 1993); Eleanore Bushnell, *Crimes, Follies, and Misfortunes: The Federal Impeachment Trials* (Urbana: University of Illinois Press, 1992); Michael J. Gerhardt, *The Federal Impeachment Process: A Constitutional and Historical Analysis* (Princeton, N.J.: Princeton University Press, 1996).

76. *Nixon v. United States,* 506 U.S. 224 (1993).

77. Irene A. Tesitor and Dwight B. Sinks, *Judicial Conduct Organizations,* 2d ed. (Chicago: American Judicature Society, 1980).

78. This information is from a table and article in the *Judicial Conduct Reporter* 17/18 (Winter–Spring 1996), 1–3, 7. Because of reporting methods, the figures in this paragraph should be treated as approximate rather than exact.

79. Ken Armstrong, "More Bite Sought from Judicial Watchdogs," *Chicago Tribune,* June 23, 1996, sec. 1, 1, 8.

80. Harriet Chiang, "Similar Scandals—Different Results," *San Francisco Chronicle,* April 21, 1994, A6. See William Carlsen and Harriet Chiang, "Secret Justice for State's Judges," *San Francisco Chronicle,* April 20, 1994, A1, A4; and Chiang and Carlsen, "California Trails the Nation in Judging Wayward Judges," *San Francisco Chronicle,* April 21, 1994, A1, A6

81. See Volcansek, *Judicial Impeachment,* 68–119.

82. Sandra Chereb, "College Teaches Jurists How to Wear Black Robes," *Los Angeles Times,* December 15, 1996, B4.

6

Trial Courts: Criminal Cases

It would be difficult to estimate the number of hours that the American public collectively has devoted to the O.J. Simpson cases, but that number surely is enormous. His criminal trial itself attracted extraordinary interest, and long after it ended, the large stack of books written about the trial continued to grow.

The attention given to the Simpson trial reflected a unique set of circumstances. Perhaps most important, it had been a long time since anyone so famous was charged with murder. In another sense, however, the interest in O.J. Simpson's trial illustrates a general rule. Criminal cases hold an interest for people that is far greater than anything else that courts do. When Americans think about courts, it is primarily about the criminal side of their work.

This interest in criminal courts creates a basic tension in the way they operate. Judges and attorneys in trial courts often feel considerable pressure from their audiences to handle criminal cases in particular ways. But to a considerable degree, they resist this pressure. The practices they use to process criminal cases reflect their own goals and interests, and they usually have strong reasons to maintain those practices. Moreover, they value for its own sake their considerable freedom to shape the criminal law in its actual operation.

This chapter examines the work of trial courts in criminal cases (for convenience, referred to here as criminal courts). I discuss their handling of cases, emphasizing the conditions and motivations that shape their practices. Efforts to "reform" criminal courts also receive attention in this chapter—particularly the impact of the reforms that are actually adopted. It should become clear that criminal courts are complex institutions, and those who seek to change them must accept and deal with this complexity.

Criminal courts vary a good deal. The chapter describes general patterns in their operation and differences among them. Since the great majority of criminal cases go to state courts, the focus is primarily on that level. But the discussions of processes and outcomes in the chapter take federal cases into account as well.

After a general examination of criminal courts, the chapter explores four key processes: bringing cases to court, plea bargaining, trials, and sentencing.

AN OVERVIEW OF CRIMINAL COURTS

To provide an overview of criminal courts, this section surveys three matters—types of criminal cases, participants in criminal proceedings, and procedures for the handling of cases.

Types of Criminal Cases

The line between criminal and civil cases is not entirely clear-cut. In general, however, criminal cases are those in which government charges people with offenses for which they may be punished if found guilty.[1]

Congress and the state legislatures determine through statutes what acts are defined as criminal offenses. For this reason, the coverage of the criminal law should be viewed as a product of political decisions. This political character is hardly visible for offenses such as murder and robbery, which always have been treated as criminal by consensus. But such a consensus does not exist for acts such as gambling, for which the laws have varied among states and changed over time. One of the most heated national debates today is about the circumstances under which abortion should be treated as a criminal offense. The number of criminal offenses tends to grow over time as legislators react to perceptions of new problems, such as the use of computers to interfere with the operation of data systems.

The criminal and civil sides of the law overlap. A single act or incident often can lead to either type of case, or both. Moreover, cases that are formally criminal sometimes look more like civil proceedings. Prosecutions for writing checks with insufficient funds, for instance, often are resolved when the defendant agrees to pay restitution to the business that initiated the criminal proceeding.

The criminal statutes create three types of cases: felonies, misdemeanors, and juvenile proceedings.

Felonies   The most serious criminal offenses, those punishable with the most severe sanctions, are called felonies. Some states define felonies as offenses for which a defendant may be sentenced to death or to imprisonment in the state penitentiary (as opposed to a local jail). Other states and the federal government define felonies as offenses for which at least one year's imprisonment is possible. Violent offenses are almost always treated as felonies, while relatively minor crimes such as petty theft and gambling are usually misdemeanors. But the line between the two categories is arbitrary and varies from state to state.

Felonies constitute only a minority of criminal cases, but their seriousness gives them an importance far beyond their numbers. For that reason, and because we know the most about them, this chapter gives primary attention to felonies. Typically, felony cases are tried in the major trial courts of a state system, so the chapter focuses chiefly on those courts.

Misdemeanors   Offenses that are not classified as felonies are misdemeanors. These cases typically go to minor trial courts in the states, and most federal misdemeanors are handled by magistrates rather than judges.

Nearly all traffic and parking offenses are classified as criminal misdemeanors, sometimes in a separate category. These cases greatly outnumber all others in the criminal courts. But because most are relatively minor in seriousness and possible sanctions, I give little attention to them.

Juvenile Offenses   Crimes allegedly committed by younger people constitute a special category, which may be called juvenile offenses. Each state has established juvenile courts, sometimes as divisions of other courts. When juvenile courts were created, the goal was to emphasize treatment rather than punishment; indeed, juvenile cases were no longer defined as criminal. Below a designated age, usually eighteen to twenty-one, defendants generally go to juvenile courts. In recent years, however, an increasing number of states have allowed juveniles who are charged with the most serious offenses to be tried in adult courts if they are older than a minimum age. That change is one indication that the idea of treatment rather than punishment has lost support. Besides the criminal offenses that apply to both adults and juveniles, most states have created other offenses that apply only to juveniles, such as truancy and incorrigibility.

Participants in Criminal Courts

Of all the people who take part in the work of criminal courts, the most important are those who hold three positions: judges, prosecutors, and defense attorneys. Together, these three sets of participants have the greatest impact on the processing of cases and on their outcomes. Typically, the judges and lawyers who handle criminal cases do so on a regular basis. As a result, they get to know each other well and often develop close working relationships. To use two terms suggested by students of criminal courts, lawyers and judges are at the center of the "courtroom work group" and the "courthouse community."[2]

The closeness of relationships within this community differs from court to court, based in part on the stability of the work group. Relations are likely to be most cooperative and shared understandings strongest where all the lawyers and judges are frequent rather than occasional participants in criminal cases. In general, the smaller the set of judges and lawyers who come together in criminal courts, the closer their working relationships. For this reason, courts in small and medium-sized counties typically feature tighter work groups than do big-city courts. But even in big cities, members of the work group can become familiar with each other and develop strong norms and expectations about what each participant will do. In any event, judges, prosecutors, and defense attorneys—whether or not they cooperate—are all so central to criminal cases that the actions each takes and the interactions among them are crucial to what happens in court.

Judges   Most trial judges hear criminal cases at least part of the time. On multijudge courts, some judges are assigned permanently or for long periods to hear only criminal cases.

Judges, of course, play a central role in criminal cases. Simply by presiding in court, they influence the proceedings before them. But they also make several kinds of decisions about cases. Before the trial, they determine whether there is sufficient evidence to maintain a case against a defendant; in addition, they set bail and decide whether to accept a defendant's guilty plea. In a nonjury trial, the judge decides whether to convict or acquit. If a defendant pleads guilty or is convicted after a trial, a judge usually makes the sentencing decision.

This list of responsibilities may exaggerate the judge's importance somewhat; even where a judge holds the ultimate power of decision, the actual exercise of that power is influenced by prosecutors and defense attorneys. In interactions among the three work group members, judges have the advantage of higher legal status. But as one set of commentators has suggested, the judge's "dominance in formal status does not invariably translate into actual influence."[3] Judges may even find themselves in a relatively weak position to exert control; sentencing decisions, for instance, are often constrained by plea bargaining agreements between the prosecutor and defense attorney. Even so, judges hold great power over case processing and outcomes.

Prosecutors   In minor cases, police officers sometimes act as prosecutors, but with that exception the government is represented by attorneys in criminal cases. Some prosecutors work in offices that deal only with criminal cases, but it is common for those offices to handle other government legal work as well.[4]

Prosecutors' offices generally follow the same geographical lines as courts. In the federal court system, for instance, each judicial district has an office of the United States Attorney as well as a district court. Where a state court serves a county, there is usually a county prosecutor's office. But in Alaska, Connecticut, and Delaware, the state attorney general is responsible for prosecution throughout the state.

The structure of a prosecutor's office varies with its workload. In state systems, many rural counties have only a single part-time prosecutor. In contrast, most metropolitan counties have large offices with scores of full-time assistants to the chief prosecutor. The largest offices include several hundred assistants. Larger offices often feature specialization by individual assistants in specific kinds of cases. And in such offices, power over the handling of cases may be highly decentralized.

The official who heads a prosecutor's office in a state system may have any of several titles—most often district attorney, county attorney, or prosecuting attorney. U.S. Attorneys are appointed by the president and confirmed by the Senate. In the states, nearly all chief prosecutors are elected, most for four-year terms. Many prosecutors win a series of elections, holding office for considerable time, but their visibility also makes them vulnerable to defeat. In 1996, prosecutors lost re-election bids in San Francisco and Chicago. Also defeated in 1996 was a Michigan county prosecutor who was criticized because of his expensive and unsuccessful prosecutions of Dr. Jack Kevorkian for assisting in suicides.

Most often, assistant prosecutors take this position shortly after graduation from law school and move on to private practice after a few years. Because of this initial inexperience and fairly rapid turnover, at any given time a significant proportion of prosecutors are still in the process of learning their jobs. But the large numbers of cases they handle reduce the time required to develop expertise.

Like judges, prosecutors make important decisions at several stages in the processing of criminal cases. Initially, they decide which cases will go to court and on what charges. Prosecutors present the government's case throughout the pretrial and trial stages, and they also make plea bargaining agreements with defendants. Finally, if defendants are convicted, the prosecutor's recommendation usually influences the judge's sentencing decision and often is the primary influence on that decision.

These roles give the prosecutor a power that is rivaled only by that of the judge. In many courts, perhaps most, the prosecutor is even more important than the judge. On the basis of his experiences, one convict concluded that "the person who runs the show is the prosecutor."[5] Developments such as the growing use of sentencing rules that restrict judges' discretion have strengthened prosecutors further in recent years. One legal scholar argued in 1992 that "prosecutors wield vastly more power than ever before."[6]

Defense Attorneys   In the most minor cases, such as those involving routine traffic offenses, a defendant is unlikely to have an attorney. But defense attorneys are seldom absent from more serious cases. According to one estimate, only "25 or so" defendants each year—a very small fraction of the total—represent themselves in Cook County (Chicago) circuit court.[7]

Defense attorneys can be put into three categories: public defenders, private attorneys paid by their clients, and private attorneys who are assigned and paid by courts to represent indigent defendants. Public defenders share several characteristics with prosecutors. They generally work out of local offices, which are part of statewide systems in some states. Some public defenders are full-time, others part-time. Like assistant prosecutors, most public defenders move on to private practice after a few years.

Some private attorneys handle criminal cases only occasionally, while others spend much or even most of their time in the criminal field. A small proportion of the lawyers who do substantial work in criminal defense are both prosperous and well regarded. But most criminal lawyers receive lower incomes and less prestige than most other attorneys because their clients typically are people with low incomes and even lower social status.[8]

Defense attorneys have less control over the processing of cases than do judges and prosecutors. But they automatically exert an impact as the representatives of defendants in plea bargaining and in court. Along with judges and prosecutors, they make up the core of the criminal court work group.

Other Court Personnel   Other people who work in the courts also influence the handling of cases. Courtroom clerks schedule and arrange cases, and their scheduling decisions may affect the disposition of cases by giving one side a tactical advantage. Parajudges such as magistrates sometimes act in place of judges, usually in minor cases and in the preliminary stages of other cases.

Probation officers also work in the courts, supervising convicted defendants who have been given probation rather than a prison sentence. Within the court, they produce presentence reports that judges use in determining their sentencing decisions.

Defendants   Defendants occupy the most ambiguous position of all the participants in court proceedings. Although defendants must approve their lawyers' decisions, including any plea bargains, they stand outside the core work group of the court. As a result, they may have only limited impact on the course of events in their cases. Depending on the extent of their prior experience with the criminal courts, they may have considerable expertise in the workings of the courts, or they may be heavily dependent on their lawyer's expertise.

Defendants affect the course of their case not only with their responses to lawyers' advice but through their testimony if they appear as witnesses and through their behavior in court proceedings. Their impact is most obvious when they make bad choices. A Massachusetts defendant in a drug case listed his occupation as "drug dealer" in his application for release without bail; his request was denied.[9]

Defendants are not, of course, a random sample of the population. The great majority are male, a highly disproportionate number are members of racial minority groups, and they stand relatively low in socioeconomic status. Among a sample of state prison inmates in 1991, 34 percent had graduated from high school and only 12 percent had any college education; prior to entering prison, a slight majority had annual incomes of less than $10,000.[10] All those figures are far below the average for the population as a whole. In a study of nine felony courts, from 53 percent to 90 percent of the defendants had attorneys provided by programs for the indigent.[11]

The Prosecutor's Clients   In the abstract, the prosecutor's clients are the government and the citizenry as a whole. But prosecutors have two more direct clients: law enforcement agencies and the people who bring complaints of crimes. Since police departments and other agencies make the arrests that allow criminal prosecutions, prosecutors' activities depend on the kinds of arrests police make and the quality of the evidence they gather. Police officers often are important witnesses in court as well. They also serve as a significant audience for the criminal courts, one that is inclined to be critical when it perceives leniency in the treatment of defendants.

People who make criminal complaints are generally the victims of the crimes involved. Prosecutors depend on their cooperation to make effective cases against defendants, yet victims traditionally have been excluded from decisions about the handling and disposition of their cases. In recent years, however, the federal government and most states have changed their laws to give victims fuller rights to participate in cases. (There is also a strong campaign for an amendment to the U.S. Constitution to guarantee certain rights to crime victims.) Most states now allow a victim to make a statement, usually in writing, at a sentencing hearing. Several require consultation with the victim in the plea bargaining process. These rights seem to have some impact on the outcomes of cases and on the feelings of victims, though the impact is complex and variable.[12]

Witnesses and Jurors   In general, law enforcement officers and complainants are the most important witnesses in trials. Of course, other people also serve as witnesses. They are not given a high priority in the concerns of courtroom professionals, who often fail to inform them about what they need to do. They may appear in court only to find cases postponed, and repeated postponements can discourage them from reappearing—which is often the goal of the defense attorney who seeks postponements.

Two sets of jurors, members of *grand juries* and *petit,* or *trial, juries,* also take part in criminal cases. Both are selected from the general population. Trial jurors (and in most states, grand jurors) are chosen through methods intended to produce a fairly representative cross section of the public.

Grand juries exist in the federal system and in most states to determine whether there is sufficient evidence to indict a defendant and thus bring the defendant to trial. Unlike trial juries, they sit continuously for a substantial period of time and hear large numbers of cases. They have little independent power, because they are guided through cases by the prosecutor and nearly always follow the prosecutor's recommendations. A New York City prosecutor reported that "even the most independent-minded grand juries were eventually numbed into unquestioningly doing our bidding."[13] A former chief judge of the New York court of appeals once said that most grand juries would "indict a ham sandwich" if the prosecutor asked them to do so.[14]

Trial juries have more impact on the outcomes of cases. In the cases that actually go to jury trials, the jury decides whether to convict the defendant and, in some states, determines the sentence for a defendant it finds guilty. Only a small proportion of criminal cases culminate in jury trials, but the handling of other cases is affected by predictions of jurors' potential behavior. For instance, if a jury would be unlikely to convict a particular defendant, perhaps because the evidence was ambiguous, the prosecutor might be inclined to drop the case or offer a relatively favorable plea bargain.

Criminal Courts and Their Environments   The judges and attorneys who handle criminal cases have considerable freedom to act on the basis of their own goals and interests. One reflection of that freedom is their continued use of plea bargaining despite its unpopularity. But by no means are criminal courts entirely free from external influences.

These influences generally favor severity toward criminal defendants. In a 1994 national survey, respondents were asked: "In general, do you think the courts in this area deal too harshly or not harshly enough with criminals?" Altogether, 3 percent thought that the courts were too harsh, 85 percent not harsh enough. There were few differences among different types of people, and the results differed little from past surveys.[15]

As noted earlier, law enforcement officers also criticize the courts for what they see as undue leniency, and even prosecutors sometimes make such criticisms of judges. Responding in part to their reading of public opinion, politicians frequently label the courts as too "soft" on crime. In the 1990s, both judges and those who appointed them are attacked regularly by opponents on this ground.

Sometimes the pressures on judges are quite direct. Early in 1996, Harold Baer, a federal district judge in New York, ruled that narcotics seized by the police in New York City could not be used as evidence against a defendant. His opinion also expressed some criticism of police behavior in that part of the city. Baer was widely denounced, there were calls for his impeachment, and the Clinton administration hinted that it might seek his resignation—though Clinton himself had appointed Baer to the district court. Ten weeks after his original decision, Baer reversed himself and apologized for his criticism of the police.[16]

Baer did not say that he was reacting to the pressures that had been put on him, but occasionally a judge acknowledges the impact of such pressures. A Nevada judge said that he had refrained from advising the jury to acquit a murder defendant because he had been pressured by a prosecutor and a police detective not to advise an acquittal; the judge said that he felt "threatened" and "intimidated" by the prosecutor.[17] Sometimes, of course, the effects of criticism are obvious even if they are not acknowledged:

> Repeat offender Isaac Peterson, in jail in Birmingham, Alabama, happened to have his bail hearing set for the morning . . . after district judge Jack Montgomery had become fed up with criticism from the mayor that he sets bail too low. Peterson's bail was raised from $5,000 to $9 trillion.[18]

A Summary of Court Procedures

Criminal courts operate under laws and rules that establish a series of formal procedures for the handling of cases. These procedures serve as a framework for court action, but that action is also shaped by informal procedures and routines. Thus both the formal procedures and the ways they operate in practice are important.

Formal Procedures   Formal criminal court procedures differ a good deal across the country, and no general description could apply fully to all the systems that exist. But it is possible to provide a broad description of the stages through which cases usually go.[19] Exhibit 6.1 summarizes a typical set of procedures for felony cases, procedures that are the basis of the discussion that follows.

Court handling of felony cases usually begins with an arrest by the police. This arrest can be based on a formal complaint by a citizen, on a warrant (an authorization to arrest that is issued by a judge to the police), or on police observation of a possible crime.

The suspect makes an initial appearance in court shortly after arrest. If the arrest was made without a warrant, as it usually is, the police must convince the judge that there is sufficient basis for holding the suspect. At the initial appearance, the suspect is informed of the criminal charges and of the applicable procedural rights. Counsel may be appointed for an indigent defendant, and bail is likely to be set.

At the preliminary hearing or preliminary examination, the prosecution must show probable cause to believe that the defendant committed the crime indicated by

EXHIBIT 6.1   Typical Major Stages of Formal Action in Felony Cases

1. Arrest
2. Initial appearance by the defendant in court
3. Preliminary hearing or examination
4. Grand jury indictment or filing of information by the prosecutor
5. Arraignment of the defendant
6. Procedures to prepare the case for trial: discovery, motions, conference
7. Trial
8. Verdict
9. Sentencing (where defendant has been found guilty).

the charge. To do so, the prosecutor presents evidence that the defense may then contest. If the judge finds probable cause, the defendant is held for further proceedings.

In federal court and in the states that use the grand jury, the prosecutor then presents evidence to that body. On the basis of this evidence, the grand jury decides whether to indict the defendant and on what charges. In states that do not use grand juries, the prosecutor simply files what is called an information, attesting that there is sufficient evidence to try the defendant.

In states where the early stages of felony cases are handled in a minor trial court, the case now moves into a major court. The next stage is arraignment, at which the defendant is formally presented with the charge or charges. The defendant can enter a plea to the charge either at the arraignment itself or at a later time.

After the arraignment, several procedures are undertaken to prepare the case for trial. Discovery allows the defendant to examine the prosecution's evidence. If the defendant does so, the prosecutor may in turn examine the defense evidence. In the federal courts and in some states, either side or the judge may initiate a pretrial conference to clarify the issues. The prosecution and defense can also make pretrial motions. For example, the defense may move to suppress evidence on the ground that the police obtained it illegally.

The last three stages of court action are the most familiar. At the trial, both sides present evidence and arguments on the issue of the defendant's guilt. When the trial has ended, the judge or jury reaches a verdict, convicting or acquitting the defendant. If there are multiple charges against a defendant, the jury can convict on some charges and acquit on others. After the verdict, if the defendant is found guilty, the judge or jury (usually the judge) pronounces a sentence.

During a trial, the judge may intervene by granting a defense motion for acquittal on the ground that the evidence is insufficient to sustain a conviction. After the trial, on such a motion, the judge may override a conviction by the jury. (A judge cannot override a jury acquittal.) After a conviction, the judge may grant a defense motion for a new trial on the basis of a serious flaw in the original trial.

The formal procedures for misdemeanors are less extensive than those for felonies. Grand juries are not used, and other pretrial stages such as the preliminary hearing are often omitted. For relatively minor misdemeanors, states may dispense with the right to a jury trial.

The premise that juvenile offenders should be treated rather than punished led to some important differences between juvenile and adult courts. In general, juvenile courts were intended to be governed less fully by formal rules and procedures. Juvenile courts remain less formal than adult courts today. But this difference has been narrowed, in part because of a 1967 Supreme Court decision that gave juvenile defendants most of the procedural rights granted to adults under the Constitution.[20] Growing concern about serious crimes by juveniles has led not only to the sending of some cases to adult courts but to pressures against leniency in the treatment of juvenile defendants.

Court Procedures in Practice   As noted earlier, this description of formal procedures gives only a partial picture of how cases are actually processed. Several characteristics of case processing merit emphasis.

First, cases go through a winnowing process, in which most drop out at some point between arrest and trial. This winnowing occurs primarily in two forms. In one, cases are eliminated through a prosecutor's decision not to file charges or through dismissal, usually at the initial appearance or the preliminary hearing. Some cases that began with felony arrests reappear as misdemeanors. The point at which cases usually drop out in a particular court depends largely on where prosecutors have the best opportunity to screen arrests.

The other form of winnowing comes from guilty pleas by defendants. Strictly speaking, a guilty plea constitutes only a waiver of trial and any pretrial proceedings that remain when the plea is made. But by telescoping the proceedings and terminating cases early, guilty pleas have the effect of dropping cases out of court.

The combined winnowing effect of decisions not to file charges, dismissals, and guilty pleas is overwhelming. The attrition of cases is illustrated by Figure 6.1, which is based on data from thirty jurisdictions across the United States in 1987 or 1988 (primarily counties). As the figure demonstrates, only 3 percent of the cases were actually tried in the felony court (a small proportion were tried in other courts). As low as this figure is, the proportions of misdemeanor cases going to trial is even lower. In the misdemeanor court of New York City, it was reported in 1996 that fewer than 0.3 percent of the cases went to trial.[21]

A second important aspect of court procedure in practice is the frequent bypassing or abbreviation of the prescribed procedures. Even defendants who plead not guilty may waive some preliminary procedures, such as the pretrial hearing and the grand jury's consideration of indictment. Just as important, formal procedures may be undertaken with far more speed and less care than the rules would suggest.

FIGURE 6.1   Typical Attrition of One Hundred Felony Arrests Brought by the Police for Prosecution

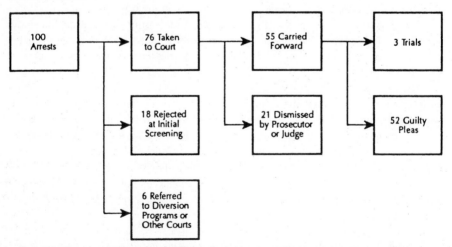

Source: Adapted from Barbara Boland, Paul Mahanna, and Ronald Sones, *The Prosecution of Felony Arrests, 1988* (Washington, D.C.: U.S. Department of Justice, 1992), 3. Based on data from thirty jurisdictions in either 1987 or 1988.

"Fast food justice"[22] has become speedier and more common with recent growth in court caseloads.

The most extreme abbreviation occurs in busy misdemeanor courts, which often carry out their business so rapidly that the formal stages become virtually unrecognizable. One observer of misdemeanor proceedings in New Haven, Connecticut, reported that "defendants came and went in rapid succession. While a few cases took up as much as a minute or two of the court's time—and a small handful involved the court in protracted proceedings—the overwhelming majority of cases took just a few seconds."[23]

A third important procedural matter is the length of time between an arrest and the final disposition of a case. Criminal courts have both legal and practical reasons to keep this time short. The Constitution guarantees the right to a speedy trial, and Congress and many state legislatures have backed this right by setting limits on the time for disposition of cases. Delay also penalizes defendants who are jailed prior to trial. On the other hand, delay often makes convictions more difficult as witnesses become unavailable or their memories fade.

Yet many courts, especially in big cities, face more cases than they can handle comfortably without undue delay. Judges and prosecutors must resort to a variety of measures to overcome this problem. Criminal cases are given priority over civil cases (with the result that civil litigants often endure very long delays before trial). And the goal of avoiding trials through dismissals and guilty pleas takes a very high priority. But delay remains a problem. In state felony cases in 1992, the median length of time from arrest to conviction was more than five months, and nearly nine months in cases with jury trials.[24] The existence of this problem has a pervasive effect on criminal courts.

BRINGING CASES TO COURT

The large volume of criminal cases in many courts obscures a very important reality: only a small fraction of the cases that might be brought to court actually get there and last beyond the earliest stages of court action. The reasons for this phenomenon lie chiefly in the domains of the police and of prosecutors.

The Police: Making Arrests

Relatively few crimes result in arrests. Indeed, one study estimated that of every thousand serious felonies committed in the city of New York, only sixty-five produced arrests.[25] A three-state study estimated probabilities of arrest that ranged from about one in four for aggravated assaults to about one in a thousand for drug deals.[26]

Opportunities for Arrests   Most criminal offenses do not result in arrests simply because there is no opportunity to make them: the police are unable to detect a crime or apprehend a likely suspect.

Unless a crime is committed in the presence of a police officer, law enforcement agencies must rely on others to inform them of it. But even when crimes involve great injury, victims often do not make complaints to the police. A national survey in 1993 found that only 35 percent of all victims reported crimes to the police, with reporting rates generally highest for the most serious crimes.[27] For crimes that have no direct victims, such as drug sales and highway speeding, the rate of reports to police undoubtedly is very low. Thus only through active surveillance can the police detect these kinds of offenses.

Even when the police are aware of an offense, they cannot always apprehend a suspect. When an officer observes a crime directly or when a complainant singles out a suspect who is easily located, the task is easy. But in other cases, it is usually much more difficult to identify and locate a suspect—far more difficult than detective stories would suggest. For the most serious criminal offenses in 1994, the proportion of offenses known to the police that were "cleared" through an arrest was only 21 percent; as with the reporting of crimes, the clearance rate was higher for more serious offenses.[28]

The Arrest Decision   When police officers identify a likely suspect, they generally make an arrest. Indeed, they often have reasons to do so even when a conviction is far from certain. For example, an arrest may seem an appropriate way to deal with an immediate problem, such as a fight, or it may allay public concern about a well-publicized crime. And police departments and individual officers are judged in part by the volume of arrests they make and the proportion of crimes they solve through arrest.

Yet there are also pressures against making every possible arrest. Police resources are often stretched thin, so officers may choose not to arrest suspects in cases that appear to be relatively trivial. Reasons of policy may also militate against making arrests in particular cases. The police recognize, for instance, that the general public does not support the full enforcement of some laws. Thus, to take one example, they seldom arrest those who are engaged in social gambling where it is illegal. And officers may agree not to arrest a suspect in exchange for information about criminal activity.

These kinds of judgments give the police tremendous power. Arrest in itself constitutes a kind of punishment, and it can lead to additional punishments in the criminal justice system. By the same token, a decision not to arrest ordinarily leaves a person free from possible punishment.

The Prosecutor: Charging Decisions

When a case comes to the attention of a prosecutor's office, usually through an arrest, that office must decide whether to carry the case forward or drop it. There are several points at which a prosecutor can make such a decision. In what is probably the most common pattern, prosecutors do most of their screening when they decide whether to file charges against someone who has been arrested. But in some places the police file felony charges themselves, and prosecutors then decide whether to maintain those cases in court or to dismiss them. For convenience, I refer to the prosecutor's screening of cases as the charging decision, though the screening may actually come at a later point.

The prosecutor has more choices than simply charging the suspect or dropping the case. If a suspect is to be charged, the prosecutor must also decide what charges to bring. After a felony arrest is made, one critical decision is whether to charge the suspect with a felony or reduce the case to a misdemeanor.[29] The prosecutor may also take action other than criminal prosecution. For instance, in some cases it may seem preferable to institute a civil case against a suspect.

The proportion of cases in which prosecutors make and carry forward charges varies from place to place, but in most courts prosecutors screen out a high proportion of the cases that are brought to them. As Figure 6.1 shows, in one sample of jurisdictions about half the arrests were carried forward to felony court. Most of the others were rejected or dismissed, chiefly by prosecutors.

Criteria for Charging Decisions   The charging decisions of prosecutors are based on many criteria, which one scholar has arranged into three categories: evidential, pragmatic, and organizational.[30]

Evidential criteria have to do with the likelihood of conviction. The question for the prosecutor is how certain a conviction seems to be in light of the available evidence. To take a case to trial and then lose it constitutes a waste of time and effort. And because prosecution puts heavy burdens on a defendant, the decision to prosecute someone who will probably be acquitted often seems unfair. Further, defeats in court hurt prosecutors by lowering the winning percentage of both individual prosecutors and their offices. Defeats also weaken the prosecutor's position in plea bargaining with defense attorneys.

Studies consistently show that evidential criteria rank high in charging decisions.[31] In 1988, 45 percent of the case rejections by Portland prosecutors were for problems in the evidence; in Manhattan, the proportion was 79 percent.[32] These studies also show that conviction may be doubtful for any of several reasons. Sometimes it is simply uncertain that the defendant committed a crime, but problems may arise even when a prosecutor is confident that the defendant is guilty. A great many dismissals, for instance, result from the withdrawal of a complaint because of the complainant's relationship with the defendant, because of fear, or for some other reason. The unwillingness of other witnesses to testify, sometimes because of intimidation, may also weaken the case against a defendant.[33] And since prosecutors are more concerned with the likelihood of a conviction than with factual guilt, a case is unlikely to go forward without a cooperative complainant and necessary witnesses.

This screening on the basis of evidential criteria helps to create an unofficial presumption of guilt in the minds of most people in the criminal courts. Knowing that prosecutors generally reject weak cases, judges and even defense attorneys often assume that if the prosecutor has chosen to carry a case forward, the defendant is probably guilty and is likely to be convicted if the case goes to trial. This presumption affects the ways that cases are perceived and handled at later stages, especially in plea bargaining.

Pragmatic criteria for charging decisions involve efforts to individualize justice. Most frequently, pragmatic criteria relate to judgments about the severity of felony charges as applied to individual cases. For instance, a case may fit the legal definition of a felony but involve only minor wrongdoing, so a prosecutor will not file a felony charge. Often the characteristics of the defendant also come into play. First offenders, for example, are likely to be treated more leniently than repeat offenders.

Aside from dropping a case, prosecutors have other alternatives from which to choose. One common choice is to charge a suspect with a misdemeanor in order to provide leniency without freeing that person from all sanctions. Noncriminal action, such as arranging restitution to the victim or psychiatric treatment for the suspect, sometimes seems appropriate. These kinds of actions can result from plea bargains, but frequently prosecutors take them on their own.

Organizational criteria for charging decisions have to do with the needs of the prosecutor's office. In one sense, all criteria for prosecution decisions have an organizational component, but some are more directly organizational than others.

One organizational concern is relationships with other policymakers and with the general public. As noted earlier, prosecutors may respond to pressures from their political environments. Especially important on a day-to-day basis is the need to maintain cooperation with law enforcement officials. One effect is that prosecutors may feel obliged to bring charges in cases that are important to the police.

Another organizational concern is the prosecutor's workload. Some offices are seriously overburdened. Even in more fortunate offices, people prefer to reduce workloads in order to ease pressures and limit the length of their workdays. This concern has the effect of tightening the standards for charging suspects. Thus cases that might not appear trivial in the abstract may be treated as trivial in light of competing demands in the prosecutor's office. Reduction of a felony to a misdemeanor is especially attractive when misdemeanors are prosecuted by a different office.

Charging Decisions and the Power of Prosecutors   Just as discretion in arrest decisions gives power to the police, so too does a similar discretion in charging decisions give power to prosecutors. This power extends beyond the fates of individual suspects: in establishing and applying criteria for charging suspects, prosecutors in effect rewrite the criminal law.

Indeed, the rewriting is often formal. For instance, the federal statute dealing with bribery of bank employees was somewhat vague in its limitations on bank employees' acceptance of gifts from people with whom they do business. To provide greater clarity, the Justice Department gave U.S. Attorneys guidelines under which "occasional receipt of meals, entertainment or other gifts of modest or nominal value" should not be prosecuted.[34] Individual prosecutors' offices may develop their own guidelines, with resulting variation in policy from place to place. A study of seven U.S. Attorneys' offices found that each office prosecuted certain offenses only if at least a minimum amount of money was involved, but the minimum varied a good deal—from $500 to $5,000 for bank fraud, embezzlement, and the interstate transportation of stolen property.[35]

Such guidelines, as well as prosecution decisions in individual cases, reflect the attitudes of prosecutors and the pressures they may feel. Thus prosecution policies are likely to change as social values change. Until recently, for example, most prosecutors were reluctant to bring charges in cases involving violence within the family, in part because they believed that such matters were best kept out of the criminal justice system. Today, however, many prosecutors are more willing to bring charges in domestic violence cases because of a growing belief that criminal sanctions are appropriate and desirable.

The power that flows from charging decisions is illustrated by decisions whether to charge that aggravating circumstances exist in first-degree murder cases, thereby making a death sentence possible. Prosecutors' policies concerning such charges vary considerably from one city to another. The deputy district attorney responsible for homicide cases in Pittsburgh estimated in 1995 that his office filed a notice that it might seek the death penalty in about one-quarter of the eligible cases. In Philadelphia, operating under the same state laws, prosecutors in the mid-1990s filed such a notice and actually sought the death penalty in nearly all eligible cases. Although only a small proportion of those attempts actually resulted in death sentences, a murder suspect in Philadelphia was far more likely to face the possibility of execution and the consequences that follow from that possibility than was one in Pittsburgh.[36]

Prosecutors are often attacked for alleged abuses of their charging powers. Both federal and state prosecutors, for instance, are frequently suspected of "political" motivations—particularly an eagerness to prosecute political opponents and a reluctance to prosecute friends and allies. In recent years, there have been many complaints of overzealous and inappropriate litigation tactics by federal prosecutors.[37] Such attacks are reminders of the discretion involved in charging decisions, as well as the power that flows from that discretion.

PLEA BARGAINING

Every criminal defendant must choose whether to plead guilty or not guilty. Typically, at least in serious cases, the defendant initially pleads not guilty. The choice then is whether to change the plea to guilty at some point before trial. (Occasionally, a defendant pleads *nolo contendere,* or no contest. This plea, like a guilty plea, waives the right to trial, but it does not constitute an admission of guilt.)

In most courts, the great majority of felony cases carried forward by the prosecutor are resolved through guilty pleas. This means that convictions generally result from guilty pleas rather than trials. In federal courts in 1995, and in state courts in a sample of three hundred counties in 1992, 92 percent of all convictions resulted from guilty pleas rather than trials.[38] In some courts, trials seldom occur. Indeed, this is generally true of misdemeanor courts. In 1989, 173,000 misdemeanor cases were filed in Los Angeles; about 800 were tried.[39] In one county, according to a former public defender, trials in either felony or misdemeanor cases were "rare and precious events, like Christmas, or one's wedding day, or going off to war."[40]

A defendant may plead guilty for a variety of reasons. In minor cases, for instance, the likely penalty may be so light that it would not be worth the expense and trouble of going to trial. But the most common reason is that the defendant expects to receive a more favorable sentence by pleading guilty rather than being convicted at trial.

This expectation may be based on an explicit agreement in which the defendant is promised benefits related to the sentence in exchange for a guilty plea. Even if there is no explicit agreement, the defendant still may perceive that a guilty plea will produce a more advantageous sentence. This calculation, sometimes called an implicit bargain, is especially common in misdemeanor cases.

We can define plea bargaining to include only explicit bargains or to encompass implicit bargains as well. The question of definition is more than a technical matter, as it affects judgments about such issues as the practicality of eliminating plea bargaining. I think it is generally appropriate to use the broader definition because a defendant who pleads guilty in the belief that a more favorable sentence will result is in effect making a bargain. When prosecutors and judges give signals that guilty pleas indeed are rewarded, as they often do, it is not just the defendant who perceives that a bargain is occurring.

The practice of plea bargaining affects every aspect of the adjudication of felony cases. The handling of cases in their early stages is influenced by the expectation of bargaining, and the existence of a bargain constrains judges in their sentencing decisions. And the knowledge that a case was *not* settled by a bargain can influence its handling. Judges, for instance, often impose heavier sentences on defendants who refused to plead guilty and were convicted at trial.

Forms of Plea Bargaining

The implicit bargain represents one form of plea bargaining.[41] Explicit plea bargains take a variety of forms, which can be placed in three categories. Exhibit 6.2 presents some basic characteristics of each type of plea bargaining. The first is the *charge bargain,* in which the prosecutor reduces the defendant's potential sentence liability by reducing the package of charges. This reduction may be horizontal, with the number of multiple charges for an offense such as burglary reduced in exchange for a guilty plea to the remaining charges. Or the reduction may be vertical, with the highest charges dropped in exchange for a guilty plea to lesser ones. The latter may be charges already in existence or new ones brought in as substitutes.[42] Reduction of felony charges to a misdemeanor is especially common. Police officers and prosecutors sometimes set the

EXHIBIT 6.2   Characteristics of Major Types of Plea Bargaining

Type	Primary Bargainer with Defense	Constraint on Judge's Power?	Certainty of Sentence
Charge bargain	Prosecutor	Yes	Variable
Prosecutor's sentence bargain	Prosecutor	Yes	Moderate
Judge's sentence bargain	Judge	No	Very high
Implicit bargain	None	No	Very low

Source: Based primarily on John F. Padgett, "The Emergent Organization of Plea Bargaining," *American Journal of Sociology* 90 (January 1985), 756–760.

stage for charge bargains by "overcharging" defendants initially—bringing some charges that they have little intention of carrying forward.

Because the defendant's sentence liability is reduced in order to make a guilty plea attractive, the charges to which a defendant pleads guilty may bear little relationship to the original charges or even to the actual offense. Indeed, according to one commentator, "it is no oversimplification to say that courthouse personnel first decide what a defendant's punishment shall be and then hunt around to find a charge that is consistent with their decision."[43] In New York City, shoplifting and assault often are reduced to disorderly conduct, and assault may become harassment.[44] Armed robbery frequently turns into unarmed robbery, a process known as "swallowing the gun." Some years ago a Wisconsin prosecutor who reduced an auto speeding charge to driving the wrong way on a one-way street was embarrassed by the discovery that his town had no one-way streets.[45]

The second category is the *prosecutor's sentence bargain.* Here the prosecutor gives the defendant some assurance about the sentence that a judge will hand down. Most often, the prosecutor agrees to recommend a particular sentence, with the expectation that the judge will follow that recommendation. The judge, however, is not obliged to do so, and judges sometimes reject bargains where they deem the terms to be inadequate. In a 1995 case involving serious violations of housing laws in Washington, D.C., lawyers for the city recommended a sentence of twenty-one days in jail, to be served on weekends; the judge instead sentenced the defendant to more than five years in jail.[46] Some sentence bargains involve less direct concessions by the prosecutor, such as an agreement to make no sentence recommendation or to allow the defendant to go before a lenient judge.

The final category is the *judge's sentence bargain.* A judge may indicate the likely sentence that would follow a guilty plea, and the defendant pleads guilty on the assumption that this sentence will actually be imposed. This is almost surely the least common form of bargaining in felony cases, and its legitimacy is not fully accepted. For instance, in one case the Massachusetts Supreme Court sought "to remind judges that they are not to participate as active negotiators in plea bargaining discussions."[47] A failed bargaining session in 1992, described in Exhibit 6.3, suggests that not all

EXHIBIT 6.3   An Unsuccessful Effort at Sentence Bargaining

Bruce Damon, attempting to work a plea bargain in February to charges that he knocked off a bank in Whitman, Mass., argued to the judge that the 8-to-15-year term suggested by the prosecutor was way too long. First of all, Damon said, when he robbed a bank in 1987, he only got 3-to-5. Second, he said, citing an article from the Brockton Enterprise newspaper, the bank had enjoyed record earnings despite the robbery and expected to do well in 1992, also. Said Damon, "I didn't hurt this bank at all." When the judge asked Damon if he would rob banks again if he were free, Damon replied, "I'd like to plead the Fifth Amendment on that." The judge refused to accept the plea and scheduled Damon for trial.

Source: Quoted from Chuck Shepherd, "News of the Weird," *Funny Times,* July 1992, 21.

judges have complied with this ruling. In any case, judicial sentence bargaining flourishes in New York City. Special courtrooms have been set up in New York for judges to achieve plea bargains in drug cases by working directly with defense attorneys and prosecutors.[48]

Multiple forms of bargains sometimes are combined in a particular case. For instance, a prosecutor may reduce the charges against a defendant and offer to recommend a particular sentence in exchange for a guilty plea. Each courthouse community develops its own practices, with different kinds of bargains dominant in different places.

The Bargaining Process

The process of plea bargaining varies as much as its form. Much of that variation stems from the different forms themselves, which determine whether the defendant and defense attorney negotiate primarily with the prosecutor or with the judge—or, in the case of implicit bargaining, reach a decision to plead guilty without any negotiation. Defense attorneys usually bargain on behalf of their clients. In cases involving minor misdemeanors, however, defendants often represent themselves and negotiate or choose to plead guilty on their own. Plea bargaining most often occurs shortly before the trial is scheduled to begin, but it can come earlier or even later. One Virginia murder defendant agreed to a sentence of forty years even while, as it turned out, the jury was in the process of acquitting him.[49]

In each court, routines develop for the initiation and transaction of bargains. In some places, prosecutors "hold court" prior to court sessions in order to negotiate with attorneys who have cases scheduled for trial that day. Some courts use pretrial conferences as a forum for bargaining. But bargaining is not necessarily restricted to a single point in the proceedings; the two sides may negotiate at several points along the way to trial until they reach a mutually acceptable result.[50]

To a considerable extent, there is also a routine to the *terms* of plea bargains. Although every criminal case might be regarded as unique in some respects, basic patterns recur. Members of the courtroom work group become accustomed to the most common forms of particular offenses, such as burglary and assault. For these "normal crimes," as one scholar has called them,[51] standard terms of bargains— "going rates"—are likely to develop. These standard terms can then be adjusted for special circumstances in cases.

The terms of bargains are likely to be quite standardized in misdemeanor cases, and political scientist Malcolm Feeley has argued that we should adjust our image of plea bargaining to reflect that reality:

> Discussions of plea bargaining often conjure up images of a Middle Eastern bazaar, in which each transaction appears as a new and distinct encounter, unencumbered by precedent or past association. Every interchange involves higgling and haggling anew, in an effort to obtain the best possible deal. The reality of American lower courts is different. They are more akin to modern supermarkets, in which prices for various commodities have been clearly established and labeled in advance. . . . To the extent that there is any negotiation at all, it usually focuses on the nature of the case, and the establishment of relevant "facts."[52]

Although Feeley focused on misdemeanor courts, bargaining in felony courts also follows the supermarket model to a degree.[53]

Both the going rates and the terms of bargains in specific cases reflect multiple factors. One of them is the participants' sense of justice and fairness, as applied to a specific offense and defendant. Perhaps more fundamental is the bargaining power of the participants, which rests largely on their estimates of what would happen if a case went to trial. Thus one important consideration is the estimated likelihood of conviction after a trial. Federal prosecutors usually have very strong cases because they carefully screen out the weaker ones; partly for this reason, they need to yield relatively little in exchange for guilty pleas.[54] Similarly, when the sentence will be handed down by a judge who tends to be severe, the prosecutor's position is strengthened. Other considerations also can affect bargaining power. Heavy caseloads, for instance, put prosecutors and judges under pressure to dispose of cases quickly and thus give the defense additional leverage.

Explaining the Prevalence of Plea Bargaining

If plea bargaining is so common, it must serve important goals for people in the criminal courts. Observers of the courts disagree on the relative importance of different motivations for plea bargaining, but two broad motivations clearly are dominant: reducing the time required to dispose of cases and achieving outcomes that seem desirable.

Saving Time and Other Resources   One basic motivation for plea bargaining is the desire of lawyers and judges to save time. Time is required to reach bargains and ratify them in court, but trials ordinarily require even more time—especially jury trials in serious cases. This difference is fundamental to plea bargaining. Indeed, historical research suggests that bargaining became popular partly because trials became more time consuming. For example, the large flow of cases involving liquor offenses during Prohibition in the 1920s helped to increase the reliance of federal courts on guilty pleas.[55]

Judges and full-time prosecutors and public defenders gain obvious advantages from reducing the time required to dispose of cases. Plea bargaining allows them to work shorter days, handle more cases in the same workday, or achieve some combination of the two.

Part-time prosecutors and private defense attorneys gain financially from speedy disposal of cases. The less time that part-time prosecutors devote to their public duties, the more they can devote to their private practices. For private defense attorneys, quick turnover of cases is the most profitable mode of practice. Ordinarily, the attorney's fee—whether paid by the client or by the court—will not increase enough to pay for the extra time required to try a case rather than to avoid trial through a guilty plea.

Where there are heavy caseload pressures on judges, prosecutors, and public defenders, the incentive to dispose of cases quickly is especially strong. Indeed, in some cities it would be impossible to hold full-dress trials in more than a small proportion of cases; hence plea bargaining, or some equivalent, is necessary to avoid complete chaos. In Manhattan, one judge said, "We go to plea bargaining out of necessity, not out of desire. It is inescapable."[56] But an interest in speed is not confined to courts with burdensome caseloads. As one scholar put it, "regardless of caseload, there will always be *too many cases* for many of the participants in the system, since most of them have a strong interest in being some place other than in court."[57] Some prosecutors in Chicago reportedly like to end proceedings early on summer days so that they can escape to Wrigley Field for baseball games.[58]

Not only do trials require more time than guilty pleas; they require more effort. Attorneys and judges work much harder in trying cases than they do in resolving cases through bargains. Understandably, many lawyers and judges prefer the easier route to the more difficult one, whether their workloads are light or heavy.

Thus, contrary to widespread belief, plea bargaining is not a recent response to growing caseloads in big-city courts. Rather, it was common decades ago, when courts generally were less burdened. And it is common not just in cities but also in suburban and rural courts, whose caseload pressures often are relatively light.[59]

Achieving Desirable Results   For its participants, plea bargaining serves purposes that go beyond speed. Most important, plea bargains are a means for both the prosecution and the defense to secure acceptable results in cases, thus eliminating the possibility of highly undesirable outcomes.

In a plea bargain, the prosecutor gains a guaranteed conviction. Any case that goes to court carries at least a small risk of an acquittal, and some carry a substantial risk. By eliminating this risk, a plea bargain helps to build high winning percentages for the individual prosecutor and the prosecutor's office. By reaching bargains and helping to set their terms, prosecutors can also bring about what they see as appropriate outcomes in terms of the kinds of sanctions that defendants receive.

On the other side, the defense attorney and the defendant gain what they perceive as advantages in sentencing. Virtually all the participants in the criminal courts assume that, all else being equal, a defendant who pleads guilty will receive a lighter sentence than one who has been convicted at trial. Indeed, some judges announce such a policy openly. One New York City judge said that he might tell a defendant the following:

> I'm prepared to give you one to three years instead of three to nine years, not because you deserve it but because I have other things I have to do that require my attention more than you do. So I will give you a sentence that is below what you should get. Of course, if you go to trial and you're convicted, I won't punish you, because that was your choice. But I will give you what you deserve.[60]

According to a reporter, another New York City judge made the same point in a different way:

> Once, three young men who made their living by robbing people in the subway spurned the deal they were offered by the arraigning judge. They went all the way to trial, and got convicted. Seeing what a menace to society they were, the trial judge gave them 5–to-15 years in prison. "How can you do that?" cried one of the defendants. "The judge downstairs offered us a year!"
>
> The trial judge replied: "At one time I could have bought Xerox at three dollars a share. I missed the market, and so did you."[61]

The primary rationale for rewarding defendants who plead guilty is that they aid the court in processing cases quickly. As one Chicago judge remarked of a defendant who might go to trial, "He takes some of my time—I take some of his."[62] Another rationale is that defendants who plead guilty have taken responsibility for their offenses rather than hoping for a lucky acquittal. The defendant who has good reason to go to trial may not be punished, but others can expect to pay for their trials. As one Pennsylvania judge put it, "I don't mind worthwhile trials, where there's actually some question about what happened—then I get to feel like a real judge. But some people are just jerking around the system. You can't have that. It's not really a penalty for the trial, it's more that they've abused the system. . . ."[63]

Among studies designed to measure the impact of guilty pleas on the severity of sentences, there is some disagreement in findings. But most of the evidence supports the perception that defendants who plead guilty are rewarded at sentencing—at least in comparison with defendants who are convicted in jury (rather than bench) trials.[64] Quite aside from whatever actual rewards exist, a plea bargain generally eliminates the risk that a judge will hand down an unusually heavy sentence. When a bargain ensures that a defendant will not go to prison, this assurance is especially attractive. And since defense attorneys (like other court participants) believe that the great majority of defendants would have little chance of victory at trial, pleading guilty in exchange for a sentencing benefit typically appears to be an excellent bargain.

Because defense attorneys have multiple reasons to resolve cases through plea bargains, there is a risk that they will induce clients to accept bargains that are not in their best interests. Certainly attorneys tend to emphasize the advantages of guilty pleas; one public defender tells "my clients they can have a trial, but they have to understand they are gambling with their lives, and the state has two dice and they have one."[65] Defense attorneys may put considerable pressure on clients to plead guilty. Yet defendants often are quite willing, even eager, to plead guilty. In most cases, to both defendants and their attorneys, a guilty plea seems to offer a significant benefit—a lighter sentence—at little cost.

Thus the prevalence of plea bargaining reflects the combined effects of participants' interest in saving their resources and their interest in achieving acceptable outcomes. That combination is reflected in the plea bargain in a case that was quite unusual in most other respects, the one that arose from the injuring of figure skater Nancy Kerrigan in 1994. That bargain is described in Exhibit 6.4.

The Impact of the Work Group   As already noted, the people who make up the core of the courtroom work group—attorneys and judges—tend to develop close working relationships through their constant interaction and interdependence. Indeed, as one lawyer observed of public defenders and prosecutors, "It's like prison guards and prisoners: They're all locked in together."[66] Plea bargaining is facilitated by these relationships, which foster the development of regular bargaining procedures and tacit understandings about feasible terms under particular circumstances.

The interdependence of work group members also strengthens the pressures for plea bargaining. Not all lawyers and judges like plea bargaining, and many come to their jobs expecting to bring most cases to trial. But they generally adapt to a system that is dominated by such bargaining,[67] primarily because they learn its advantages from veteran lawyers and judges.

In January 1994, figure skater Nancy Kerrigan was hit on the knee with a metal baton prior to the competition in Detroit for places on the U.S. Olympic team and was forced to drop out of the competition. Tonya Harding, another leading American skater, won the competition and went to the Olympics. So did Kerrigan, who was given a place on the team despite her nonparticipation in the competition. In February, Kerrigan finished second at the Olympics and Harding eighth.

Soon after the attack, suspicion centered on people connected with Harding. Among them were Harding's ex-husband Jeff Gillooly and, ultimately, Harding herself. Harding denied involvement, but she seemed likely to face prosecution.

Then, in March, the district attorney's office in Portland, Oregon (Harding's home) reached a plea bargain with Harding and her attorney. Under the agreement, Harding pled guilty to hindering prosecution of the case. She agreed to three years of supervised probation and a $100,000 fine; she also agreed to other provisions, including establishment of a $50,000 fund to benefit the Special Olympics and surrendering her membership in the U.S. Figure Skating Association. In return, she would not be prosecuted for other, more serious offenses in Portland. She was also guaranteed that state prosecutors in Detroit and federal prosecutors would not bring cases against her.

From Harding's perspective, the value of the bargain seems clear. She avoided the possibility of going to prison. Although she was paying a good deal of money, her notoriety had brought her the ability to earn a great deal. She was giving up her chance to participate in major figure skating events, but she might well have lost that opportunity through action by the Figure Skating Association. She also was able to put the criminal justice process behind her. "She had to come to the end," said her lawyer, "if she was going to move on with her life."

But what about the prosecution perspective? For one thing, the plea bargain saved considerable time and resources. According to the prosecutor in the case, "Her indictment would have led to a prolonged, disruptive media frenzy that would have tied up the court and this office for a year." The prosecutor insisted that there was "substantial evidence to support Ms. Harding's involvement prior to the assault," but it was uncertain that he could have won a jury conviction on that charge. "In any prosecution," he said, "there are a number of goals you want to accomplish to secure what you believe is justice. We did not achieve each and every goal. But we did achieve many of them. Whether we could have achieved more of them at trial, even though the evidence is clear, is problematical." Thus the district attorney's office accepted a plea to a lesser charge and a sentence that did not include time in prison.

News stories barely mentioned the judge in the case; he apparently ratified the plea bargain without raising any questions about it.

Sources: Newspaper and magazine stories. The quotations are from these sources, respectively: Michael Janofsky, "Plea Bargain Is Called Time-Saver," *New York Times,* March 18, 1994, B13; Janofsky, "Plea Bargain," B11; Johnette Howard, "Harding Admits Guilt in Plea Bargain, Avoids Prison," *Washington Post,* March 17, 1994, A20; Janofsky, "Plea Bargain," B13.

EXHIBIT 6.4   Tonya Harding Makes a Plea Bargain

This adaptation is made more certain by the pressures that other members of the work group can place on a lawyer or judge who is reluctant to bargain. Sometimes this pressure is quite direct, making it clear that a participant will suffer for failing to engage in plea bargaining. Defense attorneys are especially vulnerable to direct pressure because judges can penalize their clients by giving them unusually heavy sentences if they are convicted after failing to plead guilty. One judge went further; not only would he threaten "draconian" sentences in cases that a public defender wanted to take to trial, but

> the attorney's supervisors would be called into chambers and "advised" to get their assistants to work out a deal. Having one's boss called on the carpet by a politically powerful judge was an embarrassment and an effective control mechanism.[68]

More often, however, the pressure that people feel is subtle, even unintentional. The reluctant bargainer simply recognizes that other members of the work group depend on bargaining to do their jobs and that it makes sense to go along. One Pennsylvania judge was usually willing to accept plea bargains even when the sentences that were agreed upon struck him as too light. As he explained, "The system is set up so that the prosecutor plea bargains. And he plea bargains because the system demands him to plea bargain. Otherwise the system fails. So I've got to live with that, even though I don't approve of it."[69]

Exceptions to the Dominance of Plea Bargaining

Prevalent as plea bargaining is, its dominance is not total. In some courts, a high proportion of cases go to trial; in all courts, some cases go to trial. How can we explain these phenomena in light of the strong incentives that exist to avoid trials?

Trials in High-Bargaining Systems   Even in courts that rely overwhelmingly on plea bargaining, some felony cases are resolved through trials. Probably the most common reason is a bargaining failure.[70] Where bargains are negotiated between the prosecutor and the defense attorney, as they usually are in felony cases, the two may assess a case so differently that they cannot reach agreement. For instance, they may disagree on the likelihood of conviction or on the weight to be given any special circumstances. And both sides want to avoid yielding too much to reach a bargain in one case in order to maintain a strong bargaining position in future cases.

Sometimes bargaining fails because the defendant refuses to accept the bargain reached by the prosecutor and the defense attorney. Some defendants see themselves as innocent and balk at admitting guilt; others think the proposed bargain is a bad one. Some kinds of cases simply do not lend themselves to bargains. Most often these are cases that are viewed as very serious, in terms of the offense and the defendant's prior record. In such cases, even a bargain probably would lead to a lengthy prison term. For this reason the defense may see an advantage in going to trial, even if the chances of acquittal seem fairly slim.

Another small but important set of cases go to trial because one or both sides have political goals that are best served by a trial. In trials of defendants with notorious reputations, for instance, the prosecutor is unlikely to bargain because a trial will help satisfy public demands for retribution and allow the prosecutor to obtain favorable publicity. On a more routine level, prosecutors are less likely to engage in bargaining when cases have received heavy publicity, for a bargain might expose the prosecutor to criticism for perceived leniency.[71]

On the other side, some defendants refuse to bargain because they find trials attractive as forums in which to proclaim their political beliefs and perhaps to gain additional support. This is one reason for the general absence of plea bargains in cases arising from arrests of people in antiabortion protests.[72]

Beyond the characteristics of particular cases, many judges and attorneys get satisfaction from participating in at least occasional trials. It is in trials that they can make best use of their legal skills, and many enjoy the trial setting. A prosecutor or defense attorney who is successful in trials gains a stronger bargaining position in the future. But there is considerable variation among individuals in this respect. Some defense lawyers, for instance, look for opportunities to try cases; others do all they can to avoid them.

High-Trial Systems   Trials are relatively common in some courts. These have included, during at least some periods, the felony courts of Los Angeles, Baltimore, Pittsburgh, and Philadelphia. Between the 1960s and the 1980s, for instance, only 30 to 40 percent of the cases carried forward by Philadelphia prosecutors were resolved by guilty pleas.[73] In each of these cities, however, there are relatively few jury trials; rather, trials are generally conducted before a judge alone.

Observers of bench trials in some of these cities have concluded that many of them are perfunctory, in that only a limited defense to the charges is offered. Lynn Mather reported that in Los Angeles, abbreviated bench trials often served the same function as guilty pleas, with prior agreement that the defendant would be convicted of a lesser charge or with a prior commitment by the judge as to the likely sentence.[74] Such a trial has been called a "slow plea of guilty,"[75] and perhaps it should not be classified as a trial at all.

Legal scholar Stephen Schulhofer offered a different perspective on courts that make heavy use of bench trials.[76] Schulhofer concluded from his study of the Philadelphia felony court that bench trials in that court generally are "real" trials, in which the defense makes a significant effort to secure an acquittal. Yet bench trials in Philadelphia tend to be brief, apparently requiring less than an hour in most cases. As a result, lawyers and judges would save relatively little time by plea bargaining rather than trying a case before a judge. Jury trials would be far more burdensome, and judges seek to discourage their use. Most important, judges tend to give defendants who are convicted at jury trials much heavier sentences than they give those who plead guilty or who choose bench trials.[77] As a result, jury trials are uncommon. Observers might disagree about just how "real" bench trials are in Philadelphia, but it seems clear that the Philadelphia court can operate with a relatively limited reliance on guilty pleas only by using speedy bench trials and largely avoiding jury trials.

Attacks on Plea Bargaining

Some participants and observers of criminal courts defend the regular use of plea bargaining. For some of its defenders, plea bargaining is simply a necessity: the system could not function without plea bargains as a means to avoid full-scale trials. But others take a more positive view, depicting bargains as a rational and desirable way to resolve criminal cases. According to one scholar, "Plea bargaining is our predominant method of concluding criminal cases because it is fair and just; happily, it also increases court efficiency."[78]

But defenders of plea bargaining are in the minority. The many critics of widespread bargaining rest their criticisms on different premises. Some oppose it on principle as a departure from the formal model of criminal procedure. As they see it, trials are the fairest means to resolve criminal cases and the best way to reach an appropriate result.

A related argument is that plea bargaining victimizes defendants. In the view of some observers, lawyers and judges put heavy pressure on defendants to give up their fundamental rights and accept bargains. Innocent people are sometimes pressured to plead guilty. But whether they are innocent or guilty, defendants who might be acquitted at trial give up that chance in favor of a bargain that may not be advantageous.

The most common criticism, however, is that plea bargaining allows criminals to escape full punishment. In this view, prosecutors and judges weaken the criminal law by reducing sentences in exchange for guilty pleas. The law loses some of its deterrent effect because the cost of committing a crime is reduced, and the victim and the community are deprived of adequate retribution for criminal acts.

The last two criticisms are not necessarily inconsistent. In one common view, summarized by a New York City public defender, plea bargaining in that city has opposite effects on different kinds of defendants: "The guilty are getting great breaks. But the innocent are put under tremendous pressure to take a plea and get out. The innocent suffer, and the community suffers."[79]

In a number of places, opponents of plea bargaining have secured limitations on bargaining practices. In 1996, for instance, the district attorney in one borough of New York City prohibited charge bargaining after indictment. In 1995, the governing body of the New Jersey courts prohibited judges from accepting plea bargains after the pretrial conference under most circumstances. In 1995, a new prosecutor in Indianapolis barred charge bargaining in felony cases and prohibited plea bargains in cases from some city districts with high crime rates.[80] In 1982, California voters adopted a ballot proposition that established major restrictions on plea bargaining for offenses designated as serious felonies.[81]

In some places, efforts have been made to eliminate plea bargaining altogether. Local courts or prosecutors have established policies of refusing to accept or participate in bargains. The most noteworthy such effort occurred in Alaska. In 1975, the state attorney general, who supervises all prosecutors, prohibited them from bargaining. This action was reinforced by a 1977 state supreme court decision that disallowed bargaining by judges. Both prohibitions remained in effect until 1994, when the attorney general serving at that time adopted a policy that allowed bargaining with some limitations.[82]

A different line of attack, quite widespread in recent years, is the adoption of laws that provide mandatory minimum sentences for certain offenses or that reduce judicial sentencing discretion in general. Often one purpose of these laws is to limit bargaining.

Our evidence on the effectiveness of these measures is incomplete. But the evidence that does exist depicts a complex reality. It appears that some kinds of prohibitions, if seriously enforced, can substantially reduce the incidence of explicit bargaining. But it also appears that plea bargaining has strong survival powers, because of a combination of two powerful factors: the great incentives that people have to bargain and the means that exist to circumvent prohibitions.

The most extensive evidence exists on the severe restrictions on plea bargaining in California and on the effort to eliminate it altogether in Alaska. As described in Exhibit 6.5, the restrictions in California changed the practice of plea bargaining but did not prevent its continuation as a common practice.

EXHIBIT 6.5   Restricting Plea Bargaining in California

In 1982, California voters approved a ballot proposition that was called the "Victims' Bill of Rights." One provision of the proposition stated:

> Plea bargaining in any case in which the indictment or information charges any serious felony . . . is prohibited, unless there is insufficient evidence to prove the people's case, or testimony of a material witness cannot be obtained, or a reduction or a dismissal would not result in a substantial change in sentence.

This provision was presented to Californians as a prohibition of plea bargaining, and undoubtedly most voters who noticed the provision thought that is what they were considering. But the exceptions listed in the provision would seem to provide considerable room for the continuation of plea bargaining if prosecutors wanted to use them. An even bigger exception was more difficult to discern: the provision did not affect plea bargaining prior to indictment or information, while felony cases are still in Municipal Court (they later go to Superior Court). At least some of the sponsors of this provision understood the significance of this exception, but they did not communicate it to voters.

Adoption of this provision had considerable effect on the process of plea bargaining in California, particularly in counties where most bargaining prior to 1982 had occurred in Superior Court. But it did not seem to reduce the incidence of bargaining. Indeed, because of growing court caseloads and other developments, guilty pleas became even more common. The proportion of felony defendants pleading guilty was reported to have increased from 78 percent in 1982 to 90 percent in 1991.

Conceivably, participants in California criminal cases might have used the Victims' Bill of Rights as an occasion to limit their use of plea bargaining. In light of all their incentives to bargain, however, that was never a real possibility in most places. Instead, when the ballot proposition gave them room to continue bargaining at high rates, they did so. So Californians who had thought they were voting to eliminate plea bargaining—or at least to reduce its incidence substantially—did not get what they expected.

Sources: Candace McCoy, *Politics and Plea Bargaining: Victims' Rights in California* (Philadelphia: University of Pennsylvania Press, 1993); Ted Rohrlich and Ed Chan, "Plea Bargaining Thrives Despite Proposition 8 Ban," *Los Angeles Times,* April 20, 1983, sec. 1, 1, 18–20. The data on rates of guilty pleas are from Philip Hager, "Fewer Felony Trials in State Despite a Rise in Caseload," *Los Angeles Times,* September 27, 1992, A1.

The abolition effort in Alaska achieved partial success.[83] The attorney general's 1975 prohibition reduced the incidence of explicit bargaining drastically. But high proportions of defendants continued to plead guilty, largely because they believed that they would receive more severe sentences if they lost at trial. In this sense, explicit plea bargaining was largely replaced by implicit bargaining. Some charge bargaining continued despite the ban, and it became much more common over time. The main reasons for this increase apparently were a reduced commitment to the ban in the attorney general's office and state revenue problems that made the avoidance of trials more attractive. When the attorney general's prohibition on bargaining was rescinded in 1994, one commentator explained that this change was "designed to bring the Department's written policies into line with the actual practices of the last ten years."[84]

Recent efforts to reduce judges' sentencing discretion are discussed later in the chapter. But it should be noted that these efforts have neither eliminated nor, it appears, even reduced plea bargaining. Rather, bargaining practices have been maintained or adapted to fit new sentencing rules.

Thus it appears that plea bargaining is very difficult to eliminate, especially if we define it to include implicit bargaining. The proportion of cases resolved by bargains *can* be reduced, at least under some circumstances, and some courts operate with relatively low rates of guilty pleas. But at least in courts with heavy caseloads, such low rates seem to require the standard use of short bench trials, which achieve some of the same goals as plea bargaining for lawyers and judges. This fact underlines the lesson that people who participate in criminal courts shape court practices on the basis of their own incentives, and efforts to change these practices must take this reality into account.

CRIMINAL TRIALS

Of all the activities in criminal courts, trials receive by far the most attention. In one sense, this attention is undeserved because few cases are actually tried. Yet trials are an important part of what happens in criminal courts. First of all, many cases—including a disproportionate number of the most serious ones—do go to trial. Trials also set standards for other court processes; decisions by prosecutors on whether to bring charges and the terms of plea bargains are both based largely on estimates of what would happen at trial.

Trials merit attention for another reason as well. Much of the criticism of plea bargaining is based on a belief that trials are a better means to resolve the issue of guilt. But comparison of trials and bargains is often based on an idealized version of the criminal trial. Instead, it needs to be based on trials as they actually operate. For that reason, this section focuses primarily on the effectiveness of trials in reaching decisions about guilt and innocence.

The Trial Process

Under the Constitution and Supreme Court decisions, a criminal defendant has the right to a jury trial in cases in which imprisonment of more than six months is possible.[85] Federal courts use twelve-member juries in criminal cases, while two-thirds of the states allow for smaller juries (as small as six) in at least some courts. Most defendants who go to trial in felony cases opt for juries, though the proportion of bench trials varies a good deal from place to place. Bench trials are more common in less serious cases.

In jury trials, the first important step is the selection of jurors. The selection process begins with a pool of potential jurors, who are chosen from sources such as voter registration lists and drivers' license lists. Selection from this pool centers on the voir dire, in which either the lawyers or the judge questions prospective jurors about matters deemed relevant to the trial. A lawyer may ask that the judge dismiss a juror for cause if possible bias or incompetency has been established. Each side also has a certain number of peremptory challenges, which are used to dismiss a juror without showing cause. In felony cases in the federal courts, the government has six peremptory challenges and the defendant ten.

At the start of a jury trial, each attorney may make an opening statement. The prosecutor then presents evidence, primarily through testimony by witnesses; the defense attorney may cross-examine these witnesses. After the prosecution has presented its case, the defense offers its own case in the same manner. Throughout this process, the attorneys may make motions and object to questions or the introduction of other evidence, and the judge rules on these matters. The trial ends with closing arguments by attorneys for each side.

After the closing arguments, the judge instructs the jury on the legal rules that are relevant to the decision. The jury then retires to discuss the case and reach a verdict. (In all but four states, a unanimous vote is required in criminal cases.) Finally, the jury's verdict is announced. If the jury cannot reach a decision, it will be dismissed and a mistrial declared. The prosecutor can then initiate a retrial.

Bench trials are generally simpler, briefer, and less formal than jury trials, primarily because procedures used to select jurors and to aid them in reaching a decision are absent. This difference is highlighted by the extreme example, the speedy bench trials of routine traffic offenses in misdemeanor courts. But both jury and bench trials tend to be brief. Even in federal court, where trials are relatively formal and lengthy, most criminal cases in 1995 required three days or less to try.[86] Some trials extend over several months, but they are exceptional.

The Effectiveness of Trial Decision Making

How effectively do trials operate to produce correct judgments about guilt or innocence? The concept of a correct judgment is a slippery one. In every case, there is a factual reality and a set of applicable legal rules. Occasionally, the law and the facts combine in such a way that they leave the correct verdict uncertain. But in most cases, a decision maker who was omniscient, learned, and objective would invariably reach the correct verdict. The issue here is the extent to which real judges and juries, functioning in real trials, can reach correct verdicts.

Decision Making in Trials   Judges and juries decide cases on the basis of the information they are given. In practice, this information is often both incomplete and inaccurate.

Incomplete information is a widespread problem. In some cases, important evidence may not exist; for instance, there might be no witnesses to a burglary. Witnesses or physical evidence that do exist may go undiscovered. Other evidence may not get to court because of logistical problems.

Witnesses, the primary sources of information in most cases, illustrate the problem of inaccuracy. People are far from perfect in their capacities to perceive, recall, and relate what they have seen and heard. The identification of suspects is especially prone to error. In one experiment, a film of a mugging and a subsequent six-person lineup were shown on a television news program. Of the viewers who called in their identifications after the program, choosing among the six suspects or rejecting all six, 14.1 percent were accurate—about the proportion that could be expected solely on the basis of chance.[87] Other studies of eyewitnesses have also found high rates of error.[88]

Thus a judge or juror may be handicapped by inadequate information. Processing that information to reach a verdict adds further difficulties. First of all, jurors and judges are, in effect, the witnesses of trials, and their recollections too may be both incomplete and inaccurate.

The judge or jury must also analyze the evidence to choose the most credible version of the facts. In some trials, this process is fairly easy, because there is only one credible version. But in trials where several interpretations of the facts are possible, the choice may be exceedingly difficult. For instance, assessing the truthfulness of witnesses is often one critical part of the task. Such assessments are highly prone to error. Summarizing the relevant research, one scholar said that "decisions about whether a statement is the truth or a lie are made about as well as if one were tossing a coin."[89]

For all these reasons, a judge or jury is likely to do a highly imperfect job of ascertaining the relevant facts. Jerome Frank, a legal scholar and judge, summarized this imperfection bluntly: "Facts are guesses."[90]

The final step for a judge or juror is to apply legal rules to the facts—rules that frequently are ambiguous and difficult to apply. Perhaps most important, it is necessary to determine whether the defendant is guilty beyond a reasonable doubt, but the meaning of "reasonable doubt" is murky. The Supreme Court has approved several different explanations of that meaning, and it has also said that judges need not define the concept at all for jurors.[91] Judges' instructions to jurors on the law are often very difficult to understand—or, as one judge put it, "Most jurors cannot understand the pompous language thrust on them by the legal caste."[92]

A decision-making task of high difficulty and ambiguity, such as the task faced by judges and juries in close cases, provides fertile ground for irrelevant information to influence judgments. "In a trial-advocacy lecture," one prosecutor reported, "we were warned never to ask jurors after a trial how they had reached their verdict. Their answers would be too disturbingly unrelated to the facts."[93]

The Impact of the Adversary System   The problems that have just been identified need to be put in the context of the *adversary system,* in which two sides contest at trial, because this system is designed to minimize such problems. Ideally, the trial operates as a kind of marketplace of ideas: if each side presents the strongest possible case, the truth will emerge from the confrontation of those cases.

Unquestionably, the adversary system in practice goes some distance toward meeting this ideal. For instance, the desire of prosecutors and defense attorneys to win cases gives them an incentive to ferret out relevant information. But the clash between the two sides cannot eliminate the inherent difficulty of reaching a correct verdict, and one or both sides may be incapable of presenting anything resembling the strongest possible case.

Moreover, the adversary system has negative as well as positive effects. The desire to make a strong case can cause an attorney to obscure the facts rather than illuminate them or to increase prejudice rather than reduce it. Each side, after all, is not fighting for the truth to emerge; it is fighting to win.

This problem is illustrated by jury selection, in which lawyers work hard to obtain jurors who are inclined to support their side. As one attorney put it, "If we can't get a jury which is biased in our favor, or at least a jury which is biased against [the other side], we will accept an impartial jury."[94] Lawyers traditionally have reacted to potential jurors in terms of their judgments about how characteristics such as age, occupation, or nationality might affect perceptions of a case. Increasingly, lawyers make use of "scientific jury selection," in which mechanisms such as public opinion surveys and focus groups are used in an effort to determine how people with particular characteristics might respond to a case. There is considerable disagreement about the effectiveness of these efforts. Perhaps the most reasonable judgment, offered by one expert on juries, is that jury consulting "clearly isn't a science, but it is an art that might make a difference in some marginal case."[95]

Another example is the defendant's appearance. Defense lawyers often take care to make their clients look respectable and sympathetic. Defendants who can afford "trial consultants" may get advice on such matters as what to wear and how and when to smile. The consultant will tell the defendant to have friends at the trial for the jury to see. "If he has none," according to one account,

> the trial consultant will often pay the law firm's clerical staff about $50 daily (on top of their regular salary), plus a wardrobe stipend, to pose as friends. They sit behind the defendant looking concerned and talk to him during breaks.[96]

Such tactics are understandable, but they have nothing to do with the facts of a case.

The adversary system also affects the testimony of witnesses. Not surprisingly, attorneys prepare witnesses to testify in the manner that will be most favorable to their side. Feeling a stake in the outcome, witnesses generally go along. For instance, expert witnesses generally act as advocates for the side that hires them. This was true of a psychiatrist who testified for the defense against an injured worker; the psychiatrist differed from most experts only in his candor. Asked whether the worker was a "malingerer," the psychiatrist replied, "I wouldn't be testifying if I didn't think so, unless I was on the other side, then it would be a post traumatic condition."[97]

Sometimes, witnesses simply lie. Indeed, some judges view perjury as commonplace. According to a federal district judge in Atlanta, "I think people would be shocked if it were truly known how many witnesses lied under oath in a court of law every day."[98]

Ideally, cross-examination serves to bring the truth to light, but in practice it may create additional problems. According to Judge Rudolph Gerber, "Cross-examination by harassment is one of the greatest impediments to the truth. An all-too-frequent occurrence . . . is the use of insult and innuendo to obscure the truth by obstructing its mouthpiece—the witness."[99]

The adversary system is especially problematic when one side has an advantage over the other in the ability to make its case effectively. One source of such an advantage, of course, is the quality of the attorneys on the two sides. The aphorism that a jury has the job of deciding which side had the better lawyer exaggerates but highlights an important reality: advocacy skills can make a critical difference.

Just as important, one side may have a better opportunity to prepare the case for a trial, a difference that often reflects economics. A prosecutor may have more time and resources to develop a strong case than an overburdened public defender. On the other hand, the rare defendant with access to large sums of money—such as O.J. Simpson or the Menendez brothers in Los Angeles—can afford preparations that go well beyond what any prosecutor could undertake. Of course, the side with the more skilled attorneys and the greater resources for trial preparation does not always win, but it gains advantages that can prove decisive.

Judges and Juries as Decision Makers   Thus far I have not distinguished between judges and juries as trial decision makers. Many people make a sharp distinction between the two, arguing that juries do a bad job of deciding cases. Jury verdicts in well-publicized cases often outrage observers who favored a different result, and their outrage sometimes extends to criticism of jurors' competence in general. In offering that criticism, they enter a long historical debate over the relative merits of judges and juries.

There are several issues in this debate. Critics of juries argue that their lack of experience and expertise puts them at a great disadvantage in assessing the facts of a case and applying the law under the difficult circumstances of a trial. One experienced observer of the criminal justice system reported, "I am coming closer and closer to the conclusion . . . that jurors simply cannot be expected to do what they are required to do."[100] Critics also argue that when the law conflicts with a decision maker's personal sense of justice, a juror is less capable than a judge of adhering to that law. On the other side, supporters of juries see a virtue both in their freshness—unlike many judges, they have not built up an assumption that defendants are guilty—and in their independence from the obligations and pressures that judges may feel. One student of juries has argued that their tendency to follow "commonsense justice" rather than the "law on the books" is desirable.[101]

We know a good deal about the factors that affect jury behavior.[102] One major theme of the research is that jurors in effect modify the law to fit their own sense of equity. They resist convicting defendants under unpopular laws, take the victim's conduct into account in judging the defendant, and consider whether what they perceive to be the potential punishment for an offense is more than a defendant merits. This concern with equity is reflected in the three acquittals of Dr. Jack Kevorkian for criminal offenses based on his assistance in suicides; jurors apparently were willing to depart from the applicable legal rules because they thought it inappropriate to punish Kevorkian for his activities.[103] Another theme is that jurors are sometimes swayed by irrelevant or even illegitimate considerations, such as racial bias. As both these themes suggest, the social and political attitudes of jurors can have considerable impact on their verdicts.

The existing research, however, does not tell us much about the extent to which judges differ from juries in these respects. In one study from the 1950s, judges were asked to compare jury verdicts with those that the judges themselves would have reached.[104] There was a 22 percent rate of disagreement, which the judges ascribed chiefly to jury departures from the law that no judge would have made. Yet these determinations were made by judges who had disagreed with the juries—not the most objective observers. Nor should we assume that judges are highly superior to jurors in their capacity to reach the right decisions.

This study found that juries were considerably more likely to acquit than were judges. More recently, the conviction rate in jury trials seems to have risen substantially, and there is some evidence that juries now are at least as likely to convict as judges. Political scientist James Levine has argued that this change in jury behavior reflects increased public concern about crime.[105] And because of changing attitudes, jurors today may be more willing to convict for some offenses that traditionally had high acquittal rates in jury trials—most notably drunken driving and sexual assault.[106]

These findings do not provide a clear picture of the relative merits of judges and juries. There is some evidence that juries have greater deficiencies as decision makers. But this disadvantage should not be exaggerated. The commentator whose despair at the weaknesses of jurors was quoted earlier also underlined the limitations of judges: "Experience on the bench may teach judicial temperament—even a little law—but I have yet to be persuaded that it sharpens the skills of detecting honest error and conscious falsehood in the renditions of strangers."[107] As suggested earlier, jurors' "amateur" status may have its advantages. And research in social psychology suggests that a multimember body has real strengths in reaching decisions in comparison with a single person. Those strengths may be illustrated by the admittedly unrepresentative case described in Exhibit 6.6. In any event, evidence that takes into account the different mixes of cases heard by judges and juries remains too limited to allow firm judgments.

Some Concluding Thoughts on Criminal Trials   The journalist H. L. Mencken once defined a courtroom as "a place where Jesus Christ and Judas Iscariot would be equals, with the betting odds in favor of Judas."[108] Mencken sought to underline the very real imperfections of trials as means to reach the correct judgments—imperfections reflected in the occurrence of clearly mistaken verdicts in some cases.[109]

In assessing the impact of these imperfections, we should make a distinction between clear cases and close cases. In many trials, the facts and the law are such that one result is virtually guaranteed, and all the imperfections of trials are unlikely to have any effect. In many other cases, however, there is enough uncertainty that the process can have an effect and the wrong verdict may be reached.

The realities of trials should be taken into account in assessing other methods for resolving cases, especially plea bargaining. The weaknesses of plea bargaining must be balanced against the weaknesses of trials, and certainly neither should be idealized. It is a mistake to criticize plea bargaining in comparison with an ideal trial process that always produces the correct verdict. But it is also a mistake to prefer plea bargaining on the ground that it avoids the imperfections of the criminal trial. Since

A criminal defense lawyer is making his closing argument to the jury. His client is accused of murder, but the body of the victim has never been found. He dramatically withdraws his pocket watch and announces to the jury, "Ladies and gentlemen, I have some astounding news. We have found the supposed victim of this murder alive and well, and, in exactly one minute, he will walk through that door into this courtroom."

A hushed silence falls over the courtroom, as everyone waits for the momentous entry. Nothing happens.

The lawyer then says, "The mere fact that you were watching that door, expecting the victim to walk into this courtroom, suggests that you have a reasonable doubt whether a murder was committed." Pleased with the impact of the stunt, he then sits down to await an acquittal.

The jury is instructed, files out and files back in 10 minutes later with a verdict finding the defendant guilty. Following the proceedings, the astounded lawyer chases after the jury foreman to find out what went wrong. "How could you convict?" he asks. "You were all watching the door!"

The foreman explains, "Most of us were watching the door. But one of us was watching the defendant, and he wasn't watching the door."

Source: Quoted from Rodney R. Jones, Charles M. Sevilla, and Gerald F. Uelman, *Disorderly Conduct: Verbatim Excerpts from Actual Cases* (New York: W. W. Norton, 1987), 143.

EXHIBIT 6.6   A Case of an Effective Jury

some of the same weaknesses affect both, and since trials set standards by which plea bargains are negotiated, the two processes differ less in result than they do in form.

SENTENCING DECISIONS

If any single stage of the criminal court process is the most critical, it is sentencing. Most cases that prosecutors carry forward result in convictions, either through guilty verdicts or through guilty pleas. For defendants who are convicted, sentencing is the ultimate court decision that helps determine their fate. From the perspective of society as a whole, sentencing decisions largely determine the pattern of sanctions that actually operates in the criminal justice system.

Formal sentencing power lies primarily with trial judges. Except for cases involving a possible death sentence, only six southern and border states provide for sentencing by juries. Even in those states, juries generally set sentences only in the small minority of cases involving jury trials, and judges have some power to revise jury recommendations for sentences. The federal government and an increasing number of states allow some appeals of judges' sentences,[110] but in most states sentences still cannot be appealed if they are consistent with the applicable statutes.

Sentencing Systems

Congress and the state legislatures each select their own statutory systems for sentencing. The most important difference among these systems is in the amount of discretion that is lodged with two decision makers, the sentencing judge and the parole board that sets release dates for prisoners.[111]

For most of this century, American sentencing systems generally granted broad discretion to judges. They could impose a variety of sanctions, including prison or jail, fines, probation, community service, and restitution. If judges did impose a prison sentence, they were given a wide range of sentence lengths from which to choose for any specific offense.

Most states retain the essential features of these "high-discretion" systems today. In Alabama, for example, a defendant who is convicted of a Class A felony, such as the most serious arsons and burglaries, can receive a prison sentence of ten years to life. In Alabama, as in most other states, a judge can impose probation, under which defendants are free from imprisonment but generally must accept a degree of supervision and some restriction on their activities. In reality, then, the possible sentence for an offense sometimes can range from life in prison to no prison time at all. The actual range is not as great as it appears, because parole systems usually shorten actual prison sentences, but it is still quite considerable.

The freedom held by judges in high-discretion systems is also reflected in the range of alternative sentences and conditions for probation that they can impose. The list in Exhibit 6.7 suggests how far judges' freedom extends by describing some examples of unusual requirements that judges have imposed on convicted defendants.

EXHIBIT 6.7   Examples of Unusual Conditions of Probation Imposed Upon Convicted Defendants

Offense	Condition
Assistance in burglaries	Finishing college
Selling cocaine	Moving out of his mother's home
Child abuse	Not becoming pregnant for four years
Drug offense	Attending church services every Sunday for a year
Manslaughter, armed robbery	Prohibition of "any activity, of any nature, which can generate profit to you for the crimes you committed"

Sources: Peter Morrison, "Sentenced to (Dorm) Life," *National Law Journal,* July 11, 1994, A27; Gail Diane Cox, "Apron Strings Ordered Cut," *National Law Journal,* May 20, 1996, A23; Janan Hanna, "Judge's No-Pregnancy Order Made News, but Ignored Rights," *Chicago Tribune,* January 14, 1996, sec. 2, 5; "U.S Judge Orders Woman to Go to Church for a Year," *New York Times,* February 11, 1994, B12; Garrett Epps, "Free Speech, Even for Kathy Power," *Washington Post,* March 4, 1994, A22.

In recent years, every state and the federal government have amended their sentencing systems in an effort to reduce judges' discretion. (The federal government and five states have also eliminated parole, and other states have reduced the discretion of parole boards.) One widespread approach is to adopt sentencing guidelines for judges.[112] The guidelines may be optional (as in Wisconsin and Virginia) or "presumptive" in the sense that departures from them must be justified (as in Minnesota, Pennsylvania, and the federal system). By one count in 1994, six states have optional guidelines, ten others presumptive guidelines.[113] If they are presumptive, the prosecutor or defendant can appeal a decision that falls outside the guidelines. Systems of presumptive guidelines differ in the extent to which judges can depart from the guidelines if they provide justification.

Another approach, which has been used everywhere, is to set mandatory minimum sentences for certain specific offenses. For instance, Michigan requires an additional two-year prison term for possessing a gun while committing a felony, and New York requires prison sentences for narcotics offenses. A popular variant of mandatory minimum sentences, widely adopted since 1993, is the "three-strikes" laws that typically require long sentences after the third conviction for a serious felony. In states without presumptive sentencing guidelines, these laws are efforts to reduce sentencing discretion selectively within high-discretion systems. Where such guidelines exist, mandatory minimum sentences further limit judges' discretion.

The Sentencing Process

The process by which judges hand down sentences varies considerably, particularly in its timing. Sometimes, most often in misdemeanor cases, the sentence is announced immediately after the trial or the acceptance of a guilty plea. But in felony cases, sentencing generally follows a sentencing hearing, held some time after the trial.

Before a sentencing hearing, the judge typically receives a presentence report that has been compiled by a probation officer. This report contains background information on the defendant, including such matters as prior criminal record and family situation. The report usually recommends whether to impose a prison sentence or probation and sometimes makes a more specific sentence recommendation.

At the hearing itself, the judge usually hears from both the prosecutor and the defense attorney. Defendants are generally allowed to speak and sometimes do so. In some states, the victim of the defendant's crime also may speak. After these presentations, the judge usually imposes the sentence immediately. The judge may offer a brief oral justification of the sentence, but anything more extensive or more formal is unusual.

Sentencing Choices: A First Look

As we have seen, most states give judges a great deal of discretion in choosing sentences. Even in states that limit discretion severely, judges make significant choices. How do they go about making these choices?

To begin with, a judge's real options in any specific case are often considerably narrower than the applicable statute suggests. First of all, judges develop views about the sentences that are appropriate under common circumstances; thus, they may consider only a limited range of possible sentences. Of course, these conceptions of appropriate sentences are affected by their interactions with other members of the work group.

The judge's response to a specific case is also influenced by other court participants. Probation officers have some impact with their reports and recommendations. Indeed, the current federal sentencing system gives considerable importance to the framing of facts in presentence reports by probation officers. Prosecutors are even more important; their recommendations often carry great weight with judges, especially when they have reached a sentence bargain with the defense attorney. In such cases, although there is no compulsion to accept the prosecutor's recommendation, a judge who supports plea bargaining almost invariably does so. Thus it is not surprising that prosecutors sometimes think of themselves as the sentencers. One New York City prosecutor reportedly told a judge that, if the defendant accepted a bargain immediately, "I'll give him a year." The judge bristled at having his authority usurped—and then gave the defendant a one-year sentence.[114]

People outside the work group also seek to influence the sentence in some cases. Judges may receive letters on behalf of a defendant. Police officers often attempt to exert some pressure on sentencing judges. In one New York City case, in which a defendant had wounded several police officers in a gun battle but was convicted only of illegal gun possession, a thousand police officers paraded around the courtroom for almost two hours in a demonstration demanding the maximum sentence.[115] Undoubtedly, these efforts sometimes affect the judge's decision in a specific case. More generally, judges often feel pressure to impose heavy sentences in order to protect themselves from public criticism and possible electoral defeat.

Significant as all these influences are, judges still have considerable control over sentences. The recommendations of other participants and the terms of sentence bargains constrain judges less than it might appear, because both are tailored in part to fit a judge's preferences. Judges, after all, are free to reject recommendations and bargains that they find unacceptable. Besides, there are many cases in which no sentence bargain has been reached. In such cases, judges often have wide ranges from which to choose in practice as well as in law. Finally, only in a small minority of cases do judges feel pressures from outside the court system that are too strong to resist.

Thus judges must make choices, and the task of choosing among alternative sentences is difficult. Sentences can be used to serve any of several goals, including *retribution* (giving offenders their "just deserts"), *general deterrence* (discouraging other people from committing crimes), *rehabilitation* (changing the attitudes and capabilities of offenders so they will not commit more crimes), and *incapacitation* (confining offenders so they cannot commit crimes outside of prison). A judge may support several of these goals but find that they point in different directions. Further, it is often unclear what kind of sentence best serves these goals.

These problems would make sentencing difficult in any case, but judges often have to make choices under conditions that are far from ideal. Time pressures may limit the care with which they can consider a sentence, and they may lack the information that they should have. In 1993, a Georgia judge attracted unfavorable attention when he sentenced a seventeen-year-old first offender to three years in prison for burglary of ice cream bars from a school. The judge later defended himself in part by saying that he had not been informed of the defendant's age or what he allegedly had stolen.[116]

Further, practical problems often make some possible sentences less attractive. Prisons may be overcrowded. Probation services may be inadequate to provide real supervision of offenders. Fines may be difficult to collect; it was reported in 1995 that the federal government collected between 1 and 5 percent of the money it was owed in fines.[117] As a result, judges may feel that they are only choosing among a set of bad alternatives.

If judges are unhappy with their alternatives, many observers of the courts have been unhappy with the choices that judges make. Some of this feeling relates to the general severity or leniency of sentencing. This issue is difficult to assess, because people differ considerably in their views about how severe sentences should be. Two other issues, both fundamental to sentencing, are more amenable to evaluation: the criteria on which sentences are based and the consistency with which they are meted out.[118]

Criteria for Sentences

Judges can base their sentencing decisions on many criteria, either consciously or unconsciously. These criteria include attributes of both the criminal offense and the defendant. Some of these attributes, such as the seriousness of the offense and the defendant's criminal record, are generally regarded as legitimate bases for decisions. Others, such as the race and economic status of the defendant, are almost universally regarded as illegitimate. Still others, such as the defendant's employment status and family situation, are subjects of disagreement.

One critical issue in sentencing is the relative importance of legitimate and illegitimate criteria. Although the evidence on this issue is incomplete and ambiguous, we have considerable information about the impact of some criteria.

Seriousness of the Offense and the Defendant's Prior Record   Most people would agree that sentences should be based primarily on the seriousness of the offense and the defendant's prior criminal record. The research on sentencing indicates that most of the variation in the severity of sentences can in fact be explained by these factors, especially by the seriousness of the offense.[119] Exhibit 6.8 illustrates the significance of the offense in determining whether defendants go to prison and the length of their prison sentences, though there might be disagreement about whether all the offenses are in the appropriate order.

The importance of these two criteria is not surprising. Sentencing statutes virtually guarantee a relationship between the seriousness of offenses and the severity of sentences by setting different ranges for different offenses. The effects of these statutory ranges are reinforced by the consensus among judges and other members of the courtroom work group that more serious offenses call for stronger sanctions. Some legislatures have also established sentencing penalties based on defendants' prior records. Even where they have not, agreement in the courtroom on the relevance of this factor ensures that it will be important.

The significance of this finding should not be overstated, for there is a good deal of variation in the severity of sentences that cannot be explained by offense

Offense	Percentage Sentenced to Prison or Jail (%)	Mean Maximum Sentence for Persons Sentenced to Prison or Jail (months)
Murder	97	238
Rape	87	130
Robbery	88	101
Burglary	75	56
Aggravated assault	72	56
Drug trafficking	75	50
Larceny	65	34

Note: Death sentences treated as sentences to prison, but death sentences and life imprisonment not included in mean sentence lengths. "Murder" includes nonnegligent manslaughter; "larceny" includes auto theft.
Source: Patrick A. Langan and Helen Grazidei, *Felony Sentences in State Courts, 1992* (Washington, D.C.: U.S. Department of Justice, 1995), 2–3.

EXHIBIT 6.8   Sentences Imposed by State Courts in 300 Counties for Felony Offenses, 1992

seriousness and prior record. If illegitimate criteria such as race have an impact on sentences, even an impact overshadowed by that of legitimate criteria, then a serious problem exists.

Race and Economic Status   For those who fear that illegitimate criteria influence sentences, the primary concerns have been race and economic status. Actually, concerns about discrimination by race and wealth extend to every stage of the criminal justice process, from arrest to release from prison. It is widely believed, both by experts and by the general public, that racial prejudice and the advantages of high economic status produce disparities in the treatment of different groups throughout the process.[120] Hence an examination of sentencing addresses only one aspect of possible discrimination in the criminal justice system.

Some trial judges openly express prejudice against defendants who are members of racial minority groups, and this prejudice undoubtedly affects their sentencing decisions. But concerted research has not produced any consensus about the overall impact of the defendant's race on sentencing. Most recent studies have sought to isolate the impact of the defendant's race by controlling for other factors that may influence sentences. Some studies have found significant racial discrimination, while others have not. Thus one recent study concluded that there was no racial bias in sentencing by federal judges in the western Ninth Circuit; another study concluded that black and Hispanic defendants received unduly severe sentences in New York state courts.[121] At least in part, these differences reflect differences in actual sentencing practices. Discrimination appears to exist in some places, for some types of crimes, and for some judges, but not universally.[122]

Discrimination may be related to the race of the victim as well as that of the defendant. This issue has been studied most intensively for capital punishment. In several states, it appears that people who have been convicted of murdering whites are more likely to receive the death penalty than those convicted of murdering blacks, even if other factors relevant to the sentence are taken into account.[123] Though the evidence on nondeath sentences is limited, it also supports the conclusion that crimes with white victims are punished more severely.[124]

On the economic status of defendants, there is reason to think that people with higher status tend to receive more lenient sentences than do people with lower status who are convicted of the same offenses. This result seems likely because higher-status people have more resources to defend themselves and because they are more likely to enlist the sympathies of judges and other participants in sentencing. It is unclear from the existing research whether higher-status people actually obtain lower sentences across the whole range of offenses.[125] But economic status apparently has a decisive impact on the use of one sanction—the death penalty. One defender of capital punishment acknowledged, "I don't know of any affluent people who have been sentenced to death"; a lawyer with long experience in capital cases concluded that "the death penalty is for poor people."[126]

Perhaps the most important issue concerning economic status and sentencing decisions is the treatment of *white-collar crime.* The concept of white-collar crime is difficult to define, but it generally refers to offenses "committed by nonphysical means and by concealment and guile" for economic gain.[127] These offenses, such as embezzlement, mail fraud, income tax fraud, and forgery, are more likely than most other crimes to be committed by people of high socioeconomic status. Corporations can also be charged with white-collar crimes such as price fixing.

Defendants and potential defendants in white-collar cases appear to enjoy advantages in all stages of the criminal justice process, based in part on their economic resources and high social status.[128] These advantages are symbolized by the successful lobbying of large businesses to obtain favorable sentencing rules for federal crimes committed by corporations. As one commentator pointed out, such groups as "drug smugglers" and "bank robbers" were not in a position to engage in similar lobbying.[129]

Prosecutors may also be reluctant to take strong action against people suspected of white-collar crime. The federal Justice Department has been charged with unwillingness to take a strong stand against criminal violations of the environmental laws. In one case, members of a grand jury were so unhappy with a federal prosecutor's decision not to charge individuals with criminal offenses stemming from toxic pollution at a Colorado nuclear plant that they sought unsuccessfully to bring indictments themselves.[130] One Justice Department official tried to justify the lack of indictments with this explanation: "Environmental crimes are not like organized crime or drugs. There, you have bad people doing bad things. With environmental crimes, you have decent people doing bad things. . . . They might lose their house, their car. It will change their lives."[131]

Critics charge that the advantages of white-collar defendants extend to sentencing—that judges treat them with undue leniency, especially if they are well respected or hold high positions. These critics point to cases such as those involving a financier who was convicted of $1.2 million in tax evasion and a banker who looted his company of millions of dollars, neither of whom went to prison; the banker was required only to pay a fine of $30,000 over twenty-five years.[132] To some extent, such sentences can be explained by the high socioeconomic status of judges themselves, which makes them sympathetic toward defendants with similar backgrounds. As one federal judge said of his colleagues: "Probably the most important factor in sentencing in cases of white-collar crime is the empathy factor. Most of the judges in this district are white and middle-class. When they see a white-collar defendant they no doubt say to themselves, 'There, but for the grace of God, go I.' "[133] As suggested by the quotation in the preceding paragraph, prosecutors may share that feeling.

The available data indicate that, on the whole, individuals convicted of white-collar crimes receive lighter sentences than those convicted of other crimes, even crimes that seem comparable.[134] This difference is difficult to interpret because it might result chiefly from factors other than judicial favoritism. For example, white-collar crime by definition involves no violence, and its perpetrators usually have no prior record and appear to be good candidates for rehabilitation. Judges and others generally consider leniency to be appropriate when these conditions exist.

In recent years, there have been some signs that prosecutors are more willing to bring cases and that judges are more willing to impose significant sanctions on prominent white-collar offenders.[135] For instance, New York hotel owner Leona Helmsley was sentenced to four years in prison and fined $1.7 million for tax fraud; the owner of a company found guilty of defrauding government contractors was sentenced to five years in prison and required to forfeit $2.2 million.[136] But critics continue to argue that white-collar crime is treated with undue leniency. "The more you steal, the less time you do," said Ralph Nader, "as long as you do it on the 20th floor."[137] In part, different perceptions of sentencing in white-collar cases reflect disagreements about the appropriate severity of sanctions in such cases.

Consistency in Sentencing

The issue of consistency in sentencing is about whether cases with the same characteristics end with the same sentences. Inconsistencies can arise at three levels. First, patterns of sentencing may differ among courts. Second, judges in the same court may adopt different sentencing practices. Finally, an individual judge may operate with no firm standards, dispensing different sentences in similar cases.

The severity of sentencing varies considerably from place to place, based partly on differences in state laws and partly on the characteristics of particular courts and localities. For instance, people convicted of offenses such as burglary in the South are considerably more likely to go to prison, and those sentenced to prison typically serve much longer sentences, than their counterparts in the North.[138] Such variation might be considered appropriate. But it is difficult to justify variation within a single court, either among judges or in a single judge's decisions.

We do not have a clear picture of sentencing consistency and inconsistency within courts. It appears that the development of going rates in sentencing for particular crimes produces considerable uniformity in the treatment of similar cases. But it appears that a good deal of inconsistency exists as well.

Variation Among Judges   Some sentencing variation among judges on the same court seems inevitable. Judges do not approach sentencing with the same premises; one survey of federal district judges found fundamental disagreements about the importance of various goals for sentencing.[139] And even judges who share the same premises cannot be expected to apply them in identical ways.

Lawyers who handle criminal cases are well aware of sentencing differences among judges, both in general severity and in their responses to particular crimes or types of defendants. Thus, when defendants in a New York federal court had an opportunity to choose the judge who would sentence them after a guilty plea, so many preferred one judge "that they almost needed a reservation."[140]

Comparisons of sentences by different judges support these perceptions. Especially significant are studies in which several judges proposed sentences in the same cases. One study of federal judges in New York and Chicago drew data from sentencing councils in which judges recommend sentences in pending cases. The study found that a group of three judges who independently assessed the same cases agreed on whether to impose a prison sentence only 70 percent of the time. When the three judges did agree that a defendant should be given a prison term, they agreed on the length of the term only about 10 percent of the time.[141] These results provide strong evidence that the identity of the sentencing judge in a case can make a considerable difference.

Inconsistent Judges   A few years ago, a District of Columbia judge advised a group of new public defenders, "Don't go before me at the end of the day. And Friday afternoon is a poor time to have anybody sentenced." A member of his audience later offered his own observations: "Sometimes a trend sweeps through the courthouse and all the judges start hitting harder, as when a high-profile murder has aroused the community; at other times, they all lighten up—around Christmas, for instance."[142]

These assessments suggest that even an individual judge may be inconsistent in responding to similar cases. It is impossible to measure such disparities systematically. Yet inconsistencies in a judge's sentences seem almost inevitable. When asked to apply abstract and often conflicting goals, judges—or anyone else—will find it difficult to do so consistently.

This difficulty is suggested by the behavior of another District of Columbia judge. In the same month, the judge sentenced two people who were convicted of carrying a gun without a license, both with previous related convictions. One defendant received probation, while the other was given a sentence of fifteen years to life in prison. In explaining the difference in these sentences, the judge merely cited his "gut reaction" to the two defendants.[143] We might criticize the judge for his sentences, yet he was probably doing his best to assess the two defendants' prospects for rehabilitation. Whatever his motives, most people would regard the result as unfortunate, and it illustrates the sentencing inconsistencies that can arise in practice.

Sentencing Reform Through New Systems

The available evidence supports a mixed evaluation of judges' sentencing practices. On the positive side, most judges seem to use their discretion well in some respects, giving the greatest weight to factors that most people regard as legitimate. On the negative side, illegitimate factors sometimes affect sentences, and inconsistency seems to be widespread.

These are not the only reasons for criticisms of sentencing systems and practices. Criminologists and others have become disillusioned with the goal of rehabilitation and the resulting emphasis on individualized justice. This disillusion has led to greater concern with retribution and general deterrence, goals that point toward more uniform sentencing for particular crimes. Conservatives argue that judges introduce too much leniency into the criminal law through their sentencing decisions.

These criticisms differ in their implications, but each leads to an interest in reducing the sentencing discretion of judges. As noted earlier, the result has been a widespread alteration of sentencing systems to channel or limit judicial discretion.

Like other institutional changes in the courts, the effects of these alterations are not obvious. For one thing, judges may resist efforts to limit their discretion because they prefer the freedom to make their own choices. By the same token, both judges and attorneys may prefer to maintain sentencing practices that produce what they regard as good results rather than changing them. Further, major changes in sentencing systems can have unexpected effects on sentencing outcomes and on the functioning of the courts. Although the impact of sentencing reforms is uncertain and disputed, we do have some sense of their effects.

Voluntary sentencing guidelines seem to have only limited effects. Reportedly, "few judges" in Denver and Philadelphia "made significant efforts to comply with the guidelines."[144] This lack of response is understandable, because judges and lawyers are unlikely to change their practices substantially when they are left free to continue those practices.

Systems that actually limit judges' discretion would seem likely to achieve a much greater impact. In states with presumptive sentencing guidelines, judges are required to justify departures from the mandated range of possible sentences. Studies suggest that high proportions of sentences are within the mandated range, largely because departures from that range can be appealed and reversed. As a result, variation in sentences for specific offenses has declined. But the decline often is lower than might be expected, in part because guidelines usually leave judges with considerable leeway. The evidence on reduction in unjustified sentencing disparities among defendants is ambiguous.[145]

Mandatory minimum sentences for specific offenses introduce a degree of compulsion, particularly where judges are not allowed to make exceptions. But sometimes judges simply impose a sentence that is more lenient than the minimum required by the law; such noncompliance was found to be common for drunk-driving laws in Indiana and New Mexico.[146] For their part, prosecutors can refuse to charge a defendant with an offense for which there is a mandatory sentence, as they apparently do most of the time under the New York gun possession law.[147]

Washington State was the first to adopt a "three-strikes" law in 1993. Within three years, twenty-one other states and the federal government had adopted similar laws. Judges and prosecutors have some discretion in their use of these laws, and a 1996 study found that—with the exception of California—the states with three-strikes laws had applied them rarely or not at all.[148] This result appears to reflect the availability of other laws to obtain long sentences for habitual offenders and a feeling that the sentences mandated by the three-strikes laws often are inappropriate.

The California law is a stringent one. It doubles the sentence for a defendant con-victed of a felony if the defendant had a prior conviction for a serious or violent felony. On a third conviction, the law mandates a long sentence, most often twenty-five years to life. Prosecutors can decide whether to "charge" a defendant with prior convictions, and their practices differ a good deal from county to county.[149] But enough prosecutors made regular use of the three-strikes law in the first two years of its operation that thousands of defendants received penalties under the law. In 1996, the California supreme court ruled that judges could disregard prior convictions, a change that may reduce use of the three-strikes penalties.[150] One effect of the frequent use of the California law has been a substantial increase in the number of trials, as defendants who face long sentences for a second or third conviction decide to take their chances with juries rather than pleading guilty.[151]

Congress has made two major changes in the federal sentencing system since the 1980s, and together they have had a greater impact than many of the changes in state systems. One change is the establishment of mandatory minimum sentences for more than sixty federal offenses since 1984.[152] Although most of these provisions have never been used, four (three involving drug offenses) have been employed a good deal. And in 1984, Congress created the U.S. Sentencing Commission to write rules for federal sentencing that would narrow judges' discretion substantially. A detailed and complex set of presumptive guidelines became effective in 1987, and a number of amendments have been added since then. The basic structure of the rules is sum-marized in Exhibit 6.9.

Because these two changes are intertwined, the separate impact of each is diffi-cult to ascertain. There is also disagreement among observers as to how the guidelines have worked. But it is possible to reach some tentative conclusions on the basis of the experience thus far.[153]

First, the changes seem to have reduced considerably judges' discretion over sen-tences. Sentences fall within the range established by the Sentencing Commission in a substantial majority of cases because the rules are relatively tight and deviating sen-tences can be appealed and overturned if they have insufficient justification.[154] Judges have complained a good deal about the constraints imposed on them by the commis-sion rules and the mandatory minimums, constraints that they see as requiring them to hand down unjustifiable severe sentences. The Supreme Court may have been influenced by these complaints when it ruled in 1996 that courts of appeals should review sentences departing from the guidelines by a standard that gives some weight to the judgment of district judges.[155] One sign that the guidelines create significant constraints for judges is the substantial increase in sentence severity that occurred after the guidelines went into effect.[156]

Second, the power lost by judges has shifted primarily to prosecutors. Since charges against defendants translate more directly into sentences than in the past, prosecutors' original charges and charge bargains gain much greater impact. Under

1. In imposing a sentence, a district judge must consider the guidelines of the Sentencing Commission, a body established by the statute. Under these guidelines, the possible sentence ranges are based on 43 offense level categories (determined from the offense, adjusted for factors such as the type of victim and the defendant's role in the offense) and six criminal history categories (determined primarily from the number and characteristics of past convictions). For each combination of offense and criminal history categories, a range of possible imprisonment lengths (for instance, 57 to 71 months) is indicated. Other guidelines indicate when probation may be substituted for a prison sentence and the amounts of monetary fines appropriate for each offense level.

2. In each case the judge must impose a sentence within the range established by the Sentencing Commission unless the judge finds a relevant aggravating or mitigating circumstance that the Commission did not adequately take into account. Not ordinarily relevant are such personal characteristics as age, education, employment record, and family and community ties; never relevant are race, sex, religion, and socio-economic status. A judge can depart from the guidelines if the prosecution states that the defendant has provided substantial assistance in the investigation or prosecution of another offender.

3. If the sentence is above the range established by the Sentencing Commission, the defendant may appeal the sentence; if it is below the range, the prosecution may appeal. If the court of appeals finds that the sentence is unreasonable, it may return the case to the district judge for resentencing or amend the sentence itself.

Sources: United States Code, Title 18; United States Sentencing Commission, *Federal Sentencing Guideline Manual, 1995 Edition* (Saint Paul, Minn.: West Publishing Co., 1995)

EXHIBIT 6.9 A Summary of Federal Sentencing Rules Under the Sentencing Reform Act of 1984

the commission rules, prosecutors can have considerable effect through their reporting of case-related facts to judges, particularly the assistance that defendants have provided with other cases. Most sentences departing from the commission's range actually result from prosecutors' motions based on "substantial assistance" by defendants. One commentator said flatly that "prosecutors—not judges—now hold the power over sentencing."[157]

Third, the adoption of tighter rules for sentencing does not necessarily eliminate inconsistency or arbitrariness. Although judges' decisions have become more consistent in relation to the cases presented to them, some inconsistency remains. Additional inconsistency can arise through prosecutors' decisions about which cases to present and in what form. As a result, to take one important example, racial discrimination may continue to exist.[158]

Furthermore, statutes and sentencing rules themselves may incorporate arbitrary features. For instance, drug "kingpins" can come out better than small-time violators because they have more information with which to assist prosecutors and the sentencing rules give weight to this consideration. One mandatory minimum sentence provision, as interpreted by the Supreme Court, causes sentences for trafficking in

LSD to vary by many years depending on the weight of the medium (such as blotter paper) in which the drug is carried.[159]

Most of what we know about state efforts to change judicial sentencing practices suggests the difficulties of securing such changes. The federal experience thus far indicates that these practices *can* be changed. But it also shows that altering judges' behavior does not necessarily eliminate problems in sentencing.

CONCLUSIONS

The widespread effort to change sentencing practices in recent years reflects a broader concern about the handling of criminal cases. Nearly everyone is unhappy with some aspects of what criminal courts do; as a result, attempts at reform are common.

Those who engage in reform often ignore the realities of criminal courts. What courts do largely reflects the goals and needs of people in the courthouse community. As long as these goals and needs remain the same, efforts to alter court practices significantly are likely to face resistance. This is often true of attempts to eliminate plea bargaining and to change sentencing patterns.

These attempts have not always failed. New sentencing rules, for instance, have had considerable impact in the federal courts. Even such successes, however, are not total. And major changes in one element of the work of criminal courts often affect other elements of their work in unexpected—and perhaps undesired—ways.

Thus an understanding of criminal courts is useful for reasons other than mere intellectual curiosity. With this understanding, one can do a better job of evaluating both current practices and proposed alternatives. The lesson is not that people should be satisfied with the current workings of the criminal courts. Rather, we should be careful and realistic in considering what should be changed and how the changes should be made. Otherwise the effects of reforms are most unlikely to meet our expectations.

FOR FURTHER READING

Abramson, Jeffrey. *We the Jury: The Jury System and the Ideal of Democracy.* New York: Basic Books, 1994.

Baldus, David C., George Woodworth, and Charles A. Pulaski Jr. *Equal Justice and the Death Penalty: A Legal and Empirical Analysis.* Boston: Northeastern University Press, 1990.

Finkel, Norman J. *Commonsense Justice: Jurors' Notions of the Law.* Cambridge: Harvard University Press, 1995.

Griset, Pamela. *Determinate Sentencing: The Promise and the Reality of Retributive Justice.* Albany: State University of New York Press, 1991.

McCoy, Candace. *Politics and Plea Bargaining: Victims' Rights in California.* Philadelphia: University of Pennsylvania Press, 1993.

Tonry, Michael. *Sentencing Matters.* New York: Oxford University Press, 1996.

Uviller, H. Richard. *Virtual Justice: The Flawed Prosecution of Crime in America.* New Haven, Conn.: Yale University Press, 1996.

Wheeler, Stanton, Kenneth Mann, and Austin Sarat. *Sitting in Judgment: The Sentencing of White-Collar Criminals.* New Haven, Conn.: Yale University Press, 1988.

NOTES

1. See Henry J. Abraham, *The Judicial Process,* 5th ed. (New York: Oxford University Press, 1986), 21.
2. On "work groups," see James Eisenstein and Herbert Jacob, *Felony Justice: An Organizational Analysis of Criminal Courts* (Boston: Little, Brown, 1977), ch. 2. On "courthouse communities," see Peter F. Nardulli, James Eisenstein, and Roy B. Flemming, *The Tenor of Justice: Criminal Courts and the Guilty Plea Process* (Urbana: University of Illinois Press, 1988), ch. 5.
3. James Eisenstein, Roy B. Flemming, and Peter F. Nardulli, *The Contours of Justice: Communities and Their Courts* (Boston: Little, Brown, 1988), 37.
4. This discussion is based in part on Carol J. DeFrances, Steven K. Smith, and Louise van der Does, *Prosecutors in State Courts, 1994* (Washington, D.C.: U.S. Department of Justice, 1996).
5. Jonathan Casper, *American Criminal Justice: The Defendant's Perspective* (Englewood Cliffs, N.J.: Prentice-Hall, 1972), 135.
6. Bennett L. Gershman, "The New Prosecutors," *University of Pittsburgh Law Review* 53 (Winter 1992), 393.
7. Terry Wilson, "Defendants Fight Odds as Own Lawyers," *Chicago Tribune,* June 14, 1992, sec. 2, 1.
8. John P. Heinz and Edward O. Laumann, *Chicago Lawyers: The Social Structure of the Bar* (New York: Russell Sage Foundation, 1982), 319–333. On private defense lawyers in two cities, see Henry Allen, "A Full Plate of Justice," *Washington Post,* December 5, 1996, B1, B2; and Anne Keegan, "Men of Monadnock," *Chicago Tribune Magazine,* March 3, 1996, 14–20.
9. "Beyond Dumb," *Akron Beacon Journal,* July 24, 1992, D6.
10. Allen Beck et al., *Survey of State Prison Inmates, 1991* (Washington, D.C.: U.S. Department of Justice, 1993), 3.
11. Roger A. Hanson, Brian J. Ostrom, William E. Hewitt, and Christopher Lomvardias, *Indigent Defenders Get the Job Done and Done Well* (Williamsburg, Va.: National Center for State Courts, 1992), 14.
12. Leslie Sebba, *Third Parties: Victims and the Criminal Justice System* (Columbus: Ohio State University Press, 1996).
13. David Heilbroner, *Rough Justice: Days and Nights of a Young DA* (New York: Pantheon Books, 1990), 249.
14. Maurice Carroll, "Wachtler Urges Legislators to Approve Court Changes," *New York Times,* April 23, 1985, B2.
15. Kathleen Maguire and Ann L. Pastore, eds., *Sourcebook of Criminal Justice Statistics 1995* (Washington, D.C.: U.S. Government Printing Office, 1996), 172–173.
16. Don Van Natta Jr., "Judge Assailed over Drug Case Issues Reversal and an Apology," *New York Times,* April 2, 1996, A1, A10.
17. *Haupt v. Dillard,* 17 F.3d 285, 287 (9th Cir. 1994). See Timothy Egan, "A Murder Defendant Is Not Guilty, and Not Satisfied," *New York Times,* April 15, 1994, B10.
18. Chuck Shepherd, "News of the Weird," *The Reader* (Chicago), May 10, 1991, sec. 3, 51.
19. Sources of information for this description include William P. McLauchlan, *American Legal Processes* (New York: Wiley, 1977), 105–123; David W. Neubauer, *America's Courts and the Criminal Justice System,* 3d ed. (Monterey, Calif.: Brooks/Cole, 1988), 26–34; and Barbara Boland, Paul Mahanna, and Ronald Sones, *The Prosecution of Felony Arrests, 1988* (Washington, D.C.: U.S. Department of Justice, 1992), 3–9.

20. *In re Gault,* 387 U.S.1 (1967).
21. Jan Hoffman, "Criminal Court Judges: Vital Unglamorous Role," *New York Times,* January 8, 1996, B12.
22. Deborah Nelson, "Juvenile Injustice," *Chicago Sun Times,* March 22, 1992, 1.
23. Malcolm M. Feeley, *The Process Is the Punishment: Handling Cases in a Lower Court* (New York: Russell Sage Foundation, 1979), 11.
24. Maguire and Pastore, *Sourcebook of Criminal Justice Statistics 1995,* 509.
25. Hans Zeisel, *The Limits of Law Enforcement* (Chicago: University of Chicago Press, 1982), 18.
26. Joan Petersilia, *Racial Disparities in the Criminal Justice System* (Santa Monica, Calif.: Rand Corporation, 1983), 45.
27. Lisa Bastian, *Criminal Victimization 1993* (Washington, D.C.: U.S. Department of Justice, 1995), 3. See Martin S. Greenberg and R. Barry Ruback, *After the Crime: Victim Decision Making* (New York: Plenum Press, 1992).
28. Maguire and Pastore, *Sourcebook of Criminal Justice Statistics 1995,* 425–426.
29. See Celesta A. Albonetti, "Charge Reduction: An Analysis of Prosecutorial Discretion in Burglary and Robbery Cases," *Journal of Quantitative Criminology* 8 (September 1992), 317–333.
30. George F. Cole, *The American System of Criminal Justice,* 5th ed. (North Scituate, Mass.: Duxbury Press, 1975), 323–326.
31. Zeisel, *Limits of Law Enforcement,* 111–112; Richard S. Frase, "The Decision to File Federal Criminal Charges: A Quantitative Study of Prosecutorial Discretion," *University of Chicago Law Review* 47 (1980), 263–265; Celesta A. Albonetti, "Prosecutorial Discretion: The Effects of Uncertainty," *Law and Society Review* 21 (1987), 291–313.
32. Boland, Mahanna, and Sones, *Prosecution of Felony Arrests, 1988,* 35–36. These proportions include what are classified as "witness" reasons.
33. See Toni Locy, "Judges Vow Action Against Intimidation," *Washington Post,* June 24, 1994, D1, D6.
34. Donald K. White, "When Cookies Are OK and VCRs Are a Crime," *San Francisco Chronicle,* August 21, 1985, 28.
35. United States Comptroller General, *Greater Oversight and Uniformity Needed in U.S. Attorneys' Prosecutive Policies,* General Accounting Office Report GAO/GGD-83-11 (1982), 8.
36. Tina Rosenberg, "Deadliest D.A.," *New York Times Magazine,* July 16, 1995, 24, 42, 46.
37. Jim McGee, "War on Crime Expands U.S. Prosecutors' Powers," *Washington Post,* January 10, 1993, A1, A17, A18; Jim McGee, "Misconduct Cases Rise at Justice Department," *Washington Post,* April 23, 1996, A15.
38. Administrative Office of the United States Courts, *Judicial Business of the United States Courts: Report of the Director* (1995) (Washington, D.C.: Administrative Office of the United States Courts, n.d.), 225; Patrick A. Langan and Robyn L. Cohen, *State Court Sentencing of Convicted Felons, 1992* (Washington, D.C.: U.S. Department of Justice, 1996), 44.
39. David Freed, "Plea Bargaining Becomes the Currency of the Courts," *Los Angeles Times,* December 20, 1990, A42.
40. David Lynch, "The Impropriety of Plea Agreements: A Tale of Two Counties," *Law and Social Inquiry* 19 (Winter 1994), 127.
41. This discussion of forms of plea bargaining is based in part on John F. Padgett, "The Emergent Organization of Plea Bargaining," *American Journal of Sociology* 90 (January 1985), 753–800.
42. Alfred Blumstein, Jacqueline Cohen, Susan E. Martin, and Michael H. Tonry, eds., *Research on Sentencing: The Search for Reform,* 2 vols. (Washington, D.C.: National Academy Press, 1983), I, 43.
43. Donald R. Cressey, "Doing Justice," *The Center Magazine* 10 (January/February 1977), 23.
44. E. R. Shipp, "How the Criminal Court Fails: 8 Crucial Areas," *New York Times,* June 30, 1983, B4.

45. Donald J. Newman, *Conviction: The Determination of Guilt or Innocence Without Trial* (Boston: Little, Brown, 1966), 182.

46. Wendy Melillo, "D.C. Landlord Given Nearly 6 Years in Jail," *Washington Post,* September 20, 1995, B1, B6; "Judge Sticks by Landlord's Sentence," *Washington Post,* October 13, 1995, B5.

47. *Commonwealth v. Gordon,* 574 N.E.2d 974, 976 n. 3 (Mass. 1991).

48. Howard Kurtz, "In New York Courts, Next Drug Plea, Please," *Washington Post,* October 8, 1988, A1, A16.

49. Don Nunes, "Acquitted Defendant Faces Years in Prison," *Washington Post,* August 20, 1982, A1, A10.

50. Debra S. Emmelman, "Trial by Plea Bargain: Case Settlement as a Product of Recursive Decisionmaking," *Law & Society Review* 30 (1996), 335–360.

51. David Sudnow, "Normal Crimes: Sociological Features of the Penal Code in a Public Defender's Office," *Social Problems* 12 (Winter 1965), 255–276.

52. Malcolm Feeley, "Pleading Guilty in Lower Courts," *Law and Society Review* 13 (Winter 1979), 462.

53. See Nardulli, Eisenstein, and Flemming, *The Tenor of Justice,* especially ch. 8.

54. James Eisenstein, *Counsel for the United States: U.S. Attorneys in the Political and Legal Systems* (Baltimore: Johns Hopkins University Press, 1978), 178–182.

55. John F. Padgett, "Plea Bargaining and Prohibition in the Federal Courts, 1908–1934," *Law & Society Review* 24 (1990), 413–450.

56. Harold J. Rothwax, *Guilty: The Collapse of Criminal Justice* (New York: Random House, 1996), 145.

57. Feeley, *Process Is the Punishment,* 272 (emphasis in original).

58. Personal communication to the author.

59. Relevant comparative and historical evidence can be found in Milton Heumann, *Plea Bargaining: The Experiences of Prosecutors, Judges, and Defense Attorneys* (Chicago: University of Chicago Press, 1978), 24–33; Feeley, *Process Is the Punishment,* ch. 8; and Lawrence M. Friedman, "Plea Bargaining in Historical Perspective," *Law & Society Review* 13 (Winter 1979), 247–259.

60. Rothwax, *Guilty,* 154.

61. Timothy Crouse, "Plea Bargains: Making a Sweet Deal with Justice," *The Village Voice,* January 17, 1977, 21.

62. Albert W. Alschuler, "The Trial Judge's Role in Plea Bargaining, Part I," *Columbia Law Review* 76 (November 1976), 1089.

63. Jeffery T. Ulmer and John H. Kramer, "Court Communities Under Sentencing Guidelines: Dilemmas of Formal Rationality and Sentencing Disparity," *Criminology* 34 (1996), 396.

64. David Brereton and Jonathan D. Casper, "Does It Pay to Plead Guilty? Differential Sentencing and the Functioning of Criminal Courts," *Law and Society Review* 16 (1982), 45–70; Thomas M. Uhlman and Darlene N. Walker, "'He Takes Some of My Time; I Take Some of His': An Analysis of Judicial Sentencing Patterns in Jury Cases," *Law & Society Review* 14 (Winter 1980), 323–341; Nardulli, Eisenstein, and Flemming, *Tenor of Justice,* 244–245.

65. Martin Berg, "Playing the Chaos Game," *California Lawyer* 12 (August 1992), 37.

66. Jonathan Barzilay, "The D.A.'s Right Arms," *New York Times Magazine,* November 27, 1983, 121.

67. See Heumann, *Plea Bargaining.*

68. Lynch, "Impropriety of Plea Agreements," 120.

69. Eisenstein, Flemming, and Nardulli, *The Contours of Justice,* 31.

70. Sources of information for this discussion include Lynn Mather, *Plea Bargaining or Trial?: The Process of Criminal-Case Disposition* (Lexington, Mass.: Lexington Books, 1979), 142–144; and David W. Neubauer, *Criminal Justice in Middle America* (Morristown, N.J.: General Learning Press, 1974), 286–287.

71. David Pritchard, "Homicide and Bargained Justice: The Agenda-Setting Effect of Crime News on Prosecutors," *Public Opinion Quarterly* 50 (Summer 1986), 143–159.

72. Felicity Barringer, "Abortion Foes Clog Vermont Courts," *New York Times,* May 7, 1990, A9; Steven Pressman, "Cyrus Zal, Missionary-at-Law," *California Lawyer* 10 (March 1990), 17–18, 104–106.

73. See Stephen J. Schulhofer, "Is Plea Bargaining Inevitable?" *Harvard Law Review* 97 (March 1984), 1037–1107. The figure for Philadelphia is on p. 1096.

74. Mather, *Plea Bargaining or Trial?* 55–56.

75. Ibid., 55.

76. Schulhofer, "Is Plea Bargaining Inevitable?"

77. Uhlman and Walker, "He Takes Some of My Time," 323–341.

78. Candace McCoy, *Politics and Plea Bargaining: Victims' Rights in California* (Philadelphia: University of Pennsylvania Press, 1993), xiv.

79. James Mills, *On the Edge* (New York: Doubleday, 1975), 132.

80. Andrew Blum, "'No Plea' Policies Sprout Across U.S.," *National Law Journal,* September 9, 1996, A1, A20.

81. McCoy, *Politics and Plea Bargaining,* 37. See McCoy, "Crime as a Boogeyman: Why Californians Changed Their Constitution to Include a 'Victims' Bill of Rights' (and What it Really Did)," in *Constitutional Politics in the States: Contemporary Controversies and Historical Patterns,* ed. G. Alan Tarr (Westport, Conn.: Greenwood Press, 1996), 128–146.

82. Michael L. Rubinstein, Stevens H. Clarke, and Teresa J. White, *Alaska Bans Plea Bargaining* (Washington, D.C.: U.S. Department of Justice, 1980); Teri Carns, "Plea Bargaining Policy Rescinded by Cole," *Alaska Bar Rag,* March–April 1994, 9, 20.

83. Rubinstein, Clarke, and White, *Alaska Bans Plea Bargaining;* Teresa White Carns and John A. Kruse, "Alaska's Ban on Plea Bargaining Reevaluated," *Judicature* 75 (April–May 1992), 310–317.

84. Carns, "Plea Bargaining Policy Rescinded by Cole," 9.

85. The discussion of rules for jury trials in this paragraph and the next one is based in part on V. Hale Starr and Mark McCormick, *Jury Selection: An Attorney's Guide to Jury Law and Methods,* 2d ed. (Boston: Little, Brown, 1993), 37–55.

86. Administrative Office of the United States Courts, *Judicial Business of the United States Courts (1995),* 364.

87. Robert Buckhout, "Nearly 2000 Witnesses Can Be Wrong," *Social Action and the Law* 2 (1975), 7; reported in Elizabeth F. Loftus, *Eyewitness Testimony* (Cambridge: Harvard University Press, 1979), 135.

88. Brian L. Cutler and Steven D. Penrod, *Mistaken Identification: The Eyewitness, Psychology, and the Law* (New York: Cambridge University Press, 1995).

89. Michael J. Saks, "Enhancing and Restraining Accuracy in Adjudication," *Law and Contemporary Problems* 51 (Autumn 1988), 263.

90. Jerome Frank, *Courts on Trial: Myth and Reality in American Justice* (Princeton, N.J.: Princeton University Press, 1949), ch. 3.

91. *Victor v. Nebraska,* 511 U.S. 1 (1994). See Amy K. Collignon, "Searching for an Acceptable Reasonable Doubt Jury Instruction in Light of *Victor v. Nebraska,*" *Saint Louis University Law Journal* 40 (Winter 1996), 145–172.

92. Rudolph J. Gerber, *Lawyers, Courts, and Professionalism: The Agenda for Reform* (New York: Greenwood Press, 1989), 81. See Shari S. Diamond, "Instructions Frequently Baffle Jurors," *National Law Journal,* June 6, 1994, C1, C7, C9.

93. Heilbroner, *Rough Justice,* 95.

94. *For the Defense,* January 1988, 14; quoted in Gerber, *Lawyers, Courts, and Professionalism,* 114.

95. Reynolds Holding, "New Breed of Advisers Picks Juries," *San Francisco Chronicle,* July 7, 1993, A4; a less positive judgment is offered in Jeffrey Abramson, *We, the Jury: The Jury System and the Ideal of Democracy* (New York: Basic Books, 1994), 145.

96. Lynda Edwards, "Charm School for the Accused," *Mademoiselle,* July 1993, 122.

97. *Ladner v. Higgins,* 71 So. 2d 242, 244 (La. Ct. of Appeals 1954). The case is noted in Charles M. Sevilla, *Disorder in the Court: Great Fractured Moments in Courtroom History* (New York: W. W. Norton, 1992), 81. See also Anthony Champagne, Daniel

Shuman, and Elizabeth Whitaker, "Expert Witnesses in the Courts: An Empirical Examination," *Judicature* 76 (June–July 1992), 7.

98. Mark Curriden, "The Lies Have It," *American Bar Association Journal,* May 1995, 69.

99. Gerber, *Lawyers, Courts, and Professionalism,* 111.

100. H. Richard Uviller, *Virtual Justice: The Flawed Prosecution of Crime in America* (New Haven, Conn.: Yale University Press, 1996), 310.

101. Norman J. Finkel, *Commonsense Justice: Jurors' Notions of the Law* (Cambridge: Harvard University Press, 1995). The quotations are from p. 2.

102. This evidence is summarized well in James P. Levine, *Juries and Politics* (Pacific Grove, Calif.: Brooks/Cole, 1992), chs. 4–8. See also Reid Hastie, ed., *Inside the Juror: The Psychology of Juror Decision Making* (New York: Cambridge University Press, 1993).

103. Edward Walsh, "Kevorkian Critics Left with Dilemma," *Washington Post,* May 18, 1996, A3.

104. Harry Kalven Jr. and Hans Zeisel, *The American Jury* (Boston: Little, Brown, 1966).

105. Levine, *Juries and Politics,* 123–127. On judge-jury differences, see Martha Myers, "Judges, Juries, and the Decision to Convict," *Journal of Criminal Justice* 9 (1981), 289–303.

106. See Kalven and Zeisel, *The American Jury,* 249–254, 293–296. An anonymous reviewer of the manuscript for an earlier edition of this book pointed out this possibility.

107. Uviller, *Virtual Justice,* 242.

108. H. L. Mencken, *A Mencken Chrestomathy* (New York: Alfred A. Knopf, 1949), 623.

109. Martin Yant, *Presumed Guilty: When Innocent People Are Wrongly Convicted* (Buffalo, N.Y.: Prometheus Books, 1991); Hugo Adam Bedau and Michael L. Radelet, "Miscarriages of Justice in Potentially Capital Cases," *Stanford Law Review* 40 (November 1987), 21–179.

110. See Susanne Di Pietro, "The Development of Appellate Sentence Review in Alaska," *Judicature* 75 (October–November 1991), 143–153.

111. Sources of information for this discussion of sentencing systems include Blumstein et al., *Research on Sentencing,* I, chs. 1, 3.

112. See Bureau of Justice Assistance, *National Assessment of Structured Sentencing* (Washington, D.C.: U.S. Department of Justice, 1996); and Richard S. Frase, "State Sentencing Guidelines: Still Going Strong," *Judicature* 78 (January–February 1995), 173–179.

113. Bureau of Justice Assistance, *National Assessment of Structured Sentencing,* 17.

114. Mills, *On the Edge,* 136.

115. William G. Blair, "Larry Davis Gets 5 to 15 Years for Conviction on Weapons," *New York Times,* December 16, 1988, A1, B5.

116. "Judge Defends Sentence for Ice Cream Theft," *San Francisco Chronicle,* September 9, 1993, A9. After a long series of events, the defendant ended up with a sentence that included no imprisonment. Hollis R. Towns, "Ice Cream Caper Thaws," *Atlanta Journal and Constitution,* September 30, 1994, C1.

117. Lauren Frank, "National Fine Center Centralizes Payment Collection," *Judicature* 79 (September–October 1995), 92.

118. See Blumstein et al., *Research on Sentencing,* I, 72–75.

119. Ibid., I, 83–87; Jo Dixon, "The Organizational Context of Criminal Sentencing," *American Journal of Sociology* 100 (March 1995), 1157–1198.

120. See Coramae Richey Mann, *Unequal Justice: A Question of Color* (Bloomington: Indiana University Press, 1993); and Michael Tonry, *Malign Neglect—Race, Crime, and Punishment in America* (New York: Oxford University Press, 1995).

121. William Carlsen, "Study on Sentences Finds No Racial Bias in Western Judges," *San Francisco Chronicle,* August 21, 1996, A3; Clifford J. Levy, "Minority Defendants Handed Harsher Sentences, Study Says," *New York Times,* April 10, 1996, A13.

122. Martha A. Myers and Susette M. Talarico, "The Social Contexts of Racial Discrimination in Sentencing," *Social Problems* 33 (February 1986), 236–251; Stephen Klein, Joan Petersilia, and Susan Turner, "Race and Imprisonment Decisions in California," *Science* 247 (February 16, 1990), 812–816.

123. David C. Baldus, George Woodworth, and Charles A. Pulaski Jr., *Equal Justice and the Death Penalty: A Legal and Empirical Analysis* (Boston: Northeastern University Press, 1990); Samuel R. Gross and Robert Mauro, *Death and Discrimination: Racial Disparities in Capital Sentencing* (Boston: Northeastern University Press, 1989).

124. Ruth Marcus, "Racial Bias Widely Seen in Criminal Justice System," *Washington Post,* May 12, 1992, A4.

125. Stevens H. Clarke and Gary G. Koch, "The Influence of Income and Other Factors on Whether Criminal Defendants Go to Prison," *Law and Society Review* 11 (Fall 1976), 57–92; Blumstein et al., *Research on Sentencing,* I, 110–114.

126. Bob Egelko, "Rich Never Face Death Sentence," *San Francisco Examiner,* August 15, 1994, A2.

127. Herbert Edelhertz, *The Nature, Impact, and Prosecution of White Collar Crime* (Washington, D.C.: U.S. Department of Justice, 1970), 3; quoted in Stanton Wheeler, "White-Collar Crime: History of an Idea," *Encyclopedia of Crime and Justice,* ed. Sanford H. Kadish (New York: Free Press, 1983), 1653.

128. Kenneth Mann, *Defending White-Collar Crime: A Portrait of Attorneys at Work* (New Haven, Conn.: Yale University Press, 1985); Jack Katz, "Legality and Equality: Plea Bargaining in the Prosecution of White-Collar and Common Crimes," *Law and Society Review* 13 (Winter 1979), 431–459.

129. Fred Strasser, "Corporate Sentences Draw Fire," *National Law Journal,* March 12, 1990, 3, 9. See also John C. Coffee Jr., "Big Corporations, Off the Hook," *Legal Times,* May 6, 1991, 22, 26.

130. Sharon LaFraniere, "The Grand Jury That Couldn't," *Washington Post,* November 10, 1992, A1, A4. See Jim McGee, "Environmental Crimes Controversy Still Shadowing Reno," *Washington Post,* April 7, 1994, A25.

131. "DOJ Says House Rocky Flats Report 'Inaccurate, Misleading, Incomplete,'" *Daily Environment Report,* January 16, 1993, A9; quoted in David Burnham, *Above the Law: Secret Deals, Political Fixes, and Other Misadventures of the U.S. Department of Justice* (New York: Scribner, 1996), 69.

132. See, respectively, Robert Kuttner, "Why Do We Send Our White-Collar Criminals to 'Country Club' Prisons?" *Chicago Tribune,* April 13, 1988, sec. 1, 17; and Milton Moskowitz, "Justice Comes in Strange Patterns," *San Francisco Chronicle,* September 6, 1975, 29.

133. Stanton Wheeler, Kenneth Mann, and Austin Sarat, *Sitting in Judgment: The Sentencing of White-Collar Criminals* (New Haven, Conn.: Yale University Press, 1988), 162.

134. Bureau of Justice Statistics, *White Collar Crime* (Washington, D.C.: U.S. Department of Justice, 1987), 4–5; Donald A. Manson, *Tracking Offenders: White-Collar Crime* (Washington, D.C.: U.S. Department of Justice, 1986), 3. See also Robert Tillman and Henry N. Pontell, "Is Justice 'Collar-Blind'?: Punishing Medicaid Provider Fraud," *Criminology,* 30 (1992), 547–573.

135. Bureau of Justice Statistics, *White Collar Crime,* 6–7.

136. William Glaberson, "Helmsley Gets 4–Year Term in U.S. Prison for Tax Fraud," *New York Times,* December 13, 1989, 19; "Write-Off Bid Works; Company 'Executed'," *National Law Journal,* August 22, 1994, A13.

137. Stuart Taylor Jr., "Stiffer Sentences," *New York Times,* May 9, 1985, D4.

138. Langan and Cohen, *State Court Sentencing of Convicted Felons, 1992,* 57–58.

139. Brian Forst and Charles Wellford, "Punishment and Sentencing: Developing Sentencing Guidelines Empirically from Principles of Punishment," *Rutgers Law Review* 33 (Spring 1981), 805.

140. David Margolick, "At the Bar," *New York Times,* December 18, 1987, B6.

141. Shari Seidman Diamond and Hans Zeisel, "Sentencing Councils: A Study of Sentencing Disparity and Its Reduction," *University of Chicago Law Review* 43 (Fall 1975), 118–124.

142. James S. Kunen, *"How Can You Defend Those People?" The Making of a Criminal Lawyer* (New York: Random House, 1983), 37, 106.

143. Leon Dash, "Sentences Tied to 'Gut Reaction,'" *Washington Post,* June 26, 1975, D5.

144. Jacqueline Cohen and Michael H. Tonry, "Sentencing Reforms and Their Impact," in Blumstein et al., Research on Sentencing, II, 417.
145. Bureau of Justice Assistance, *National Assessment of Structured Sentencing,* 82–98. See Lisa Stolzenberg and Stewart J. D'Alessio, "Sentencing and Unwarranted Disparity: An Empirical Assessment of the Long-Term Impact of Sentencing Guidelines in Minnesota," *Criminology* 32 (May 1994), 301–310.
146. H. Laurence Ross and James P. Foley, "Judicial Disobedience of the Mandate to Imprison Drunk Drivers," *Law & Society Review* 21 (1987), 315–323.
147. Francis J. Flaherty, "How 'Mandatory' Are Tough Gun Laws?" *National Law Journal,* February 11, 1985, 3.
148. William Claiborne, "New 'Three Strikes' Laws Rarely Applied, Study Says," *Washington Post,* September 10, 1996, A3.
149. Steven Pressman and Jennifer Kaae, eds., "Three Strikes," *California Lawyer,* October 1996, 33–41, 83–87.
150. *People v. Superior Court,* 917 P.2d 628 (Calif. 1996).
151. William Claiborne, "'Three Strikes' Tough on Courts Too," *Washington Post,* March 8, 1995, A1, A14.
152. United States Sentencing Commission, *Mandatory Minimum Penalties in the Federal Criminal Justice System* (Washington, D.C.: U.S. Government Printing Office, 1991).
153. Michael Tonry, *Sentencing Matters* (New York: Oxford University Press, 1996); Ilene H. Nagel and Stephen Schulhofer, "A Tale of Three Cities: An Empirical Study of Charging and Bargaining Practices Under the Federal Sentencing Guidelines," *Southern California Law Review* 66 (1992), 501–561; U.S. Sentencing Commission, *Mandatory Minimum Penalties.*
154. Marc Miller, "Rehabilitating the Federal Sentencing Guidelines," *Judicature* 78 (January–February 1995), 185.
155. *Koon v. United States,* 135 L. Ed. 2d 392 (1996).
156. Douglas C. McDonald and Kenneth E. Carlson, *Federal Sentencing in Transition, 1986–90* (Washington, D.C.: U.S. Department of Justice, 1992).
157. Marcia Chambers, "Prosecutors Take Charge of Sentences," *National Law Journal,* November 26, 1990, 13.
158. U.S. Sentencing Commission, *Mandatory Minimum Penalties,* 76–82; United States General Accounting Office, *Sentencing Guidelines: Central Questions Remain Unanswered* (Washington, D.C.: Government Printing Office, 1992), 111–142.
159. Jim Newton, "Long LSD Prison Terms—It's All in the Packaging," *Los Angeles Times,* July 27, 1992, A1, A20, A21. The decision was *Chapman v. United States,* 500 U.S. 453 (1991).

7

Trial Courts: Civil Cases

There is a fundamental excitement to criminal cases. The courthouse visitor who wanders into a criminal trial is likely to find drama, even if the trial concerns a relatively minor crime.

In civil cases, by no means is drama guaranteed. Indeed, someone who wanders into a civil trial may find the proceedings positively boring. A dispute over the terms of a contract, to take one example, is likely to be dominated by technical detail.

Yet civil cases have an undeniable importance. Lawsuits for personal injuries involve disputes over billions of dollars each year. The outcomes of civil proceedings determine whether people can be evicted from their homes, whether they are committed to mental institutions, and who gains custody over children. Collectively, civil cases have a far greater direct impact on the lives of Americans than do their criminal counterparts.

The diversity of civil cases makes it difficult to generalize about them. For that reason, much of this chapter focuses on individual types of cases rather than civil cases as a whole. Taken together, the types of cases that are considered in the chapter provide a sense of what courts do and how they operate in civil cases.

In discussing civil courts—shorthand for trial courts in civil cases—I give some emphasis to two issues involving links between courts and the larger society in which they work. The first issue concerns litigation, or the use of civil courts, and its alternatives. Matters that might be taken to court can be handled in a variety of other ways, and only a small minority of potential civil cases actually go to court. Whether or not potential cases go to court can be quite important, because the outcomes of these matters may depend on whether they are resolved in court or elsewhere. Yet the possibility of litigation affects the ways in which problems are handled outside of court; much of the negotiation through which people resolve disputes occurs "in the shadow of the law."[1] Thus an examination of civil courts must take into account actions and decisions outside the courts as well as within them.

The second issue concerns the benefits and burdens that civil courts allocate. Court decisions affect a great many individuals and institutions. For this reason, it makes a good deal of difference who wins cases and who is favored by the legal rules that courts establish. Litigation aimed at winning individual cases and shaping general rules often involves contention between parties of vastly unequal economic resources—for example, injured individuals and insurance companies or debtors and finance companies. We might expect advantaged interests to do much better than the weaker interests with which they contend; the extent to which this result actually occurs is an important concern of the chapter.

Both these issues relate to a central reality of the civil courts: they are the focus of a great deal of political contention. Because civil cases have such high stakes, every group in American society wants a favorable position in court. Ideally, any group—whether manufacturers or labor unions or consumers—would like to have the maximum access to the courts when its members would gain an advantage by using them. By the same token, each group would like to eliminate access to the courts for those who could bring its members into court. In other words, everyone wants the chance to be a *plaintiff,* the party that brings a lawsuit; nobody wants to be a *defendant,* the party against whom a suit is brought. For cases that do go to court, every group wants rules that give it the best possible chance of winning. Groups do not leave all this to chance; they expend considerable effort to gain a favorable position. Thus civil courts cannot be understood in isolation from the larger political process that shapes them.

AN OVERVIEW OF CIVIL COURTS

With civil cases, as with criminal cases, it is useful to begin with a general look at trial courts and their work. This section examines the purposes behind civil cases, surveys the most common types of cases, and discusses the participants and procedures in civil courts.

The Purposes of Civil Courts

People go to civil courts to seek *remedies*—things they are asking the courts to give them.[2] The most common remedy is *damages* to compensate for a loss. The loss may be something concrete, such as the cost of a car repair after an accident, or more abstract, such as damage to a reputation resulting from a libelous publication. Closely related to damages is *restitution,* the return of something belonging to a person such as land or corporate bonds.

Another kind of remedy is *coercion,* in which a party asks the court to require that another party either take a particular action or refrain from an action. The major form of this remedy is an injunction, in which a court orders action such as the halting of a labor strike. The final type of remedy is a *declaration* of legal rights or status, such as the termination of marriage through divorce or a ruling that a statute is unconstitutional.

For what purposes are the courts given the power to provide these remedies? Two broad goals, each tied to a general function of the courts discussed in Chapter 1, underlie this power.[3] The first is *dispute resolution:* the law offers remedies to people who have grievances in order to secure the peaceful and orderly settlement of conflicts. The second is *behavior modification:* the law imposes costs on certain kinds of behavior with the intent of discouraging that behavior.

These broad goals enjoy general acceptance, but more specific issues elicit heated disagreement. For instance, commentators today are engaged in a debate about how well courts do in resolving disputes, and this debate affects policies that give people incentives either to go to court or to stay out. There is even more contention about what kinds of behavior the law should discourage and how it should do so.[4] In order to prevent drunken driving, should party hosts and bartenders be held liable for damage caused by drivers to whom they have served excessive amounts of alcohol? Should people injured by defective products be able to obtain extra, "punitive" damages if a company has acted irresponsibly in making a product, so that companies have a stronger incentive to make safe products? Not surprisingly, both issues have been the subject of considerable conflict.

These and other issues about the availability of legal remedies are resolved in part by legislatures through statutes. But the courts play a major role by interpreting these statutes, which often are ambiguous in their application to specific situations. In some areas of law, called "common law" fields, appellate courts have been primarily responsible for establishing legal rules, with legislatures intervening only to a limited degree. Thus, for example, the rules about when people must be compensated for personal injuries have been determined chiefly by court decisions. Not surprisingly, on many issues the law varies a great deal from state to state. For instance, in some states, landlords have a legal duty to provide reasonable protection against crime to their tenants, but in other states they do not. Of course, the legal rules that exist in any state at a given time reflect the political processes that shape every aspect of the civil courts.

Major Types of Civil Cases

Among the wide range of cases handled by civil courts, some occur much more frequently than others. The preponderance of cases fall into four categories.

Contract cases arise when one party to a contract claims that the other party has violated its terms. Such cases can involve the whole array of agreements that exist in our society. But most are brought by businesses against individuals on the basis of contracts for the sale or rental of goods and services or for the lending of money. In these cases, the business alleges that it has not received the money owed to it and seeks restitution in the form of direct payment or through some other means, such as the foreclosure of a mortgage on property. I refer to this kind of contract case as *debt collection.*

Personal injury, property damage, and wrongful death cases can be lumped together under the heading of *personal injury* cases. In turn, personal injury cases constitute the largest part of the field called tort law. In these cases, the party who has suffered a loss seeks damages in compensation. Personal injury cases typically result from accidents, which can be triggered by everything from the use of a household product to the receipt of medical care. The majority of these cases arise from accidents involving motor vehicles.

Domestic relations cases concern marriage and matters related to it. Courts provide the administrative service of granting marriage licenses and performing marriages. Even if we leave this service aside, the work of trial courts in domestic relations is still sizable. Most of this work concerns divorce: awarding divorces, determining child custody, and allocating economic resources between the former wife and husband.

Finally, most *estate* cases concern the assets of people who have died. In these cases, courts supervise the administration of wills and handle the estates of people who have died without wills. Also in this category are guardianships for people who are declared mentally incompetent to handle their own affairs.

These four types of cases all come under the heading of private law. Only a small minority of civil cases can be considered public law, which involves the government acting as government. But the number of public law cases is growing with the scope of government activity. Because public law cases are more prominent at the appellate level, they are discussed primarily in Chapters 8 and 9.

Public law cases are likely to go to federal court. But the great majority of all civil cases are handled in state courts. For that reason this chapter, like the preceding one, focuses chiefly on the state level. The processes involved in civil litigation are similar at the state and federal levels, and I generally do not distinguish between the two sets of courts.

Participants in Civil Courts

As in criminal courts, the most important participants in civil courts are lawyers and judges. In both settings, they are the core of the courtroom work group. Another similarity is that the closeness of the relationships among these people depends on the regularity with which a set of lawyers comes before a particular judge. Thus, in rural courts and in courts (and court divisions) that handle a narrow range of civil cases, a judge may deal frequently with a relatively small group of lawyers. In urban courts with a broad jurisdiction, judges may encounter a much larger group of lawyers, and close working relationships are less likely to develop.

Judges   The great majority of judges spend at least part of their time hearing civil cases. Many judges sit on courts that hear only civil cases. Some specialize more narrowly, serving permanently on courts or divisions that handle only probate, domestic relations, or bankruptcy cases.

In most respects, the powers and responsibilities of judges in civil cases are similar to those in criminal cases. One difference is the greater frequency of bench trials compared with jury trials in civil cases. In federal district courts, 45 percent of all civil trials in 1995 were before judges, as against only 20 percent of criminal trials.[5] This difference, of course, increases the judge's role as a decision maker. Another difference is that judges participate in negotiations between civil parties more often than they do in plea bargaining. But unlike criminal litigants who must await the judge's sentencing decision, civil parties who settle out of court ordinarily determine the specific terms of the settlement themselves.

Attorneys   As in criminal cases, attorneys usually appear in civil cases with greater than minimal stakes. In many areas of law, the lawyers who participate in cases are primarily specialists in those areas. But in common and nontechnical areas, such as estates, much of the work is done by lawyers who are not specialists. This is particularly true outside of big cities.

Some areas of law on the civil side resemble criminal law in the sense that lawyers specialize by the "side" they represent. For example, in areas that pit the government against private parties, such as taxes and economic regulation, the government is represented by its own full-time employees, while private attorneys serve private parties on a permanent or case-by-case basis. In areas that typically involve conflicts between businesses and individuals, such as debt collection and personal injury cases, the attorneys who represent businesses generally are a separate group from those who represent individuals. In some other areas, however, most lawyers work on both sides. For instance, a divorce lawyer is likely to represent both husbands and wives.

Parties   Civil cases pit plaintiffs against defendants. Cases often have multiple plaintiffs, defendants, or both. Under some conditions a case may be brought as a class action, in which one or more people sue on behalf of a larger set of people who share the same situation. A common example is consumers who allege that they were overcharged for a product.

The parties to civil cases can be classified in several ways, but three related distinctions are especially important. One is the obvious distinction between individuals and organizations, primarily businesses and governments. A second, made by Marc Galanter, is between "one-shotters," or "those claimants who have only occasional recourse to the courts," and "repeat players . . . who are engaged in many similar litigations over time."[6] (Typical repeat players include insurance companies, finance companies, and some government agencies.) Galanter has also distinguished among litigants by their economic status, dividing them into "haves" and "have-nots." These classifications are linked, in that organizations tend to be repeat players and to have substantial economic resources, while individuals tend to be one-shotters and to possess fewer resources.

Galanter argues that the haves generally "come out ahead" in litigation.[7] Most obviously, and perhaps most importantly, they can afford more and better legal services. This advantage is related to the distinction between the corporate and personal sectors of the bar that was discussed in Chapter 3. On the whole, the lawyers who represent businesses and governments can provide better services to their clients than can those who represent individuals.

Further, haves are repeat players far more often than have-nots, and repeat player status itself confers some advantages over one-shotters. One major advantage is the ability of repeat players to structure transactions in ways put themselves in a favorable position if disputes result. For instance, a lease for an apartment within a large complex typically is written by lawyers for the company that owns the complex, and its terms favor that company in disputes with renters. Exhibit 7.1 describes the advantages gained by one set of repeat players, the owners of cruise lines, in their agreements with passengers.

Repeat players also can make choices in specific cases that help them in future cases. It is common for companies that have been sued for defective products to reach settlements that forbid the plaintiffs from sharing information they have gained about the products in question. Post-trial settlements are sometimes conditioned on a plaintiff's agreement to join the defendant in a motion to the court for "vacatur," which causes a decision that favored the plaintiff effectively to disappear. A legal scholar who studies vacatur has said that it is used primarily by parties such as insurance

The cruise line industry operates under long-standing principles of law that put it in an advantageous position. For instance, a passenger who receives substandard medical care from a ship's doctor cannot sue the cruise line, since these doctors are treated as independent contractors rather than employees.

Cruise lines seek to increase their advantage with the provisions they write on their tickets. A line may designate the country whose laws would apply to a dispute with a passenger, choosing the country with the most desirable rules from its perspective. Cruise lines also designate the place in which any legal dispute must be adjudicated, often choosing the country in which its ship is registered. Courts have upheld provisions that, for instance, require American passengers who bought their tickets from an American company to bring any lawsuit in Italy.

A ticket from one cruise line contained twenty-five "terms and conditions" in fine print, many of them highly advantageous to the line. A prospective passenger who objected to those provisions would have little recourse, since—under paragraph 16(a) of the terms and conditions—the ticket was nonrefundable once it was purchased by the passenger. One of the clauses required that any disputes be litigated in Florida; when a passenger challenged that requirement, the Supreme Court upheld it.

Sources: Thomas A. Dickerson, "Laws Leave Passengers Shipwrecked," *National Law Journal*, May 29, 1995, B9, B11, B12; *Hodes v. S.N.C. Achille Lauro ed Altrigestione*, 858 F.2d 905 (3d Cir. 1988); *Carnival Cruise Lines v. Shutts*, 499 U.S. 585 (1991).

EXHIBIT 7.1   Structuring of Transactions by Cruise Lines

companies and governments, "repeat players" that "have a stake not just in a particular case but in controlling the law as it develops."[8]

Galanter's analysis leads to predictions about the outcomes in civil cases that pit different types of parties against each other. In most debt collection cases, for example, merchants and financial institutions sue low-income individuals. In most personal injury cases, individuals sue defendants who are represented by insurance companies. On the basis of Galanter's arguments, we would expect the organizational parties in these cases—as repeat players and haves—to win most of what they seek. The last section of this chapter examines the evidence on these predictions.

Other Participants   Of the other participants in criminal courts, some—such as witnesses and court clerks—play similar roles in the civil courts. Law enforcement officers are far less important, although they often serve as witnesses in auto accident cases. Grand jurors and probation officers, of course, are absent altogether.

As noted earlier, trial juries are less common in civil cases than in criminal cases. When a jury does appear, its position is somewhat different from that of the criminal jury. In suits for damages, civil court juries determine the amount to be paid if they find the defendant liable. Thus they exercise the equivalent of the judge's sentencing power in criminal cases. But the trial judge has more power in civil cases to override a jury's verdict or to take a decision away from a jury.

A Summary of Court Procedures

Both formal and actual procedures for civil cases vary a good deal. The basic and most common set of procedures is the one ordinarily used in suits for damages and restitution. I focus on those procedures, discussing other sets of procedures more briefly.[9]

The Basic System   In a typical set of procedures for civil cases, as shown in Exhibit 7.2, court action begins with the filing by the plaintiff of a *complaint* making legal allegations against the defendant. (For the sake of simplicity, I assume that the case has only a single plaintiff and a single defendant.) The next step is notification of the defendant, called *serving process*. The defendant may then file an *answer* to the complaint. This answer offers defenses to the complaint, and it may also make counterclaims against the plaintiff—in effect, making the plaintiff a defendant as well. The complaint and the answer are called the *pleadings*.

A series of pretrial procedures follows the pleadings. In *discovery,* the parties gather evidence from each other, primarily in three forms. The first is *depositions,* in which the lawyer for one side questions the other party and the witnesses for the other side. The second is *interrogatories,* in which one party presents questions to the other party for more extensive written responses. The third is the *discovery of documents and other materials* held by the other party. The judge does not supervise discovery directly but settles any disputes that may arise at this stage.

Discovery is intended to eliminate the surprise element at trial, but in the process it has developed its own problems. Lawyers sometimes seek to wear down their opponents through extensive and costly discovery demands and through abusive questioning of witnesses at depositions. In one case, the Delaware Supreme Court strongly condemned as "outrageous and unacceptable" the conduct of a lawyer who heaped abuse on the opposing attorney at the depositions in the case.[10] Parties sometimes fail to provide documents that are sought in discovery. In a case in Washington State, two documents that were critical to the case and that had not been produced in discovery

EXHIBIT 7.2   **Typical Stages of the Processing of Civil Suits for Damages or Restituion**

1. Filing of a complaint by the plaintiff
2. Serving of process on the defendant
3. Filing of an answer to the complaint by the defendant
4. Discovery of evidence: depositions, interrogatories, and discovery of materials
5. Pretrial conference and order
6. Trial
7. Verdict on liability and (where liability is found) the remedy
8. Post-trial motions: for a judgment notwithstanding the verdict, to set aside the verdict
9. Compliance with or enforcement of the judgment

came to light only when someone anonymously sent them to the lawyer on the other side.[11]

After discovery is completed, the judge may schedule a *pretrial conference* with the parties. In some courts, the conference is mandatory. During the conference, the judge seeks to clarify the issues in the case and ready it for trial. Afterwards, the judge makes up a pretrial order listing the evidence that the parties will present.

Like criminal cases, civil cases can drop out along the way to trial. The plaintiff can dismiss the case voluntarily, perhaps because of a perception that a favorable outcome is unlikely or because filing the lawsuit was a symbolic action to express anger or dissatisfaction.[12] Frequently, the parties reach a settlement out of court. Typically, judges accept such settlements. One reason is that civil settlements have the same advantages for judges as criminal plea bargains: in particular, they save time and trouble. And in most cases judges feel that settlements involve only the interests of the two sides; if *they* are satisfied, the matter is resolved.

But judges occasionally reject settlements when they think that all relevant interests are not served. In a few cases, judges have rejected settlements of class action suits, concluding that the rejections serve the defendants and the plaintiffs' lawyers well but do little for the plaintiffs themselves. In 1995, a federal district judge rejected a proposed settlement of the government's antitrust suit against the Microsoft Corporation, based on a statute requiring that any settlement by the government in an antitrust case be in "the public interest." Four months later, however, a court of appeals overruled the district judge—and took him off the case on the ground that he had given the appearance of bias.[13] That action symbolizes the general tendency of courts to approve settlements that the parties find acceptable.

Sometimes the judge reaches a decision in the case before it comes to trial. The judge may dismiss the case because of the plaintiff's failure to pursue it adequately. Similarly, the judge may issue a *default judgment* against the defendant for failure to file an answer or to meet other procedural requirements. Either party may also ask for a *judgment on* the basis of *the pleadings,* which the judge can grant if the other party has failed to make sufficient allegations to support a case. And the judge can grant a *summary judgment* to one party on the ground that there are no genuine issues of fact and that the law compels a decision in favor of that party.

In most areas of the law, the great majority of cases do drop out prior to trial. One study examined tort, contract, and property cases in major trial courts in the country's seventy-five largest counties in 1992. Of all cases, 62 percent were settled by the parties prior to trial, 11 percent were dismissed, and 18 percent were resolved through a default judgment or summary judgment. Of the civil cases resolved in federal district courts in 1995, only 3 percent reached trial.[14]

The trial itself resembles a criminal trial. As it proceeds, the plaintiff seeks to prove the defendant's liability and the appropriateness of the desired remedy. In response, the defendant may contest either or both issues; on the remedy, the question usually is the amount of money to be paid in damages if liability is found. The standard of proof for liability generally is a *preponderance of the evidence,* a standard that is easier to meet than the proof beyond a reasonable doubt required of criminal prosecutors.

During a jury trial, the judge may grant a *directed verdict* in favor of one party at the close of the other party's case, on the ground that the evidence allows only one outcome. If there is no directed verdict, the judge or jury decides the contested issues after the trial. Where damages or restitution are to be provided, the amount is determined.

After a jury decision, the losing party can ask the judge for what is called a *judgment notwithstanding the verdict,* on the ground that there was insufficient basis for the jury's decision. A party can also ask the judge to set aside the verdict and order a new trial on the basis of problems in either the trial or the verdict.

If the court's judgment requires one party to provide a remedy to the other, that party may comply readily with the judgment. If voluntary compliance does not occur, the winning party can seek enforcement of the judgment by the sheriff or another official through a variety of methods, including garnishment (a process in which an employer withholds part of the losing party's wages and turns it over to the winning party) and the forced sale of the loser's property to pay the judgment.

Cases may take a long time to go through these stages. At an extreme, a 1990 study found that litigants in Los Angeles waited an average of five years from filing to a jury trial.[15] Some cases require even more time for resolution. A Florida divorce case filed in 1966 was finally resolved by a trial court in 1993. A suit by a Virginia bar against a college student that stemmed from their dispute over a five-dollar tab was finally resolved after fourteen years, though the student's own lawsuits against the bar and its lawyer continued.[16]

Other Sets of Procedures   In civil cases with small stakes, as in similar criminal cases, formal procedures can be relatively simple. This is particularly true of small claims courts, which are usually special divisions of trial courts designated to hear cases in which plaintiffs seek relatively small amounts of money or (in some states) such remedies as evictions. A significant proportion of all civil cases, about 20 percent in one survey of four states,[17] are heard under small claims procedures.

Small claims courts were created to handle cases at relatively little expense to the parties and with less delay than in other civil courts. In line with these goals, small claims courts operate under specially simplified procedural rules. Pretrial procedures are shortened and simplified, and trials are held before judges with considerable informality. Often lawyers do not even participate in the proceedings. Indeed, some small claims courts prohibit their appearance.

Cases in which the plaintiff seeks a coercive remedy are handled under a different set of procedures, which can be illustrated with injunctions. Prior to trial the plaintiff may ask for a *temporary restraining order,* sometimes without giving notice to the defendant. Later the plaintiff may seek a *preliminary injunction,* which the defendant can contest. Both are intended to prevent the defendant from taking irreversible action, such as demolishing a building. The trial itself, in which the plaintiff seeks a permanent injunction, is held before a judge alone. In many cases, it is relatively short because much of the relevant evidence was presented in the pretrial hearings. If an injunction is awarded, it can be enforced with a motion to hold a noncomplying party in contempt of court. If a judge holds that party in contempt, the judge can impose a fine or prison sentence.

Cases involving divorces and the estates of deceased people have their own procedures as well. In both categories, most cases are uncontested: for example, nobody disputes a will, or a husband and wife both want a divorce and agree on the terms of the settlement. Such cases must go to court for approval of the uncontested action, but the hearings are generally routine and abbreviated. Of course, when divorce and estate cases are contested, they must go through adversarial proceedings before a judge.

DECIDING WHETHER TO LITIGATE

Of all the images that people hold of Americans, one of the strongest is that we are a litigious people. In this image, people in the United States—or at least a great many people—look eagerly for opportunities to file lawsuits. Trivial or nonexistent injuries turn into claims for large amounts of money. This eagerness has grown enormously over the years, resulting in a litigation "explosion." The courts themselves have encouraged this explosion by awarding damages in highly questionable circumstances. The result has been considerable damage to the American economy and American society: billions of dollars each year are drained from productive use to pay legal costs, companies stop making useful products to avoid potentially disastrous lawsuits, and everyone suffers.

This section considers the accuracy of that image: to what extent can it be said that Americans are litigious, and how much of a litigation explosion is actually occurring? But before those questions can be addressed directly, we need to take a broader look at decisions whether to engage in litigation.

As individuals or members of organizations, people often decide whether to take cases to court—that is, to litigate. These decisions emerge from situations in which a person develops a grievance or recognizes an opportunity that might be handled through litigation.

In such situations, people may do nothing at all, choosing to live with the grievance or to forgo the opportunity, or they may choose to take action in some form other than litigation. But they might decide to go to court, either as a first action or after trying one or more alternatives. Going to court itself involves two steps: filing a lawsuit and taking a case to trial. Although both steps are important, the second is the more decisive, for it means that the parties are putting their dispute before a court rather than settling it in another forum.

Some Types of Litigation

The considerations that influence litigation decisions and the decision process itself vary from one area of the law to another. To provide some sense of how people make litigation decisions, I explore three somewhat different areas: discrimination, personal injuries, and disputes between businesses.

Discrimination   Discrimination cases are much less common than some other categories of litigation, but this area tells a good deal about conditions that affect whether potential cases go to court. When commentators speak of today's Americans as litigious, they sometimes use discrimination claims to illustrate their arguments. Such references have some support in reality, in that the volume of discrimination cases has grown rapidly. To take one example, the number of employment discrimination cases filed in federal court tripled between 1980 and 1995.[18]

Yet the discrimination cases that come to court constitute only a small fraction of those that might be brought. One survey identified people who felt that they had been the victims of discrimination in such areas as employment, education, or housing. Of these people, fewer than three in five complained about the matter, fewer than one in thirty hired a lawyer, and fewer than one in a hundred filed a lawsuit.[19] In a 1990 survey, 10 percent of those who recalled an incident of employment discrimination had complained to a government agency, and 2 percent consulted an attorney or filed a lawsuit.[20]

This pattern of behavior appears to have several sources.[21] One is lack of knowledge about how to proceed in a discrimination case. Because the legal remedies are not well publicized, many people do not know what action they can take if they are denied an apartment or a job and feel that the denial was discriminatory. As a result, they may simply live with their grievance.

Second, it is generally difficult to get favorable legal action on discrimination complaints. Discrimination in such matters as hiring of employees and rental of housing is often difficult to prove in court. The administrative agencies that handle discrimination problems, either by taking cases to court themselves or by helping complainants, typically have limited legal powers and inadequate staffing. In turn, the difficulty of getting favorable action and adequate fees discourages lawyers from representing complainants, who often find it difficult to obtain representation.[22] And those who are charged with discrimination frequently resist complaints rather than trying to satisfy the complainant, because they see themselves as blameless and because the prospects of unfavorable court action are limited.

Finally, seeking to redress discrimination entails costs, and these costs are especially high when the action extends to litigation. Some costs are monetary, such as paying for the services of a lawyer who will not take a case on a purely contingent basis. Other costs are psychological. To press a discrimination claim is to become involved in a conflict, to be identified as a complainer, and to live with uncertainty. Such problems are especially serious when people complain of discrimination by those with whom they must continue to deal, such as employers and school administrators. In these cases, to put it mildly, a lawsuit can lead to strained relations. A successful lawsuit hardly mends such frayed connections. According to one consultant on employment discrimination, "Most of the women I know who have filed these suits say they would never do it again."[23]

Despite all these difficulties, people bring a good number of discrimination cases to the courts—primarily to federal courts. But these cases are only a fraction of the cases that could be brought.

Personal Injuries   People frequently experience physical injuries or damage to their property as a result of mishaps. Any incident that produces a significant physical injury or costly property damage might seem likely to go to court. One reason is that the party who could sue and the party who could be sued (the other driver, for example, or the manufacturer of a product) are generally strangers, thus reducing greatly the element of personal conflict.

Furthermore, most people are aware that they have legal remedies for personal injuries, and a potential plaintiff who has a strong case involving a substantial amount of money can usually find a lawyer who is willing to take the case on a contingent fee basis. Advertising by attorneys helps to publicize remedies and identifies lawyers who might take a case. And lawyers increasingly make direct contact with people who have been involved in accidents.

Considerable litigation does arise from personal injuries. Yet this litigation, like litigation over discrimination, represents only a very small proportion of the cases that could have gone to court. One of the studies cited in the discussion of discrimination found that, in torts involving $1,000 or more, 3.8 percent actually resulted in court filings.[24] A study of accidental injuries that caused restricted activity or doctor visits found a 2 percent rate of filing.[25]

The processes that keep potential cases out of court differ with the type of personal injury, and automobile accidents and medical malpractice provide two contrasting examples. After auto accidents, at least a large minority of people who suffer significant physical injuries or property losses make claims against the party they see as responsible.[26] But auto accident claims ordinarily are resolved before a lawsuit is filed. (Some states have "no-fault" systems that restrict lawsuits for relatively minor claims based on auto accidents, but suits are the exception to the rule in other states as well.)

The potential defendant in these cases is the party that allegedly caused the injury, but any settlement or court judgment would ordinarily be paid by that party's insurance company. Thus the claim quickly becomes one against the insurance company, which takes over for its client in handling the case. Insurance companies generally want to settle claims quickly, in part because they prefer to reach an agreement with an injured party who has not yet hired an attorney.

Insurance companies frequently succeed in securing early agreements, largely because people who have suffered injuries or property damage also wish to settle their cases quickly. These settlements usually involve payments to the injured party, although the adjuster sometimes convinces that party to accept the lack of a payment and take no further action.

If the two sides do not reach an easy settlement and the injured party remains dissatisfied, more often than not that party will hire an attorney. In one study of bodily injury claims, 55 percent of all injured parties eventually used a lawyer.[27] Although this step escalates the conflict to a degree, it also facilitates a settlement. The lawyers who represent injured parties are usually experienced in personal injury cases; indeed, they are often specialists in that area. On the other side, the insurance company's adjusters or attorneys are also specialists. Thus, as in plea bargaining, the two sides share an understanding of how to negotiate these cases. Another similarity is that the two sides share a degree of agreement on the general terms for settlements of common types of cases, terms that are shaped by the participants' predictions of what would happen if the case were brought to trial.

In a substantial minority of cases, the lawyer for the injured party eventually files suit, and serious negotiations may not occur until the scheduled trial date is close. But the two sides can usually reach a mutually agreeable settlement at some point. This success is facilitated by the experience and expertise of most negotiators and by some of the same conditions that help produce successful plea bargaining. One is that both sides want to avoid the risks of a trial—in which an insurance company might be required to pay high damages or an injured party might lose and collect nothing. Another is that both insurance companies and lawyers who represent injured parties want to avoid spending the time that is required to take cases to trial. In cases based on bodily injuries in auto accidents, a study found that 18 percent of all claims led to lawsuits, but only 1 percent of the claims actually went to trial—and half of those were settled before a verdict.[28]

The cases that do go to trial are not a representative sample of all auto accidents. Rather, as one study shows, they tend to involve conditions that make negotiated settlements relatively difficult or unattractive.[29] One example is cases in which the damages are serious but the liability issue seems favorable to the defendant. In such a case, the insurance company is likely to offer a settlement that is relatively small in comparison with the damages, and the plaintiff may see a trial as a worthy gamble on the possibility of a much bigger recovery. In very big cases, insurance company employees may be unwilling to take responsibility for a large settlement, and the costs of a trial in such cases are insignificant compared with the stakes. Thus the company may refuse to settle.

The litigation rate in medical malpractice has risen enormously in the last thirty years, but it is still low. A New York study estimated that only 3 percent of the people who suffered significant injuries from negligent medical care in hospitals even filed claims that might eventually lead to lawsuits. (The study also found that most potential lawsuits are initiated by people who were *not* the victims of medical negligence, though many of these people did suffer significant injuries through medical care.[30]) Other studies have produced similar findings.[31] And like other kinds of cases, most malpractice litigation is settled or dropped before trial.[32]

One reason for the low rate of malpractice suits is that many people with potential lawsuits simply take no action. They may not recognize the possibility of malpractice or know how to make a claim. Alternatively, they may decide that such action is not a good idea. But lawyers also play an important screening role, typically turning down far more malpractice cases than they accept.[33] In part, that screening role reflects the difficulty of obtaining a favorable outcome in malpractice cases. People are less likely to bring cases to lawyers when their injuries are minor, and such cases are also less attractive to lawyers.

Thus medical malpractice operates differently from auto accidents. In auto accident cases, the relative rarity of litigation reflects primarily the effectiveness of negotiation in settling legal claims out of court. In malpractice, it reflects primarily the infrequency of claims. The results—at least for use of the courts—are similar. These results, especially those for medical malpractice, diverge considerably from the image of the highly litigious American.

The Business World   Like individuals, businesses frequently face decisions about whether to engage in litigation. In particular, legal issues arise almost continuously in the interactions between businesses, issues that could lead to lawsuits. If a manufacturer promises to deliver goods to a wholesaler by a given time and fails to do so, or the wholesaler orders goods and then cancels the order, the offended party could bring a suit for breach of contract. Or if one manufacturer initiates a process that overlaps with one that a competitor has patented, that competitor could sue for patent infringement.

Certainly, businesses do file a good many lawsuits against each other. Indeed, one scholar has argued that businesses exhibit the same kind of litigiousness that is usually ascribed to individuals.[34] As in other areas, however, the volume of such litigation is quite small when compared with all the situations in which litigation is possible. This difference is especially striking because large and medium-sized businesses could bear the monetary costs of litigation with relative ease. Why, then, do they not take each other to court more often?

One part of the answer lies in the disadvantages of litigation. The length of time it requires is disruptive to business operations. Its monetary costs may be affordable, but they are still unwelcome. Perhaps the most important disadvantage is that litigation would jeopardize relationships on which businesses depend. Virtually any company relies on amicable relations with other companies, particularly for buying and selling of goods and services. Such relations are unlikely to survive a lawsuit, and a firm's readiness to litigate may discourage other businesses from dealing with it. Legal scholar Stewart Macauley found that the need to maintain business relationships militated even against putting disputes over contracts in a legal context. As one purchasing agent told Macauley, "You don't read legalistic contract clauses at each other if you ever want to do business again."[35]

Another part of the answer is the existence of alternative methods to resolve disputes. Close relationships between people in firms that deal with each other facilitate informal settlements; people can work out problems without assistance because of their mutual trust and their shared understandings about appropriate terms of settlement. Ranchers in one California county have developed norms for the handling of situations in which one rancher's cattle trespass on the land of another—norms that have little to do with the applicable legal rules.[36]

When the parties cannot settle disputes by themselves, they can turn for help to other people. The lawyers for two businesses often reach an agreement on behalf of their clients. Businesses also make considerable use of *mediation* (in which a mediator helps the parties reach a mutually acceptable resolution of their dispute) and *arbitration* (in which the parties turn a dispute over to an arbitrator, who imposes a binding decision on them). Mediation is especially attractive because the parties retain control over the outcome, but even arbitration often provides speed, economy, and flexibility that litigation lacks. The American Arbitration Association and trade associations in specific industries provide mediation and arbitration services, and companies that work together often arrange in advance to use these services if disputes arise.

Mediation and arbitration have become more common in the business world, reflecting the increasing monetary costs and delays associated with litigation. Within several fields, such as commercial insurance and the food industry, companies have signed agreements to go through alternative dispute resolution for a ninety-day period before filing suits against each other.[37]

Of course, some disputes between businesses do end up in court. Litigation is more likely when two firms lack a continuing relationship and thus have less ability and incentive to work out their differences. In some situations, usually involving direct competitors, the stakes are simply so high that the possible benefits of litigation outweigh its costs. Revlon and Procter & Gamble are major competitors in the cosmetics business. In 1994, Revlon introduced a new lipstick with the claim that it would not rub off, and its share of the market increased considerably. A year later, Proctor & Gamble challenged Revlon to substantiate its claim, possibly in preparation for a lawsuit; Revlon responded by filing its own lawsuit asking a court to rule that its claim was accurate.[38]

Perhaps the largest category of business litigation is quite different from these high-stakes cases: one business falls into financial difficulties and fails to meet its contractual obligations to another company, which sues to recover what it is owed.[39] In this situation, the company that initiates a lawsuit probably does not expect to have further dealings with the company in trouble. For that reason the suit carries little risk.

In the evolution of industries, the volume of litigation is likely to decline over time. Early in the development of an industry, typically a great many companies struggle for a foothold. The relationships among the companies that deal with each other and their understandings with each other about appropriate business practices are weak. And relevant legal rules may not yet be clear. As a result, it is difficult to settle disputes without litigation. In addition, litigation may be attractive as a means to gain a decisive advantage over competitors.

Thus there has been a great deal of litigation in the computer industry under a wide array of laws. In recent years, for instance, the Nintendo company has been plaintiff or defendant in a variety of lawsuits in which the issues ranged from copyright infringement to breach of contract to antitrust violations. In 1997, Digital Equipment sued Intel for alleged infringement of patents on the design of chips for microprocessors, a suit involving stakes of billions of dollars.[40]

Later on, when the industry is more stable—when there are firmer relationships between companies and better mechanisms for resolving disputes—it is both easier and more desirable to avoid litigation. Consequently, lawsuits become less common. But litigation never disappears altogether. New sources of instability, such as changes in technology or the entry of a major new competitor, can bring companies to court more often.

The Incidence of Litigation

In each of the areas surveyed so far, litigation is substantial in absolute numbers but uncommon when compared with the number of potential cases. In this respect, these areas are typical. The study cited in the discussion of personal injuries and discrimination looked at individuals with significant grievances, generally involving $1,000 or more, across a wide range of legal areas. Only 5 percent of these grievances led to the filing of lawsuits, a substantial majority of which were settled out of court.[41] Yet civil suits are hardly rare: more than 15 million civil cases are filed every year.[42]

The Disadvantages of Litigation   The discussion thus far suggests why most potential cases do not go to court: litigation has several features that generally make it unattractive. Three of these features are especially important:

1. Litigation is expensive. The costs required to prepare and try a case make all but the simplest trials unaffordable for most individuals and many organizations, unless a special device such as the contingent fee is operating. Even those who can afford litigation would still prefer to avoid its costs.
2. Litigation means that the parties lose control over the outcome. In the hands of a judge or jury, a case might produce a result that is highly unfavorable to one of the parties. As with plea bargaining, then, it often seems far safer to reach a settlement that is at least palatable to both sides.
3. Litigation creates or exacerbates conflict between the parties. The contest element in trials pits people against each other in a very direct and serious way. For most people, this conflict is unpleasant in itself, and it often has practical consequences as well. If the parties had a relationship before the trial—such as two neighbors or two businesses that deal with each other—it is doubtful the relationship will survive intact.

Taken together, these attributes of litigation create powerful reasons to avoid it. Justice Richard Neely of the West Virginia Supreme Court concluded that "once anyone actually sets foot in a court, any court, he is a loser—even if he comes out of the litigation a technical winner."[43] Ambrose Bierce, a nineteenth-century writer and social critic, put the matter in more vivid terms when he defined litigation as "a machine which you go into as a pig and come out of as a sausage."[44]

These statements exaggerate the disadvantages of litigation, but they give appropriate emphasis to the negative consequences of going to court. Because people generally recognize at least some of these consequences, most of the time they avoid litigation; those who do litigate, as Sally Engle Merry reported, "usually turn to court reluctantly and only as a last resort."[45]

When Litigation Is Attractive   In view of these disadvantages, the many cases that do go to court require explanation. Part of the explanation lies in conditions that reduce or negate the disadvantages.

Under some circumstances, for instance, the monetary costs of litigation are limited. In personal injury cases, the contingent fee makes it possible for many people to afford bringing a lawsuit. The streamlined procedures of small claims courts minimize the costs of bringing a case and arguing it in court.

Similarly, in some situations the conflict element in litigation is greatly reduced. Most important, there may be no relationship that would be damaged by litigation. In the United States, as one scholar said, "litigation tends to be between parties who are strangers."[46] In other instances, the relationship from which litigation arises may have been destroyed before a lawsuit is filed.

Another part of the explanation for litigation is that under some circumstances its benefits seem particularly great. First, there are people for whom the conflict or the risk involved in litigation is an attraction rather than a deterrent. In her study of family and neighborhood problems, Merry found people who gained satisfaction from suing acquaintances.

> Some plaintiffs come to use the law as an arena for manipulation and play, a place to toy with enemies and to gain strategic successes by pummeling one's opponents with legal charges and summonses. . . . Some come to regard the court as enter-

tainment, as a place to try out dominance games with others and to see what will happen.[47]

Such people are exceptional, but their numbers are not negligible. In California, a 1990 statute allowed judges to declare that specific individuals are "vexatious litigants" and bar them from filing new lawsuits without court permission. By 1995, judges had used that power against 225 people.[48] One litigant filed or attempted to file more than seven hundred cases with the federal district court in Philadelphia—all between late 1993 and late 1994.[49]

Second, litigation is sometimes perceived as a last resort, the only way left to deal with an intolerable situation. This is true of most divorces and many personal bankruptcies. Divorce is a kind of special case: if one or both partners wish to terminate their marriage officially, they have no alternative but to go to court. Similarly, owners of companies may sue other businesses that they see as responsible for their eroding positions or impending failures.

Third, people may file lawsuits simply because litigation offers the potential for very substantial gains that cannot be achieved in other ways. One example is bankruptcy filings by corporations that are not in dire financial straits. Such a company may be using bankruptcy to overturn labor contracts or to gain protection from claims by people whom its products have injured.[50] Another example is lawsuits for personal injuries that are filed in the hope of gaining a "windfall" settlement. At the extreme, people who have not been injured at all bring suits. When the state of New Jersey staged several minor bus accidents to ferret out fraudulent claims, officials found that substantial numbers of people entered the buses after the accidents and claimed that they had been injured. People who never reached the buses also filed injury claims.[51] Undoubtedly, some false claims of that type result in lawsuits.

The potential gains from litigation may be political. Interest groups such as the American Civil Liberties Union regularly engage in "political litigation" to secure court rulings that advance their policy goals; these activities are examined in the next chapter. In recent years there has been considerable growth in Strategic Lawsuits Against Public Participation (SLAPPs), civil cases filed against people and organizations that had sought to influence government policy. Such lawsuits, brought most often by businesses with economic stakes in government decisions, typically are intended to punish opponents and to deter opposition in the future. George Pring and Penelope Canan, scholars who coined the term *SLAPPs*, "conservatively estimate that thousands have been sued into silence."[52] Some examples appear in Exhibit 7.3.

Alternatives to Litigation

Whether people go to court depends in part on the availability of alternatives to litigation. Most of the time people do have alternatives, and a great many alternatives exist in various situations.

The Array of Alternatives   These alternatives differ in several ways, of which two are particularly important.[53] The first is how public they are: to what extent is the issue between the parties opened up to wider participation and scrutiny? The second is the formality of the process by which the issue is handled. These two factors

Five Illinois homeowners picketed in front of their subdivision's model homes to indicate their unhappiness about the construction of their roofs. The company that owned the subdivision sued them, seeking an injunction against the picketing and monetary damages.

A Rhode Island resident wrote a letter to a state agency in which she said that hazardous waste from a dump site was polluting underground water. The company that owned the dump sued her for interfering with the company's contractual relationship with the agency and for defamation.

A city council member in a California city was removed from office in a recall election. He sued a great many people for libel and slander, including one person who apparently did nothing other than sign a recall petition. The former council member included several unnamed defendants, "John Does," and wrote a letter to a local newspaper in which he warned, "Be careful, John Does."

Sources: Hugh Dellios, "Builder's Suit Quiets Picketing Residents," *Chicago Tribune,* April 4, 1990, sec. 1, 8; Chris Poon, "Anti-SLAPP Law Fails to Protect Dump's Critic from Defamation Suit," *Providence Journal-Bulletin,* August 5, 1994, 5B; Eve Pell, "Lawsuits That Chill Local Politics," *California Lawyer,* February 1984, 43.

EXHIBIT 7.3   Examples of Lawsuits to Deter Political Criticism and Activity

overlap to some extent, in that more formal processes tend to be more public as well. Thus, as Figure 7.1 shows, litigation and its major alternatives can be listed in the order of their "publicness" and formality.

Direct negotiation between the parties is a simple and routine means to handle legal issues, by far the most common way in which people deal with disputes that might otherwise go to court. Aggrieved consumers take their complaints to store managers. A driver whose car has been damaged talks to the owner of the other car and to the owner's insurance company. Neighbors who disagree over their property line discuss the problem between themselves.

Slightly more formal is negotiation in which attorneys represent the parties. The use of lawyers widens the scope of the negotiation, especially for individuals and businesses that do not employ lawyers regularly. Attorneys often introduce an element of legal formality as well, and their knowledge of the law and courts means that the way in which a court might respond to the dispute becomes more relevant to the negotiation.

Mediation and arbitration have already been discussed in the context of business disputes, but both are used in other areas as well. Mediation can be fairly informal (when, for example, parish priests and other religious authorities help individuals resolve their disputes) or more formal (as in the work of professional mediators in negotiations between labor and management). Arbitration is less common than mediation because it is more formal, with the arbitrator reaching a binding decision. But it is used a good deal in disputes between businesses, in consumer complaints, and in labor-management relations. In some arbitration programs, the parties agree not to "appeal" from the arbitration judgment to a court.

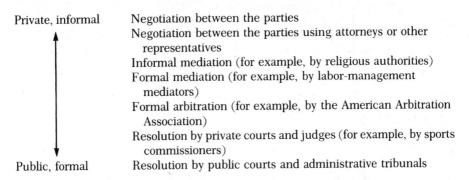

Private, informal   Negotiation between the parties

Negotiation between the parties using attorneys or other
representatives

Informal mediation (for example, by religious authorities)

Formal mediation (for example, by labor-management
mediators)

Formal arbitration (for example, by the American Arbitration
Association)

Resolution by private courts and judges (for example, by sports
commissioners)

Public, formal   Resolution by public courts and administrative tribunals

FIGURE 7.1   Litigation and Some Major Alternatives to Litigation

Sources: Adapted from formulations in Marc Galanter, "Why the 'Haves' Come Out Ahead: Speculations on the Limits of Legal Change," *Law & Society Review* 9 (Fall 1974), 124–135; and Austin Sarat and Joel B. Grossman, "Courts and Conflict Resolution: Problems in the Mobilization of Adjudication," *American Political Science Review* 69 (December 1975), 1201–1208.

A variant of arbitration is the use of private courts and judges.[54] Some organizations have their own forums to resolve disputes within the organization. Such forums are common within colleges, religious bodies, and sports associations. It was American League president Gene Budig, acting as a judge, who chose a five-game suspension as the sanction for baseball player Roberto Alomar in 1996 after Alomar spat in an umpire's face. In other instances, forums are set up to resolve disputes between members of an organization and people outside it. An example is the tribunals that resolve complaints between automobile manufacturers and consumers. In some states, litigants can hire a private judge to reach a decision in lieu of the regular court, and the private judge's decision has the same official and binding status as that of the court. Perhaps inevitably, this device has become known as the "rent-a-judge" system.

At the furthest distance from simple two-party negotiation is the resolution of a legal issue in a court or in another government tribunal, such as an administrative court in the executive branch. Courts generally reach decisions in a fully public setting on the basis of formal procedures through the application of legal rules. These characteristics distinguish courts at least marginally from all the alternative forums and fundamentally from most.

Growth in the Use of Alternatives   In recent years, interest in alternatives to litigation has burgeoned, often under the heading "alternative dispute resolution." Government has given strong encouragement to the use of alternatives. Statutes and court rulings require litigants and potential litigants to undertake mediation or arbitration under some circumstances. The Federal Arbitration Act, enacted in 1947, establishes the general rule that private agreements to resolve disputes through arbitration are enforceable. In 1996, President Clinton issued an executive order strongly endorsing the use of alternative dispute resolution by lawyers for the federal government.[55]

This burgeoning interest is reflected in the growth of organizations that provide mediation and arbitration services.[56] The American Arbitration Association, a long-standing organization, has been joined by several others. The largest is Judicial Arbitration and Mediation Services (JAMS), based in California. JAMS and some other organizations use ex-judges as arbitrators, competing for the services of the most prestigious ex-judges and sometimes inducing them to leave the bench. In 1993, the chief justice of the California Supreme Court used JAMS to resolve the property settlement in his divorce. Apparently he found the results satisfactory; three years later he retired from his position, and shortly afterwards he went to work for JAMS.[57]

In and out of the legal community, most observers view the movement toward alternatives to litigation as a highly desirable development. It may reduce court case-loads, helping courts to keep up with their work and reducing delays for those who go to court. More important, it is seen as allowing people to avoid the disadvantages of litigation. Clearly, this is a real benefit. Most potential litigants are better off if they stay out of court, and the heavy use of some alternatives indicates that they serve real needs.

Yet some observers express skepticism about the growing movement toward alternatives to litigation. There is concern that the removal of disputes from public to private forums is part of a general trend toward "privatization." This trend is viewed as favoring people and institutions that can afford the better services offered by the private sector over those who have no choice but to use public services. In 1996, a California judge pointed with alarm to what she saw as the creation of a two-tiered system of justice, an inadequately funded public system and "a private system restricted to the wealthy."[58]

The most widely expressed concern is quite different: that people increasingly are required to use alternatives to litigation when those alternatives may be to their disadvantage. In particular, consumers and employees sign contracts with provisions under which they give up their right to go to court, agreeing that they will go to arbitration instead. If consumers want to obtain certain goods or services, or if prospective employees want a particular job, they have no choice but to accept those provisions; frequently, they are unaware that the provisions exist. Employees in the securities industry cannot sue their employers, even for violations of the federal civil rights laws. Customers of the Bank of America cannot go to court over disputes about their accounts or credit cards. Members of the Kaiser Permanente health maintenance organization in some states give up their right to sue for malpractice.

Why do companies require their customers and employees to accept such agreements? One reason is the perception that arbitration is less expensive and more efficient than litigation, characteristics that presumably are good for both sides. "Our goal and our customers' goal is the same," according to a Bank of America representative. "We want to see a fair and just resolution as quickly and inexpensively as possible."[59]

Yet the decision to rule out litigation is effectively one-sided, made by the party that would be required to defend its actions in court. And the alternatives to litigation that businesses require often are operated by the businesses themselves or the industries of which they are a part. Thus there is some reason to conclude that decision makers in those businesses think they will get more favorable outcomes by requiring that disputes be settled through arbitration. Kaiser Permanente requires arbitration in only three of the seventeen states in which it does business. Its choice of those three states was based in part on the company's assessment of where it would be more successful in court and where it would do better out of court.[60]

All this does not mean that the movement for alternatives to litigation is simply an effort to gain an advantage for groups that want to avoid being sued, and certainly it does not mean that litigation is necessarily preferable to such alternatives as mediation and arbitration. But the choice between litigation and its alternatives is not necessarily a neutral one; the benefits that result from staying out of court may not accrue equally to the two sides in a dispute.

Paths to—and Away From—the Courts   By taking the array of potential alternatives into account, we can map out several routes to the courts. When people hold a grievance or opportunity that might be litigated, some of them go directly to court. Others employ alternatives, usually starting with those that are least public and formal and therefore least likely to share the disadvantages of litigation. After one or more alternatives fail to produce a satisfactory result—if, say, the negotiations stall or a mediator suggests an unacceptable solution—these people then go to court.

But a much larger number of people follow paths that do not take them to court. Many people do nothing. Consumers who feel they have suffered discrimination or who find that a product is defective often simply live with their grievance. Others obtain a satisfactory result through some alternative to litigation, most often negotiation with the other party. Still others accept unsatisfactory outcomes from alternatives rather than taking on litigation with its negative elements. A consumer who finds a merchant unyielding in negotiations and who gets no satisfaction from mediation by the Better Business Bureau may give up at that point. Through a combination of these routes, most possible litigation never occurs.

The Impact of Government on Litigation

The discussion of litigation thus far has dealt almost entirely with individuals and institutions in the private sector. But government institutions significantly affect both the volume and the types of litigation that occur. Most directly, government agencies themselves are involved in a great many actual and potential court cases. In 1995, for instance, the federal government was a party in about one-fifth of the civil cases filed in federal district courts.[61] As a result, their conduct of these matters—particularly their decisions whether to go to court—has considerable impact.

Just as important, courts and the other branches of government can influence private-sector litigation in a variety of ways. Some effects of government policy on litigation have been noted at several points, but the breadth and depth of these effects merit more extensive consideration.

First and most fundamentally, legislative and judicial policies create and define legal remedies, thereby determining who has the right to go to court under what circumstances. Thus changes in the law can change the potential for litigation. In 1997, for instance, the Supreme Court ruled that citizens could sue under the Endangered Species Act if they felt that enforcement of the act caused them economic harm.[62] This ruling undoubtedly will lead to new litigation against environmental regulations. Changes in the law can close off avenues of litigation as well as opening them. After a lawsuit was brought against charitable institutions, challenging their practices under the securities and antitrust laws, Congress in 1995 passed two statutes to rule out such litigation.[63] Such changes can have enormous effects. Since the 1960s, civil rights laws newly enacted by Congress and interpretations of older laws by the Supreme Court have created essentially a new area of litigation, one in which the federal courts hear more than seventy thousand cases a year.

Second, government decisions help determine the attractiveness of litigation. In recent years, many state legislatures have changed legal doctrines and procedures in personal injury law in ways that are unfavorable to injured parties. For example, some states have established the rule that a manufacturer is not liable for injuries caused by a product if that product adhered to the "state of the art" when it was made. States have also placed limits on the damages that can be awarded to plaintiffs under certain circumstances. Such changes are likely to discourage lawsuits.

To take a different kind of example, federal laws that allow plaintiffs' lawyers to win attorneys' fees from defendants have encouraged litigation. The Civil Rights Act of 1991 made it possible for plaintiffs to win monetary damages in cases brought under the major federal law against employment discrimination. Not surprisingly, that provision increased substantially the interest of lawyers in bringing those cases.[64] By the same token, judicial rules allowing monetary sanctions for the bringing of frivolous lawsuits, such as Rule 11 of the Federal Rules of Civil Procedure, have made it riskier to file cases that a judge might interpret as frivolous.[65]

Finally, legislatures and courts can help determine whether potential and actual cases are resolved at trial or in other ways. As discussed earlier, they increasingly encourage alternatives. Trial judges have long promoted settlements in civil cases, and their efforts have intensified with growing caseloads. Some courts go further, providing mediators to help settle cases. Several legislatures have passed statutes requiring mediation or arbitration in certain kinds of cases, such as medical malpractice claims and divorce; many state and federal courts have adopted rules mandating arbitration before trial.

This development is illustrated by the reactions of courts to mandatory arbitration clauses in contracts. Some courts have ruled that these clauses cannot be enforced under certain circumstances.[66] For the most part, however, courts have upheld provisions that prevent people from litigating. In 1993, a California court of appeals ruled on a contract in which a physician's patients gave up their right to sue for malpractice, not only for themselves but for their children, "born or unborn." The court held that this provision applied to children who were not yet conceived when the contract was signed.[67] The Supreme Court has reached several decisions favoring arbitration requirements. In 1996, for instance, the Court ruled on a Montana statute requiring that mandatory arbitration clauses in contracts "be typed in underlined capital letters on the first page of the contract." The Court held that the statute was void because it conflicted with the Federal Arbitration Act.[68]

Courts' approval of mandatory arbitration clauses also illustrates the fact that rules affecting the use of courts usually favor some groups in society over others. As a result, such rules are often the subject of fierce contention between groups. In 1995,

Congress enacted a statute that limited and discouraged lawsuits by investors for securities fraud.[69] It did so after sustained and intensive lobbying by the groups that would benefit, including brokers, accounting firms, and the business community generally. On the losing side were consumer groups and the lawyers who bring lawsuits for securities fraud. The lobbying by the two sides extended as far as newspaper advertisements arguing for and against the legislation. The groups that opposed the legislation secured a veto by President Clinton, but those that favored it had sufficient political strength and sympathy from a conservative Congress that the veto was overridden.

In debates over such proposals, the combatants often argue broadly that courts should remain open to citizens with grievances or that litigation exacts unacceptable costs on the country. In reality, however, every group favors opening up the courts or limiting litigation depending on where its interest lies. The Farm Bureau, the nation's largest agricultural group, has argued for limits on the budget and activities of the federal Legal Services Corporation, which funds lawyers for low-income people and sometimes brings lawsuits against farm owners. At the same time, the Farm Bureau supports the enactment of statutes that would allow food producers to bring lawsuits for "food disparagement," defined in Georgia as "the willful or malicious dissemination to the public in any manner of false information that a perishable food product or commodity is not safe for human consumption." Thirteen states had adopted such laws by 1997, and Texas cattle ranchers sued Oprah Winfrey for remarks on her television show about "mad cow" disease.[70]

In making policies that influence the use of litigation, government affects its own interests as a potential litigant. For the most part, governments have the power to determine under what circumstances suits can be brought against them. The North American Free Trade Agreement (NAFTA) includes a variety of provisions that people might use to challenge actions of the federal or state governments, arguing that those actions are inconsistent with NAFTA. When Congress adopted legislation to implement NAFTA in 1993, it simply prohibited such suits.

Litigation and the American Culture

As I have noted, Americans often are portrayed as a litigious people, eager to sue whenever the opportunity arises. Indeed, one legal scholar has argued that "we are the most litigious people in the world."[71] A prominent judge went one step further, concluding that "Americans are the most litigious nation in human history."[72]

Commentators often seize on anecdotal evidence about lawsuits to support this conclusion, and it is not difficult to find such evidence. A softball coach in Roanoke, Virginia, sued the city for $4 million after he was ejected from a game, claiming—among other things—that he "has been and will forever be hampered in his pursuit of happiness." A Detroit resident sued the city's two newspapers for $9 million on the ground that following their horoscope columns had done harm to his life. A Virginia man wrote Ann Landers to tell why he murdered his wife, she included the letter in her column, and he sued her for $100 million for slander.[73]

Yet we have seen that people in the United States avoid most opportunities to go to court; the number of civil cases is a very small fraction of what it could be if

Americans undertook litigation whenever they had a possible case. This fact alone suggests that Americans are not highly litigious.

The best way to explore the issue is through direct comparisons between the United States and other nations. Although truly comparable data are difficult to obtain, Marc Galanter pulled together some estimates of litigation rates for the United States and some other industrialized nations—with surprising results.[74] According to these estimates, the United States has far more cases per capita than nations such as Japan and Italy. But the American litigation rate is fairly comparable to that in some other nations, including England and Denmark. On the other hand, Robert Kagan concluded that comparable matters, especially those involving government policy, are more likely to go to court in the United States than in other industrialized democracies.[75]

To the extent that litigation is relatively common in the United States, characteristics of the American culture are not entirely responsible. Rather, legal rules and structures that encourage litigation also play a significant role.[76] The radical difference in litigation rates between the United States and Japan, often cited as evidence of cultural differences in the use of the courts, may actually result from a complex interaction between cultural values and government policies that affect use of the courts.[77] For instance, the Japanese government keeps the number of lawyers low by establishing very high standards for the bar exam, standards that produce a pass rate of 3 percent.[78]

A Litigation Explosion?

"There was a time," a commentator wrote in 1989,

> when an aggrieved party was usually content to turn the other cheek or request an apology or simply tamper with the brakes of his antagonist's car—in short, to take advantage of any number of options before seeking the services of a lawyer. No longer. One tiny affront or injustice, real or imagined, and attorneys are being retained and witnesses duly sworn in before you can say "in the matter of the application of."[79]

Whether or not the United States is a particularly litigious society, this commentator is typical of many who believe the country has become more litigious in recent years. Indeed, it is common to refer to a "litigation explosion." In general, that explosion is seen as centering on lawsuits by individuals, particularly suits for personal injuries.

The perception of a growth in litigiousness stems from several factors.[80] The rapid growth in the legal profession suggests that lawsuits are also increasing rapidly. Groups such as doctors, insurance companies, and local governments all complain about floods of litigation against them, and judges regularly complain about growing caseloads in their courts. Major events such as the Oklahoma City bombing of 1995 and developments such as the growth in repetitive stress injuries seem inevitably to produce litigation. Accounts of seemingly trivial or bizarre lawsuits, such as those cited earlier, make it appear that litigation is running out of control.

These indications of growth can be deceptive. For instance, a spate of lawsuits in an area may appear unprecedented because we fail to recall similar episodes in the past. According to a sportswriter in 1992, "Baseball had the dead ball era followed by the live ball era. This is the litigious era."[81] He did not realize that baseball in the early twentieth century was marked by a volume of litigation—involving players, teams, and leagues—that almost surely surpassed its volume in the 1990s.[82]

It is difficult to determine just how accurate the perceptions of an explosion actually are. One problem is that historical data on litigation are incomplete. Another problem is that the data we have are susceptible to differing interpretations.

These data do suggest that there has been substantial growth in the number of civil cases over the past few decades. Federal courts hear only a small proportion of all cases, but data on their caseloads are unusually good. There were 117,000 civil cases filed in federal district courts in 1975 and 248,000 in 1995—an increase of 120 percent. On the other hand, all this growth came in the first half of that period. Between 1985 and 1995, the number of civil cases actually dropped 9 percent.[83] Over the long term, it appears that the cases filed in court have become increasingly likely to be settled prior to trial. The percentage of federal civil cases that actually reached trial dropped from 15 percent in 1940 to 3 percent in 1995.[84]

Perceptions of a litigation explosion focus primarily on tort cases, even though those cases do not stand out as a source of growth in litigation.[85] The number of tort cases has grown considerably over time, but the trends are complex and open to differing interpretations. And this growth seems to have leveled off in recent years. Between 1986 and 1993, the number of tort cases filed in twenty-two states and in federal court changed very little.[86] The lack of growth during that period is striking, because this was a time of widespread perceptions that people were increasingly willing to bring lawsuits for personal injuries

Some scholars have sought to provide a broader perspective by looking at litigation trends over the course of U.S. history. They have found a tendency for litigation per capita to rise over time, but the increases generally have been moderate, and some courts had higher rates in some past periods than in recent years.[87] Summarizing these studies, one writer concluded that the thesis of "the country's growing legal dementia . . . could be true except it overlooks one salient point: It used to be worse."[88] Though not entirely conclusive, this research indicates that Americans have not developed a new inclination to litigate in the current era.

Views about the existence of a litigation explosion are based less on what we know about the reality than on self-interest and ideological position. On one side, many people in the business community see themselves as beset by lawsuits that hurt the interests of their organizations and of society as a whole. Understandably, they emphasize the concept of a litigation explosion and the harm it does as a way of building support for changes in legal rules that might protect them from lawsuits. On the other side, lawyers who represent individual plaintiffs and groups representing such interests as consumers see lawsuits as an important tool to protect individual rights and, in the case of lawyers, to advance their own professional interests. Accordingly, they downplay the idea of an explosion in an effort to blunt the drive for legal changes that they oppose. More broadly, because of the interests involved, political conservatives generally argue that a litigation explosion is occurring, while liberals deny its existence. The two groups also differ in how they depict the outcomes of tort cases, a subject considered later in the chapter.

THE LITIGATION PROCESS

Whatever we conclude about the propensity of Americans to litigate, a great many lawsuits are actually filed in court. Like criminal cases, civil cases can take many different paths; to a great extent, the paths that cases take vary among fields of law.[89] This section focuses on three major types of cases that generally follow different routes; the routes are summarized in Exhibit 7.4.

Pretrial Settlement and Full Trials: Personal Injuries

In some types of civil cases, the parties are in conflict, but they generally try to reach a settlement before trial and usually succeed. Cases in which the parties do not reach a settlement typically go to full-scale trials, often before juries. The largest category of such cases is personal injury suits.[90] Injury cases arise from a wide range of situations, but a majority of potential and actual cases involve auto accidents. More than 90 percent of personal injury cases are brought by individuals, most often against individuals but frequently against businesses.[91]

In most personal injury cases, as noted earlier, an insurance company is respon-

EXHIBIT 7.4   Paths Through Court for Three Types of Civil Cases

	Personal Injury	Debt Collection	Divorce
Pretrial Stage			
Typical length of time	Lengthy	Brief	Moderate
Incidence of settlements between parties	Most cases	Some cases	Most cases
Trial Stage			
Typical length of time	Relatively lengthy	Quite brief	Quite brief
Incidence of uncontested trials	Few cases	Most cases, resulting from defaults by defendants	Most cases, resulting from agreements between parties
Post-Trial Stage			
Noncompliance with judgments	Uncommon	Common	Common

Source: Based in part on David M. Engel and Eric H. Steele, "Civil Cases and Society: Process and Order in the Civil Justice System," *American Bar Foundation Research Journal,* Spring 1979, 311–317

sible for paying any judgment against the defendant and therefore takes charge of the defendant's case. The defendants themselves play no significant part either in negotiations or in setting strategy.

The great majority of potential injury cases are never filed in court. The filing of a personal injury lawsuit may reflect the inability of the two sides to reach an early settlement. But the filing is not a signal of failure so much as a punctuation of negotiations, an indication of seriousness by the lawyer for the injured party. Most suits eventually are settled out of court. Because of such settlements and other methods of pretrial disposition, such as dismissals, verdicts by judges or juries are unusual. A study of the seventy five largest counties in the United States found that three-quarters of the tort lawsuits were settled between the parties; only 3 percent were resolved through a verdict after trial.[92]

In most respects, the negotiation process after the filing of lawsuits is similar to earlier negotiation. There is a long period between filing and trial in most civil courts, a median of about two years in the seventy-five largest counties.[93] Thus the act of filing usually brings no urgency to the negotiations. As the trial date comes closer, lawyers concentrate more on efforts to reach a settlement. As Herbert Kritzer has pointed out, the prospect of trial not only shapes the terms of settlement but helps to make settlement possible.[94] When Vermont established a moratorium on civil jury trials because of budget problems, one unexpected effect was that lawyers stopped negotiating on cases.[95]

The filing of a lawsuit gives the parties additional means to test and challenge each other's positions. For example, lawyers use discovery to learn about the content and strength of the other party's case, and what they learn can affect the bargaining power of the two sides. Lawyers can also draw out the pretrial period for tactical purposes, seeking to wear down the other side.

Another frequent effect of filing is to bring the court into the settlement process. Judges in civil cases play an active role in encouraging settlements, primarily during pretrial conferences. These direct efforts are supplemented by broader mechanisms to encourage settlements. One example is a federal rule that gives plaintiffs an incentive to accept settlement offers by assessing court costs against a plaintiff who rejects a formal offer and then does no better at trial.[96] Another is the mandatory arbitration systems used for certain cases in some states and federal districts. Some of these systems also provide financial incentives to the parties to accept the arbitrator's decision rather than go to trial.

Typically, negotiations are neither long nor complex. One study of federal and state cases found that in the typical tort case there were only two rounds of bargaining, and on the average lawyers spent less than three hours in negotiation. This pattern results from the ease with which lawyers usually reach settlements and the low monetary stakes, which make it counterproductive for lawyers to expend a great deal of time to reach a settlement.[97]

Although trials are exceptions to the rule in personal injury cases, they are not rare. Indeed, the overwhelming majority of civil jury trials result from personal injuries.[98] As in criminal law, the formality and length of trials in personal injury cases vary a great deal.

Bench trials and jury trials are both common in personal injury cases. In civil cases, like criminal cases, some observers perceive substantial differences between the behavior of judges and juries. It is widely believed that civil juries are more sympathetic toward plaintiffs than are judges because, like criminal juries, they tend to elevate equity over law. In personal injury cases, emphasizing equity means providing compensation for people who have suffered losses. But the available evidence suggests that, overall, juries differ little from judges in their support for plaintiffs.[99] There is also some evidence that jurors as a group are not particularly sympathetic toward the injured parties. "Like the public," one scholar concluded, "civil jurors are deeply suspicious of plaintiffs who bring lawsuits against businesses."[100]

One reason may be that business groups seek to convince the public that there has been a litigation explosion with negative effects on society. Another tactic has been to publicize allegedly outrageous jury decisions in favor of plaintiffs. That tactic is exemplified by the case of McDonald's coffee, discussed in Exhibit 7.5. One lawyer who represents defendants in medical malpractice cases said that "an advertising campaign and a public relations campaign mounted by insurance companies" has "had an impact on the public, who make up juries, on the way they view malpractice cases."[101]

The limitations of criminal trials as a mechanism to reach the truth were examined in Chapter 6. These weaknesses are also relevant to civil trials, including those in personal injury cases. In some respects, the weaknesses are more serious on the civil side. For instance, the period of time from a personal injury to a trial is usually far longer than the period from a criminal offense to a trial, which is significant because the recollections of witnesses deteriorate with time. In such areas as product liability, civil cases can involve issues of technical complexity that create special problems of understanding for both judges and juries.

As in criminal law, some commentators regard juries as less capable than judges in personal injury cases. Indeed, some judges and lawyers have proposed that the right to jury trials be eliminated in some civil cases, particularly those involving highly complex issues. But one scholar derived from the available evidence on civil and criminal cases "the unexpected conclusion that juries are one of our society's most reliable decision-making institutions."[102]

Successful personal injury plaintiffs may face difficulties in collecting the money they have been awarded. Sometimes it is simply impossible to collect that money. Individual defendants often have limited assets. As a result, plaintiffs cannot collect money beyond the level of the individual's insurance coverage—if the individual does have coverage. Although O.J. Simpson was hardly a typical defendant, the collection difficulties faced by the plaintiffs who won a judgment aginst him in 1997 were not unusual.[103] This problem is less common when businesses are defendants, because they typically have more assets. When Kmart Corporation did not immediately post a required bond with the court after losing an age discrimination case, the plaintiffs had federal marshals go to two Kmart stores in Florida and gather $45,000 from their cash registers.[104] But business defendants, like individuals, may delay payment through appeals and use the threat of appeal as a device to secure a post-trial settlement that reduces the amount they have to pay. And trial judges and appellate courts frequently modify jury awards or reverse them altogether.

For all these reasons, plaintiffs as a group do considerably less well in the final outcome than they do in the jury verdict. One study of California and Illinois jury tri-

In 1992, seventy-nine-year-old Stella Liebeck sat in a car and tried to open a cup of McDonald's coffee while holding it between her knees. The coffee gushed out on her, and she suffered third-degree burns. Ultimately Liebeck sued McDonald's for her injuries, and in 1994 a jury awarded her $2.9 million.

The verdict garnered headlines. It also brought outrage against Liebeck and the jury. One journalist put Liebeck in the same category as two people who killed their children and as the Menendez brothers, who killed their parents. According to one newspaper, it was "one of the most outrageous jury awards on record." A commentator said the verdict was "confirmation that the earth had slipped off its axis." Business groups that sought legislation limiting awards to tort plaintiffs publicized the case. One radio ad asked, "Is it fair to get a couple of million dollars from a restaurant just because you spilled your hot coffee on yourself? Of course not. It's ridiculous. But it happened."

But some commentators, including people on the other side of the debate over tort law, argued that the jury's verdict was far from outrageous. Liebeck had spent a week in a hospital and later returned for painful skin grafts. She contacted McDonald's and asked only for her expenses and the wages that her daughter had lost staying home with her during recuperation; apparently, McDonald's offered $800. Only then did Liebeck contact a lawyer, who unsuccessfully sought a settlement with McDonald's.

When the case went to trial, at least some jurors initially thought that the case was frivolous. But they learned that McDonald's kept its coffee at a very high temperature and had continued to do so despite seven hundred complaints of burns from the coffee over a decade. Ultimately the jury awarded Liebeck $200,000 in compensatory damages, which they reduced by 20 percent because she was partially at fault. They added $2.7 million in punitive damages as a way, they thought, of making McDonald's take the problem seriously. Thus there seems room for disagreement about whether the jury's verdict was indeed outrageous.

Liebeck and her lawyer did not actually get $2.9 million. The trial judge reduced the jury's award to $640,000. Later the two sides reached an out-of-court settlement that was not disclosed but that reportedly was for less than $600,000.

Sources: Aric Press, "Are Lawyers Burning America?" *Newsweek,* March 20, 1995, 32–35; other newspaper and periodical reports. The quotations are from, respectively, "McHot Coffee Award" (editorial), *Indianapolis News,* September 21, 1994, A12; Cynthia Tucker, "Ridiculous School Suits Instill Fear in Teachers," *Montgomery Advertiser,* October 8, 1996, 8A; and Saundra Torry, "Tort and Retort: The Battle over Reform Heats Up," *Washington Post,* March 6, 1995, F7.

EXHIBIT 7.5   The Case of McDonald's Coffee

als found that defendants in personal injury cases ultimately paid an average of 79 percent of the original amount awarded by the jury.[105] For the largest verdicts, the proportion is even lower—less than 20 percent in one study of twenty-five cases with large jury awards in 1993.[106]

Some personal injury cases stand out for their massive size.[107] These cases can stem from major accidents, such as fires in public places and airline crashes. Some of the largest cases involve "toxic torts"—injuries allegedly caused by products such as drugs and medical devices. These "cases" actually are composed of many individual cases—in a few instances, hundreds of thousands of cases. Because they involve similar claims, the outcome of a single case often affects what happens to other cases.

Mass personal injury cases are very difficult for courts to handle, because of the number of individual cases and the connections among them. Cases may be spread across many courts, creating problems of coordination. (Under some circumstances, however, they can be consolidated in single courts.) With many lawyers involved and high monetary stakes, settlement negotiations tend to be difficult, and what appears to be a final agreement among the parties may not fully settle the issues. The most complicated of these cases can take years, even decades, to resolve fully. Where settlements are not reached, trials are likely to be long and complex. The spillage of dioxin in a train derailment resulted in an Illinois trial that lasted for three and a half years, a U.S. record.

Brief Trials and Defendant Defaults: Debt Collection

Civil cases involving small amounts of money often go through pretrial stages quickly, with a small proportion of settlements and little involvement on the part of the court. Most trials are abbreviated and relatively informal, and many defendants lose by default because they fail to take the required actions before trial or fail to appear at the trial. Cases often go to small claims courts, which process cases quickly through fairly simple procedures. Most cases of this type fall in the general category of debt collection, in which businesses seek to recover money that is allegedly owed to them by individuals or seek another remedy such as eviction of a tenant. Debt collection actions are quite common, one of the largest categories of civil court cases. Indeed, one study of major trial courts in three cities found that a majority of all cases filed were for debt collection.[108]

Students of the courts give little attention to debt collection cases, because there is nothing very exciting about them. The controversies that exist in other areas of the law, the arguments about litigiousness and a litigation explosion, have little to do with debt collection. There was a flurry of interest in these cases during the 1960s and 1970s, because the defendants typically have low incomes and there was widespread concern about poverty in that period. That concern receded, and attention turned to other segments of the courts' work. But debt collection cases are important to the large number of people involved in them. They are also important for an understanding of how the courts allocate benefits and burdens, since they typically involve contention between two parties with highly unequal resources. Within the limits of what we know about these cases, then, they merit consideration.

Like other categories of cases, those involving debt collection constitute only a small portion of the total that might be filed as lawsuits. Most disputes are settled through some means other than litigation. But there are so many disputes over debts that even the relatively small proportion that result in litigation constitute a large number. Dockets in many small claims courts consist primarily of actions by businesses to collect debts from individuals; although small claims courts were created to facilitate litigation by individuals, they have also provided attractive forums for business creditors. One study of twelve small claims courts found that two-thirds of the cases filed in 1990 were for debt collection, even though some of the courts had rules that limited the filing of those cases.[109]

In the pretrial stage of debt collection cases, a great many defendants fail to take the action needed to protect their positions in court. Defendants are supposed to receive a summons and then appear in court to file an answer, but in practice a good deal of slippage occurs. A study of debtor defendants in Chicago, Detroit, and New York found that 30 percent of the defendants claimed that they had not received a summons. The proportion was highest in New York, where there is considerable evidence that process servers routinely fail to perform their duty. (In one case, a New York process server swore under oath that he had served a subpoena on a person at his residence, when that person had moved to Los Angeles a month earlier.)[110] But even when people were served with a summons, only 28 percent of them appeared in court, and only 26 percent of those who appeared actually filed an answer. Altogether, then, the proportion of defendants who filed an answer in court was only 5 percent.[111]

Aside from the absence of a summons, the failure of a defendant to file an answer can result from several conditions: the debtor may not understand what is required, may fear going to court, or may feel that no effective defense is possible. The low proportions of defendants with attorneys and the high proportions with low incomes and limited education help to account for these conditions.

The defendant's failure to file an answer to the complaint allows the plaintiff to win a default judgment. Cases can be resolved without full trials in several other ways. Some defendants who have filed answers nonetheless lose default judgments because they do not appear for the trial. The creditor may win a summary judgment if the defendant's answer is judged to be inadequate, which is likely if the defendant has drafted that answer without a lawyer's help. Some debtors contact their creditors and reach a settlement prior to trial.

Faced with heavy caseloads, judges often make active efforts to avoid trials. Increasingly, courts that hear debt collection cases divert these cases either to mandatory or to voluntary arbitration systems. Some judges pressure litigants who appear for trial to reach settlements instead. In the small claims court in Washington, D.C., according to a reporter, "Defendants with the temerity to show up are quickly shuffled outside to negotiate a payment plan or make some kind of deal—mediation encouraged by the court."[112]

Some cases do go to contested trials, although the proportion is fairly small. In the study of Chicago, Detroit, and New York that was discussed earlier, that proportion was estimated to be as low as 1 percent.[113] Jury trials are quite uncommon. Nonjury trials usually are informal, and they typically require only part of a court day. All this is especially true of small claims courts, in which the frequent absence of attorneys further speeds proceedings. A debt collection case in a small claims court may require only a few minutes to try, and according to a 1996 report, a typical eviction trial in Chicago lasted three minutes.[114]

Victorious plaintiffs often find it difficult to collect judgments against defendants in debt collection cases. Many debtors lack the money to pay a judgment readily, and some are unwilling to pay even if they can do so. Creditors then must resort to formal mechanisms to recover what they are owed. For example, the garnishment of wages from debtors who are employed is a common action. Despite the use of these mechanisms, many judgments simply cannot be collected. In one study of Iowa small claims courts, only 28 percent of the businesses that won cases against individuals collected all the money they were awarded, and 61 percent collected none at all.[115]

Court Ratification of Pretrial Settlements: Divorce

Divorce is an unusual type of litigation, in that people who wish to terminate a marriage officially must file a case in court. Traditionally, the laws of most states required not only that divorce cases go to court but also that they take the appearance of a contest; a divorce could be granted only when one spouse proved that the other was at fault under the law. But the spouses often worked together to frame the evidence in order to prove the necessary fault.

Because of legal changes since the late 1960s, about half the states no longer have the traditional fault-based grounds for divorce. *Every* state now allows divorces (sometimes called dissolutions) without the showing of fault.[116] Some states allow a divorce on the ground that the marriage has broken down irretrievably or that there are irreconcilable differences between the spouses. Others grant a divorce on the ground that the couple has lived apart for a specified period of time. Still others have adopted both of these no-fault grounds. If only one of the spouses seeks a divorce, the other may have the right to contest it, but the new grounds make it difficult to oppose a divorce petition successfully. If the spouses agree to obtain a divorce, under some circumstances in some states they need not actually appear in court.

Aside from granting a divorce, the courts must deal with the economic issues of property division and alimony. Where children are involved, their custody and support must also be determined. Judges approve or disapprove agreements between the spouses on these issues and adjudicate cases in which no agreement is reached.

In the overwhelming majority of divorce cases, the parties reach agreement on all the issues outside of court. In a study of two counties, 10 percent of the Virginia cases and 5 percent of the Wisconsin cases went to trial.[117] A California study found that in divorces with children, only in 1.5 percent of the cases did a judge have to make a decision about child custody.[118] Agreements often are achieved after long and difficult negotiation, because divorce and the issues associated with it usually have enormous concrete and emotional stakes for the parties. Some states seek to facilitate out-of-court settlement by requiring mediation between the parties. This requirement has aroused opposition from those who see mandatory mediation as giving an advantage to the stronger partner in the marriage.[119] It is uncommon for judges to disapprove agreements between the parties. In one sample of three hundred Wisconsin cases, judges refused to approve the couple's agreement in only one instance.[120] The judge's scrutiny of an agreement is usually perfunctory.

In part because of this limited scrutiny, expectations of what would happen if a case went to court do not fully govern settlements. This is especially true when there seems little chance that a case actually will be contested in court. Other factors, such as the bargaining skills of the two sides, come into play.

In the minority of cases that do go to trial, the law gives judges a great deal of discretion over issues such as alimony and child custody. Inevitably, their decisions about these issues are influenced by their personal values on such matters as the relative fitness of mothers and fathers as parents. Judges are also affected by the terms of the settlements they approve in uncontested cases, which help set their expectations about how they should decide cases.[121] Thus, as in other areas of law, out-of-court settlements and judges' decisions affect each other in significant ways.

Noncompliance with court decrees in divorce cases is a common problem. Parents frequently violate agreements concerning custody and visitation rights, and "child stealing" to overcome court judgments has become a highly visible phenomenon. A large proportion of people who are required to pay alimony or child support meet that obligation only in part or not at all, and noncompliance becomes more common over the years after a divorce. Of the parents who are required to pay child support, in any given year about one-half pay the full amount due; one-quarter, part of the amount due; and the other one-quarter, nothing at all. Overall, parents in 1991 paid 67 percent of the child support they were ordered to pay.[122]

Traditionally, courts and other government agencies did little to secure compliance with the terms of divorce decrees. But these efforts have increased substantially in recent years. This is especially true of child support. Between 1984 and 1996, Congress enacted four statutes with provisions to improve compliance with child support orders. The 1988 law mandated that, for child support orders beginning in 1994, states would have to require that child support payments be deducted directly from wages and forwarded to custodial parents. About two-thirds of the states now allow suspension of drivers' licenses for parents who have failed to pay child support.[123] These mechanisms have had some effect. But they have not come close to eliminating noncompliance, in part because they are not fully enforced. One sign of the continuing problems is that some private firms now offer to track down noncompliant parents for a fee—though the owner of such a firm in Houston was arrested in 1996 for failure to pay child support.[124]

The difficulties involved in securing compliance are symbolized by the case of a wealthy divorced father who spent the years between 1990 and 1995 evading his child support obligations through expedients such as moving from state to state, claiming not to be the father of his three children, and allegedly hiding assets. Improvements in enforcement of child support orders are symbolized by the fact that he ultimately was apprehended and served time in state and federal jails—although it seemed quite unlikely that he would ever fully repay the hundreds of thousands of dollars that he owed.[125]

Both noncompliance with court orders and other problems can create conflicts between the former spouses after a divorce is granted. These conflicts frequently lead one or both parties to seek court action, and several studies suggest that such action occurs in 20 percent or more of all divorces.[126] Thus divorce illustrates particularly well the fact that legal decrees may not fully resolve the problems that brought people to court.

WINNERS AND LOSERS

Political scientist Harold D. Lasswell defined politics as "who gets what, when, how."[127] In the sense of that definition, American civil trial courts are deeply enmeshed in politics. One of their main functions is the allocation of gains and losses.

And the prospect of action by civil courts affects a much larger number of allocations that are made outside of court. Thus it is important to look at the patterns of outcomes in cases that go to court and those that might have gone to court.

Earlier in the chapter, I discussed Marc Galanter's argument that "the 'haves' come out ahead"—that those who come to court with more resources than their opponents tend to prevail in court. Galanter's argument directs our attention to the relationship between resources and success, not only in cases that go to court but also in the cases that could have gone to court. The available evidence is both limited and ambiguous, but it allows some partial and tentative conclusions.

Personal Injuries

In most fields, the cases that courts actually decide are a small sample of the matters that could have gone to court. Since some kinds of matters are more likely to end up in court than others, these cases are also unrepresentative of all potential cases. For that reason, we must be careful about our inferences from court decisions. Still, it is useful to look at what we know about jury decisions on personal injuries, which constitute the great majority of court decisions in this field.[128]

Overall, injured parties win about half the time in jury verdicts, but the success rate for plaintiffs varies considerably from one type of case to another. One study of 1992 cases found a 73 percent success rate in cases involving toxic substances but only a 30 percent success rate in medical malpractice cases. The low rate in malpractice is noteworthy, because this is an area in which juries often are criticized for undue generosity to injured parties.[129] Similarly, the mean amount awarded to successful plaintiffs in those cases varied from $1.5 million in product liability cases to a little over $200,000 in auto accident cases and those involving slander or libel. (Because the mean is affected heavily by the largest awards, the median is much lower: $51,000 overall, as against a mean of $408,000.) There is a widespread perception that plaintiffs in personal injury cases frequently are awarded high levels of punitive damages, but such awards were made in only 4 percent of all cases in which a plaintiff won any damages.[130]

Patterns in jury decisions over time are of particular interest. On the one hand, there is a widespread perception that jurors have become increasingly willing to give large awards to plaintiffs. On the other hand, business groups have worked in recent years to reduce jurors' sympathy toward plaintiffs. One study examined jury verdicts in nineteen counties across five states between 1970 and 1990. The patterns varied from place to place, with plaintiffs' success rates remaining stable in two states but increasing somewhat in the other three—apparently because of major changes in the relevant legal rules in those states. For successful plaintiffs, the median size of the jury's award (controlling for inflation) increased substantially in some counties, remained fairly stable in others, and actually dropped in a few.[131]

Some studies have looked more broadly at the outcomes of personal injury claims, whether or not these claims result in trials. Auto accidents, the most common source of personal injury cases, have also been the subject of the most research of this type.

The research on auto accidents that result in injuries points to several conclusions.[132] First, most people recover something for their injuries—through a settlement with another party, through other sources such as their own insurance, or both. But at least a substantial minority of people with serious injuries receive nothing from the other party, sometimes because they lose in court.

Second, the law has considerable effect on what people recover, even in the cases that do not go to trial. Where a defendant seems to be legally liable for an accident, the injured party is more likely to receive something in an out-of-court settlement and tends to receive a larger amount. Similarly, people with the greatest expenses for their injuries generally are entitled to recover the most under the law, if the defendant is found liable; they also receive the most when they settle out of court.

Third, despite this tendency, in an important sense those with the most serious injuries do least well. While people with minor losses frequently recover more money than they lost, thereby gaining some compensation for their nonmonetary costs, the people who are most seriously hurt typically receive only a fraction of their costs from the other party—though other sources of payment reduce this gap somewhat.[133] One reason is that minor claims have nuisance value: it is cheaper for insurance companies to offer generous settlements than to bear the costs of going to court. In contrast, people with more severe losses suffer from the opposite situation: insurance companies can discount their offers in such cases because the injured party wishes to avoid the costs of going to court to receive full compensation. Besides, the costs of a serious accident may exceed the limits on the defendant's insurance coverage.

Fourth, lawyers have conflicting economic effects. Injured parties who are represented by attorneys do better than unrepresented parties, presumably because lawyers are effective in bargaining and in threatening court action. But lawyers' fees take up a significant part of what clients recover, a part that averages a quarter or more of the settlement.[134]

Overall, according to one study, people injured in auto accidents recover 70 percent of their costs from some source, and about one-third of this total comes from legal claims against other parties. The 70 percent recovery was somewhat better than the 62 percent rate for all personal injuries.[135]

Personal injury claims generally pit prosperous insurance companies against individuals of varying incomes. Do insurance companies—the haves—usually come out ahead? Personal injury plaintiffs certainly hold their own in court, and they receive a good deal of money from actual and potential defendants through their insurance companies. But on the whole, payments for personal injury claims leave a considerable gap between the costs that individuals bear for accidents and their compensation for those costs. Even the relatively high rate of recovery for auto accidents means that nearly one-third of all costs are not recovered. Thus the overall picture is mixed and ambiguous, and it is not clear how to evaluate the success of the haves and have-nots.

Debt Collection

As noted in the preceding section, defendants in debt cases frequently fail to protect their rights by making necessary court appearances and taking other required actions. Consequently, creditors win a great many cases without opposition. Even when debtors do contest claims at trial, their creditors usually win.

On the whole, then, creditors do quite well in court. Studies of debt collection cases consistently have found very high rates of success—over 95 percent—for business creditors through favorable judgments in trials or, more often, default judgments.[136] In a study of major trial courts in Cleveland, Milwaukee, and Baltimore, Craig Wanner calculated that business creditors as a group recovered more money than what they originally claimed was owed to them. This seemingly impossible result resulted chiefly from court penalties against defendants for such items as interest, late-payment charges, and attorneys' fees.[137] That study may overstate the success of business creditors, but their success is clearly quite substantial.

However, the difficulty of actually collecting what the courts award must be taken into account. Although businesses do better than individuals in this regard, a significant proportion of money awarded to them does not get collected. This slippage is an important exception to the general effectiveness with which businesses use the courts for debt collection.

Business success in debt collection can be interpreted in quite different ways. On the one hand, we might see it as meaning simply that a set of litigants with very strong cases are able to use the courts effectively to secure their rights. According to this interpretation, consumers and borrowers agree to pay money; they fail to do so; and when creditors turn to the courts, they can enforce debtors' obligations to them. Thus the courts are operating as they should in cases where there is little ambiguity about the law and the facts.

But under another interpretation, the courts are not operating in so benign a fashion. From this perspective, business creditors have strong cases partly because they have shaped the law in their favor through lobbying in the legislature and through past advocacy in the courts, partly because they can arrange transactions in a way that leaves debtors with little basis for a defense. Furthermore, some debtors have potentially strong defenses under the law, but they cannot protect their interests in the courts because they lack legal knowledge and access to lawyers and because court personnel are unsympathetic to them. In contrast, creditors develop expertise in using the courts and credibility with judges. And because of their backgrounds and experiences, many judges begin with a predisposition to favor creditors. Given all these factors, some commentators view the success of business creditors as not entirely appropriate. Indeed, one student of small claims courts referred to their "persecution and intimidation of the low-income litigant" in debt collection cases.[138]

This second interpretation fits neatly into Galanter's framework of analysis. Debt collection cases are a particularly clear example of a conflict between haves and have-nots. Business creditors enjoy all the advantages of haves, including their status as repeat players, while the defendants are primarily low-income individuals and one-shotters with limited resources and capacities to use the courts. Because of this disparity, the haves are quite successful.

People who see the success of business creditors as less than fully justified have sought to improve the position of debtors in court. They have made several kinds of proposals, many of which have been adopted to some degree. For example, federally funded legal services for the poor have given some debtors a better chance to defend themselves. Many courts have made procedural changes, such as improvements in the serving of summonses. In addition, some states have made the law more favorable to consumers and debtors. For instance, the inadequacy of goods and the failure to repair an apartment have been adopted as defenses in debt cases. These changes apparently have had limited impact, because they have been insufficient to overcome the cumulative advantages of creditors over debtors.[139] The high rate of victories that creditors secure in court may or may not be desirable, depending on our perspective. In either case, we can expect this rate to continue.

Divorce

One outcome of divorce proceedings is that people who want divorces usually get them. Depending on the circumstances, the ease of divorce can favor either or both parties.

A second outcome is that mothers usually receive physical custody of children (that is, children are to live only or primarily with their mothers), perhaps 85 to 90 percent of the time.[140] Although many states now encourage joint legal custody arrangements, under joint custody most children live with the mother most of the time.[141] Since custody is contested in only a small proportion of cases, it is difficult to judge what this outcome means in terms of winners and losers. Traditionally, courts gave preference to mothers, particularly for younger children. There is some evidence that this preference has declined, but it has not disappeared altogether. For this reason, even a father who would like to obtain custody might not seek it. But some fathers do not seek custody because they do not want it.

The economics of divorce are also complex. In most instances, if the court transferred no money from one partner to the other, the woman would be at a great disadvantage. Even if a woman is employed full-time when the divorce occurs, her income is likely to be lower than that of her husband. Many women have no career at the time of divorce. If they take a full-time job after divorce, the level of pay probably will be low. Those women who have custody of children also bear the costs of their care.

This situation is alleviated by the payment of alimony and child support, but only to a limited degree. Alimony is awarded in less than one-quarter of all divorces, generally it is awarded for relatively short periods, and the amounts awarded tend to be low.[142] Most divorced women with custody of children are awarded child support. But the levels of child support awarded, like the levels of alimony, tend to be low. In 1991, the mothers who were entitled to child support for one or more children would have received $3,375. Because of noncompliance with support orders, the average received was actually $2,298.[143]

As a result, on average, the money transferred from former husbands to former wives is insufficient to compensate for the differences in their earnings from employment and for the costs of raising children. Indeed, a number of studies have shown that—at least for the first few years after divorce—former husbands generally end up in a considerably better economic position than do former wives.[144]

If larger awards of alimony and child support are necessary to produce economic equality between the former spouses, why are they not typically made? Some observers argue that no-fault divorce laws are a major cause of this situation, because they reduced the bargaining leverage and economic rights of women who were "innocent parties" in a divorce; other observers disagree.[145] It does appear that most divorced women have ended up worse off economically under both fault and no-fault rules for divorce. In the words of one scholar, "The economic situation of women and children . . . was bad before no fault, and it continues to be bad now."[146] Thus the economic disparity between women and men after divorce seems to have more fundamental sources: the more limited earnings of women from employment and judges' reluctance to require that men pay a large share of their income in alimony and child support, a reluctance that affects negotiated settlements as well.[147]

In recent years, policymakers have taken some steps to improve the economic situation of divorced women. Largely as a result of federal rules, many states have increased their efforts to enforce child support orders and have established guidelines for judges that tend to increase the levels of support. One study of three states found that guidelines did increase the average level of child support by proportions ranging from 5 percent in Colorado to 28 percent in Hawaii. Since the level of support had been highest in Colorado and lowest in Hawaii, the guidelines had an equalizing effect.[148]

In most divorces, husbands can be considered the "haves" because of their superior earning power. Courts reallocate substantial resources from former husbands to former wives, but that reallocation is insufficient to produce economic equality. This result can be interpreted in different ways.

An Overview

The three areas of court activity considered in this section, though each is quite significant, are not a random sample of everything that civil courts do. In particular, each is a private-law area, and I have not discussed areas in which government plays a prominent role.

At the least, these three surveys suggest the difficulty of analyzing success in court and in matters affected by the courts. Depending on our concept of success and how we apply it, we might reach different conclusions about the success enjoyed by a particular group of litigants.

The area of personal injuries is perhaps the most ambiguous. It is not entirely clear what should be the benchmark for success in negotiations and in court for people who have been injured. The results are so mixed that any benchmark would be difficult to apply.

Divorce is also ambiguous. In divorce cases, a great deal of money is transferred from men to women, but divorced women on average seem to end up much less well off than the men. Which group is more successful in court? I interpret the results to mean that former husbands are more successful in the financial aspects of divorce, but some might disagree.

Debt collection seems clearest. Creditors have some difficulty in collecting the money that courts award them. With that exception, creditors appear to be highly successful in their use of the courts. Whether that success is desirable is a more difficult and more debatable issue.

Because of the ambiguities that I have noted, as well as the gaps in what we know, some caution in assessing winners and losers is appropriate. But in one of the three areas that has been discussed, and probably in a second, it seems reasonable to conclude that the litigants starting out with an economic advantage generally enjoy success in court. In none of these areas do the litigants with an economic disadvantage achieve a general record of success. If these three areas are fairly typical in this respect, it seems reasonable to conclude that in civil litigation the haves do tend to come out ahead.

CONCLUSIONS

This chapter has stressed the links between civil trial courts and American society as a whole. The discussion of winners and losers underlines the strength of these links.

The field of personal injury law illustrates the effects of courts on actions outside the judicial system. A very small proportion of injuries are the subject of court trials; the remainder are handled elsewhere. Yet the laws that courts apply and the decisions they reach influence the resolution of claims and disputes that never come to court— because a dispute that is not settled outside of court would be resolved on terms imposed by the courts. Although negotiated settlements do not mirror court decisions perfectly, they are shaped by predictions of what would happen if cases went to court. It is through this indirect impact that the courts help allocate far more gains and losses than the number of trials suggests.

Conversely, the field of debt collection illustrates the impact of social realities on the courts. As we have seen, the outcomes of debt collection cases can be interpreted in different ways. But it is clear that creditors are far better able to defend their interests in court than are debtors. In turn, this advantage stems primarily from the differences in economic and social status between the two groups.

These kinds of links, of course, are not unique to the civil side of the law. As Chapter 6 indicates, the work of criminal courts is also linked to events and forces outside of court. But the ties between trial courts and their environments seem especially close in civil cases. Certainly, they make it clear that we can understand what courts do only in the context of the larger society in which they operate.

FOR FURTHER READING

Daniels, Stephen, and Joanne Martin. *Civil Juries and the Politics of Reform.* Evanston, Ill.: Northwestern University Press, 1995.
Ellickson, Robert C. *Order Without Law: How Neighbors Settle Disputes.* Cambridge: Harvard University Press, 1991.
Greenhouse, Carol J., Barbara Yngvesson, and David M. Engel. *Law and Community in Three American Towns.* Ithaca, N.Y.: Cornell University Press, 1994.
Harr, Jonathan. *A Civil Action.* New York: Random House, 1995.
Kritzer, Herbert M. *Let's Make a Deal: Understanding the Negotiation Process in Ordinary Litigation.* Madison: University of Wisconsin Press, 1991.
Litan, Robert E., ed. *Verdict: Assessing the Civil Jury System.* Washington, D.C.: Brookings Institution, 1993.
Merry, Sally Engle. *Getting Justice and Getting Even: Legal Consciousness Among Working-Class Americans.* Chicago: University of Chicago Press, 1990.
Ross, H. Laurence. *Settled Out of Court: The Social Process of Insurance Claims Adjustment,* rev. 2d ed. New York: Aldine, 1980.

Vidmar, Neil. *Medical Malpractice and the American Jury.* Ann Arbor: University of Michigan Press, 1995.

Weiler, Paul C., et al. *A Measure of Malpractice: Medical Injury, Malpractice Litigation, and Patient Compensation.* Cambridge: Harvard University Press, 1993.

NOTES

1. Robert H. Mnookin and Lewis Kornhauser, "Bargaining in the Shadow of the Law: The Case of Divorce," *Yale Law Journal* 88 (April 1979), 950–997.
2. See Dan B. Dobbs, *Dobbs Law of Remedies,* 2d ed. (St. Paul: West Publishing, 1993), 1–3.
3. Kenneth E. Scott, "Two Models of the Civil Process," *Stanford Law Review* 27 (February 1975), 937–950.
4. See Peter H. Schuck, ed., *Tort Law and the Public Interest: Competition, Innovation, and Consumer Welfare* (New York: Norton, 1991).
5. Administrative Office of the United States Courts, *Judicial Business of the United States Courts: Report of the Director (1995)* (Washington, D.C.: Administrative Office of the United States Courts, n.d.), 162, 225.
6. Marc Galanter, "Why the 'Haves' Come Out Ahead: Speculations on the Limits of Legal Change," *Law & Society Review* 9 (Fall 1974), 97.
7. Ibid., 97–124.
8. Saundra Torry, "It's a Magical History Tour at 'Vacatur Center'," *Washington Post,* March 10, 1997, Washington Business section, 7. See Jill E. Fisch, "Rewriting History: The Propriety of Eradicating Prior Decisional Law Through Settlement and Vacatur," *Cornell Law Review* 76 (March 1991), 589–642; and *Agee v. Paramount Communications, Inc.,* 932 F. Supp. 85 (S.D.N.Y. 1996).
9. See Mary Kay Kane, *Civil Procedure in a Nutshell,* 4th ed. (St. Paul: West Publishing, 1996).
10. *Paramount Comunications Inc. v. QVC Network Inc.,* 637 A.2d 34, 55 (Del. 1994).
11. *Washington State Physicians Insurance Exchange & Association v. Fisons Corporation,* 858 P.2d 1054 (Wash. 1993). See Stuart Taylor, Jr., "Sleazy in Seattle," *American Lawyer,* April 1994, 5, 74–79.
12. Frank A. Sloan et al., *Suing for Medical Malpractice* (Chicago: University of Chicago Press, 1993), 157.
13. *United States v. Microsoft Corporation,* 159 F.R.D. 318 (D.D.C. 1995), 56 F.3d 1448 (D.C. Cir. 1995).
14. Carol J. DeFrances, Steven K. Smith, and Patrick A. Langan, *Civil Jury Cases and Verdicts in Large Counties* (Washington, D.C.: U.S. Department of Justice, 1995), 1; Administrative Office of the United States Courts, *Judicial Business of the United States Courts (1995),* 162.
15. James S. Kakalik, Molly Selvin, and Nicholas M. Pace, *Averting Gridlock: Strategies for Reducing Civil Delay in the Los Angeles Superior Court* (Santa Monica, Calif.: Rand Corporation, 1990), 1.
16. "Court Says 'Enough' in 26–year Divorce," *Chicago Tribune,* May 23, 1993, sec. 1, 7; Jeff Leeds, "14–Year Battle over $5 Bar Tab Comes to an End," *Washington Post,* November 25, 1994, C4.
17. Victor E. Flango, Robert T. Roper, and Mary E. Elsner, *The Business of State Trial Courts* (Williamsburg, Va.: National Center for State Courts, 1983), 33.
18. *Annual Report of the Administrative Office of the United States Courts (1980)* (Washington, D.C.: Administrative Office of the U.S. Courts, n.d.), 374; Administrative Office of the United States Courts, *Judicial Business of the United States Courts (1995),* 139.
19. Richard E. Miller and Austin Sarat, "Grievances, Claims, and Disputes: Assessing the

Adversary Culture," *Law & Society Review* 15 (1980–81), 544; Herbert M. Kritzer, Neil Vidmar, and W. A. Bogart, "To Confront or Not to Confront: Measuring Claiming Rates in Discrimination Grievances," *Law & Society Review* 25 (1991), 883.

20. Randall Samborn, "Many Americans Find Bias at Work," *National Law Journal,* July 16, 1990, 1.

21. See Kristin Bumiller, *The Civil Rights Society: The Social Construction of Victims* (Baltimore: Johns Hopkins University Press, 1988), 27–28.

22. Sharon Walsh, "The Vanishing Job-Bias Lawyers," *Washington Post,* July 6, 1990, C1, C2.

23. Amy Saltzman, "Life After the Lawsuit," *U.S. News & World Report,* August 19, 1996, 57.

24. Miller and Sarat, "Grievances, Claims, and Disputes," 544.

25. Deborah R. Hensler et al., *Compensation for Accidental Injuries in the United States* (Santa Monica, Calif.: Rand Corporation, 1991), 122.

26. This discussion of auto accident cases draws from Miller and Sarat, "Grievances, Claims, and Disputes"; Hensler et al., *Compensation for Accidental Injuries;* All-Industry Research Advisory Council, *Compensation for Automobile Injuries in the United States* (Oak Brook, Ill.: AIRAC, 1989); and especially H. Laurence Ross, *Settled Out of Court: The Social Process of Insurance Claims Adjustment,* rev. 2d ed. (New York: Aldine, 1980).

27. All-Industry Research Advisory Council, *Compensation for Automobile Injuries,* 115.

28. Ibid., 115.

29. Ross, *Settled Out of Court,* 215–224.

30. Paul C. Weiler et al., *A Measure of Malpractice: Medical Injury, Malpractice Litigation, and Patient Compensation* (Cambridge: Harvard University Press, 1993), 61–76.

31. Stephen Daniels and Joanne Martin, *Civil Juries and the Politics of Reform* (Evanston, Ill.: Northwestern University Press, 1995), 117–119; Frank A. Sloan and Chee Ruey Hsieh, "Injury, Liability, and the Decision to File a Medical Malpractice Claim," *Law & Society Review* 29 (1995), 413–435; Michael J. Saks, "Malpractice Misconceptions and Other Lessons About the Litigation System," *Justice System Journal* 16 (1993), 7–13.

32. Neil Vidmar, *Medical Malpractice and the American Jury* (Ann Arbor: University of Michigan Press, 1995), 49–57.

33. Mark Crane, "Lawyers Don't Take *Every* Case," *National Law Journal,* January 25, 1988, 1, 34.

34. Ross E. Cheit, "Corporate Ambulance Chasers: The Charmed Life of Business Litigation," *Studies in Law, Politics, and Society* 11 (1991), 119–140.

35. Stewart Macauley, "Non-Contractual Relations in Business: A Preliminary Study," *American Sociological Review* 28 (February 1963), 61.

36. Robert C. Ellickson, *Order Without Law: How Neighbors Settle Disputes* (Cambridge: Harvard University Press, 1991), 52–55.

37. Mike France, "More Big Businesses Ask: Can We Talk, Not Sue?" *National Law Journal,* March 13, 1995, B1, B2.

38. Martha M. Hamilton, "Smear Campaign?" *Washington Post,* December 13, 1995, F1, F10.

39. Ross E. Cheit, "Patterns of Contemporary Business Litigation in Rhode Island" (paper presented at the 1990 meeting of the Law & Society Association in Berkeley, California), 36–38.

40. Laurence Zuckerman, "Suit by Digital Says Intel Stole Pentium Design," *New York Times,* May 14, 1997, C1, C7.

41. Miller and Sarat, "Grievances, Claims, and Disputes," 544; Joel B. Grossman, Herbert M. Kritzer, Kristin Bumiller, Austin Sarat, Stephen McDougal, and Richard Miller, "Dimensions of Institutional Participation: Who Uses the Courts and How?" *Journal of Politics* 44 (February 1982), 105.

42. Court Statistics Project, *State Court Caseload Statistics: Annual Report 1990* (Williamsburg, Va.: National Center for State Courts, 1992), 4; Court Statistics Project, *State Court Caseload Statistics, 1994* (Williamsburg, Va.: National Center for State Courts, 1995), 137.

43. Richard Neely, *How Courts Govern America* (New Haven: Yale University Press, 1981), xiv.

44. Ambrose Bierce, *The Devil's Dictionary: A Selection of the Bitter Definitions of Ambrose Bierce* (Mount Vernon, N.Y.: Peter Pauper Press, 1958), 37.

45. Sally Engle Merry, *Getting Justice and Getting Even: Legal Consciousness Among Working-Class Americans* (Chicago: University of Chicago Press, 1990), 3.

46. Marc Galanter, "Reading the Landscape of Disputes: What We Know and Don't Know (and Think We Know) About Our Allegedly Contentious and Litigious Society," *UCLA Law Review* 31 (October 1983), 24.

47. Merry, *Getting Justice and Getting Even,* 142–143.

48. William Carlsen, "Judge Reins in S.F. Woman Who Filed 30 Lawsuits," *San Francisco Chronicle,* January 2, 1996, A1, A8. The statute is codified at *California Code of Civil Procedure,* sec. 391.7 (West Annotated California Codes, 1997 ed.).

49. *In re Bryant,* 1994 U.S. Dist. LEXIS 16540 (E.D. Pa. 1994).

50. Kevin J. Delaney, *Strategic Bankruptcy: How Corporations and Creditors Use Chapter 11 to Their Advantage* (Berkeley: University of California Press, 1992).

51. Peter Kerr, "'Ghost Riders' Are Target of an Insurance Sting," *New York Times,* August 18, 1993, A1, C2.

52. George W. Pring and Penelope Canan, *SLAPPs: Getting Sued for Speaking Out* (Philadelphia: Temple University Press, 1996), 3.

53. See Austin Sarat and Joel B. Grossman, "Courts and Conflict Resolution: Problems in the Mobilization of Adjudication," *American Political Science Review* 69 (December 1975), 1200–1217.

54. See Marc Galanter and John Lande, "Private Courts and Public Authority," *Studies in Law, Politics, and Society* 12 (1992), 400–407.

55. Executive Order 12988, published at 61 *Federal Register* 4729 (1996).

56. See Karen Donovan, "Searching for ADR Stars," *National Law Journal,* March 14, 1994, A1, A20, A21.

57. "Justice Lucas's JAMS," *California Lawyer,* October 1993, 26; Harriet Chiang, "Ex-Chief Justice Joins Private Mediation Firm," *San Francisco Chronicle,* July 17, 1996, A14.

58. *McMillan v. Superior Court,* 57 Cal. Rptr. 2d 674, 681 (Cal. 2d Dist. 1996). See Doris Marie Provine, "Justice a la Carte: On the Privatization of Dispute Resolution," *Studies in Law, Politics, and Society* 12 (1992), 345–366.

59. Barry Meier, "In Fine Print, Customers Lose Ability to Sue," *New York Times,* March 10, 1997, C7.

60. Ibid. See Jane Bryant Quinn, "Is Arbitration an Investment in Frustration?" *Chicago Tribune,* May 11, 1997, sec. 5, 3.

61. Administrative Office of the United States Courts, *Judicial Business of the United States Courts (1995),* 138.

62. *Bennett v. Spear,* 137 L. Ed. 2d 281 (1997).

63. *Philanthropy Protection Act of 1995,* P.L. 104–62; *Charitable Gift Annuity Antitrust Relief Act of 1995,* P.L. 104–63.

64. David Segal, "Lawyers Stake a Claim on Bias Lawsuits," *Washington Post,* January 27, 1997, A1, A12; Kirstin Downey Grimsley, "Worker Bias Cases Up 20 Pct. a Year," *Washington Post,* May 12, 1997, A1, A10.

65. See Thomas E. Willging, *The Rule 11 Sanctioning Process* (Washington, D.C.: Federal Judicial Center, 1988); and Stephen B. Burbank, *Rule 11 in Transition: The Report of the Third Circuit Task Force on Federal Rule of Civil Procedure 11* (Chicago: American Judicature Society, 1989).

66. See *Prudential Insurance Co. of America v. Lai,* 42 F.3d 1299 (9th Cir. 1994).

67. *Pietrelli v. Peacock,* 16 Cal. Rptr. 2d 688 (Cal. 1st Dist. 1993).

68. *Doctor's Associates, Inc. v. Casarotto,* 134 L. Ed. 2d 902 (1996). See Paul D. Carrington and Paul H. Haagen, "Contract and Jurisdiction," *Supreme Court Review,* 1996, 331–402.

69. *Private Securities Litigation Reform Act of 1995,* P.L. 104–67.

70. Marianne Lavelle, "Food Abuse: Basis for Suits," *National Law Journal,* May 5, 1997, A1, A21. The quoted language in the Georgia statute is at *Official Code of Georgia Annotated* sec. 2–16–2 (1) (1996).

71. Bayless Manning, "Hyperlexis: Our National Disease," *Northwestern University Law Review* 71 (January–February 1977), 772.

72. Lois Forer, *The Death of the Law* (New York: David McKay, 1975), 133.

73. See, respectively, "Softball Coach Sues in Search of Happiness," *Washington Post,* June 11, 1993, C2; Debra Carr, "Lawsuit: Newspapers' Horoscopes Turn Into Horrorscope for Detroit Man," *National Law Journal,* March 23, 1992, 47; and Victoria Benning, "Dear Ann Landers, I Take It All Back," *Washington Post,* April 18, 1997, B3.

74. Galanter, "Reading the Landscape of Disputes," 51–61.

75. Robert A. Kagan, "Adversarial Legalism and American Government," *Journal of Policy Analysis and Management* 10 (1991), 369–406.

76. Ibid., 386–397.

77. See V. Lee Hamilton and Joseph Sanders, *Everyday Justice: Responsibility and the Individual in Japan and the United States* (New Haven, Conn.: Yale University Press, 1992), 186–202.

78. Mary Jordan, "Raising the Bar for Japan's Lawyers," *Washington Post,* February 14, 1996, A1, A17.

79. George Kalogerakis, "Those Who Can, Sue," *Spy Magazine,* June 1989, 94.

80. Galanter, "Reading the Landscape of Disputes," 10–11.

81. Murray Chass, "There's No Joy in Mudville? Sue for Mental Anguish," *New York Times,* August 21, 1992, B9.

82. Harold Seymour, *Baseball: The Golden Age* (New York: Oxford University Press, 1971).

83. *Annual Report of the Director of the Administrative Office of the United States Courts, 1975* (Washington, D.C.: Government Printing Office, n.d.), 346; *Annual Report of the Administrative Office, 1985* (Washington, D.C.: Government Printing Office, n.d.), 280; Administrative Office of the United States Courts, *Judicial Business of the United States Courts (1995),* 138.

84. Galanter, "Reading the Landscape of Disputes," 4; Administrative Office of the United States Courts, *Judicial Business of the United States Courts (1995),* 162.

85. Court Statistics Project, *State Court Caseload Statistics, 1990,* 25.

86. Steven K. Smith, Carol J. DeFrances, and Patrick A. Langan, *Tort Cases in Large Counties* (Washington, D.C.: U.S. Department of Justice, 1995), 2. See also Thomas B. Marvell, "Tort Caseload Trends and the Impact of Tort Reforms," *Justice System Journal* 17 (1994), 193–206; and Deborah R. Hensler, "Reading the Tort Litigation Tea Leaves: What's Going on in the Civil Liability System?" *Justice System Journal* 16 (1993), 139–154.

87. Wayne McIntosh, "150 Years of Litigation and Dispute Settlement: A Court Tale," *Law & Society Review* 15 (1980–1981), 823–848; Lawrence M. Friedman and Robert V. Percival, "A Tale of Two Courts: Litigation in Alameda and San Benito Counties," *Law & Society Review* 10 (Winter 1976), 267–301; Stephen Daniels, "Caseload Dynamics and the Nature of Change: The Civil Business of Trial Courts in Four Illinois Counties," *Law & Society Review* 24 (1990), 299–320.

88. William Mullen, "U.S. Seeks a Cure to Legal Dilemma," *Chicago Tribune,* July 26, 1991, sec. 1, 1.

89. David M. Engel and Eric H. Steele, "Civil Cases and Society: Process and Order in the Civil Justice System," *American Bar Foundation Research Journal,* Spring 1979, 307–311.

90. This discussion is based in part on Herbert M. Kritzer, *Let's Make a Deal: Understanding the Negotiation Process in Ordinary Litigation* (Madison: University of Wisconsin Press, 1991); Miller and Sarat, "Grievances, Claims, and Disputes"; and Ross, *Settled Out of Court.*

91. Smith, DeFrances, and Langan, *Tort Cases in Large Counties,* 2, 4, 5.

92. Ibid., 3.

93. Ibid., 4.

94. Kritzer, *Let's Make a Deal,* 130.

95. Ted Rohrlich, "The Case of the Missing Jurors . . ." *Los Angeles Times,* May 19, 1990, A27.

96. 28 *United States Code,* Federal Rules of Civil Procedure, Rule 68.

97. Kritzer, *Let's Make a Deal,* 32, 38, 65.

98. DeFrances et al., *Civil Jury Cases and Verdicts in Large Counties,* 2.

99. Kevin M. Clermont and Theodore Eisenberg, "Trial by Jury or Judge: Transcending Empiricism," *Cornell Law Review* 77 (July 1992), 1124–1177.

100. Valerie P. Hans, "The Contested Role of the Civil Jury in Business Litigation," *Judicature* 79 (March–April 1996), 248.

101. Richard Pérez-Peña, "Study Finds Sharp Drop Last Year in Awards for Medical Malpractice Cases," *New York Times,* January 27, 1995, B16.

102. Michael J. Saks, "Do We Really Know Anything About the Behavior of the Tort Litigation System—and Why Not?" *University of Pennsylvania Law Review* 140 (April 1992), 1239.

103. See B.J. Palermo, "The Race for O.J.'s Assets Is On—and It Is Tortuous," *National Law Journal,* April 14, 1997, A9.

104. Karen Testa, "Court Orders Assets Seizure at 2 Florida Kmart Stores," *Washington Post,* February 14, 1996, D4.

105. Michael G. Shanley and Mark A. Peterson, *Posttrial Adjustments to Jury Awards* (Santa Monica, Calif.: Rand Corporation, 1987), 36.

106. Maura Dolan, "Huge Jury Awards Seldom Live Up to Their Billing," *Los Angeles Times,* November 26, 1996, A1, A20, A21. See also "Verdicts Revisited," *National Law Journal,* September 26, 1994, C1–C16.

107. See Deborah R. Hensler and Mark A. Peterson, "Understanding Mass Personal Injury Litigation: A Socio-Legal Analysis," *Brooklyn Law Review* 59 (1993), 961–1063.

108. Craig Wanner, "The Public Ordering of Private Relations. Part One: Initiating Civil Cases in Urban Trial Courts," *Law & Society Review* 8 (Spring 1974), 422.

109. John A. Goerdt, *Small Claims and Traffic Courts: Case Management Procedures, Case Characteristics, and Outcomes in 12 Urban Jurisdictions* (Williamsburg, Va.: National Center for State Courts, 1992), 47.

110. John Gregory Dunne, *Quintana and Friends* (New York: Dutton, 1978), 243–244.

111. David Caplovitz, *Consumers in Trouble: A Study of Debtors in Default* (New York: Free Press, 1974), 215.

112. Doug Struck, "In a 'People's Court' of Quirky Cases, Even Patience is Tried," *Washington Post,* July 14, 1997, A1.

113. Caplovitz, *Consumers in Trouble,* 220.

114. Ed Sacks, "Report Concludes Most Tenants Are Unsuccessful in Eviction Court," *Chicago Sun-Times,* November 17, 1996, Housing section, 2.

115. Project, "The Iowa Small Claims Court: An Empirical Analysis," *Iowa Law Review* 75 (January 1990), 521.

116. See Herbert Jacob, *Silent Revolution: The Transformation of Divorce Law in the United States* (Chicago: University of Chicago Press, 1988).

117. Margaret F. Brinig and Michael V. Alexeev, "Trading at Divorce: Preferences, Legal Rules and Transactions Costs," *Ohio State Journal on Dispute Resolution* 8 (1993), 294.

118. Eleanor E. Maccoby and Robert H. Mnookin, *Dividing the Child: Social and Legal Dilemmas of Custody* (Cambridge: Harvard University Press, 1992), 137.

119. Florence Hamlish Levinsohn, "Breaking Up Is *Still* Hard to Do," *Chicago Tribune Magazine,* October 21, 1990, 23.

120. Marygold S. Melli, Howard S. Erlanger, and Elizabeth Chambliss, "The Process of Negotiation: An Exploratory Investigation in the Context of No-Fault Divorce," *Rutgers Law Review* 40 (Summer 1988), 1145.

121. Ibid., 1147.

122. U.S. Bureau of the Census, Current Population Reports, Series P60–187, *Child Support*

for Custodial Mothers and Fathers: 1991 (Washington, D.C.: U.S. Government Printing Office, 1995), 6–10.

123. Charles Babington, "Md. Targets Child-Support Delinquents," *Washington Post,* May 1, 1996, D3.

124. Gary Taylor, "You Reap What You Sow," *National Law Journal,* May 20, 1996, A23.

125. Malcolm Gladwell and Nancy Reckler, "Recalcitrant Father Jailed in New York," *Washington Post,* August 19, 1995, A1, A4; Lynda Richardson, "Failure to Support Children Earns Man 6 Months in Jail," *New York Times,* November 7, 1996, B23.

126. Miller and Sarat, "Grievances, Claims, and Disputes," 544–546; Kressel, *Process of Divorce,* 10–13.

127. Harold D. Lasswell, *Politics: Who Gets What, When, How* (New York: P. Smith, 1950).

128. See Daniels and Martin, *Civil Juries and the Politics of Reform,* 66.

129. See Neil Vidmar, *Medical Malpractice and the American Jury* (Ann Arbor: University of Michigan Press, 1995).

130. Brian J. Ostrom, David B. Rottman, and John A. Goerdt, "A Step Above Anecdote: A Profile of the Civil Jury in the 1990s," *Judicature* 79 (March–April 1996), 235, 238, 239.

131. Daniels and Martin, *Civil Juries and the Politics of Reform,* 87–90.

132. This discussion is based on several studies, including U.S. Department of Transportation, *Economic Consequences of Automobile Accident Injuries* (Washington, D.C.: Government Printing Office, 1970); Hensler et al., *Compensation for Accidental Injuries;* and All-Industry Research Advisory Council, *Compensation for Automobile Injuries.*

133. See All-Industry Research Advisory Council, *Compensation for Automobile Injuries,* 31, 129.

134. See James S. Kakalik and Nicholas M. Pace, *Costs and Compensation Paid in Tort Litigation* (Santa Monica, Calif: Rand Corporation, 1986).

135. Hensler et al., *Compensation for Accidental Injuries,* 105–108.

136. Caplovitz, *Consumers in Trouble,* 221; Goerdt, *Small Claims and Traffic Courts,* 51–52; Sacks, "Report Concludes Most Tenants Are Unsuccessful," 2.

137. Craig Wanner, "A Harvest of Profits: Exploring the Symbiotic Relationship Between Urban Civil Trial Courts and the Business Community" (paper presented at the 1973 meeting of the American Political Science Association in New Orleans, Louisiana).

138. Beatrice A. Moulton, "The Persecution and Intimidation of the Low-Income Litigant as Performed by the Small Claims Court in California," *Stanford Law Review* 21 (June 1969), 1657–1684.

139. See Marilyn Miller Mosier and Richard A. Soble, "Modern Legislation, Metropolitan Court, Miniscule Results: A Study of Detroit's Landlord-Tenant Court," *Journal of Law Reform* 7 (Fall 1973), 6–70.

140. Diane Shrier, Sue K. Simring, Judith R. Grief, Edith T. Shapiro, and Jacob J. Lindenthal, "Child Custody Arrangements: A Study of Two New Jersey Counties," *Journal of Psychiatry and Law* 17 (Spring 1989), 9–20; Barbara R. Rowe and Jean M. Lown, "The Economics of Divorce and Remarriage for Rural Utah Families," *Journal of Contemporary Law* 16 (March 1990), 314. On custody decisions generally, see Maccoby and Mnookin, *Dividing the Child,* 98–114.

141. See Marsha Garrison, "Good Intentions Gone Awry: The Impact of New York's Equitable Distribution Law on Divorce Outcomes," *Brooklyn Law Review* 57 (Fall 1991), 717.

142. Gordon H. Lester, *Child Support and Alimony: 1987,* U.S. Bureau of the Census, Current Population Reports, Series P-23, No. 167 (Washington, D.C.: Government Printing Office, 1990), 8, 11; Garrison, "Good Intentions Gone Awry," 697–699.

143. Bureau of the Census, *Child Support 1991,* 9.

144. Suzanne Bianchi and Edith McArthur, *Family Disruption and Economic Hardship: The Short-Run Picture for Children,* U.S. Bureau of the Census, Current Population Reports, Series P-70, no. 23 (Washington, D.C.: Government Printing Office, 1991); Rowe and Lown, "Economics of Divorce and Remarriage," 322–325; Maccoby and Mnookin, *Dividing the Child,* 249–265; Richard R. Peterson, "A Re-Evaluation of the Economic Consequences of Divorce," *American Sociological Review* 61 (June 1996), 528–536.

145. Lenore J. Weitzman, *The Divorce Revolution: The Unexpected Social and Economic Consequences for Women and Children in America* (New York: Free Press, 1985); Herbert Jacob, "Faulting No-Fault," *American Bar Foundation Research Journal,* Fall 1986, 773–780; Stephen D. Sugarman, "Dividing Financial Interests on Divorce," in *Divorce Reform at the Crossroads,* ed. Stephen D. Sugarman and Herma Hill Kay (New Haven: Yale University Press, 1991), 130–165.
146. Marygold S. Melli, "Constructing a Social Problem: The Post-Divorce Plight of Women and Children," *American Bar Foundation Research Journal,* Fall 1986, 770.
147. See Marsha Garrison, "How Do Judges Decide Divorce Cases? An Empirical Analysis of Discretionary Decision Making," *North Carolina Law Review* 74 (January 1996), 473–475.
148. Jessica Pearson, Nancy Thoennes, and Patricia Tjaden, "Legislating Adequacy: The Impact of Child Support Guidelines," *Law & Society Review* 23 (1989), 569–590.

8

Appellate Courts: The Process

Most court cases start and end in trial courts. More often than not, cases are resolved prior to trial. In those that do go to trial, the losing party often accepts defeat rather than appealing the verdict. But many cases do get appealed—more than one hundred thousand a year. Those cases allow appellate courts to reconsider the treatment of litigants at their trials. More important, the cases give appellate judges the chance to make policy that affects the courts below them and, sometimes, the country as a whole.

The final two chapters of this book focus on appellate courts. This chapter examines matters of process: how cases flow to and through appellate courts and how and why courts reach their decisions. Chapter 9 considers appellate courts as policymakers, discussing the policies they produce and the impact of those policies.

Trial and appellate courts are closely linked. Cases move back and forth between the two sets of courts, which apply the same body of law in deciding them. Yet in some respects the appellate process differs fundamentally from the trial process. Indeed, as suggested in Chapter 1, trial and appellate courts each may resemble some nonjudicial institutions more closely than they resemble each other.

In this context, it is important to distinguish between first-level and second-level appellate courts. First-level courts stand directly above trial courts and review their decisions. Second-level courts stand above the first-level courts and review *their* decisions. Eleven states have only a single appellate court, usually called a supreme court, that serves as a first-level court. The remaining states and the federal system each have one or more intermediate appellate courts (most often called courts of appeals) as first-level courts and a supreme court as a second-level court.

It is second-level appellate courts that differ most sharply from trial courts. The stately pace of proceedings in second-level courts symbolizes the attention that their judges give to individual cases, in contrast with the routine and rapid processing of individual cases that is often found in trial courts. First-level appellate courts are between trial courts and second-level appellate courts in this respect. Growing caseload pressures in recent years have increased their resemblance to trial courts. In response to the greater volume of appellate litigation, there is more emphasis on processing cases, and some cases are handled in a relatively routine fashion. In turn, these procedural changes have affected the outcomes of cases and subtly changed intermediate appellate courts as institutions.

AN OVERVIEW OF APPELLATE COURTS

Consideration of appellate courts can begin with some general matters: the purposes that underlie appellate courts, their business, their major participants, and their procedures for handling appeals.

The Purposes of Appeal

Appellate courts exist, and dissatisfied litigants are permitted to appeal, primarily to serve two purposes.[1]

First, appellate courts can correct errors in application of the law to individual litigants and thus further the cause of justice. Because individual judges and juries can err, review of their judgments seems necessary so that their mistakes do not cause injustice to litigants. That is why litigants in trial courts nearly always have the right to a single appeal.

Appellate courts enjoy some advantages in reaching the right result under the law: they often have more information, and they can operate at a slower pace. A trial judge may make a procedural ruling with little time for reflection or study in the emotional and chaotic conditions of a trial. An appellate court has the luxury of reviewing that ruling with the assistance of extensive written briefs and oral arguments and with weeks or months to make a judgment. And because appellate decisions are made by multiple judges rather than a single one, the chance of an erroneous decision is reduced.

A second purpose of appellate courts is to make the law clearer and more consistent with their decisions. Clarity and consistency are important because they give people and their attorneys greater certainty about the legal consequences of their actions—whether a contract will be declared valid if it is challenged or whether a corporate merger might be disapproved under the antitrust laws. Clarity and consistency also serve the goal of equal justice by helping to ensure that the law is applied in the same fashion to different cases.

One way that appellate courts reduce ambiguity and inconsistency is by resolving conflicting interpretations of the law. If federal district judges in the Sixth Circuit interpret the federal sentencing laws in different ways, the Sixth Circuit Court of Appeals can adopt a single interpretation for them to follow. Even in the absence of a conflict, an appellate court can overturn what its members see as a lower court's mistaken interpretation of a legal provision. By correcting interpretations of the law and the law's application to specific cases, appellate courts can supervise trial courts and keep them on what appellate judges see as the right path.

Where there are both first-level and second-level courts, each has a primary purpose. Courts of appeals directly review trial court decisions, so they do most of the error correction. As the head of a whole court system, the supreme court concentrates on developing and clarifying the law. This is one way in which the two sets of courts differ.

The Business of Appellate Courts

To a considerable extent, as we would expect, the mix of cases in appellate courts mirrors the mix in trial courts. Most important, the diversity of cases in trial courts is reflected at the appellate level. But there are some differences, which have several sources.

First, the jurisdiction of appellate courts differs from that of trial courts in a few important respects. Appeals from some administrative agencies go directly to appellate courts, bypassing the trial level entirely. In most states, appeals from minor trial courts go first to major trial courts, and few of these cases ever get to appellate courts. Prosecutors cannot appeal acquittals in trial courts.

A different jurisdictional matter is the discretionary jurisdiction of second-level appellate courts. To varying degrees, these courts can choose which cases they will hear and decide from those that litigants bring to them. With this discretion, their judges can choose to hear some kinds of cases rather than others. At the extreme, a state supreme court might turn away a whole category of cases.

Third, litigants in different kinds of cases are not equally likely to appeal. Patterns of appeals and the use of discretionary jurisdiction are examined in the next two sections.

Finally, the content of cases is often transformed at the appellate level. The factual questions that dominate most trials are largely irrelevant to appellate courts, which generally accept the conclusions about facts reached by trial judges and juries. Rather, appeals from trial decisions usually emphasize issues of legal interpretation. Ordinarily, such issues must be raised at the trial level in order to be considered on appeal, but they may receive considerably more attention in the appellate court. As a result, a case in which the trial focused on whether the defendant was the person who robbed a store may be transformed on appeal into a case about whether the police followed the proper procedures in searching the defendant's car. Broad legal issues tend to receive even greater emphasis as cases move up to second-level appellate courts.

By no means do all appeals come after trials. Many result from pretrial rulings, and in some states a criminal defendant who pled guilty can appeal the sentence or procedures used in the case. According to one study, only one-quarter of the cases decided by the Arizona court of appeals in Phoenix resulted from trials.[2]

The Participants

Cases on appeal involve a narrower range of participants than do trials. Judges are the central figures, and attorneys play integral roles as well. Other participants are important because they affect what judges and lawyers do: law clerks influence judges, and the parties to cases influence their attorneys.

Judges   Appellate courts are judge centered. Most cases that come to an appellate court are ultimately decided by the court—by judges—rather than settled outside of court. In reaching their decisions, members of appellate courts are influenced by other participants in the courts. But more than trial judges, they are the primary decision makers. Thus it is the goals and motives of judges that determine most directly what appellate courts do.

Yet in one respect individual appellate judges are less important than trial judges. Because appellate courts almost always decide cases collectively, the power of any single judge is diluted. Trial judges can put their individual stamp on courtroom proceedings and decisions. As a result, federal district judges in particular can make a good deal of difference by themselves. Appellate judges can also make a great deal of difference, but they do so as part of a group rather than by acting alone. Unlike trial judges, they must have the support of colleagues if they are to make law and policy.

Law Clerks   Appellate judges are assisted by attorneys who serve as law clerks.[3] (Law clerks should not be confused with court clerks, who help to administer and manage courts.) Many appellate courts also have central staffs of law clerks who carry out major functions for the court as a whole. Members of these staffs are sometimes called staff attorneys.

Most law clerks are recent law school graduates who take their positions for a relatively short period, often only a year. At the appellate level, many of these short-term clerks are high-ranking graduates of prestigious law schools. Some clerks, particularly those on central staffs, serve for longer periods. For the young attorneys who serve individual judges, clerkships can be considered a form of apprenticeship in which close contact between judge and clerk helps to socialize clerks and prepare them for elite positions in the legal system—including, in some instances, judgeships of their own later in life.[4]

The number of law clerks has grown with the caseloads of appellate courts. (Increasingly, trial judges have law clerks as well.) In the federal court system, Supreme Court justices are now allowed to hire four personal law clerks each, and court of appeals judges are allowed three. Central staffs of clerks did not become common until the 1970s, but they now exist in every federal court of appeals and in many state appellate courts.

Caseload growth has also led judges to give clerks more responsibility. One example is the role of central staff attorneys in many intermediate appellate courts. These law clerks categorize cases and perform preliminary work in those deemed to be relatively simple and straightforward—preliminary work that often extends to proposing decisions and opinions to the judges. Law clerks who serve individual judges are delegated such important functions as summarizing the written materials in cases and drafting opinions, though there is considerable variation in judges' use of clerks.[5]

Commentators have expressed several concerns about the influence of law clerks. One concern is that their availability and interests lead appellate judges to write more concurring and dissenting opinions than they otherwise would.[6] Conservatives charge that clerks are predominantly liberal and that they subtly move judges in a liberal direction.[7] The broadest and most widely shared concern is that clerks do too much of judges' work. In a survey of judges on the federal courts of appeals, 32 percent said that they sometimes relied on clerks to do work that judges should do themselves, while another 31 percent said they often or usually did so. One judge noted that "in this circuit, a judge has to turn out 150 opinions a year to stay current. It is not possible to do that without excessive reliance on the law clerks."[8] The importance of law clerks to judges is suggested by the elaborate efforts that many federal judges undertake to hire those whom they identify as the best candidates for clerkships, efforts in which—according to one observer—"the law of the jungle reigns and badmouthing, spying and even poaching among judges is rife."[9]

But the shift of power from judges to law clerks should not be exaggerated. Delegation of responsibility in appellate courts remains far more limited than in many other government organizations; more than cabinet secretaries and members of Congress, appellate judges still do their own work. Moreover, judges retain the greatest control over the most important cases and decisions.

Attorneys   Ordinarily, parties in appellate courts are represented by attorneys. Parties that can afford to hire lawyers nearly always do so. Indigent criminal defendants are provided with free attorneys for their first appeal from a conviction, if they have a right to that appeal (as they almost always have). Indigent defendants often must petition second-level appellate courts to hear their cases without a lawyer's help, but a court that does grant a hearing will then supply an attorney to argue the case.

The attorneys who handle appeals are a mixture of appellate specialists and nonspecialists. Many of the specialists work for government. Appellate specialists in the U.S. Department of Justice are responsible for some federal government litigation in the courts of appeals and nearly all of the government's legal work in the Supreme Court. Some states operate public defenders' offices that handle only appeals. The private sector also has some lawyers who are full or partial appellate specialists, among them attorneys who work with interest groups such as the National Association for the Advancement of Colored People (NAACP) Legal Defense Fund and the American Federation of Labor–Congress of Industrial Organizations (AFL-CIO).

But it is the general rule in the private sector and common in the public sector for a lawyer who has tried a case to handle it on appeal as well. One result is that a good deal of appellate work is done by lawyers with little experience at that level. Most lawyers who argue cases before the Supreme Court do so only once, and occasionally a lawyer who has never even filed a petition with the Court argues a significant case before it. The inexperience shared by many appellate lawyers is often reflected in their work. Appellate judges sometimes complain about the limited competence of the lawyers who argue before them, focusing chiefly on the nonspecialists. Even a nonlawyer who watches several oral arguments in an appellate court is likely to be struck by the weaknesses of some advocates.

At the appellate level, as in trial courts, attorneys play crucial roles in developing and presenting cases. But their roles differ considerably between the two levels. Trial lawyers generally negotiate settlements outside of court and orchestrate the presentation of evidence at trial. Appellate lawyers do much less negotiation, and rather than orchestrate evidence, they offer legal arguments directly through written *briefs* (detailed presentations of their line of reasoning in the case) and through oral argument.

Parties   The parties to appellate cases, like the cases themselves, are quite diverse. Criminal defendants appear frequently because there are so many appeals from criminal convictions. Government agencies appear in criminal cases and an array of civil cases. A variety of other litigants, both individuals and institutions, are parties in appellate cases.

The parties that are represented by attorneys do not participate directly in appellate court proceedings. (Indeed, in one Supreme Court case, Justice Potter Stewart asked an attorney to verify that his reclusive client actually existed.[10]) Their roles in appellate litigation vary considerably. At one end of the continuum, some parties supervise their attorneys closely; at the other end, some are distant spectators as their lawyers develop and carry out strategies in appellate court.

A Summary of Appellate Court Procedures

Like trial procedures, appellate procedures vary among courts and types of cases. The most important distinction is between a traditional system of full appellate procedure and a collection of procedures that depart from it, chiefly by abbreviating the traditional process.[11]

The Traditional System   The traditional system of appellate procedure has two versions. One applies when a case falls under mandatory jurisdiction, under which a court must decide a case; the other applies when a case falls under discretionary jurisdiction, under which a court can choose whether or not to accept a case for decision. Because first-level appellate courts have mostly mandatory jurisdiction and second-level courts mostly discretionary jurisdiction, they generally use different versions of the traditional procedure. As Exhibit 8.1 shows, however, these two versions have much in common.

Where a court's jurisdiction is mandatory, the process begins when one side (or, occasionally, both sides) decides to appeal a lower-court verdict or another ruling.

EXHIBIT 8.1   Typical Stages of Processing in Appellate Courts (Traditional Procedures)

Mandatory Jurisdiction	Discretionary Jurisdiction
a. Filing of an appeal and brief by the appellant	a. Filing of a petition for a hearing by the petitioner
b. Submission of a brief by the appellee	b. Submission of a brief in opposition to this petition by the respondent
c. Submission of a reply brief by the appellant	c. Court decision on whether to grant a hearing
	d. Submission of additional briefs by the parties

1. Prehearing conference (in some courts)
2. Court rulings on motions by the parties (such rulings may also come at other points)
3. Oral argument by the attorneys before the court
4. Court conference to reach a tentative decision
5. Writing of opinion(s) and continuing discussion of the case
6. Announcement of the decision and opinion(s)
7. Further action by the lower court in response to the appellate decision (in most cases)

The party who files an appeal generally is required to have the transcript of the trial proceedings and other parts of the record of the case prepared and transmitted to the appellate court. The costs of preparing both the transcript and the rest of the record make appeals expensive for those who must pay the full costs. But these costs are waived for indigent criminal defendants.

The party making the appeal, the *appellant,* submits a written brief arguing in favor of the appellant's position. This brief generally focuses on legal issues, alleging errors by the lower court that require overturning of its decision. In opposition, the other party, the *appellee,* submits a brief supporting the lower-court decision and taking issue with the appellant's contentions. The appellant may then submit a reply brief.

In a case falling under a court's discretionary jurisdiction, these early stages take a somewhat different and more extended form. The process begins when the party that is dissatisfied with a lower-court decision, the *petitioner,* asks the appellate court to call up the case and hear it. This petition takes different legal forms in different courts. In the Supreme Court, a petitioner asks the Court to issue a *writ of certiorari* to the court that last decided the case; if the writ is issued, it requires that the record of the case be sent up to the Supreme Court. The petitioner submits a brief in support of the request for a hearing, which is accompanied by the record of the case. The other party, the *respondent,* may then submit a brief in opposition to the request.

After receiving these materials, the court considers and rules on the petition. Courts typically require a majority vote or a near majority—four of nine on the Supreme Court—to accept a case. If the court rejects the petition, it reaches no decision in the case and simply allows the lower court to make its ruling final. But if the petition is accepted, the case is called up for decision. The parties then submit additional briefs on the merits of the case.

From this point on, cases under mandatory and discretionary jurisdiction are treated in the same way. After receiving the briefs in a case, some courts allow for a conference with the parties to help prepare the case for a hearing or to promote a settlement. Whether or not the court encourages settlements, in some first-level appellate courts, a large minority of cases—primarily civil cases—drop out through settlement or dismissal.[12]

Before the hearing, the court may need to rule on motions by the parties. The subjects of such motions can include the release of prisoners while their appeals are pending, permission for indigents to proceed without paying court fees, and exceptions to the court's procedural rules.

An appellate hearing takes the form of oral argument, in which the attorneys for the two sides make presentations that highlight and supplement their briefs. The judges may interrupt these presentations to ask questions, and in some courts such interruptions are frequent. The length of the oral argument varies, but one common practice is to divide an hour equally between the two sides. Sometimes the argument is dramatic. As one judge has cautioned, however, it "is for the most part intensely boring."[13]

After the hearing, the judges meet in conference to consider the case and reach a tentative decision. Here their choice is whether to uphold, or *affirm,* the lower-court decision, or to overturn it either completely or in part. In general, a court *reverses* a decision when it overturns the decision completely, and it *modifies* a decision by overturning the decision in part. The court might, for example, uphold a verdict for a personal injury plaintiff but rule that the damages awarded by the trial court were too high. A court may also *vacate,* or make void, a lower-court decision. The Supreme Court sometimes uses this procedure when a recent change in the law calls into question the validity of a lower-court decision.

At some point, usually after the conference, one judge is assigned to write the opinion that will describe the court's decision and the reasoning on which that decision is based. This opinion has several purposes: to justify the decision to the parties and any other audience; to instruct the lower court on what to do if it must reconsider the case; and to announce the rules of law that determined this decision, rules that subordinate courts are bound to follow in future decisions.

The assigned judge works to produce a draft opinion for the consideration of the other judges, whose comments may cause the opinion to be modified in minor or major ways. Meanwhile, other judges may be writing and circulating alternative opinions, which reach a different result from the assigned opinion or offer different rationales for the same result. Whether or not there are multiple opinions, judges may engage in a process of compromise and bargaining. The heart of this process is an effort by opinion writers to gain the support of colleagues through the way they word their opinions. One judge may say to another, "You take out this sentence, or put in this footnote, and I will sign."[14]

The process of decision ends when each judge takes a final position. The court's decision is then announced, and the opinion that represents the majority is issued on the court's behalf. Judges who disagree with the court's decision in the case, in that they favored a different outcome for the parties, may cast dissenting votes. If a vote in the Supreme Court is announced as 7–2, the two are justices who dissented from the decision.

When judges dissent, one or more usually write *dissenting opinions,* in which they explain their differences with the majority. Other dissenters may sign on to a judge's dissenting opinion. Such opinions have no direct impact on the law, but they allow judges to express their views and perhaps influence future court decisions.

Judges can also write *concurring opinions.* One type of concurring opinion expresses agreement with the court's decision, its treatment of the parties, but disagrees with the rules of law that the court uses to justify its decision. Because the long-term impact of an appellate decision lies chiefly in the rules of law that it announces, the disagreement expressed in concurring opinions often is as significant as the disagreement in dissenting opinions. Another type of concurring opinion agrees with both the decision and the rules of law in the court's opinion but expresses the judge's individual views about some matter—perhaps an interpretation of the court's opinion or a point of disagreement with a dissenting opinion.

Occasionally, because of disagreement about the rationale, no opinion gains the support of a majority of judges. In this situation, there is a decision but no authoritative interpretation of the legal issues in the case. The absence of a majority opinion in some of the Supreme Court's decisions on affirmative action has led to considerable confusion among lower-court judges and other people.

What happens after an appellate court decision depends primarily on the content of the decision. If the court affirms the lower court's decision, it notifies the lower court that it can make its ruling final. If the court overturns the lower-court decision in some way, it may make a final disposition of the case itself or direct the lower court to reach a particular final decision. Frequently, however, an appellate court that has reversed, modified, or vacated a decision sends the case back (*remands* it) to the lower court for further consideration in light of the appellate court decision and opinion. The lower court then has at least some freedom to resolve the case as it sees fit.

Alternative Procedures   Many appellate courts follow this traditional set of procedures closely in at least a portion of their cases. But there have always been deviations from this model, primarily as means to expedite case processing and to reduce judges' workloads. These deviations have become far more common since the 1960s. In first-level courts today, two scholars note, "the traditional appellate process exists, if at all, in most courts for only a small portion of appeals."[15] Most of the alternative procedures can be placed in three categories.

The first concerns opportunities for the parties to make their case. Most courts have reduced the length of oral argument or, in some cases, eliminated it altogether. Of the cases decided on the merits by federal courts of appeals in 1995, oral argument was held in only 40 percent.[16] The Hawaii Supreme Court announced in 1994 that because of caseload pressures, it would hear arguments only in cases "of such extraordinary complexity or importance that oral argument is the only way to reach an understanding of the issues involved."[17] Courts with discretionary jurisdiction sometimes decide cases solely on the basis of the petition for hearing and the brief in opposition, dispensing both with further briefing and with oral argument.

The second category involves the court's decision-making process. Judges sometimes dispense with conferences to consider cases collectively, and a few courts announce some of their decisions immediately after oral argument. Some courts assign a case to a single judge at an early point, and other judges largely defer to the assigned judge. An even more radical departure is delegation to nonjudges. As noted earlier, many courts give central staff attorneys major responsibilities for some decisions.

The final category of alternative procedures concerns the court's opinion. Decisions may be announced with no opinion. Alternatively, the court may issue an opinion that is relatively brief—sometimes so brief that it is essentially no opinion at all. Shorter opinions are often designated as *per curiam,* "by the court," rather than being signed by a single judge. This form avoids individual responsibility for opinions that may not be as carefully developed as longer, signed opinions. Such practices have become quite common; in one period, a Florida court of appeals issued an opinion in only one-third of its decisions.[18] Finally, courts can direct that opinions not be published, which means that the rules of law in those opinions are not binding in future cases. Opinions that are not intended for publication may require less care and thus less time to write.

Often these alternative procedures are used in combination. In some courts, certain cases are decided without oral argument, are given tentative decisions by central staff attorneys, and are handed down with brief unpublished per curiam opinions written primarily by staff attorneys. Many appellate courts have created two tracks, with some cases handled under a system that resembles the traditional one and others given more limited consideration and treatment.

APPEALS

With a few exceptions, cases come to appellate courts because one or more of the parties take cases there. Thus the work of appellate courts is based on the composition
of appeals and petitions for hearings. For the sake of simplicity, I refer to all cases as
appeals in the discussion that follows.

Factors That Affect the Decision to Appeal

In many respects, opting to appeal is like going to court in the first place. In both
instances, people who are not entirely satisfied with their situation—in this case, an
unfavorable court ruling—must decide whether to accept the situation or seek redress.

But there are differences between the two decisions. Perhaps most important,
appealing an adverse decision is less momentous than the original decision to litigate:
the case is already in the court system, and the parties have already experienced the
disadvantages of going to court. This difference helps explain why a higher proportion of potential cases are filed and why cases are less likely to be settled out of court
at the appellate level.

Decisions to appeal, like decisions to go to court initially, are based on many factors. But three considerations seem to be especially important: the degree of dissatisfaction with the lower-court decision, the chances of success on appeal, and the
monetary cost.

Dissatisfaction with a Decision   Almost nobody is happy to lose a court case.
Yet the intensity of the loser's unhappiness can vary a good deal, depending chiefly
on how much has been lost. A criminal defendant who was granted probation and one
who was sentenced to death are likely to have very different feelings about their
defeats. Similarly, the amount of money a civil defendant has lost in a trial verdict or
that a losing plaintiff had sought conditions their reactions.

These prosaic observations suggest an obvious conclusion: litigants who have
lost the most generally appeal at the highest rates. Not surprisingly, the available evidence supports this conclusion. A California study found, for example, that the rate
of criminal appeals increased with the seriousness of the offense.[19]

As a result, even appellate courts that must hear all appeals deal disproportionately with cases that have relatively large stakes. Another result is that minor trial
courts, whose cases involve relatively small stakes, generally are subject to little
appellate scrutiny. Finally, since the average case at the federal level involves bigger
stakes, the rate of appeal there is higher than in state courts.

Chances of Success   In one survey of lawyers, by far the most important factor in deciding whether to appeal federal district court rulings was the likelihood of
success on appeal.[20] This finding is not surprising. In any appellate court, the odds
are against a successful appeal. But the odds vary from case to case, and we would
expect people to appeal most often where they see the chances of victory as relatively
great.

Litigants typically lack the experience with which to estimate the chances of a favorable outcome. Thus one important role for lawyers can be to offer such an estimate. Attorneys discourage some appeals by indicating that success is unlikely, but they may exaggerate the prospects for a favorable result in some cases because an appeal will bring them additional fees.

Of course, perceptions of the prospects for success are heavily influenced by past decisions; in this way, appellate courts affect decisions whether to bring appeals. The Supreme Court's growing conservatism in recent years, for instance, has discouraged some people with civil liberties claims from bringing those claims to the Court. At the same time, prosecutors and others whose claims might appeal to conservative justices have become more willing to go to the Court. Courts sometimes offer more specific invitations to potential litigants, indicating in opinions that they would look favorably on cases raising a particular legal claim.

Some appeals are brought even though the chances of success seem slim. Sometimes litigants or their attorneys simply miscalculate. At other times, the stakes are so large—a possible death penalty, for instance—that an appeal seems justified. For some litigants, it is important to take a last opportunity to express their grievance and to seek what they see as justice.[21]

In some cases, the appellant can win even by losing. For example, a corporation that lost in trial court and was ordered to pay substantial damages to the other party often makes money in interest by delaying the time when the damages actually must be paid. Appeals also can be used as a weapon to wear down opponents who have fewer resources for continued litigation, sometimes forcing them to accept compromise settlements or making enforcement of trial court judgments more difficult.

Financial Costs   As noted earlier, appeals generally are expensive. It is costly not only to prepare a trial record but also to compensate lawyers for their time in preparing and presenting an appeal. The remand of a case after a successful appeal frequently results in a new trial, exacting additional costs from the appellant.

As a result, at least in civil cases, individuals and institutions with the most resources are the most likely to appeal. In the absence of special arrangements such as a contingent fee or legal aid, a nonwealthy litigant whose funds have already been depleted by the costs of a trial may be reluctant to undergo the additional expense of an appeal. In contrast, litigants who are in a stronger financial position can bring an appeal if the potential gains from a successful appeal or from delay are sufficient.

Personal financial resources have much less impact on criminal appeals. Most people convicted of serious crimes are indigent. As a result of Supreme Court rulings, the costs of a first appeal ordinarily are waived for indigent defendants. Second-level courts typically allow indigent people to petition for hearings without paying the usual fees and costs for preparing the necessary materials. This, of course, is one way that courts influence decisions whether to appeal.

Thus, in one important respect, criminal defendants are freer to appeal than are large corporations. Accordingly, a defendant who has received a heavy sentence may see little reason not to appeal, whatever the chances of victory: much might be gained, and there is little harm in trying. Not surprisingly, then, a high proportion of criminal defendants appeal from defeats at trial—a far higher proportion than of those who lose civil cases.

Appeals by the Government

In deciding whether to bring appeals, government officials consider the same factors as do other litigants. But those officials often operate somewhat differently from most other parties. Most distinctive is the federal government, whose approach to appeals merits some attention.[22]

The federal government in appellate courts is a good example of the "repeat player" in litigation that Marc Galanter has described. Indeed, one scholar has argued, in the Supreme Court, the lawyers who represent the government "are the definitive Repeat Players."[23] Because of the large and continuing flow of cases, in any given field of law the government has a great many cases that it could appeal. Decisions to appeal are centralized: government cases generally cannot be filed in the courts of appeals or the Supreme Court without the authorization of the solicitor general's office within the Justice Department. These lawyers can take a long-term view, with a focus more on achieving rules of law that favor the government's interests than on winning individual cases; put another way, they have the capacity to act strategically. It helps that the government faces fewer financial constraints in its litigation than do most private parties.

One example of strategic action is the use of selective appeals to help shape the law. The government sometimes forgoes an appeal in a tax case because the court of appeals to which the appeal would go seems unfavorable to the position of the Internal Revenue Service. Instead, it waits for a case in a circuit whose court of appeals seems likely to be more sympathetic.

Another example of strategy is the rationing of petitions for hearings in the Supreme Court. The solicitor general's office is far more selective in asking for hearings than are private litigants as a group. This restraint allows the government generally to take only its strongest cases to the Court. One benefit is that the justices expect government petitions to be meritorious.

The federal government's repeat player status also allows its attorneys to develop expertise in handling appeals. In the Supreme Court, the preponderance of the government's legal work is handled by the small staff of attorneys in the solicitor general's office. Those lawyers gain a good deal of experience in writing briefs and arguing cases before the Court—experience that few other attorneys can match.

The skill that they develop through this experience, combined with the government's ability to act strategically, helps to produce extraordinary success for the federal government both in getting the Court to accept its cases and in winning cases that the Court does hear. The government does especially well in the case selection process. In its 1995–1996 term, the Court accepted twenty-four of the thirty-two cases that the solicitor general asked it to hear, a 75 percent success rate. In contrast, other litigants brought more than six thousand cases to the Court and secured hearings in only seventy-five, a 1 percent success rate.[24]

As a government participating in appellate litigation, the federal government is something of an extreme case. Some state governments lack centralized control over appeals. Particularly in smaller cities and counties, local governments may have too few cases to act strategically and to develop experience in their attorneys. Financial constraints on appeals also may be more severe at the state and local levels. But many of the larger state and local governments share enough similarities with the federal government to distinguish them from most private litigants in the ways that they operate in appellate courts.

Interest Groups and Political Litigation

When people file lawsuits, or when they appeal unfavorable decisions, they are usually acting on behalf of themselves alone. People file divorce cases because they want to end their marriages. Individuals sue for personal injuries and businesses bring debt collection cases in order to recover money. Such cases can be considered *ordinary litigation.*

In contrast, cases may be brought and moved upward through the courts on the basis of broader goals. Rather than advancing their personal interests, people may seek to achieve racial equality or limit government regulation or protect free speech. This kind of activity can be labeled *political litigation.*

Cases can involve a mix of ordinary and political motives. The party to a case might want simply to win admission to law school, but her lawyers want to attack affirmative action as an admissions policy. A business may fight environmental rules in order to advance its economic interests, but its executives also oppose those rules on ideological grounds. The array of recent and current lawsuits involving the tobacco industry, described in Exhibit 8.2, encompasses a complicated set of motives.

EXHIBIT 8.2   Litigation Involving the Tobacco Industry

Since the 1950s, hundreds of individuals have sued tobacco companies, alleging that the companies were liable for health damage that resulted from smoking. The companies have enjoyed enormous success: few cases have gone to trial, plaintiffs have won only three of those cases, and two of the three verdicts were overturned on appeal (the third was under appeal in mid-1997). In large part, those results reflected the substantial resources that companies devoted to fighting lawsuits.

In the past few years, however, there has been a more concerted drive to recover money from the tobacco industry. In 1994 more than fifty law firms that handled mass tort litigation pooled their resources and expertise to bring a class-action lawsuit against the major tobacco companies, alleging that the companies addicted people while concealing the fact that cigarettes were addictive. In 1995, a federal district judge in New Orleans certified the case as a class action, but in 1996 the Fifth Circuit Court of Appeals threw out the case as inappropriate for a nationwide class action. In response, the plaintiffs' lawyers filed class action cases in individual states.

In 1994, the state of Mississippi filed a lawsuit against the major tobacco companies, seeking to recover what it alleged to be costs to the state Medicaid program resulting from illnesses caused by smoking. Additional states joined in the lawsuit; a majority had done so by 1997. States hired private attorneys on a contingency basis to carry out the legislation. One relatively small company, Liggett, reached a limited settlement with five states in 1996 and a broader settlement with twenty-two states in 1997; in the settlement, it agreed to pay substantial sums to the states over twenty-five years.

The tobacco industry was also in conflict with the federal government. The federal Food and Drug Administration (FDA) adopted rules in 1996 to regulate tobacco in a number of ways. The major tobacco companies, advertising agencies, and retailers brought a lawsuit to challenge the FDA's right to undertake that regulation. In 1997, a federal district judge in North Carolina upheld several of the FDA's rules while striking down others. Meanwhile, the Justice Department was investigating the tobacco industry with the possibility of bringing criminal charges against its executives and trade groups.

As a result of all these pressures, in 1997 the two largest tobacco companies began negotiations to achieve a broader settlement of the claims against them by states and individuals. After several months a settlement was reached, one in which tobacco companies would pay $368 billion over twenty-five years and accept heavier government regulation of tobacco in exchange for some limits on regulation and substantial limits on lawsuits and damage awards against the industry. Federal legislation was required to put the settlement into effect, and in the summer of 1997 it was uncertain what Congress and the president would do.

What has spurred all this litigation? To a great extent, it is the economic interests of the participants: individuals and state officials who want to win money from tobacco companies, lawyers who could gain very substantial fees if the suits against the companies were successful, and tobacco company officials who want to avoid such payments and to protect their industry's well-being. But many of the participants are also motivated by the hope of affecting national policy on smoking and tobacco. And that is the central concern of most of the groups that have joined the litigation as amici. Thus the lawsuits over tobacco, like many other lawsuits, can be considered a combination of ordinary and political litigation.

Sources: Castano v. American Tobacco Company, 84 F.3d 734 (5th Cir. 1996); *Coyne Beahm, Inc. v. Food and Drug Administration,* 958 F. Supp. 1060 (M.D.N.C. 1997); other court decisions; newspaper articles.

EXHIBIT 8.2   *(Continued)*

Only a very small proportion of the cases filed in trial courts can be classified as purely political litigation, and even litigation with a political element is relatively rare. Political litigation is more common at the appellate level, because litigants with political motives often seek to win favorable legal rules that apply to a whole state, a whole federal circuit, or—best of all—the country as a whole. For that reason, political litigation is best discussed in the context of appellate courts.

Interest Groups   Political litigation can be undertaken by determined individuals and lawyers who act on their own. But most political litigation involves interest group activity. Of course, interest groups play a central part in American politics as a whole. Groups were always active in the courts, and the level of group activity has grown considerably. This active role is inevitable: courts are important policymakers, so interest groups have a strong incentive to influence the courts.

These efforts at influence operate through several channels. As discussed in Chapter 4, one channel is the selection of judges. This may be the most effective way to shape a court's policies, since those policies heavily reflect judges' attitudes. Thus groups contribute money to candidates for state judgeships and lobby senators over federal court nominations.

Interest groups can also lobby courts indirectly, through the mass media, public statements, and even marches and demonstrations. Groups on both sides of the abortion debate have used all these methods in their efforts to influence Supreme Court decisions. Business groups fund programs to educate judges about economics, and liberal groups have argued that such programs are mechanisms to advocate conservative and pro-business positions.[25]

But most common is interest group participation in litigation itself. A wide range of groups involve themselves in litigation. So do other entities such as companies and individuals (for example, government officials) that act as interest groups at particular times.

Like political litigation, interest group litigation activity is more prominent in appellate courts. Interest groups sometimes involve themselves in cases at the trial level, but their participation becomes increasingly common at each step up the ladder of appellate courts. One reason is that groups sometimes become aware of cases, and join them, only at the appellate level. Another is that cases with broad implications for public policy are most abundant in the highest courts. Indeed, it is sometimes group efforts that get cases to those courts.

Interest Group Roles   Interest groups that participate in litigation can take three kinds of roles. The first is direct sponsorship of cases. Rules of *standing* require that a litigant have a direct stake in a case. As a result, an interest group usually cannot file a suit in its own name. But a group can begin with a general or specific policy goal and look for potential clients whose cases could be used to advance that goal. Thus local chapters of the American Civil Liberties Union (ACLU) take complaints from individuals that their civil liberties have been violated and use some of these complaints as vehicles for lawsuits.

In the second role, groups locate a case that is already in the courts and belatedly sponsor or support one side. After a criminal defendant has been convicted at trial, for example, the NAACP Legal Defense Fund may learn that the case involves a challenge to racial discrimination in the selection of jurors, an issue with which the group is concerned. It might then offer to finance any appeals, and such financing gives the Legal Defense Fund an opportunity to shape the case in ways that serve its own goals.

A group can play a third, more limited, role in a case by submitting an *amicus curiae* ("friend of the court") brief. An amicus brief supplements material provided by the litigant that the group supports in order to strengthen that party's case or suggests a resolution of the legal issues different from those favored by the parties. The submission of an amicus brief usually requires a court's permission, but that permission is generally granted. An amicus brief can cost tens of thousands of dollars to prepare, but it is less expensive than sponsoring a case and avoids the logistic difficulties of sponsorship.

The Goals of Interest Group Litigation   From the perspective of an interest group, government offers a number of possible forums in which to exert influence. A group will devote some of its efforts to the courts when courts provide a means to advance the group's goals. Litigation can serve interest group goals in several ways.

Most obvious and most important, litigation provides a means to obtain a definitive judicial ruling that favors the group's position. The Public Citizen Litigation Group has helped to bring cases challenging the Gramm-Rudman-Hollings "budget-balancing" law and the 1996 legislation that allowed presidents to veto specific items in budget bills; the group's goal has been to obtain Supreme Court decisions overturning these policies in order to maintain what it views as the appropriate separation of powers between Congress and the executive branch.[26] In recent years several groups have worked to achieve decisions that expand the rights of private property owners who are subject to government regulation.[27]

At the other end of the spectrum is litigation undertaken for tactical purposes, with little concern for judicial doctrine. Environmental groups sometimes file lawsuits against proposed projects in order to delay the projects and thus make them less feasible. In the 1980s, the Southern Poverty Law Center brought a series of lawsuits against Ku Klux Klan organizations as a means to weaken the Klan financially and more generally. This campaign achieved considerable success: in 1993, the center won all the assets of the largest Klan group in the settlement of a civil rights case.[28]

Groups differ in the regularity with which they participate in litigation.[29] One reason is that the courts are more relevant to some groups than to others. Courts can do little for a farm organization that seeks increased crop subsidies, but they can do a great deal for an insurance group that seeks changes in rules of liability for products that cause injuries. Another reason is that some groups see the courts as more sympathetic to their positions than the other branches, while others perceive the legislature and executive branch as more friendly.

For both these reasons, the most prominent interest groups in the courts between the 1940s and the 1960s were the NAACP Legal Defense Fund and the ACLU. The NAACP sought protection for the constitutional rights of black citizens, and so the courts were an appropriate forum. Moreover, until the 1960s the Supreme Court was far more willing to support civil rights than were Congress and the president. Similarly, the ACLU's focus on protection of civil liberties drew it to the courts, and many of its "clients"—criminal defendants, political extremists, unconventional religious denominations—attracted little sympathy in the other branches.

Both these groups remain important, but they stand out less because there has been a burgeoning of activity from other groups. Some of these groups share with them a liberal ideological orientation. The NAACP Legal Defense Fund provided a model for groups representing women, Hispanics, and the disabled. Environmental groups such as the Sierra Club have engaged in a good deal of litigation. *Public interest law firms,* inspired by legal reformer Ralph Nader, were created specifically to bring cases on issues such as employment discrimination, occupational safety, and consumer rights.

A number of groups with conservative goals have also become frequent participants in litigation. Several conservative public interest law firms have been established since 1973; these firms litigate on a wide array of issues. Other conservative groups focus on such matters as abortion, criminal justice, and labor-management relations.[30] One spur to this conservative activity is a perceived need to counter the efforts of liberal groups. Another is the growing conservatism of the federal courts that resulted from appointments by Republican presidents. The new conservative groups contribute to a growing diversity of groups using the courts, a diversity illustrated by the sampling in Exhibit 8.3.

Alongside the groups that emphasize use of the courts are many others that engage in litigation as a limited part of their political activities. This category includes major economic groups such as the U.S. Chamber of Commerce and the AFL-CIO, whose goals and political strength lead them primarily to the executive branch and the legislature. Frequently, however, they turn to the courts to protect gains or redress losses elsewhere.

Most of the litigation in which governments engage has political elements. In enforcing environmental laws or contesting challenges to criminal convictions, a government is seeking to shape policy. But some government litigation is even more clearly political. The solicitor general frequently submits amicus briefs to the Supreme Court to press the administration's views about a policy issue raised in cases involving other parties. In amicus briefs, the Clinton administration has defended state laws that prohibit doctor-assisted suicide, argued that state-imposed term limits for Congress are unconstitutional, and supported businesses whose contracts with local governments are cut off in retaliation for criticism of those governments.[31] California governor Pete Wilson has brought several lawsuits in support of his policy positions on issues such as immigration and affirmative action. Some observers have perceived that his primary goal was to strengthen his popularity as governor and potential presidential candidate.[32]

The level of interest group activity in the courts has increased a great deal over the years, spurred by a growing recognition that courts can serve group purposes. The Supreme Court now receives amicus briefs in most of the cases that it considers fully. Interest group activity has also burgeoned in the state supreme courts. Across sixteen supreme courts, the average proportion of cases that had at least one amicus brief increased from 3 percent in 1965 to 13 percent in 1990.[33] A Minnesota study indicates that even in federal district courts, groups are associated with the plaintiffs in a significant proportion of cases.[34]

One result is that cases with important policy implications increasingly involve battles between competing interest groups. When a state's voters adopt a controversial initiative on insurance rates or campaign finance, one set of groups is likely to challenge the initiative in the courts while another set supports the state's efforts to defend it.[35] On issues ranging from abortion to environmental protection, groups on both sides use the courts to advance their positions. In this way courts have become an integral part of the contention among interest groups that is an enduring feature of American politics.

Interest Group Influence   Most activity of interest groups in litigation is aimed at obtaining favorable judicial decisions. To what extent can groups actually affect the courts' decisions?

Probably the most powerful form of influence for groups is making litigation possible. Many cases that raise important legal and policy questions would not arise without the assistance of interest groups, simply because no individuals have the resources and the incentives to carry such cases forward on their own. To take a few of many such examples, this is true of most challenges to school segregation, lawsuits

American Civil Liberties Union. The ACLU was founded after World War I, gradually gaining a large membership (currently about 275,000 people). Throughout its history it has been heavily involved in litigation as a means to protect civil liberties, with some emphasis on freedom of expression. It has established special projects to undertake litigation in areas such as women's rights and national security. The ACLU frequently participates in Supreme Court cases. In the Court's 1996–1997 term, the ACLU sponsored a challenge to the federal statute prohibiting the display of "indecent" materials over the Internet if they are available to minors, and it submitted briefs in cases with issues ranging from the scope of federal civil rights laws to government aid to religious schools.

American Center for Law and Justice. The ACLJ was founded in 1990 by Reverend Pat Robertson's Christian Coalition to litigate on behalf of conservative Christian values. It was modeled in part on the ACLU, reflecting a view that a counterbalance to that organization was needed. Among a wide range of concerns, two major issues for the ACLJ are abortion and school religious activities. On abortion, Chief Counsel Jay Alan Sekulow has argued in two Supreme Court cases against restrictions on protest activities at abortion clinics. The ACLJ is also a major participant in the legal debate over religious observances at public school graduations.

NAACP Legal Defense and Educational Fund. The NAACP created a Legal Defense Fund in 1939 to focus on litigation, reflecting the organization's belief that the rights of black citizens could be advanced significantly through court decisions. The fund has since become a separate organization, with no mass membership. Under the leadership of Thurgood Marshall, it orchestrated the legal attack on school segregation, including a series of cases that resulted in major Supreme Court decisions—most important, *Brown v. Board of Education* (1954). In recent years, the fund has used litigation to enforce federal laws against discrimination in voting and in employment, and it has continued its long-standing involvement in capital punishment cases based on the racial implications of the death penalty.

Public Citizen Litigation Group. Consumer advocate Ralph Nader helped create this organization in 1972 as a "public interest law firm." The group litigates on many issues, including consumers' rights and election reform. Its most visible activity has been a series of challenges to federal laws on the ground that they breached the Constitution's separation of powers among the three branches. These challenges have resulted in major Supreme Court decisions on congressional vetoes of administrative rules, the Gramm-Rudman-Hollings budget deficit reduction law, and guidelines for sentencing by federal judges. Most recently, in 1997, a lawyer from the group argued in the Court on behalf of members of Congress who challenged the constitutionality of legislation allowing presidents to veto individual items within appropriation bills; the Court did not reach a decision on that issue.

Washington Legal Foundation. The foundation was created in 1977 as a conservative counterpart and counterbalance to liberal public interest law firms, and it grew into an organization with 200,000 members. The foundation frequently submits amicus briefs. It also sponsored Senator Barry Goldwater's lawsuit against President Carter's termination of a treaty with Taiwan and a lawsuit against John Hinckley by a secret service agent who was shot in Hinckley's attempt to assassinate President Reagan. Among its positions in recent years are support for a House of Representatives

EXHIBIT 8.3   Some Interest Groups That Are Active in the Courts

rule requiring a three-fifths majority to approve tax increases; for a construction company's claim that its contract with the government was terminated without adequate compensation; and for victims of the Oklahoma City bombing who wanted to attend Timothy McVeigh's trial while maintaining their right to testify on McVeigh's penalty if he was convicted.

Sources: Karen O'Connor and Lee Epstein, *Public Interest Groups: Institutional Profiles* (New York: Greenwood Press, 1989); Lee Epstein, *Conservatives in Court* (Knoxville: University of Tennessee Press, 1985); newspaper reports; court cases and decisions.

EXHIBIT 8.3   *(Continued)*

to achieve stronger enforcement of environmental laws, and efforts to advance the rights of children.[36] Just by getting such cases to court, interest groups make a considerable difference.

The capacity of groups to affect what courts decide is less certain. Groups potentially can influence courts through the quality of their arguments, which may affect judges' perceptions of issues. For example, an amicus brief may suggest to a court a basis for its decision that might otherwise have gone unnoticed. But there are limits to this kind of influence. Judges often have strong views about the issues that come before them, so they are not very susceptible to persuasion. On the whole, the ACLU has enjoyed less success in the Supreme Court since the 1970s than it did in the 1960s. This does not necessarily mean that the ACLU has become less influential; rather, the justices who serve on the Court now are less sympathetic to the group's positions.

To the degree that judges *are* open to persuasion, there is reason to think that interest groups can affect a court's choices. Though the evidence is mixed, research has indicated that group participation in cases sometimes has an impact.[37] But that impact should not be exaggerated. In particular, it should not be assumed that a group whose position in a case coincided with the court's decision was responsible for that favorable result.

The connections between interest group activities in the courts and elsewhere in government should be emphasized. Groups that want to shape policy in a particular area usually divide their efforts between the courts and the other branches, and they often work simultaneously in both. Groups that suffer a defeat in a state legislature may take the issue to the courts, and the losing side in the Supreme Court may seek redress in Congress. In this respect, as in others, courts are closely linked with other government institutions.

Growth in Appeals

Appellate caseloads have grown rapidly in the last few decades.[38] Figure 8.1 shows the extent of this growth in two intermediate appellate courts, those of Illinois and the federal system.

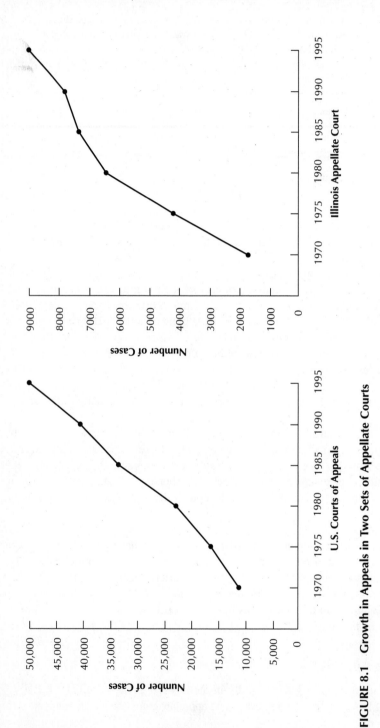
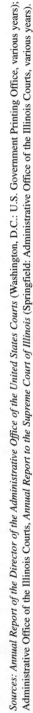

FIGURE 8.1   Growth in Appeals in Two Sets of Appellate Courts

Sources: Annual Report of the Director of the Administrative Office of the United States Courts (Washington, D.C.: U.S. Government Printing Office, various years); Administrative Office of the Illinois Courts, *Annual Report to the Supreme Court of Illinois* (Springfield: Administrative Office of the Illinois Courts, various years).

In part, this growth simply reflects an increase in the numbers of cases resolved in trial courts and in administrative agencies: there are more decisions that can be appealed now. But there has also been an increase in the proportion of decisions that are appealed. The rise in the rate of appeal for criminal cases is especially striking. In 1950, less than one in one hundred of the criminal cases that were resolved in federal district courts resulted in an appeal. In 1989, one in five criminal cases were appealed.[39] (These figures include all criminal cases, not just those that went to trial. As early as 1970, more than half of all the defendants who were found guilty after trials brought appeals,[40] and that proportion is probably higher today.)

The primary source of this change is the court decisions and legislation that have made appeals much easier for criminal defendants. Indeed, one commentator concluded that the Supreme Court's decisions assuring free counsel for indigent defendants on appeal "undoubtedly caused most of the increase" in appeals over the next two decades.[41] This conclusion underlines the impact courts can have on their own caseloads.

In the federal courts, the sentencing guideline system that went into effect in 1987 has provided additional bases for appeal, even by defendants who pled guilty. Undoubtedly, new sentencing statutes have had similar effects in some states. This example is a reminder of the extent to which the other branches shape court caseloads.

SCREENING CASES

The growth in appeals over the past few decades has accelerated a long-term trend: most appellate courts in most periods experience an increase in their caseloads. At various times, the caseloads of most courts reach a point at which their judges no longer feel they can give full attention to each case without creating an intolerable backlog. The primary response to this problem has been to adopt systems under which some cases receive full judicial consideration while others receive more limited consideration.

These screening systems take two quite different forms. One involves the exercise of discretionary jurisdiction, under which some cases are given no decision on the merits at all. This form is found primarily in second-level appellate courts. In the other form, which predominates in first-level courts, some cases that must be decided on the merits under mandatory jurisdiction are handled with expedited procedures.

Discretionary Jurisdiction

The discretionary jurisdiction held by some appellate courts is linked to the creation of appellate systems with two levels. Most supreme courts began as the only full appellate courts in their systems. Because of the belief that litigants are entitled to one appeal, most of the supreme courts' jurisdiction was mandatory. But as a supreme court's caseload grew and became burdensome, its justices sought relief. The legislature responded by creating an intermediate appellate court and giving the supreme court discretionary jurisdiction over a large share of the cases that come to it. As caseloads continued to grow, some supreme courts were given discretionary jurisdiction over a broader set of cases.

Under discretionary jurisdiction, a court can simply deny a hearing in any case that it chooses, thereby allowing the lower-court decision to become final. A court's refusal to hear a case cannot be appealed elsewhere. (However, the U.S. Supreme Court can agree to hear a case that a state supreme court has refused to hear.) Thus courts with discretionary jurisdiction hold an impressive power to set their agendas as they see fit.

Screening Procedures   Courts use a variety of procedures in deciding on requests for hearings. In general, the courts that receive the largest volume of cases have developed the most elaborate screening procedures.

The U.S. Supreme Court receives more petitions than any other court, currently more than six thousand each year. To deal with these petitions, it has created a two-stage screening process.[42] In the first stage, the Court identifies cases that seem to deserve closer scrutiny by putting them on its *discuss list.* Petitions for certiorari that fail to reach this list are denied without collective consideration.

The chief justice is primarily responsible for creating the discuss list, although another justice can add cases to it. In practice, at this stage the justices delegate to law clerks most of the work of evaluating petitions, and most justices personally read only a small portion of the petitions and supporting materials. As of 1997, all but one of the justices pool their law clerks so that a single clerk summarizes a particular petition for all the justices who participate in the pool. Later, a justice's own clerks do additional work on the petitions.

A small proportion of cases, perhaps one in eight, reach the discuss list.[43] The justices vote in conference on whether to hear these cases, usually without much discussion. As noted earlier, four votes from the nine justices are necessary to accept a case.

State supreme courts vary a good deal in their screening procedures. The procedure used by the California Supreme Court resembles the U.S. Supreme Court's process in most respects: a staff attorney prepares a "conference memo" on each petition for review for the justices and their clerks to consider, and petitions are placed on a "B list" if no justice thinks they deserve discussion by the court in conference. The key difference with the Supreme Court is that a majority vote—four of the seven justices—is required to accept a case.[44]

Courts differ in their propensities to accept cases; in general, those that receive the largest numbers of cases reject the largest proportions. Some cases are neither rejected nor fully accepted but receive summary decisions on the merits. In recent years, the Michigan Supreme Court has rejected nearly 90 percent of what are called petitions for leave to appeal, disposed of another 8 percent through summary decisions, and fully decided about 3 percent.[45]

Screening Criteria   Many considerations influence court decisions whether to accept cases. In broad terms, judges are motivated both by perceptions of their court's responsibilities and by policy goals. More specifically, several criteria appear to be important.[46]

One is the significance of the legal issues involved in a case. A supreme court can do the most to make the law clear and consistent, and its members can best advance their policy goals, by selecting cases with broad legal and practical significance. It usually makes little sense to accept a tort case with a narrow issue related to the facts of that case, an issue that may never arise again. But it makes a great deal of sense to accept a tort case involving general requirements for the safety of products, requirements that will be relevant to any product liability case in the future. Many petitions for hearings can be denied almost automatically because the narrowness of their issues is self-evident. This does not mean that all significant cases are accepted, but those with the greatest potential impact have an unusually good chance to gain a hearing.

Another important criterion is conflict or uncertainty in the law. Conflict can arise when two lower courts interpret a legal provision differently or when a lower court seems to depart from the supreme court's interpretation. Uncertainty can arise from an ambiguous provision of law. In practice, judges give high priority to resolving conflict and uncertainty. But as the numbers of laws and lower-court decisions proliferate, so too does the volume of legal conflicts and uncertainties. As a result, at least some supreme courts, including the U.S. Supreme Court, are unable to accept all the cases in which the law needs to be clarified. Still, a conflict or uncertainty on a significant issue, such as the meaning of a major tax provision or a basic principle of divorce law, is very likely to gain consideration.

An impression that the lower court has made an error in the decision under review often impels supreme court justices to accept certain cases. Though error correction is not the primary purpose of second-level courts, justices feel better about allowing a lower-court decision to stand if they think it was the right one. Because of this consideration, the U.S. Supreme Court reverses lower-court decisions in most of the cases it hears, despite the general tendency of appellate courts to affirm. Of course, different justices may not agree on whether a lower court erred, and their judgments are colored by their ideological predispositions. Thus liberals are more inclined to accept cases brought by criminal defendants than are conservatives.

Judges' policy preferences may be manifested in a more complicated way when they act on their predictions about what would happen if their court accepted a case. If a supreme court justice thinks that the lower court interpreted the law incorrectly but that the supreme court would still affirm the lower court, the justice might prefer to leave the decision standing rather than give it supreme court approval. This practice is so common on the U.S. Supreme Court that it has a standard label: "defensive denials."[47]

As this discussion suggests, judges frequently disagree about whether a case should be heard. In the Supreme Court, a great many cases are accepted with only four or five votes, and occasionally justices are so unhappy with decisions to deny hearings that they announce their dissents from those decisions. A study of the Georgia Supreme Court suggests one explanation for such disagreements: different justices seem to weight criteria for accepting a case quite differently.[48]

As these disagreements indicate, the agendas of courts with discretionary jurisdiction reflect the goals and perspectives that are dominant among their justices at a given time. As a court's membership changes, so will its case-screening decisions.

Screening of Mandatory Cases

When judges on supreme courts find their caseloads burdensome, they can seek discretionary jurisdiction. But judges on intermediate courts lack that option; their jurisdiction will remain mandatory. Working within this constraint, judges on these courts have taken several kinds of actions to cope with growing caseloads. One is to request additional judges and supporting personnel. Another is to use prehearing conferences to encourage the settlement of cases.

Most important, courts have made staffing and procedural changes that allow them to dispose of cases with smaller expenditures of judicial time. The most significant of these changes are the creation of central staffs and the regular use of abbreviated alternatives to traditional procedures. In most courts, the two innovations go together: central staff members screen cases to determine which will receive abbreviated consideration and do much of the work in the cases that are given abbreviated consideration. In courts that regularly use abbreviated procedures, those procedures can become the rule rather than the exception.

Case Screening and the Use of Abbreviated Procedures   Different courts screen cases and abbreviate their consideration in different ways. But certain patterns exist, in part because courts have copied practices from each other. The approach taken by most courts follows the general lines of the following model:[49]

1. After the court receives the full set of written materials in a case, these materials are routed to its central staff. Either the chief staff attorney or another member of the staff then reviews each case and decides tentatively whether it should receive full court consideration or more limited treatment. Cases assigned to the limited-treatment category are those viewed as easy to decide, usually because the appellant seems to have a weak case. Full-consideration cases are sent to a panel of judges for a decision; in most courts, the panel usually holds oral argument in these cases. The cases designated for abbreviated treatment are retained within the central staff for further work.
2. A staff attorney examines more fully each case that has been retained. At this point, the staff member may decide that the case actually requires full court consideration. Ordinarily, however, the staff member proceeds to write a memorandum on the case, usually with a recommendation as to how it should be decided. In many courts, the staff member also writes a proposed opinion for the court.
3. The cases that the staff has considered are assigned to a court panel, often a special "screening" panel, and the case materials are forwarded there as well. The judges on the panel, usually three in number, review each case individually or as a group. If any judge feels that oral argument is necessary, it can then be scheduled. Otherwise the panel considers the case and reaches a decision on the basis of the written materials. This decision is issued with an opinion, usually a brief per curiam one that is based on the staff attorney's work. This opinion generally goes unpublished.

The Impact of Case Screening and Abbreviated Procedures   Appellate courts screen mandatory cases and reach decisions through abbreviated procedures primarily in order to improve their efficiency. By deciding a high proportion of cases with less of its judges' time, a court potentially can dispose of more cases with the same number of judges. Screening does seem to have this impact. In the intermediate courts of Illinois and New Jersey, for example, the adoption of screening systems helped to produce measurable increases in output.[50]

Screening can have other effects on a court and its work, some of them unintended and undesired. One concerns the quality of the court's decision making. Advocates of staff involvement in decisions argue that preparatory work by staff attorneys provides busy judges with a better basis for their decisions, and undoubtedly there is some truth to this claim. Yet some commentators argue that processing of cases by the staff limits the care with which judges consider those cases. In 1993, a member of a federal court of appeals issued a broader indictment of screening and the procedures associated with it.

> Those who believe we are doing the same quality work that we did in the past are simply fooling themselves. We adopt more and more procedures for "expediting" cases, procedures that ensure that individual cases will get less attention. . . . The use of these makeshift procedures ensures that many cases do not get the full attention they deserve, and the quality of our work suffers. It is a most unsatisfactory way for us to have to do our job.[51]

Thomas Davies concluded from his study of a California court of appeal that central staff involvement in cases is unlikely to improve the quality of decision making. Indeed, in his view the "assignment of an appeal to staff processing normally ensures that the case will be treated as 'routine' or 'frivolous,'" and so it is given relatively little scrutiny.[52] Two legal scholars with experience on appellate courts suggested that "there is a substantial risk that central staff case processing may lead to premature judgment based upon information inaccurately filtered by staff."[53]

Another possible effect is to reduce judges' control over decisions. Although abbreviated procedures are designed to ensure that judges determine how cases are decided, practical realities may undermine this goal. When pressed for time, judges are strongly tempted to accept a staff attorney's analysis of a case rather than engage in the laborious task of examining and considering case materials themselves. A study of the Michigan Court of Appeals found "high levels of agreement between staff recommendations and the judges' decisions, strongly suggesting that the judges rely almost entirely on staff recommendations to reach their decisions."[54] A staff attorney on the Kansas Court of Appeals interpreted high agreement rates differently: "The judges agreed with me most often simply because they had no choice—there was only one answer possible."[55] Yet the concerns that judges express about the roles of central staffs indicate that they too perceive a loss of control, and some shift of power from judges to staff members seems inevitable.

A final consequence is that staff screening may weaken the vitality of the right to appeal. Most cases to which courts give abbreviated consideration are put in this category because the appellant's case seems weak. Yet in light of such an initial perception and the absence of oral argument, does this mean that appellants are effectively denied the opportunity to make their case? A study of the federal Fifth Circuit Court of Appeals found that the court affirmed district courts at a higher rate after the introduction of screening procedures.[56] This finding suggests that such procedures can exert a subtle but significant—and perhaps troubling—impact on the outputs of the appellate courts. Yet a study of the Ninth Circuit Court of Appeals indicated that assignment of cases to screening panels did not affect the likelihood of reversal— though it did decrease the likelihood of a published opinion.[57]

This issue underlines a more general point: structural and procedural changes adopted for seemingly neutral reasons such as efficiency can affect the substance of what courts do. Judges have not adopted abbreviated procedures in order to change the patterns of the decisions that they reach; they are simply trying to keep up with their caseloads. Yet the changes they have made may be producing different outcomes for some litigants and different court policies.

DECISION MAKING

Whether its jurisdiction is chiefly mandatory or discretionary, the heart of an appellate court's work is its decisions in the cases it hears. These decisions produce victories and defeats for individual litigants. More important, they establish rules of law that influence future court cases and activity elsewhere in government and society. For this reason, explanation of appellate court decisions is one of the central issues in the study of courts.

Perspectives on Decision Making: An Overview

The explanations for court behavior presented in Chapter 1 suggest that appellate court decisions can be understood from several perspectives: the legal perspective, which views decisions as the product of legal rules; the personal perspective, which explains decisions in terms of the judges themselves; and the environmental perspective, which emphasizes influences from the larger society. The relevance of each perspective differs somewhat between first-level and second-level appellate courts.

First-Level Courts   Because first-level courts have mandatory jurisdiction, they must decide both "easy" and "difficult" cases. Judges on these courts frequently express the view that most of their cases are easy to decide because the merits clearly lie on one side. Legal scholar and Supreme Court justice Benjamin N. Cardozo concluded that perhaps 90 percent of appeals could be decided only one way.[58]

When judges speak of easy cases, for the most part they are referring to appeals that have little merit, so that affirmance is the obvious result. The chief judge of the federal Eighth Circuit Court of Appeals in St. Louis estimated that about one-quarter of all appeals his court receives are "frivolous."[59] A judge on a California court of appeal commented that "if 90 per cent of this stuff were in the United States Post Office, it would be classified as junk mail."[60]

In effect, these judges are saying that the law is the dominant element in the courts' decision making: most of the time, only one result can be justified under the law. This belief helps judges to feel comfortable about delegating responsibility over seemingly easy cases to central staffs. It also helps to explain the low rates of dissent in most first-level appellate courts: in a high proportion of these cases, it would be difficult for judges to disagree about the result.

In some cases, probably more than most judges recognize, the decision is not so clear-cut, and judges must exercise discretion. In doing so, they are seldom subject to much external pressure. Most first-level courts are intermediate courts, less visible to the public than the courts above or below them. Particularly at the state level, intermediate courts typically receive little attention and thus limited scrutiny from the mass media and interest groups.

Certainly these courts are influenced by their environments, but the influence is primarily indirect and fairly subtle. Because external pressures are fairly weak, judges' personal characteristics are especially important in shaping their judgments within the constraints of the law. And because appellate decisions are made by groups of judges, their interaction helps to determine how individual predilections translate into collective decisions.

Second-Level Courts   Second-level courts usually have some mandatory jurisdiction; as a result, they decide some relatively easy cases. But their jurisdiction is mainly discretionary. Because there would be little reason to hear cases with obvious results, the cases that a court selects generally involve more difficult and uncertain questions. Thus existing legal rules constrain second-level courts to only a limited degree. Indeed, cases often require that courts establish new rules in order to clarify ambiguities and fill in gaps in the law.

Of course, the law is relevant to decisions in these courts. The state of the law often pushes a court strongly toward some results and away from others. This legal influence helps to explain why the nine justices on the U.S. Supreme Court, who typically hold widely varying perspectives, make a good many unanimous decisions. By the same token, the frequency of dissent in the Supreme Court and in many state supreme courts reflects the difficulty of the legal questions they resolve.[61]

On the whole, the U.S. Supreme Court and state supreme courts enjoy much less insulation from their environments than do intermediate appellate courts. Some supreme courts are the subject of extensive newspaper coverage, and interest groups often participate in cases before them. Legislators also pay considerable attention to the activities of supreme courts. As a result, supreme court justices feel more direct pressure than do intermediate appellate judges. But even in supreme courts, a great many decisions receive only limited attention. And even when supreme court justices receive intense scrutiny, they are generally less vulnerable to external pressures than are legislators and chief executives.

Thus the law and the environment leave judges on second-level courts with considerable freedom to take the directions they wish in their decisions. As a consequence, perhaps more than in any other courts, judges' characteristics and their interactions with colleagues shape judicial decisions. For this reason, explanations of decisions by supreme courts must focus chiefly on their justices.

The rest of this section looks more closely at three key factors shaping appellate court decisions: judges' policy preferences, group processes, and the political and social environment.

Policy Preferences

In voting on cases over the course of a year, the justices on the U.S. Supreme Court divide along a variety of lines. In the eleven 5–4 decisions in the Court's 1995–1996 term, there were six different combinations of justices in the majority.[62] But the pattern of justices' votes in cases is far from random. Rather, justices tend to line up in systematic ways. In five of the eleven 5–4 decisions in the 1995–1996 term, the same four justices—John Paul Stevens, David Souter, Ruth Bader Ginsburg, and Stephen Breyer—were the dissenters. That degree of clustering among the justices could hardly be the result of chance.

Nor are the bases for that clustering random. In all five times that Stevens, Souter, Ginsburg, and Breyer lined up against their colleagues, those four justices took a more liberal position than the Court majority. And they all cast a higher proportion of liberal votes during the term than did any of the other five justices.

Preferences, Ideology, and Decisions   What accounts for that kind of pattern? Differences in the responses of justices to the same case result primarily from their personal attitudes toward the policy issues in the case. External pressures and the law may move the whole Court in one direction or the other, but disagreements among the justices stem chiefly from their preferences about policy. We know this is true because those disagreements reflect fairly well the views that justices expressed before they became judges. To take one good example, William Rehnquist had established a record of strong conservatism for two decades before he joined the Court in 1971, and in the time since, he has amassed a consistently conservative record as a justice. For this reason, the general ideological positions that justices will support can usually be predicted with some accuracy as soon as they are appointed.[63] Further, the views that justices express away from the Court typically are consistent with the positions they take in cases. Among the current justices, Clarence Thomas and Antonin Scalia are especially willing to offer their views about social issues in speeches and other forums, and those views are as conservative as the opinions they write on the Court.

Justices' policy preferences often change marginally, and they sometimes change substantially. On the whole, however, they are fairly stable. In turn, this stability gives predictability to the Court's divisions. It would be fairly safe to predict at the beginning of any term that Justice Stevens will cast more liberal votes during that term than any of his colleagues.

There is another element of consistency that runs through the Court's decisions. Most of the policy issues that courts address can be characterized in liberal-conservative terms. A justice who takes a liberal position on one issue is likely to take liberal positions on most others. Justice Stevens has complex views, and occasionally he stands alone in taking a conservative position in a case. Leaving aside such anomalies, however, he tends toward the liberal side on a wide range of economic and civil liberties issues. In the same way, Justice Thomas tends toward the conservative side across the same range of issues. Some other justices are less consistent in this sense, taking more liberal positions on some issues than on others, but it is quite rare for a justice to stand at the liberal end of the Court on one set of issues and at the conservative end on another.

Based on the frequency with which they cast liberal and conservative votes, the justices can be placed on a continuum ranging from the most liberal to the most conservative. Figure 8.2 shows how the members of the Court in 1997 might be placed, based on their liberal and conservative votes on civil liberties cases in the Court's 1995–1996 term. The figure also shows the divisions between justices on the two

Liberal ◄───► Conservative

Stevens	Ginsburg		Kennedy	O'Connor		Scalia
	Breyer			Rehnquist		
	Souter			Thomas		

Cases with Divisions That Were Entirely Consistent with the Continuum

Board of County Commissioners v. Umbehr (1996): Does the right to freedom of speech under the First and Fourteenth Amendments protect a business from termination of a contract with a local government in retaliation for criticism of that government?
Yes: Stevens, Ginsburg, Breyer, Souter, Kennedy, O'Connor, Rehnquist
No: Thomas, Scalia

Romer v. Evans (1996): Does a state constitutional amendment that prohibits laws against discrimination on the basis of sexual orientation violate the equal protection clause of the Fourteenth Amendment?
Yes: Stevens, Ginsburg, Breyer, Souter, Kennedy, O'Connor
No: Rehnquist, Thomas, Scalia

United States v. Ursery (1996): Did the combination of a defendant's prosecution of a drug offense and the seizure of his house under the forfeiture laws violate the Fifth Amendment's prohibition of double jeopardy for an offense?
Yes: Stevens
No: Ginsburg, Breyer, Souter, Kennedy, O'Connor, Rehnquist, Thomas, Scalia

Cases with Divisions That Were Partially Inconsistent with the Continuum

Montana v. Egelhoff (1996): Does a state law that prohibits judges and juries from taking the defendant's "intoxicated condition" into account in determining his mental state and thus whether he was guilty of a crime violate the due process clause of the Fourteenth Amendment?
Yes: Stevens, Breyer, Souter, O'Connor
No: Ginsburg, Kennedy, Rehnquist, Thomas, Scalia

Carlisle v. United States (1996): Can a federal district judge acquit a criminal defendant after a guilty verdict even though the defendant did not file a motion for acquittal within the time limit for such motions?
Yes: Stevens, Kennedy
No: Ginsburg, Breyer, Souter, O'Connor, Rehnquist, Thomas, Scalia

FIGURE 8.2   Positions of 1997 Supreme Court Justices on a Liberal-Conservative Continuum in Civil Liberties Cases, with Divisions of Justices in Selected Cases

Note: The places of the justices on the continuum and the width of the distances between them are based on the proportions of liberal and conservative votes cast by each justice in civil liberties cases in the 1995–1996 term. Justices in the same position on the continuum cast about the same numbers of liberal and conservative votes in the term as each other.

sides in some civil liberties decisions during the term. Most divisions were fully consistent with the positions of the justices on the overall continuum. But some cases divided justices in ways that we would not predict from the continuum.

The impact of ideology on the justices' behavior should not be exaggerated.

Some issues that come to the Court, such as disputes between states over their borders, do not have much ideological content. Cases involving economic issues do not have as clear an ideological content as they once did, so that the patterns of votes in those cases are less systematic than those in civil liberties cases. More important, even justices with strong preferences on particular issues sometimes take positions that seem to deviate from these views. Such deviations may result from their reading of the law or an interest in achieving unanimity. All this being true, however, justices' policy preferences are the factor that influences their behavior most fundamentally.

So far I have focused on the U.S. Supreme Court, but policy preferences tied to ideology influence judges' positions on other appellate courts as well. This is especially true of state supreme courts with discretionary jurisdiction, since the law is quite uncertain in most of the cases they hear. It is less true of first-level appellate courts because they hear so many cases with seemingly obvious results; in such cases, judges' policy preferences can have little impact. But the minority of cases in which ideology is relevant tend to be the most important—the ones in which the court's decision affects people other than the parties.

Indeed, there is a variety of evidence that judges' preferences influence decisions at all levels of appellate courts. As in the Supreme Court, for instance, lower-court judges who bring well-established views on legal issues to their positions typically follow the same path on the bench. A good example is Richard Posner, a noted law professor at the University of Chicago, who was appointed to the federal court of appeals for the Seventh Circuit. As a professor, Posner had staked out strong conservative positions on legal issues involving economic questions; as a judge, he has taken similarly conservative positions.

There are some appellate courts in which judges do not seem to follow ideological lines in the positions they take. In 1990, one observer said of the Maryland Court of Appeals, the state's highest court: "I can't think of anyone on the court who is ideological one way or the other."[64] But in general, from the Supreme Court to state intermediate courts, judges' preferences on individual issues and their overall positions on the liberal-conservative spectrum go far toward determining their behavior on the bench.

Court Policies and the Selection of Judges   It follows that the general direction of an appellate court's policies reflects its membership. A state supreme court whose members are mostly liberal in their policy preferences is very likely to take liberal positions on most issues. The positions of federal courts of appeals on controversial issues vary with the mix of liberals and conservatives in the various circuits. Change in a court's position can be explained in similar terms. The U.S. Supreme Court has shifted a good deal in the ideological tenor of its policies over the past half century, and these shifts result chiefly from the departure of some justices and their replacement by justices with different views.

In turn, this means that the people who select judges have considerable power to shape the courts' direction. Presidents and governors are in the most powerful positions, because presidents nominate federal judges and governors choose a high proportion of state judges through regular and interim appointments. Given enough opportunities, sufficient care, and some good luck, a chief executive can have a fundamental effect on court policies.

We are most familiar with the impact some presidents have had on the Supreme Court. With eight appointments, Franklin Roosevelt was largely responsible for making the Court a liberal force in American life. In turn, Richard Nixon used his four appointments to moderate the Court's liberalism.

Presidents have similar effects on the lower federal courts. Although Jimmy Carter was the only president in the twentieth century who filled no Supreme Court vacancies, he did appoint more judges to the lower federal courts than any of his predecessors. Carter and his aides in the Justice Department selected judges with attention to their policy views. As a result, his appointments made the courts of appeals and the district courts more liberal.

The impact of Ronald Reagan and George Bush on the federal courts is particularly clear. On the Supreme Court, Reagan's elevation of William Rehnquist to chief justice in 1986 brought the Court's most conservative member into that leadership position. Reagan's three appointments of associate justices (Sandra Day O'Connor, Antonin Scalia, and Anthony Kennedy), followed by Bush's selection of David Souter and Clarence Thomas, tilted the Court in a more conservative direction.

Reagan and Bush also had considerable effect on the courts of appeals and district courts. By the time that Bush left office in 1993, about two-thirds of all federal judges were their appointees. As a result, federal judicial policy moved substantially, though unevenly, in a conservative direction. Although this movement was most visible in civil liberties law, it was also reflected in economic fields such as antitrust and environmental protection.[65]

As discussed in Chapter 4, Bill Clinton has had less impact because he has favored appointees who are fairly moderate in their views. His appointments of Ruth Bader Ginsburg and Stephen Breyer had only limited effects on the Supreme Court, because the two moderate liberals replaced a more liberal justice (Harry Blackmun) and a moderate conservative (Byron White). Clinton's appointments to the lower courts have reversed the conservative shift in those courts to a degree, but much less than they might have. And Republican control of the Senate during Clinton's second term ensures that his appointees as a group will not be strongly liberal.

Governors increasingly affect the ideological positions of state courts, because they are paying more attention to the policy views of their appointees than they did in the past. For example, some recent Republican governors have moved their supreme courts in a conservative direction on economic and civil liberties issues.[66]

California is perhaps the closest parallel to the federal courts in this respect.[67] Appointments by Democratic governor Jerry Brown (1975–1983) made a liberal supreme court even more liberal in its collective point of view, resulting in doctrinal positions strongly favorable to groups such as injured people and criminal defendants. A series of appointments by Brown's Republican successor, George Deukmejian (1983–1991), created a strong conservative majority. As a result, the court reversed its decisional tendencies in civil liberties and economic policy—overturning several of its precedents in the process.[68] The most striking indication of the court's shift is the proportion of death sentences that it reversed: 94 percent between 1977 and 1986, as against 16 percent between 1987 and 1994.[69] Deukmejian was succeeded by a more moderate Republican, Pete Wilson, and Wilson's appointments have moved the Court a bit closer to the ideological center.

Of course, there are limits to the impact of the appointment power. Some judges disappoint the chief executives who appointed them, either because their views were misunderstood or because they changed after appointment. Even a judge who generally performs as expected will cast some votes that the judge's appointer dislikes.

These limits are reflected in the work of the five Reagan and Bush appointees to the Supreme Court. On the whole, the positions taken by those appointees have been considerably more conservative than liberal; in that sense, the appointments were successful. But three of the five appointees (Sandra Day O'Connor, Anthony Kennedy, and David Souter) have been relatively moderate in their positions, and Souter could be said to lean toward the liberal side of moderate. The moderation of these three justices is symbolized by their decisive joint opinion in 1992 that maintained significant limits on state regulation of abortion.[70] O'Connor's moderation has not been very surprising, but Kennedy and Souter have surprised a good many people—including, in all likelihood, the presidents who appointed them.

In the states that elect judges, voters can also change the courts' direction. In Texas, Ohio, and Alabama, the voters have moved their supreme courts to the right in recent years. With most voters strongly favorable to conservative policies on criminal justice, candidates who espouse such policies have some advantage in winning judicial elections today. As a result, appellate courts in other states are also likely to become more conservative in the near future.

Group Processes

In the classic image of an appellate court, judges work closely together on decisions, discussing and arguing about the issues, drafting and redrafting opinions, until the court reaches its collective judgment. Thus group processes are integral to the court's choices.

This image has considerable accuracy for some cases in some courts. On the whole, however, it exaggerates what might be called the group element in appellate court decisions. The more complex reality reflects conditions that work in favor of group influence on decisions and others that work against it.

One condition that favors the group element is the desire to reach consensus. Judges strive to produce an opinion that can be accepted by at least a majority, so that the court issues an authoritative statement of legal principles. Judges have an interest in achieving even greater consensus—ideally, unanimity on the outcome of the case and the court's opinion—because unanimity may give their decisions greater authority.

Also favoring the group element is another motivation that may be even more powerful. Because of their reading of the law and their policy preferences, judges often feel strongly that a particular outcome and a particular set of doctrinal rules in an opinion would be desirable. Thus they have good reason to work at winning their colleagues' support for their position.

One force working against the group element in decisions is the strength of judges' views on the issues they face. When a court comes to a case involving product liability or criminal procedure, its members may not be amenable to persuasion. Judges who recognize this reality might see little point in trying to shift their colleagues' positions.

Perhaps more important is time pressure. Most appellate courts have more to do than their members can handle comfortably. Thus judges may find it difficult to work at length with colleagues, discussing and negotiating cases, in order to produce a true group product.

Because of the strength of judges' views and the time pressure they feel, the conferences that courts hold after arguments on a case typically are much less lively than we might expect. "When I first came on the court," reported a federal court of appeals judge,

> I imagined that conferences would be reflective, refining, analytical, dynamic. Ordinarily they are none of these. We go around the table and each judge, from junior to senior, states his or her bottom line and maybe a brief explanation. Even if the panel is divided, the discussion is exceedingly crisp. The conference changes few minds.[71]

Chief Justice Rehnquist has reported a similar pattern in the Supreme Court.[72]

As a result of differences in these conditions, the importance of group processes varies among courts. On the whole, that importance is greater in second-level courts. Discretionary jurisdiction reduces time pressures on judges, and the average case is likely to seem more important to judges than the average case in a first-level court. Moreover, most second-level courts decide every case with the same full set of judges, who thus interact regularly and come to know each other well. The Supreme Court, for example, has some resemblance to the classic image of an appellate court: although the justices engage in little face-to-face discussion of cases, they communicate with draft opinions and memos. The importance of these interactions is indicated by frequent changes in the language of opinions and occasional shifts in the majority between the Court's first tentative vote on a case and its final decision. One study found that the side that lost in the Court's first vote in the case ended up winning about 9 percent of the time.[73]

By the same token, fundamental departures from the classic image occur most often in first-level courts. Judges on these courts may work under enormous time pressure. In courts with constantly shifting three-judge panels, such as large federal courts of appeals, it is difficult for any particular set of three judges to develop the sorts of relationships and routines that facilitate effective group decision making. According to a judge on a federal court of appeals, "the difference in the collegial atmosphere between sitting with all of one's colleagues each month and sitting with each only once or twice or even three times a year is enormous."[74] And because many cases seem both unimportant and "easy," judges have less reason to discuss and argue about them.

The result can be a strong tendency to defer to a single judge who has primary responsibility for a case. In many courts, a case is assigned to one judge early in the decision process, with the implicit understanding that this judge will take primary responsibility for the decision. The other judges pay less attention to the case and generally defer to the assigned judge's view. As a result, the court's decision sometimes depends largely on the random assignment of a case to one judge rather than another.

Even when a court does not use early assignment procedures, its judges may be reluctant to disagree with the position of the judge who writes the opinion in a case. "I hate to say this," one California judge conceded, "but just the workload alone may encourage one judge to agree with the others, because otherwise he or she would have to write a dissenting opinion."[75] Several judges on one federal court of appeals reported that they limited their dissents to cases in which they disagreed strongly with the majority—when they felt what one judge called "outrage"—primarily because of a lack of time.[76] In extreme form, this deference to a single judge produces what has been called a one-judge decision.[77]

Beyond the difference between first-level and second-level courts, a court's traditions and mode of operation may affect the group element in decisions. One element of a court's operation is the amount of time that judges spend together. On most federal courts of appeals, judges reside and work in different cities, and on some state supreme courts the judges do most of their work in their home cities rather than in the capital. Although this separation does not preclude group interaction, it does limit such interaction. In contrast, the judges on some courts work in close proximity to each other. When the Illinois Supreme Court is in session, for about six months a year, its members "work, eat and sleep in the same building, a situation that keeps them in almost constant contact."[78]

A member of the New York Court of Appeals, the state's highest court, has argued that this close interaction and the absence of panels have considerable impact on her court:

> The fact that we are a nonresident, plenary bench promotes quick bonding. In Albany, we are all away from hearth and home, with a huge caseload and the same seven of us to work our way through it. Every case is a matter to be resolved in common. We spend a major part of our Albany days in conference, engaged in the sometimes bruising but miraculously solidifying process of trying to reach a consensus.[79]

Within any specific court, of course, group elements may play a greater role in some decisions than others. The key source of variation is the perceived importance of a case. Even on a court with a high division of labor, judges will not defer to a single colleague on a case in which the court is asked to resolve major issues concerning abortion or the death penalty.

On the whole, group processes are distinctly secondary to judges' individual attitudes and perspectives. Even in the Supreme Court, justices' votes on the outcome of cases typically stay the same over the course of the decision process, and most of the Court's opinions look similar in final form to the way they looked in their initial draft. Still, the group element sometimes makes a critical difference for the decisions of the Supreme Court and other courts: the language of opinions changes in important ways, a minority becomes a majority.[80]

Influence of Individual Judges In the group processes that shape decisions, we can expect some judges to exert more influence than others. One source of special influence is the judge's position. Each court has a chief judge or chief justice who holds certain powers within the court. Especially where the position is permanent rather than rotating among judges, it may also carry a degree of prestige. On appellate courts that divide into panels, the most senior judge on each panel generally acts as a kind of temporary chief who directs the panel's work.

The powers of chief judges vary considerably from court to court.[81] Of the powers that chief judges hold, among the most important is presiding over conference discussions of cases. The conference leader can formulate the alternatives to be considered and channel the discussion of those alternatives, thereby helping to move the court in a particular direction.

Also useful is the power to designate who will write the court's opinion. On most appellate courts, assignment of opinions generally is random. But in some courts the chief judge assigns opinions. (In a few of these courts, including the U.S. Supreme Court, chief justices assign opinions only when they were part of the majority in the court's initial vote on a case.) By assigning an opinion to an ideological ally or writing the opinion personally, the chief judge can secure a desired rationale for the decision. By assigning the opinion to an ideologically moderate judge, the chief judge can increase the likelihood of achieving consensus. On the Supreme Court, chief justices have taken both these approaches.[82]

The influence of a chief judge depends not only on formal powers but also on leadership skills and the inclinations of other judges. Some chief justices of the Supreme Court have exerted considerable influence over the Court's direction, while others have played much more limited roles. It seems clear, for instance, that William Rehnquist is more influential than his predecessor, Warren Burger (1969–1986).

Of course, judges who lack the chief's formal position can also have a disproportionate influence on their colleagues—an influence often stemming from extraordinary legal or persuasive skills. On the Supreme Court, William Brennan (1956–1990) was an important leader because he worked effectively to build majorities for liberal positions. Brennan's leadership has been credited with solidifying the liberal majority on the Warren Court and with achieving some victories for liberal positions in an increasingly conservative Court under Warren Burger and William Rehnquist.

Some judges, in contrast, exert little influence over their colleagues. They make no effort to sway other judges, or their personal characteristics or situations blunt their effectiveness. John Purtle, a member of the Arkansas Supreme Court from 1979 to 1990, found himself completely at odds with the other six justices because of strong ideological disagreement and their disapproval of some of his conduct on and off the bench. Purtle resigned from the court, saying, "There is no need to keep butting my head against the wall. . . . There is no likelihood that either the majority or I will change."[83]

But the small size of appellate courts and panels produces a considerable equality of influence. Simply casting one vote out of nine provides a good deal of leverage in itself, and one out of three provides even more. On any court, then, influence is likely to operate in all directions.

Interpersonal Relationships   In appellate courts, as in other groups, interpersonal relations can vary from harmonious to highly conflictual. But because interaction among judges generally occurs in private, it is often difficult for people outside a court to discern the character of that interaction.

We might take frequent disagreement in cases as evidence of internal conflict, but this is not necessarily so. High dissent rates may reflect a court's ideological lineup and its traditions rather than the relations among justices. One sign of conflict is heated language in opinions. But as suggested by Exhibit 8.4, even judges who criticize each other sharply in opinions may have an amicable working relationship. On

The federal Ninth Circuit Court of Appeals on the West Coast includes several judges with strong ideological views. The most outspoken judges on the court are conservative Alex Kozinski and liberal Stephen Reinhardt, both strong-minded judges who proclaim their views articulately on and off the bench.

Opinions by Kozinski and Reinhardt sometimes criticize opposing views in strong language. In a 1991 case, Kozinski wrote a dissenting opinion in which he said that the result reached by the majority was "so preposterous it would be laughable if it were not so scary." Reinhardt wrote a concurring opinion in which he called Kozinski's judgment "a remarkable comment considering that the dissent not only flagrantly misconstrues an elementary legal principle . . . but does so 'in a dangerous and unprecedented way.'"

In 1995, the court struck down Arizona's constitutional amendment making English the state's official language, on the ground that the amendment abridged the free speech rights of government employees. Reinhardt wrote the court's opinion. Kozinski wrote a dissenting opinion in which he ridiculed the court's ruling, arguing that its logic had broad and highly undesirable implications: "This case is about whether state employees may arrest the gears of government by refusing to say or do what the state chooses to have said or done." Reinhardt responded with a separate concurring opinion attacking Kozinski's dissent; its tone is suggested by one passage in which Reinhardt wrote that "Judge Kozinski's views of the rights of non-English speaking persons would make the Statue of Liberty weep."

But Kozinski and Reinhardt are not mortal enemies. They make public appearances together, sometimes debating issues of legal policy. One observer concluded that they are "best of friends" off the bench. Thus their example underlines the need for caution in making inferences about interpersonal relations from the language of court opinions.

Sources: The decisions were *Sanders v. Parker Drilling Company,* 911 F.2d 191 (9th Cir. 1991); and *Yniguez v. Arizonans for Official English,* 69 F.3d 920 (9th Cir. 1995). The quotation in the last paragraph is from Kenneth Jost, "Supreme Court v. Ninth Circuit," *The Recorder,* July 29, 1996, 1.

EXHIBIT 8.4   Judge Reinhardt and Judge Kozinski

the current Supreme Court, justice Antonin Scalia stands out for the strong terms in which his opinions criticize the writers of competing opinions, but he has argued that such language does not necessarily indicate or produce personal frictions.[84]

Occasionally, though, the conflict within a court is so intense that it becomes visible even to outsiders. A member of the Indiana Supreme Court accused the court's chief justice of personal misbehavior shortly before the chief justice faced a retention election. (The chief judge of the state's intermediate court went further, hiring a private detective to investigate the chief justice. The investigation apparently included checking the contents of the chief justice's garbage.)[85] There has been a series of battles on the Nevada Supreme Court. In the most recent episode, precipitated by disagreement over discipline of a trial judge, "justices are publicly accusing each other of cover-ups, conspiracies, corruption and temporary insanity."[86] Feuds on the Pennsylvania Supreme Court have featured a takeover of some of the chief justice's administrative powers by his colleagues, charges and countercharges of ethical misdeeds, and some justices who did not speak to each other for many years.[87]

One court that has experienced strong conflicts over a long period of time is the federal court of appeals for the District of Columbia; those conflicts are described in Exhibit 8.5. The primary source of these conflicts has been ideological differences. In some other courts, political rivalries have been responsible for conflicts. Of course, personal enmities can also foster or exacerbate bad feelings.

Interpersonal relations are likely to affect a court's functioning. Good relations facilitate consensus in cases and enhance a court's efficiency in handling its work, while bad relations may have just the opposite effect. Even efforts to prevent conflict may have an impact. The Rhode Island Supreme Court of the early 1970s, for instance, seemed to avoid major policy issues in order to maintain harmony among justices with diverse views.[88] This example suggests both that active involvement in difficult issues may be a source of conflict and that willingness to face conflict may allow a court to address such issues.

EXHIBIT 8.5   Conflict in the Federal Court of Appeals for the District of Columbia

> The federal court of appeals for the District of Columbia hears an unusually large number of cases that involve significant political and policy issues. Partly for this reason, there have been serious frictions between liberal and conservative judges on the court. During the 1960s, the two ideological factions ate separately in the judges' dining room, and one moderate judge ate elsewhere because it was "more comfortable over here, away from the feuding."
>
> During the 1980s and 1990s, strong conflicts within the court surfaced once again. The language in some opinions was bitter, and in one incident a judge told a colleague that "if you were ten years younger I would be tempted to punch you in the nose." The leak of a draft opinion in 1991 created difficulties for Clarence Thomas, a member of the court, during the battle over his confirmation to the Supreme Court. The next year the court's liberals and conservatives feuded publicly—in part through press releases—over investigation of the leak.
>
> A new chief judge in 1994 worked to ease tensions on the court. By no means, however, did conflicts disappear altogether. A dispute within the court continued over a task force study of possible racial, ethnic, and gender bias in the federal courts in the District of Columbia; one judge testified before a Senate committee that a vacancy on the court need not be filled; and another judge criticized some of the court's environmental decisions in an article. It remains to be seen whether the level of conflict can be reduced further or at least kept at a relatively low level.

Sources: Newspaper and periodical reports. The quotations are from, respectively, Joseph C. Goulden, *The Benchwarmers: The Private World of the Powerful Federal Judges* (New York: Weybright and Talley, 1974), 253; and Ann Pelham, "Silberman, Dogged by Story, Provides Details of Outburst," *Legal Times,* March 11, 1991, 7.

The Court's Environment

Ultimately, everything that courts do can be traced to external forces. Judges' policy preferences, for instance, reflect social influences on them. Even with a degree of insulation from their environment, courts are also subject to more direct influences from external forces.

The Legal Environment   Appellate courts are part of a legal community that includes lawyers and other courts. One effect of the legal community is to reinforce the influence of legal rules and legal considerations on judges. This community exerts other kinds of influences as well.

Judges are obliged to follow legal rules established by courts above them, but they pay attention to the positions of other courts as well. The opinions of state and federal appellate courts constitute a body of doctrine from which judges on any court can draw ideas. Like legislators and administrators, judges look to their counterparts elsewhere for solutions to policy problems. When the Oregon Supreme Court faces a contract issue that is new to it, its members will be interested in how other state supreme courts have dealt with the same issue. If several courts have addressed an issue and the weight of judicial opinion lies primarily on one side, that weight may sway another court that faces the issue. This is particularly true of the federal courts of appeals, because disagreements among the circuits create a conflict in federal law. As one judge said, "If the circuits are split, then I'm on my own, but if they've only gone in one direction, I'll generally go along. It would have to be an off-the-wall position for me to disagree."[89]

The opinions of lawyers can also influence a court. Of course, the lawyers who argue cases affect specific decisions. Supreme Court justice David Souter reported that, when he was on the New Hampshire Supreme Court, he kept track of his tentative positions in cases before and after oral argument; there were enough shifts "to indicate to me that oral argument was a matter of substantial importance to me in deciding cases."[90] Lawyers may have their greatest influence on cases that judges do not see as critical, so that they rely heavily on the arguments before them.

Lawyers' advocacy can have broader effects as well. In the late nineteenth and early twentieth centuries, some of the most skilled attorneys in the country represented businesses that sought to have government regulations of business practices declared unconstitutional, and their efforts influenced the views of federal judges on such regulations.[91] In the last half century, the lawyers representing civil rights and civil liberties groups have played a similar role. The skilled advocates who handle cases for the ACLU and the NAACP Legal Defense Fund have done much to shape Supreme Court policy, and their effectiveness spurred competing groups to develop their own legal expertise in order to achieve a comparable impact.

Another influence on judges is the general pattern of opinion within the bar on social and political issues. Not only do law school and legal practice shape the attitudes of people who later become judges, but judges continue to interact with lawyers and to read what lawyers are saying about legal issues. As a result, judges are drawn toward prevailing opinions within the bar. Traditionally, the predominant viewpoint of the legal profession was conservative, but in recent years that viewpoint has become more liberal; one sign of this change is a striking shift in the positions taken by the American Bar Association on political issues. The more liberal legal profession may be one force helping to sustain judicial liberalism.

The Political Environment   In a speech in April 1996, federal appellate judge Stephen Reinhardt referred to the pressures felt by elected appellate judges on the death penalty. "I have spoken with judges who must stand for election, and I have heard them say that they cannot afford to reverse capital convictions in cases that engender heated community passions."[92] Other observers have reported a similar fear among elected judges about capital punishment cases, and there is some evidence indicating that the prospect of election affects judges' votes in those cases.[93] Indeed, that is the intention of some people who attack judges for votes to overturn death sentences. In 1996, a Tennessee judge failed to win retention after an opposition campaign based on the death penalty. Afterward, the state governor said, "Should a judge look over his shoulder about whether they're going to be thrown out of office? I hope so."[94]

The impact of the voters on death penalty decisions underlines the effects of the political environment on appellate courts. In a variety of ways, elements of that environment can help to shape judges' votes and opinions.

First of all, voters' impact can extend beyond the death penalty. Elected judges have reason to fear that any decisions overturning criminal convictions can be used by opponents to attack them as "soft on crime," and this fear undoubtedly has some effect on judges' choices.[95] There is no other area in which public feelings run as deep as they do in criminal justice, but judges may take the voters into account in other areas when they anticipate that an opponent might use their position in a case as an issue. Judges also may think about the effect of their positions on their ability—and that of a potential opponent—to raise campaign money.

Whether or not they are elected, judges have good reason to pay attention to another part of their environment: the other branches of government. Legislatures and chief executives affect appellate courts in several ways: they determine court budgets, they adopt legislation that has an impact on judges' working conditions, they can act to overturn or limit court decisions, and they can help determine whether decisions are enforced.

Judges may modify their positions in an effort to avoid having their decisions overturned. More important, they want to avoid attacks on their court as an institution. State courts are especially vulnerable to such attacks, because legislators and governors tend to be less hesitant about acting against courts than are their federal counterparts. As a member of the Utah Supreme Court said, "We live down the hall from the house and the senate and up the stairs from the governor's office. The things we do that have an impact on the law and on the other branches of government have immediate repercussions for us."[96]

The Supreme Court illustrates judicial efforts to minimize confrontations with the other branches. The Court has struck down nine times as many state and local laws as federal laws;[97] in part, this ratio reflects the Court's dependence on Congress and its independence from state legislatures and city councils. In this century, the Court has twice retreated under fire from the other branches. In 1937, it escaped the threat of President Roosevelt's proposal to "pack" the Court with additional members when two justices shifted position by upholding major New Deal legislation as constitutionally acceptable. With the Court no longer a roadblock to Roosevelt's program, support for the proposal waned. In the late 1950s, the Court defused a congressional drive to attack its liberal policies on civil liberties issues by taking a more conservative tack.

The clearest evidence that appellate courts are influenced by their environments comes from instances in which a court reverses its decision in a specific case after receiving strong criticism for that decision. There have been several examples of such action in recent years:

- The Illinois Supreme Court in 1994 established an exception to the attorney-client privilege that shields communication between the two (and sometimes their communication with other people) from disclosure in court. After "an outpouring of criticism from bar groups," the court agreed to rehear the case. A year later, it reached the opposite decision, with several justices switching sides.[98]
- A Georgia statute allows prosecutors to ask for mandatory life sentences for people convicted of second drug offenses. In 1995, the state supreme court issued a decision that gave prosecutors more responsibility to show that their decisions about when to seek life sentences were not based on racial discrimination. The Georgia attorney general and all forty-six district attorneys in the state attacked the ruling. One month later the court issued a new decision in the case. One judge switched sides, and a 4–3 majority in one direction became a 4–3 majority in the other.[99]
- In 1996, the Louisiana Supreme Court held that state laws prohibiting the sale of alcoholic beverages to people who were between eighteen and twenty years old was unconstitutional as a form of age discrimination. Groups concerned with drunk driving protested, and the state also faced a monetary cost: a federal statute penalizes states with drinking ages under twenty-one by withholding a portion of their federal highway funds. The state attorney general asked the court to reconsider the case, and the legislature put a proposition on the ballot to overturn the Court's decision unless the Court reversed itself. Four months later the Court *did* reverse itself, in part because one justice changed his position.[100]

The Limits of Environmental Influence Having considered the ways in which external forces can influence appellate courts, I should emphasize once again the general autonomy of these courts. For the most part, judges are free to choose their own policy directions. Pressure from the environment is seldom so strong that it forces judges into a particular position. If they wish, judges can resist pressure rather than bow to it.

There is abundant evidence of this freedom. State appellate judges often adhere to positions that may arouse the wrath of voters. Several state supreme courts have used their state constitutions to expand the rights of criminal defendants; some justices have voted to overturn large numbers of death sentences despite overwhelming public approval of capital punishment. The Supreme Court has adopted some policies that were highly unpopular both in Congress and in the nation as a whole, such as its prohibition of laws that punish flag burning. As Exhibit 8.6 describes, the Illinois

In June 1994, the Illinois Supreme Court ruled on a dispute over parental rights for a three-year-old boy who was given the pseudonym "Richard." The facts of the case aroused considerable sympathy for the "Does," the couple who sought to adopt Richard and with whom Richard had lived since shortly after his birth. This sympathy was reflected in several amicus curiae briefs submitted on behalf of the Does. Nonetheless, the court held that the Does did not have the right to adopt Richard. In the court's view, Richard's birth father had effectively met the statutory requirements for objections to adoption and thus retained his parental rights.

The decision aroused considerable opposition. A *Chicago Tribune* columnist named Bob Greene, who had already written about the case, wrote six columns in which he strongly condemned the court. Greene gave particular attention to Justice James Heiple, the author of the court's opinion. Titles of the columns included "Supreme Injustice for a Little Boy" and "The Sloppiness of Justice Heiple." The Illinois legislature and governor acted with unusual speed to enact a statute with the goal of overturning the result in this case. Meanwhile, the Does sought a rehearing in the supreme court.

A month after its original decision, however, the supreme court denied a rehearing. Heiple wrote a supplemental opinion in which he denounced the governor, the legislature, and especially Greene. During the next six months the Does unsuccessfully sought a hearing from the U.S. Supreme Court; meanwhile, criticism of the Illinois court and Justice Heiple continued. Despite this criticism, the state supreme court ruled in January 1995 that the Does must return Richard to his birth father. After the Does failed in more efforts to secure action from the U.S. Supreme Court, that decision stood.

Greene continued to write frequently about the case and the court, focusing on Justice Heiple. In 1996, allegations were made that Heiple had sought to use his position to avoid speeding tickets. After a complicated series of proceedings, in 1997 he was censured by the state Courts Commission. In addition, a legislative committee studied whether impeachment was appropriate for Heiple's behavior in the traffic incidents as well as for actions he had taken in administering his court and the judicial system after he became chief justice. Heiple stepped down as chief justice during the impeachment investigation but remained on the court. Ultimately, the committee voted not to recommend impeachment but condemned Heiple's conduct.

Leaving aside the merits of the charges against Heiple, some observers concluded that the impeachment investigation largely reflected negative reaction to Heiple's role in the custody case. If this was true, Heiple paid a considerable price for adhering to his position in the case and perhaps for lashing out at his critics.

Sources: *Petition of Doe,* 638 N.E.2d 181 (Ill. Sup. Ct. 1994); other court decisions; newspaper stories and columns, primarily in the *Chicago Tribune.*

EXHIBIT 8.6   The Illinois Supreme Court Refuses to Retreat

Supreme Court that bowed to the feelings of bar groups on the lawyer-client privilege resisted immense pressure in a child adoption case.

The strongest external forces on the courts are likely to be the most subtle and the least visible. Most important, currents of opinion in the legal and political communities create constraints that rule out some possible policies and influence judges' choices among other policies. In this sense, the environments of courts are similar to the state of the law these courts apply. Each directs appellate judges toward some decisions rather than others, but both leave considerable room for judges to put their own stamp on the decisions they reach.

CONCLUSIONS

This chapter examined the processes by which appellate courts makes decisions and the forces that shape those decisions. As I have emphasized, the decisions of appellate courts—like those of trial courts—reflect a complex set of influences. The relative importance of these influences differs among courts and cases, so that it is difficult to generalize about explanation of judges' choices.

Another concern of this chapter should be underlined: to a degree, caseload pressures have transformed appellate courts. Most important, these pressures have created distinctions between types of cases. While some cases continue to receive close attention from judges, others are handled in more routine ways, with judges' law clerks and central staff attorneys doing much of the work. In second-level courts, many petitions for hearings are denied with little consideration by judges, and in first-level courts, many appeals are decided largely by staff attorneys.

The differentiation among cases has allowed judges to concentrate on the cases that seem to deserve the greatest attention rather than give all cases limited consideration. Thus judges can continue carrying out their traditional functions of correcting lower-court errors and enunciating legal principles in the face of growing caseloads. Yet the differentiation also may have produced some unintended and undesirable effects, such as weakening the right to appeal. One thing is clear, however: as appellate courts increasingly adopt new procedures to cope with greater workloads, they are subtly altering their own characteristics as institutions.

FOR FURTHER READING

Coffin, Frank M. *On Appeal: Courts, Lawyering, and Judging.* New York: Norton, 1994.

Epstein, Lee, and Joseph F. Kobylka. *The Supreme Court and Legal Change: Abortion and the Death Penalty.* Chapel Hill: University of North Carolina Press, 1992.

Grodin, Joseph R. *In Pursuit of Justice: Reflections of a State Supreme Court Justice.* Berkeley: University of California Press, 1989.

Lawrence, Susan E. *The Poor in Court: The Legal Services Program and Supreme Court Decision Making.* Princeton, N.J.: Princeton University Press, 1990.

Perry, H. W. Jr. *Deciding to Decide: Agenda Setting in the United States Supreme Court.* Cambridge: Harvard University Press, 1991.

Salokar, Rebecca Mae. *The Solicitor General: The Politics of Law.* Philadelphia: Temple University Press, 1992.

Schwartz, Bernard. *Decision: How the Supreme Court Decides Cases.* New York: Oxford University Press, 1996.

Segal, Jeffrey A., and Harold J. Spaeth. *The Supreme Court and the Attitudinal Model.* New York: Cambridge University Press, 1993.

Simon, James F. *The Center Holds: The Power Struggle Inside the Rehnquist Court.* New York: Simon & Schuster, 1995.

Wasby, Stephen L. *Race Relations Litigation in an Age of Complexity.* Charlottesville: University Press of Virginia, 1995.

NOTES

1. Federal Judicial Center, *Structural and Other Alternatives for the Federal Courts of Appeals* (Washington, D.C.: Federal Judicial Center, 1993), 7–9.
2. Joy A. Chapper and Roger A. Hanson, *Intermediate Appellate Courts: Improving Case Processing* (Williamsburg, Va.: National Center for State Courts, 1990), 6–7.
3. This discussion draws from John Bilyeu Oakley and Robert S. Thompson, *Law Clerks and the Judicial Process* (Berkeley: University of California Press, 1980).
4. Susan E. Grogan, "Judicial Apprentices? Law Clerks in the United States" (paper presented at the 1991 meeting of the American Political Science Association, Washington, D.C.).
5. Frank M. Coffin, *On Appeal: Courts, Lawyering, and Judging* (New York: Norton, 1994), 74–75.
6. Anthony T. Kronman, *The Lost Lawyer: Failing Ideals of the Legal Profession* (Cambridge: Harvard University Press, 1993), 346–347.
7. "Attacking Activism, Judge Names Names," *Legal Times,* June 22, 1992, 16.
8. *Report to the Federal Courts Study Committee of the Subcommittee on the Role of the Federal Courts and Their Relation to the States* (Washington, D.C.: duplicated, 1990), 72–73.
9. David Margolick, "At the Bar," *New York Times,* March 17, 1989, B4.
10. Frank J. Sorauf, *The Wall of Separation: The Constitutional Politics of Church and State* (Princeton, N.J.: Princeton University Press, 1976), 136.
11. See Daniel John Meador and Jordana Simone Bernstein, *Appellate Courts in the United States* (St. Paul: West Publishing, 1994), 70–88.
12. Chapper and Hanson, *Intermediate Appellate Courts,* 10–11.
13. Joseph R. Grodin, *In Pursuit of Justice: Reflections of a State Supreme Court Justice* (Berkeley: University of California Press, 1989), 19.
14. Ibid., 65.
15. Chapper and Hanson, *Intermediate Appellate Courts,* 16. See Thomas E. Baker, *Rationing Justice on Appeal: The Problems of the U.S. Courts of Appeals* (St. Paul: West Publishing, 1994), 106–150.
16. Administrative Office of the United States Courts, *Judicial Business of the United States Courts: Report of the Director* (1995) (Washington, D.C.: Administrative Office of the United States Courts, n.d.), 87.
17. "Quiet! Justices at Work," *National Law Journal,* September 26, 1994, A10.
18. Chapper and Hanson, *Intermediate Appellate Courts,* 87.
19. Thomas Y. Davies, "Affirmed: A Study of Criminal Appeals and Decision-Making Norms in a California Court of Appeal," *American Bar Foundation Research Journal* (Summer 1982), 566.
20. Gregory J. Rathjen, "Lawyers and the Appellate Choice: An Analysis of Factors Affecting the Decision to Appeal," *American Politics Quarterly* 6 (October 1978), 387–405.
21. See Scott Barclay, "Posner's Economic Model and the Decision to Appeal," *Justice System Journal* 19 (1997), 77–99.

22. See Rebecca Mae Salokar, *The Solicitor General: The Politics of Law* (Philadelphia: Temple University Press, 1992).

23. Ibid., 31; see Marc Galanter, "Why the 'Haves' Come Out Ahead: Speculations on the Limits of Legal Change," *Law and Society Review* 9 (Fall 1974), 97–125.

24. These data are from a statistical report compiled by the Office of the Solicitor General, U.S. Department of Justice.

25. Jay Mathews, "Business Tries to Shape Legal System, Report Says," *Washington Post,* May 19, 1993, F4.

26. *Immigration and Naturalization Service v. Chadha,* 462 U.S. 919 (1983); *Raines v. Byrd,* 138 L. Ed. 2d 849 (1997).

27. H. Jane Lehman, "Owners Aren't Giving Ground in Property Battles," *Chicago Tribune,* February 9, 1992, sec. 16, 1–2.

28. Lynne Duke, "Klan Unit Surrenders Assets to Settle Rights Suit," *Washington Post,* May 20, 1993, A1, A6. See Bill Stanton, *Klanwatch: Bringing the Ku Klux Klan to Justice* (New York: Grove Weidenfeld, 1991).

29. See Kim Lane Scheppele and Jack L. Walker Jr., "The Litigation Strategies of Interest Groups," in Jack L. Walker Jr., *Mobilizing Interest Groups in America* (Ann Arbor: University of Michigan Press, 1991), 157–183.

30. Karen O'Connor and Lee Epstein, "The Rise of Conservative Interest Group Litigation," *Journal of Politics* 45 (May 1983), 479–489; Lee Epstein, *Conservatives in Court* (Knoxville: University of Tennessee Press, 1985).

31. The cases were, respectively, *Vacco v. Quill,* 138 L. Ed. 2d 834 (1997); *U.S. Term Limits, Inc. v. Thornton,* 514 U.S. 779 (1995); and *Board of County Commissioners v. Umbehr,* 135 L. Ed. 2d 843 (1996).

32. Victoria Slind-Flor, "Calif. Governor Sues His State," *National Law Journal,* August 28, 1995, A6; Reynolds Holding, "Governor's Legal Antics Laughed Out of Court," *San Francisco Chronicle,* October 30, 1995, E1, E3; Reynolds Holding, "U.S. Court Rejects State Suit over Costs of Illegal Immigration," *San Francisco Chronicle,* January 8, 1997, A3.

33. The cases included are those that were decided with a signed opinion. See Lee Epstein, "Exploring the Participation of Organized Interests in State Court Litigation," *Political Research Quarterly* 47 (June 1994), 348.

34. Susan M. Olson, "Interest-Group Litigation in Federal District Court: Beyond the Political Disadvantage Theory," *Journal of Politics* 52 (August 1990), 869–870.

35. See Nancy McCarthy, "Lawsuits Become Integral to State's Initiative Process," *California Bar Journal,* February 1997, 1, 13.

36. On children's rights, see Susan Gluck Mezey, *Children in Court: Public Policymaking and Federal Court Decisions* (Albany: State University of New York Press, 1996).

37. See Lee Epstein and C. K. Rowland, "Debunking the Myth of Interest Group Invincibility in the Courts," *American Political Science Review* 85 (March 1991), 205–217; Kevin T. McGuire and Gregory A. Caldeira, "Lawyers, Organized Interests, and the Law of Obscenity: Agenda Setting in the Supreme Court," *American Political Science Review* 87 (September 1993), 717–726; and Donald R. Songer and Ashlyn Kuersten, "The Success of Amici in State Supreme Courts," *Political Research Quarterly* 48 (March 1995), 31–42.

38. This discussion of growth in appeals is based in part on Richard A. Posner, *The Federal Courts: Challenge and Reform* (Cambridge: Harvard University Press, 1996), 53–79, 110–121.

39. Federal Judicial Center, *Structural and Other Alternatives,* 25.

40. Jerry Goldman, "Federal District Courts and the Appellate Crisis," *Judicature* 57 (December 1973), 212.

41. Thomas B. Marvell, "Appellate Court Caseloads: Historical Trends," *Appellate Court Administration Review* 4 (1982–1983), 9. The main decision was *Douglas v. California,* 372 U.S. 353 (1963).

42. See H. W. Perry Jr., *Deciding to Decide: Agenda Setting in the United States Supreme Court* (Cambridge: Harvard University Press, 1991), 41–91.

Notes   **307**

43. See Ruth Bader Ginsburg, "Remarks for American Law Institute Annual Dinner May 19, 1994," *Saint Louis University Law Journal* 38 (Summer 1994), 884.
44. Grodin, *In Pursuit of Justice,* 59–60.
45. Maurice Kelman, "Case Selection by the Michigan Supreme Court: The Numerology of Choice," *Detroit College of Law Review* (Spring 1992), 1–2.
46. See Perry, *Deciding to Decide;* Gregory A. Caldeira and John R. Wright, "Organized Interests and Agenda Setting in the U.S. Supreme Court," *American Political Science Review* 82 (December 1988), 1109–1127; and Grodin, *In Pursuit of Justice,* 60–61.
47. Perry, *Deciding to Decide,* 198–207. See Robert L. Boucher Jr. and Jeffrey A. Segal, "Supreme Court Justices as Strategic Decision Makers: Aggressive Grants and Defensive Denials on the Vinson Court," *Journal of Politics* 57 (August 1995), 824–837.
48. Victor E. Flango, "Case Selection in the Georgia and Illinois Supreme Courts," *Justice System Journal* 12 (Winter 1987), 398–401.
49. Chapper and Hanson, *Intermediate Appellate Courts,* 15–22; Donna Stienstra and Joe S. Cecil, *The Role of Staff Attorneys and Face-to-Face Conferencing in Non-Argument Decisionmaking* (Washington, D.C.: Federal Judicial Center, 1989), 1–3.
50. Daniel J. Meador, *Appellate Courts: Staff and Process in the Crisis of Volume* (St. Paul: West Publishing, 1974), 104–105.
51. Stephen Reinhardt, "A Plea to Save the Federal Courts—Too Few Judges, Too Many Cases," *American Bar Association Journal,* January 1993, 52.
52. Thomas Y. Davies, "Gresham's Law Revisited: Expedited Processing Techniques and the Allocation of Appellate Resources," *Justice System Journal* 6 (Fall 1981), 397–398.
53. Robert S. Thompson and John B. Oakley, "From Information to Opinion in Appellate Courts: How Funny Things Happen on the Way Through the Forum," *Arizona State Law Journal* (1986), 41.
54. Mary Lou Stow and Harold J. Spaeth, "Centralized Research Staff: Is There a Monster in the Judicial Closet?" *Judicature* 75 (December–January 1992), 220.
55. David J. Brown, "Facing the Monster in the Judicial Closet: Rebutting a Presumption of Sloth," *Judicature* 75 (April–May 1992), 291.
56. Charles R. Haworth, "Screening and Summary Procedures in the United States Courts of Appeals," *Washington University Law Quarterly* (Spring 1973), 309–319.
57. Jerry Goldman, "Appellate Justice Economized: Screening and Its Effect on Outcomes and Legitimacy," in *Restructuring Justice: The Innovations of the Ninth Circuit and the Future of the Federal Courts,* ed. Arthur D. Hellman (Ithaca, N.Y.: Cornell University Press, 1990), 136–162.
58. Benjamin N. Cardozo, *The Growth of the Law* (New Haven, Conn.: Yale University Press, 1924), 60. See also Harry T. Edwards, "The Judicial Function and the Elusive Goal of Principled Decisionmaking," *Wisconsin Law Review,* 1991, 856–858; and Coffin, *On Appeal,* 275.
59. Douglas O. Linder, "How Judges Judge: A Study of Disagreement on the United States Court of Appeals for the Eighth Circuit," *Arkansas Law Review* 38 (Summer 1985), 498 n. 72.
60. John T. Wold, "Going Through the Motions: The Monotony of Appellate Court Decisionmaking," *Judicature* 62 (August 1978), 61–62.
61. Henry R. Glick and George W. Pruet Jr., "Dissent in State Supreme Courts: Patterns and Correlates of Conflict," in *Judicial Conflict and Consensus,* ed. Sheldon Goldman and Charles M. Lamb (Lexington: University Press of Kentucky, 1986), 202–203.
62. "The Supreme Court, 1995 Term," *Harvard Law Review* 110 (November 1996), 370.
63. Jeffrey A. Segal and Albert D. Cover, "Ideological Values and the Votes of U.S. Supreme Court Justices," *American Political Science Review* 83 (June 1989), 557–565; Jeffrey A. Segal, Lee Epstein, Charles M. Cameron, and Harold J. Spaeth, "Ideological Values and the Votes of U.S. Supreme Court Justices Revisited," *Journal of Politics* 57 (August 1995), 812–823.
64. Lisa Leff, "You Can't Accuse Md. High Court of Playing Politics," *Washington Post,* February 15, 1990, E1.

65. William E. Kovacic, "Reagan's Judicial Appointees and Antitrust in the 1990s," *Fordham Law Review* 60 (October 1991), 49–124; William E. Kovacic, "The Reagan Judiciary and Environmental Policy: The Impact of Appointments to the Federal Courts of Appeals," *Boston College Environmental Affairs Law Review* 18 (Summer 1991), 669–713.
66. Loren Stein, "State Courts Tilt to Right Under GOP Governors," *Christian Science Monitor,* March 27, 1996, 1, 18.
67. See John H. Culver, "The Transformation of the California Supreme Court" (paper presented at the 1995 meeting of the Western Political Science Association, Portland); and Barry Latzer, "California's Constitutional Counterrevolution," in *Constitutional Politics in the States: Contemporary Controversies and Historical Patterns,* ed. G. Alan Tarr (Westport, Conn.: Greenwood Press, 1996), 149–177.
68. Some overturnings of precedents are described in Culver, "Transformation of the California Supreme Court." More recent overturnings came in *Freeman & Mills, Inc. v. Belcher Oil Company,* 900 P.2d 669 (Calif. Sup. Ct. 1995); and *Peterson v. Superior Court,* 899 P.2d 905 (Calif. Sup. Ct. 1995).
69. Culver, "Transformation of the California Supreme Court," 18. See Craig F. Emmert and Carol Ann Traut, "The California Supreme Court and the Death Penalty," *American Politics Quarterly* 22 (January 1994), 41–61.
70. *Planned Parenthood v. Casey,* 505 U.S. 830 (1992).
71. Patricia M. Wald, "Some Real-Life Observations About Judging," *Indiana Law Review* 26 (1992), 177.
72. William H. Rehnquist, *The Supreme Court: How it Was, How it Is* (New York: William Morrow, 1987), 294–295.
73. Saul Brenner, "Fluidity on the Supreme Court: 1956–1967," *American Journal of Political Science* 26 (May 1982), 390. See Forrest Maltzman and Paul J. Wahlbeck, "Strategic Policy Considerations and Voting Fluidity on the Burger Court," *American Political Science Review* 90 (September 1996), 587.
74. Coffin, *On Appeal,* 216.
75. Wold, "Going through the Motions," 64.
76. Linder, "How Judges Judge," 484–486.
77. Robert S. Thompson, "One Judge and No Judge Appellate Decisions," *California State Bar Journal* 50 (November–December 1975), 476–480, 513–519.
78. Daniel Egler, "Hallowed Chambers," *Chicago Tribune,* March 12, 1984, sec. 2, 8.
79. Judith S. Kaye, "My 'Freshman Years' on the Court of Appeals," *Judicature* 70 (October–November 1986), 166.
80. See Bernard Schwartz, *The Unpublished Opinions of the Rehnquist Court* (New York: Oxford University Press, 1996).
81. Sanford S. McConkie, "Decision-Making in State Supreme Courts," *Judicature* 59 (February 1976), 337–343.
82. See Forrest Maltzman and Paul J. Wahlbeck, "Hail to the Chief: Opinion Assignment on the Supreme Court" (paper presented at the 1995 meeting of the American Political Science Association, Chicago).
83. David Margolick, "A Judicial Maverick Is Worn Down in Arkansas," *New York Times,* March 16, 1990, B11.
84. Antonin Scalia, "The Dissenting Opinion," *Journal of Supreme Court History,* 1994, 41.
85. Terry Horne, "Former Judge Hired Private Detective," *Indianapolis News,* November 17, 1994, B1; "Judge Checks Out Colleague's Trash," *National Law Journal,* December 5, 1994, A10.
86. Stephen Magagnini, "Nevada's Top Court Hogtied by Feud," *Sacramento Bee,* March 17, 1996, A1.
87. Roger Stuart, "Top Court Splits Duties, Cuts Nix Clout," *Pittsburgh Post-Gazette,* October 12, 1993, A1, A8; Joseph A. Slobodzian, "High Court Hi-jinks Irk Bar," *National Law Journal,* October 25, 1993, 1, 45, 46.
88. Edward Beiser, "The Rhode Island Supreme Court: A Well-Integrated Political System," *Law and Society Review* 8 (Winter 1973), 167–186.

89. David E. Klein, "The Adoption and Rejection of Legal Doctrines: Explaining the Choices of Federal Appellate Court Judges" (Ph.D. dissertation, Ohio State University, 1996), 114.

90. "Decision Process 'Helps to Discipline the Mind,'" *Legal Times,* September 24, 1990, 17.

91. Benjamin Twiss, *Lawyers and the Constitution* (Princeton, N.J.: Princeton University Press, 1942).

92. Quoted in *Congressional Record,* vol. 142 (daily edition), H12262 (October 2, 1996).

93. See Melinda Gann Hall, "Constituent Influence in State Supreme Courts: Conceptual Notes and a Case Study," *Journal of Politics* 49 (November 1987), 1117–1124; and Hall, "Justices as Representatives: Elections and Judicial Politics in the American States," *American Politics Quarterly* 23 (October 1995), 485–503.

94. Stephen B. Bright, "Political Attacks on the Judiciary," *Judicature* 80 (January–February 1997), 166.

95. See Reynolds Holding, "U.S. Courts Find Flaws in State Justice," *San Francisco Chronicle,* May 8, 1995, A1, A6.

96. Lawrence Baum and David Frohnmayer, eds., *The Courts: Sharing and Separating Powers* (New Brunswick, N.J.: Eagleton Institute of Politics, Rutgers University, 1989), 21–22.

97. Lawrence Baum, *The Supreme Court,* 5th ed. (Washington, D.C.: CQ Press, 1995), 201, 204.

98. *People v. Knuckles,* 650 N.E.2d 974 (Ill. Sup Ct. 1995). The quotation is from "Court to Revisit Privilege," *National Law Journal,* June 20, 1994, A8.

99. *Stephens v. State,* 456 S.E.2d 560 (Ga. Sup. Ct. 1995). See Bill Rankin, "Flip-Flop on Life Sentence," *National Law Journal,* April 24, 1995, A6.

100. *Manuel v. State,* 677 So.2d 116 (La. Sup. Ct. 1996). See "High Court of Louisiana Reverses Self on Drinking," *New York Times,* July 3, 1996, A9.

9

Appellate Courts: Policy and Impact

Without question, appellate courts are important policymakers. If they were not important, they would not get so much attention from interest groups, legislators, and others who want to influence their policies. But there is little agreement about the extent of their influence. Are they equal in impact to the other branches of government, as some observers suggest, or are they distinctly secondary players in the making of national and state policy?

This chapter considers the role of appellate courts in policymaking. The first part of the chapter deals with what appellate courts do as policymakers. The second part of the chapter examines what happens after appellate courts act—the impact of their policies elsewhere in government and in society as a whole. On the basis of those surveys, it will be possible to reach a tentative judgment about the significance of the Supreme Court and other appellate courts in American life.

APPELLATE COURT DECISIONS AS POLICIES

We can think of appellate court decisions as having two components, corresponding to the functions of these courts that were discussed in Chapter 8. The first is a review of how the lower court treated the parties to the case, a review that is important primarily to those parties. The second is a judgment about the principles of law that are applicable to the case. Those judgments, expressed in opinions, give appellate courts an important role in the making of public policy. After a brief discussion of review of lower courts, I will focus on the policies made by appellate courts through their opinions: the content of courts' agendas, the ideological direction of their policies, and the extent of their activism in policymaking.

Review of Lower-Court Decisions

In review of lower-court decisions, what appellate courts do most of the time is to leave those decisions standing. First-level appellate courts review trial courts directly, and in a substantial majority of cases they affirm the decisions that are appealed to them. In the cases they decided on the merits in 1995, the federal courts of appeals affirmed the trial court decision or dismissed the appeal 88 percent of the time.[1] Put another way, the courts of appeals "disturbed" the trial court decision only 12 percent of the time.

Moreover, many decisions that disturb trial decisions modify decisions in limited ways rather than overturning them altogether. A study of criminal appeals in five state courts found a 21 percent disturbance rate, but a majority of those disturbances were partial wins for defendants—most often, a corrected sentence or a new sentencing hearing. Only 8.5 percent of the defendants who appealed had their convictions overturned, and three-quarters of those successful defendants faced the possibility of a new trial rather than having their cases dismissed.[2]

These low disturbance rates can be explained by a combination of several forces.[3] Widely accepted legal doctrines give a strong presumption of validity to trial court decisions. This presumption is strengthened in practice by the experience of appellate judges, who learn that most cases are suitable for affirmance. And frequent reversals would exacerbate conflict between trial and appellate judges and increase appellate caseloads by encouraging appeals.

Unlike first-level appellate courts, those at the second level disturb lower-court decisions in a high proportion of the cases they decide. In its 1995–1996 term, the U.S. Supreme Court affirmed the lower court in only 32 percent of the decisions for which it provided full opinions. But that figure is deceptive because Supreme Court justices and judges on other second-level courts are inclined to accept cases in which they think that the lower court erred in its decision. If we take into account all the cases the Supreme Court refused to hear in its 1995–1996 term, the actual disturbance rate was only 2.4 percent.[4]

Because of this low disturbance rate and because many decisions are not appealed, the great majority of decisions by trial courts and intermediate appellate courts become final. In this respect, then, appellate courts intervene rather little into the work of the courts below them.

Of course, this is only one aspect of the relationship between higher and lower courts. Even though appellate courts overturn relatively few decisions, the opinions they write influence what the courts below them do in a much larger number of cases. For example, one state supreme court decision on liability rules in auto accident cases can shape hundreds of trial court decisions. Only after considering the roles and impact of appellate courts more broadly can we fully assess the relationship between higher and lower courts.

Appellate Court Agendas

The potential impact of courts on the rest of government and society is determined, first of all, by the types of issues they address. We can begin to sketch out the roles of appellate courts in policymaking by examining the sets of cases they hear and decide with opinions—their agendas. The more work that a court does in a particular field, the greater its potential to shape public policy in that field. As suggested in Chapter 8, the agendas of appellate courts reflect rules of jurisdiction, patterns of litigation and appeals, and judges' choices of cases in which to write opinions. The 1996 agendas of three appellate courts at different levels are summarized in Exhibit 9.1.

The agendas of state supreme courts reflect the work of state courts generally. Because state court litigation is quite diverse, so too is the business of state supreme courts and thus their activity as policymakers. That diversity is reflected in the agenda of the Pennsylvania Supreme Court. As that example shows, however, supreme courts focus far more on public law—cases that arise from government policy in a fairly direct way—than do the trial courts below them. In particular, criminal cases stand out as a major part of supreme court agendas.

The agendas of federal courts of appeals show both similarities to and differences from those of state supreme courts. As the example of the Sixth Circuit in Exhibit 9.1 indicates, the courts of appeals concentrate on public law even more than do the state appellate courts. Criminal law is not as prominent, partly because criminal justice is still primarily a state activity. The higher proportion of cases resulting from economic regulation reflects the broad sweep of regulation by the federal government.

The agenda of the U.S. Supreme Court is distinctive.[5] Broadly speaking, the Court devotes itself overwhelmingly to public law issues; as Exhibit 9.1 shows, all other cases account for only a small minority of its opinions. Within this category, the Court is primarily a civil liberties specialist. Indeed, in recent years, about half its opinions have involved civil liberties issues. The largest number of these cases concern criminal procedure, but the Court also decides a great many cases on the right to equal treatment under the law and other individual liberties, such as freedom of expression and freedom of religion. As Exhibit 9.1 shows, economic regulation is another significant public law area. A third major area, which overlaps the first two,

EXHIBIT 9.1   Subject Matter of Cases Decided with Published Opinions by Three Appellate Courts in 1996

Category of Cases	Pennsylvania Supreme Court (%)	Federal Court of Appeals Sixth Circuit (%)	U.S. Supreme Court (%)
Debt and contract	12.8	8.1	4.8
Torts	9.0	10.5	9.5
Family and estates	1.5	1.6	0.0
Public law			
Criminal	44.4	29.8	33.3
Regulation of economic activity	18.0	27.4	22.6
Other	14.3	22.6	29.8

Note: Many cases could have fit into multiple categories depending on the coding rules, so the percentages should be viewed only as general descriptions of the three courts' agendas. The table includes cases decided by the Pennsylvania Supreme Court in January-September 1996 (one unclassifiable case was omitted), cases decided by the Sixth Circuit in January-April 1996, and cases decided by the U.S. Supreme Court in its 1995-1996 term (October 1995-June 1996).

is federalism—that is, the constitutional relationship between national and state governments.

Even this brief discussion suggests something about the potential roles of appellate courts as policymakers. Although the various state and federal courts cover a broad range of issues, there are some important areas of public policy in which appellate courts are largely inactive. The outstanding example is foreign policy, which state courts barely touch and in which federal courts make relatively few decisions. Even in fields where they are active, the courts may not deal with the most fundamental issues. In economic regulation, for instance, courts focus primarily on the details of regulatory policy rather than on the general form and scope of regulation.

Ideological Patterns in Appellate Court Policy

The agendas of appellate courts indicate the areas to which they devote the most attention. Just as important is the content of the policies that courts make in those areas. That content is most easily summarized in ideological terms: the distribution of liberal and conservative policies.

At any given time, the policies of appellate courts are certain to be quite diverse ideologically. But this does not mean that they are random. For most of American history, appellate courts as a whole were fairly conservative in their policies, by the current definition of that term. In the past sixty years, in contrast, their policies have been quite mixed.

The traditional conservatism of appellate courts was best reflected in economic policies. Federal and state courts addressed a wide range of legal issues affecting the interests of economically powerful groups, and the dominant theme in their decisions was support for those interests.

The U.S. Supreme Court did much to protect property rights and the freedom of business enterprises from restrictions by state and federal governments. As legislation to regulate and restrict business practices grew early in this century, the Court frequently struck laws down as unconstitutional. Ultimately, the Court overturned much of President Franklin Roosevelt's New Deal economic program in the 1930s.

The economic policies of state courts also had a conservative emphasis.[6] As the industrial economy developed, state courts did much to protect the business sector from threats to its economic well-being. For instance, they adopted a set of rules for personal injury law that favored businesses over injured individuals.

This conservative emphasis in appellate court policy is not difficult to understand. Judges came primarily from economically advantaged sectors of society and were imbued with the values of those sectors. They were trained in a legal profession in which conservative values predominated, and they often embarked on legal careers that involved service to business enterprises. Further, the most skilled advocates in court generally represented businesses and other institutions with conservative goals. Because of all these forces, perhaps it was inevitable that the dominant element in judicial policy was conservative.

In the past half century, judicial conservatism has been replaced by an ideologically mixed pattern of policy, in which the liberal element has often been more prominent. Across a range of issues, the courts have given significant support to the interests of relatively weak groups in society, groups that possess far fewer social and

economic resources and far less conventional political power than the business interests that courts tended to favor in the past. Pat Buchanan, candidate for the
Republican presidential nomination in 1996, complained that the Supreme Court's
beneficiaries are "members of various minorities, including criminals, atheists, homo-
sexuals, flag-burners, illegal aliens including terrorists, convicts and pornographers."[7]
Although some might quarrel with Buchanan's characterization of the Court, his list
captures the Court's departure in the past few decades from its traditional pattern of
policy. Conservatives have made similar complaints about lower federal courts and
state appellate courts.

  This ideological change has been most visible in the Supreme Court. Beginning
in 1937, the Court quickly abandoned its earlier support for business interests that
sought protection from government regulation. More slowly, and culminating in the
1960s, it began to provide support for the civil liberties of relatively powerless groups
in American society. It extended the constitutional rights of criminal defendants to
state proceedings and established new controls on police investigations and trial procedures. It required the desegregation of southern public schools and protected the
rights of racial minority groups in other areas of life. It strengthened freedom of
expression both for the mass media and for people who express their views through
vehicles such as pamphlets and marches.

  Since the 1970s, the Supreme Court has supported civil liberties with less consistency. It narrowed the rights of criminal defendants, and it became more reluctant
to establish new rights in any area. But even in the 1990s, when the Court's membership is its most conservative in several decades, it has maintained a surprising degree
of support for individual liberties. It was in 1996, after all, that Patrick Buchanan
complained about the Court's support for the liberties of weak and unpopular groups.
And despite some hints of a new direction, the Court has continued to accept active
government regulation of the economy.

  Over the past few decades, the ideological positions of the federal courts of
appeals have varied over time and differed from court to court. On the whole, however, they too have been distinctly more liberal than in earlier periods. Certain courts
have stood out for their liberal policies. From the 1960s to the 1980s, the court of
appeals for the District of Columbia gave strong support to the rights of criminal
defendants and the mentally ill, the interests of consumers, and protection of the environment. The Fifth Circuit in the Deep South championed racial equality under the
law in the 1950s and 1960s despite the anti–civil rights pressures in that region. In the
1980s and 1990s, the Ninth Circuit on the West Coast has been distinctly more liberal
than the Supreme Court. The result has been several conflicts over policy between the
two courts, most dramatically on capital punishment.

  Early in this century, state supreme courts began to move away from their long-
standing support for business in tort law by expanding rights to recover compensation
for personal injuries.[8] This trend gradually gained momentum as courts increasingly
eliminated old rules that had favored defendants. Most dramatically, supreme courts
in the 1960s and 1970s largely eliminated the requirement that those who are injured
by defective products must prove that the manufacturer was negligent. In the past
decade, the movement to expand the rights of injured people has slowed considerably,
and to some degree state courts have become more favorable to the interests of tort
defendants,[9] but for the most part the revolution in personal injury law remains intact.

State courts have taken decidedly mixed positions in civil liberties. In the 1950s and 1960s, some supreme courts openly resisted the Supreme Court's expansions of individual liberties, interpreting the Court's decisions narrowly. Since the 1970s, as the Supreme Court itself has narrowed some liberties, some state courts have accepted this direction enthusiastically.[10] But others, particularly in the West and Northeast, have undertaken their own expansions of liberties by finding independent sources of protections in their state constitutions.[11] This activity has extended to areas ranging from freedom of expression to sex discrimination, but the largest part has concerned criminal justice. In the 1990s, for instance, several state courts have established protections from police searches and seizures that go beyond the protections of the U.S. Constitution.[12] On the whole, state supreme courts today give much more support to individual rights than they did in past eras.

The relative liberalism of appellate courts in the current era is more difficult to explain than was their traditional conservatism. Undoubtedly, the recent liberalism has roots in a changing pattern of social values. In this century, support by the general public and political leaders for protection of business enterprises from government regulation has declined. Meanwhile, some civil liberties—especially those related to equality—have gained more support. This change in values is reflected in judges' own attitudes and in the kinds of litigation and arguments that come to appellate courts.

Another source of this ideological change is the kinds of people who become judges. Like judges in the past, most current judges come from families with high status. But there are more exceptions today; as a result, the attitudes of judges on economic and social issues are less likely to be conservative.

More directly, the people who select judges are themselves more liberal than they were in earlier periods. At the federal level, liberal Democratic presidents have sought out appellate judges who shared their liberalism. Franklin Roosevelt's appointments turned the Supreme Court away from its traditional economic conservatism, and appointments by Kennedy and Johnson in the 1960s helped solidify its commitment to civil liberties. Similarly, Roosevelt, Johnson, and Jimmy Carter all used their appointments to move the lower federal courts in a liberal direction. At the state level, growing Democratic strength in the North from the 1930s on brought more liberal governors into office; in turn, these governors influenced the direction of state appellate courts with their own appointments.

To some extent, this shift to greater liberalism has been self-reinforcing. The courts' support for civil liberties encouraged interest groups to bring new cases, seeking further expansions of liberties. When the Supreme Court in the 1960s played a strong role in expanding civil liberties, many lawyers gained an appreciation for that role, and those who reached the bench themselves sought to follow it. As the changes in tort law demonstrate especially well, a trend in judicial policy tends to gain a certain momentum of its own.

The partial reversal of this liberal trend in the past decade reflects events outside the courts. The success of Republican presidential candidates from 1968 through 1988 brought more conservatives into the federal courts, with an inevitable impact on judicial policy. In part because of activity by interest groups, fears about negative effects of expanded rights for injured people became widespread, and these fears undoubtedly influenced state court decisions in tort law.

Of course, future directions in appellate court policies will reflect further developments in their political environments, developments as broad as trends in social thinking and as specific as the outcomes of presidential and gubernatorial elections. The policy shifts that have occurred in this century should remind us that the ideological stance of the courts is always subject to change.

Judicial Activism

Observers of the courts sometimes contrast what they call *judicial activism* and *judicial restraint.* Of the two, restraint has the more positive connotation; in contrast, activism sounds like something inappropriate. Indeed, critics of the courts frequently attach the label of activism to judges and decisions with which they disagree. "Basically," according to one scholar, "judicial activism is what the other guy does that you don't like."[13]

Thus the concept of judicial activism might be dismissed as nothing more than political rhetoric. But activism does have real meaning. Policymaking is inherent in the work of the courts, but judges have some control over the *extent* of their involvement in policymaking. In deciding cases, judges often face a choice between alternatives that would enhance their court's role in policymaking and those that would limit its role. A court might decide a tort case on the basis of a narrow rule, or it might announce a broad rule that affects a whole class of tort cases. When facing a longstanding issue, a court may follow the legal rules it laid down earlier or overturn precedent and establish new rules. When a policy of the legislature or executive branch is challenged, a court can uphold that policy and allow it to continue, or it can overturn the policy and make it inoperative. When judges choose to increase their impact as policymakers, they can be said to engage in activism; choices to limit that impact can be labeled judicial restraint. The level and forms of judicial activism tell us much about the role that courts play in policymaking.

The examples in the preceding paragraph indicate that activism has several different elements. A decision that appears to be activist by one criterion might not be activist by another.[14] Perhaps the most important element of activism is intervention into policies made by the legislative and executive branches. This kind of intervention often takes the form of striking down statutes or other government policies as unconstitutional. It may also involve giving detailed directions to the other branches for their policy choices.

In any era, judicial activism may be primarily liberal or primarily conservative in its content. Today, in contrast with the first part of this century, most activism favors liberal policies. As a result, conservatives tend to attack activism, while liberals defend it. Indeed, congressional Republicans in 1997 announced that they would consider seeking impeachment of some federal judges for engaging in activism by making specific liberal decisions that had activist elements.[15] Nevertheless, judicial activism raises a serious set of issues that transcend the substance of activist policies at any given time.

Supporters of judicial restraint argue that activist policymaking is undesirable on several grounds. They perceive activism as illegitimate because the courts are relatively free from popular control and accountability—particularly the federal courts, whose judges are appointed for life. They also see activism as risky because it puts the courts into confrontations with more powerful policymakers and thus threatens their autonomy. Some commentators have attacked activism on a more practical level, arguing that the courts are not well equipped to make good policy choices on complex social issues.

Defenders of activism counter these arguments in several ways. Some minimize the alleged weaknesses of the courts—arguing, for instance, that their capacity to make good policy is greater than the critics have suggested. Many view the courts' freedom from popular control as a virtue rather than a weakness because that freedom allows the courts to protect important but often unpopular values such as civil liberties.

This debate is impossible to resolve definitively, because the issues involved are so complex and because some of them involve disagreements about values. In light of this difficulty, perhaps it is inevitable that most people react to activism on an ideological basis. In any case, it is uncertain that the debate over judicial activism has much effect on the actual behavior of courts.

Judicial Activism Today   As I have suggested already, American courts have always engaged in activism. But the level of activism has been unusually high in the past few decades, perhaps higher than in any earlier period. The best single quantitative indicator of activism is the number of laws that the Supreme Court declares unconstitutional. Between 1960 and 1996, by one count, the Court struck down 63 federal statutes and 549 state and local laws.[16] Both figures constitute nearly one-half of the total for the Court's entire history.

These figures reflect the Supreme Court's involvement in a wide range of important policy questions. Some examples will underline the extent of that involvement:

- The Court has been a central participant in public policy on race. In decisions over the past half century, the Court has established rules about when school segregation is unconstitutional and what action is required when it is. The Court's decisions since the 1970s have indicated when affirmative action by government and private institutions is legally acceptable. In the 1990s, the Court has limited the leeway of state governments in drawing legislative district lines to maximize representation for racial minority groups.

- In *Roe v. Wade* (1973), the Court intervened in the developing debate over abortion law with a ruling that effectively struck down the laws of at least forty-six states. Since then the Court has handed down a series of decisions on abortion issues ranging from the legality of restrictions on government funding for abortion to the legality of restrictions on protests at clinics that perform abortions.[17]

- Since the 1960s, the Court has been an active overseer of criminal procedure in the United States. The Court decides the acceptability of police procedures for searches and questioning of suspects, determines the circumstances under which defendants can be sentenced to death, and rules on a myriad of other procedural issues under the Constitution.

- The Court intervenes in the political process as well. Most important, a series of decisions from 1976 through 1996 has severely limited government regulation of campaign finance.[18] The result has been to make meaningful limitations on campaign spending impossible.

Lower federal courts have engaged in their own activism, often following the lead of the Supreme Court but sometimes taking their own initiatives. To take a few examples from recent years, the courts of appeals have made decisions that prevented new federal rules for local telephone competition from going into effect on schedule; that limited the federal government's ability to bring criminal cases for "insider training" in stocks; and that allowed lawsuits for damages against people outside the United States for violations of international law on human rights.[19] In a 1996 decision that received considerable attention, a Fifth Circuit panel ruled that affirmative action programs in university admissions were unconstitutional, despite a 1978 Supreme Court decision that had allowed such programs.[20]

Activism in the federal courts extends to the trial level. With some encouragement from appellate courts, federal district judges frequently intervene in the governance of public institutions such as schools, prisons, and mental institutions, holding existing conditions to be unconstitutional and then supervising closely the task of reforming them. Frank Johnson of Alabama was a leader in this development.[21] In at least one important instance, this supervisory role extended to the private sector: Between 1982 and 1996, Harold Greene of the District of Columbia exercised considerable control over the structure of the telephone industry through his administration of an antitrust consent decree involving AT&T.[22]

District judges frequently make decisions of other types that have substantial effects on public policy temporarily or permanently. In recent years, judges in one district—Washington, D.C.—have held that the North American Free Trade Agreement (NAFTA) could not go into effect until an environmental impact study was completed; ruled that long-standing procedures for extraditing criminal suspects to other countries are unconstitutional; and struck down the 1996 statute allowing the president a "line-item veto" of portions of appropriations bills.[23]

State supreme courts have also engaged in an impressive level of activism. The increased use of state constitutions as independent protections for civil liberties by some supreme courts is a significant expansion in their roles. Perhaps the most striking example is the series of supreme court rulings on school funding. In 1973, the U.S. Supreme Court rejected the argument that systems based on local property taxes violated the equal protection clause of the Fourteenth Amendment even though those systems produced substantial differences in funding levels across school districts within a state.[24] Litigants had already begun to challenge these funding systems under state constitutions, and after 1973 they focused solely on state-level challenges. While many supreme courts have upheld their states' funding systems, courts in fifteen states have struck down those systems as unconstitutional at least once.

One indication of activism at all court levels in the current era is judicial responses to laws adopted by the voters. In about half the states, voters can adopt statutes or constitutional amendments independently through the initiative. Initiative measures adopted by the voters are often challenged, most often on the ground that they violate the U.S. Constitution. Courts have struck down initiatives in many instances, even though they are running directly against voter sentiment in doing so. Exhibit 9.2 provides some examples of these decisions.

What accounts for the relatively high level of activism today? To a degree, it simply reflects the policy goals of judges, particularly those whose commitment to civil liberties leads them to invalidate policies of the other branches. The Supreme Court

English as the Official Language of Arizona. In 1988, Arizona voters adopted an initiative that made English the state's official language: "the language of the ballot, the public schools and all government functions and actions." In 1990, a federal district court ruled that the initiative violated the constitutional free speech rights of state employees, and the Ninth Circuit Court of Appeals affirmed that decision. In 1997, however, the Supreme Court ordered that the case be dismissed because it had become moot. Undoubtedly there will be a new challenge to the initiative in the future.

Gay Rights in Colorado. In 1992, Colorado voters approved an initiative that barred the state and local governments from adopting or enforcing any law that prohibited discrimination on the basis of sexual orientation. A Colorado trial court held that the initiative violated the equal protection clause of the Fourteenth Amendment, and the state supreme court affirmed its judgment. The state brought the case to the U.S. Supreme Court, which heard the case and agreed with the state courts that the initiative was unconstitutional.

Term Limits for Members of Congress. Since 1990, voters in twenty-one states have approved limits on the length of time that members of Congress could remain in office. These measures were challenged on several constitutional grounds. In suits to challenge those measures, a federal district court in Washington State and the Arkansas Supreme Court held that term limits initiatives that voters had adopted were unconstitutional, and the Nevada Supreme Court prevented a term-limits measure from going on the ballot. The Arkansas case went to the U.S. Supreme Court, which agreed with the state supreme court—though only by a 5–4 vote—that states could not add to the requirements in the Constitution for membership in Congress. The Court's decision makes it impossible to impose term limits on Congress without a constitutional amendment.

Sources: Court decisions, newspaper articles.

EXHIBIT 9.2   Some Examples of Voter-Passed Initiatives Struck Down by Courts

undoubtedly helps to foster activism in the lower courts through its own example, and the lower courts set examples for each other. It is easier for a federal judge to order major prison reforms when a dozen judges in other districts have already done so.

The high level of activism also reflects forces outside the courts. Perhaps its most fundamental source is the growth in government action at all levels. Because government policies now touch people more often and more deeply than in past eras, it is inevitable that more questions about the legal validity of government action arise. Today the Supreme Court strikes down more laws than it did in the past, but there are more laws on the books now. The 1940 edition of the *United States Code,* the compilation of federal statutes, was forty-five hundred pages long. In contrast, the current edition contains more than twenty-five thousand pages.

Growth in government action also increases conflicts within government that courts are called upon to decide. When a legislature and chief executive bring their dispute over the veto power to the courts, for instance, judges may be required to make a judgment that affects the balance of power between the two branches. Since

1995, the Mississippi Supreme Court has heard a series of cases involving the powers of Governor Kirk Fordice in several areas: use of the item veto, application of rules for administrative procedure, appointment of officials, and control over litigation for the state.[25] No matter what the court did, the cases gave it a significant part in determining the governor's position in state government.

There also has been growth in interest group litigation to challenge government action. Interest groups cannot force activism on a reluctant court, but they can facilitate activism by providing opportunities and by constructing arguments for it. Groups such as the American Civil Liberties Union have played a critical role in bringing civil liberties cases to court, just as groups such as the Sierra Club have done on environmental issues. Courts have encouraged interest groups and others to challenge government action through decisions responding positively to such challenges. Judicial activism, like so much about the courts, results from an interaction between judges and the larger society in which they work.

THE IMPACT OF APPELLATE COURT POLICIES

The activity of courts in resolving public policy issues gives them great potential influence over the rest of government and American society as a whole. In an era of considerable activism in the courts, that potential role is heightened.

But the actual impact of the courts depends on how people respond to their decisions. To take one example, the Supreme Court has made several major decisions interpreting the scope of federal laws against employment discrimination. The ultimate impact of those rulings depends on a wide range of actions in government and the private sector: whether Congress allows the rulings to stand, how enforcement agencies interpret them, decisions by individuals whether to file lawsuits for discrimination, and decisions by employers whether to change their practices. As this example suggests, we cannot determine the effects of appellate court decisions from a reading of the decisions themselves; the responses of individuals and institutions to those decisions must be taken into account.

Implementation by Lower Courts and Administrators

An appellate court's impact depends in part on responses to its decisions by lower courts and administrators. When a court rules on a legal issue, the courts and administrative bodies below it are responsible for applying that ruling, where it is relevant, to other cases and other situations. (Such administrative bodies include all the agencies in the executive branch of government, ranging from federal regulatory commissions to police departments and school systems.) Their actions help to determine how far a ruling radiates in the legal system as a whole.

The Implementation Record   In responding to decisions by appellate courts, lower-court judges and administrators have choices to make. Most fundamentally, they must decide how fully they will put those decisions into effect. Responses to appellate court decisions differ a great deal.

At one end of the spectrum, some officials directly refuse to follow rulings that apply to them. In 1997, the Social Security Administration ordered its administrative judges to follow the agency's policies rather than the rulings of federal courts. According to an internal memorandum, "An administrative law judge is bound to follow agency policy even if, in the administrative law judge's opinion, the policy is contrary to law."[26] In 1996, a federal district judge in the District of Columbia announced in an opinion that his court of appeals had interpreted a procedural rule badly, so "this court is compelled to disavow District of Columbia precedent."[27]

At the other end of the spectrum, officials often comply fully with the legal rules that appellate courts lay down. This compliance typically receives little attention, because it is undramatic and accords with people's expectations. But it merits some emphasis, because it suggests that appellate courts have considerable power to shape the choices of officials below them in the legal hierarchy.

Perhaps the most important characteristic of responses to appellate court decisions is variation in the degree of compliance—variation among decisions and among different policymakers responding to the same decision. That generalization can be illustrated by examining some major areas of appellate court policy.

The first is school desegregation.[28] In *Brown v. Board of Education* (1954), the Supreme Court required that school districts with separate schools for black and white students desegregate their systems. In the Deep South, the federal Fifth Circuit Court of Appeals followed the *Brown* decision faithfully. But federal district judges, who had ultimate responsibility for applying the decision to specific cases, generally allowed successive delays in desegregation. Meanwhile, many southern school administrators and other public officials flatly refused to follow the Supreme Court's ruling. As a result, schools in the Deep South remained almost as segregated in 1964 as they had been ten years earlier. Only after Congress and the federal executive branch intervened, chiefly by providing financial incentives, did significant desegregation begin in the Deep South.

Desegregation followed a different path in the rest of the country. The border states, such as Maryland and Missouri, also were subject to the *Brown* decision. Their school districts gradually desegregated while the Deep South maintained its resistance. In the 1970s and 1980s, the Supreme Court required elimination of the more complex segregation found in many northern school districts to the extent that it was caused by government action. On the whole, northern federal judges followed the Court's rules, and school districts generally followed court desegregation orders.

The second area is police procedure.[29] In the 1960s, the Supreme Court applied the "exclusionary rule" to state proceedings, holding that illegally seized evidence could not be introduced in court. It also established major new restrictions on searches and seizures. In another set of decisions, the Court laid down rules for police interrogation of suspects; its key decision in this regard was *Miranda v. Arizona* (1966), which required that certain warnings be read prior to questioning. Since then, several state supreme courts have gone even further than the Supreme Court in restricting these types of police practices.

Some lower courts, especially at the trial level, have applied these rulings reluctantly and narrowly. For their part, police officers have engaged in a good deal of partial and full noncompliance with court-imposed restrictions. Officers seem to follow the rules for questioning of suspects reasonably well in a literal sense, but they sometimes try to limit the impact of those rules. For instance, detectives may make efforts to discourage suspects from making use of their rights. Police officers follow legal rules for searches far more than they did before the exclusionary rule was established, but their compliance is still well short of complete.

The final area is school religious activities.[30] Over the past half century, federal courts have limited religious observances in public schools. Especially important were the decisions by the Supreme Court in 1962 and 1963 that prohibited schools from engaging in organized prayer or Bible reading exercises, a position that the Court reiterated and extended in later decisions. A great many schools eliminated observances that the courts struck down, but others maintained them despite their illegality. It appears that noncompliance with the Court's rulings has increased in the 1990s. For instance, many schools have failed to follow the Court's 1992 ruling that clergy could not lead prayers in graduation ceremonies.

How can we account for imperfections in the implementation process? What causes variation in responses to appellate court rulings? Several factors are relevant.

Attitudes Toward Policy   Every appellate court decision embodies a position on a policy issue, whether it be school desegregation, liability for personal injuries, or government regulation of air pollution. The judges and administrators who deal with these issues do not respond to decisions of higher courts as neutrals. Indeed, their personal attitudes are perhaps the most powerful forces in determining their responses to the policies they are asked to implement. More specifically, two kinds of attitudes are important, *policy preferences* and *self-interest.*

The policy preferences of judges and administrators have an obvious relevance to their implementation of decisions. If asked to carry out an appellate court decision with which they agree, they can be expected to do so with alacrity. By the same token, it is unlikely that they will react enthusiastically if they strongly disagree with a decision. When faced with an appellate court order that violated her "moral and ethical conscience," for instance, one federal district judge withdrew from the case rather than carry it out.[31]

This point helps to explain how decisions have been implemented in the three policy areas that were just discussed. The Supreme Court's decisions in each of these areas have been viewed as very bad policy by many of those responsible for carrying them out, and understandably people with that view have often balked at following the Court's lead. This has been true, for instance, of teachers and school administrators who think that prayers are an essential part of school activities. This factor also helps to explain differences in responses to the same decision: the border states desegregated their schools more quickly than the Deep South largely because their school officials were not as strongly opposed to the idea of desegregation.

It follows that the implementation of appellate court decisions has an ideological dimension. As we have seen, the major thrust of activist judicial policies in recent years has been liberal; not surprisingly, conservative officials are the most likely to resist these policies. Similarly, the Supreme Court's conservative policies on some issues in the 1980s and 1990s have aroused resistance from liberal judges on the federal Ninth Circuit Court of Appeals on the Pacific Coast.[32]

Self-interest is also relevant to the implementation process. Appellate court rulings can affect the self-interest of judges and administrators in several ways. These rulings may threaten or reinforce practices that officials find advantageous, such as the rapid processing of cases in trial courts. Or they may ask elected officials to take positions that are highly popular or unpopular with their constituents. Most of the public favors cutting back on the procedural rights of criminal defendants, so most state prosecutors and judges can be expected to carry out decisions that narrow those rights more effectively than decisions that expand them.

The early failure to achieve school desegregation in the Deep South resulted in large part from local pressures. School officials typically had overwhelmingly white constituencies because of restrictions on voting by black citizens, and most southern whites were strongly opposed to desegregation. Federal district judges held lifetime positions, but they faced likely ostracism and possible violence if they demanded speedy desegregation.

Similarly, resistance by law enforcement officials to court decisions that limit investigative practices can be understood chiefly in terms of self-interest. Police officers have the inherently difficult job of solving crimes by identifying suspects and obtaining physical evidence. Court rulings that limit searches and seizures of evidence or the questioning of suspects complicate this job and threaten to make it even more difficult. Thus most officers initially take a negative view of these rulings.

Ultimately, their compliance with such decisions depends largely on how much difficulty the decisions seem to cause. Police have found that court-imposed rules for searches and seizures often prevent them from obtaining the evidence they want, and so their compliance with these rules has been quite imperfect. In contrast, officers gradually learned that literal compliance with *Miranda* did not make their job appreciably more difficult, because most suspects are willing to answer questions despite hearing the prescribed warnings—particularly when officers encourage them to do so. As a result, *Miranda* has become a part of police routines.

Any court decision that requires major changes in policy is likely to conflict with the policy preferences or self-interest of many judges and administrators. One reason is that people and institutions left on their own choose the policies that accord with their preferences and self-interest. Hence, when an appellate court intervenes to demand a change, it is usually demanding that officials do what they find less desirable. Perhaps just as important, officials tend to resist any major change that is imposed on them because it is easier to continue doing things the same way than to adopt new routines.

Judicial Authority   If officials' self-interest and policy preferences may work against the full implementation of court decisions, other factors facilitate effective implementation. One is acceptance of appellate court *authority,* the right of those courts to bind legal subordinates with their rulings.

It appears that most people accept an obligation to follow the legal rules laid down by courts above them as part of the general obligation to obey the law. Lawyers are directly imbued with this duty through their training. Because most judges are lawyers and because they themselves benefit from judicial authority, judges tend to accept higher-court authority even more than do administrators.

The impact of court authority can be seen in the response to some unpopular decisions. A great many teachers and school administrators, for instance, have eliminated religious observances that they personally favored. This willingness to follow the courts' lead despite disagreement with their decisions stems chiefly from acceptance of the obligation to do what the Court asked.[33]

The impact of authority is sometimes quite explicit, when judges proclaim their willingness to apply a higher-court precedent despite their disapproval of the policy expressed in that precedent. In one typical instance, a federal district judge in Louisiana wrote in a 1990 opinion that he was "respectfully disagreeing" with a ruling by the court of appeals above him but that this ruling was "binding and controlling in this cause," so that he had to follow it.[34]

Despite the authority of appellate courts, judges and administrators sometimes fail to carry out an applicable decision. Although judicial authority may be strong, it is not absolute, and a public official's disagreement with the substance of a policy may outweigh the authority of the court that issued the policy. Such intense disagreement is most likely to arise on issues that arouse strong feelings, such as abortion and the death penalty. And officials may disagree with the general tenor of an appellate court's decisions sufficiently that they accord less authority to those decisions. A liberal judge on a federal court of appeals said, "I follow the law the way it used to be, before the Supreme Court began rolling back a lot of people's rights."[35]

More important, officials can often reconcile their acceptance of a court's authority with evasion of its ruling. They may, for instance, seize upon the ambiguity in an appellate court opinion to avoid following its spirit. This was the response of many federal district judges to *Brown v. Board of Education,* in which the Supreme Court required that schools be desegregated "with all deliberate speed."[36] Judges who opposed desegregation interpreted this language as allowing them to delay the initiation of desegregation for many years, so long as any practical difficulties could be shown.

Similarly, officials may evade the spirit of a decision by engaging in narrow compliance with it. One trial judge described informally his narrow compliance with appellate court decisions protecting the rights of criminal defendants:

> I've got to find some way to get around some rule that some court has pronounced about something, and I don't think we should have to admittedly—okay. I'm not great on defendants' rights. . . . So, you can argue until you're blue in the face. I'll agree with you that it is a close call, but I don't choose on close calls to read it in favor of the defendant. I just don't see that we have to do that.[37]

Another way to reconcile a court's authority with a failure to follow its ruling is to engage in selective misperception of the ruling. Some school personnel believe that they are in compliance with the Supreme Court's school prayer decisions when they allow students to absent themselves from prayer recitations. Such misperception is fostered by the poor communication of decisions to many administrators, who may learn of relevant decisions from imperfect reports by the mass media or by superiors. When communication is incomplete or erroneous, officials often can interpret decisions as they see fit.

Sanctions   If the authority of appellate courts does not overcome resistance to their rulings, we might expect them to employ *sanctions,* penalties designed to force compliance. Appellate courts do possess some meaningful sanctions that they can threaten or actually employ against disobedient judges and administrators. But these sanctions are fairly weak in comparison with those that exist in most other organizations. The Supreme Court, for instance, cannot fire a district judge who refuses to follow its decisions.

For lower-court judges, the most common sanction is reversal of decisions that fail to follow an applicable ruling. Judges do not like to have their decisions reversed because this suggests that they have erred, and a judge who is frequently reversed may be perceived as incompetent. Hence judges have an incentive to apply appellate court rulings properly to the cases they decide.

Yet reversal has limited practical consequences—usually only the requirement that a judge rehear a case. For this reason, judges who strongly oppose an appellate policy may be willing to accept reversals as a consequence of following their inclinations. Despite several reversals, a federal district judge in Virginia has continued to depart from sentencing guidelines that she sees as deeply flawed.[38] And reversals do not always follow disobedient decisions, in part because such decisions might not be appealed and reviewed.

For many administrative bodies, the most significant sanctions involve being taken to court and becoming subject to a court order that requires a change in policies. If a school continues to hold prayer exercises despite the Supreme Court's decisions, an unhappy parent can file suit and secure an order against such practices. The monetary costs of going to court and the embarrassment of an adverse court order can deter a certain amount of noncompliance. But like reversal, this is not a very powerful set of sanctions. One reason is that someone with legal standing must go to court to seek an order requiring compliance with a decision, and frequently no one does so. Thus many school districts can continue religious observances because no lawsuit has ever been filed against them.

For administrative bodies that depend more directly on the courts, judges have a stronger sanction: the refusal to give needed support to agency policies. This sanction applies to some regulatory agencies, such as the National Labor Relations Board, that require court enforcement of their rulings. Less directly, police departments are dependent on courts to convict the defendants they arrest. Thus noncompliant behavior that jeopardizes enforcement of agency rulings or conviction of defendants carries real costs. For instance, police officers want to follow court requirements for obtaining evidence so that it will not be ruled inadmissible in court. But achieving a conviction is not always of great importance to individual police officers, who are judged chiefly on their ability to make "good arrests" rather than on the convictions of people they arrest. For this reason, they may be willing to jeopardize a conviction by violating judicial rules.

Faced with what they see as noncompliance, appellate courts can take stronger measures. For one thing, they can try to embarrass noncompliant officials by rebuking them. The chief judge of the Court of Veterans Appeals used a speech to criticize officials in the Department of Veterans Affairs for ignoring his court's rulings.[39] A federal district judge said that the National Credit Union Administration had attempted to "circumvent" his ruling in a case, and he called it a "rogue federal agency."[40]

When judges or administrators violate a direct court order, those officials or their governments may be cited for contempt of court and given a monetary penalty. Though judges often are reluctant to use such a strong sanction, contempt citations against governments are not rare. A state trial judge held New York City in contempt several times over what he saw as its failure to provide adequate shelter for homeless families.[41] Contempt citations against the District of Columbia government have been common in recent years during a series of conflicts between judges who seek reform in local institutions and administrators who operate those institutions. Exhibit 9.3 examines the relationship between the courts and the District.

Taken together, the sanctions that appellate courts can employ are significant but quite imperfect. Lower-court judges and administrators often hold attitudes that incline them against faithfully carrying out appellate court policies. Although the authority of appellate courts and their sanctions do overcome some resistance, they are not strong enough to produce perfect compliance. As a result, the policies of

EXHIBIT 9.3   Courts and the District of Columbia Government

The District of Columbia government has been the defendant in a large number of lawsuits challenging its operation of a wide range of programs. Many of these suits have resulted in court-imposed decrees against the District or consent decrees in which the government agreed to certain actions. Judges have issued orders to the District on issues ranging from recycling to fire code violations in schools.

Judges frequently have ruled that the District failed to meet its obligations under decrees, and they have sometimes taken strong measures to secure compliance. In a number of instances the courts found the District or its officials in contempt of court for noncompliance with decrees, and they sometimes imposed substantial monetary penalties. Monitors were appointed to oversee the operation of several programs. In 1997, officials chosen by judges actually ran programs in foster care, public housing, and prison medical services. Altogether, the judicial intervention in the operation of the District government is extraordinary.

Much of this intervention involves the operation of the District's correctional facilities. Since 1971, a series of lawsuits has been filed in federal district court against the District for conditions in its prisons. Several consent decrees have been reached, requiring specific changes in conditions. Since 1993, the court has used a special master to monitor compliance with court decrees involving prison conditions. The government or its officials have been held in contempt at least twice for failure to comply with decrees.

A 1985 lawsuit involving conditions in the District's juvenile correctional facilities resulted in a 1986 consent decree. Two years later, the District was found in contempt for noncompliance with the decree, and it has been assessed millions of dollars in fines for failure to comply with limits on the number of people housed at its juvenile detention center. In a case involving sexual harassment of prison employees, a federal judge in 1996 ordered a prison warden and another official jailed for contempt for retaliating against a complainant. That order underlined the extent of the conflict that had developed between the District and the courts.

Sources: Toni Locy, "In D.C., It's Often Government by Decree," *Washington Post,* October 3, 1994, A1, A6, A7; Vernon Loeb, "District Wants Relief from Cost of Court Orders," *Washington Post,* April 7, 1997, B1, B3; other articles in the *Washington Post..*

appellate courts—like other government policies—are subject to implementation problems.

Responses by the Legislative and Executive Branches

Legislatures and chief executives have considerable power to affect the impact of court decisions. They also hold power over courts themselves. Thus it is important how they use these powers in practice.

Responding to Statutory Interpretations   Most decisions by appellate courts interpret statutes, the laws that legislatures enact. Such decisions give additional form to the policies that are laid down in the legislation itself. In this way, state courts help to shape legislative policy on such matters as divorce and occupational licensing, just as federal courts affect congressional policy on taxes and civil rights.

Most court interpretations of statutes attract little attention in the other branches of government because they are uncontroversial. But some statutory decisions arouse opposition from legislators or officials in the executive branch, who conclude that the court has misinterpreted their intent or simply that it has reached an undesirable result. These opponents can use a straightforward remedy: adoption of new legislation that overrides the offending court decision.

Bills to undertake such overrides are introduced quite often in Congress. Like other legislation, most of these bills fall by the wayside at some point, but many are enacted. One study found that between 1967 and 1990, Congress overturned 121 statutory decisions of the Supreme Court and 220 decisions of lower courts.[42] Although no comparable figures are available on state legislatures, it is clear that they also respond to statutory decisions with some frequency. Exhibit 9.4 describes some recent overturnings of statutory decisions at the federal and state levels.

State legislatures can also supersede court decisions in areas such as property and torts, where the law has developed through court-made rules independent of statutes. Legislatures have been especially active in the tort field in recent years.[43] After state supreme courts adopted new doctrines expanding the legal rights of injured parties, legislatures often adopted statutes to negate or limit these doctrines. Several legislatures, for instance, overturned decisions making social hosts liable for injuries caused by their serving of liquor to guests. This action has come at the behest of groups that must defend against lawsuits, particularly the insurance companies that usually pay any damages awarded against defendants.

Legislatures sometimes use overrides to influence specific cases. In a long-running dispute over child custody and visitation in the District of Columbia courts, the mother has aroused sufficient sympathy in Congress to gain two statutes favoring her position. After she was jailed for contempt of court for failure to provide visitation to the father or disclose her child's whereabouts, a 1989 statute secured her release. After the mother took the child to live with her family in New Zealand, a provision was inserted into a 1996 budget bill with the goal of ensuring that she could maintain custody and withhold visitation rights if she returned to the United States.[44] Similarly, the victims and survivors of victims in the Oklahoma City bombing of 1995 enlisted congressional help in the form of two statutes that overrode pretrial rulings by the judge in Timothy McVeigh's case: that there could not be a closed-circuit broadcast

Legislative (Year)	Decisions Overridden
Congress (1996)	1992 and 1993 decisions of the federal court of appeals for the District of Columbia; each decision had held that a policy of the Environmental Protection Agency failed to meet statutory requirements for solid waste disposal.
Congress (1996)	A 1990 Supreme Court decision that allowed migrant farm workers to sue their employers for injuries that were covered by workers' compensation.
Virginia (1995)	A 1994 state supreme court decision that gave employees broad rights to sue for discrimination under state law.
Ohio (1995)	A 1982 state supreme court decision that allowed injured workers to sue employers for "intentional torts" even if they were covered by workers' compensation (partial override).

EXHIBIT 9.4   A Sampling of Recent Legislation Overriding Court Decisions

of the trial and that people who intended to testify at the penalty phase of the trial if McVeigh was convicted could not attend the phase of the trial in which guilt or innocence was determined.[45]

The discussion so far may suggest that legislation in response to judicial interpretation of a statute always involves direct conflict between the two branches, but this is not the case. The legislation that follows a statutory decision may ratify that decision, at least in part, rather than overturn it. And a court sometimes invites the legislature to overturn its decision if legislators see fit.

In any event, legislative overrides of judicial decisions are only one aspect of the process through which the statutory law develops. In fields such as criminal law and environmental protection, each branch helps to shape and reshape public policy through a series of actions and decisions. Legislation, executive branch implementation, and judicial interpretations modify and build on each other, creating a body of law that reflects the initiatives of all three branches.

Responding to Constitutional Interpretations   Ordinarily, a court decision that overturns a statute on constitutional grounds can itself be overturned only by a constitutional amendment. The federal and state constitutions have intentionally been made difficult to amend. Under the usual procedures, amendment of the United States Constitution requires the agreement of two-thirds of each house of Congress and three-quarters of the state legislatures. Since the Bill of Rights was adopted in 1791, only seventeen amendments have survived this process. State constitutions are usually amended through another two-stage process, which involves a proposal by the legislature and its ratification by the voters. This process is less cumbersome than its federal counterpart, but it is still difficult.

At both the state and federal levels, some constitutional amendments overturn court decisions. Four amendments to the federal Constitution clearly were aimed at overturning Supreme Court decisions, and five others can also be put in that category. The most recent such amendment was the Twenty-sixth, which overturned a 1970 decision limiting congressional power to lower the legal voting age.[46] In the states, several constitutional amendments have been adopted in recent years to overturn court decisions—most often on the death penalty and other criminal justice issues.

But these instances are exceptional. Because the amendment process is so difficult, even highly unpopular constitutional decisions generally are not overturned. The rarity of such action is especially striking at the federal level. In response to the liberal activism of the Supreme Court since the 1950s, members of Congress have introduced dozens of amendments designed to overturn particular decisions, yet only two of these resolutions have received the necessary two-thirds majority in either house of Congress. These two resolutions, approved by the House in 1995 and 1997, were to overturn the Court's decisions striking down laws against flag burning. The Senate's defeat of the 1995 resolution despite the great unpopularity of the Court's decisions reflects congressional reluctance to amend the Constitution—though the 1997 resolution or a successor might yet win congressional approval as a proposed amendment.

Under some circumstances, a legislature can negate or limit the effect of a constitutional decision through statutory action. When the Supreme Court struck down state death penalty laws in *Furman v. Georgia* (1972), its ambiguous decision seemed to indicate that redrafted versions would be constitutionally acceptable if they established clearer standards for imposing the death penalty. In response, most states did redraft their statutes, and the Court upheld some of the new statutes in 1976.[47] After *Roe v. Wade* (1973), the Supreme Court decision that struck down state prohibitions of abortion, Congress and many state legislatures adopted provisions that limited government funding of abortion; these provisions were also found acceptable under the U.S. Constitution.[48] (Some state supreme courts have held, however, that their own constitutions require state funding of abortion.)

Other statutory responses have been in more direct conflict with the court decisions in question. After *Brown v. Board of Education*, for example, southern states adopted a variety of laws to prevent desegregation, most of which were clearly unconstitutional and which were struck down by federal courts. Legislatures have also enacted statutes that directly contravened Supreme Court decisions on school prayer and abortion.

The issue of marriage between men or between women has produced a complicated legislative response. In 1993, the Hawaii Supreme Court held that the state's prohibition of same-sex marriage would have to meet a high standard to be found acceptable under the state constitution. The supreme court sent the case challenging that prohibition back to a trial court for reconsideration under that standard. In reaction, eighteen states enacted statutes indicating that they would not recognize same-sex marriages performed in other states. In 1996, Congress adopted a statute allowing states to take such action, though it was unclear whether the Constitution allowed states to deny recognition to valid marriages even with congressional permission. The Hawaii trial court in 1997 ruled that the state's ban on same-sex marriages violated the state constitution. While the case was on appeal, the state leg-islature approved a state constitutional amendment proposal that would prohibit same-sex marriage while giving some rights and benefits to gay and lesbian couples. If the state's voters approved the amendment, as they were expected to do, any court ruling to the contrary would be overruled.

Influencing the Implementation Process   In several ways, legislatures and chief executives can help determine how court decisions are put into practice. First, they may influence the behavior of implementers by taking positions on controversial decisions. For example, the strong and active opposition of some southern governors to school desegregation contributed to the lack of meaningful desegregation in the Deep South during the decade after *Brown v. Board of Education.*

Second, the legislature and executive can provide—or fail to provide—tangible help in achieving effective implementation. After a decade of inaction in the Deep South, Congress in 1964 gave the executive branch the power to withhold federal funds from school districts that refused to desegregate. The Johnson administration used this power with some vigor, and the result was that real desegregation finally began in that region. Ironically, Congress took several actions to try to impede deseg-regation of northern schools in the 1970s and 1980s, although these actions seemed to have little impact. In a different kind of action, Presidents Eisenhower and Kennedy each used federal troops in one instance to enforce school desegregation in the South.

Finally, some court decisions require compliance by legislatures or chief execu-tives themselves. Perhaps the most famous example was the Supreme Court decision in *United States v. Nixon* (1974), which required that President Nixon turn over tape recordings of his conversations to a federal court. After some hesitation, Nixon com-plied, even though material in the recordings forced his resignation. His compliance, like that of some predecessors, suggests that the president's legitimacy might be seri-ously damaged by a failure to obey court rulings.

In recent years, state legislatures have frequently been faced with court rulings that required them to make major changes in public institutions. In many states, fed-eral judges have ordered improvements in prisons and mental hospitals, and several state supreme courts have ordered changes in state systems for the financing of pub-lic schools. Legislators have good reasons to try to carry out these orders; most impor-tant, if they fail to do so, courts may take more drastic action, such as requiring that a prison be closed. But budgetary constraints may make effective implementation of a sweeping decision very difficult, and legislators often resent court rulings that require institutional change.

As a result of these conflicting considerations, the record of legislative action in response to those decisions is mixed. For instance, state legislatures have responded very differently to court decisions that require fundamental changes in school fund-ing systems. At one end of the spectrum, the Kentucky legislature responded enthu-siastically to a 1989 state supreme court decision that struck down the state's funding system.[49] At the other end, the New Jersey Supreme Court has battled with the state legislature since 1973 over changes in school funding mandated by the court. That battle is described in Exhibit 9.5.

In *Robinson v. Cahill* (1973), the New Jersey Supreme Court ruled that the state's system of school funding, based primarily on local property taxes, failed to meet the state constitution's mandate that "the legislature shall provide for the maintenance and support of a thorough and efficient system of free public schools." The court indicated that the school funding system resulted in inadequate educational opportunity in districts with limited tax bases. The court required the state legislature to develop a new funding system and set deadlines for it to do so. The legislature adopted a new system in 1975 but failed to finance it, and the court prohibited the state's schools from operating after July 1, 1976 unless funding was provided. The legislature acquiesced early in July and adopted an income tax to provide funding.

A new lawsuit was filed in 1981, based on the claim that the new funding system failed to remedy the deficiencies of the old system. After a series of preliminary proceedings, the supreme court ruled on the lawsuit in 1990. The court held that the state funding system remained unconstitutional because it did not provide adequate resources to the state's poorest urban districts. The court required the state to ensure that those districts had at least as much to spend per student as the state's wealthiest districts and that the resources provided were adequate to address the "special educational needs" of the poorest districts.

The legislature soon adopted an income tax increase advocated by the governor to meet that mandate. However, after great public criticism—criticism that ultimately led to the governor's defeat for re-election—the legislature in 1991 pulled back some of the education funding from the tax increase. In 1994, the supreme court held that the legislature's response was inadequate and ordered the legislature to adopt legislation providing the needed funding by September 1996. After the court provided a three-month extension, the legislature acted in December 1996, but in May 1997 the supreme court ruled that the action was inadequate and issued a new order concerning school funding. Thus, two dozen years after the first ruling in the case, the legislative and judicial branches remained in conflict.

Sources: Richard Lehne, *The Quest for Justice: The Politics of School Finance Reform* (New York: Longman, 1978); Russell S. Harrison and G. Alan Tarr, "School Finance and Inequality in New Jersey," in *Constitutional Politics in the States: Contemporary Controversies and Historical Patterns,* ed. G. Alan Tarr (Westport, Conn.: Greenwood Press, 1996), 178–201; *Abbott v. Burke,* 693 A.2d 417 (N.J. Sup. Ct. 1997); other court decisions and newspaper articles.

EXHIBIT 9.5   The Legislature, the Supreme Court, and School Funding in New Jersey

Attacking the Courts as Institutions   Legislatures and chief executives typically control court jurisdiction, budgets, and staffing. If they are unhappy with court policies they can use these powers to attack the courts, either to limit what the courts can do as policymakers or simply to exact a measure of revenge.

At the federal level, the president and Congress frequently threaten to use their powers against the courts, but such an attack is seldom carried out. In 1937, for example, President Franklin Roosevelt proposed legislation that would allow him to "pack" the Supreme Court with six new members, thereby changing the Court's policy direction. The proposal died in Congress, partly because the Court retreated under this threat. Only once, in 1869, has Congress narrowed the Supreme Court's jurisdiction to keep the Court out of a controversial area—in that instance, Reconstruction of the South after the Civil War. Indeed, in the past thirty years, a multitude of bills have been introduced to remove the jurisdiction of the Court or of all federal courts over such areas as abortion and school busing, but none was adopted.

In a number of instances, state legislatures have actually used their institutional powers to attack courts. In 1991, the California Supreme Court upheld an initiative measure that cut the state legislative budget by 38 percent; its opinion seemed to endorse the view that the legislature needed reform. In response, the legislature cut the supreme court's budget by the same 38 percent. One person who discussed that cut with legislators "discovered they had memorized the 'offensive' passages in the high court opinion, and quoted them back to her in the hallways of the Legislature."[50]

Another instance of financial retaliation was reported by a lawyer who argued a case before the Nevada Supreme Court during a rainstorm and found that rain was pouring into the courtroom itself. The chief justice explained that the court had asked the legislature for money to fix the problem, but the legislature refused because of its unhappiness with some of the court's decisions.[51]

Significant though these attacks are, some nineteenth-century legislatures took stronger action. Early in that century one legislature reportedly expressed its displeasure with a decision of the state supreme court by reducing the justices' annual salaries to twenty-five cents.[52] The Kentucky legislature went even further in the 1820s. Unhappy with decisions that had struck down two statutes, some legislators sought to remove all the judges on the Kentucky Court of Appeals. After they failed to obtain the necessary two-thirds majority to achieve the judges' removal, they acted by a simple majority to abolish the court and create a replacement for it. The old court refused to disband, and litigants and trial judges had to decide which court to pay attention to. At one point, the governor prepared to use military force to prevent the old court from recovering its papers that had gone to the new court. The conflict was settled after two years when the legislature rescinded its establishment of the new court.[53]

The Courts and the Other Branches: The General Relationship   The other branches of government take action against courts and court decisions less frequently than we might expect. This is especially true at the federal level. Congress and the president have vast powers to undo court decisions through legislation and the proposal of constitutional amendments, and equally vast powers to attack the courts as institutions. Why have they not used these powers more extensively?

One reason is the sheer difficulty of such action. On controversial matters—and serious action against a court is almost always controversial—it is usually difficult to get past the many potential roadblocks in the legislative process. Senator Russell Long perhaps expressed this best: "It is absolutely beyond the power of any human mind to assess the various ways that something which appears destined to become law can fail to become law, but it happens all the time."[54] Because constitutional amendments require more than simple legislative majorities, they are even more difficult to adopt.

Another reason is the tinge of illegitimacy that is attached to many forms of anti-court action, particularly attacks on the courts as institutions. Even the adoption of constitutional amendments may seem illegitimate if the provisions to be amended are themselves regarded as sacrosanct. Amendments to overturn Supreme Court decisions that expanded civil liberties can be seen as cutting into the Bill of Rights, and such a step would bother many members of Congress a good deal.

Thus the relationship between the courts and the other branches is somewhat different in practice from what formal legal powers would suggest. Legislatures and chief executives would seem to be dominant over the courts, but they do not employ their powers very fully. This restraint increases the courts' role in making public policy.

The courts' own restraint also has an impact. Judges often avoid conflict with the other branches of government by limiting their intervention on policy questions. In particular, they limit the number of laws that they declare unconstitutional. And courts sometimes retreat from their past policies in order to ease conflicts with the other branches.

Finally, we should keep in mind the narrow area of policy interventions that appellate courts make. The willingness of other policymakers to live with judicial initiatives in some fields may result in part from the courts' inactivity in others.

The Impact of the Courts on Society

The most important impact that any government institution can have is on society as a whole—on people's behavior as individuals and on social institutions such as the family and the economy. The courts have been given credit, or blame, for a wide range of effects on society:

1. Many people view the Supreme Court's 1973 decision in *Roe v. Wade* as the source of massive growth in the rate of legal abortions.[55]
2. *Roe v. Wade* and the Court's decisions on school prayer have been cited as important stimuli for development of the religious right as a major political movement.[56]
3. Supreme Court decisions in support of racial equality are widely seen as a major spur to the civil rights revolution in the 1950s and 1960s and improvement in the status of African American citizens since that time.[57]
4. One legal scholar concluded that the Supreme Court's decisions "upholding personal rights secured by the Constitution" have "enhanced the liberties of many individuals and produced substantial consequences."[58]
5. Some commentators argue that state court decisions expanding the right to sue for personal injuries have resulted in a long list of bad effects, including enormous economic costs.[59]
6. A number of commentators assert that court decisions expanding the legal rights of public school students, mandating compensatory treatment for disadvantaged students, and prohibiting school prayer have damaged the educational process and had adverse effects on students.[60]
7. Supreme Court justice Clarence Thomas has argued that the "rights revolution" fostered by the courts has produced "a culture that declined to curb the excesses of self-indulgence" and "has affected the ideal of personal responsibility."[61]

If most of those assertions are accurate, courts make a great deal of difference for American society.

Types of Impact Those who conclude that the courts exert significant effects are making causal arguments about links between court decisions and social behavior, links that take two forms. In the first form, courts directly affect behavior by changing people's incentives. Thus expansion of the right to sue for personal injuries may have increased the economic incentives for individuals and lawyers to bring lawsuits. In turn, the growing volume of lawsuits may have increased the financial risk of making products that are subject to lawsuits for personal injuries, thereby leading manufacturers to stop making those products.

In the second, less direct link, courts trigger broader social change by influencing people's thinking and the structures in which they operate. For instance, the Supreme Court decisions favoring freedom of speech may have underlined that freedom as a value for some people and thereby stimulated them to speak on political matters. Similarly, the Court's decisions on school prayer and abortion may have aroused people who opposed those decisions to mobilize for political action against the broader policies that the decisions represented. By expanding the legal rights of students, the courts may have changed the attitudes of students toward authority, both within the schools and in the larger society.

This second form of impact is often linked to the first. If court decisions expanding the legal rights of students have made it less risky for them to challenge the actions of school administrators, the accumulation of such challenges over time might weaken the authority of those administrators and thus affect the general pattern of behavior by students.

Limits on the Impact of Courts When commentators claim that courts have had enormous effects, good or bad, the links that they posit usually make sense. Still, there is often reason to be skeptical about those claims, because courts are only one of many influences on social behavior and social institutions.

First, policymakers in the other branches also act on issues that courts address. Choices by those policymakers channel and often reduce the impact of courts. *Brown v. Board of Education* did not produce much desegregation in the Deep South for a decade because school administrators and other officials resisted the Supreme Court's ruling. When desegregation did occur later, the direct source was enforcement actions by Congress and the Johnson administration.

More broadly, the policies made by courts in any field coexist with policies of the other branches of government. Those policies have their own impact, and effects that are ascribed to courts may result largely from legislative and executive branch action. Thus the great increase in legal abortion rates during the 1970s resulted in considerable part from action by state legislatures before *Roe v. Wade*.[62] A tremendous array of government policies might influence the education and behavior of young people, and it is the other branches rather than the courts that operate the schools.

Second, forces other than government policies also shape society. One important lesson of the past three decades for both politicians and scholars is that the capacity of government to do either good or ill is constrained by more fundamental influences on individual behavior and the structure of society. Racial discrimination has proved at least moderately resistant to government action, in part because it is deeply rooted in some people's perceptions and attitudes. Government has an impact on American culture, but so do family socialization, the mass media, and other influences. Courts are limited by these conditions just as the other branches are.

We can probe the limits on the impact of courts by looking at two examples of potential impact, the incidence of crime and the status of women.

The Incidence of Crime   Beginning in the 1950s and then more concertedly in the 1960s, the Supreme Court expanded the procedural rights of criminal defendants in several areas. The most important of these expansions were its requirements that indigent defendants in any serious case be provided with attorneys, that suspects be warned of their rights prior to police questioning, and that evidence seized illegally be excluded from use in court. Since the 1970s, the Court has been less supportive of defendants' rights, but it has maintained substantial protections for those rights. And courts in several states have expanded procedural rights for defendants under their own constitutions.

The judicial expansion of defendants' rights—particularly restrictions on police practices—has aroused a good deal of criticism. The 1992 Republican party platform argued that widespread violent crime was, in part, "the legacy of a liberalism that elevates criminals' rights above victims' rights."[63] "If we're looking for root causes of the crime explosion," said presidential candidate Bob Dole in 1996, one of them clearly is "the crisis in our courts."[64]

How might this have happened? As critics see it, appellate court decisions make it more difficult to obtain and use needed evidence against criminals, thus reducing the likelihood that they will be convicted. As people who are contemplating criminal acts become aware that their chances of conviction and punishment have decreased, they are more willing to commit such offenses.

This analysis cannot be evaluated with confidence because the information we have is both limited and conflicting, but some very tentative judgments are possible. The first issue is the effect of expanded defendants' rights on conviction rates. Scholars disagree vehemently about the number of convictions that are "lost" because suspects are read their *Miranda* rights. Even the scholars who have the most negative view of *Miranda*'s effects, however, believe that it affects less than 4 percent of all cases.[65] Studies indicate that a smaller proportion of potential arrests and convictions are lost as a result of restrictions on searches and seizures.[66] Of course, these small proportions translate into substantial numbers of cases.

In any event, it is likely that policymakers who participate more directly in the criminal justice system actually affect conviction rates a good deal more than do appellate courts. Police officers, prosecutors, and trial judges have more direct control over what happens in specific cases. They also put appellate court policies into effect, reshaping and sometimes weakening these policies in the process. Legislatures have considerable impact through their funding decisions.

If court rulings reduce the number of arrests and convictions, it is unclear how much that reduction affects the incidence of criminal behavior. A direct effect is that guilty people who go free may commit additional offenses. But if appellate courts have the massive impact that some people ascribe to them, this impact must result from calculations by potential criminals: substantial numbers of people would choose to commit crimes because they perceive that the chances of conviction have declined.

Rational calculations appear to play a part in many, if not most, decisions to commit crimes. But emotional and moral factors are involved as well.[67] If a moderate reduction in the likelihood of conviction has resulted from rulings of appellate courts, it is not clear that this reduction is sufficient to change many decisions whether to engage in crime—even if those decisions are based largely on rational considerations.

This issue is far from settled, and those who believe that appellate court policies have produced substantial increases in crime might be right. But there are reasons to question the judgment that these decisions have had significant effects on the crime rate. Moreover, it seems unlikely that those decisions have had an impact that outweighs other forces and trends in government and society.

The Status of Women   Until the 1960s, courts generally ratified and accentuated the inequalities between women and men that were established by other institutions in society. The Supreme Court, for instance, upheld state laws that excluded women from the legal profession, restricted other employment opportunities, and prevented women from voting.

In the last three decades, courts have responded to society's changing attitudes toward women's status and roles. Through interpretations of the federal and state constitutions, courts have struck down a variety of legal rules that distinguished between women and men. The Supreme Court has been the most visible participant in this process. Although the Court's record is mixed, it is clear that the Court will hold unconstitutional any law that discriminates directly against women. That position was exemplified by the Court's 1996 decision requiring the admission of women to state-run colleges with a military orientation.[68]

This wave of court decisions has overturned a large number of laws and legal rules that put women at a disadvantage, including provisions that limited the rights of women in marriage and laws that treated female criminal defendants in special ways. These decisions have also speeded the elimination of other laws that discriminate by sex, and they have made unenforceable many laws that remain on the books. During the same period, the status of women in American society has changed substantially; one example is the growing representation of women in such professions as law and medicine.

To what extent are appellate courts responsible for these changes? On the whole, it appears that they have played only a minor part.[69] One reason is that judges have not been entirely fervent or even consistent in attacking sex discrimination. But even a more concerted effort would have had only a limited effect when compared with other forces. Recent changes in the status and roles of women reflect a general social revolution in American society, a revolution that has been spurred chiefly by changes in such matters as women's educational attainments rather than by government action. To the extent that government has encouraged this revolution, legislatures and chief executives have done more than appellate courts, mainly because they are better situated to take actions with a major impact.

Employment provides a good illustration of these general points.[70] The concentration of women in certain occupations and the relatively low wages of the average female worker result from a wide range of conditions, including the education of girls, the conflict between caring for children and professional careers, and discrimination by employers. Recent improvements in the employment status of women also derive from several sources. Government policies, especially prohibitions of employment discrimination, have played a part in these improvements. But these policies have come from the legislative and executive branches, not from the judiciary. Courts have made some important interpretations of antidiscrimination laws, yet the effects of their decisions appear to be quite limited in comparison with action by the other branches of government and with nongovernmental forces. In this area, and more generally, courts have played only a small part in changing the roles of women.

   The Impact That Courts Do Have   The examples of crime and women's status underline the need for caution about ascribing massive effects to court decisions. But even in these two areas and others like them, courts have significant effects. Although appellate courts may not have a substantial influence on the incidence of crime, their decisions have changed the treatment of suspects and defendants by the criminal justice system. At least some people have escaped police searches, obtained more favorable terms in plea bargains, and avoided convictions because of the rights established in appellate court decisions. Court decisions have affected the status of women by making it easier for students to challenge sex discrimination in court and by interpreting sexual harassment as a form of discrimination in employment, to take two important examples. These effects cannot be dismissed as trivial.

   Similarly, the courts are not among the most important forces shaping the structure of industries or relations between labor and management, but they have some impact. Interpretations of the antitrust laws by the federal courts since the 1970s have reduced the legal barriers to mergers, thereby reinforcing more basic sources of the trend toward larger and fewer companies in particular industries. A 1938 Supreme Court decision allowed employers to hire permanent replacements for striking workers; the belated use of this power by companies in the 1980s and 1990s was one reason for the weakening of the labor movement.[71]

   Another example concerns abortion. The impact of the Supreme Court's 1973 decision in *Roe v. Wade* is often exaggerated because people do not take into account the changes in social attitudes and legislative policies that preceded *Roe*. Yet the Court greatly speeded up the process of legal change with its original decision and with later rulings that limited state regulation of abortion. *Roe v. Wade* provided a focal point for the debate over abortion; the Court inadvertently helped to bring about a large-scale antiabortion movement. Thus the Court had a major effect on both the numbers of abortions that are performed and the political contention over abortion. The Court's decisions since 1989 have expanded the states' power to regulate and restrict abortion. At the least, those decisions have given state legislatures a more central role in the conflict over abortion policy.

   The effects of the Supreme Court on the antiabortion movement underline the potential impact of the courts on political action. Court decisions can become a focal point for action because they create the promise of favorable results in the future.[72] In addition, decisions such as *Roe v. Wade* can serve as negative symbols that rally people in counterreaction.

   Perhaps the most important example of the courts' impact in recent years concerns the status and roles of African American citizens. It is important not to overstate this impact; indeed, some commentators argue that the courts have had little effect in this area.[73] For one thing, change in the situations of African American citizens has been limited in important respects. A good deal of racial segregation remains in schools and colleges, and the average income of blacks continues to be far below that of whites. Nor were courts the primary source of the changes that have occurred. As with changes in women's rights, the most important sources were outside government. Moreover, much of the government policy supporting racial equality came from the legislature (such as prohibitions of employment discrimination) or was initiated by the courts but became effective only when the other branches of government acted (such as school desegregation and protection of the right to vote in the Deep South).

Yet courts played a major part in facilitating change. Although court decisions were insufficient to desegregate southern schools without congressional help, they did make desegregation possible. Perhaps more important, *Brown v. Board of Education* and other decisions were significant symbols; they declared that government support for discrimination was constitutionally unacceptable and encouraged other efforts to achieve racial equality. Once the civil rights movement became active, the Supreme Court took extraordinary steps to protect it, striking down convictions of people arrested in demonstrations and overturning state laws intended to cripple civil rights organizations. The Court's decisions were neither necessary to sustain the movement nor sufficient to protect it from harassment, but they may have strengthened it significantly.

Thus the courts, and especially the Supreme Court, have been important contributors to the process of social change in this area. Although court decisions would have had little impact in themselves, they served to bolster and stimulate other forces for change. Because the civil rights revolution itself has been so important, this example should dispel any doubt that the courts can make a difference in American society.

CONCLUSIONS

This chapter has examined the roles of appellate courts as policymakers from several perspectives. As we have seen, those roles are complex and difficult to characterize, but a few conclusions are possible.

Perhaps the most important conclusion concerns limitations on the power of courts as policymakers. The Supreme Court and other courts have a significant impact on the rest of government and society, but their impact is not nearly as great as it is sometimes depicted. For one thing, the courts focus on some kinds of policy issues rather than others; as a result, to take one important example, they generally can have only a limited effect on foreign policy. Even in the areas where they are active, the courts often endorse rather than overturn policies of the other branches. Finally, where courts do act independently and decisively to create new policies, the impact of those policies may be limited severely by the actions of people in other government institutions.

Both this chapter and the book as a whole stress that the courts are closely linked with the rest of government and society. Those links largely determine the roles that courts play in the making of public policy. The opportunities that judges have to make policy decisions depend heavily on the jurisdiction that legislatures give them and on the cases that individuals and groups bring them. What judges do with those opportunities is shaped by their own socialization within the legal system and the larger society and by their perceptions of what their legal and political audiences will accept. And the ultimate impact of a court decision depends on the ways that other policymakers and people outside of government react to it.

It should be clear by now that the roles of the courts are not static. Over the course of time, both the ideological pattern of appellate court policies and the extent of judicial activism have varied. The contribution of the courts to public policy today looks rather different from their contribution half a century ago. As relevant conditions continue to change, we can expect further changes in what the courts do—in some instances, changes that we cannot predict today.

FOR FURTHER READING

Chilton, Bradley Stewart. *Prisons Under the Gavel: The Federal Court Takeover of Georgia Prisons.* Columbus: Ohio State University Press, 1992.

Gates, John B. *The Supreme Court and Partisan Realignment: A Macro- and Microlevel Perspective.* Boulder, Colo.: Westview Press, 1992.

Haar, Charles M. *Suburbs Under Siege: Race, Space, and Audacious Judges.* Princeton, N.J.: Princeton University Press, 1996.

Johnson, Charles A., and Bradley C. Canon. *Judicial Policies: Implementation and Impact.* Washington, D.C.: CQ Press, 1984.

Keynes, Edward, with Randall K. Miller. *The Court vs. Congress: Prayer, Busing, and Abortion.* Durham, N.C.: Duke University Press, 1989.

McCann, Michael W. *Rights at Work: Pay Equity Reform and the Politics of Legal Mobilization.* Chicago: University of Chicago Press, 1994.

Pacelle, Richard L. Jr. *The Transformation of the Supreme Court's Agenda from the New Deal to the Reagan Administration.* Boulder, Colo.: Westview Press, 1991.

Rosenberg, Gerald N. *The Hollow Hope: Can Courts Bring About Social Change?* Chicago: University of Chicago Press, 1991.

NOTES

1. Administrative Office of the United States Courts, *Judicial Business of the United States Courts: Report of the Director* (1995) (Washington, D.C.: Administrative Office of the United States Courts, n.d.), 110.
2. Joy A. Chapper and Roger A. Hanson, *Understanding Reversible Error in Criminal Appeals* (Williamsburg, Va.: National Center for State Courts, 1989), 34–35. See also Thomas Y. Davies, "Affirmed: A Study of Criminal Appeals and Decision-Making Norms in a California Court of Appeal," *American Bar Foundation Research Journal* (Summer 1982), 576.
3. See Davies, "Affirmed."
4. "The Supreme Court, 1995 Term," *Harvard Law Review* 110 (November 1996), 372.
5. Richard L. Pacelle Jr., *The Transformation of the Supreme Court's Agenda from the New Deal to the Reagan Administration* (Boulder, Colo.: Westview Press, 1991); Pacelle, "The Dynamics and Determinants of Agenda Change in the Rehnquist Court," in *Contemplating Courts,* ed. Lee Epstein (Washington, D.C.: CQ Press, 1995), 251–274.

6. See Lawrence M. Friedman, *A History of American Law,* rev. ed. (New York: Simon & Schuster, 1985); Stanton Wheeler, Bliss Cartwright, Robert A. Kagan, and Lawrence M. Friedman, "Do the 'Haves' Come Out Ahead? Winning and Losing in State Supreme Courts, 1870–1970," *Law and Society Review* 21 (1987), 403–445; Melvin I. Urofsky, "State Courts and Progressive Legislation During the Progressive Era: A Reevaluation," *Journal of American History* 72 (June 1985), 63–91; and Gary T. Schwartz, "Tort Law and the Economy in Nineteenth-Century America: A Reinterpretation," *Yale Law Journal* 90 (July 1981), 1717–1775.

7. "Delivers Remarks at the Heritage Foundation, Washington, D.C." (transcript by FDCH Political Transcripts, January 29, 1996).

8. Lawrence Baum and Bradley C. Canon, "State Supreme Courts as Activists: New Doctrines in the Law of Torts," in *State Supreme Courts: Policymakers in the Federal System,* ed. Mary Cornelia Porter and G. Alan Tarr (Westport, Conn.: Greenwood Press, 1982), 83–108.

9. James A. Henderson Jr. and Theodore Eisenberg, "The Quiet Revolution in Products Liability: An Empirical Study of Legal Change," *UCLA Law Review* 37 (February 1990), 479–553; Eisenberg and Henderson, "Inside the Quiet Revolution in Products Liability," *UCLA Law Review* 39 (April 1992), 731–810.

10. Barry Latzer, "The Hidden Conservatism of the State Court 'Revolution,'" *Judicature* 74 (December–January 1991), 190–197.

11. See G. Alan Tarr, "The Past and Future of the New Judicial Federalism," *Publius* 24 (Spring 1994), 63–79.

12. Examples include *State v. Savva,* 616 A.2d 774 (Vt. Sup. Ct. 1991), on automobile searches; and *State v. Canelo,* 653 A.2d 1097 (N.H. Sup. Ct. 1995), on the exclusion of illegally seized evidence from trials.

13. Richard Willing, "'Activist' Label Actively Applied," *USA Today,* March 10, 1997, 3A.

14. Bradley C. Canon, "A Framework for the Analysis of Judicial Activism," in *Supreme Court Activism and Restraint,* ed. Stephen C. Halpern and Charles M. Lamb (Lexington, Mass.: Lexington Books, 1982), 385–419. See also Richard A. Posner, *The Federal Courts: Challenge and Reform* (Cambridge: Harvard University Press, 1996), 314.

15. Katherine Q. Seelye, "Conservatives in House Are Preparing an Impeachment List of Federal Judges," *New York Times,* March 14, 1997, A13.

16. These figures were calculated from data in Congressional Research Service, *The Constitution of the United States of America: Analysis and Interpretation* (Washington, D.C.: Government Printing Office, 1987); *1990 Supplement* (Washington, D.C. Government Printing Office, 1991); and more recent decisions.

17. See *Harris v. McRae,* 448 U.S. 297 (1980); and *Schenck v. Pro-Choice Network,* 137 L. Ed. 2d 1 (1997).

18. *Buckley v. Valeo,* 424 U.S. 1 (1976); *Colorado Republican Campaign Committee v. Federal Election Commission,* 135 L. Ed. 2d 795 (1996).

19. The decisions were, respectively, *Iowa Utilities Board v. Federal Communications Commission,* 109 F.3d 418 (8th Cir. 1996); *United States v. Bryan,* 58 F.3d 933 (4th Cir. 1995); and *Kadic v. Karadzic,* 70 F.3d 232 (2d Cir. 1995).

20. *Hopwood v. Texas,* 78 F.3d 932 (5th Cir. 1996).

21. Tinsley E. Yarbrough, *Judge Frank Johnson and Human Rights in Alabama* (University: University of Alabama Press, 1981); Larry W. Yackle, *Reform and Regret: The Story of Federal Judicial Involvement in the Alabama Prison System* (New York: Oxford University Press, 1989); Ronald Smothers, "Cursed and Praised, Retiring Judge Recalls Storm," *New York Times,* November 8, 1991, B9.

22. Caroline E. Mayer and Mike Mills, "Bells' Overseer Sees an Era End," *Washington Post,* February 13, 1996, D1, D5.

23. The decisions were, respectively, *Public Citizen v. Office of the United States Trade Representative,* 822 F. Supp. 21 (D.D.C. 1993); *United States v. Rezaq,* 899 F. Supp. 697 (D.D.C. 1995); and *Byrd v. Raines,* 956 F. Supp. 25 (D.D.C. 1997).

24. *San Antonio Independent School District v. Rodriguez,* 411 U.S. 1 (1973). On state supreme court decisions in this field, see Bill Swinford, "Shedding the Doctrinal Security

Blanket: How State Supreme Courts Interpret Their Constitutions in the Shadow of *Rodriguez*," *Temple Law Review* 67 (1994), 981–1001.

25. The cases were, respectively, *Fordice v. Bryan,* 651 So. 2d 998 (Miss. Sup. Ct. 1995); *Fordice v. Thomas,* 649 So. 2d 835 (Miss. Sup. Ct. 1995); *Fordice v. Green,* 679 So. 2d 196 (Miss. Sup. Ct. 1996); and *In re: Fordice,* 691 So. 2d 429 (Miss. Sup. Ct. 1997).

26. Robert Pear, "U.S. Challenges Courts on Disabilities," *New York Times,* April 21, 1997, A12.

27. *United States v. Sanchez,* 917 F. Supp. 29, 32 (D.D.C. 1996).

28. J. W. Peltason, *Fifty-Eight Lonely Men: Southern Federal Judges and School Desegregation,* 2d ed. (Urbana: University of Illinois Press, 1971); Charles S. Bullock III, "Equal Education Opportunity," in *Implementation of Civil Rights Policy,* ed. Charles S. Bullock III and Charles M. Lamb (Monterey, Calif.: Brooks/Cole, 1984), 55–92.

29. Richard A. Leo, "The Impact of *Miranda* Revisited," *Journal of Criminal Law and Criminology* 86 (Spring 1996), 621–692; Paul G. Cassell and Bret S. Hayman, "Police Interrogation in the 1990s: An Empirical Study of the Effects of *Miranda,*" *UCLA Law Review* 43 (February 1996), 839–931; Jerome H. Skolnick, *Justice Without Trial: Law Enforcement in Democratic Society,* 3d ed. (New York: Macmillan, 1994), 274–283; Craig D. Uchida and Timothy S. Bynum, "Search Warrants, Motions to Suppress and 'Lost Cases': The Effects of the Exclusionary Rule in Seven Jurisdictions," *Journal of Criminal Law and Criminology* 81 (Winter 1991), 1034–1066.

30. H. Frank Way Jr., "Survey Research on Judicial Decisions: The Prayer and Bible Reading Cases," *Western Political Quarterly* 21 (June 1968), 189–205; Martha M. McCarthy, "Much Ado over Graduation Prayer," *Phi Delta Kappan* 75 (October 1993), 120–125.

31. Leslie Guevarra, "Judge Won't Absolve Late Drug King," *San Francisco Chronicle,* August 14, 1987, 4.

32. Katherine Bishop, "When an Appeals Court Becomes the Big Issue in Death Penalty Cases," *New York Times,* May 22, 1992, B9; William Carlsen, "Frontier Justice," *San Francisco Chronicle,* October 6, 1996, 1, 4, 5.

33. Richard M. Johnson, *The Dynamics of Compliance* (Evanston, Ill.: Northwestern University Press, 1967); William K. Muir Jr., *Prayer in the Public Schools: Law and Attitude Change* (Chicago: University of Chicago Press, 1967).

34. *United States v. State of Louisiana,* 751 F. Supp. 606, 608 (E.D. La. 1990).

35. Carlsen, "Frontier Justice," 5.

36. *Brown v. Board of Education,* 349 U.S. 294, 301 (1955).

37. Charles M. Sevilla, *Disorder in the Court: Great Fractured Moments in Courtroom History* (New York: Norton, 1992), 108–109.

38. Alan Cooper, "10th Time Panel Reverses Maverick," *National Law Journal,* March 24, 1997, A8. See *United States v. Perkins,* 108 F.3d 512 (4th Cir. 1997).

39. *Third Annual Judicial Conference of the United States Court of Veterans Appeals,* 8 *Veterans Appeals Reporter* xxv, xxx–xxxiv (1994). See Bill McAllister, "Veterans Court Judge Assails VA Resistance," *Washington Post,* October 21, 1994, A23.

40. Michelle Singletary, "Judge Rebukes Agency Regulating Credit Unions," *Washington Post,* December 5, 1996, D1. See *First National Bank and Trust Company v. National Credit Union Administration,* 1996 U.S. Dist. LEXIS 19735 (D.D.C. 1996).

41. Celia W. Dugger, "Judge Finds New York City in Contempt over Its Care of Homeless Families," *New York Times,* September 28, 1994, A21; Matthew Purdy, "City to Revise Its Housing of Homeless," *New York Times,* February 2, 1995, B3.

42. William N. Eskridge Jr., "Overriding Supreme Court Statutory Interpretation Decisions," *Yale Law Journal* 101 (November 1991), 338.

43. See Linda Lipsen, "The Evolution of Products Liability as a Federal Policy Issue," in *Tort Law and the Public Interest: Competition, Innovation, and Consumer Welfare,* ed. Peter H. Schuck (New York: Norton, 1991), 262–271; and "Tort Revision," *National Law Journal,* December 26, 1994/January 2, 1995, C12.

44. Barton Gellman, "For Morgan Bill, a Quick Trip Through Congressional Maze," *Washington Post,* September 23, 1989, A9; Vincent J. Schodolski, "Suit Contends

Congress Acted Illegally in Child Custody Case," *Chicago Tribune,* April 27, 1997, sec. 1, 5.

45. Jeffrey Toobin, "Victim Power," *New Yorker,* March 24, 1997, 40–43; Ryan Ross, "Judge Asserts Right to Bar Okla. Victims," *National Law Journal,* April 7, 1997, A10.

46. *Oregon v. Mitchell,* 400 U.S. 112 (1970).

47. *Gregg v. Georgia,* 428 U.S. 153 (1976).

48. *Harris v. McRae,* 448 U.S. 297 (1980).

49. William Celis III, "Kentucky Begins Drive to Revitalize Its Schools," *New York Times,* September 26, 1990, B6.

50. Victoria Slind-Flor, "Calif. Bar Criticized by Judges," *National Law Journal,* October 19, 1992, 27. The decision was *Legislature v. Eu,* 54 Cal. 3d 492 (1991).

51. Lawrence Baum and David Frohnmayer, eds., *The Courts: Sharing and Separating Powers* (New Brunswick, N.J.: Eagleton Institute of Politics, 1989), 35.

52. Evan Haynes, *The Selection and Tenure of Judges* (Newark, N.J.: National Conference of Judicial Councils, 1944), 95.

53. Stephen L. Carter, *The Confirmation Mess: Cleaning Up the Federal Appointments Process* (New York: Basic Books, 1994), 105–107.

54. Peter Masley, "The Capitol," *Washington Post,* April 23, 1977, A3.

55. See Walter Isaacson, "The Battle over Abortion," *Time,* April 6, 1981, 20–28.

56. Walter Goodman, "The Deep Roots of the Religious Right," *New York Times,* September 27, 1996, B3.

57. Charles A. Johnson and Bradley C. Canon, *Judicial Policies: Implementation and Impact* (Washington, D.C.: CQ Press, 1984), 256–260.

58. Jesse H. Choper, "Consequences of Supreme Court Decisions Upholding Individual Constitutional Rights," *Michigan Law Review* 83 (October 1984), 12.

59. Peter W. Huber, *Liability: The Legal Revolution and Its Consequences* (New York: Basic Books, 1988), 3–5; Kirk W. Dillard, "Illinois' Landmark Tort Reform: The Sponsor's Policy Explanation," *Loyola University Chicago Law Review* 27 (Summer 1996), 805–817.

60. Edward A. Wynne, "What Are the Courts Doing to Our Children?" *The Public Interest* 64 (Summer 1981), 3–18; H. Wesley Smith, "Holding Court in the Schools," *Newsweek,* February 4, 1985, 12–13; "Remarks to the 47th National Conference . . . ," *Weekly Compilation of Presidential Documents* 19 (July 1, 1983), 953–954.

61. "Thomas Critiques the 'Rights Revolution,'" *Legal Times,* May 23, 1994, 23.

62. Susan B. Hansen, "State Implementation of Supreme Court Decisions: Abortion Rates Since *Roe v. Wade,*" *Journal of Politics* 42 (May 1980), 372–395; Gerald N. Rosenberg, *The Hollow Hope: Can Courts Bring About Social Change?* (Chicago: University of Chicago Press, 1991), 178–180.

63. "Party Stresses Family Values, Decentralized Authority," *Congressional Quarterly Weekly Report,* August 22, 1992, 2566.

64. "Excerpts from Speech: On the Judiciary," *New York Times,* April 20, 1996, A10.

65. Paul G. Cassell, "*Miranda*'s Social Costs: An Empirical Assessment," *Northwestern University Law Review* 90 (Winter 1996), 387–499; Stephen J. Schulhofer, "*Miranda*'s Practical Effect: Substantial Benefits and Vanishingly Small Social Costs," *Northwestern University Law Review* 90 (Winter 1996), 500–563; George C. Thomas III, "Is *Miranda* a Real-World Failure? A Plea for More (and Better) Empirical Evidence," *UCLA Law Review* 43 (February 1996), 933–959.

66. Thomas Y. Davies, "A Hard Look at What We Know (and Still Need to Learn) About the 'Costs' of the Exclusionary Rule: The NIJ Study and Other Studies of 'Lost' Arrests," *American Bar Foundation Research Journal* (Summer 1983), 611–690; Peter F. Nardulli, "The Societal Costs of the Exclusionary Rule Revisited," *University of Illinois Law Review* (Spring 1987), 223–239.

67. Daniel S. Nagin and Raymond Paternoster, "Enduring Individual Differences and Rational Choice Theories of Crime," *Law & Society Review* 27 (1993), 467–496; Raymond Paternoster and Sally Simpson, "Sanction Threats and Appeals to Morality: Testing a Rational Choice Model of Corporate Crime," *Law & Society Review* 30 (1996), 549–583.

68. *United States v. Virginia,* 135 L. Ed. 2d 735 (1996).
69. See Rosenberg, *The Hollow Hope,* 202–246.
70. Elaine Sorensen, *Exploring the Reasons Behind the Narrowing Gender Gap in Earnings* (Washington, D.C.: Urban Institute Press, 1991); Paul Burstein, *Discrimination, Jobs, and Politics: The Struggle for Equal Employment Opportunity in the United States Since the New Deal* (Chicago: University of Chicago Press, 1985), 130–154.
71. Steven Greenhouse, "Strikes Decrease to a 50–Year Low," *New York Times,* January 29, 1996, A1, A10. The decision was *National Labor Relations Board v. Mackay Radio & Telegraph Co.,* 304 U.S. 333 (1938).
72. Michael W. McCann, *Rights at Work: Pay Equity Reform and the Politics of Legal Mobilization* (Chicago: University of Chicago Press, 1994).
73. Rosenberg, *The Hollow Hope,* 39–169.

Index of Cases

In citations of court decisions, the first number is the volume of the court reports in which the decision is found, the designation of the court reports (such as "U.S." for the United States Reports) follows that number, and the second number is the first page of the decision. The year of the decision is in parentheses; except for the Supreme Court or where the name of the reporter indicates which court decided the case, the designation of that court is indicated before the year. A state name (such as "Mass.") indicates a state supreme court; a state name preceded by a district (such as "N.D. Fla.") indicates a federal district court; a circuit number (such as "9th Cir.") indicates a federal court of appeals.

Index

intermediate appellate courts
 jurisdiction and business, 47
 structure, 46, 47
major trial courts
 jurisdiction and business, 44–46
 structure, 44, 45
minor trial courts
 contrasted with U.S. Supreme Court,
  5, 6
 jurisdiction and business, 45, 46
 structure, 45
selection of judges, *see* Judicial selection
small claims courts, 225, 246–248
structure, 44–50, 52, 53
supreme courts
 decision making, 284, 292, 296–300,
  302, 303
 jurisdiction and business, 47, 48, 50,
  52, 76, 92, 93, 159, 279, 283, 284,
  311, 312
 policies, 52, 53, 60, 81, 302, 313–315,
  318, 321
 structure, 47
 unification, 43, 44, 52–54
State Department, 74
State legislatures
 legislation affecting courts, 52, 76, 148,
  166, 175, 198, 199, 206
 responses to court decisions, 10, 327–333
 selection and removal of judges, 124,
  125, 157, 158
Statutes, 2, 3
Steeh, Charlotte, 162
Steele, Eric H., 242, 259
Stein, Loren, 308
Stevens, John Paul, 130, 290, 291
Stewart, Potter, 267
Stidham, Ronald, 133
Stienstra, Donna, 307
Stolzenberg, Lisa, 216
Stone, Harlan, 65
Stookey, John A., 132
Stover, Robert V., 95
Stow, Mary Lou, 307
Strasser, Fred, 96, 98, 215
Strategic Lawsuits Against Public
  Participation (SLAPPs), 233, 234
Struck, Doug, 260
Stuart, Roger, 308
Sudnow, David, 212
Sugarman, Stephen D., 262
Supreme Court, U.S.
 backgrounds of justices, 62, 66, 138, 142,
  143, 144, 145
 compared with Congress, 7
 compared with municipal courts, 5, 6
 decision making, 9, 13, 15, 16, 269, 270,
  289–298, 300–302
 implementation and impact of decisions,
  320–338

jurisdiction and business, 32, 36–37, 312,
  313, 331, 332
 lawyers and litigants in, 80, 267, 273,
  274, 278, 279
 policies and decisions, 1, 81, 83, 88, 144,
  145, 191, 193, 207, 209, 237, 238,
  273, 278, 281, 282, 285, 311,
  313–315, 317–319
 screening of cases, 36–37, 269, 283–285
 selection of justices, 15, 104–107, 315
Suro, Roberto, 57
Swinford, Bill, 340

Taft, William Howard, 102, 142
Talarico, Susette M., 99, 215
Tapscott, Richard, 134
Tarr, G. Alan, 331, 340
Tate, C. Neal, 162
Taylor, Gary, 41, 95, 163, 261
Taylor, Stuart, Jr., 133, 215, 256
Tedin, Kent L., 162
Tennessee
 lawyers, 79
 selection of judges, 301
Tesitor, Irene A., 164
Testa, Karen, 260
Texas
 courts, 47
 judges, 151, 153
 lawyers, 60, 79
 selection of judges, 119, 121, 294
Thielemann, Greg, 133
Thoennes, Nancy, 262
Thomas, Clarence, 10, 66, 104–108, 290,
  291, 293, 299, 333
Thomas, George C., III, 342
Thompson, Robert S., 305, 307, 308
"Three-strikes" laws, 199
Thurmond, Strom, 109
Tillman, Robert, 215
Tjaden, Patricia, 262
Tobacco litigation, 15, 26, 275, 276
Tobin, Robert W., 57
Tonry, Michael W., 209, 211, 214, 216
Toobin, Jeffrey, 342
Torry, Saundra, 70, 95, 97, 99, 245, 256
Torts, *see* Personal injury cases
Towns, Hollis R., 214
Traut, Carol Ann, 308
Trial courts. *See also* Civil cases; Criminal
  cases; Federal courts; State courts;
  specific states
 contrasted with appellate courts, 5–7
 functions, 7–9
Trials
 evaluation, 192–197, 243, 244
 procedures and processes, 191, 192
Tsenin, Kay, 118, 119
Tucker, Cynthia, 245
Tuohy, James, 134, 161